Looking at
Monet

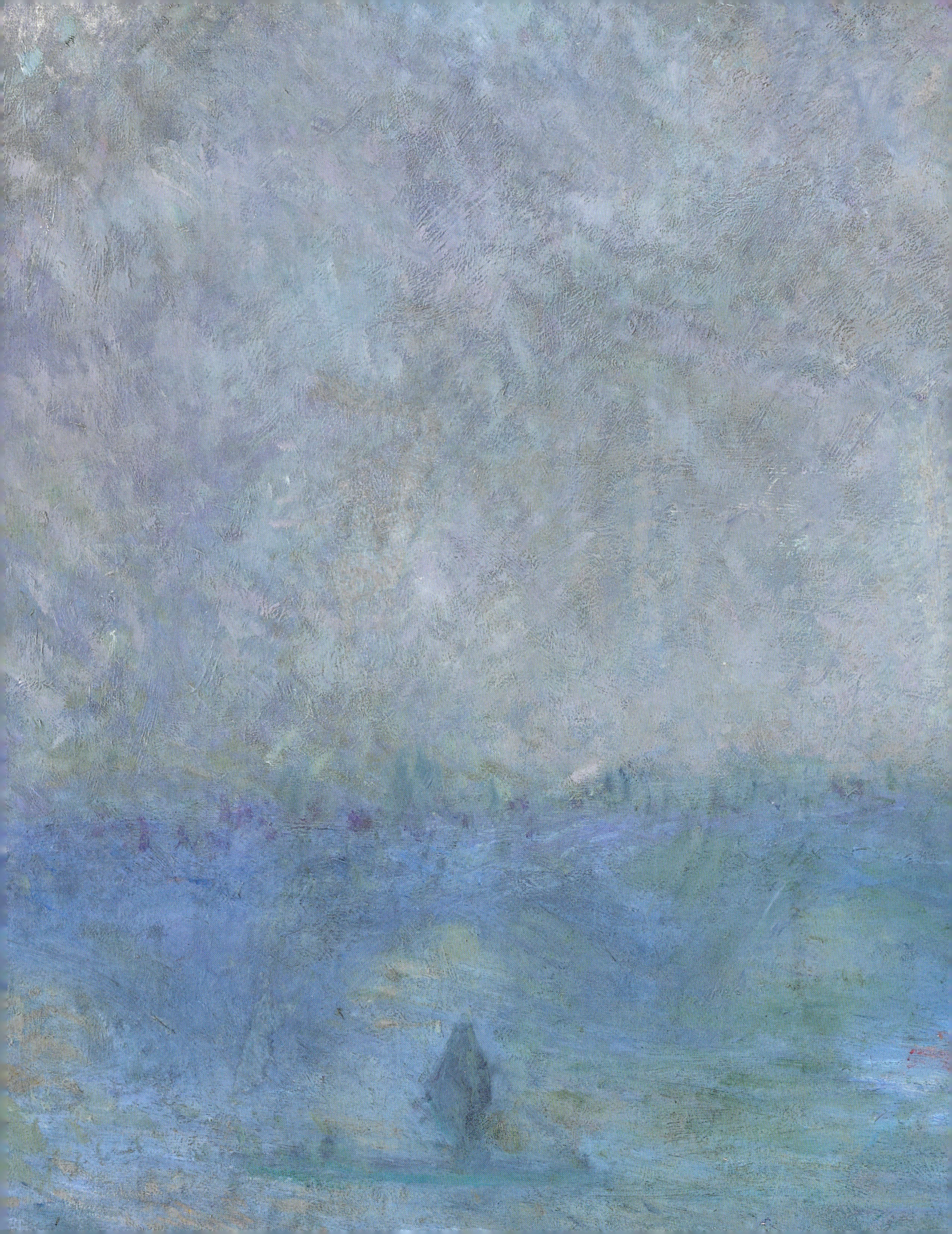

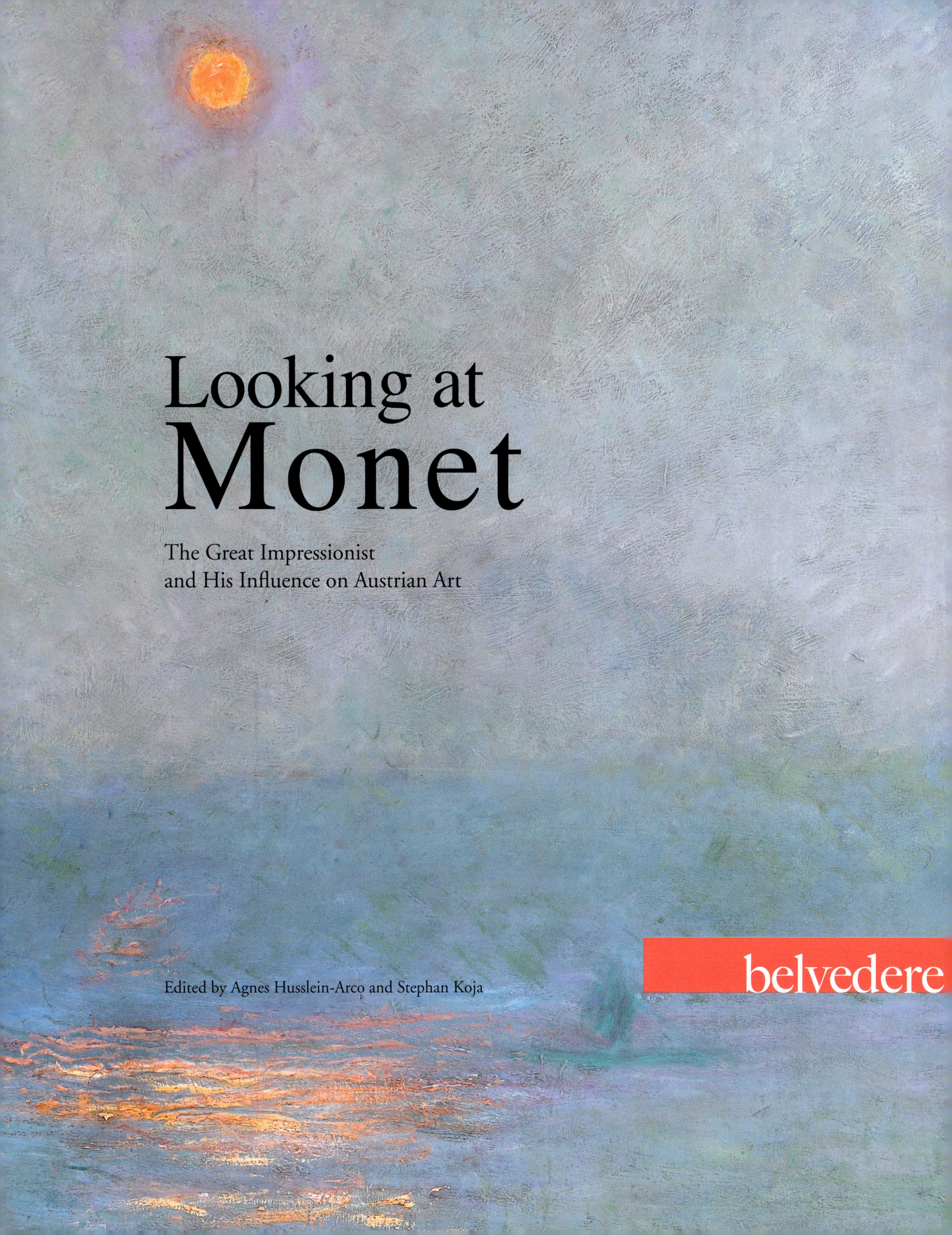

Looking at Monet

The Great Impressionist
and His Influence on Austrian Art

Edited by Agnes Husslein-Arco and Stephan Koja

belvedere

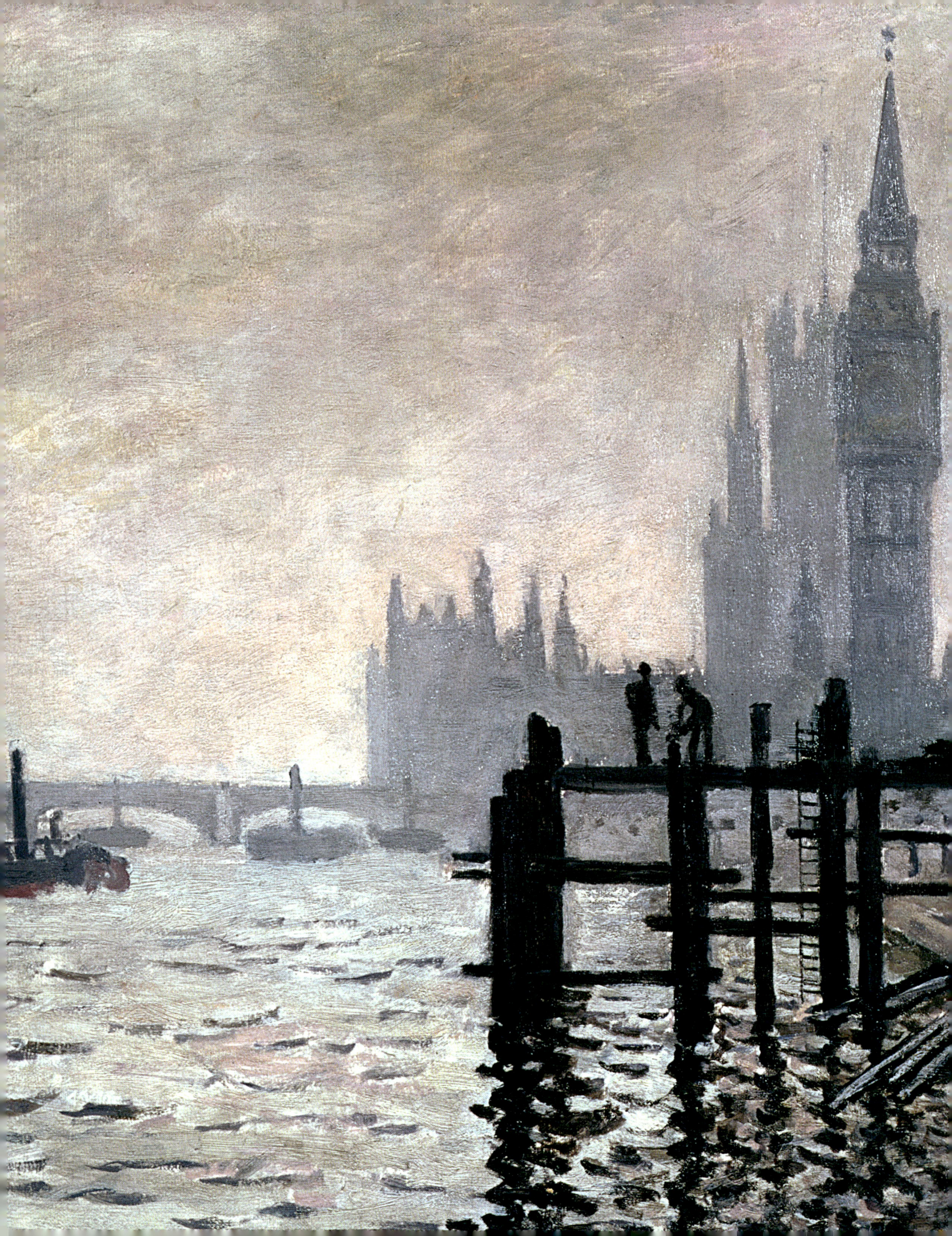

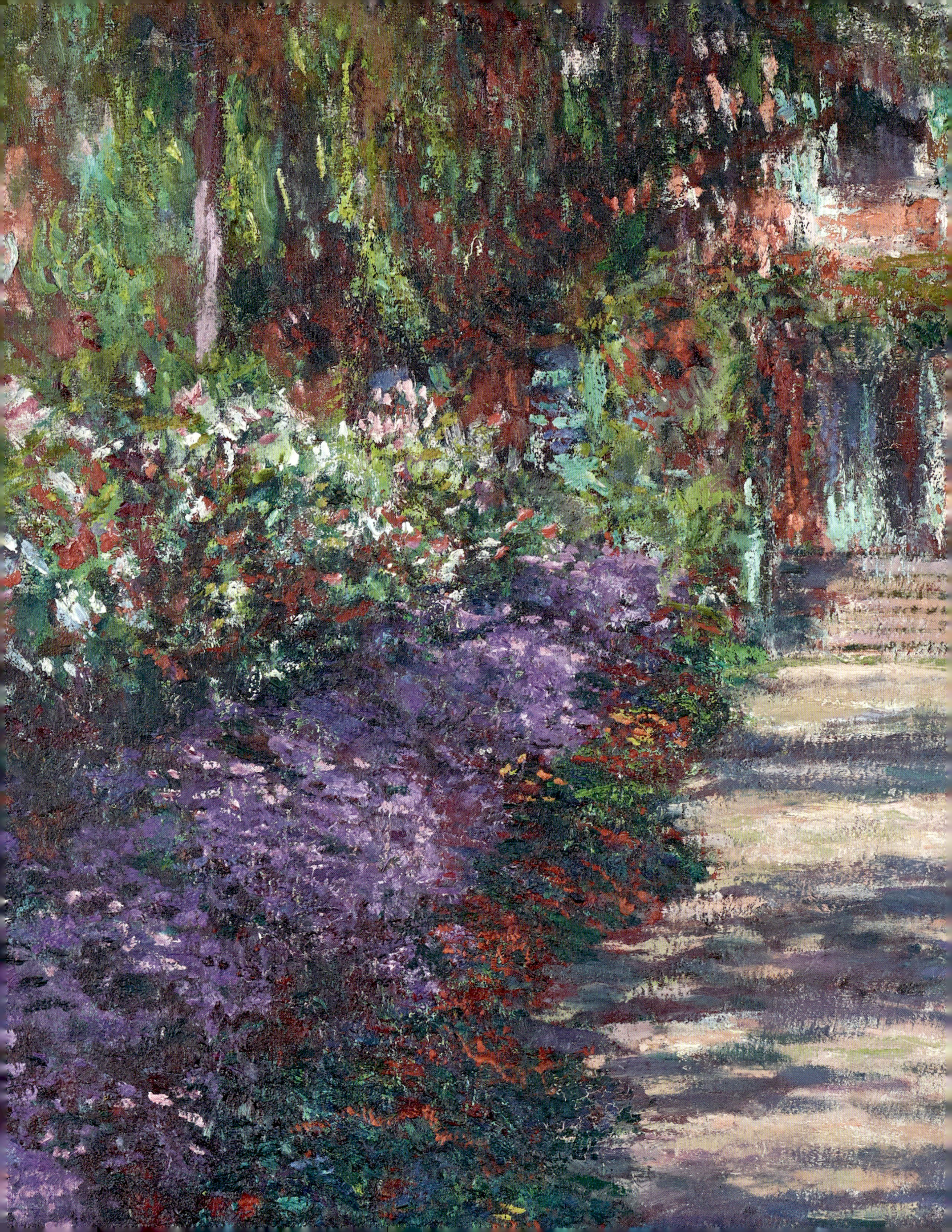

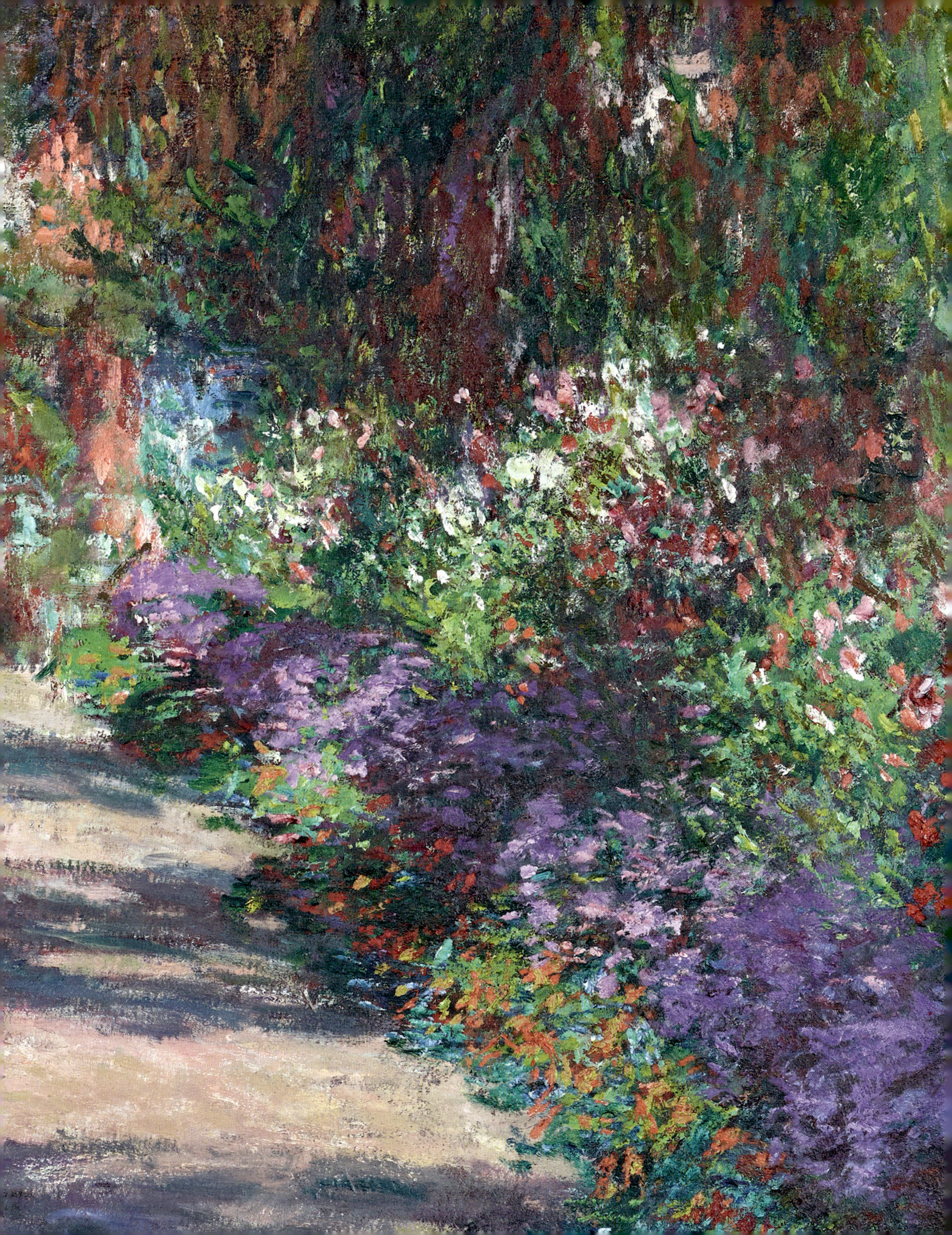

FOREWORD

"...painting in keeping with their convictions..."

Agnes Husslein-Arco

Claude Monet was an exceptional artist who left his mark on an entire epoch. His outstanding status—he became a legend in his own lifetime—made him an ever-new source of inspiration for countless artists throughout the world.

This applies equally to Austrian art; in this country, painters and photographers also profited greatly from their intense study of the works of their predecessors and contemporaries in the wider European cultural environment, and especially from the visual solutions initiated by Claude Monet. One of these artists was Theodor von Hörmann, who not only processed many impulses he had received from Monet in his own works but also wanted to give other artists and the public the opportunity for making discoveries of this kind and, therefore, passionately championed the foundation of a museum of modern art.

His ideas and tenacity are essentially to be thanked for the establishment of the Österreichische Galerie Belvedere; as early as 1894 he penned his *Thoughts on a Modern Gallery* in order to present them at a meeting of the Vienna Artists' Cooperative (Genossenschaft der bildender Künstler Wiens), "[The gallery] should include the best works from all the periods of the Austrian artists of our time, to make it possible to show the entire development of each one of them in all its phases [...] However, the developments taking place in other nations should also be illustrated with characteristic examples, so that we will continuously be able to learn and be driven forward and not fall behind any other nation."[1] Hörmann, who died in 1895 at the early age of 55, did not live to see this becoming a reality. However, the Association of Fine Artists in Vienna (Vereinigung bildender Künstler Wiens), which was founded two years later, was ultimately successful in contributing to the ideas of its forefather by making a breakthrough: the Moderne Galerie was opened in rooms in the Lower Belvedere in 1903. Works by Camille Pissarro, Pierre-Auguste Renoir, August Rodin, and Vincent van Gogh, to mention only a few of the most prominent names, were purchased with the intention of acquiring "major works by those masters" who "stand for art in Europe today" and "have left the mark of their spirit on its overall development in an indelible manner."[2] Claude Monet's painting *Paul Antoine Graff (Le Père Paul)* had already been purchased for the Moderne Galerie in 1903. In 1912, the then director Friedrich Dörnhöffer gave his reasons to the Education Ministry for acquiring an additional painting by the French master, with the following words, "It must now be seen as a historically absolutely clearly recognizable fact that French Impressionism played an extremely important role in the development of painting in the 19th century and that the entire last generation of European painters has been influenced by it to a more or less great extent. It is therefore in keeping with the established goals of the 'Österreichische Staatsgalerie' that this important epoch be represented by a number of works that comprehensively characterize its nature and ambitions. Claude Monet must be placed in the front row of the leading masters of this movement."[3] Shortly thereafter it was possible to admire Monet's painting *Anglers on the Seine near Poissy* in the collection. Thirty years later, the gallery's exquisite collection of Impressionist paintings was complemented with an additional major work when Monet's *Path in Monet's Garden in Giverny* was purchased.

The Belvedere is therefore remaining true to its tradition by focusing on the important influence the French painter had on the Austrian art of his time, as well as on following generations, in this fall's exhibition *Looking at Monet (Im Lichte Monets)*. Soon after Austrian artists had had the possibility of seeing and studying original works by Monet in exhibitions in the Künstlerhaus, the Secession, and Galerie Miethke starting in 1873, they began to

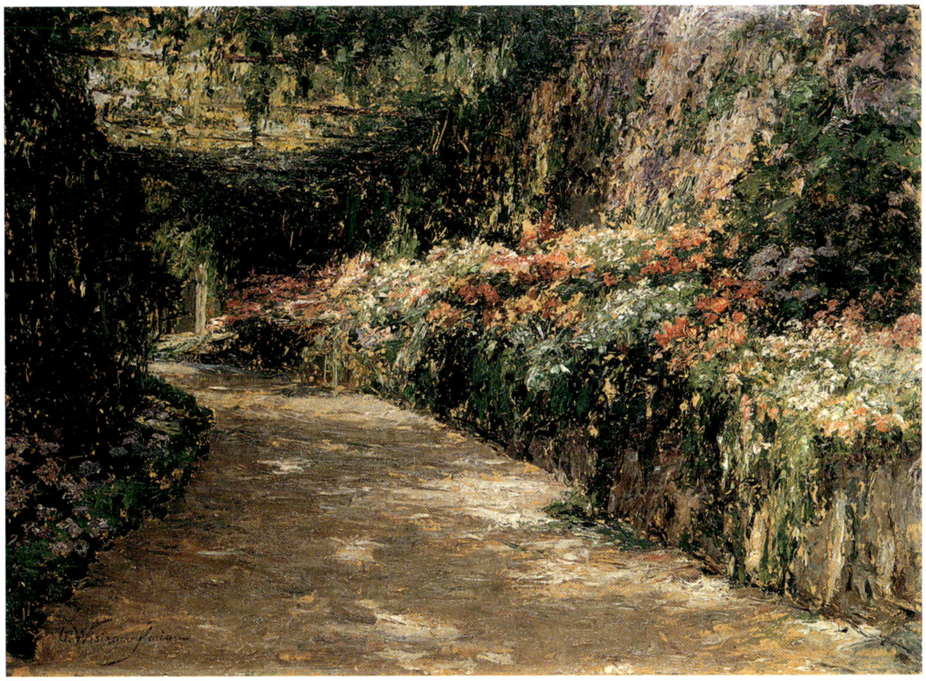

process in their own works the impressions they had received. Monet provided them with a great number of stimuli relating to motifs and technique, as well as on the compositional level, and his pictures became a source of inspiration for Austrian artists as important as Gustav Klimt, Heinrich Kühn, Carl Moll, and Emil Jakob Schindler. However, they all preserved their own individual characteristics and only absorbed those elements of Monet's work that conformed to their own objectives to the greatest degree possible. Monet was a model and personal enrichment to Hörmann and his contemporaries but none of them became mere imitators. To return to Hörmann's words, they all pursued the aim of "painting in keeping with their convictions" and "not be copiers and idol worshippers [...] but strive to give expression to the uniqueness of each individual and the individuality [of the] entire age."[4]

Here, I would like to express my deep gratitude to all who have loaned works for this exhibition; it would not have been possible to realize this without their generosity. My sincere thanks also go to the curator Stephan Koja for his commitment and expertise in preparing the exhibition and catalog, as well as to his research colleagues Irina Katnik and Kathrin Wolf for their conscientious support. Finally, I would like to thank sincerely all the authors of the contributions to this catalog that make it possible for us to have a deeper understanding of Monet's work and, at the same time, become aware of the manifold connections to Austrian art.

1 Hermann Bahr, "Der erste Secessionist. Zur Hörmann-Ausstellung in der Secession," February 1899, in: idem, *Secession*, Vienna 1900, p. 107.
2 Memorandum from the Vienna Secession to Minister of Cultural Affairs Wilhelm Ritter von Hartel, in: *Ver Sacrum*, 4th vol., issue 20, 1901, p. 343.
3 Letter dated March 10, 1912, Österreichisches Staatsarchiv, AVA, CuU, 13752/1912. The purchase for the sum of 25,000 crowns took place in April 1912 through Galerie Miethke.
4 Bahr 1900 (as in note 1), p. 106.

OLGA WISINGER-FLORIAN
Pergola near Mentone, ca. 1900
Neue Galerie am Universalmuseum Joanneum, Graz

"... I WANT THE IMPOSSIBLE..."

Claude Monet and the Renewal of Painting

Stephan Koja

"It's a great affliction, and what do I want? I pursue a dream, I want the impossible. Other painters paint a bridge, a house, a boat. They paint the bridge, the house, the boat, and are done. ... I want to paint the air in which the bridge, the house, the boat are to be found—the beauty of the atmosphere around them, and that is nothing less than impossible. Ah, if only I could be content with the possible!"[1]

When the Danish author Herman Bang recorded those words of Monet's in his diary,[2] the man who had uttered them was an established painter of international repute—one who had already left Impressionism, in the true sense, behind him. Behind him, too, lay years of tribulation and personal hardship, of exhibitions greeted with outrage and misunderstanding, but also of early triumphs and personal recognition as a leading member of the avant-garde. What remained was the ineradicable dissatisfaction of an artist with what he had accomplished, one who always aspired to greater, more difficult things, sought new challenges, was little impressed by praise and, above all, viewed public honors with total indifference.

What determined the course of young Monet's life was his meeting with Eugène Boudin in Le Havre, who introduced him to "plein-airism" and opened his eyes to the potentialities inherent in painting a subject on the spot. Boudin had a poor reputation. His "realism" had attracted ridicule and was dismissed as banal and unpoetic. That, however, was just what constituted its essential stimulus, because it taught Monet a down-to-earth approach to landscape painting devoid of false sentiment and free from many pictorial conventions. Boudin also made an almost scientific endeavor to capture natural phenomena, however fleeting, as Charles Baudelaire admiringly recounted after visiting his studio. "He will later astonish us, I am sure, with finished paintings of the marvelous magic of air and water," he wrote in *La Revue française* in 1859. His studies—such swift and faithful studies of what is transient in the extreme, of what is impossible to capture in form and color: of waves and clouds—always bear a marginal note of the date, time of day, and wind conditions, for instance: October 8, 12 noon, wind from the north-west."[3]

Boudin's procedure was diametrically opposed, as regards both subjects and their treatment, to the official taste of the Salon, where landscapes, like still lifes and genre paintings, were assigned to the lower rungs of the artistic ladder. Ever since it was founded by Colbert in 1648, the Académie des Beaux-Arts had considered it the artist's greatest challenge to depict abstract truths and human ideals drawn from history and classical art. Thus, far less importance was attached to unpretentious landscapes painted by Dutch artists of the seventeenth and eighteenth centuries than to the Mediterranean views of Nicolas Poussin or Claude Lorrain, which were still pervaded by the classical ideal.

It was during the 1830s that this artistic ukase came under attack from a group of painters based at Barbizon, a village in the Forest of Fontainebleau. Inspired by English painting, particularly that of John Constable, they abandoned grandiose classical themes and began to produce straightforward representations of the French landscape and peasant life. Their notoriety was only boosted by the fact that these novel works were rejected during the 1830s and 1840s by Salon juries of academic complexion. Charles Gleyre's pupils became acquainted with the painting of the Barbizon School through Narcisse-Virgile Diaz de la Peña, whose style alerted Monet to the possibilities afforded

Fig. 1
CLAUDE MONET
The Train Engine in the Snow (Detail), 1875
Musée Marmottan, Paris

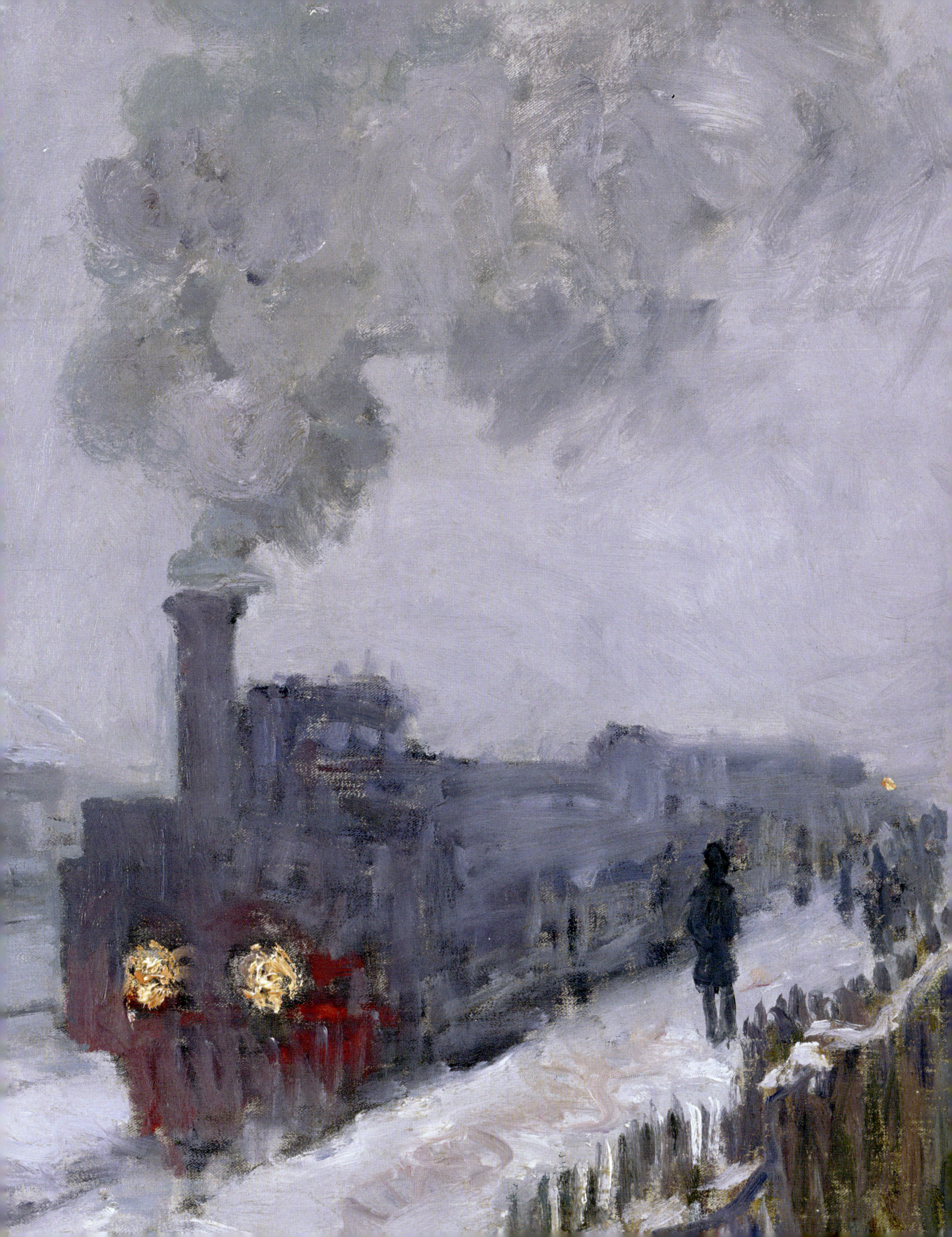

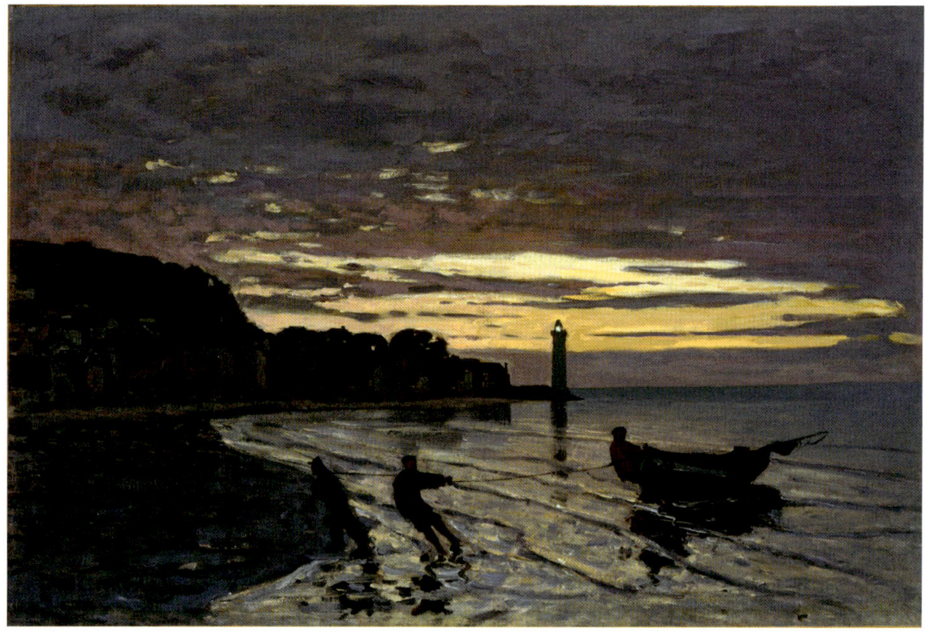

Fig. 2
CLAUDE MONET
Towing of a Boat at Honfleur, 1864
Memorial Art Gallery of the University of Rochester, New York

by highlights. Monet was lastingly impressed at the Salon of 1859 by the landscapes of Charles-François Daubigny, Théodore Rousseau, and Camille Corot, and especially fascinated by the sky in Constant Troyon's pictures. Although these painters, notably Corot and Honoré Daumier, were admired by Monet and his fellow pupils at Gleyre's studio, among them Frédéric Bazille, Pierre-Auguste Renoir, and Alfred Sisley, they themselves had little understanding of the art of their juniors. Monet was soon to transcend their conception of landscape painting. The direct approach to subjects that soon became typical of his pictures had been crucially influenced by his friendship with Johan Barthold Jongkind, whose works taught him to concentrate on essentials and ignore any details not required by the general context.

Although the young painters opposed the Salon's dictates in regard to taste, they were all tempted to win their spurs there. This was because, until well on into the nineteenth century, the Salon offered artists their only real chance of presenting new works to a wider audience. There were very few limited exhibitions and specialized dealers, so the Salon was the only real means of drawing attention to oneself and gaining a reputation. For that reason, all Monet's efforts in the early years were directed toward succeeding at the Salon. The jury of this almost annual exhibition was drawn from members of the Paris Académie des Beaux-Arts, who had always been mainly interested in history painting and successfully contrived to exclude other genres, above all those that could be termed "realistic."

There were, at the same time, plenty of attempts to break the stranglehold of official taste. At the 1855 Exhibition, Gustave Courbet, who could afford the expense, erected a pavilion of his own, "Le Réalisme," in front of the Pont de l'Alma. In 1863, in response to a storm of protest from countless artists rejected by the Salon selection committee,

Fig. 3
CLAUDE MONET
Seascape, Night Effect, 1864
Scottish National Gallery, Edinburgh

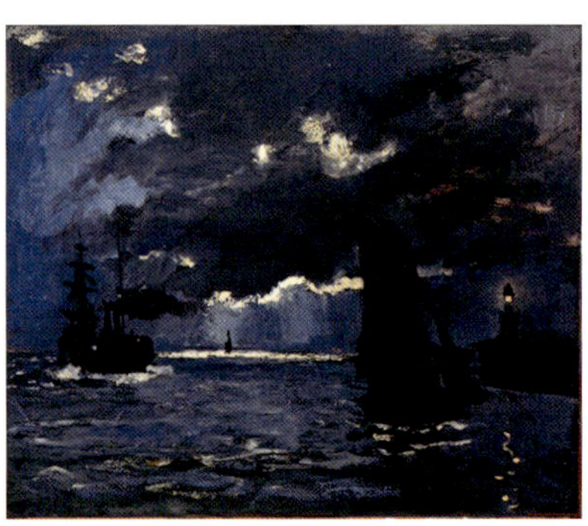

the Emperor, Napoleon III, allowed a "Salon des Refusés" to be held as an annex of the official Salon, so that members of the public could form their own opinion. The selection committee was also supplemented by some independent landscape painters such as Daubigny, Corot, and Troyon. A few years later, Manet and Courbet held exhibitions of their own, not only concurrently with the Exposition Universelle of 1867 but in open opposition to its organizers. In the same year, Monet and his youthful fellow painters appealed for a revival of the Salon des Refusés of 1863. In 1873 they had the idea of forming an artists' association of their own that would provide opportunities for showing their work without submitting it to a jury. The first show to be mounted by this group of independent painters, now celebrated as the first Impressionist exhibition, was held in 1874.

We have only to follow Monet's career during the 1860s to see how hard he strove for admission to the Salon. Works of his were shown there in 1865 and 1866, his submissions were rejected in 1867, only one of two works gained acceptance in 1868, and he was again rejected in 1869 and 1870. Thereafter he turned his back on the Salon and contributed to the Impressionist exhibitions of 1874, 1876, 1877, and 1879, which were organized as rival events. These shows were excoriated by the critics but aroused scant public interest and brought in very little money. In 1880, by which time he was in financial difficulties, Monet decided to try for the Salon once more—a course of action for which he was bitterly criticized by his fellow partisans of the *nouvelle peinture*. One of his two submissions was accepted but hung in a very bad position, even though he had deliberately selected works that were not too "modern."

But the greatest and most momentous influence on Monet as a young man was Manet. His encounter with the latter's work in 1863, initially at the Galerie Martinet but more importantly at the 'Salon des Refusés', which included Manet's *Luncheon on the Grass* (*Déjeuner sur l'herbe;* 1863), was, as Monet himself confided later, his artistic "road to Damascus" and "revelation."[4] In Manet's work he suddenly discerned the lessons to be drawn from Japanese woodcuts and their influence on modern painting. He claimed in later years that he had purchased his first Japanese woodcuts as a youth in Le Havre.[5] France had established diplomatic relations with Japan on October 9, 1858, so he may have come into contact with such works thereafter, but it is also conceivable that this statement was part of the elderly master's self-made image. Writing to Baudelaire in 1861, he mentioned that he had acquired some *japonneries* and distributed them among friends.[6] The first establishments in Paris to specialize in Japanese art opened the same year.

The off-center composition of Japanese woodcuts, their lack of spatiality and relief, their extreme simplification and stylization, their expressive linear strength, and, last but not least, the emphasis they placed on decorative planes of bright, fresh color, were features that impinged upon European painting at the very moment when it was seeking ways to renew itself.

Under the influence of Manet and the Japanese woodcut, Monet's palette, too, became distinctly brighter. He also realized more clearly than ever that color was his primary medium. Constant Troyon had recognized this strength in him when he first came to Paris as a very young man in search of advice. Monet was not, however, a draftsman par excellence, which is why many of his pictures lack the draftsman's rigor and "correctness."

Fig. 4
CLAUDE MONET
Luncheon on the Grass (central panel), 1865/66
Musée d'Orsay, Paris

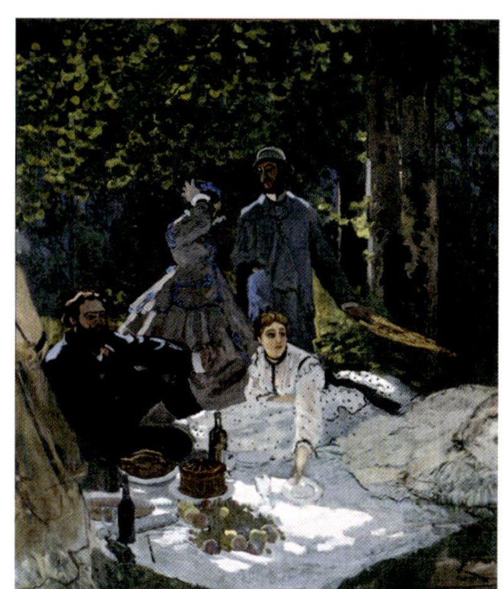

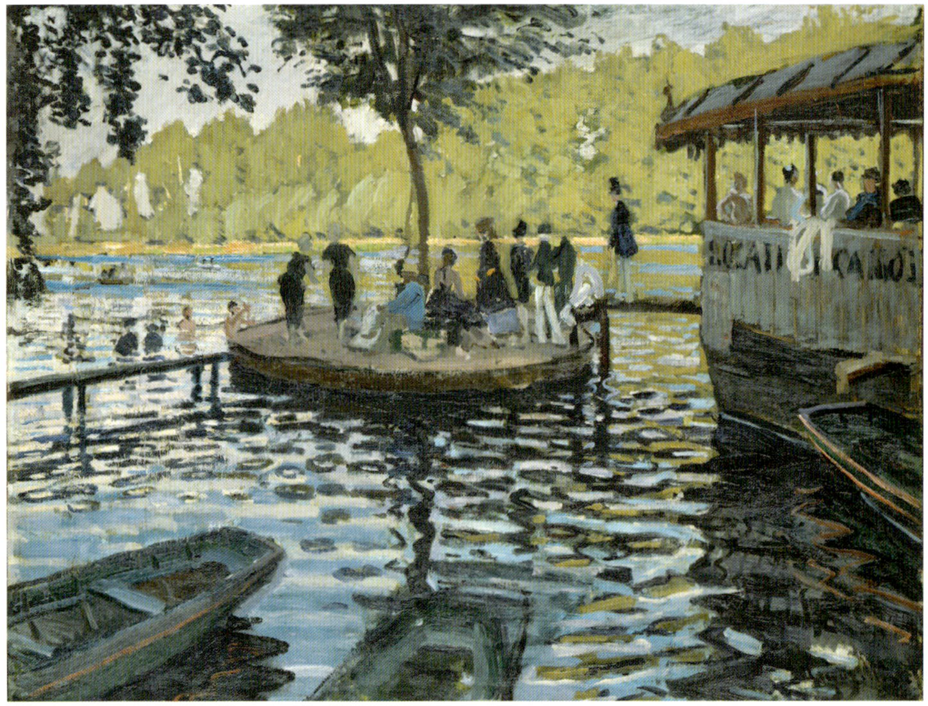

Fig. 5
CLAUDE MONET
La Grenouillère, 1869
The Metropolitan Museum of Art, New York

Monet wanted to pit himself against his great paragon by undertaking an ambitious project. Inspired by Manet's *Déjeuner sur l'herbe*, which had caused such an outcry in 1863, he planned to court attention with a large-scale painting which, though dealing with the same subject, would be wholly contemporary and up-to-date. He was particularly anxious to eliminate the gulf between art and life, painting and everyday experience, so the work had to depict a scene from daily life inhabited by people with whom he was personally acquainted. To that extent, he was more modern than Manet. Manet had liberated his palette by studying the Old Masters. Monet studied nature itself. Like Courbet (who also visited Monet's studio to inspect the progress of his work on *Le Déjeuner sur l'herbe*), Monet wanted to depict the visible alone, and to heighten its realism by exaggerating the picture's luminosity. To this end he made a series of *plein air* studies. When he came to carry these out in a life-size format, however, he had difficulty in projecting their freshness on to a canvas three or four times as big, which he found to have rules of its own. His response was to paint flatly and without detail, heightening the chromatic value of individual shades. He had learned from Eugène Delacroix, whose diaries he often consulted, that strong colors seen in shadow take on their complementary shades but never appear merely gray. Delacroix had also discovered that colors could be made more luminous by placing gradations of the same shade immediately next to them. Monet tried to observe these principles in his picture.

He never managed to finish it. Instead, on Courbet's advice, he submitted a portrait of his model and wife-to-be, Camille Doncieux, in a green dress, dashing off the picture within the space of a few days. He had perceived more clearly than ever that all painting entails transposition, the creation of something that is equivalent to what is seen but always subject to the picture's inherent laws. This realization also prompted him to transform his areas of shade into colored, sometimes brilliantly colored, areas, and to achieve his modeling by means of color—and, at the same time, to free himself from that requirement. No longer primarily to do with volume, his pictorial objects were clearly defined zones. The picture thus came more and more to be a decorative expanse structured by colors—something that was soon to provide a new generation of painters such as Vincent van Gogh and Paul Gauguin (to cite two conspicuous examples of its further development) with their essential medium of expression. As early as this, therefore, we can discern the incipient process whereby pictures threw off the demands of illusionism; the requirements of the canvas, as an expanse to be shaped and an aesthetic totality with laws of its own, became the pictorial problem. Monet had thus taken a step toward abstraction and, eventually, to the non-objective picture as reflected in his further development as a painter.

Monet's large-scale *Women in the Garden (Les femmes dans le jardin)* (1866/67), too, was painted entirely out of doors. Suspended over a trench dug specially for the purpose, it was rigged up in such a way that he could comfortably reach all parts of the canvas from a standing position.

Thereafter he began to paint scenes from city life, for example pictures of Saint-Germain-l'Auxerrois and the view across the Seine to Sainte-Geneviève, the later Panthéon, from the colonnade of the Louvre in 1867. But he concentrated more and more on landscape. He had always excluded history painting from personal consideration, but from now on genre scenes and portraits took a back seat as well. He confined himself to intimate friends or the family circle, as when he painted his young family in

Fig. 6
CLAUDE MONET
The Magpie, 1868/69
Musée d'Orsay, Paris

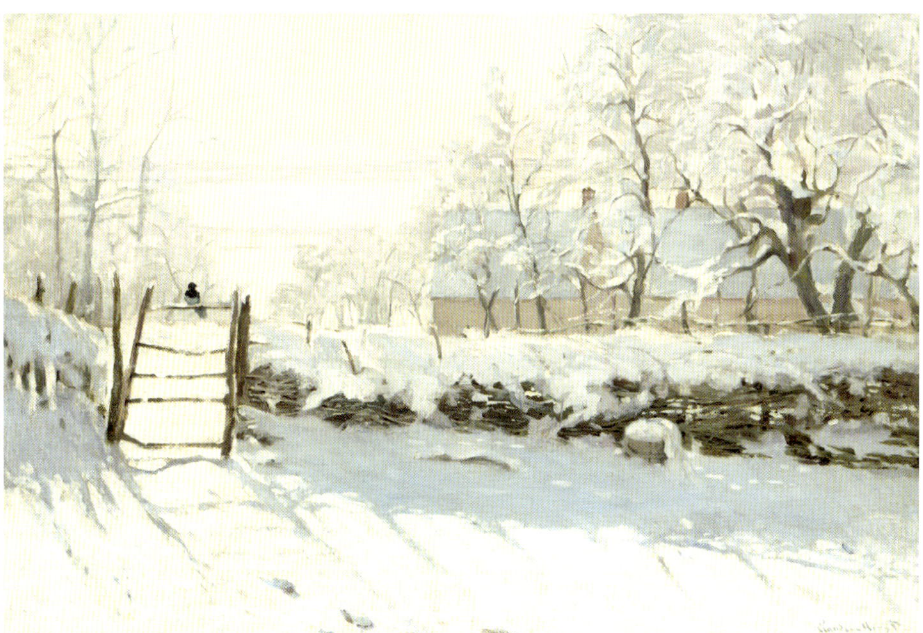

The Luncheon (Le Déjeuner) of 1868 (see fig. p. 157). Here, too, his aim was to convey what he actually perceived, to produce contemporary pictures drawn from personal experience. It was, in essence, his capturing of a particular moment in time that paved the way for Impressionism. He developed the requisite technical tool a year later, for the new pictorial language was born in the summer of 1869, when he and his friend Renoir were painting near Bougival. La Grenouillère was a well-known bathing place on the Seine downstream from there, and popular with oarsmen and canoeists as well. Monet and Renoir painted side by side, sometimes from the same viewpoint, and both dreamed of some day transposing their pictures on a monumental scale. In an unprecedented manner, these *plein air* paintings conveyed the *joie de vivre* of Parisians at leisure and the increasing popularity of the water sports to which Monet himself was addicted. But their most important feature consisted in the short, intermittent brushstrokes that were evenly distributed across the surface of the water and took precedence over details. These served mainly to render the light and reflections in the water, but they also began to encroach on other pictorial subjects such as figures. Light and shade, chromatically loud and soft, were closely juxtaposed in the shape of these brushstrokes. This gave rise a little later to the brushwork typical of Impressionism, which creates one shade out of many others. It followed that light, too, which was the main vehicle of this inimitable effect, had attained an importance hitherto unknown. Henceforth, in order to perfect his technique, Monet tried more and more often to meet the challenge presented by extremely difficult lighting conditions and delicate gradations of color, as in *The Magpie*, his unsuccessful submission to the Salon of 1869.

Working out of doors in all weathers became possible thanks to some revolutionary innovations in the field of artists' materials that had a lasting influence on the development of the *nouvelle peinture*.[7] Pre-grounded canvas was sold in London from the end of the eighteenth century and in Philadelphia and Boston from 1840 onwards. Machine-primed canvas ready-mounted on stretchers eventually became available in Europe. The collapsible tin tube was marketed in 1840 by the London firm of Robertson and a year later by Winsor & Newton. Invented by the American portrait painter John G. Rand, who lived in London and patented it in 1841, the tube delivered the painter at a stroke from all the problems posed by working out of doors with paints that had to be transported in cumbersome phials or bladders and prevented from drying out. In addition, the chemical industry offered a multitude of new shades, since many pigments could now be manufactured industrially. These abundant new paints were easy to mix, convenient to handle, and cheap into the bargain. Used in conjunction with equally inexpensive pre-primed canvases that rendered laborious grounding unnecessary, they bred an entirely novel love of experimentation on the part of painters. At the same time, the standardized dimensions of prepared canvases naturally dictated the format of the pictures painted on them and undoubtedly contributed to their framed view of the subject.

The Goncourt brothers had made the following demand of the *nouvelle peinture* a few years earlier: "There must be found a line that would precisely render life, embrace from close at hand the individual, the particular, a living, human, inward line."[8] Monet had already come very close to that ideal, but the new style would only develop to its fullest extent during his years at Argenteuil.

Fig. 7
CLAUDE MONET
The Train Engine in the Snow, 1875
Musée Marmottan, Paris

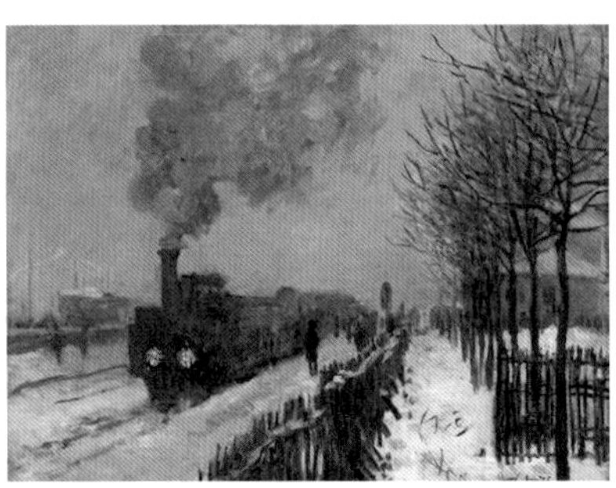

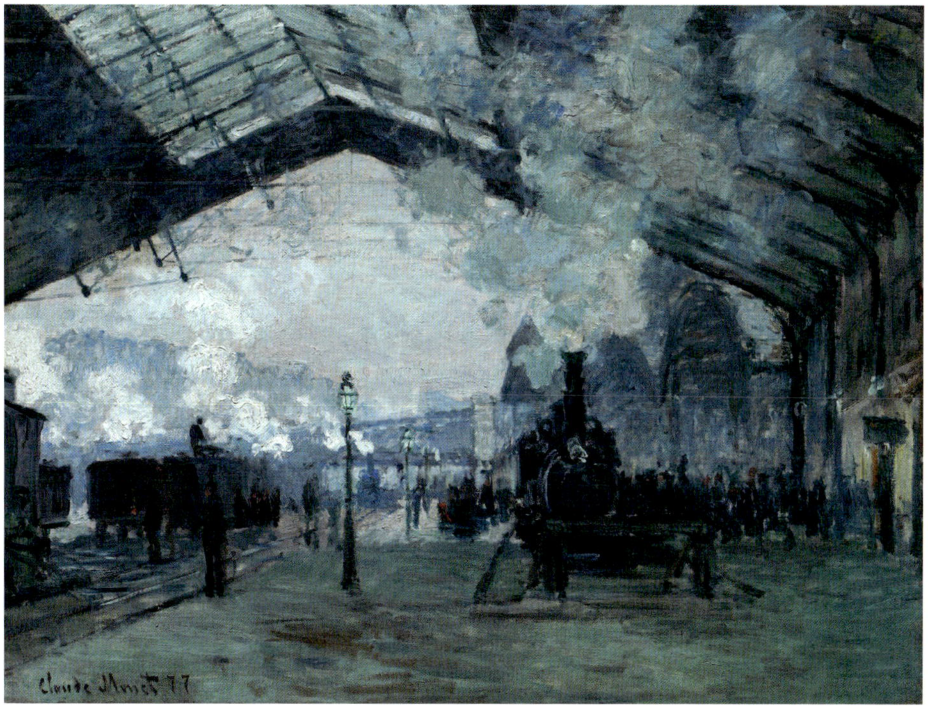

Fig. 8
CLAUDE MONET
Saint-Lazare Station, the Normandy Train, 1877
The Art Institute of Chicago

THE COMING OF IMPRESSIONISM

At the outbreak of the Franco-Prussian war in 1870 Monet and his family fled to London. Travelling via Holland he returned to France in 1871. At the end of the year Monet found himself an ideal place to live and work at Argenteuil, on the Seine, but retained a studio in Paris, only a short train ride away. His time at Argenteuil, during which he painted with a kind of carefree abandon, coincided with the few short years of true Impressionism in his œuvre. He applied himself once more to the rapid, open brushwork of Delacroix and continued, as he had already shown a fondness for doing in Holland, to observe transient phenomena and the effects of light on water. But he was more concerned than before to fix the general impression, especially of atmospheric effects, and to capture the ephemeral quality of everyday occurrences. His subjects were consistent with this. He painted railway bridges, locomotives steaming along and stations alive with movement, belching factory chimneys and bustling Parisian boulevards. They were all pursued with keen interest and treated as optical problems illustrated with reference to contemporary subjects, but without the slightest socio-political undertone. Monet also found many subjects of interest at Argenteuil itself. Understandably prominent among these, in addition to the environs of the little town, was the Seine with its boats, bridges and riverside walks, which he often painted while afloat, but he also produced family scenes inside the house, or, for choice, in his garden. Their instantaneous quality was always underscored by a markedly selective view of the subject and rapid, almost sketchy brushwork. The entire picture was subject to the dictates of time, not just its content.

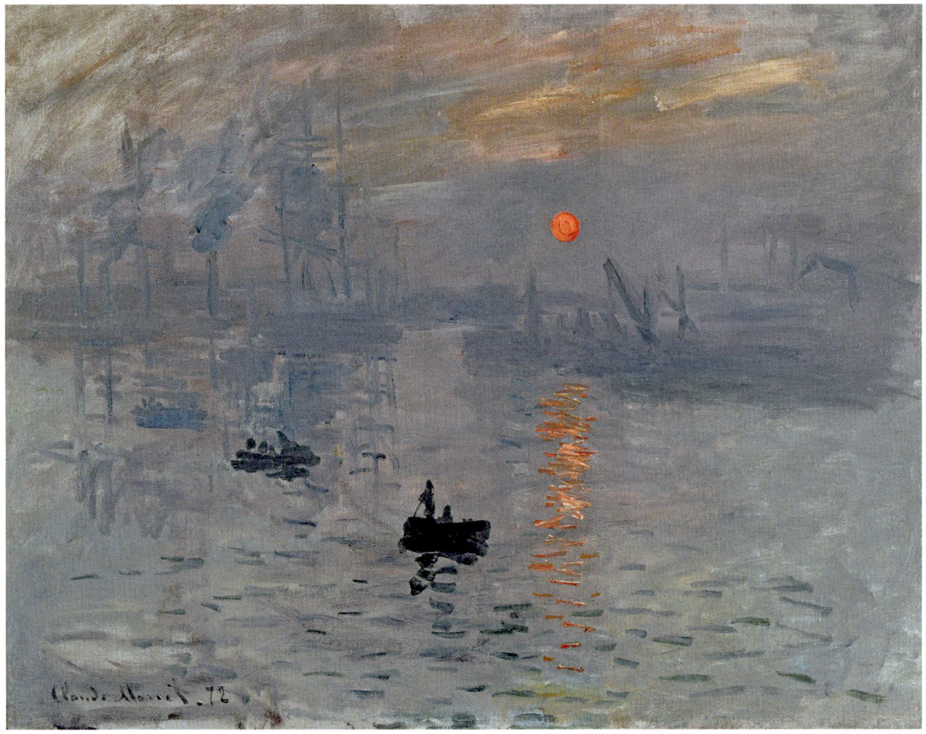

Fig. 9
CLAUDE MONET
Impression, Sunrise, 1873
Musée Marmottan, Paris

Monet's art began to embody what some, including Guy de Maupassant, termed the "new seeing," which, like someone aboard a moving train, glimpsed the landscape and its phenomena only in passing, in an instant.

This style, which manifested itself in 1873, for example in *Boulevard des Capucines*, suppressed detail with its open, dabbed brushwork, homogenized each individual form with strokes of color, and, since it had divorced itself from the precise shape of objects, merely conveyed their appearance in color. This abandonment of clear-cut outlines resulted in an entirely novel chromatic vibrancy and stressed the continuum of the picture's surface.

Baudelaire had spoken in 1863 of the speed of modern life and asserted that it called for similar speed in painting. In "Le peintre de la vie moderne," a three-part essay devoted to the painter and illustrator Constantin Guys and published by *Le Figaro* between November 26 and December 3, 1863, he encouraged painters to address contemporary subjects. "The new style," he stated, "is the transient, the fugitive, the fortuitous ... ."

The exponents of this kind of painting achieved a new, vital realism. In an endeavor to confine themselves to pure vision and free—or keep themselves free—from all prior knowledge, they made the visual process itself the subject of their pictures, not merely what they saw. No longer restricted to portrayals of clearly defined objects based on a knowledge of their nature, they conveyed their optical appearance on a canvas covered with a multitude of flecks of color. All they now trusted was the impression made on their eyes, a process that would later result in the dissolution of the pictorial subject. Cezanne's celebrated dictum "Monet is an eye, the most wonderful eye since painters have existed"[9] makes this precise point and proves how well the subsequent master of Aix had fathomed his friend's intentions. It was doubtless this awareness of his own visual process that accounted for Monet's love of painting reflections. To him, optical impression and reality were indistinguishable and laid claim to the same authenticity.

The reactions of the critics and general public in 1874, when the independent artists exhibited their work at 35 Boulevard des Capucines, premises once occupied by Nadar the photographer, are sufficiently well-known. There was a universal outcry, and the whole group—which included Renoir, Sisley, Edgar Degas, and Gustave Caillebotte as well as Monet—became the art world's "public enemies." Their contemporaries found the pictures on display unfinished and sketchy, and their subjects, which conveyed little of the sublimity that was currently *de rigueur*, were considered banal. The art critic Louis Leroy substantially helped to publicize the *nouvelle peinture* by presenting a sarcastic account of the show and labeling its participants "Impressionists" in a *Charivari* article published on April 25, and entitled "L'Exposition des Impressionnistes." Jules Castagnary's review of this first Impressionist exhibition, too, was subtitled "Les Impressionnistes"[10] and embodied the first definition of the new breed: "They are Impressionists insofar as they reproduce, not a landscape, but the impression a landscape evokes". The term "Impressionists" had been inspired by Monet's painting *Impression, Sunrise*. This means that Impressionism derived its name from a picture that may not only have been painted under the immediate impact of an effect but was also inspired by the work of James Abbott McNeill Whistler (and may also have been deliberately predated by Monet), for *Impression, Sunrise* is closely related to some views of the Thames painted by Whistler in 1872 and 1873. Although it embodies the motif of reflections in water so dear to Monet's heart at this period, its coloration is very subdued and conveys little of the luminosity found in other paintings of his.

Monet's view of landscape became more classical in his pictures of Vétheuil at the end of the 1870s, but his chromatic brilliance attained a new peak. He now painted shadows violet and enhanced the sumptuous luminosity of his shades by juxtaposing strong colors with short brushstrokes in such a way that objects were struck by light but also seemed partly to generate it from within. Completely abandoning tones weak in color, notably white and black, he stressed complementary colors in an almost exaggerated manner. His palette embraced few colors—white lead, cadmium yellow, vermilion, dark madder red, cobalt blue, and emerald green[11]—which he knew how to mix so as to produce any desired shade. Although like the other Impressionists he doubtless took account of the color theories of his time, these always played a secondary role for an artist whose use of color was essentially dependent on his precise observation of nature, and who could spend days merely contemplating and studying the effects of color and light. But immediacy was ever in the forefront of his concerns, and Georges Jeanniot records that he laid out his landscapes with a few swift strokes of "charcoal.[12] His lifelong preoccupation was color, and only in color could he express himself with confidence. 'I am very much at a loss how to answer you...', he once wrote in response to an inquiry about his drawings, 'since I always draw with brush and paint alone, and have always refused my best friends when they ask me to expose myself to a form of 'work of which I understand nothing.'"[13]

The full extent of this exposure to his extremely acute faculty of perception was abruptly

Fig. 10
CLAUDE MONET
The Rue Montorgueil, 30th of June 1878, 1878
Musée d'Orsay, Paris

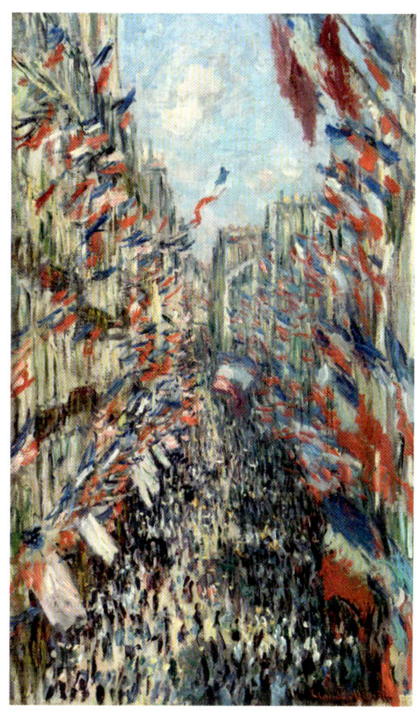

borne in on him beside the deathbed of his wife Camille: "[. . .] one day, finding myself at the deathbed of a woman who had been and was still very dear to me, I caught myself, with my eyes focused on her tragic temples, in the act of automatically searching for the succession, the arrangement of colored gradations that death was imposing on her motionless face. Blue, yellow, grey tones, who knows what else? That was the point I had reached. Nothing is more natural than the urge to record one last image of a person departing this life. But even before I had the idea of recording those features to which I was so profoundly attached, my organism was already reacting to the color sensations, and, in spite of myself, I was being involved by my reflexes in an unconscious process in which I was resuming 'the course of my daily life.'"[14]

THE 1880S
INTERPRETING THE VISIBLE

In the course of the 1880s, during which Pierre-Auguste Renoir reverted to firmly constructed, clearly defined forms, and Camille Pissarro, under the influence of Georges Seurat's Neo-Impressionism, began to flirt with the theory of divisionism and the use of pure, spectral colors, Monet's work, too, underwent a perceptible change. He was still closely tied to his subjects, with which he often sought to familiarize himself for considerable periods, and whose supervening changes sometimes prompted him to stop work, for example on two pictures of an apple tree whose fruit had been picked from one day to the next. But he stressed, in a lengthy interview published in *Gil Blas* on March 3, 1889, that a landscape's integument (*enveloppé*) of pulsating, colored light was more important to him than its concrete and objective constitution. He later expressed himself more trenchantly still: "To me, the subject is a secondary matter; what I wish to render is what is between the 'subject and myself.'"[15]

Monet strove ever harder to finish pictures at a stroke but was more and more often compelled to abandon unfinished canvases because the weather had changed too greatly.[16] At the same time, his letters more and more often liken his efforts to "struggling" and "attempting the impossible."[17]

What had happened? As Monet himself admitted, he had increasingly lost the ability to finish a picture at a stroke and leave the unique result as it stood. He now sought ever more specific effects, ever briefer moments of *instantanéité*. This necessitated working on several pictures at once and resuming work on them when the same effect returned for a short space of time. It was a concomitant of this that he more and more often finished pictures in the studio, as he had already done at Vétheuil despite his claim to be a purely *plein air* painter. His chosen light effects were so short-lived and the phenomena to be captured so ephemeral that they could not be fully rendered in one or even several on-the-spot sessions. He returned from Étretat, for example, with two dozen canvases at the end of February 1883 and fifty in 1885. On Belle-Île in 1886 he painted forty unfinished pictures that merely captured his impressions. This did, however, give him the chance to harmonize them as a group in terms of coloration.

Although the periods of time on which his effects were based grew ever shorter (and this would apply with special force to the series of the 1890s), his pictures made a less and less cursory impression; not hurriedly dashed off, they were calmly constructed and

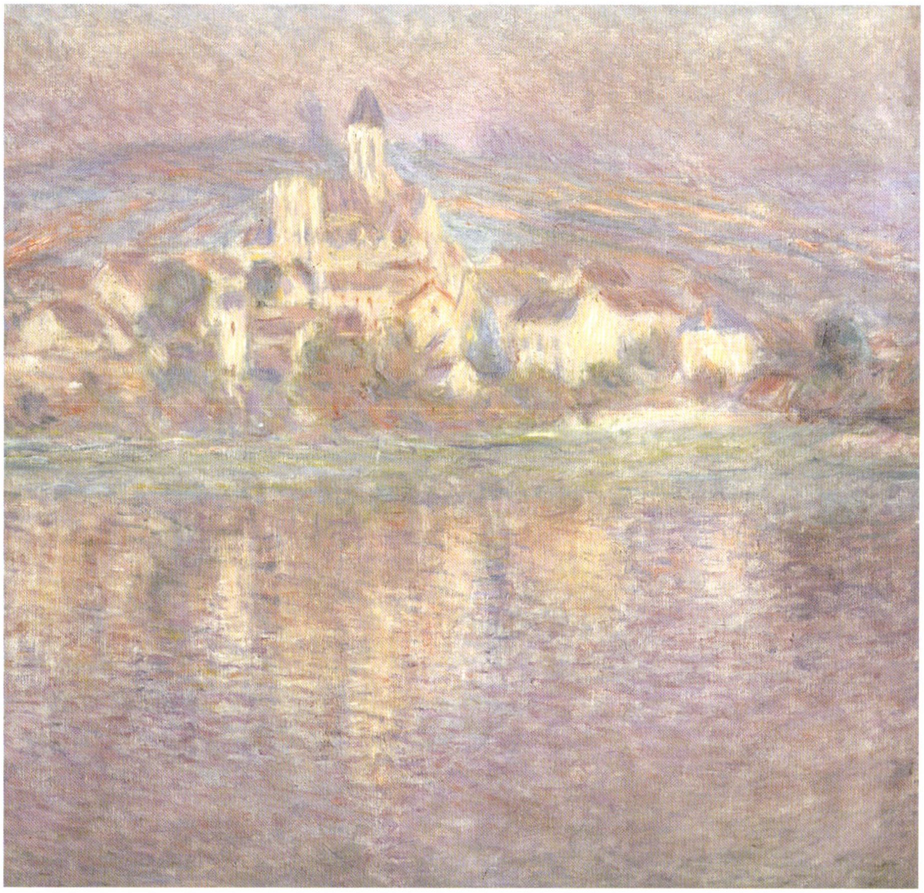

Fig. 11
CLAUDE MONET
Vétheuil, at Sunset, 1901
Musée d'Orsay, Paris

seemed to glow with splendid color effects. His struggle with time had taken on a sudden virulence, as had his struggle—not that Monet the agnostic ever voiced this—with his experience of finality, his inability to capture and hold the reality he perceived as being more and more diverse. This was the logical consequence of his form of painting, which aspired to depend solely on the visible, and thus, given the mutability of outward appearances, had to confine itself to ever shorter spaces of time. Monet's letters are eloquent of this: time was forever running away with him; the results he achieved were never sufficiently quick or valid.

His activities during these years resemble a never-ending pilgrimage, a quest for new challenges and sensations such as he found in the southern sunlight of the Mediterranean coast, the fascinating coloration of the Atlantic off Belle-Île, or the amazing diversity of snow effects in Norway. These trips were like voyages of visual exploration designed to stimulate the further development of his work. He was forever eager to discover if this or that could be recorded, this or that effect captured on canvas. Often enough it could not, hence his letters complaining that he was on the track of the impossible. Reality was always too big, always too impossibly diverse, complex, and magnificent. He could only strive, in accordance with arcane laws and harmonies, for a visual parable, an equivalent, and employ this within the autonomous framework of a picture.

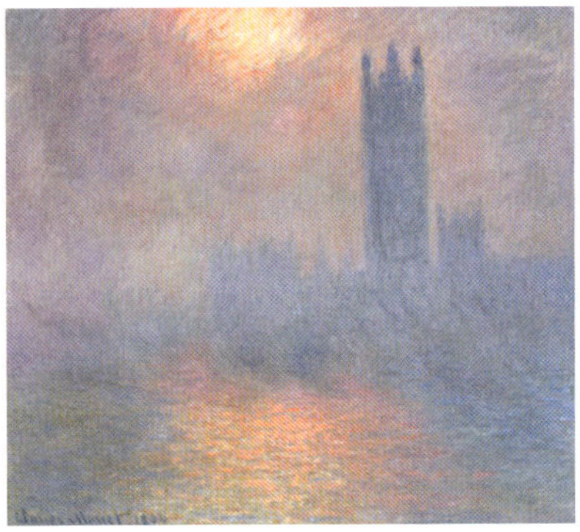

Fig. 12
CLAUDE MONET
Houses of Parliament, Effect of Sunlight in the Fog, 1904
Musée d'Orsay, Paris

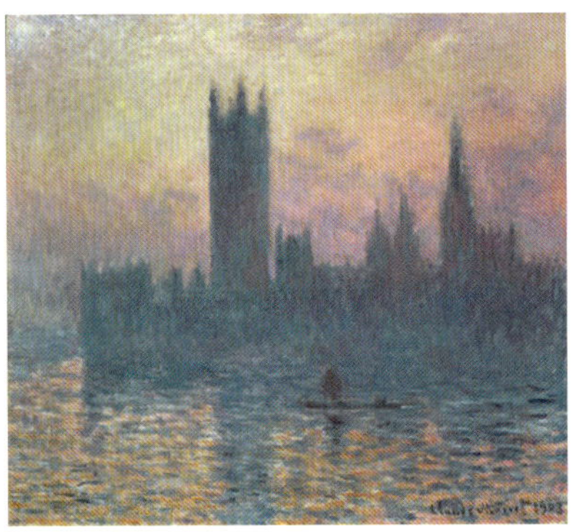

Fig. 13
CLAUDE MONET
Houses of Parliament, Sunset, 1903
National Gallery of Art, Washington, D.C.

Such must have been the basis of Monet's admiration for Cézanne, an emotion so intense that he shunned direct comparison and did not wish his pictures to be exhibited next to those of the master from Aix for fear they would fail to hold their own.[18] He suspected that Cézanne, who had spoken of art as "a harmony parallel to nature,"[19] had come closer to his own intentions and to the essence of things. Cézanne, too, had been painfully affected by this realization: "I wanted to copy nature, but I couldn't. But I was content with myself when I discovered that the sun cannot be rendered and must always be represented by something else... by means of paint."[20] Renoir and Monet had visited Cézanne at L'Estaque in 1883, and his modern pictorial approach undoubtedly provided Monet with food for thought. But Monet's pictures of the mid-1880s—and his views of the Mediterranean coast in particular—also betray compositional resemblances to works by Cézanne.

Whereas Monet's pictures up to and including the Argenteuil years had recorded modern life, attaining a notable zenith in his views of the Gare Saint-Lazare, this aspect entirely disappeared from his work thereafter. He was now interested in inherently pictorial problems, and the importance of his subjects waned. Aids to pictorial expression—color especially—thrust their way into the foreground. In the 1890s series, subjects in general become little more than a vehicle for the varied treatment of chromatic modulations and relationships in a whole set of pictures. It is this detachment from reality, this mental preoccupation with pure painting, that constitutes Monet's great modernity—a feature that set him and Cézanne apart from their contemporaries, albeit in the form of antipodes. Whereas Cézanne sought to divest appearances of their transience, used abstraction and persistent compression to attain validity, timelessness, and inner solidity, and subordinated the entire picture to a crystalline structure in his attempt to approach the essence of nature, Monet increasingly dissolved his subjects into pure color.

GENESIS OF THE SERIAL CONCEPT

Monet often complained during the 1890s that he had become too slow and could no longer paint with the freshness and carefree abandon of youth. He used to complete pictures at a stroke, he told William Fuller, "but now, I am more exacting, and it takes a long time for me to finish a picture."[21] This, as we have already mentioned, was because, in attempting to capture the instantaneous, he was enabled by the constant training of his eye to detect more and more variations and nuances and reduce a moment's work to half an hour or a few minutes only. Monet's genius consisted in his ability to discern minute differences between atmospheric effects and translate them into pictures that represented a unique moment in time. It was inevitable that the urge to capture transitory changes, together with their potentially endless series of intermediate stages and modulations, should become an obsession with him.

So Monet was forever switching canvases, pulling one out when the sun appeared and exchanging it for another when the sky clouded over, and so on. The groups of pictures he painted at Pourville and Belle-Île in the 1880s evidence a loose progression from picture to picture dictated by changes in the light—a to-ing and fro-ing, even between different subjects—whereas in series like the *Cathedrals of Rouen* (1892/94) Monet developed a regular working schedule that spanned the day and divided it, so to speak, into segments.

Monet had already reproduced different lighting conditions in his two versions of the *Boulevard des Capucines* (1873) and his four views of the *Quai du Louvre* (1876). In 1882 he had spoken of series in connection with his views of the coastguard's cottage at Petit-Ailly, near Pourville. The painters of the Barbizon School and Jongkind had decades earlier painted variations on the same theme at different times of day and Boudin had studied different light and cloud effects. Now, however, possibly under the influence of Japanese woodcuts, which could also depict a series of different aspects of the same subject, for example Hokusai's *Thirty-six views of Mount Fuji* (ca. 1830; or his three-volume work *Hundred Views of Mount Fuji*, 1834/35), Monet evolved the idea of continuous pictorial series that would render the effects of light on one and the same subject. His message could not now be conveyed in its entirety by one single picture, only by the interrelationship of several pictures and the way they complemented each other. All these series were finished off in the studio. Nature furnished the ideas that were cursorily sketched *in situ*, but the paintings themselves were almost always executed in the studio, where they were compared with an eye to their effect as an ensemble. In this way, they increasingly became subtle chromatic modulations, and Monet took to calling them by their color effects, for example *harmonie bleue*, *harmonie grise*, and so on. Originally conceived as segments of a continuous process of observation—as "'snapshots" taken after Monet's disconcerting experience with the wheatstack he had wished to

Fig. 14
CLAUDE MONET
Houses of Parliament, Sunset, 1904
Kunstmuseen Krefeld

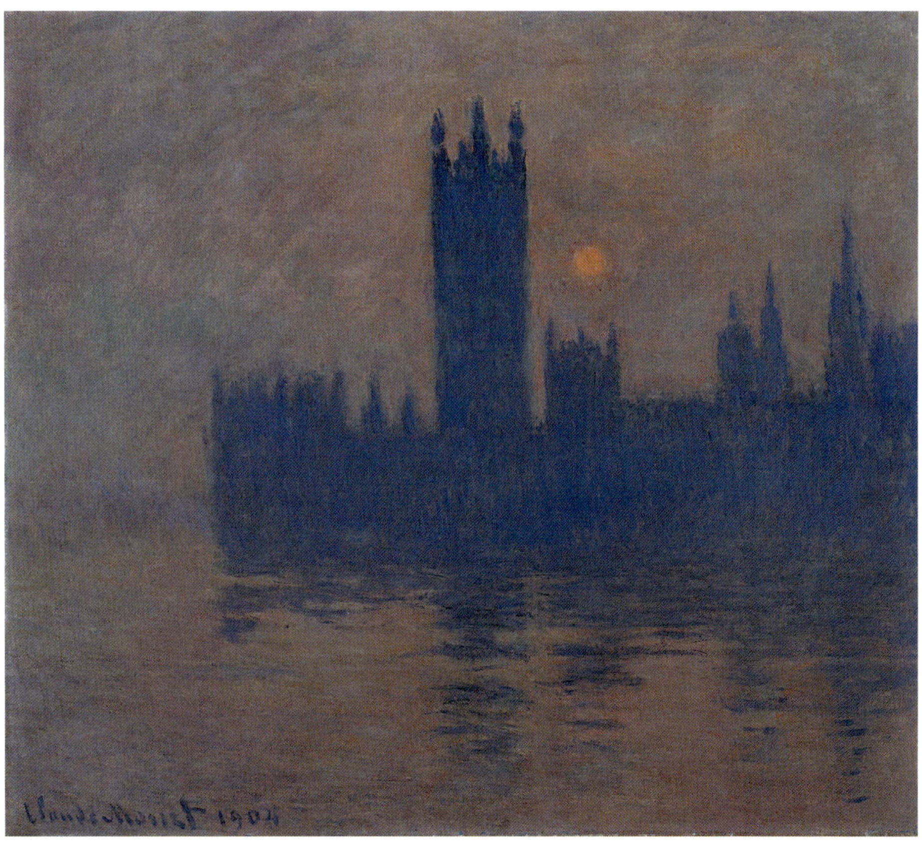

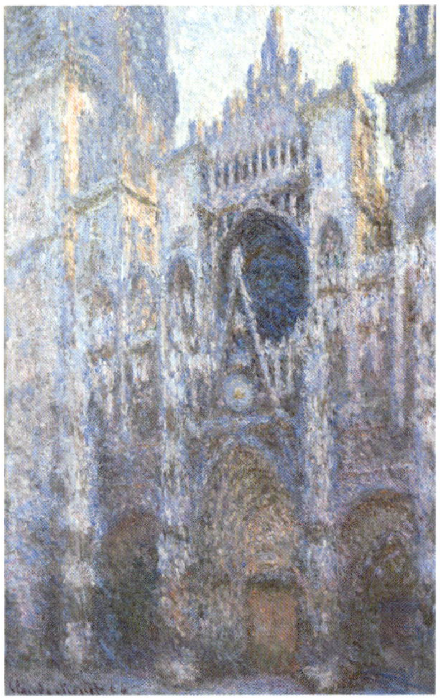

Fig. 15
CLAUDE MONET
Rouen Cathedral, West Façade, 1894
National Gallery of Art, Washington, D.C.

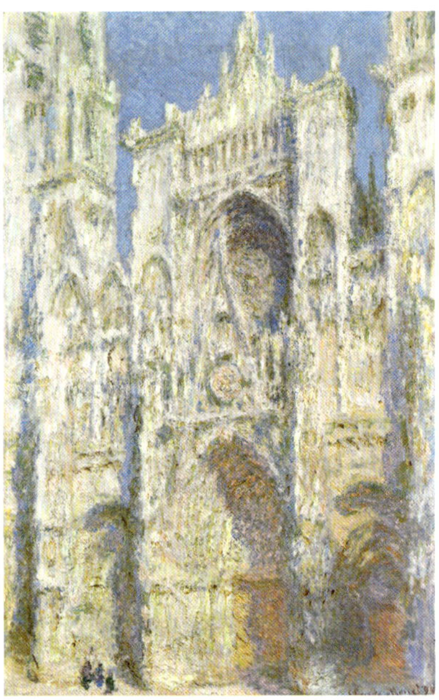

Fig. 16
CLAUDE MONET
Rouen Cathedral, West Façade, Sunlight, 1894
National Gallery of Art, Washington, D.C.

paint, only to find, after a brief interval, that its appearance had undergone a change—they soon became parts of a large decorative ensemble. It was in the harmonization of its component parts that the series attained its full coloristic subtlety. That was why Monet limited their number and included only those pictures that precisely contributed to the general impression he sought. Again and again he insisted to dealers who wished to sell them separately that there was no point in exhibiting them on their own; only as parts of an ensemble would they attain their full validity and produce an effect that transcended their individual appearance. "Anyway," he wrote to Paul Durand-Ruel, "it would be very bad to show so little of this new series, since the full effect can only be achieved by exhibiting all the pictures that belong together. Besides, I need to be able to see the things I've finished, so that I can compare them with the ones I'm working on."[22] This is what constitutes the nature of "genuine" series and helps to differentiate them from the many other groups of works in Monet's œuvre that depict the same subject at different seasons of the year or times of day.

In terms of aesthetic intention, however, this also divorced the series from nature. Monet had previously referred in his letters of 1882 to the autonomy of art in its quest for ensemble effects; now, he had clearly drawn the relevant conclusions. In his paintings of Rouen Cathedral, if not before, he demonstrated the artificiality of this proceeding and its detachment from the subject in nature, but also from the Impressionist approach. These pictures relate less to natural impressions than to each other, produce new effects in response to others already painted, and offer reflections on reflections already engaged in.

The foggy landscapes of London presented Monet with a comprehensive opportunity to dissolve his subjects and diversify them in orgies of color, as Turner had done before him. He had, after all, spoken to Theodore Robinson in 1892 of his admiration for Turner's *Rain, Steam and Speed* in London's National Gallery.[23] But, even though he derived his original inspiration from the manifold effects of fog, the creative process gained autonomy while he was finishing his pictures in the studio: "It's essential for me to have them all before me[. . .) I'm developing them all together, or at least a certain number," he wrote to Durand-Ruel in March 1905.[24] In the same year he bluntly informed his dealer: "I still have to deliver you a *Waterloo Bridge*, which will be useful to me in the future, so that afterwards I can do another with mist, the way they wanted."[25] Again, on September 17, 1912 he asked Durand-Ruel to return two pictures of the Doges' Palace because he needed them in order to complete a third version.

Paul Hayes Tucker has pointed out that Monet used to meet Joris-Karl Huysmans and Stéphane Mallarmé at the monthly Café Riche dinners from the mid-1880s onwards, and that he soon became friendly with the latter.[26] Mallarmé's love of the mysterious, particularly his belief that things can never be truly comprehended and described, only suggested, may well have left its mark on Monet. Conversely, Mallarmé was an admirer of Monet's painting in the 1990s and wrote an account of its de-materializing depictions of light. We should not, however, impute a Symbolist background to Monet's art. He was in search of color equivalents for light and ways of mutually intensifying chromatic effects.

Monet was at pains throughout his life to represent himself as a plein air painter. In an interview with Emile Taboureux in 1880 he tried to pose as a pure Impressionist who never worked indoors, even though this was already his established practice. When

Taboureux asked to see his studio, he replied: "My studio? I've never had a studio, nor, personally, can I understand why anyone would wish to shut himself up in a room. To draw, yes, perhaps, but not to paint." And a little later, in the course of conversation: "I'm still an Impressionist and will always be one."[27] Similarly, Monet still claimed never to touch any of his pictures in the studio during an interview with Georges Jeanniot, who used it as the basis of an article that appeared in *La Cravache parisienne* on June 25, 1888. Monet was correspondingly nettled by accusations that he painted from photographs, a procedure wholly inconsistent with the image he wished to convey. In 1905, for example, the painters Sir William Rothenstein and Lawrence Alexander Harrison, friends of John Singer Sargent, mentioned to Paul Durand-Ruel after a visit at the Grafton Gallery in London that Monet had painted the Rouen Cathedral from a photograph.[28] Monet's effects, which are now preserved in Paris by the Musée Marmottan, do in fact include a photograph that may possibly have served him as an aide-mémoire while developing the series in his studio at Giverny. On the same occasion Harrison insisted to Durand-Ruel that Monet had probably also done the London pictures from photographs, because the painter had asked him for some shots of the Houses of Parliament and the Thames bridges. Monet fiercely resented this imputation approached by the worried art-dealer. He did, however, concede that he had obtained a photograph of the Parliament buildings through Sargent, presumably as a guide for use when completing the series at Giverny. "Dear Monsieur Durand," he wrote to the dealer, "you're wrong to be alarmed by the matters of which you tell me. They simply betoken malice and envy, and leave me entirely cold [...] I know Mr Harrison, whom Sargent asked to get me a small photograph of Parliament which I was never able to use. But that means little, and whether or not my 'Cathedrals', my 'Londons' and other paintings are done from nature is nobody's business and of no importance. I know plenty of painters who paint from nature and turn out nothing but monstrosities."[29]

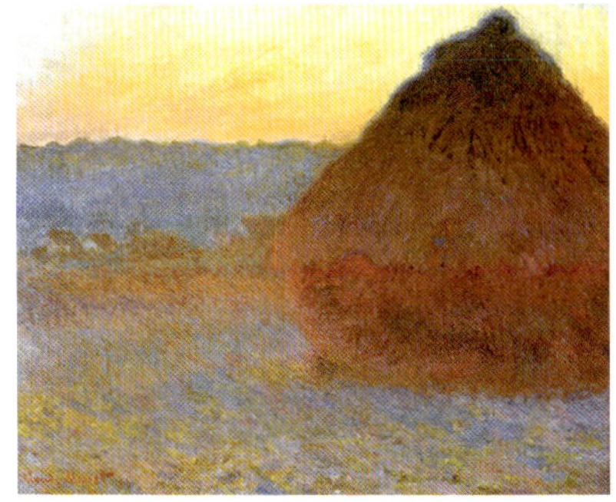

Fig. 17
CLAUDE MONET
Grainstack, 1891
Private collection

One can nonetheless cite instances, very early on, where Monet employed photographs as references or used them more than once to work out details in various pictures. Also among his effects, for example, is a photograph of a sailing boat with a sailing ship entering port beyond it, which undoubtedly served as a reference for the similar vessels in *The Jetty of Le Havre in Bad Weather* (1867). *Seascape: Storm* (1866/67) and *Entrance to the Harbour at Honfleur* (1867) may also have been painted after a similar photograph or preliminary study that was subsequently used for two different pictures. In later years Monet also liked to stress his self-taught independence and play down his periods of training under Boudin and, more especially, Gleyre.

Fig. 18
CLAUDE MONET
Poplars on the Banks of the River Epte, Overcast Weather, 1891
Private collection

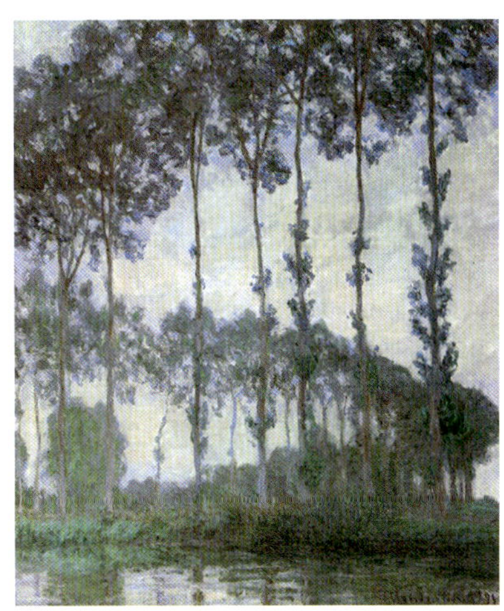

All in all, the serial concept signified a departure from tradition and represented a wholly modem idea that has retained its appeal in the art of the present day. The subject is made to disappear, because what matters is not the subject itself but the effects exerted on it and their various manifestations. At the same time, the subject is dissolved by the nature of the picture, which presents a chromatic effect rather than a clearly defined structure. Monet said as much to Willem Geertrudus Cornelis Byvanck, the Dutch art critic, who had approached him during the exhibition at Durand-Ruel's, which included fifteen of his "Wheatstacks": "To me, a landscape does not exist as a landscape, because its appearance changes moment by moment; it lives in accordance with its surroundings, with air and light, which are forever changing."[30] Monet was no longer interested in the

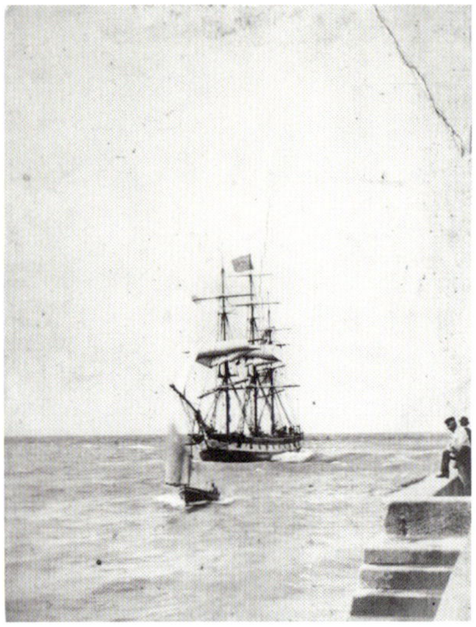

Fig. 19
JEAN-VICTOR WARNOD-MACAIRE (?)
Windjammer near Le Havre, ca. 1866

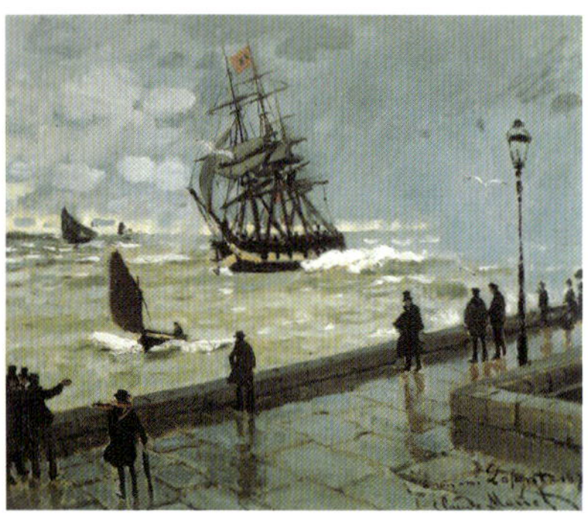

Fig. 20
CLAUDE MONET
The Jetty at Le Havre in Rough Weather, 1867
Private collection

subject per se, but in how it looked in the atmosphere, in its appearance in light and air. That was how his series became a route to abstraction, to an entirely novel conception of the picture and a new freedom in the use of his materials. Kandinsky had fully grasped this insignificance of the subject while studying a 'Wheatstack' of Monet's: "And suddenly, for the first time, I saw a *picture*. The catalogue informed me that it was a haystack. I could not recognize it myself, and this non-recognition disconcerted me. I also felt that a painter had no right to paint so indistinctly. I vaguely sensed that the subject of the picture was missing... What was entirely clear to me, however, was the unsuspected strength of the palette, which had previously been concealed from me and surpassed all my dreams. The painting acquired a magical strength and splendor. But, not that I realized it, the subject had also been discredited as an inescapable element in the picture."[31]

Monet seems, for all that, to have sensed the limits of an art in which the subject is gradually dissolved. A letter dated November 1891 mentions his desire to paint, as a product of his popular pictures, one that would be the condensation of all the rest and tied no longer to a specific time or particular weather conditions.[32] Thus, from the mid-1890s, he reverted to earlier subjects and tested his inspiration on what had previously stimulated him. But he was no longer capable of producing a single, incisive picture; instead, he continued to paint soft chromatic harmonies whose effect was to lose the subject (see fig. p. 21).

THE DREAM-WORLD OF THE WATER LANDSCAPES

From the 1880s onwards, one is struck by an incipient decline in the importance attached to the pictorial framework, the topographical definition of the beholder's viewpoint, and the spatial depth conveyed by linear or chromatic perspective. Already evident in works such as *Anglers on the Seine at Poissy* (1882; see p. 161), this becomes still more noticeable in the coastal views of Belle-Île (1882) or in the depictions of the *Rouen Cathedral* and fully manifests itself in 1897, not only in some extremely close-framed paintings of chrysanthemums seen as if from above and devoid of stems and perspective, but in Monet's first water lily pictures from the same year. These pictures began to sever their links with the beholder and present "borderless" views of a homogeneous, potentially infinite expanse, thereby depriving the beholder of an opportunity to get his bearings.

At the same time, they intensified the picture's character as a surface structured by means of color. But they also make it clear that Monet's painting during these years was ultimately becoming a form of detached observation. They remain independent of us; the totally horizonless works that succeeded the water lily pictures of 1905 ceased to be "accessible" and became pure visual impression and chromatic charm. Ever more sparsely populated, Monet's paintings finally dispensed with the human figure altogether. (It was consistent with this that, when invited to choose from a hundred photographic views of Norway during his stay there, he picked out some monochrome photographs of the rugged, impressive landscape, almost all of them entirely deserted. Anecdotal painting did not interest him, and the same applied largely to genre painting except in relation to his family.) The world thus created was highly subjective and only marginally related to objective reality. This withdrawal into an inner world, an autonomous region of harmony, is exemplified with particular clarity by the *Mornings on the Seine* series (1897) and became the true essence of Monet's art in his water-lilies and water landscapes. His treatment of color, too, is relevant. Already dominant in the late 1880s, and, more particularly, in the 1890s, are pale gradations, soft nuances, and over-subtle chromatic modulations; there are no loud notes—everything is gauzy, dreamlike, quietly contemplative. Monet projected the quest for chromatic harmonies on to his natural surroundings. The preoccupation with his garden was an essential part of this process, for there he found aimless, prodigal beauty, colors in a thousand variations, and the quasi two-dimensional vibrancy of the pure chromatic values present in a sea of flowers.

It had already been hard to tell reality from reflection in some of Monet's poplar pictures—they could be inverted without forfeiting their power of expression—and in 'Mornings on the Seine' this became a theme on which he played many variations.

Finally, in the water lily paintings, the levels of perception and reality became blurred, grass and plants below the surface were indistinguishable from the reflections of the willow trees above, and reflections could be mistaken for what they reflected.

In 1903, after some preliminary experiments in 1897, Monet had begun to paint the

Fig. 21
CLAUDE MONET
Water-Lilies, Green Harmony, 1899
Musée d'Orsay, Paris

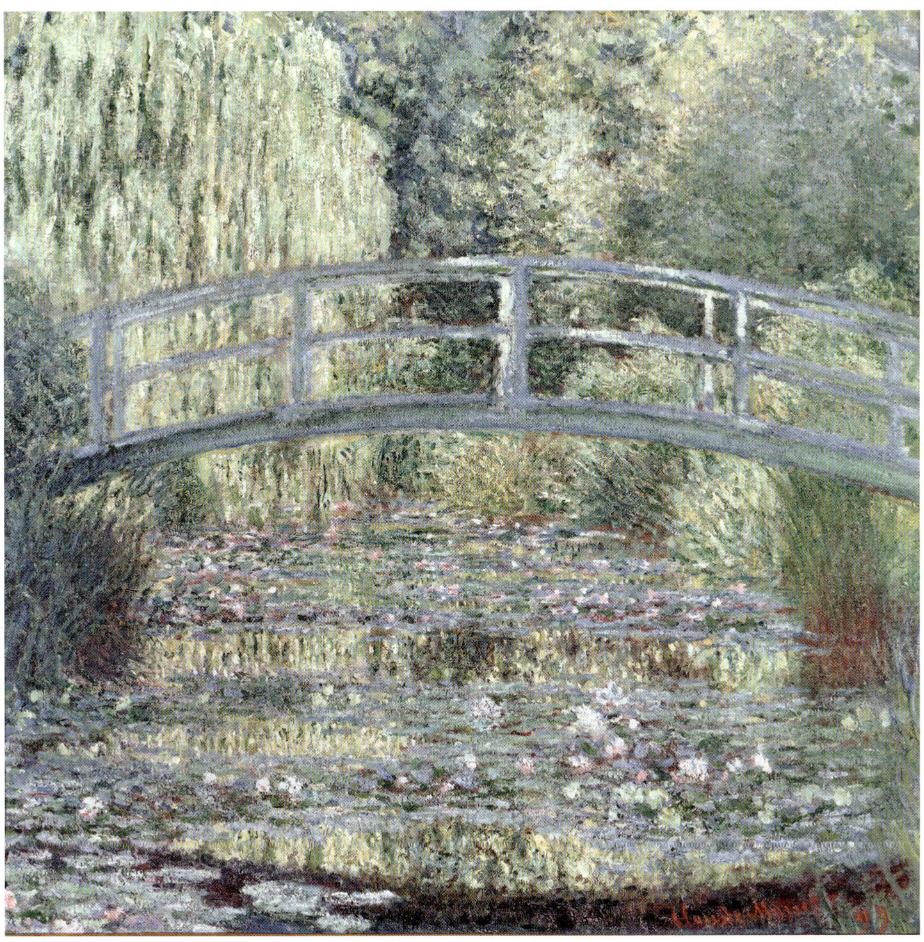

water-lilies on his enlarged pond. They were to be his only subject from now on. "I want you to know", he wrote to Geffroy in 1908, "that I'm wholly engrossed in my work. The landscapes of water and reflections have become an obsession. It exceeds an old man's strength, but I should like, for all that, to reach the stage at which I can reproduce what I feel. Some I've destroyed [...) and some I'm starting again [...] and hope that something will come of such exertions."[33] His years of work produced several large series which were shown at the Galerie Durand-Ruel in May and June 1909. The critics were enthusiastic, but some complained that these series were to be dispersed after the exhibition instead of permanently adorning a room in the form of an ensemble. This may have rekindled Monet's long-cherished desire to decorate an entire room with water-lily motifs—an idea that had often cropped up in conversation since 1897 but had never truly materialized. Even now it was to be quite a while before the idea assumed visible shape, for, quite apart from strokes of ill fortune like the deaths of his wife Alice and his son Jean, Monet was worried about his steadily deteriorating eyesight. "I was engaged on them [water-lilies and reflections in water] for eight or nine solid years," he told François Thiébault-Sisson, "and then I suddenly stopped in a panic [...] I no longer saw colors with the same intensity, I did not paint light as true to nature. Red shades seemed to me dirty, pink shades dull, and intermediate or darker shades eluded me altogether. As for shapes, I could still see them just as clearly and recorded them with the same precision. At first I steadfastly tried to cling to them. How often did I linger for hours near the little bridge [...] forced myself to resume my interrupted work and rediscover the freshness that had vanished from my palette! A vain effort. I painted more and more somberly, more and more in the manner of 'old paintings,' and when I compared my finished attempt with earlier works I was overcome with fury and cut up all my canvases with a pocket-knife [...] But there came a day, a blessed day, when I seemed to sense that the illness was temporarily in abeyance. I undertook a series of experiments aimed solely at showing me the limits and potentialities of my eyesight, and was overjoyed to discover that, although I was insensitive to the subtleties and modulations of colors at very close range, my eyes did not, at least, deceive me when I stepped back and surveyed the subject as a whole—and that was how I started on the compositions you will see in my studio."[34]

Monet's physical condition had suddenly prompted him to work on a large scale. By the end of 1914 he was painting away at his water-lily decorations like a man possessed, maintaining an incredible work-rate for someone of his age. He painted with long, sweeping movements, using broad brushes on canvases two meters high and up to eight meters in length—canvases so large that he had a studio measuring 23 by 12 meters built to accommodate them. Having spent the summer months making large-scale preliminary studies to be freely transferred to the large panels, he then created the ensemble from memory, drawing on the rich inner world of his own visual experience. These water lily decorations undoubtedly represented a development of the nineteenth-century panorama concept. Although a compromise dictated that the rooms that now house them in the Orangerie of the Jardin des Tuileries were oval, Monet's ideal would have been a circular chamber in which the beholder felt he was standing on an island in the middle of the lily pond. The water-lily decorations were an endeavor to translate his dream of the *enveloppé* into a grand, all-encompassing wall of color.

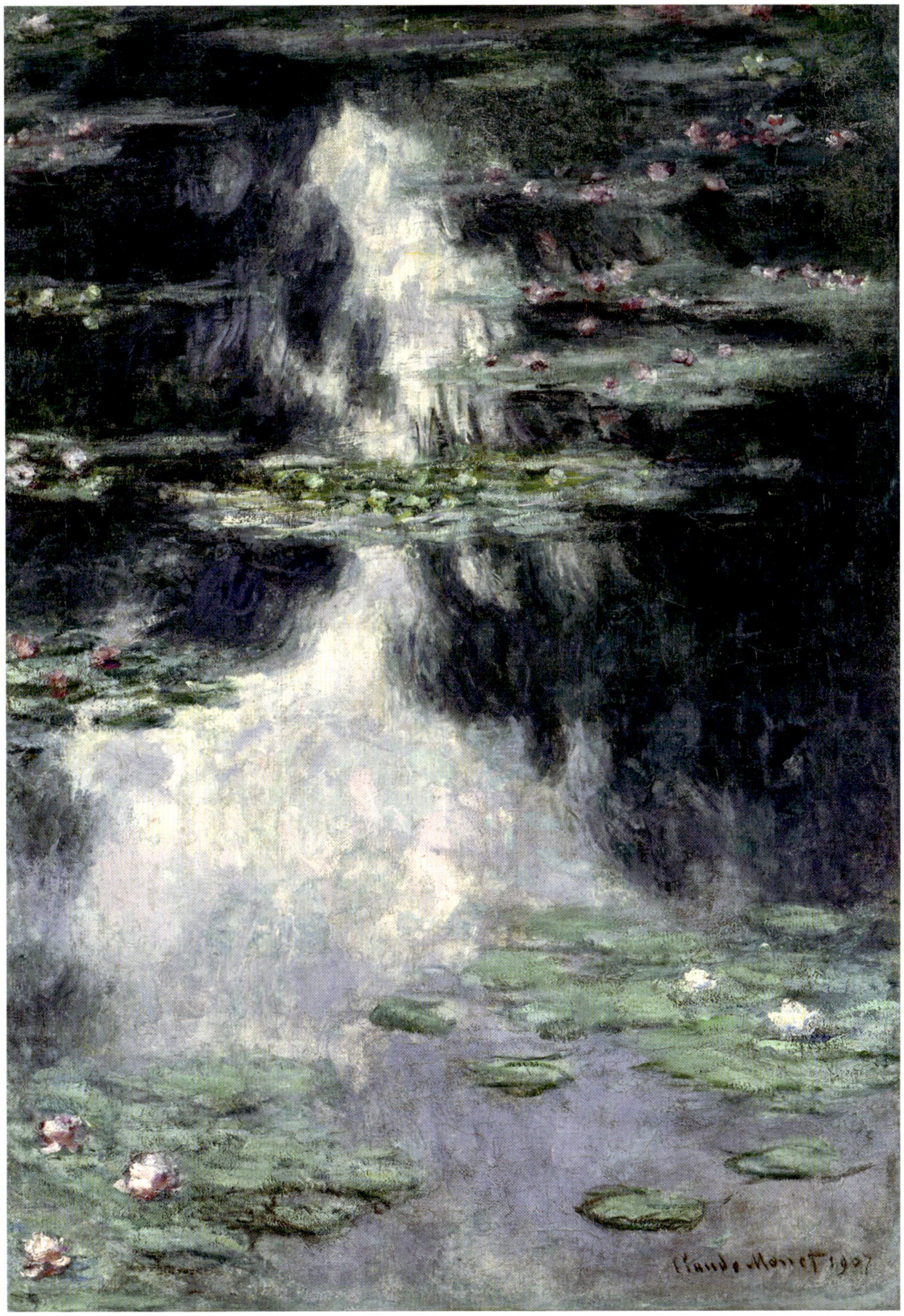

Fig. 22
CLAUDE MONET
Water-Lilies, 1907
The Israel Museum, Jerusalem

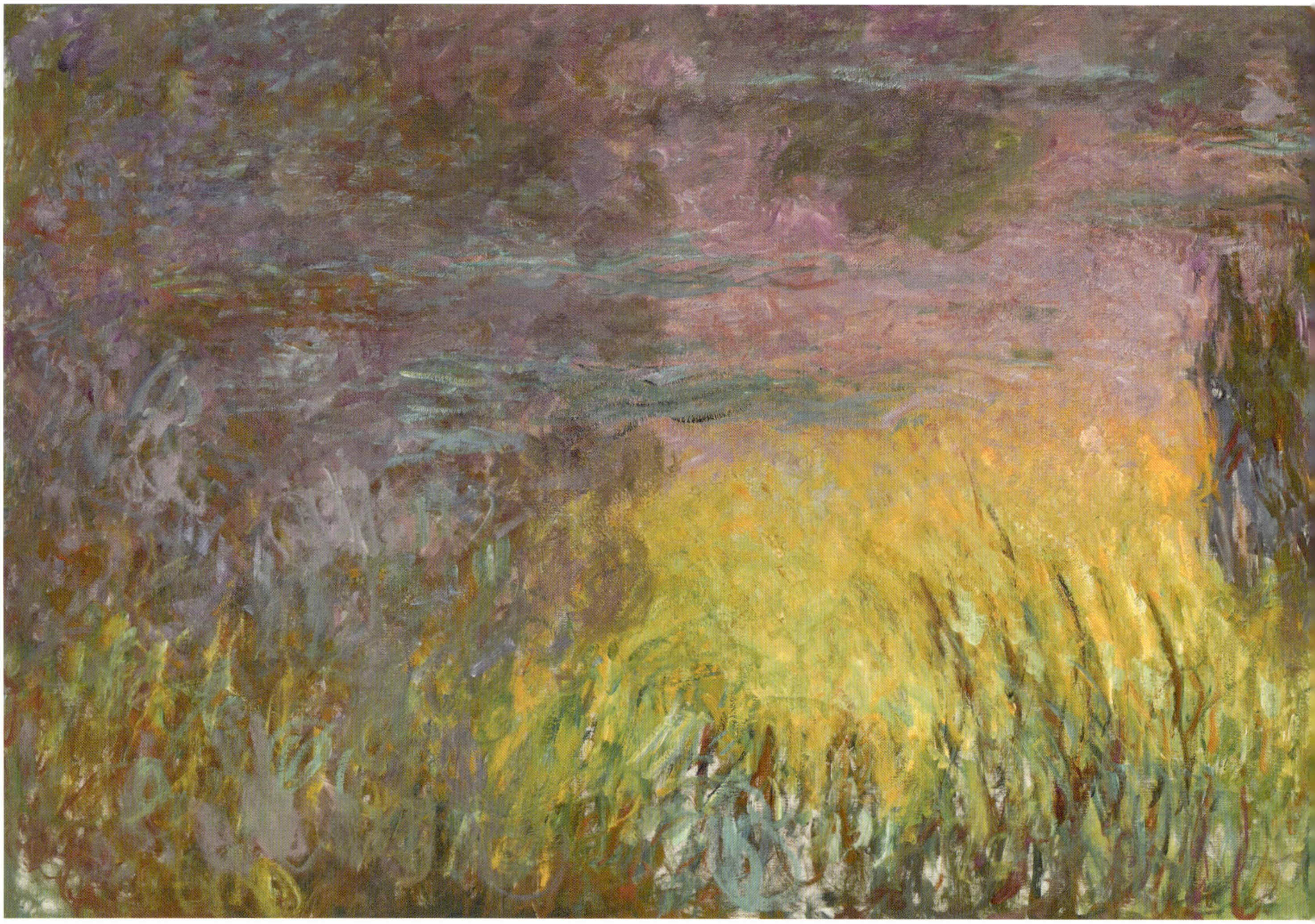

Monet's late work abandoned the direct depiction of reality in order to re-encounter or bring it to luminous life on an abstract plane. The meditative element in his contemplation of the world as reflected by his lily pond may have contributed to this. The reflection of different levels of perception posed the question of underlying validity in a new way, and it was answered by beauty of color, texture of brushwork, and the equilibrating of bright and dark planes of color. Above all, though, there was a reduction to bare essentials: the few lily pads and flowers that stand proxy for the rest are depicted in a very bold, free manner, being often only suggested.

These pictures are, at the same time, Monet's most radical transference of what he saw on to a purely two-dimensional surface which glows with its own intrinsic color, or in which the brush-stroke is left to its own dynamic. By suggesting more than they depict, they remind us how much painting, too, subsists on the imagination and requires the mind's eye to bring out what is real. No more horizon, no stabilizing lines, little coordinating structure, no perspective; just an expanse of water devoid of beginning and end. The mysterious reflections of trees and sky are sporadic and cannot be precisely located. Even the water-lily pictures dating from the first decade of this century, whose

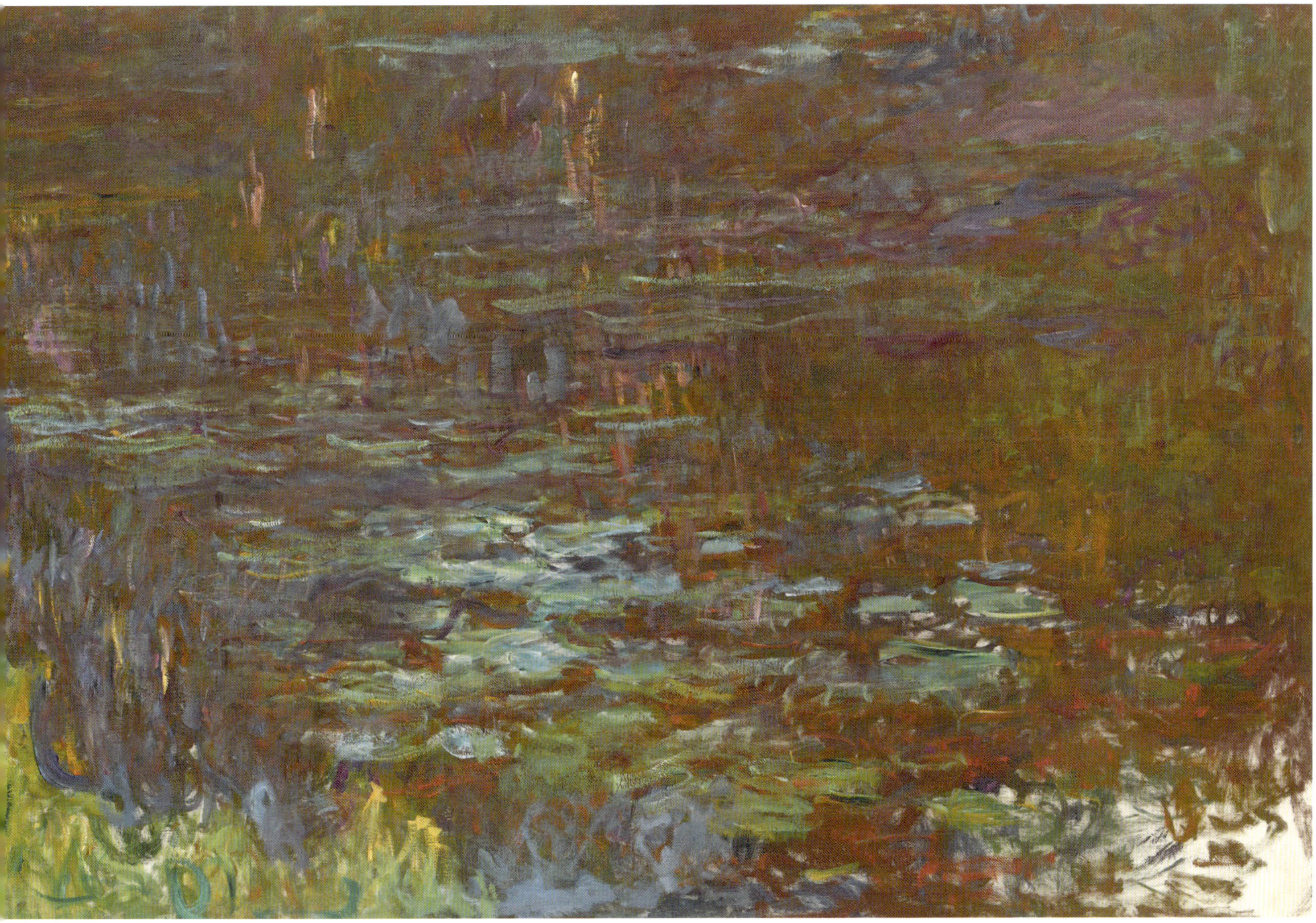

reflections inverted the traditional weighting, locating the pale areas of sky below and the darker and heavier ones above, confused those who saw them and encouraged a belief that they were upside down. Until then, a well-defined horizon had always enabled one to distinguish between reality and reflection. Now that they had merged in these horizonless pictures, the beholder seemed to be plunging into a mysterious world of purely sensuous visual experience.

Georges Clemenceau recorded a conversation in the course of which Monet said, "You philosophically seek the thing *per se*, whereas I direct my efforts simply toward a maximum of appearance in close correlation with the unknown reality. If one moves in the sphere of harmonized appearances, one cannot be far removed from reality, or at least from what we can perceive of it. All I have done is to look at what the world has shown me, so as to bear witness to it with my brush. Is that so little? Your mistake is to try to reduce the world to your dimensions, whereas your self-knowledge ought surely to grow as your knowledge of things increases. Let us help each other, hand in hand, to learn to see better and better."[35]

Those words are eloquent of the belief that characterizes Monet's œuvre: that the only

Fig. 23
CLAUDE MONET
Sunset, 1920/26
Musée de l'Orangerie, Paris

attainable certainty reposes in our observation of phenomena, but that we cannot gain possession of things themselves. We can only draw nearer to them by constantly refining our impression of them. "The concept of early Impressionism was not abandoned," writes Gottfried Boehm, "but brought to its conclusion." The earlier pictures, "despite their emphasis on outward appearance [...] did not altogether reject the question of what constituted nature over and above its impression. Monet, on the other hand, offers a monistic answer. The perception of a difference between seeing and reality, impression and actuality, became dissolved in the water-lilies, with their reflective processes."[36]

1 Hermann Bang, diary, quoted in Marianne Alphant, *Claude Monet en Norvège*, Paris 1994, p. 52; at greater length in Jean Pierre Hoschedé *Claude Monet, ce mal connu*, Geneva, 960, vol. II, pp, 111–115.

2 Their authenticity is not to be doubted, because Monet's letters often expressed a wish to achieve "the impossible."

5 Charles Baudelaire, Œuvres complètes, vol. II, Paris 1976, p. 665.

4 Cf. Virginia Spate, *The Colour of Time: Claude Monet*, London 1992, p. 26.

5 Marc Elder, *A Giverny chez Claude Monet*, Paris 1924, pp. 62–64.

6 Charles Baudelaire, *Correspondance*, vol. II (1861–66), Paris 1973, pp. 196f.

7 On this subject, see especially: Rainer Budde, „Einige Anmerkungen über den Umgang mit der Farbe bei den Impressionisten," in: exh. cat. *Landschaft im Licht. Europäische Malerei in Europa und Nordamerika*, Cologne and Zurich 1990, pp. 78–81.

8 Quoted in Joel Isaacson, *Claude Monet. Observation et Reflexion*, Oxford and New York 1978, p. 16.

9 Recorded by Joachim Gasquet in Michael Dorn (ed.), *Gespräche mit* Cézanne, Zurich 1982, p. 151.

10 Jules Castagnary, "L'Exposition du Boulevard des Capucines. Les Impressionnistes" in: *Le Siècle* (Paris), 29 April 1874.

11 In a letter from Monet to Georges Durand-Ruel, Giverny, 3 July 1905, quoted in: Daniel Wildenstein, *Claude Monet. Biographie et catalogue raisonné*, 5 vols., Lausanne/Paris 1874–1991, Vol. IV, p. 369, Letter No. 1780.

12 Georges Jeanniot, "Notes sur l'art. Claude Monet" in: *La Cravache Parisienne*, 23 June 1888.

13 Monet to (?), Giverny, 5 April 1914, quoted in Wildenstein (as in note 11), p. 390, Letter No, 2113.

14 Thus Monet to Clemenceau; quoted in: Isaacson 1978 (as in note 8), p, 210.

15 While being interviewed on 4 April 1895 for the *Oslo Dagbladed*, quoted in: Wildenstein (as in note 11), p. 65.

16 See the letter to Durand-Ruel dated 24 October 1884, quoted in: Wildenstein (as in note 11), p. 255, Letter No. 526.

17 See, for example, the letters of 1— 9 February 1888, quoted in: Wildenstein (as in note 11), pp. 227–9, Letters Nos. 824–32.

18 His respect for the other man's work was so great that, whenever he was depressed during his years at Giverny, Alice Hoschedé used to put away the Cézannes he owned because the comparison depressed him still more.

19 Paul Cézanne in a letter to Joachim Gasquet from Le Tholonet on 26 September 1897; quoted in: Françoise Cochin/Joseph J. Rishel (ed.), *Cézanne* (exh. cat., Galeries nationales du Grand Palais, Paris, September 25, 1995–January 7, 1996, Tate Gallery, London, February 8–April 4, 1996, Philadelphia Museum of Art, Philadelphia, May 26–August 18, 1996), Paris 1995, p. 17.

20 Quoted in: Karin Sagner-Düchting, *Claude Monet 1840–1926. Ein Fest für die Augen*, Cologne 1990, p. 151.

21 William Fuller, "Claude Monet and his Paintings," foreword to *Pictures by Claude Monet* (exh. cat., The Lotus Club, New York 1899); quoted in: Charles F. Stuckey, *Claude Monet 1840–1926*, Chicago and London 1995, p. 231.

22 Monet to Durand-Ruel, Giverny, 27 April 1907, quoted in: Wildenstein (as in note 11), p. 372, Letter No. 1832.

23 At dinner on 5 September 1892; Theodore Robinson, unpublished diaries, 5 September 1892, vol. I (29 March 1882 —4 February 1893), Frick Art Reference Library, New York; referred to in: Stuckey 1995 (as in note 21), p. 224.

24 Monet to Paul Durand-Ruel, Giverny, 23 March 1903, quoted in: Wildenstein (as in note 11), p. 363, Letter No. 1690.

25 Monet to Paul Durand-Ruel, Giverny, 26 October 1905, quoted in: Wildenstein (as in note 11), p. 369, Letter no. 1787.

26 Paul Hayes Tucker, *Monet in the '90s, The Series Paintings,* (exh. cat., Museum of Fine Arts, Boston, February 2–April 29, 1990, The Art Institute of Chicago, Chicago, May 19–August 24, 1990, Royal Academy of Arts, London, September 9–December 9, 1990), Boston/New Haven/London 1989, p. 101.

27 Emile Taboureux, "Claude Monet" in: *La Vie Moderne*, 12 June 1880; quoted in: Charles F. Stuckey, *Claude Monet 1840–1926*, Cologne 1994, p. 90.

28 Cf. Wildenstein (as in note 11), pp. 43f. and 428 (Doc. no. 180).
29 Monet to Durand-Ruel, Giverny, 12 February 1905, quoted in: Wildenstein (as in note 11), p. 368, Letter no. 1764; see also Letters Nos. 1765, 1767, 1768, 1779 and Doc. Nos. 180, 189.
30 Willem Geertrudus Cornelis Byvanck, *Un Hollandais à Paris en 1891: Sensations de littérature et d'art*, Paris l892, P. 177.
31 Wassili Kandinsky, *Rückblicke*, Berlin 1913, p. 14.
32 Monet to a painter at Giverny, November 1891, quoted in: Wildenstein (as in note 11), p. 263, Letter no. 1124.
33 Monet to Gustave Geffroy on 11. August 1908; quoted in: Wildenstein (as in note 11), p. 374, Letter No. 1854
34 Francois Thiébault-Sisson, "Les Nymphéas de Claude Monet à l'Orangerie des Tuileries," in *La Revue de de l'art ancien et moderne*, June 1927; quoted in: Stuckey 1994 (as in note 27), p. 290.
35 Georges Clemenceau, *Claude Monet. Betrachtungen und Erinnerungen eines Freundes*, Freiburg im Breisgau n. d., pp. 145f.
36 Gottfried Boehm, "Strom ohne Ufer. Bemerkungen zu Claude Monets Seerosen", in. *Claude Monet: Nymphéas. Impression-Vision* (exh. cat., Kunstmuseum Basel, Basel, July 7–October 10, 1986), p. 124.

The text is an adapted version of an essay first published in: Stephan Koja, *Claude Monet,* Munich/New York 1996, p. 18–35.

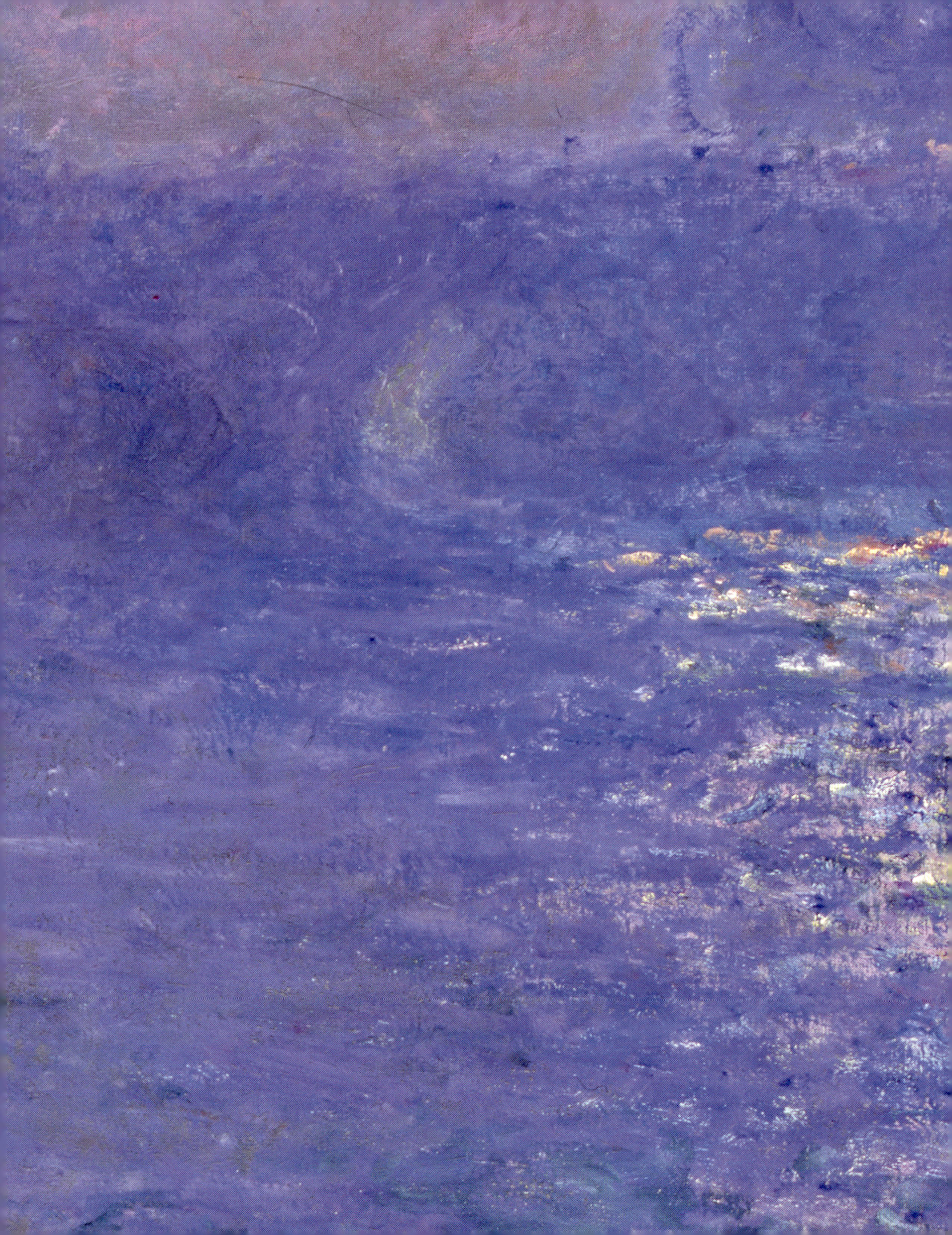

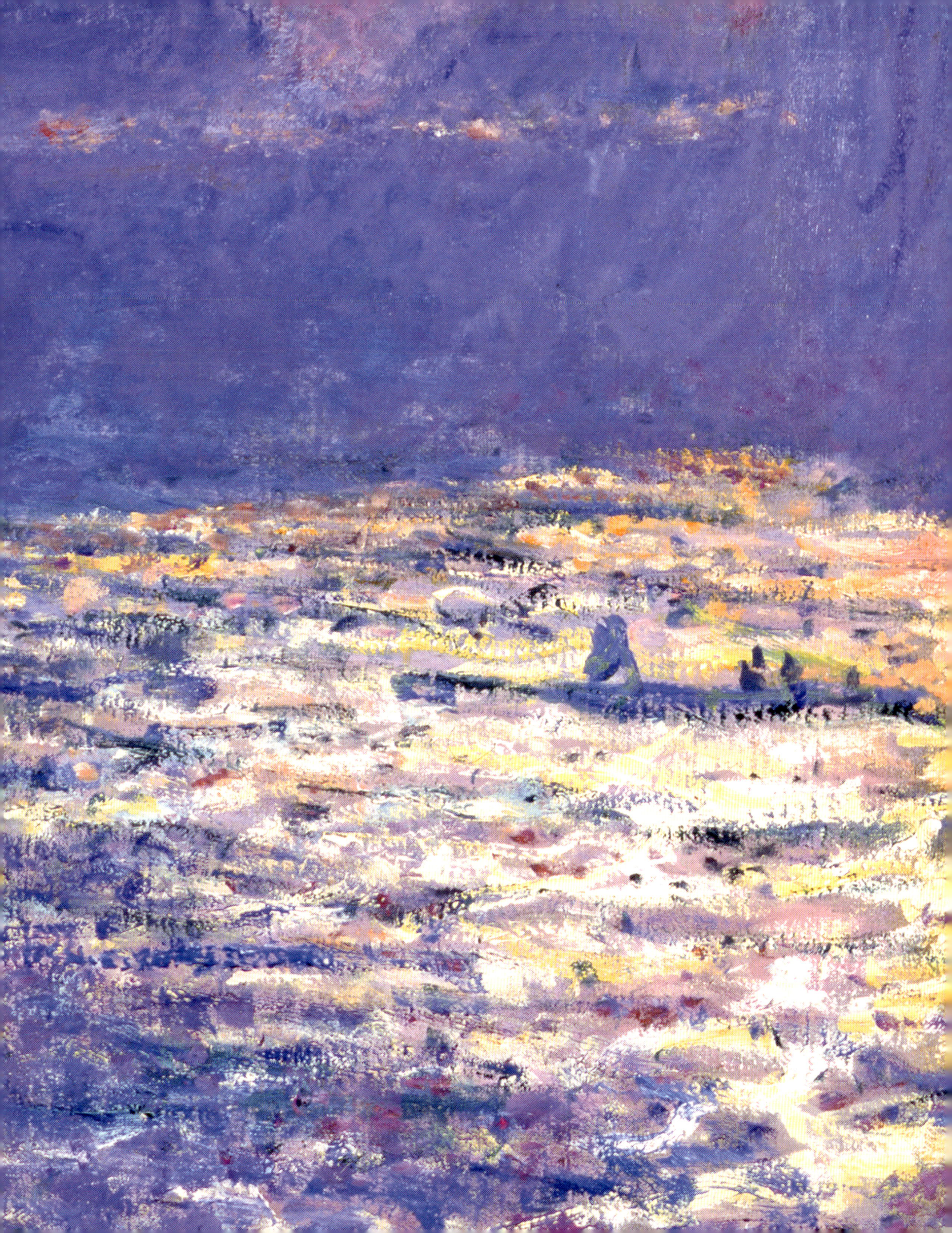

"ARE YOU ACTUALLY ALLOWED TO PAINT LIKE THAT?"

Claude Monet's Work as a Constant Source of Inspiration

Stephan Koja

Fig. 1
GUSTAV KLIMT
On Attersee, 1900
Leopold Museum – Private Foundation, Vienna

"Are you actually allowed to paint like that?"[1] Adalbert Franz Seligmann, critic for the *Neue Freie Presse*, wondered on seeing the "bold trueness to nature" and light colors in Tina Blau's painting *Spring in the Prater (Frühling im Prater)*, and the vibrancy of the hues that was felt to be radical, not very subtle, in fact verging on garish. Seligmann would have been well aware that this approach to reality, this striking transformation of color, had their origins in French painting.

It had been a revolution from below, a toppling of the hierarchy of genres affected by the unwavering pleinairism of the painters from the Barbizon School. The renewal of painting, the path to modernism, was by way of landscape painting.

Toward the end of the eighteenth and in the early nineteenth century, people's attitude to the surrounding world had started to change fundamentally. Nature was no longer regarded as a gift of the Creation but its varied phenomena became the object of exact scrutiny instead. At the same time, a burgeoning new social class aspired to new forms of visual expression. The bourgeois age had a voracious appetite for illustrations showing the world and its own ways of life—the invention in 1798 of a new printing technique, lithography, was a logical outcome of this era. As Heinrich Schwarz stated, it was also no coincidence that photography was invented in the 1830s; this enabled an even more exact capturing of the world and could also be used scientifically.[2]

At the same time, the world was in the throes of some seismic changes. Technological inventions such as the steam engine, railway, telegraph, the chemical industry, and industrial methods of production resulted in a tremendous acceleration of life. Photography could not respond to this. Although it could illustrate faces, buildings, objects, plants or landscapes with far greater precision, at first it could not capture movement. This appeared blurred, or later on, when shorter exposure times were made possible by faster lenses and more sensitive photographic materials, as a frozen moment. The representation of atmospheric effects was also largely not possible in photography.

This was where a new painting could come into its own. It could give expression to modern life, this tremendous acceleration of daily routines, and the variety of new social phenomena. And it was precisely these fleeting appearances of the weather, the atmospheres on the water's surface, fog, haze, wind, and smoke, to which it could turn its attention, making the interplay of light and color a preferred pictorial subject. In this way, it could address progress by transforming smoking factory chimneys, locomotives, steamers in ports, and so on, into subjects worthy of pictorial representation. Similarly, the amusements emerging with newly acquired leisure time—regattas, strolls, horse racing, shopping, promenades, cabarets, theaters, concerts—became subjects for this new art as well.

An aesthetic of the spontaneous, of the swiftly dashed-off depiction emerged. It harked back to the tradition of painterly brilliance, as had been cultivated by artists from the Baroque to the (then) present day—Velázquez, Frans Hals, Fragonard, Goya, Gainsborough, and Constable spring to mind, among many others.

In addition, there were the large-scale studies by the Barbizon painters, with their sketchy, open brushwork, aiming to faithfully capture their impressions before nature, as if jotting them down. After a number of painters from this generation had died, works of unanticipated boldness, previously stored in studios, suddenly appeared on the art market and young artists, Monet among them, fell under their spell. These pictures exuded an impression of immediacy and thus provided a vocabulary for painting's new tasks.

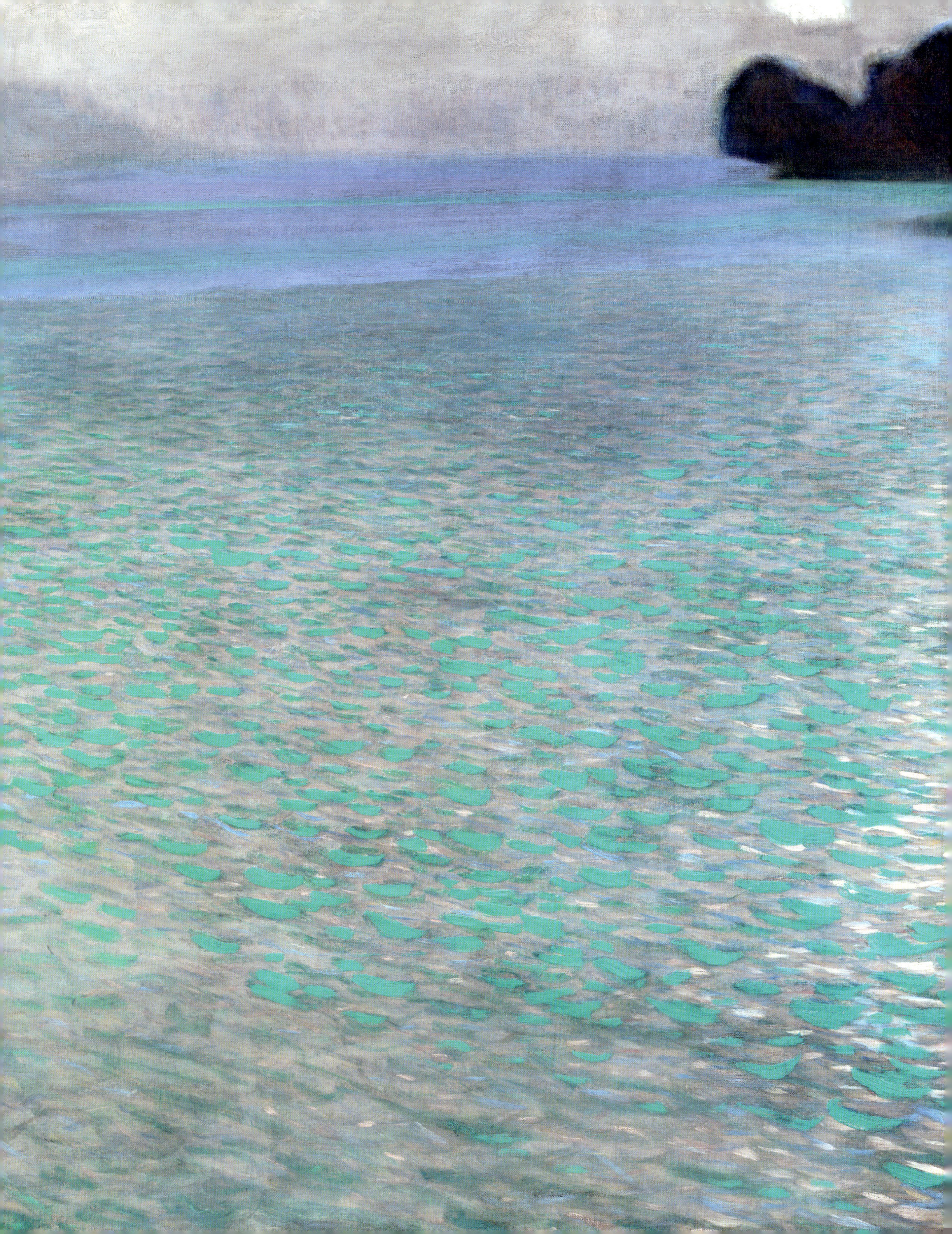

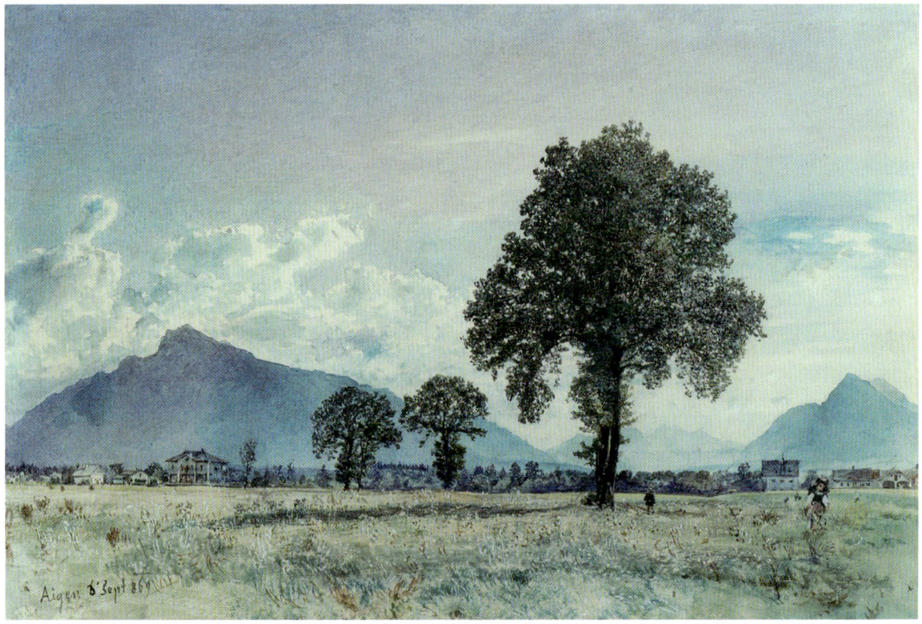

Fig. 2
RUDOLF VON ALT
View of Aigen and the Untersberg, 1869
Private collection

At the same time, scientists, philosophers, and artists were considering how people perceive their environment and came to the conclusion that one first registers optical stimuli and not the object itself. In fact, the object appears different depending on the conditions. What one perceives, therefore, is always only an impression of a moment.

It was out of these circumstances and innovative discoveries, the example of a prior tradition of open-air painting, and the results of new color theories, that a new painting arose. And Claude Monet was its most unwavering exponent, finding new ways to express the fleeting, the *instantanéité*, and capture the effects of light. He did this by working before the subject, by confining himself to visual impressions, cropping his pictures, beginning his compositions abruptly; and by using loose, spontaneous brushwork, and a bright, light-filled palette.

The challenge of how to adequately depict the phenomena of rapidly changing times was faced by Austrian artists as well. Although they too tried to provide answers, they had to contend with a far more conservative cultural environment, in which the art world was dominated by an institution that held a virtual stranglehold on taste: the Künstlerhaus in Vienna.

In Austria there had also been artists, such as Ferdinand Georg Waldmüller or Rudolf von Alt, who, in constant quest of ever-greater closeness to nature, had painted outdoors and tried to heighten the intensity of light. Yet in an environment that understood art as an interpretation of the world and sought the spiritual and poetic even in landscape, their voices generally fell on deaf ears. In Austria, too, the impetus was needed from elsewhere.

A new generation of painters led by Emil Jakob Schindler, Eugen Jettel, and Rudolf Ribarz went out into the open in quest of new expressive possibilities. When they encountered pictures by the Barbizon School in Munich at the 1869 *I. Internationale Kun-*

stausstellung they were bolstered in their efforts to devote themselves to open-air painting. Furthermore, in 1872 the Gsell collection, one of Vienna's largest private collections, was sold at auction, including works by Corot, Daubigny, Harpignies, Millet, Rousseau, and Troyon. Little later, in 1873, further paintings by the Barbizon School and possibly the first work by Monet were shown at the Vienna World's Fair. An exhibition of Courbet's art was staged at the Kunstverein at the same time. Another factor was that artists from this more mobile generation traveled—probably to a far greater extent than we envisage—in order to see exhibitions and galleries in Europe's metropolises where they found inspiration and gathered new impressions.

Gradually the work of Monet and of the other Impressionists became known in Austria. One must also bear in mind that even in the 1880s, Monet was not really recognized in France; he did not enjoy the fame we now take for granted. It was not until the end of the 1880s and the early 1890s that this started to change and his works were shown at international exhibitions with growing frequency. There was increasing awareness of his significance as the key figure of Impressionism, this painter genius whose powers of influence were a source of inspiration for generations of artists and on occasions prompted momentous changes in their artistic development. And Austria was no exception.

Initially the major influence of Monet's painting on Austrian art emerged in the sketch. As any work that was not meticulously executed was still tainted with the odor of the morally inferior among circles of art connoisseurs, many painters sought liberty in the sketch, ultimately achieving a new freedom of expression in their large-scale pictures as a result.

THE SIGNIFICANCE OF THE SKETCH

For the landscapists of the 1880s and 1890s especially, this spontaneous "bursting to life" of the subject, the immediate rendering of the visual scene, and its illustration in swift and fluid brushwork became a welcome model. Only a few artists, however, dared to transfer this style to their completed paintings—too great was their respect for the expectations of the Künstlerhaus. Similar to the Paris Salon, the Genossenschaft bildender Künstler Wiens (Vienna Artists' Cooperative), with its regular exhibitions, provided the most important opportunity for a painter or sculptor to gain attention for his work, to have it written about and published. It was not for nothing that Wilhelm Bernatzik warned Theodor von Hörmann who was always attacking the conventions and bigotry of the Künstlerhaus: "You won't achieve anything; you have, for example, always to paint everything in the same, specifically Viennese way—then you can get through."[3]

This was why painters such as Schindler, Ribarz, Egner, or Zoff created many of their boldest works in the form of sketches while they adopted a more conventional approach in their large-scale paintings.

The spontaneity and daring displayed by these painters is sometimes astounding. Open, often just suggested brushstrokes dance across the support (usually small wooden panels or cardboard). Impressions are captured in a cursory way, as if using shorthand, or in broad planes of paint, and in places, colors that pay no heed to conventions burst through. And it is precisely these sketches and studies that adopt many characteristics of Monet's painting: the rapid brushwork, appearing almost hurried, and the immediacy of the experience transferred into seemingly spontaneous strokes; the direct, almost sudden

Fig. 3
EUGEN JETTEL
Field Track in Winter, 1895
Belvedere, Vienna

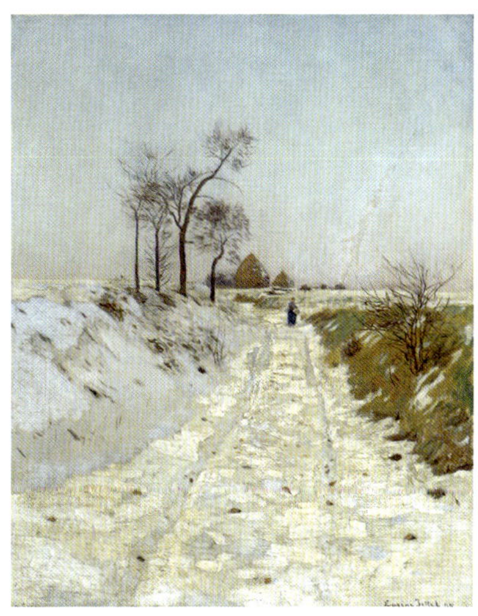

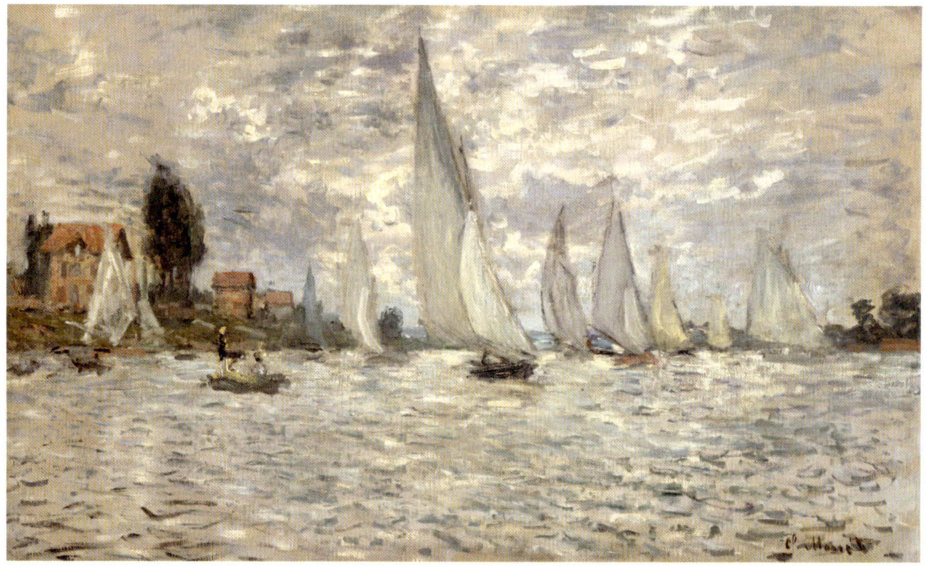

Fig. 4
CLAUDE MONET
Regatta at Argenteuil, ca. 1874
Musée d'Orsay, Paris

introduction to the compositions, as in the foreground diagonal in his riverscapes; the urban subject matter; the jotted down, sketchy people strolling by, and the unsentimental capturing of atmospheric effects with matter-of-fact directness.

This resulted in painterly approaches as similar as Monet's *Sailing Boats, Regatta at Argenteuil (Les barques, régates à Argenteuil)* (1874, W 339) and Emil Jakob Schindler's *Sylt* (ca. 1892). Monet's preference to indicate the bank at the picture's edge but devote most of his attention to the water's surface had become known to a wider public through illustrated publications such as *La Vie moderne*[4] or *Gazette des beaux-arts*[5]. A very similar painting of a *Regatta at Argenteuil* (1872, W 233) had been acquired as early as 1876 by Gustave Caillebotte, whose collection could be viewed by interested visitors.

Fig. 5
EMIL JAKOB SCHINDLER
Coast at Sylt, 1892
Belvedere, Vienna

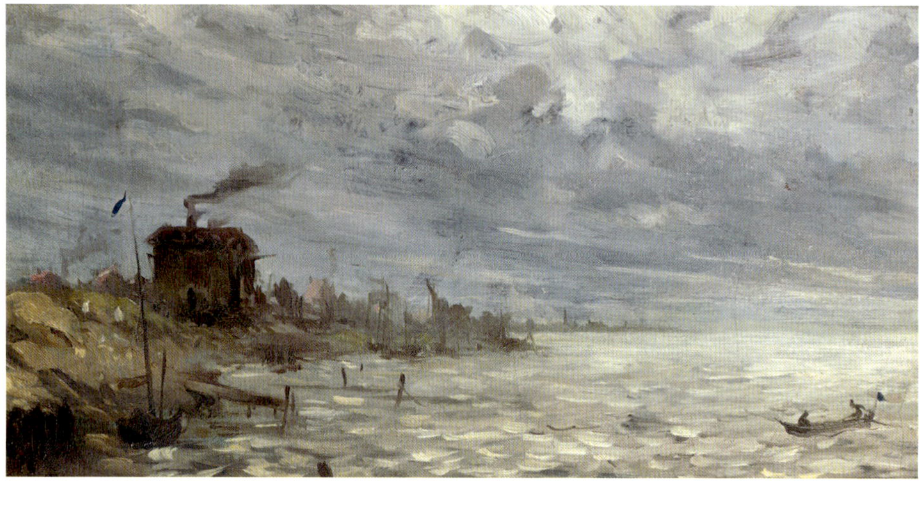

Schindler adopted the "dish-shaped" brushstrokes with a similar swiftness and verve, his suggestive strokes characterizing only the essential. He conveyed the stiff breeze of this cloudy day through the undulating short waves, the touch of paint indicating the flag on the mast, and the blurred streaks of smoke being swept away from the houses' chimneys by the wind. But it is especially the accuracy of the shades that expresses the sandy hues of the North Sea and the scudding clouds high in the sky, so that we positively feel we can smell the water and the sand.

Even Carl Moll adopted Monet's typical brushwork to represent the water in his views of Venice around 1910. It was in that year that Monet's *Anglers on the Seine at Poissy (Pêcheurs à la ligne sur la Seine à Poissy)* (1882, W 748, fig. p. 161) was shown at the Galerie Miethke, and Moll alluded to the great master in his compositions with a dominant surface of water and partially cropped subject matter. The same applies to Emil Jakob Schindler in his small study of the *Harvest Month near Plankenberg (Erntemonat bei Plankenberg)* (1890), in which the viewer's gaze is positively drawn past the half-shown haystack in the foreground into the picture's depths.

Monet's curiosity to get to grips with all weathers in his pictures and his constant quest for new challenges encouraged similar attempts by Austrian painters. The freshness and verve, the accuracy of the colors in Schindler's brilliant sketch of a *Winter in the Park (Winter im Park)* (ca. 1890) all reflect that it was evidently painted outdoors. It is a spontaneous moment showing a subject that had never been painted like that here before, but which had a prominent example in Monet's winter village scenes near Paris. Indeed, the few dark brushstrokes delineating the people out walking are closely related to Monet's figures. A sign at the left edge of the painting also adds a contemporary touch to the image, intensifying the impression of a scene observed at that very moment. Other artists, such as Emilie Mediz-Pelikan in her *Suburbs in Winter (Vorort im Schnee)* (1888, fig. p. 218), soon followed his example.

Similarly, Ribarz's *Ships in the Harbor (Schiffe im Hafen)* (1882) or Zoff's views of beaches and coasts appear like snapshots of an experienced moment. Monet's example of capturing the moment instead of making the objects comprehensible in themselves or even pondering their true essence could be achieved in sketches. What was new was this quasi-impartial view of the world as an optical phenomenon, a view that shook off tradition and called for an appropriate expression of the feel of the times.

This approach must have suited Tina Blau and her matter-of-fact objectivity. In her small pictures of the Tuileries, painted in Paris in 1883, she rendered people strolling through the gardens in brilliant sunshine and added occasional splashes of her favorite blue to the clothing, heightening the freshness of the depiction still further. After returning to Vienna, she incorporated these insights from France in a sequence of images showing the Belvedere Garden that, with similar immediacy, also emphasize the sense of a captured moment.

Marie Egner agonized over the fact that she felt she could conjure up this immediacy and freshness, this fleeting impression, and this sense of the snatching of a passing moment in her small-scale studies. But she lost her nerve when it came to her large-scale paintings and—held back by the conventions of the "perfect finish"—she could not escape a dense and detailed style of painting. "It is actually the heavy sediment in my nature which means that I cannot help but act in the same way as before. As long as my imagination is at work, then the paintbrush flies; broad planes of color are combined—

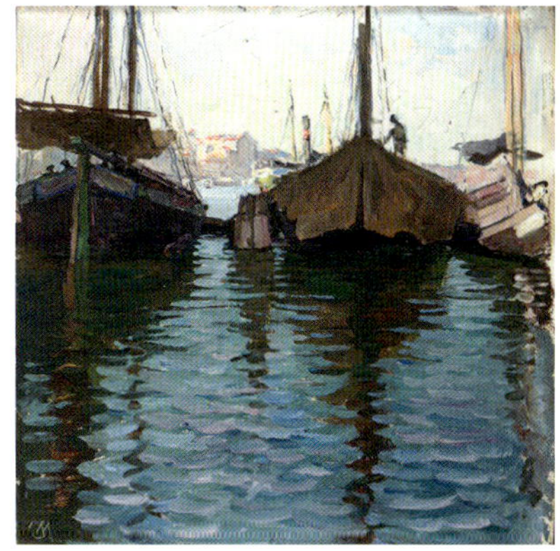

Fig. 6
CARL MOLL
Venice, ca. 1910
Private collection

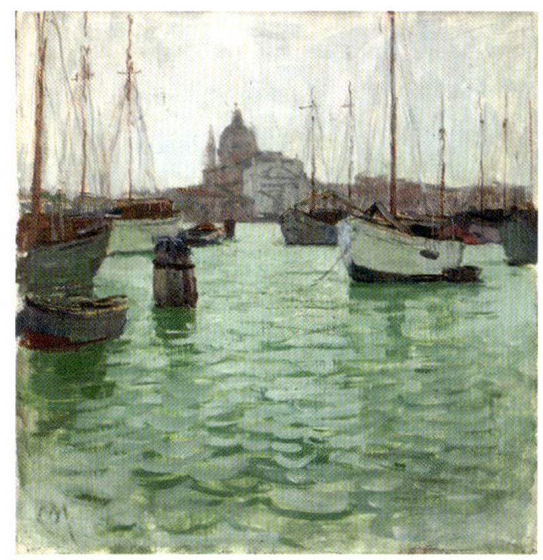

Fig. 7
CARL MOLL
Il Redentore, Venice, ca. 1910
Private collection

Fig. 8
CLAUDE MONET
Windmill near Zaandam, 1871
Ashmolean Museum, University of Oxford

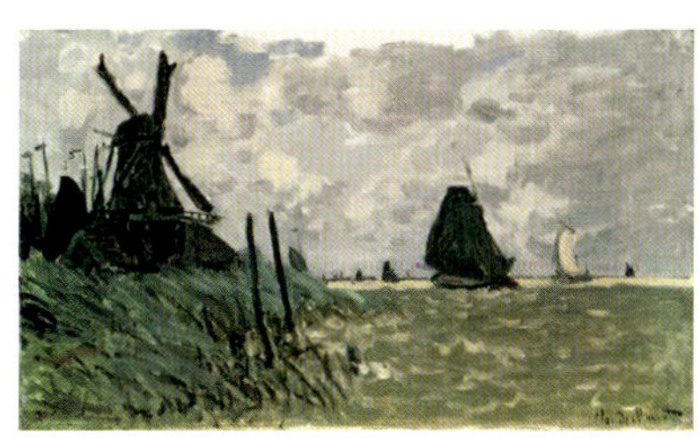

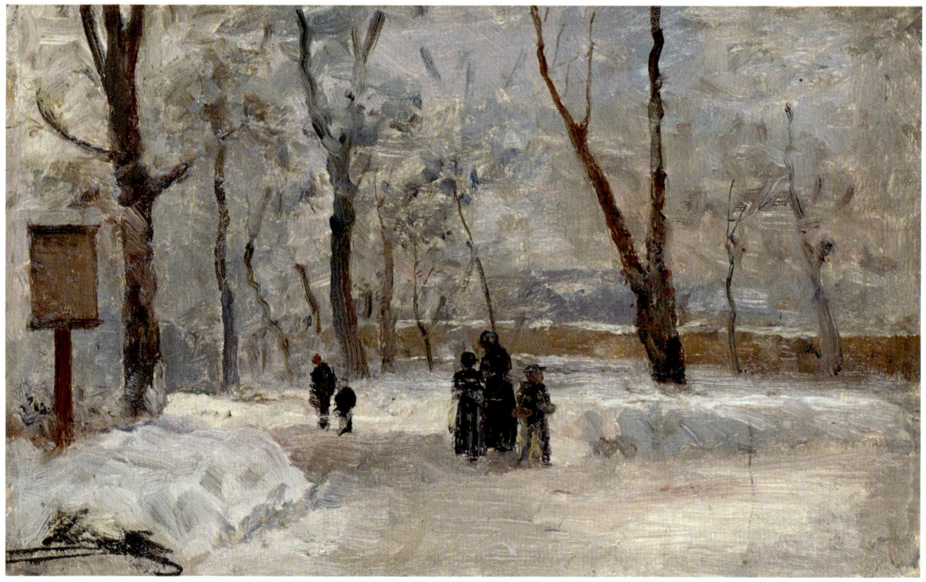

Fig. 9
EMIL JAKOB SCHINDLER
Winter in the Park, ca. 1890
Private collection, Vienna

the canvas shines; but as soon as Marie Egner picks up the paintbrush, then the old, totally darned Viennese *Pimpelmeier* is back; with the thousands of strokes and dabs and the heavy shadows."[6]

Even Rudolf Ribarz who tended to work in a compact, incisive graphic style, succumbed to the allure of concentrating on the atmospheric and ephemeral in sketches such as *Ships in the Harbor* in which the water's gleam and the smoke drifting from the ships' chimneys become the picture's true subject.

Depictions of "modern life" that exuded something "contemporary" were particularly stimulating for painters of the time. In his *Lock on the St. Denis Canal* (*Schleuse am Kanal von St. Denis*) (1883 fig. p. 228), Ribarz had not only represented all the paraphernalia for handling a boat, but also the smoking chimneys of suburban factories in the background and a train puffing across a railway bridge in the distance. Subjects such as these could be described even more spontaneously, even more hastily, as if they had only just been experienced. In Olga Wisinger-Florian's *Railway in a Landscape (Landschaft mit Eisenbahn)* (ca. 1895), a train reduced to a dark silhouette belches smoke through the picture's background, a telegraph mast stands erect against the sky, while the wind blows through the branches and the leaves of the trees on the left. The sense of the abrupt and sudden conveyed by this wonderful small painting is skillfully achieved by the long plume of smoke—the train seems to have swept into the picture at this very moment.

Exploring such subjects, previously deemed unworthy of a picture, and capturing them as a snapshot moment was undoubtedly encouraged by Monet's paintings. In 1893 Wisinger-Florian had traveled to the Chicago World's Fair, where she could see Monet's landscape with a train (1875, W 360), a composition not only characterized by the locomotive's plume of smoke but also including telegraph masts prominently placed in the image.

In a number of Seine views, Monet introduced factory chimneys rather like a vanishing point for the eye (cf. *The Promenade at Argenteuil [La promenade d'Argenteuil]*, 1872, W

Fig. 10
CLAUDE MONET
Snow Scene at Argenteuil, 1875
The National Gallery, London

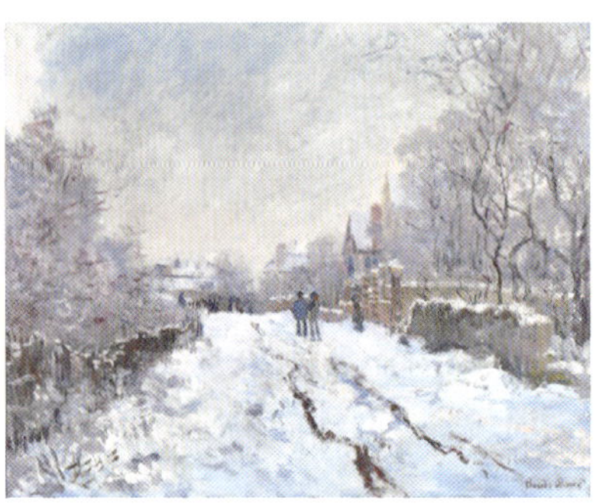

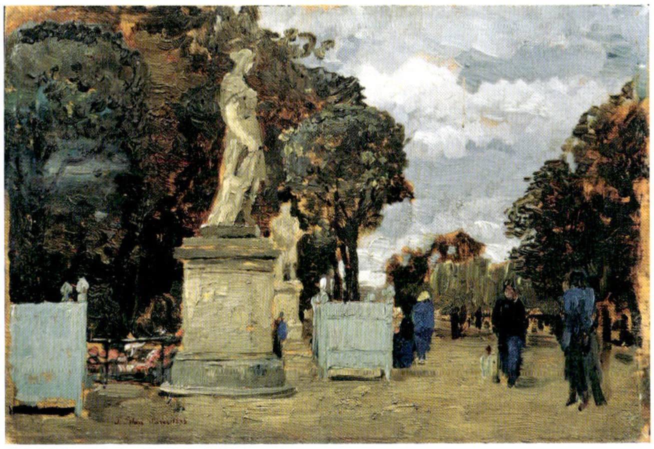

Fig. 11
TINA BLAU
From the Tuileries – Gray Day, 1883
Belvedere, Vienna

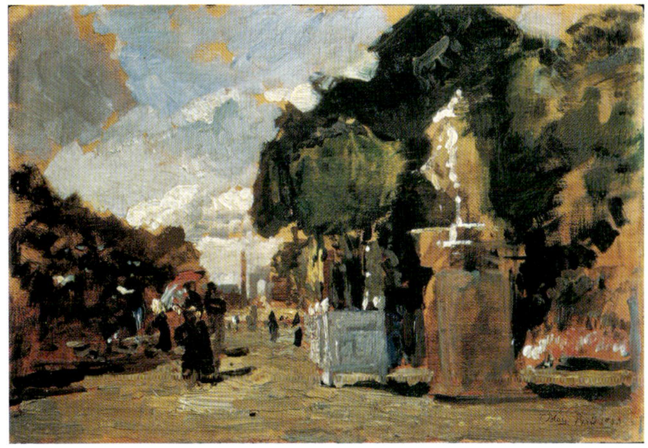

Fig. 12
TINA BLAU
From the Tuileries – Sunny Day, 1883
Belvedere, Vienna

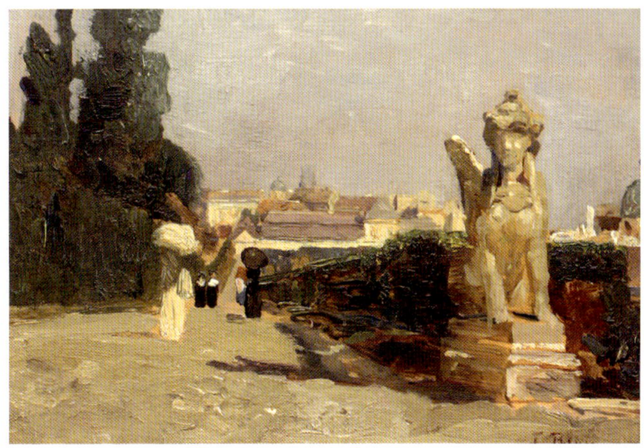

Fig. 13
TINA BLAU
In the Belvederegarden, 1883
Private collection

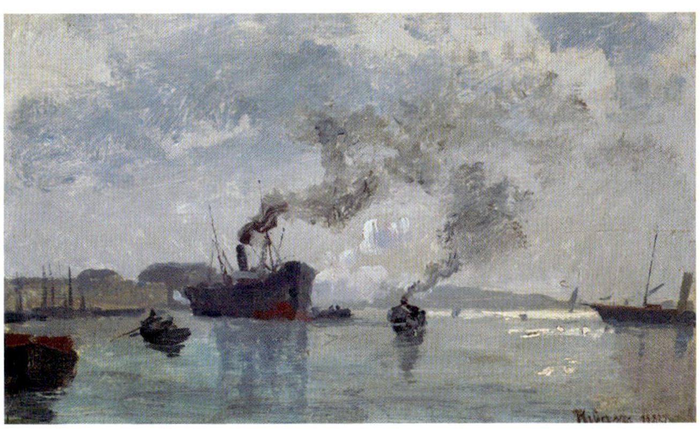

Fig. 14
RUDOLF RIBARZ
Ships in the Harbor, 1882
Belvedere, Vienna

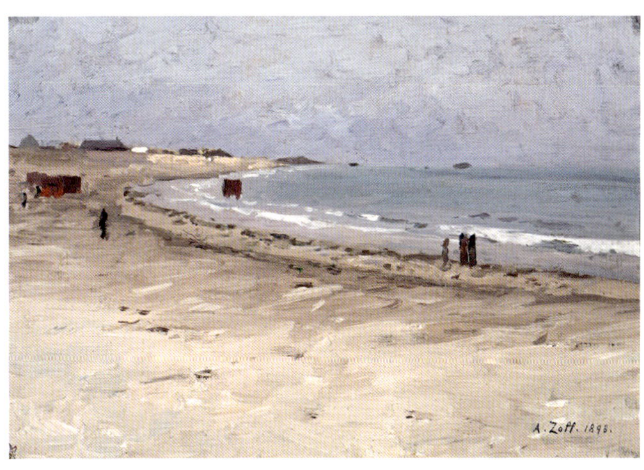

Fig. 15
ALFRED ZOFF
Sea Coast, 1893
Neue Galerie am Universalmuseum Joanneum, Graz

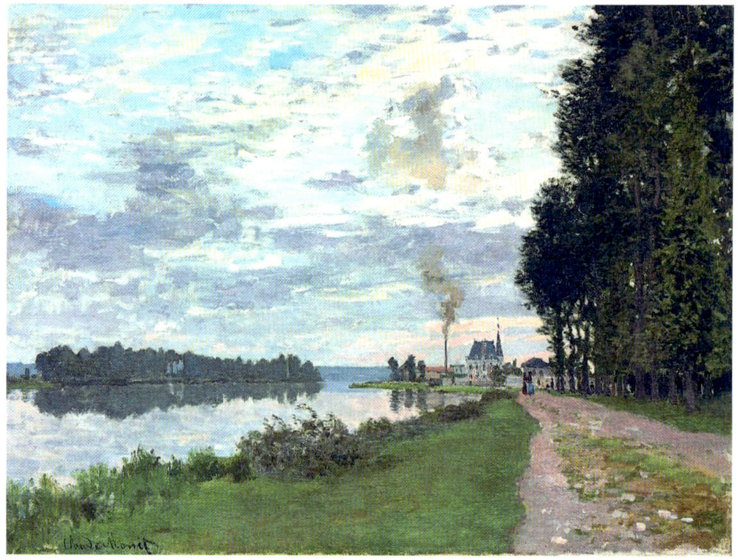

Fig. 16
CLAUDE MONET
The Promenade at Argenteuil, 1872
Private collection

Fig. 17
CARL MOLL
River Landscape, ca. 1900
Private collection, Austria

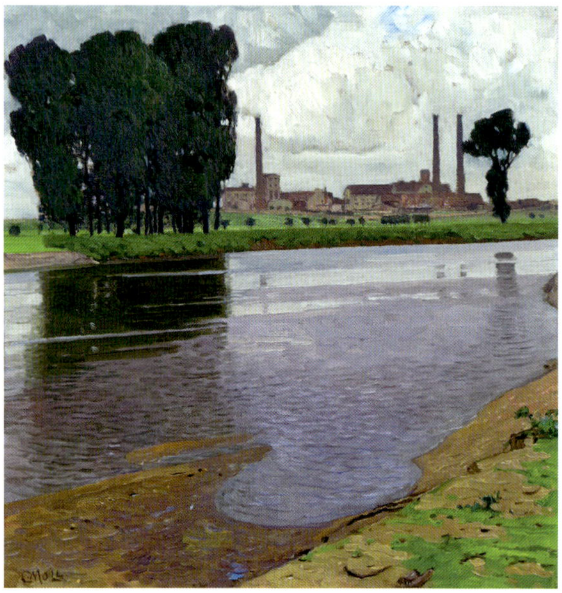

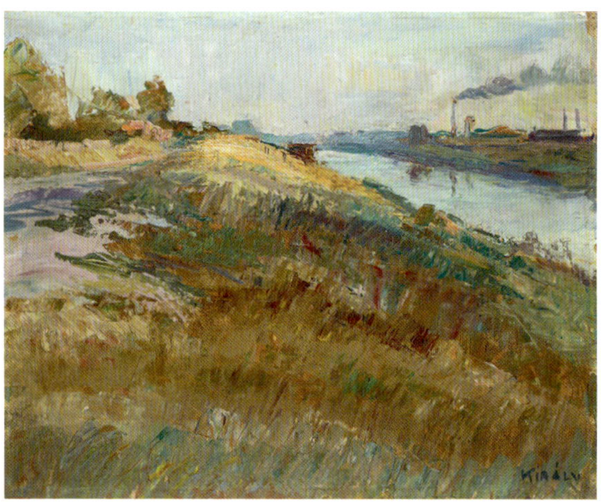

Fig. 18
Maria Kiraly
Donaulandscape, ca. 1950
Artothek des Bundes im 21er Haus, Vienna

Fig. 19
CLAUDE MONET
The Seine at Argenteuil, 1875
Private collection

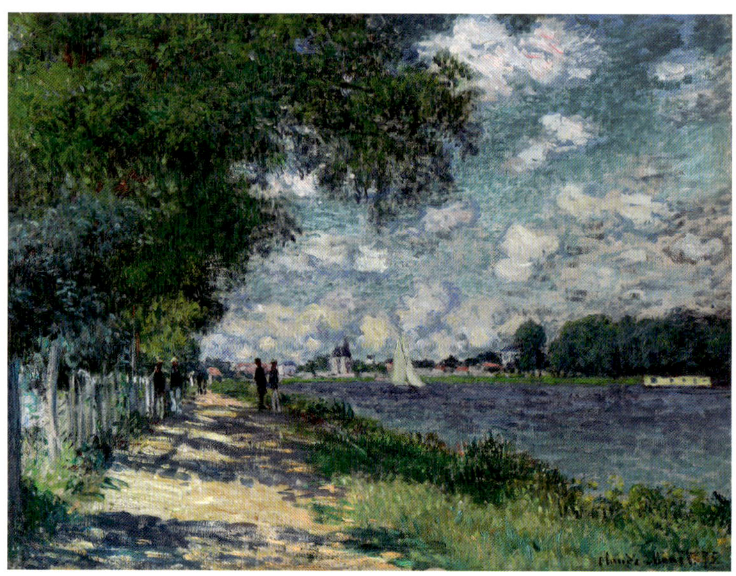

222, or *The Seine at La Grande Jatte [La Seine à la Grande Jatte]*, 1877/78, W 454). This soon caught on with other artists and lost none of its appeal until well into the twentieth century. Carl Moll's or Maria Kiraly's paintings of riverscapes are cases in point and even *fin-de-siècle* photography explored the subject of smoking chimneys towering over industrial plants.

Added to that, the bustle at stations was now regarded as a suitable pictorial subject as well[7]—and here, too, artists could look to Monet's example. The composition of Theodor Meyer's photograph of a *Classification Yard (Rangierbahnhof)*, shown at an exhibition of the Vienna Photo Club at Galerie Miethke in 1907, obviously alludes to Monet's *The*

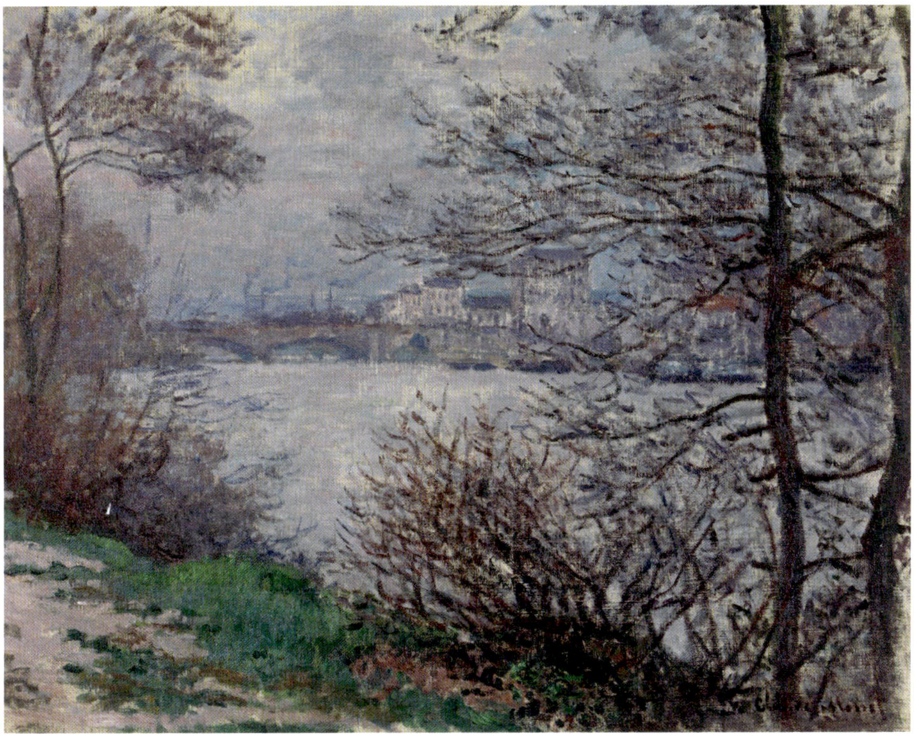

Fig. 20
CLAUDE MONET
The Seine at La Grande Jatte, 1878
Private collection, Vienna

Gare St.-Lazare of 1877 (which could, for example, have been seen by visitors to the *Exposition centennale de l'art français* at the Paris World's Fair in 1900, fig. p. 17). Similarly, in his *Freight Station (Frachtenbahnhof)* (ca. 1905) Rudolf Quittner, who had lived in Paris for many years and had been well connected in artist circles, was drawing on Monet's bold representations of stations at Argenteuil *(Argenteuil Station [La gare d'Argenteuil]*, ca. 1872, W 242) and Paris (cf. *Train Tracks at the Gare St.-Lazare [Les voies à la sortie de la gare Saint-Lazare]*, 1877, W 445, or *Outside the Gare St.-Lazare [The Signal], [La gare Saint-Lazare à l'extérieur (le signal)]*, 1877, W 448). There is no central subject, which has the effect of emphasizing the expanse of tracks and drawing attention to the smoke belching from the locomotives and the spectacle of clouds in the sky. This was an idea from Monet, just as the glow of the signals and lights suggested in just a few, brief strokes also reflects his pictorial language.

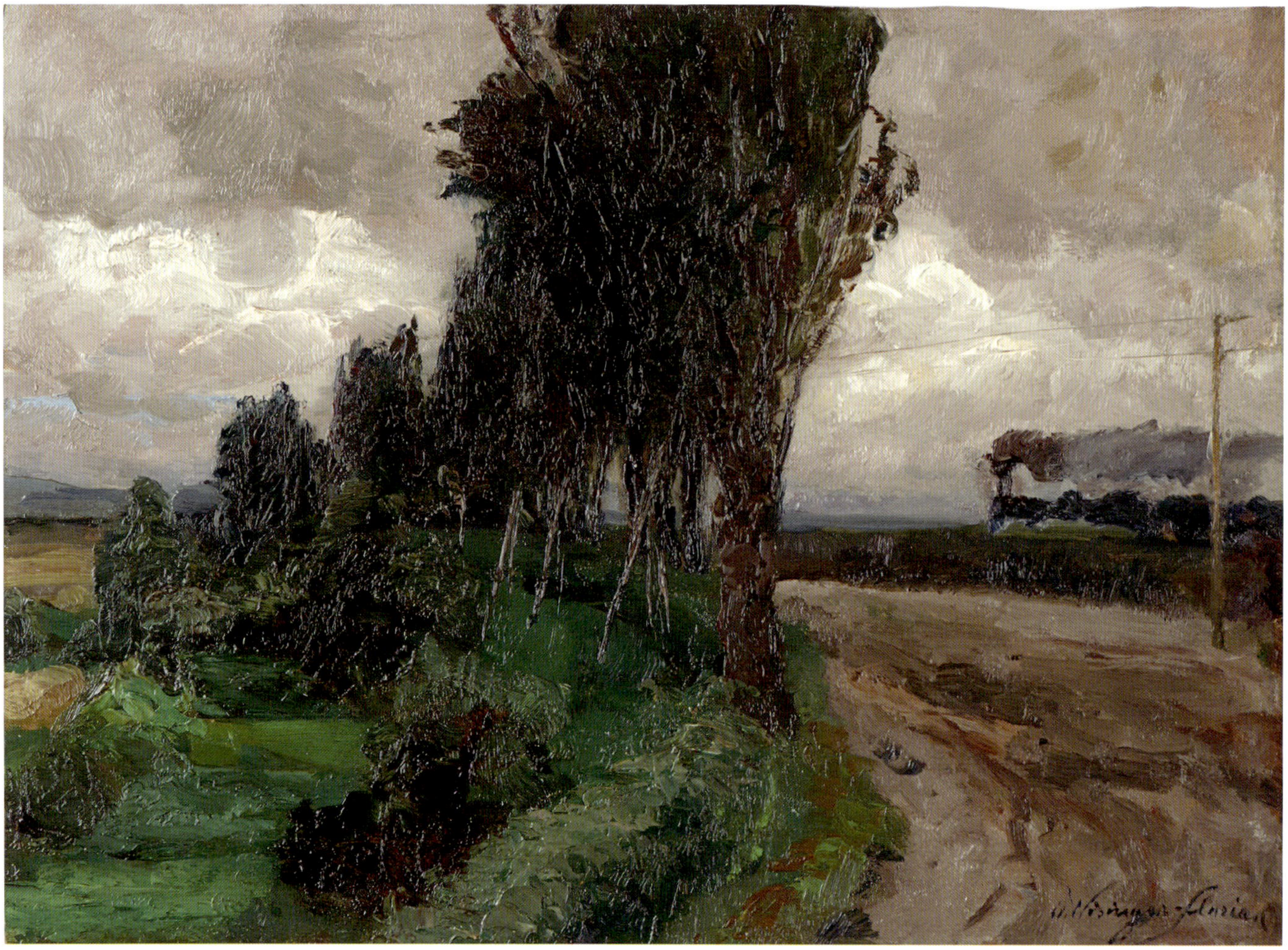

Fig. 21
OLGA WISINGER-FLORIAN
Railway in a Landscape, ca. 1895
Leopold Museum – Private Foundation, Vienna

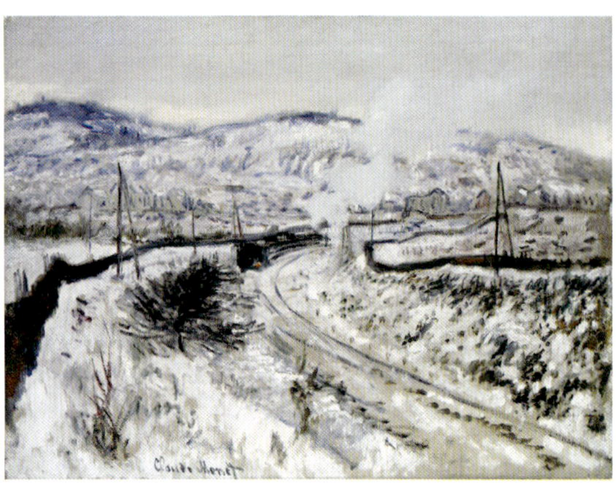

Fig. 22
CLAUDE MONET
Train in the Snow at Argenteuil, 1875
Private collection

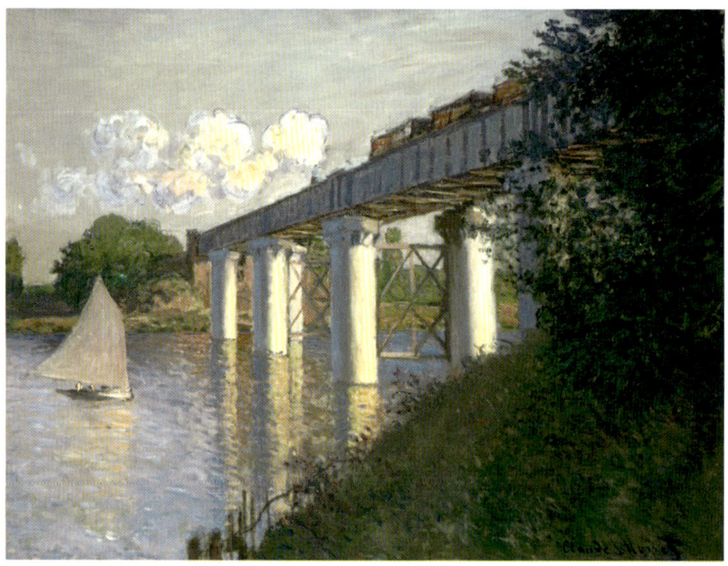

Fig. 23
CLAUDE MONET
The Railway Bridge at Argenteuil, 1874
Philadelphia Museum of Art

Fig. 24
CLAUDE MONET
Exterior of Saint-Lazare Station (The Signal), 1877
Niedersächsisches Landesmuseum, Hanover

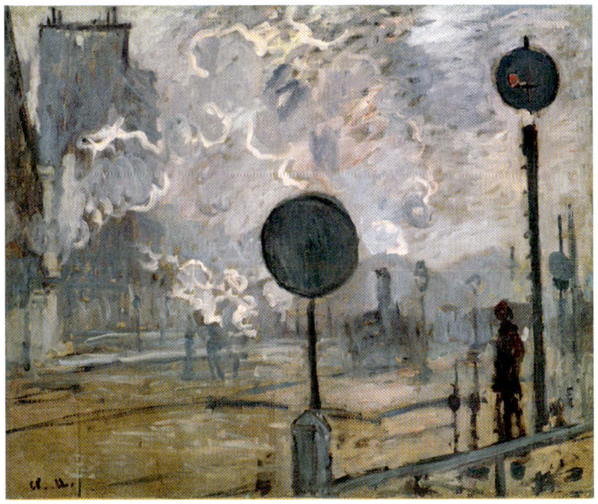

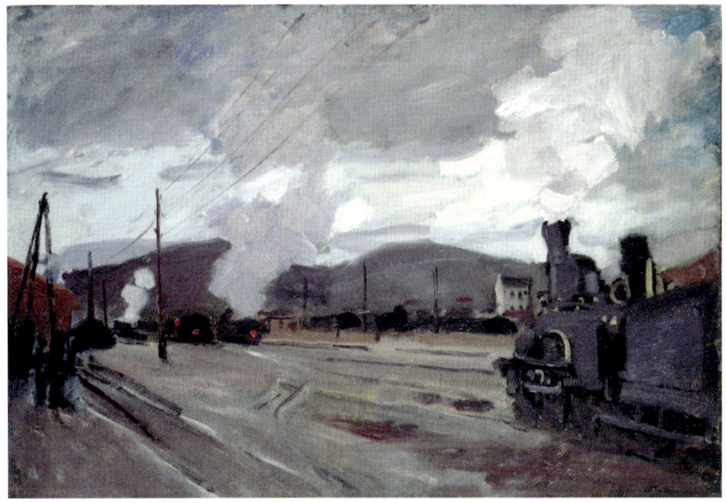

Fig. 25
CLAUDE MONET
The Railway Station at Argenteuil, 1872
Conseil Général du Val d'Oise, Cergy

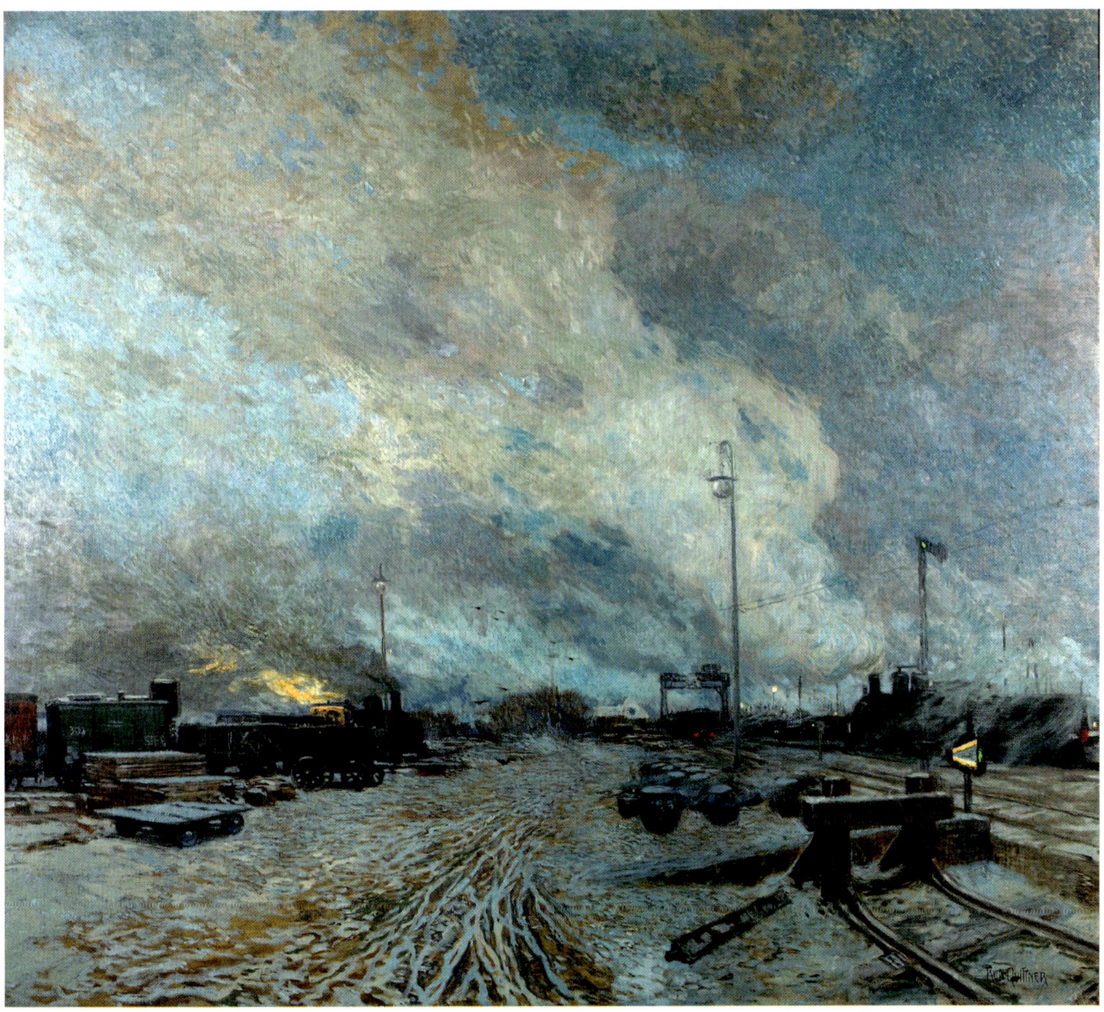

Fig. 26
RUDOLF QUITTNER
Cargo railway, ca. 1905
Belvedere, Vienna

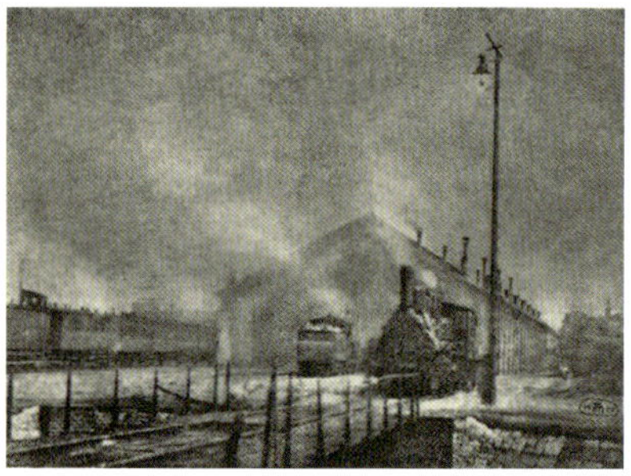

Fig. 27
THEODOR MAYER
Switch yard, ca. 1900

The focus of sketches was to capture atmospheric effects and render the experience with maximum authenticity and instantaneity in an image. And in this respect Monet's art was a recurrent point of reference. Emilie Mediz-Pelikan, who had made an intensive study of French Impressionism and especially Monet, occasionally came very close to the French master in her paintings without ever relinquishing her own signature style.

Her *Sea in the Midday Heat* (*Meer in der Mittagsglut*) (1890) pares down the depiction to the dramatic representation of color effects, dissolving the water and sky into a tapestry of open brushstrokes. With confident assurance she represented the impasto glowing sun in the haze and indicated the shining reflection in the water with a few bold strokes. Pictures such as these are unthinkable without Monet's *Impression, Sunrise (Impression, soleil levant)* (1873) (fig. p. 18). Whereas many of these artists sketched their sensations, an impression of the colors, and the composition directly in front of the motif, yet never dared take the leap to such boldness when painting larger formats, Theodor von Hörmann dedicated his life to open-air painting.

This officer from the Tyrol pursued his true talent with unwavering determination, ultimately abandoning his military career in favor of painting. Back in 1873 he had come across the landscapes by the Barbizon School at the Vienna World's Fair and discovered in these an approach that fascinated him and was profoundly in tune with his own aspirations: painting *en plein air*. Hörmann was so impressed that on two occasions he tried to gain a scholarship for Paris, only to be turned down by the committee for Vorarlberg and the Tyrol.

It was probably the summer or autumn of 1886 when the painter eventually arrived in Paris, where he would stay for the next three-and-a-half years. By this time he could look back on a rich oeuvre and had already developed his own artistic idiom.

Mainly self-taught in all essential aspects of his work—especially *plein air* painting—Hörmann had found his way to a lighter palette while working in the glaring light of the Hungarian Puszta, which now emerged in bolder contrasts (cf. fig. p. 189). It was here that his special ability blossomed, namely his sensitivity to color, and his gift for capturing light and its powers to shape a composition.

In terms of his approach to art, Hörmann was far closer to French painting than to his own tradition. He did not ask what lay behind things, was not in the least concerned to exalt the world he saw, but was interested in a precise understanding of objects' optical appearances. With indescribable fervor and indefatigable endurance he tried to come closer to this goal, and drew the veracity of his artistic ethos from this aspiration: "He essentially painted only from nature and *alla prima*, with full force and finished immediately," Ludwig Hevesi recounted. "He avoided under- and overpaintings; everything should emerge and remain as it had been inspired by the vivid moment. Only in this way could it be 'correct' ('correct' was his catchword). […] Fine-tuning everything in his studio afterward was not his thing, as in doing so he would only have lost the immediacy gained from nature through too much tinkering. In Vienna he had a particularly difficult position, as here academic art still had the greatest say. In Munich he fared better, as well as in Paris."[8]

Hörmann found affirmation of his artistic quest in France; he had, after all, independently arrived at comparable results in previous works. In France he found himself in an artistic environment that ascribed to this cause completely and presented him with some fascinating solutions.

Fig. 28
ALBERTA FRIDLÄNDER
On the Edge of the Woods, ca. 1900

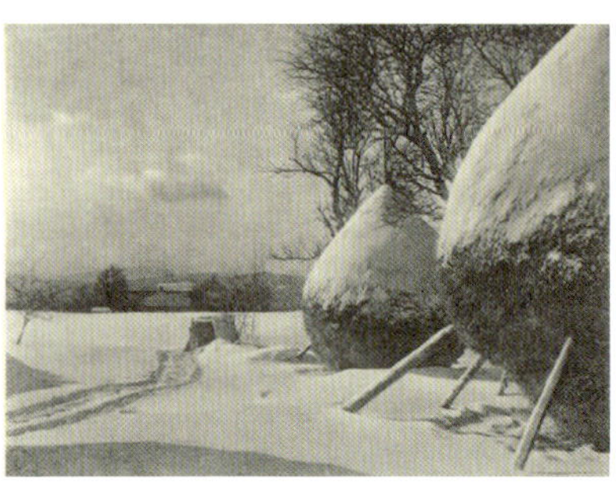

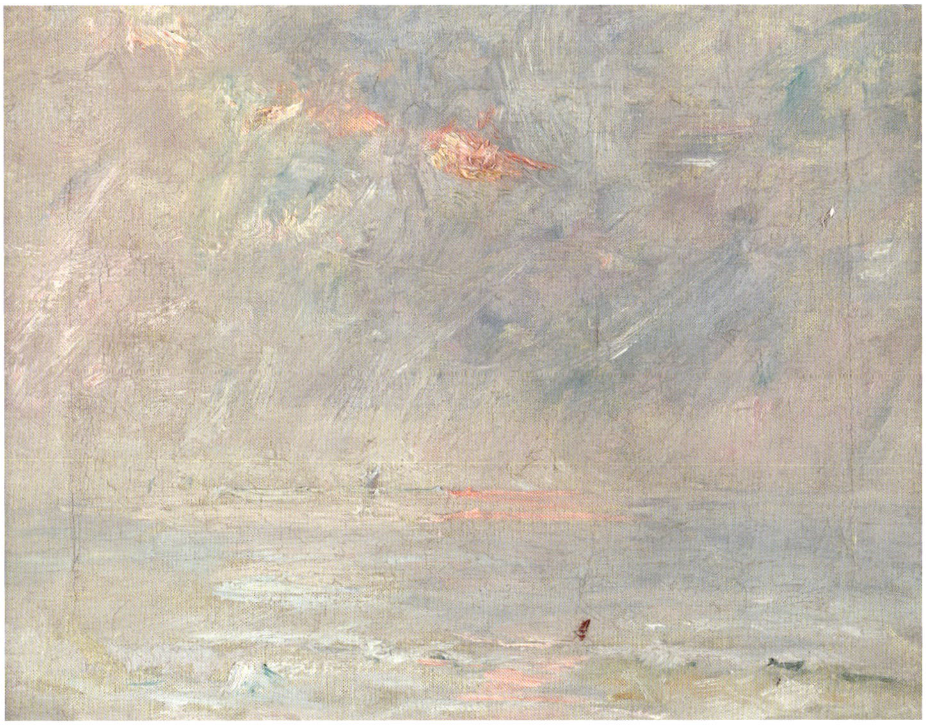

Fig. 29
EMILIE MEDIZ-PELIKAN
Sea in the Midday Heat, 1890
Private collection

A more exact rendering of color can be detected already in sketches like *Detached Houses in Jersey (Einzelstehenden Häuser auf Jersey)* (ca. 1887), emerging in the blue of the fences, the bluish-gray gate, and the bluish shimmer on the roofs. At the same time a more casual composition demonstrates an immediate, uncontrived approach to the subject. There is no "atmosphere" here, only a representation of the existing scene, pinpointing the shades with maximum possible accuracy.

In the painting *In the Tuileries, Paris (In den Tuilerien, Paris)* (ca. 1888), Hörmann came particularly close to Monet's pictures in style, subject matter, and the feel of the scene. This indicates the leisure pursuits of city dwellers, the bustling city beneath Parisian skies in late summer or autumn. It is one of Hörmann's works in which he was less concerned with pictorial depth than with a faithful rendering of color stimuli on the retina and noting the variety of color patches and impressions on this cloudy day—to such an extent that detail could be neglected. The brush loosely juxtaposes dabs or brief strokes. Even the missing faces on the figures in the foreground can be traced back to Monet, who, for example, in his *Anglers on the Seine near Poissy* (1882, fig. p. 161) omitted all physiognomical details.

In *View from the Paris Studio (Blick aus dem Pariser Atelier)* (1890), Hörmann painted the wintery city in fluid strokes, with smoke from the many chimneys rising above the rooftops. His passersby, captured in dabs on the street below, are astonishingly similar to Monet's figures in *Boulevard des Capucines* (1873, W 292) and in *Rue Montorgueil, Festival of June 30, 1878 (La rue Montorgueil à Paris. Fête du 30 juin 1878)* (1878, W 469). Hörmann must have seen both pictures in 1889 at Georges Petit's gallery, when they were

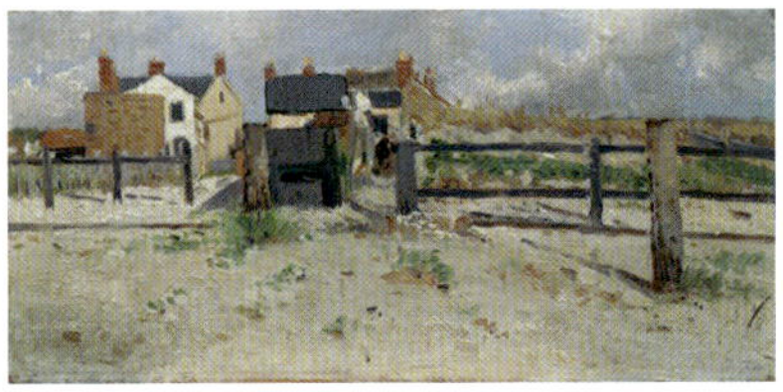

Fig. 30
THEODOR VON HÖRMANN
Houses on Jersey, 1888
Belvedere, Vienna

presented in the exhibition "Claude Monet—A. Rodin."[9] Even in the format, which was similar to the Impressionists, these loosely painted pictures emphasized the aspirations Hörmann shared with them.

During his time in Paris from 1886 through to January 1890, the painter had ample opportunity to study Monet's work. Industrious and determined as he was, one can assume that he did not miss these exhibitions. In 1887 Georges Petit's[10] presentation of Monet's dramatic coastal scenes from Belle-Île, painted the previous year, showed one of the *Pyramids of Port-Coton*. Hörmann subsequently painted a group of three striking rock stacks on the Breton coast.[11] In summer 1888,[12] Boussod, Valadon & Cie exhibited ten of Monet's works in a show with the title "Dix marines d'Antibes de M Cl. Monet," and at the aforementioned legendary exhibition "Claude Monet—A. Rodin," no less than 135 paintings by Monet were shown alongside thirty-three of Rodin's works. Three of Monet's works could be seen at the World's Fair that same year as well. Added to this, there were the exhibition spaces in galleries and collections of enthusiasts of the new art, including Paul Durand-Ruel, Jean-Baptiste Faure, or Gustave Caillebotte, that were occasionally open for viewing.

There can be no doubt that visiting exhibitions, such as the Georges Petit show of 1889, spurred Hörmann on to ever-bolder ventures. This delight in experiment is revealed, for instance, in *Nighttime Paris with the Eiffel Tower (Paris bei Nacht mit Eiffelturm)* of the same year.

Fig. 31
THEODOR VON HÖRMANN
In the Tuileries, 1888
Belvedere, Vienna

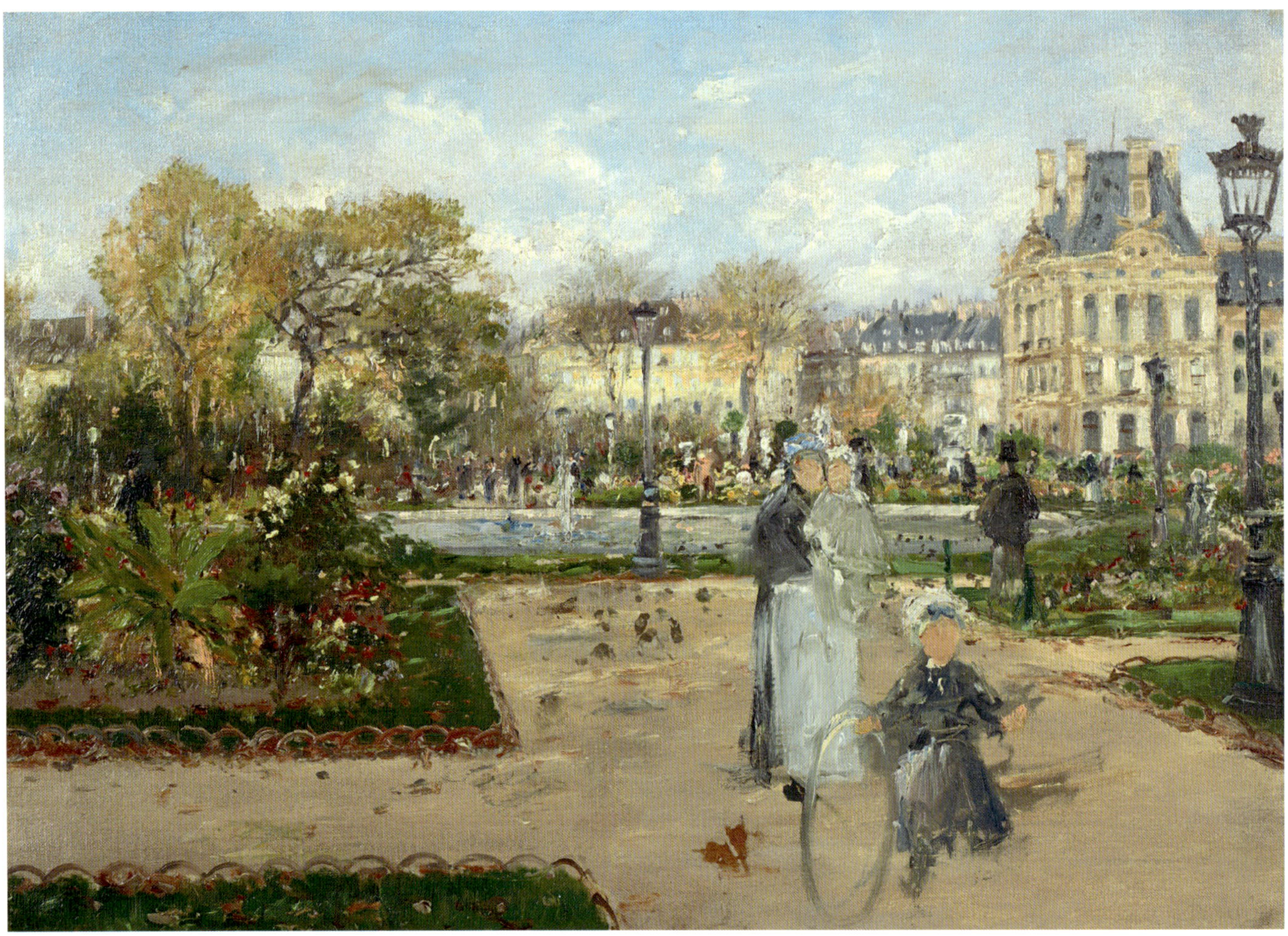

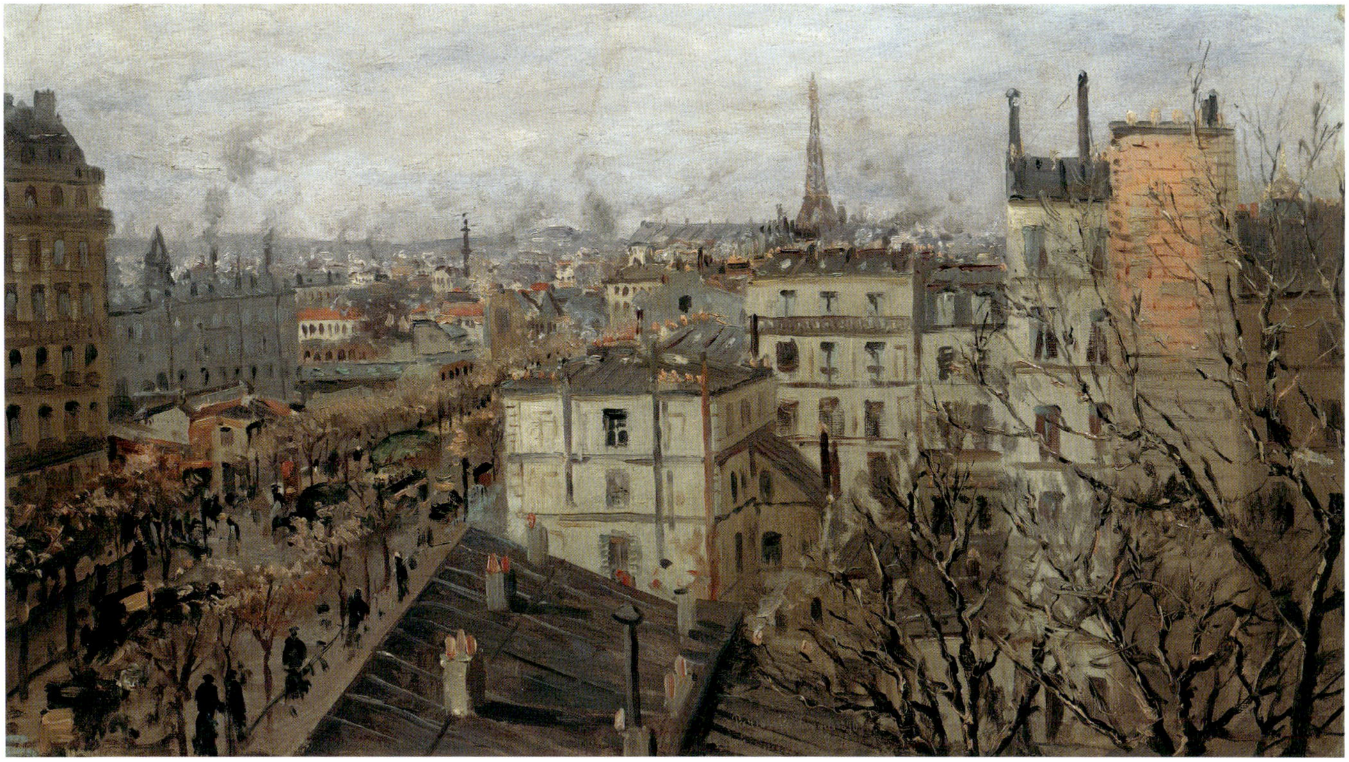

Fig. 32
THEODOR VON HÖRMANN
View of Paris, 1890
Belvedere, Vienna

The color scheme is restricted, aiming to represent the special light effects of the Eiffel Tower illuminated in red and surrounded by swathes of nocturnal clouds. Light is also cast from the window opposite onto the roof in front of the viewer. Hörmann seems to have tried to swiftly capture a nocturnal atmosphere, a record of a moment as it were, and this from the same studio where he painted his *View of Paris* somewhat later. Monet's paintings like *Train in the Snow, the Locomotive (Le train dans la neige, la locomotive)* (1875, W 356, fig. p. 11), with its glaring headlamps in the midst of all the wintery grays, could have inspired Hörmann to capture the fleeting appearances of light. On another occasion, Hörmann could even have come across paintings such as Monet's *A Seascape, Shipping by Moonlight (Marine, effet de nuit)* (ca. 1864, W 71, fig. p. 12) or *The Port of Le Havre, Night Effect (Le Port du Havre, effet de nuit)* (1873, W 264), paintings that are just as bold and immediate as his own.

Monet's *Field of Tulips in Holland (Champ de tulipes, Hollande)* (1886, W 1067), also exhibited by Georges Petit in 1889, evidently had a lasting influence on Hörmann, as around 1893 he painted his fields of sainfoin with an equally pronounced sense of depth. The Belvedere's *Large Field of Sainfoin near Znaim (Große Esparsettenfeld bei Znaim)* is dominated by the bold foreshortening of the vibrant field in the foreground and thus recalls the rectangular zones of red tulips in Monet's painting.

Hörmann's receptiveness to exploring an ice jam on the Thaya River in a painting could potentially be traced back to this exhibition visit as well, as Monet had also tried to render such rare spectacles in a pared down wintery palette.[13] Hörmann's paintings of the *Ice Jams on the Banks of the Thaya (Eisschollen am Ufer der Thaya)* (1891) convey a similar sense of the foggy chill, explore the lightless winter days in subtle gradations of gray and brown, while the warmer color scheme in one of the depictions shows an inkling of the sun's gentle glimmer piercing the hazy sky.

Fig. 33
CLAUDE MONET
Saint-Germain-l'Auxerrois, 1867
Staatliche Museen zu Berlin, Preußischer Kulturbesitz, Nationalgalerie

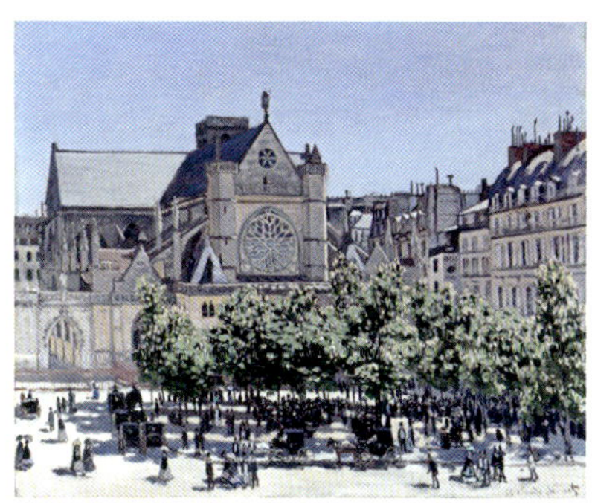

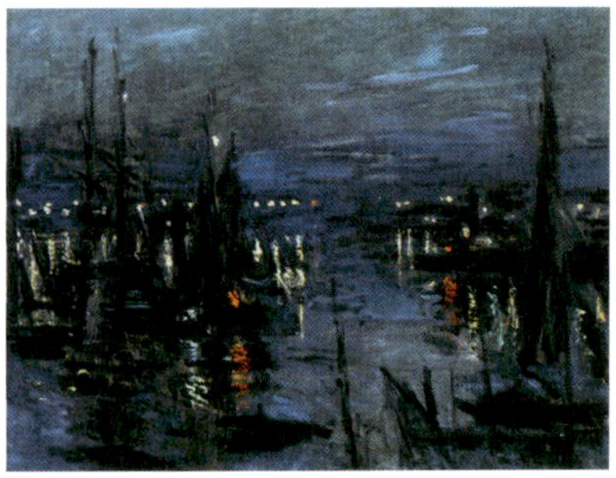

Fig. 34
CLAUDE MONET
The Port of Le Havre, Night Effect, 1873
Private collection

The manner in which Hörmann captured the event in different atmospheres of weather and light in three pictures bears a close resemblance to Monet, who had started to develop his series in precisely these years. The Georges Petit exhibition featured a considerable number of pictorial sequences, representing the same subject in different atmospheric conditions (including two versions of the ice jam on the Seine), as well as introducing one of Monet's most recent creations: his series from the *Valley of the Creuse* (1889).

Just like Monet in this series, Hörmann varied his vantage point only slightly, drawing our attention to the array of colors that altered with the changing weather.

And when, in 1895, Hörmann painted the view of the Neuer Markt from his new Vienna studio, his awareness of Monet's aforementioned paintings *Le Boulevard des Capucines* and *Rue Montorgueil* emerges in a view that leads deep into the picture's depths and the small, dark, and sketchy passersby.

In the same way as Monet, all through his life Hörmann tried out new things and sought new challenges. And like Monet, Hörmann displayed a resoluteness in which the work was all that counted. He never went easy on himself, painted outdoors in all weathers and all seasons, and did not even shrink from danger for his art, for example when he was painting the French coast. "This strong nature even defied the elements when a fury of creativity came over him. There is, for example, a picture from France showing three cliffs, which he painted in veritable mortal danger; the sea's tide rose ever higher up his body, but he continued working in the water in a frenzy, until he finally climbed up a pathless cliff with his finished study and saved himself."[14]

Fig. 35
THEODOR VON HÖRMANN
Nighttime Paris with the Eiffel Tower, 1889
Belvedere, Vienna

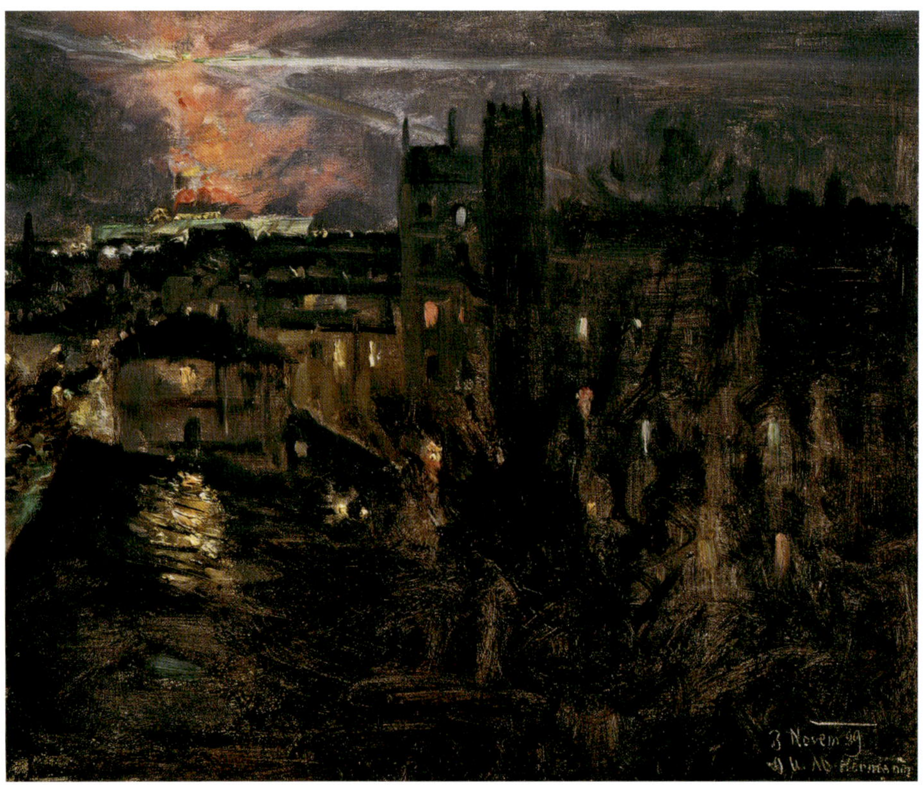

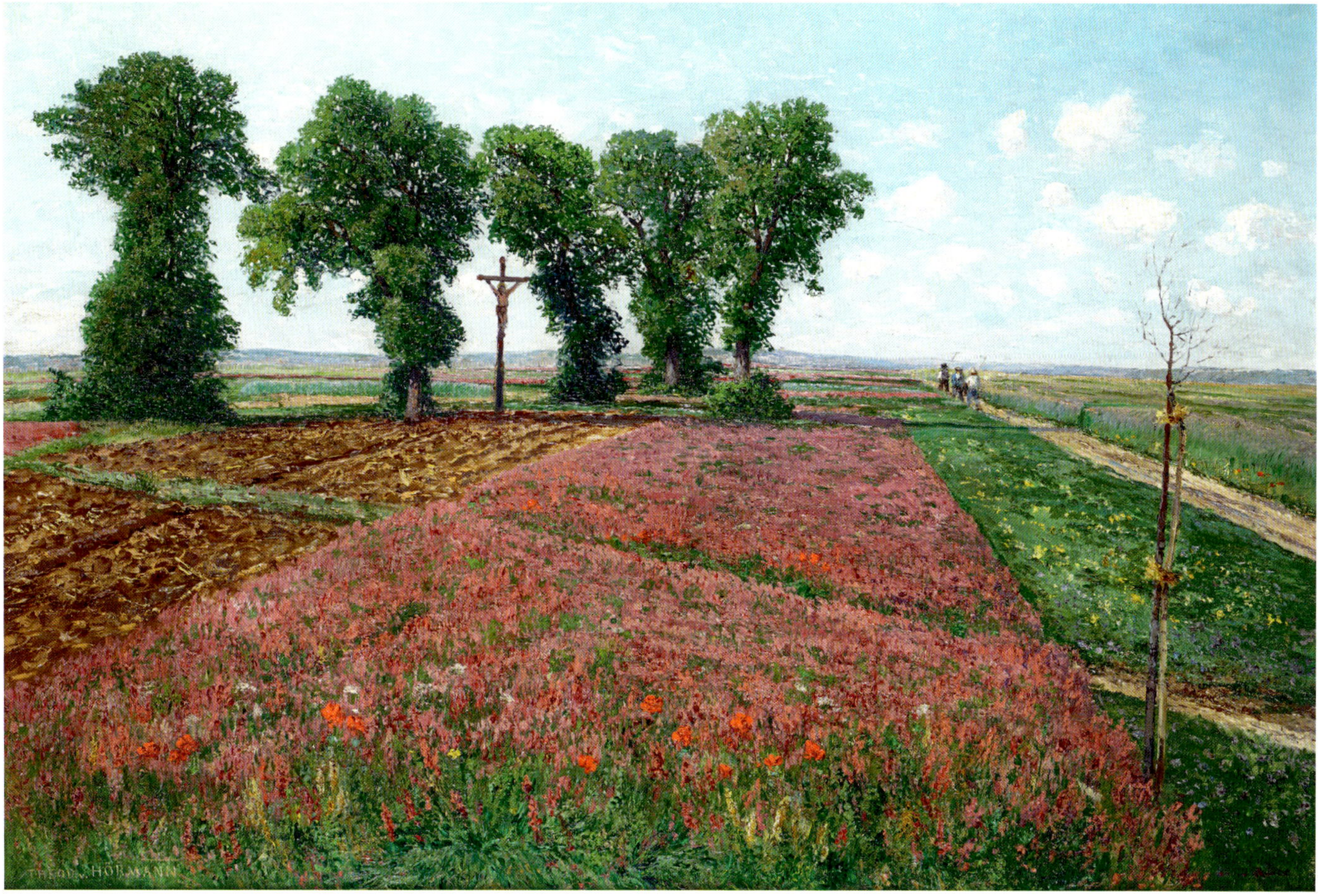

Fig. 36
THEODOR VON HÖRMANN
The Big Field of Sainfoins near Znojmo IV, 1893
Belvedere, Vienna

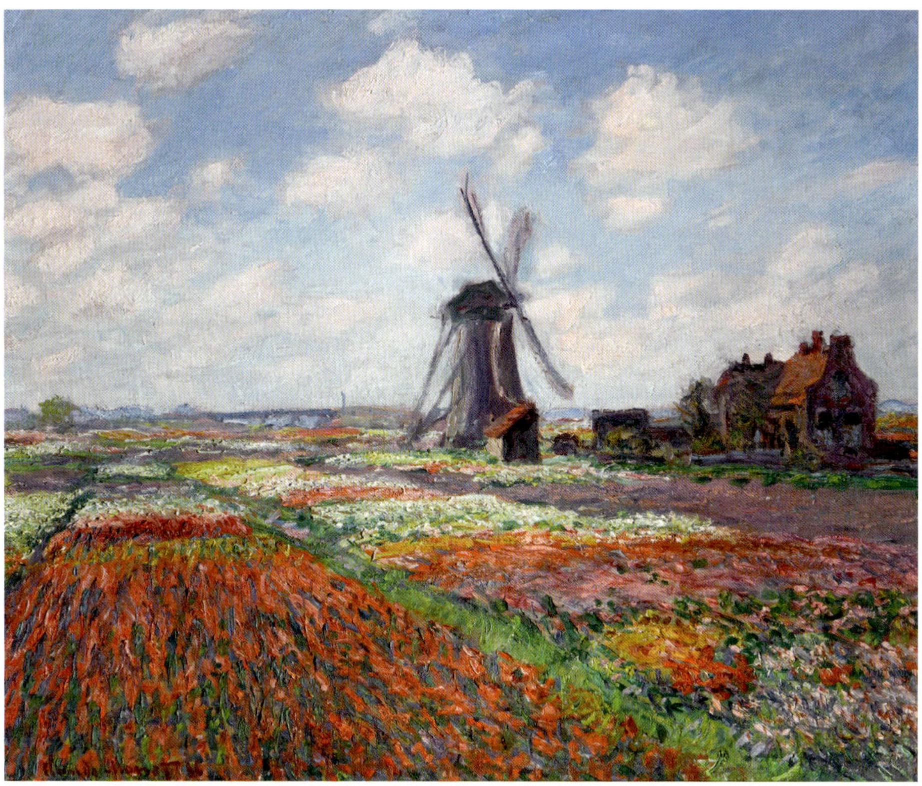

Fig. 37
CLAUDE MONET
A Field of Tulips in Holland, 1886
Musée d'Orsay, Paris

Fig. 38
THEODOR VON HÖRMANN
Ice Floes on the Banks of the Thaya I, ca. 1891
Belvedere, Vienna

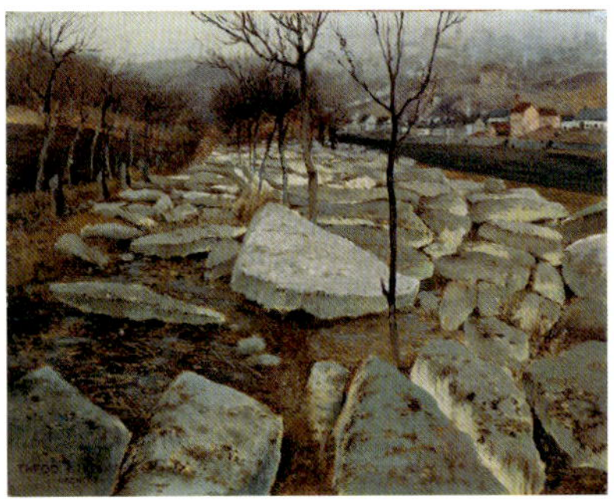

Fig. 39
THEODOR VON HÖRMANN
Ice Floes on the Banks of the Thaya II, ca. 1891
Private collection

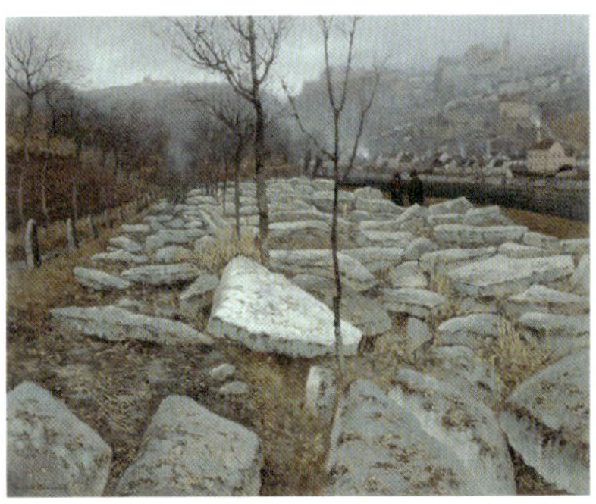

Fig. 40
THEODOR VON HÖRMANN
Ice Floes on the Banks of the Thaya III, 1891
Private collection

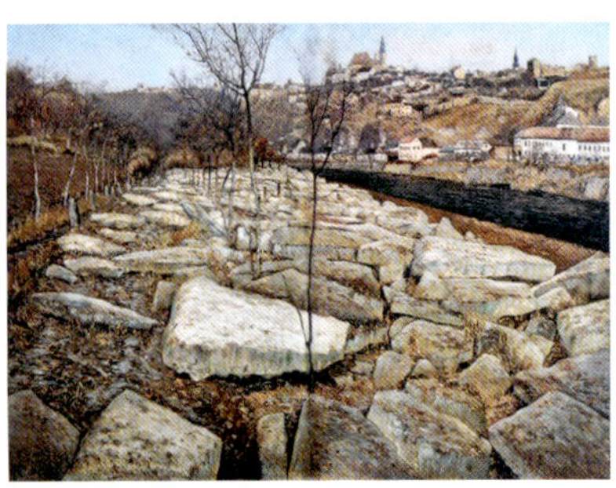

His painting *Zell am See in the Winter (Zell am See im Winter)* (1890) must also have been painted in the bitter cold. It shows the bluish-green ice of the frozen weir and conjures a sense of the foggy chill in the waning shades of gray, a chill that positively seems to creep into our bones. The unsparing way he treated himself in creating such works also contributed to Hörmann's rapidly deteriorating health and his early death.

Hörmann's immense aspiration to take the appearance of nature as the true standard also underlies his painting *Pond in a Beech Forest (Tümpel im Buchenwald)* (1892) (fig. p. 190). After the Künstlerhaus jury had grudgingly accepted it for an exhibition in March 1893, not only was it not understood by contemporaries but it also practically became a "coloristic scandal" (Hevesi).[15]

Hörmann had depicted the vibrant colors of nature with unsparing "correctness" and had tried to convey the impression of all-pervading light through a radical intensification of the dominant red shade. But he had done this without any consideration for the taste of his day or for the harmonies within the picture. He was very proud of this picture in particular. Together with the painter Peter Paul Müller from Munich, he had painted the autumnal reds of the beech forest on November 9, 1892, after both artists had spent one-and-a-half hours fishing the leaves out of the pond so they could also paint the water's surface. On hindsight, Hörmann rejoiced in his achievements: "I felt a boundless joy that my picture was totally different, bolder, more forceful in color. And he himself stated, I never would have believed it possible that two painters [...] could see and express themselves so differently, and today I know for sure that mine is more correct than his."[16]

In the immediacy and bold cropping in many of his compositions, the immense accuracy of his shades, the luminous colors and emphasis on light, Hörmann was probably the Austrian painter of the time who came closest to French Impressionism—and his artistic aspirations revealed a close affinity with Monet. However, despite the increasing differentiations in his brushwork and his use of a dappled technique, ultimately he did not go so far as to depict only the eyes' perception of light and color rather than the things themselves. In his work, things remain clearly outlined and distinguished from each other, the brushstrokes' rhythms always allude to their form, despite the fact that in his late sketches, the gestural predominates and the brushwork appears to take on a new intensity and verve.

Even an artist like Carl Schuch, who worked so independently on his masterpieces of color and his precisely orchestrated color tones, was gripped by Monet's bright colors and his quest for luminosity in his images. Schuch's pictures of Saut du Doubs, sometimes in the form of seemingly haphazard cropped scenes of unpretentious subjects, are transformed into a pageant of boldly applied shades of cobalt blue and violet, sparkling amidst the lavish array of complementary reddish-browns and green color values. At the same time, light becomes the main protagonist, accentuating things and sometimes shining upon them with unrestrained brilliance in vibrant colors. The painting is characterized by the contrast between light and dark, between what is illuminated by the warm sunlight and what lies in the shadows beneath the blue sky[17] (cf. *In the Doubs Valley [Im Tal des Doubs]*, ca. 1890, Alte Nationalgalerie Berlin or *Forest Interior near Saut du Doubs [Waldinneres beim Saut du Doubs]*, after 1890, Belvedere, Vienna).

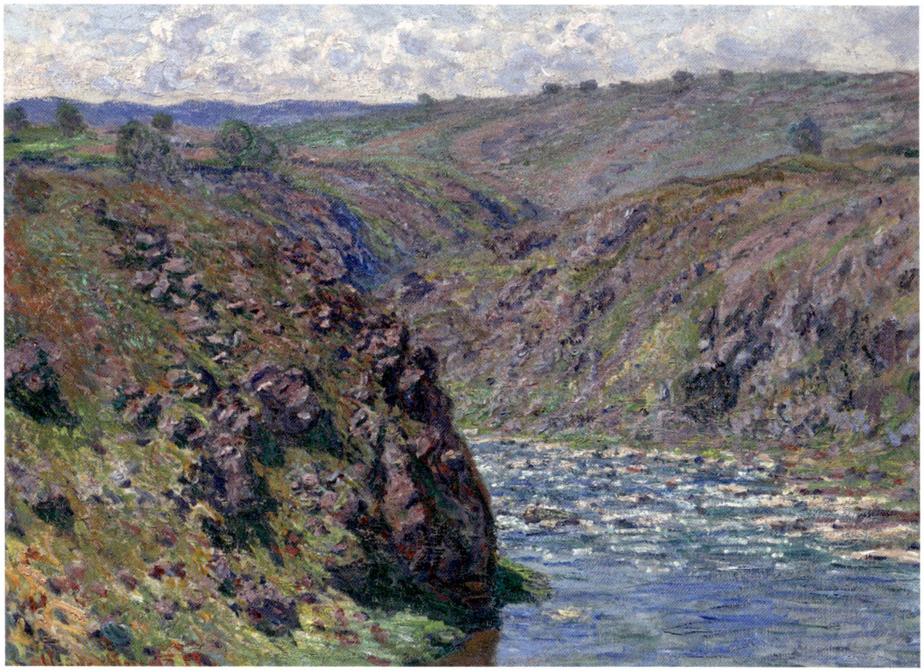

Fig. 41
CLAUDE MONET
Valley of the Creuse (Sunlight Effect), 1889
Museum of Fine Arts, Boston, Massachusetts

Fig. 42
LUDWIG HEINRICH JUNGNICKEL
View of the Danube Valley from Aggstein, ca. 1906
Landesmuseum Niederösterreich, St. Pölten

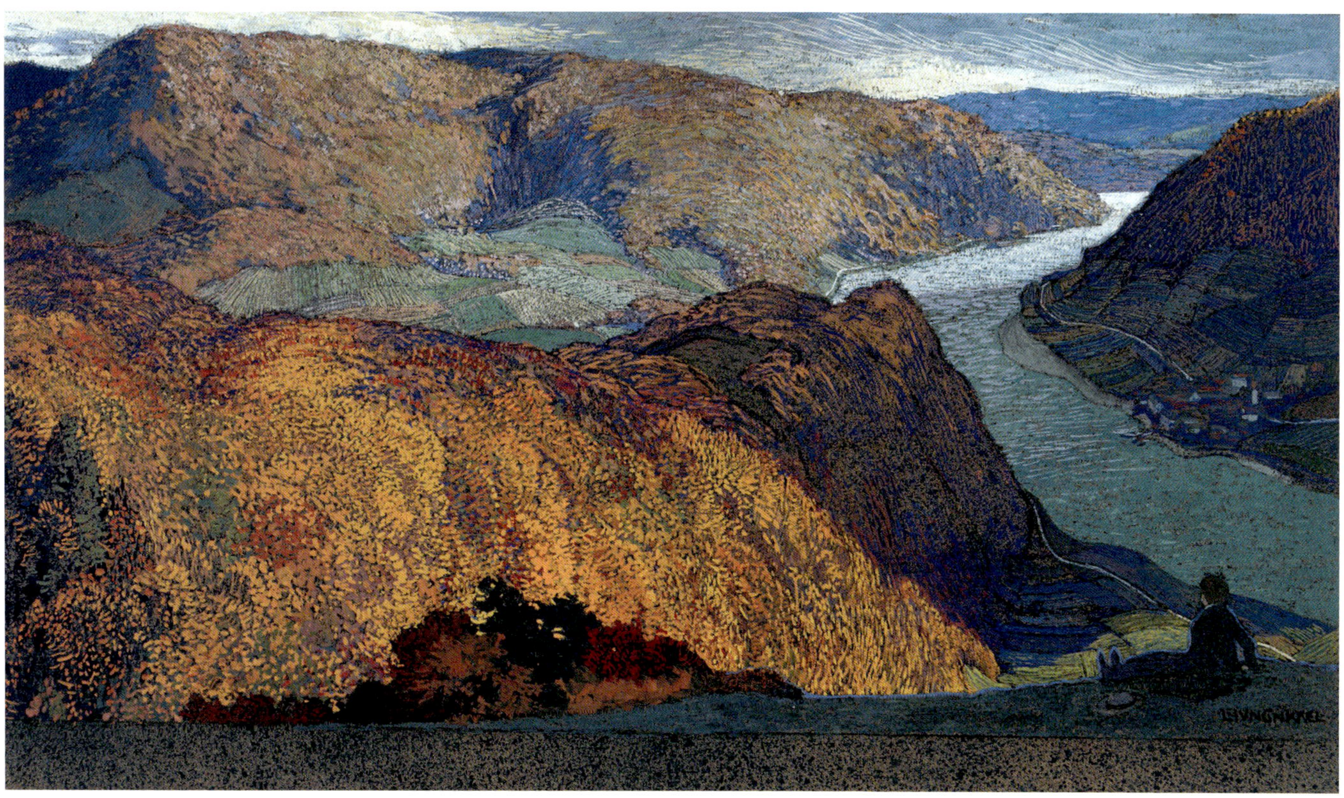

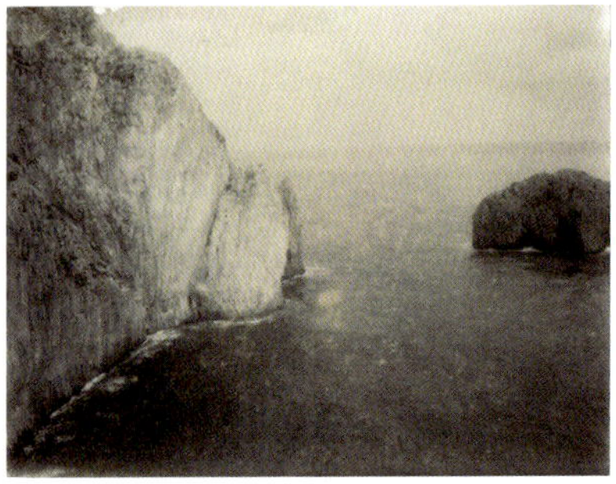

Fig. 43
ALFRED ZOFF
Coast area, ca. 1900
Archive of the Belvedere, Vienna

Fig. 44
CLAUDE MONET
Manne-Porte, Étretat, 1885
Philadelphia Museum of Art

COMPOSITIONAL AND THEMATIC INSPIRATIONS

Throughout his life, Monet was fascinated by water. He must have felt challenged in his attempts to capture its volatile nature, the continuously changing character and tones. He was to become a virtuoso in doing so.

He broke completely new ground, however, in his coastal pictures, which abandoned all traditional ideas in a radically new approach. His views of the ragged coastline and solitary needles on the Atlantic island of Belle-Île, which he painted significantly on the Côte Sauvage, the rugged coastline facing the open sea, remain among the most categorical and impressive in his oeuvre.

Coastal scenes have always been popular, and many important painters, including the likes of Eugène Boudin, Johan Barthold Jongkind, and Gustave Courbet, responded to the demand for depictions of these picturesque sites. The versions painted by Monet, however, were so new and uncompromising that they were bound to have a resounding impact.

This is evident in paintings like *The Manneporte* (W 1037) in 1885, or *The Pyramids of Port Colon (*W 1084, W 1088, W 1089) (fig. p. 124) and *La Côte Sauvage* in 1886 (W 1100)

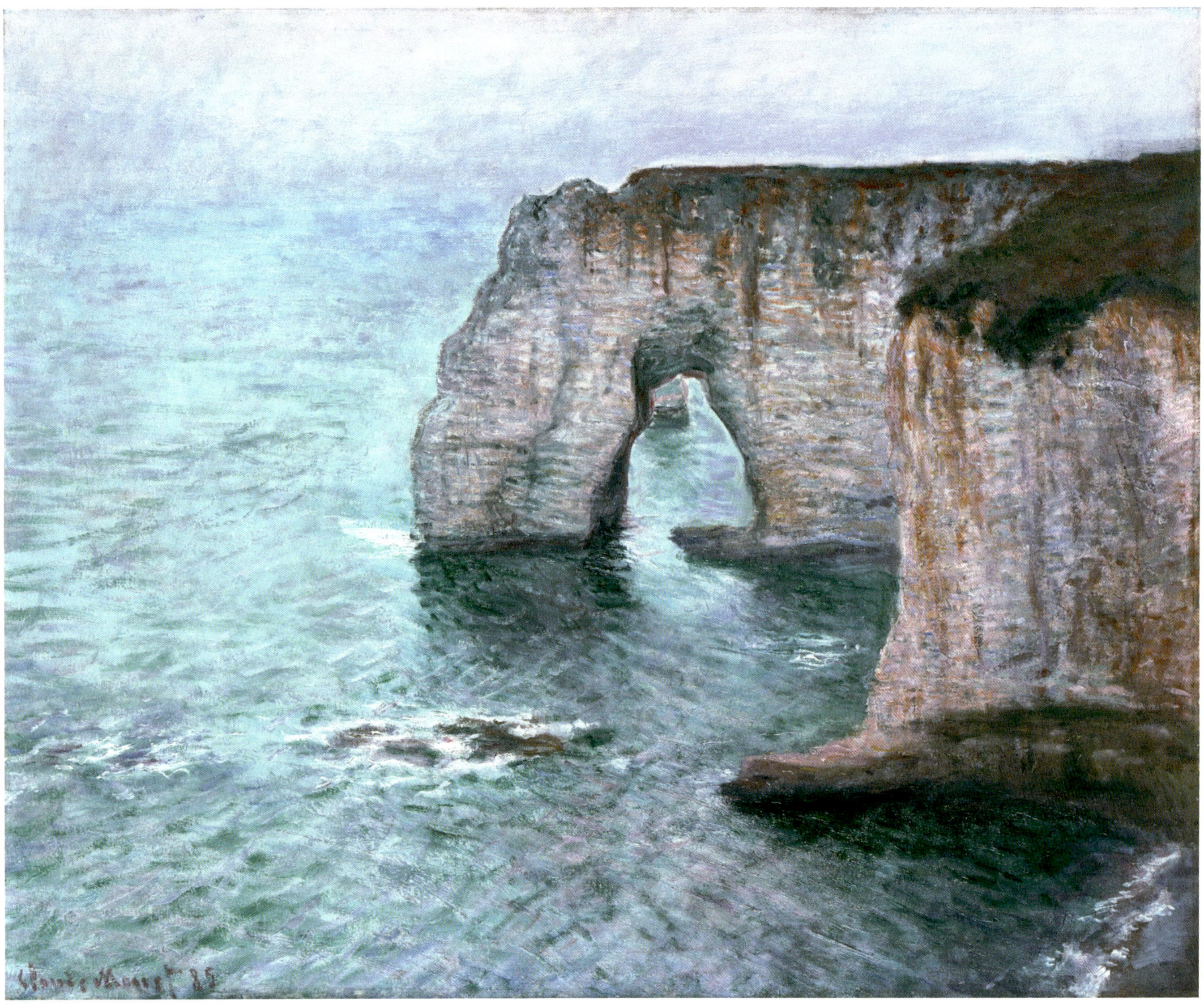

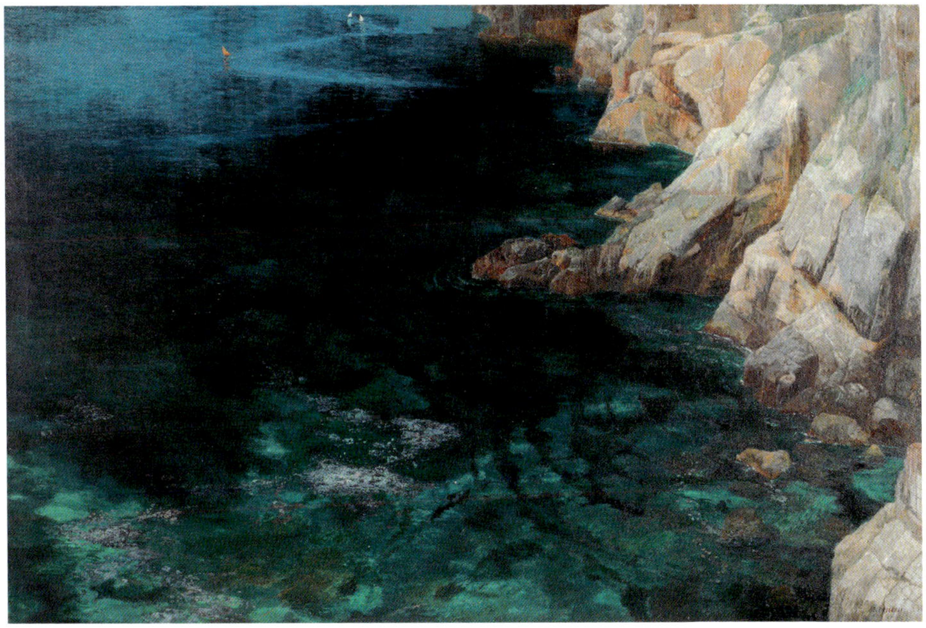

Fig. 45
EMILIE MEDIZ-PELIKAN
The Blue Coast of Duino, 1898
Private collection

with their radical perspective from above, the absence of foreground or observer's point of view, and the precipitous view down to the water. The fragmentary rock formations at the edge of the picture and the "untethered," detailed view of the sea allow the gaze to turn freely to the dramatic brushstrokes, which use a variety of tones to describe the rocks and above all the turmoil of the waves.

Pictures like this were shown in 1887 at Galerie Georges Petit, and in addition *La Côte Sauvage* was published in 1891 in the magazine *L'Art dans les deux mondes* with a gillotage on the front cover.[18]

In its structure and the drama of the rugged cliffs, Marie Egner's *Sea Surf in Dalmatia (Meeresbrandung bei Dalmatien)*, painted around the same time, reflects the impression that Monet must have made on her.

Emilie Mediz-Pelikan's coastal pictures also reference the direct view of the sea without foreground in Monet's paintings—most starkly in her masterly *Blue Coast of Duino (Blaue Küste von Duino)* (1898), where the sense of depth does not stop at the water but continues into the clear, blue-green wetness.

Finally, Alfred Zoff, whose entire artistic career was clearly influenced by Monet, applied this structural principle to a large number of his coastal pictures. He was a specialist in shores and coastlines and a master at reproducing waves, spray, and reflections, filling his sketchbooks with drawings similar to Monet's rapid, contoured pencil sketches. Here, too, the cliffs descending dramatically to the sea are at the edges of the pictures, while a large part of the pictures is devoted to the water. Zoff, who was a talented photographer and owner of two large-format cameras, reproduced this compositional scheme in his photographs, reminiscent of Monet, with dramatically plummeting cliffs or stone towers, or a view down from the cliffs into the depths of the sea.

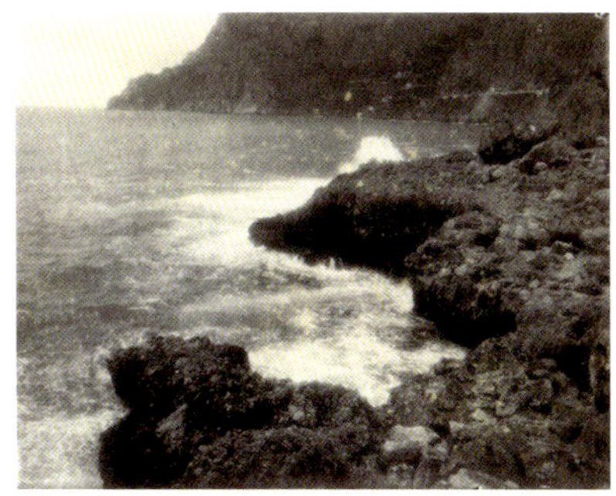

Fig. 46
ALFRED ZOFF
Coast area, ca. 1900
Archive of the Belvedere, Vienna

Fig. 47
ALFRED ZOFF
Coast areas, ca. 1908
Archive of the Belvedere, Vienna

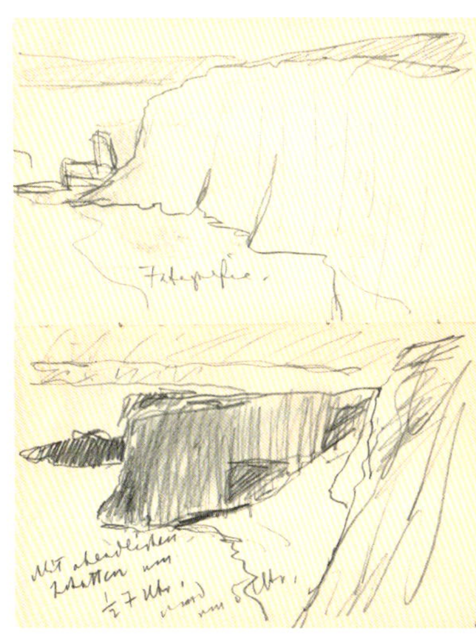

Fig. 48
CLAUDE MONET
The Côte Sauvage, 1886
Musée d'Orsay, Paris

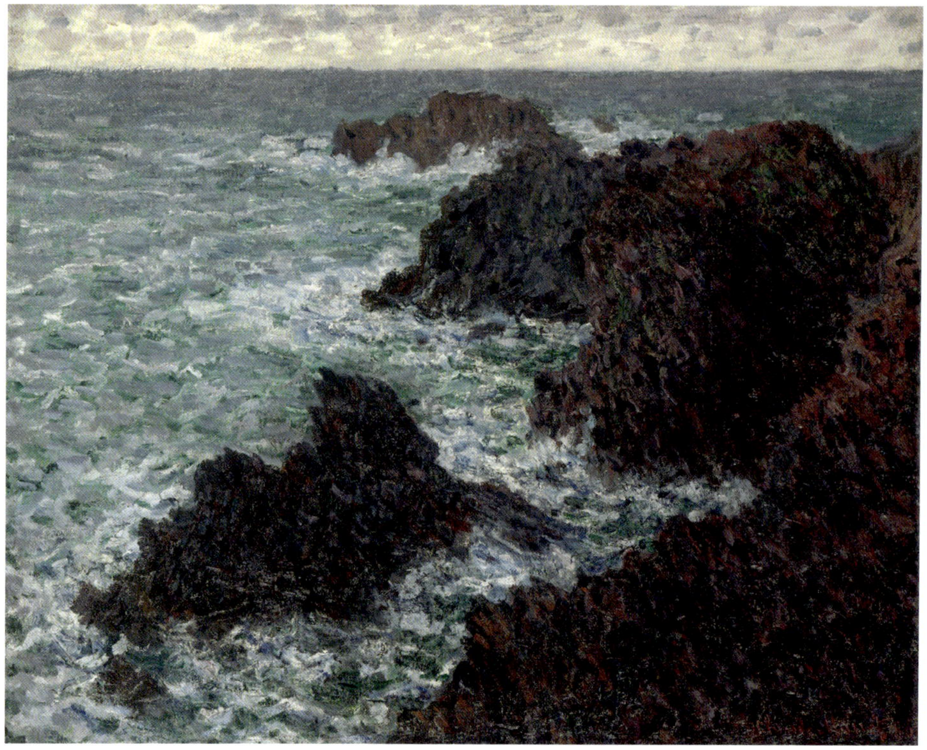

Fig. 50
MARIE EGNER
Stormy Sea in Dalmatia, 1884/90
Oberösterreichisches Landesmuseum, Linz

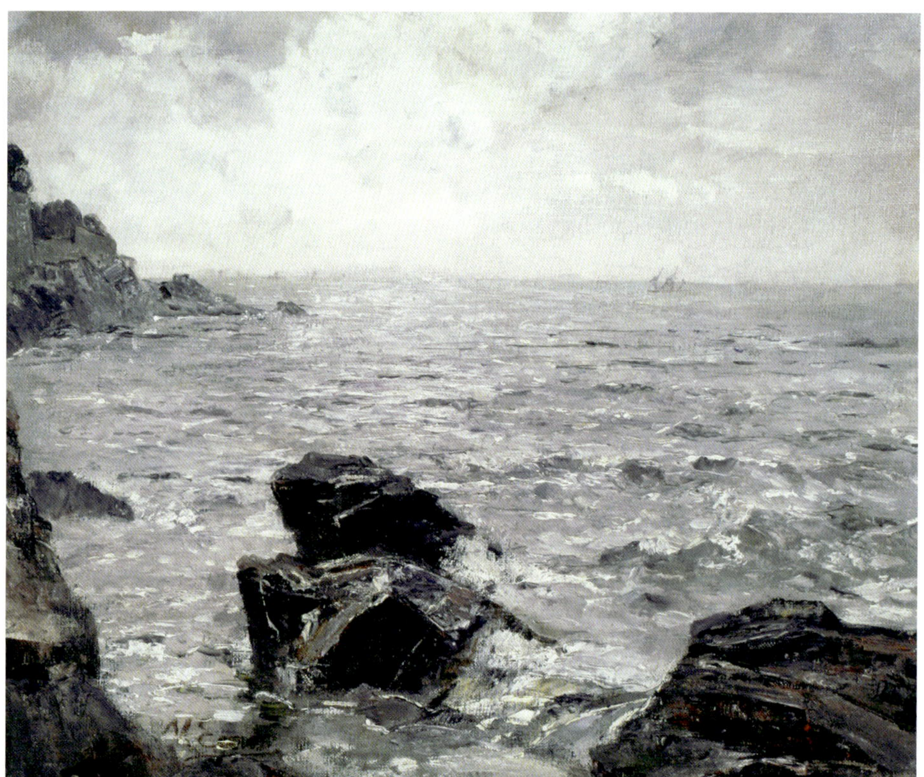

Fig. 49
Title page of *L'Art dans les deux mondes,* with
Claude Monet's *Le Côte Sauvage,* 1891

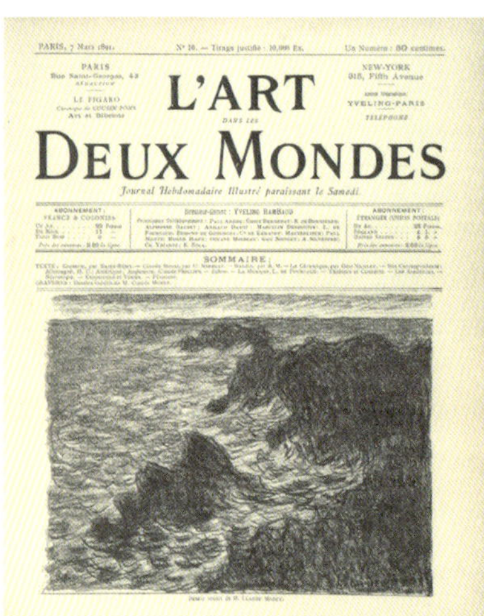

PARIS, 7 Mars 1891. — Tirage justifié : 10,000 Ex. — Un Numéro : 50 centimes.

PARIS
Rue Saint-Georges, 43

LE FIGARO

NEW-YORK
315, Fifth Avenue

YVELING-PARIS

TÉLÉPHONE

L'ART
DANS LES
DEUX MONDES

Journal Hebdomadaire Illustré paraissant le Samedi.

ABONNEMENT : FRANCE & COLONIES

ABONNEMENT : ÉTRANGER (UNION POSTALE)

SOMMAIRE :

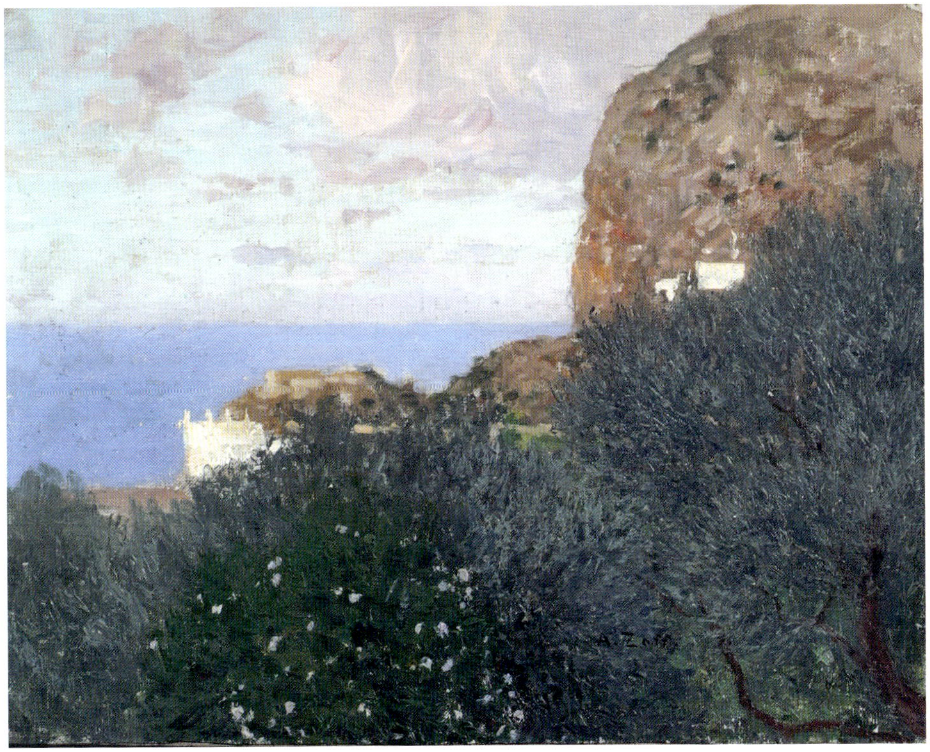

Fig. 51
ALFRED ZOFF
Capri, 1905
Belvedere, Vienna

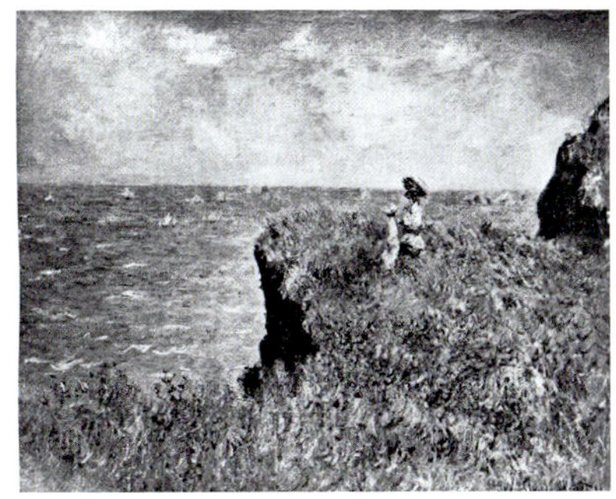

Fig. 52
CLAUDE MONET
Cliff Walk
in: Théodore Duret, *"Claude Monet and the Impressionism"*, in: *Kunst und Künstler. Illustrierte Monatsschrift für bildende Kunst und Kunstgewerbe*, 1904

In his later paintings, he also attempted to imitate Monet's color schemes by composing landscape forms using luminous, colored brushstrokes, portraying the sea with the intensity of Monet's pictures of the coastline of the South of France.
Sometimes he was able to borrow compositions directly from Monet. His *Harbor of Nieuwpoort (Hafen von Nieuwpoort)* (1910/12) is very similar to Monet's *The Seine at Rouen (La Seine à Rouen)* (1874, W 268). Pictures like this were shown in 1883 in *Gazette des beaux-arts*,[19] and in his picture of the coast of Capri he used a design principle on which Monet had based his series *Customs House (Cabane du douanier)* (1882) (fig. p. 161) and other views of the steep coast near Pourville: compact blocks of grass-covered slopes descend from the edges of the picture into the sea, while the horizon at sea cuts horizontally across the picture and divides it into different colored zones. Monet's *Cliff Walk at Pourville (Promenade sur la falaise à Pourville)* (1882, W 758) was reproduced in the February 1904 issue of *Kunst und Künstler: illustrierte Monatsschrift für bildende Kunst und Kunstgewerbe*,[20] and Zoff's small picture was painted the following year. Years later he also borrowed from Monet in his views of Dutch canals and windmills, as they had been illustrated, for example, in Camille Mauclair's book *L'impressionnisme*.[21]
Johann Victor Krämer also reacted directly to his encounter with Monet's *Church at Vétheuil (L'église de Vétheuil)* (1878, W 474), which he saw in 1910 at Galerie Miethke. Like Monet's picture, his *Ascent to the Church in Senftenberg (Aufstieg zur Kirche in Senftenberg)* (ca. 1910) has the church in the top center and the figures climbing up to it in the foreground.

Fig. 53
CLAUDE MONET
Cliff Walk at Pourville, 1882
The Art Institute Chicago

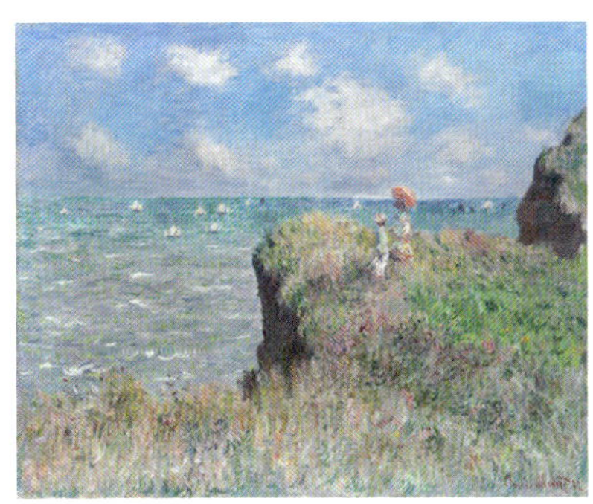

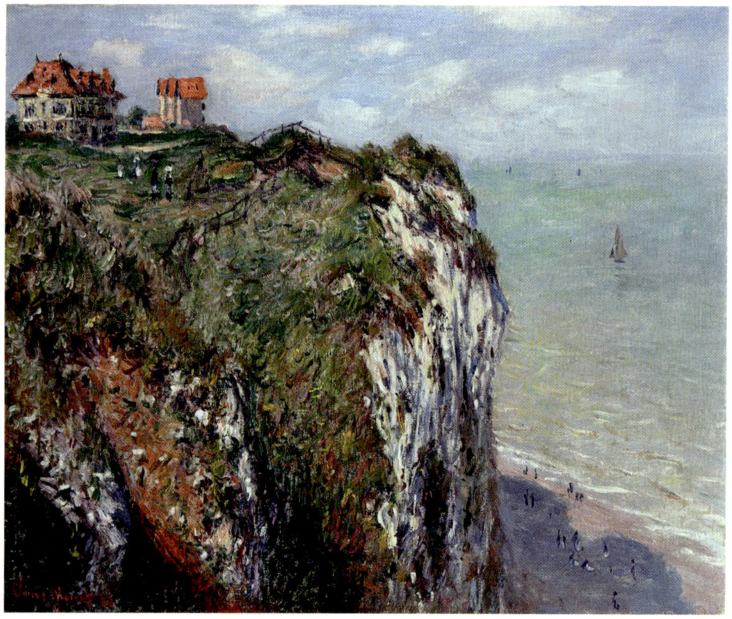

Fig. 54
CLAUDE MONET
The Cliff at Dieppe, 1882
Kunsthaus Zürich

Fig. 55
ALFRED ZOFF
Coast near Pola, undated
Private collection

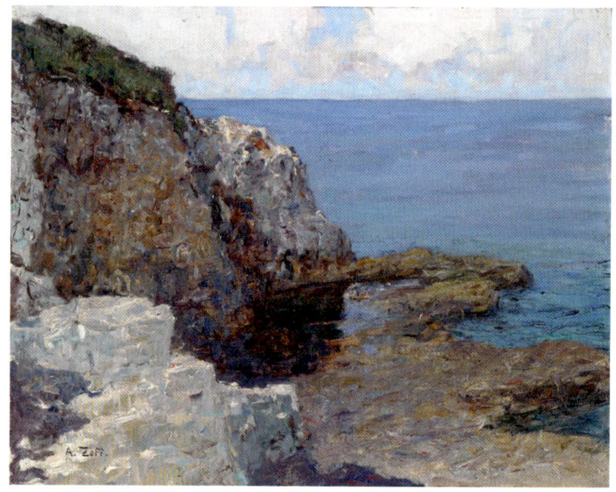

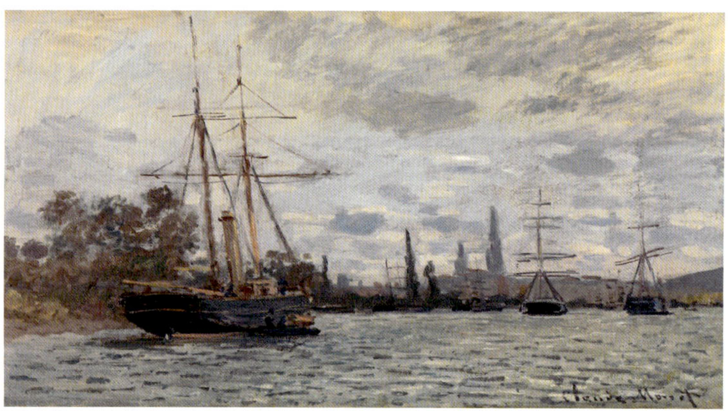

Fig. 56
CLAUDE MONET
The Seine near Rouen, 1874
Staatliche Kunsthalle Karlsruhe

Fig. 57
ALFRED ZOFF
The Harbor at Nieuwpoort, 1910/12
Private collection

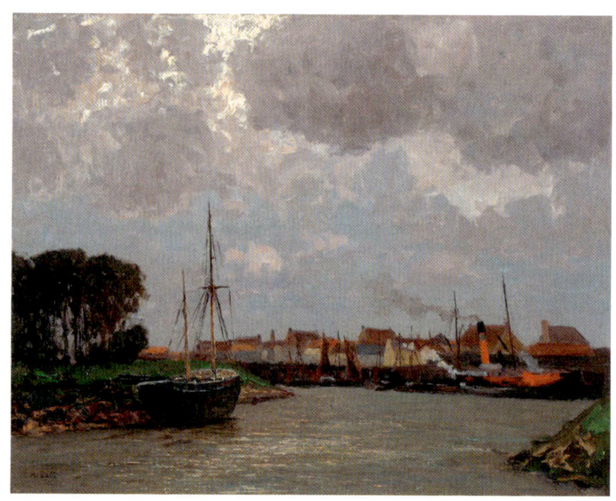

The work of Olga Wisinger-Florian also illustrates how Monet's compositions and inventions were a confrontational source of inspiration and stimulus for others. For the painter, who belonged to the generation taught by Schindler, Monet's garden pictures and flower depictions were a recurrent challenge.

Schindler's picture of his garden in Plankenberg (fig. p. 111), actually entitled *Lilacs (Flieder)* and deprived of its original effect through subsequent chemical changes to some of the colors, was astonishingly similar to Monet's two pictures of his family in the garden of his house in Argenteuil, which also featured lilacs (*Lilacs, Grey Weather [Lilas, temps gris]*, 1872, W 203; *Lilacs in the Sun [Lilas au soleil]*, 1872, W 204, fig. p. 110). As in Monet's paintings, Schindler's daughters sit and play under the branches of a lilac bush that bends over them. The picture uses the contrast between light and dark, warm and cold tones in a masterly fashion to create a sense of depth. When it was originally painted, the luminescent green coloring penetrating through the branches must have drenched the picture.

Schindler's student Olga Wisinger-Florian, who was soon to distance herself from her teacher, was far superior to her contemporaries in the quality of her pictures. Her work is that not only of an independent and self-assured woman but also of a remarkably powerful artist. Her pictures, many of them large-format, reveal not a hesitating or irresolute hand but a purposeful style, with impasto application, often with the palette knife, and strong and luminous colors. Even if her subjects appear at first glance to be conventional, on closer examination it is evident that she sought difficult and challenging themes rather than hiding behind well-tried topics.

Monet's achievements and composition resonate in her garden and flower pictures without detracting from her own distinctive style. This applies to the flower beds and paths angling deep into the pictures, the close-up view of flowers, whose blossoms appear to burst out of the paintings (see also fig. pp. 238, 239), but also to the bold colors and the characterization of the objects through a plethora of contrasting tones. The use of color in Monet's depiction of the gravel in *Main Path through the Garden at Giverny (Une allée du jardin de Monet, Giverny)* is found again not only in her *Pergola at Mentone (Pergola bei Mentone)* (1908), but also in pictures like *Falling Leaves (Fallendes Laub)* (ca. 1895, fig. p. 237) or *Praterallee in the Fall (Praterallee im Herbst)* (ca. 1900) in the dabs of luminous orange, red, rust brown, and pink juxtaposed with cobalt, light blue, and violet tones.

Pictures by Monet, such as those of his chrysanthemums, whose cropped details focus just on the luminosity of the colored flowers, are echoed in the refined depiction of blossoms using different impasto and paint application techniques (from small brush to spatula) in Wisinger-Florian's garden and flower pictures, such as *Garden Path with Hortensias (Gartenweg mit Hortensien)* in 1902 (fig. p. 239), in which the full blossoms achieve an almost three-dimensional plasticity, while the shimmering light on the surface of leaves and the red glow on their underside are depicted in masterly fashion.

Flowering poppies became fashionable at the turn of the century, suggested by Monet's pictures of meadows and fields strewn with corn poppies. They inspired not only French and American painters but also many artists from Central Europe, including the Hungarian Pál Szinyei Merse and the Czech Antonín Chittussi. The theme of fields covered with brightly colored flowers was also taken up in Austria. Olga Wisinger-Florian's *Flowering Poppies (Blühender Mohn)* (1895/1900) is like an Austrian response, in the typ-

Fig. 58
CLAUDE MONET
The Church at Vétheuil, 1878
Scottish National Gallery, Edinburgh

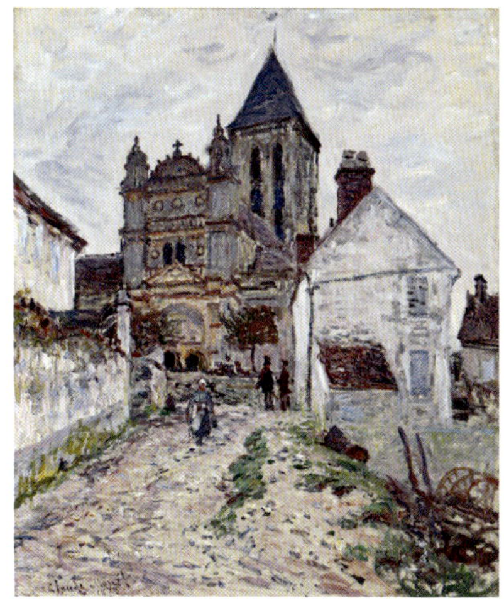

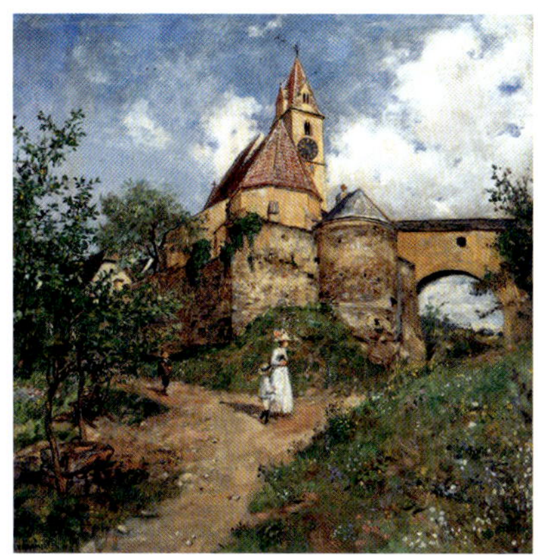

Fig. 59
JOHANN VICTOR KRÄMER
Ascent to the Church at Senftenberg, ca. 1910
Landesmuseum Niederösterreich, St. Pölten

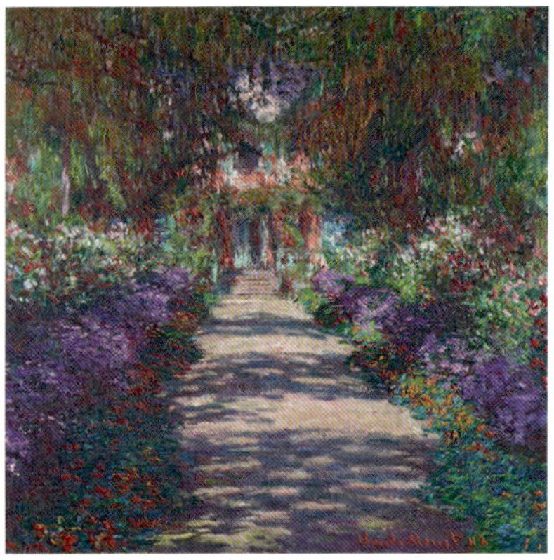

Fig. 60
CLAUDE MONET
Path in Monet's Garden in Giverny, 1902
Belvedere, Vienna

Fig. 61
OLGA WISINGER-FLORIAN
Pergola near Mentone, ca. 1900
Neue Galerie am Universalmuseum Joanneum, Graz

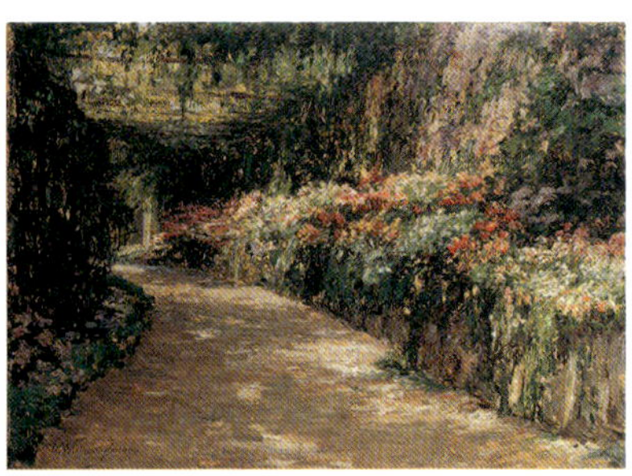

ical close-up style aptly named by Martina Haja as "*Kraut- und Rüben-Malerei*" ("cabbage and turnip painting").[22] The luminous flowers are depicted with powerful brushstrokes, giving way in the depth of the picture to softer color zones.

Marie Egner also painted flowering poppy fields, seeking unconventional details and approaches. In *Flowering Poppy Field in Styria (Blühendes Mohnfeld in der Steiermark)* (ca. 1896, see fig. p. 186) she chose a radical perspective, moving from the close-up flowers almost seamlessly to the background, where a female figure is to be seen admiring the magnificence of this natural scene. She also frequently approaches the flowers in depth and turns their colors into the main theme of the picture (see *Flowering Poppies [Blühender Mohn],* ca. 1890, fig. p. 188).

Even Gustav Klimt was not untouched by the subject. His field of poppies, painted in 1907 from the balcony of Braugasthof Litzlberg, where he and the Flöge family spent their summers, is like a subtle response to Monet's colors and pictorial world. Klimt probably exaggerated somewhat in his opulent depiction of the flowers, given that corn poppies are much rarer in the humid climate and grazing meadows of the Prealps than they are in the east of Austria. Klimt deliberately arranged the flowers in a choir-like or orchestrating setting that emphasized the fullness and contrasting complementary quality of the colors. In pictures like *Poppy Field (Mohnwiese)* everything appears to dissolve into pure color, a festive frenzy of coloristic and complementary tones.

Klimt's oeuvre took a decisive new turn shortly before the end of the century. Having paid scant attention to landscape painting hitherto, contenting himself to a few attempts at intimate portraits of fruit orchards and house façades overgrown with roses, he embarked on a new direction after 1899, without a doubt under Monet's influence.

Klimt must have seen Monet's *Morning on the Seine (Matin sur la Seine)* in the supplement to the magazine *Le Gaulois* of June 16, 1898, and recognized a potential that suited his being. Here was nature transformed, the landscape becoming two-dimensional and unapproachable. Klimt's pictures of his summer vacation in St. Agatha had still been "accessible," traditional landscape scenes painted in the spirit of *Stimmungsimpressionismus* (Atmospheric Impressionism) flourishing at the time in Austria—and no doubt inspired by Emil Jakob Schindler, who spent many summers in the neighboring Goisern.

Now Klimt discovered the "distance" in Monet's views of Vétheuil, Antibes, and later Venice, that was transformed into a "picture" through the extreme cropping.

During his summer vacation in Golling in 1899, Klimt discovered a topography that allowed him to translate what he had seen into his own pictorial language. The result was *Pond in the Morning (Ein Morgen am Teiche),* a picture that through its soft and airy transitions celebrates the reflection of trees in a pond. The trees stand darkly like a wall at the edge of the pond while the first rays of sun emerge in the background.

Like Monet, Klimt modeled the surface of the water with short, arched brushstrokes, creating the color effect through the juxtaposition of blue, pink, and violet tones, while nevertheless relying on a restrained and earthy overall color scheme. As with Monet at the turn of the century, nature was used as a starting point for achieving harmony within the picture. In Monet's *Morning on the Seine* series, the surface structure is the dominant feature. In his indulgence in the delights of delicate coloration and countless finely modulated brushstrokes, the contours become softer and the objects begin increasingly to dissolve.

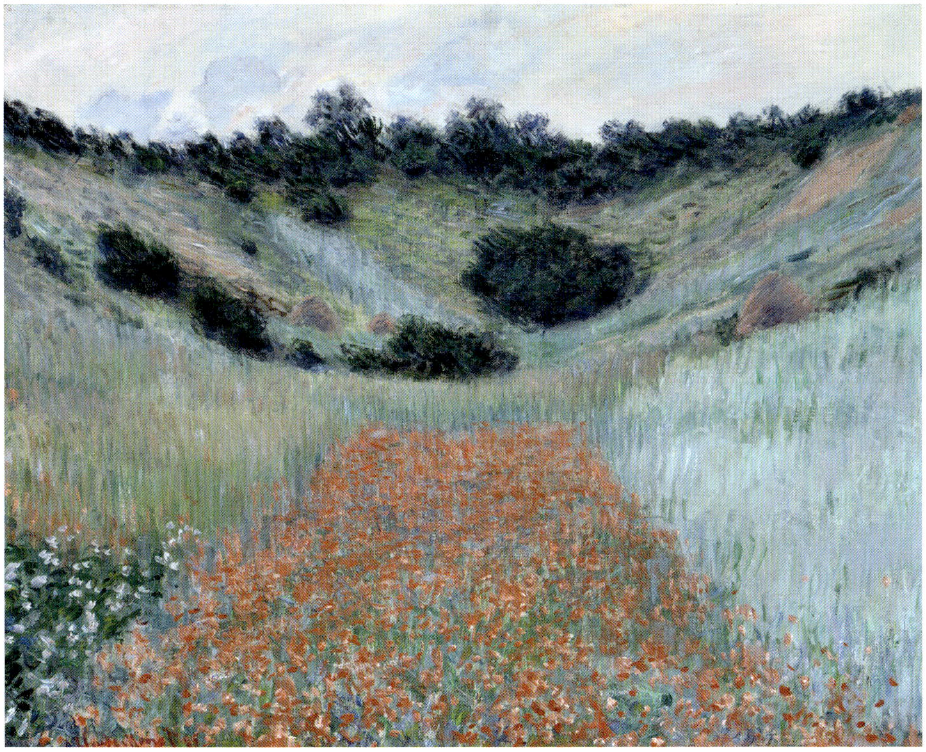

Fig. 62
CLAUDE MONET
Poppy Field in a Hollow near Giverny, 1885
Museum of Fine Arts, Boston, Massachusetts

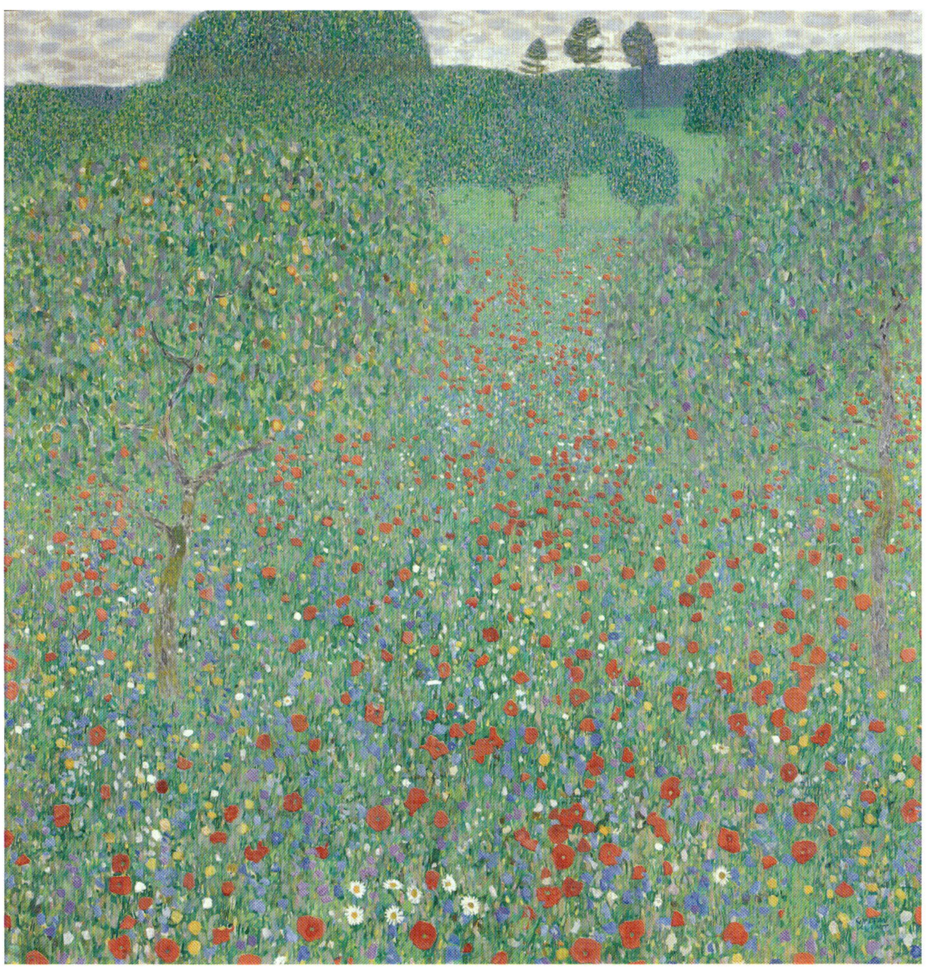

Fig. 63
GUSTAV KLIMT
Flowering Poppies, 1907
Belvedere, Vienna

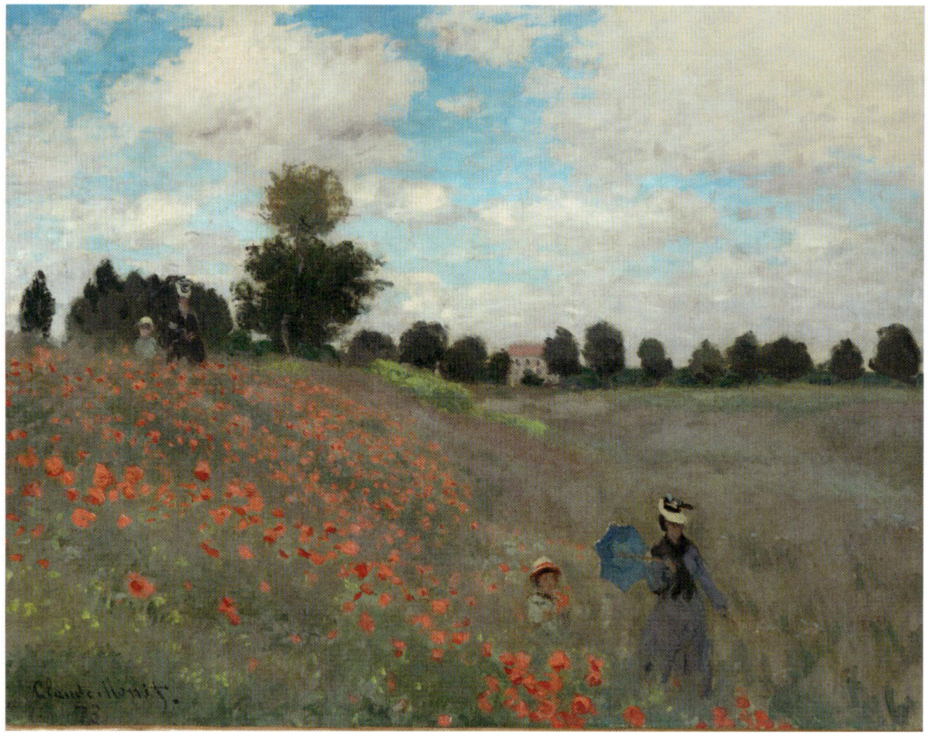

Fig. 64
CLAUDE MONET
Poppies at Argenteuil, 1873
Musée d'Orsay, Paris

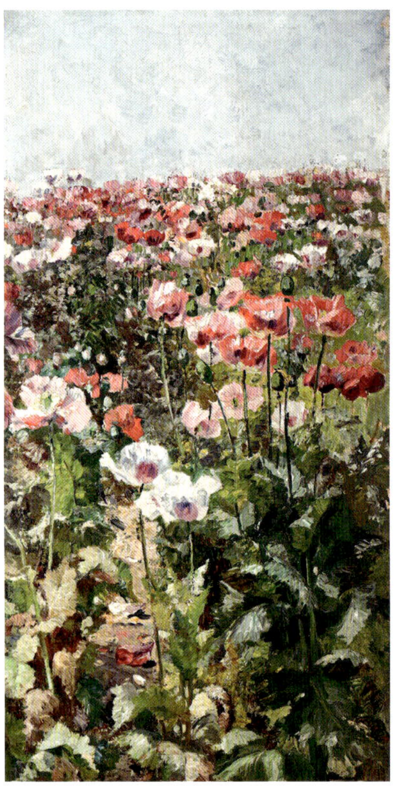

Fig. 65
MARIE EGNER
Flowering Poppies, ca. 1900
Neue Galerie am Universalmuseum Joanneum, Graz

Fig. 66
OLGA WISINGER-FLORIAN
Flowering Poppies, ca. 1895/1900
Belvedere, Vienna

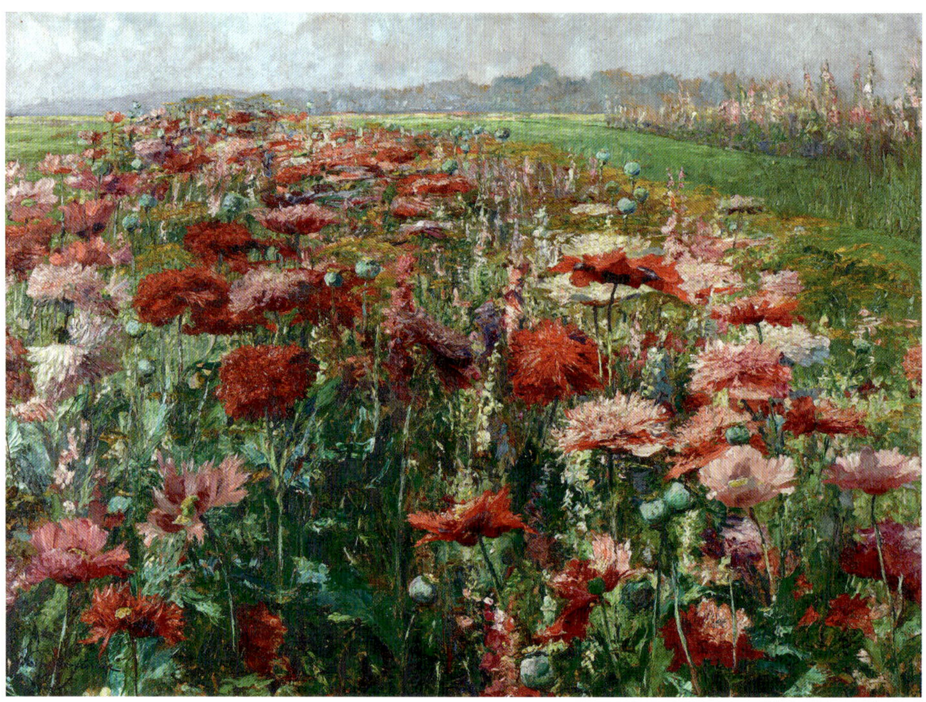

Monet's *Morning on the Seine* hit a nerve in Vienna—if only a symbolic one at first, as the picture could be read that way as well, something that resonates in Klimt's picture and also even more strongly in the paintings of Wilhelm Bernatzik and Friedrich König.

The importance of Monet for Klimt can be seen most clearly in the painting *Attersee (Am Attersee)* completed in 1900. In the Golling picture the water, cropped at the sides, occupied a large part of the canvas; in *The Swamp (Der Sumpf)* (1900) and particularly *Attersee* it became the absolutely dominant feature. Monet, who at that time was already seeking to dissolve the boundaries and organize the picture as a structured surface, as a detail from a much larger whole, influenced not only Klimt's composition but also his painting technique. The picture is characterized by short, energetic, arched brushstrokes and luminous colors that endow it with vitality and offer a balance to the reflections on the surface of the water.

Klimt's lake is extremely cropped, and the absence of any foreground denies the observer the possibility of orientation, as if he was being dangled over the water. In view of this drastic cropping of the subject on three sides and the high horizon, Ludwig Hevesi described it appropriately as a "frame full of water, Lake Attersee, nothing but short grey and green waves mingling and sliding into one another."[23]

Klimt's *Attersee* is radical—it had no precedents in Austrian landscape painting or in the artist's own work. This applies to the absence of foreground, the pure and massive surface of the water, the cut-off at the edges of the picture, the bold colors, and the brushwork. Unusually for him, Klimt used a flat brush for the short arched brushstrokes on the waves, following the form and brushstroke technique used by Monet in his early paintings of water that had made him famous. In his brochure *Les peintres impressionnistes* in 1878, Théodore Duret was already describing Monet as a painter of water "par excellence."[24]

The reproduction of *Morning on the Seine* in *Le Gaulois* already showed this direct and borderless portrayal of water. Klimt may also have seen a reproduction of Monet's *The Railway Bridge at Argenteuil* (*Le pont de chemin de fer à Argenteuil*), illustrated in 1897 in *Gazette des beaux-arts*."[25] Monet's characteristic brushstrokes to render the short waves on the water can be clearly seen here.

And yet, there are indications that Klimt might also have seen the originals of Monet's pictures and was inspired by them to paint his Attersee pictures in 1900.

It is interesting to wonder whether Klimt had the opportunity to visit the World's Fair in 1900 before the late summer. The fact that he and Emilie Flöge took French lessons from early 1897 to July 1900 would suggest that he had that intention. The award of a medal of honor at this World's Fair for Klimt's monumental ceiling painting *Philosophy (Philosophie)* (1900/07, fig. p. 202) would have provided an occasion for such a trip. The visit to Paris strongly suggests itself not least because Klimt's Attersee pictures are like a compilation of various works by Monet seen at the "Centennale", the centennial exhibition of French art at this World's Fair, and because later works by Klimt also appeared to echo the pictures by Monet that were shown there.

In Paris, Klimt would have seen the lurching view, without the support of a foreground, into the depths of a water surface framed only by the edges of the picture in the pictures of Étretat,[26] the typical brushstroke to depict the moving water with the aid of a flat brush in the pictures of Holland and Argenteuil,[27] and jarring blue, green,

Fig. 67 and 68
Annex to the journal *Le Gaulois* from June 16th, 1898 for the *Claude Monet Exhibition*

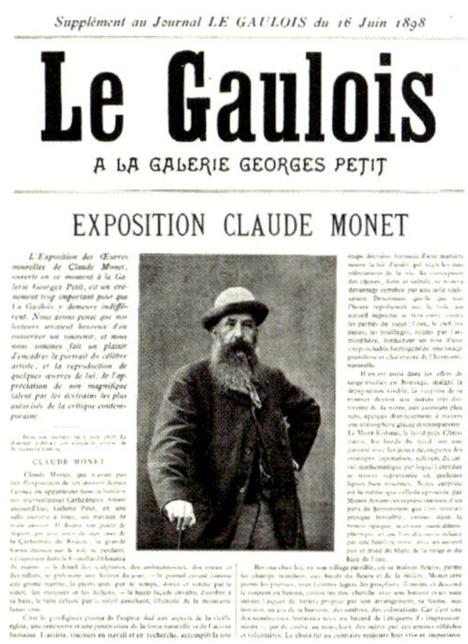
Supplément au Journal LE GAULOIS du 16 Juin 1898

Le Gaulois

A LA GALERIE GEORGES PETIT

EXPOSITION CLAUDE MONET

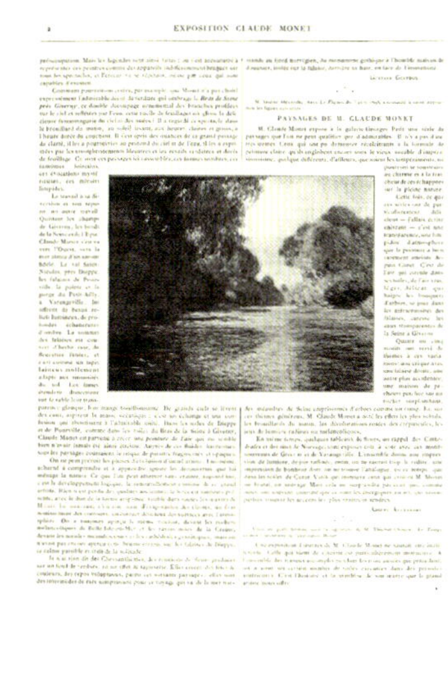
EXPOSITION CLAUDE MONET

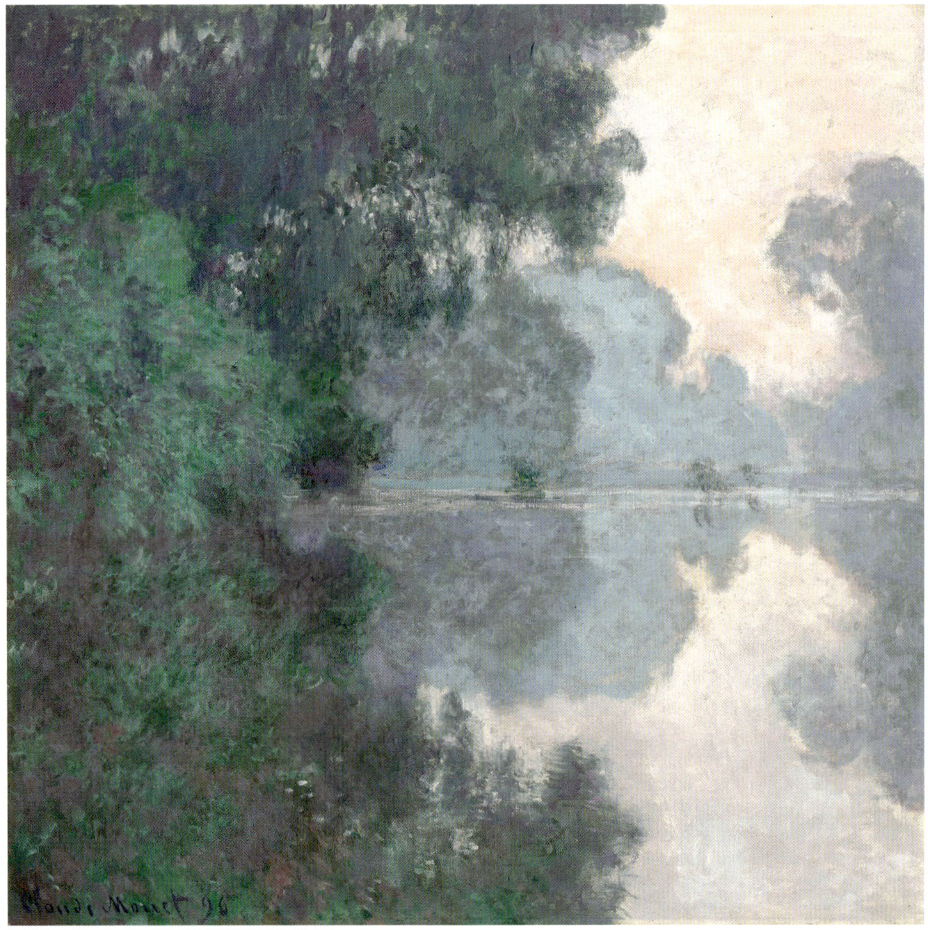

Fig. 69
CLAUDE MONET
Morning on the Seine, 1896
Private collection

and turquoise tones of Mediterranean landscapes and the colored strips far out over the sea in the pictures of Antibes.[28] In these pictures and in the views of Vétheuil[29] he will also have seen the distant view of the village as an inaccessible realm beyond the water.

At all events, Klimt's landscape painting from this time is completely transformed and takes off on a path divergent from the Austrian tradition.

Monet was also an important point of reference for Klimt's later works. His pictures of Schloss Kammer, Litzlberg, the Litzlbergkeller, or the later views of Unterach on Lake Attersee (fig. p. 205), and his pictures of Malcesine and Cassone on Lake Garda all show villages or buildings on the opposite bank, separated and inaccessibly distanced by the water.

Monet's views of villages on the opposite bank of the river, particularly his pictures of Vétheuil, use a comparable technique.[30] Whereas his earlier works from the years 1879 to 1881 (one of which was shown at the Miethke Gallery in 1910, see fig. p. 160), were more descriptive and interested in an authentic reproduction of the lighting, the villages in the later works around 1901/02 are portrayed in unrealistic, soft, shimmering, and sometimes pale tones (see fig. p. 21). Theodore Duret's article "Claude Monet und

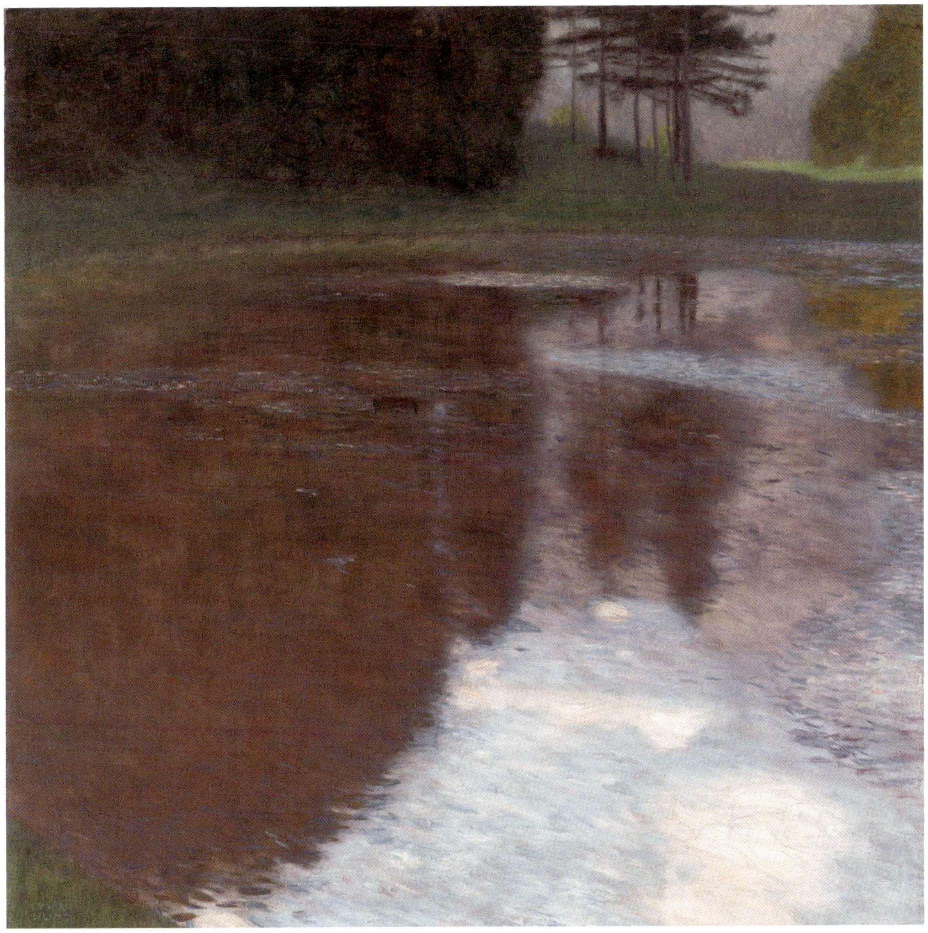

Fig. 70
GUSTAV KLIMT
A Morning on the Pond, 1899
Leopold Museum, Vienna

Fig. 71
FRIEDRICH KÖNIG
The silent Pond, ca. 1910
Belvedere, Vienna

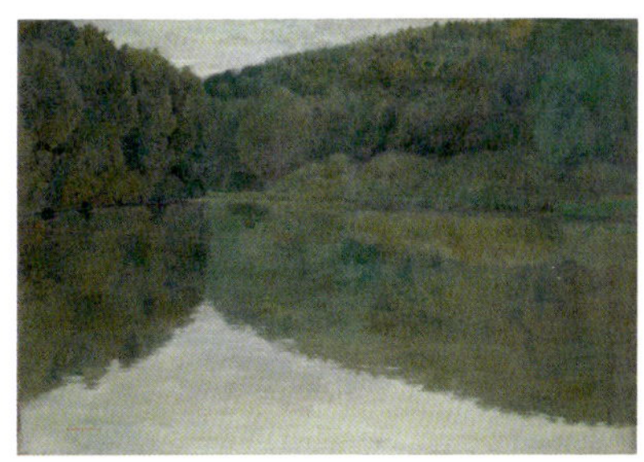

Fig. 72
WILHELM BERNATZIK
Pond, ca. 1900
Belvedere, Vienna

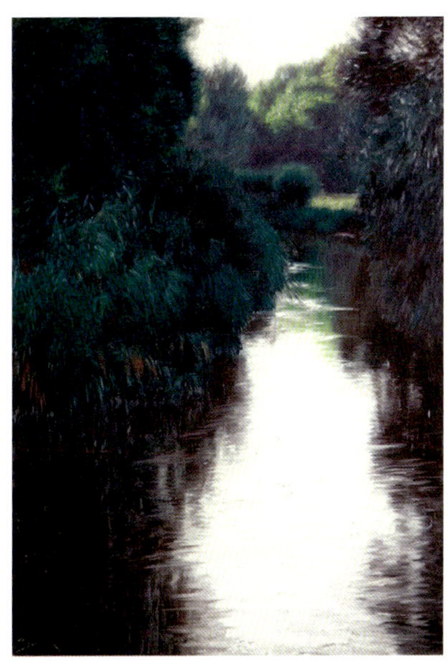

der Impressionismus" published in 1904 showed two views of Vétheuil on the other side of the river, the latter, dated 1903 in the magazine, in square form.[31] Klimt began to keep things at a distance and to make them more abstract.

In *Pond in Schloss Kammer (Schlossteich in Kammer)* (1909/10), which uses the same horizontal separation, the retreat into an autonomous area of harmony is once again emphasized through reference to Monet's water lily pictures. As with Monet, the locus itself is inaccessible, with shimmering, colored surfaces and an underlying imponderable depth. *Schönbrunn Park (Schönbrunner Park)* (1916) also follows this arrangement, dealing with the phenomenon of color through the reflection that occupies a large part of the picture. When Monet's Venice series with its strict orthogonal arrangement was presented later on, it might also have reinforced the compositional strictness of Klimt's later depictions of Schloss Kammer. Painted in 1908, Monet's series was exhibited in 1912 by Bernheim-Jeune & Cie[32] with an illustrated catalog, which the k. k. Staatsgalerie also acquired. The reproductions of Venetian palazzi have the same solemn stillness as Klimt's views of Schloss Kammer.

It was only after encountering Monet's art that Klimt recognized the potential of modern landscape painting and discovered his own talent in this area, turning him into one

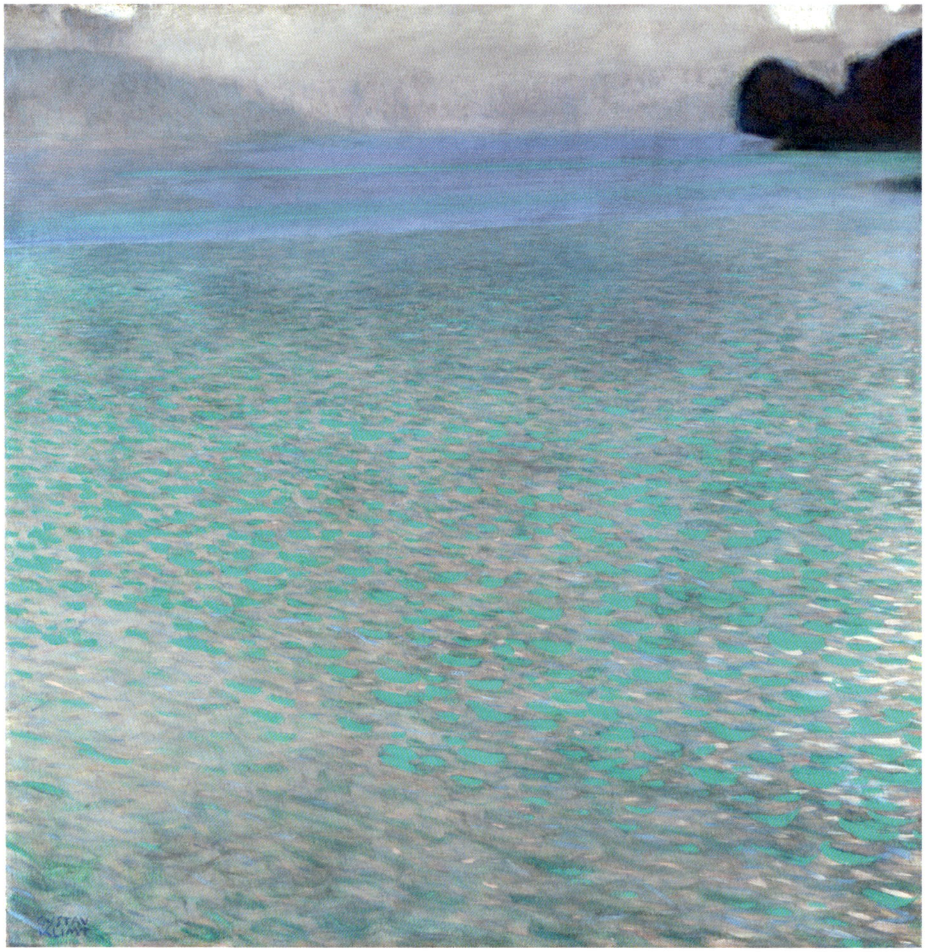

Fig. 73
GUSTAV KLIMT
On Attersee, 1900
Leopold Museum - Private Foundation, Vienna

Fig. 74
Journal
Gazette des beaux-arts, 1.1.1897, p. 97

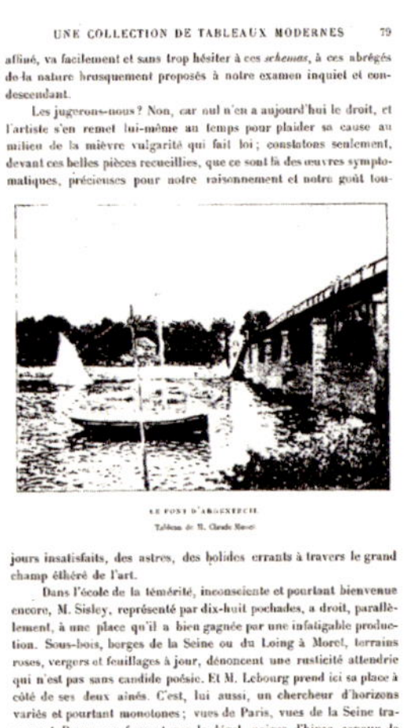

UNE COLLECTION DE TABLEAUX MODERNES 79

affiné, va facilement et sans trop hésiter à ces *schemas*, à ces abrégés de la nature brusquement proposés à notre examen inquiet et condescendant.

Les jugerons-nous? Non, car nul n'en a aujourd'hui le droit, et l'artiste s'en remet lui-même au temps pour plaider sa cause au milieu de la mièvre vulgarité qui fait loi; constatons seulement, devant ces belles pièces recueillies, que ce sont là des œuvres symptomatiques, précieuses pour notre raisonnement et notre goût toujours insatisfaits, des astres, des bolides errants à travers le grand champ éthéré de l'art.

LE PONT D'ARGENTEUIL
Tableau de M. Claude Monet

Dans l'école de la témérité, inconsciente et pourtant bienvenue encore, M. Sisley, représenté par dix-huit pochades, a droit, parallèlement, à une place qu'il a bien gagnée par une infatigable production. Sous-bois, berges de la Seine ou du Loing à Moret, terrains roses, vergers et feuillages à jour, dénoncent une rusticité attendrie qui n'est pas sans candide poésie. Et M. Lebourg prend ici sa place à côté de ses deux aînés. C'est, lui aussi, un chercheur d'horizons variés et pourtant monotones; vues de Paris, vues de la Seine traversant Rouen ou fumant par le dégel, neiges d'hiver, canaux de

of the most important Austrian landscape painters of the twentieth century. While his early attempts at landscape painting were small-format affairs, the picture size grew steadily over a decade to achieve the ideal 110 x 110 cm format.

In the decisive years when his art and preferred picture format were being defined, he was guided by Monet's solutions: apart from the compositional ideas mentioned above and the powerful luminous colors, there were the subjects—from poppy fields and water to villages on the opposite bank and alleys leading into the distance, which he transposed in his distinctive timeless and subtly balanced style, with everything anecdotal and atmospheric being omitted. Later, alongside the influences of Pointillism, van Gogh, and Japonism, which came from France, the Nabis were a further inspiration. Klimt must have been particularly interested in painters like Bonnard and Vuillard, especially their rejection of three-dimensionality in favor of patterned surfaces that merged foreground and background into a single colored structure. To achieve this effect in his landscape painting, Klimt used technical aids such as opera glasses and a powerful telescope, which brought distant objects nearer but also pushed them together and flattened them optically, emphasizing the pictorial and non-illusionist quality of his paintings (see fig. p 205). This also enabled him to address the relationship between nearness and distance effectively.

Klimt's distinctive way of characterizing objects not by modeling but through color, the weighting of tones, and the modulation of surfaces through color, was also derived from his encounter with Monet's art. In the latter's pictures, the traditional dark/light contrast, the three-dimensional penetration of space also became less significant to be replaced by the sensation of color on the retina, which he transferred to the canvas. Moreover, Klimt's encounter with *Morning on the Seine* came at a time when Monet was increasingly abandoning the mimetic and considering internal structures.

For Monet and French painting of the time, the texture of the paint was the starting point, and so Klimt, who had tended to paint with a fine glaze, began to work in a more open impasto style, enlivening the paint surfaces of his pictures through the use of different textures.

Klimt's brushwork was similar to Monet, who composed his pictures with lattice-like brushstrokes that he continued to work on and consolidate. Klimt also kept the painterly texture open so that he could rework it at any time.

Apart from Carl Schuch, Klimt was probably the only Austrian painter who understood and made use of the basic principles of the French painting aesthetics. His colors became increasingly dry, bright, subtle, and balanced without stark contrasts. These new pictures were also unvarnished. To increase the intensity of the colors, Klimt obtained the luminous tones from the local colors, but then coordinated them with the

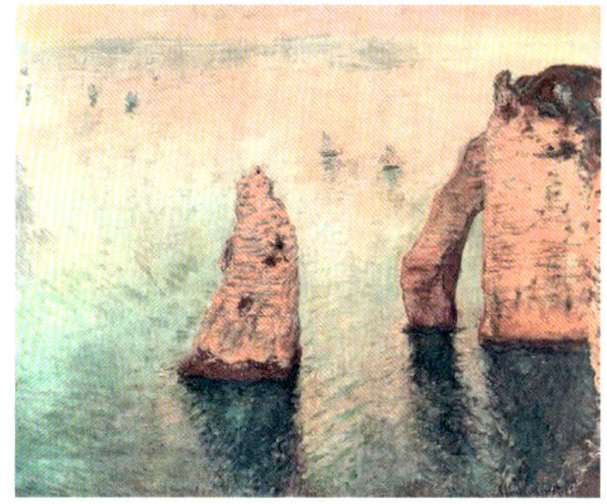

Fig. 75
CLAUDE MONET
Sailing Boats off the Rock Needle, 1885
Private collection

Fig. 76
CLAUDE MONET
The Bridge at Argenteuil, 1874
Musée d'Orsay, Paris

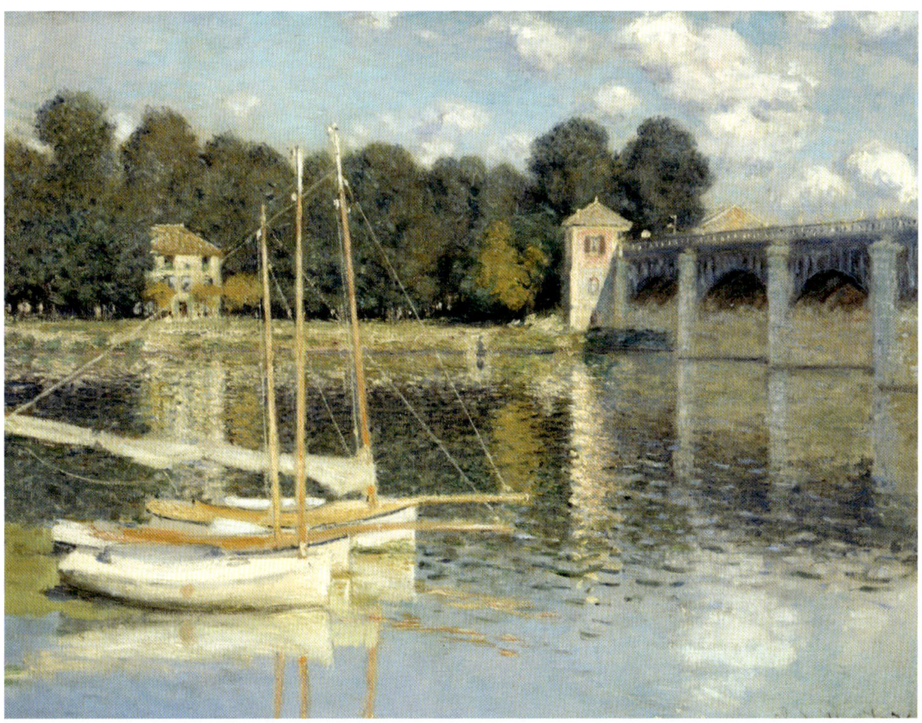

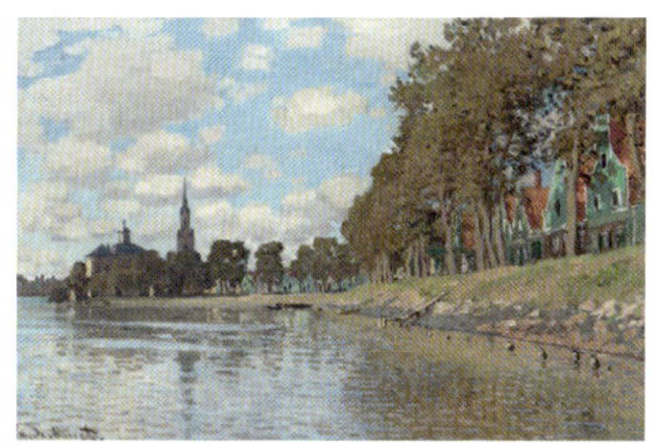

Fig. 77
CLAUDE MONET
Zaandam (Holland), 1871
Musée d'Orsay, Paris

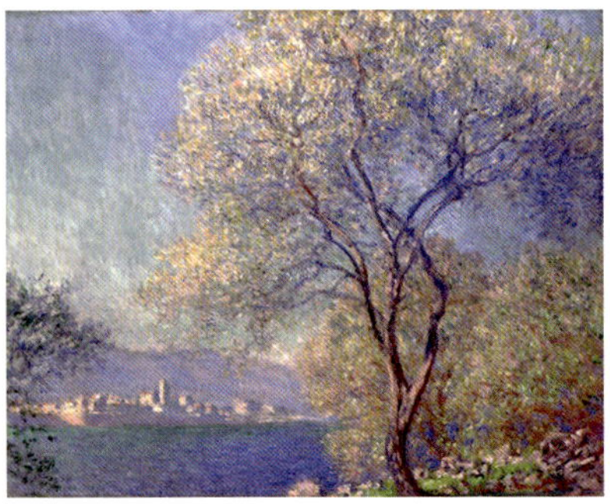

Fig. 78
CLAUDE MONET
Antibes Seen from the Salis Gardens, 1888
Toledo Museum of Art (Toledo, Ohio)

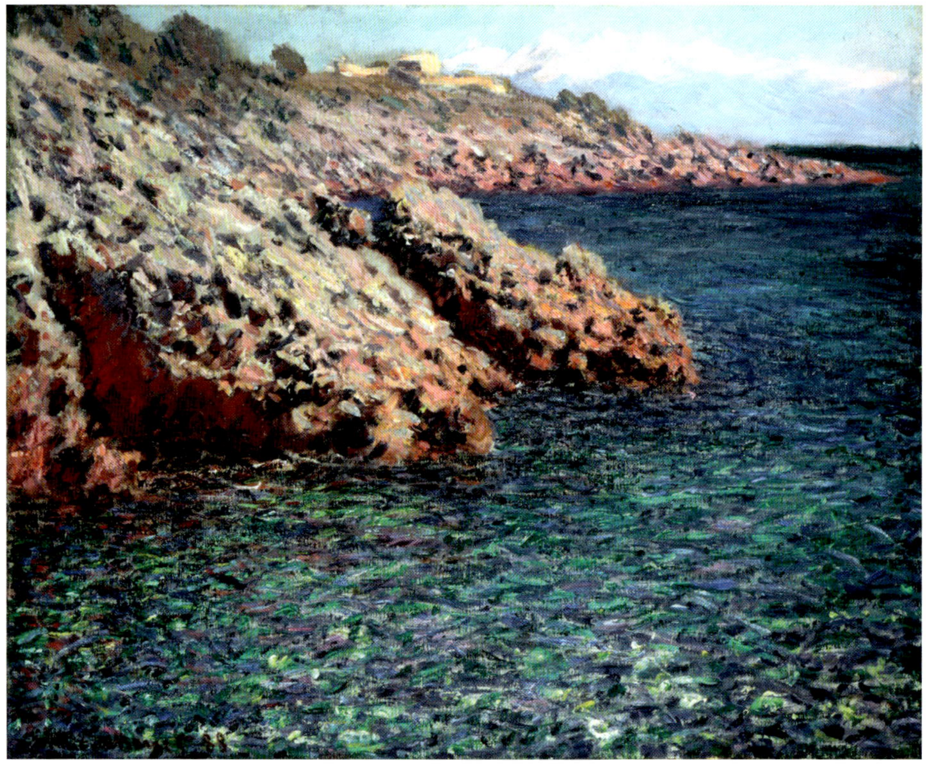

Fig. 79
CLAUDE MONET
The Mediterranean (Cap d'Antibes), 1888
Columbus Museum of Art, Ohio

Fig. 80
CLAUDE MONET
Seascape at Pourville, 1882
Columbus Museum of Art, Ohio

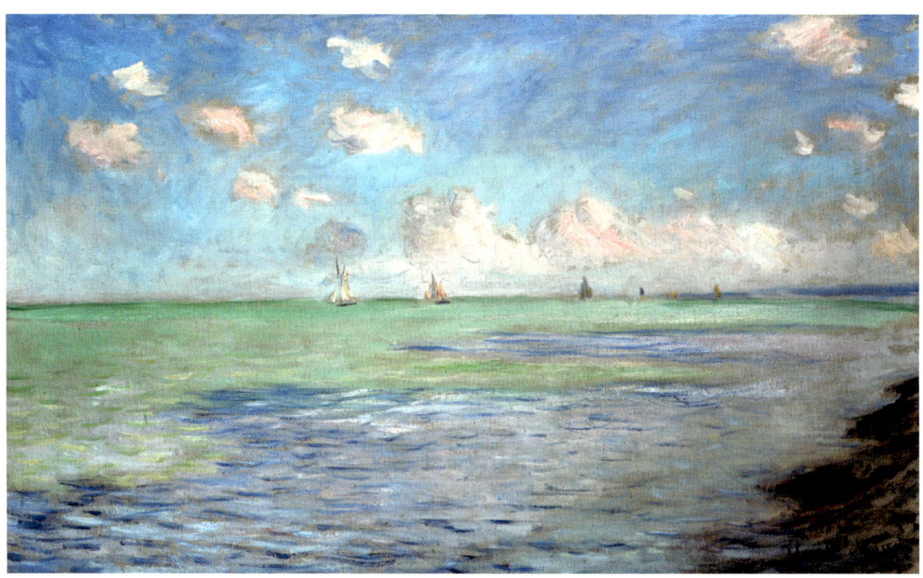

inner pictorial harmony and the rich sound of its chords. If colors were the dominating feature, light and shadow could not be emphasized. Thus there is no illuminating light in Klimt's landscapes; the colors illuminate themselves, and the light streams out from the inside. More important than the content is admiration for the relationship between form and color, the balance within the color scheme, which is developed to even greater effect through the restful pictorial structure.

Klimt's interest in optical aids might also have had something to do with his acquaintanceship with the photographers of the "Trifolium": Hugo Henneberg, Heinrich Kühn, and Hans Watzek. Heinrich Kühn also used magnifying lenses to reduce the sense of depth in his pictures.

Klimt, who painted a portrait of Henneberg's wife, was very interested in photography and ensured that it was shown in the Secession. The thirteenth exhibition taking place there in 1902 included not only works by the "Trifolium" (clover leaf) but also photos by Friedrich Viktor Spitzer.

Pictorialist photographers saw themselves as amateurs intent on reinvigorating artistic photography outside the commercial studios. Painting and Impressionism in particular informed their pictures, some of which were created with a great deal of effort. As with Impressionist paintings, the photographers sought to communicate impressions rather than a detailed reproduction. They experimented with sharp and soft focus, using diffuser lenses or smearing the lenses with grease when taking the photos, making gum prints, which did not produce sharp contours, or, if that was not enough, reprinting them and using rough paper. They claimed that their often large-format prints deserved to be considered as an art form on the same footing as painting. The subjects were similar to the Impressionist canon—water with sailing boats or ships, sun-drenched landscapes and parks with strollers, portraits, and still lifes.

One of the most innovative artists in this field was Heinrich Kühn. He experimented tirelessly to familiarize himself with the technical apparatus so as to be able to control the "tonal values" precisely and hence to design the photograph as a work of art as he imagined it. He encountered pictures by French and German artists at exhibitions in Vienna and Munich and took inspiration from them.[33]

Monet's pictures in particular were to leave visible traces in his work. This influence can be seen in photographs like *Under the Trees at the River (in Summer) (Unter den Bäumen am Fluss [Im Sommer])* (ca. 1917), which feature young female figures in lightcolored clothes with the light playing on them, the reflecting water in the background, and the emphasis on light grey tones, and in his landscapes, which quite evidently reference Monet's pictures. The painter's poppy fields and landscapes in the 1870s were clearly models for photographs like *Summer Landscape (Sommerlandschaft)* (1897), *Landscape in the South (Landschaft im Süden)* (1897), *Southern Landscape (Südliche Landschaft)* (1897), and *Southern Landscape* (1898). The influence is most evident in the Autochrome color transparencies developed by the Lumière brothers.[34]

The work with the new material that Kühn discovered in 1907 was a real challenge for a photographer so intent on fully mastering the tonal values. He had to make extensive tests to determine the quality of the material and its potential—and he had to learn to "concentrate solely on color,"[35] since "to compose on the basis of color [...] is completely different from structuring a picture or selecting a subject for a black-and-white

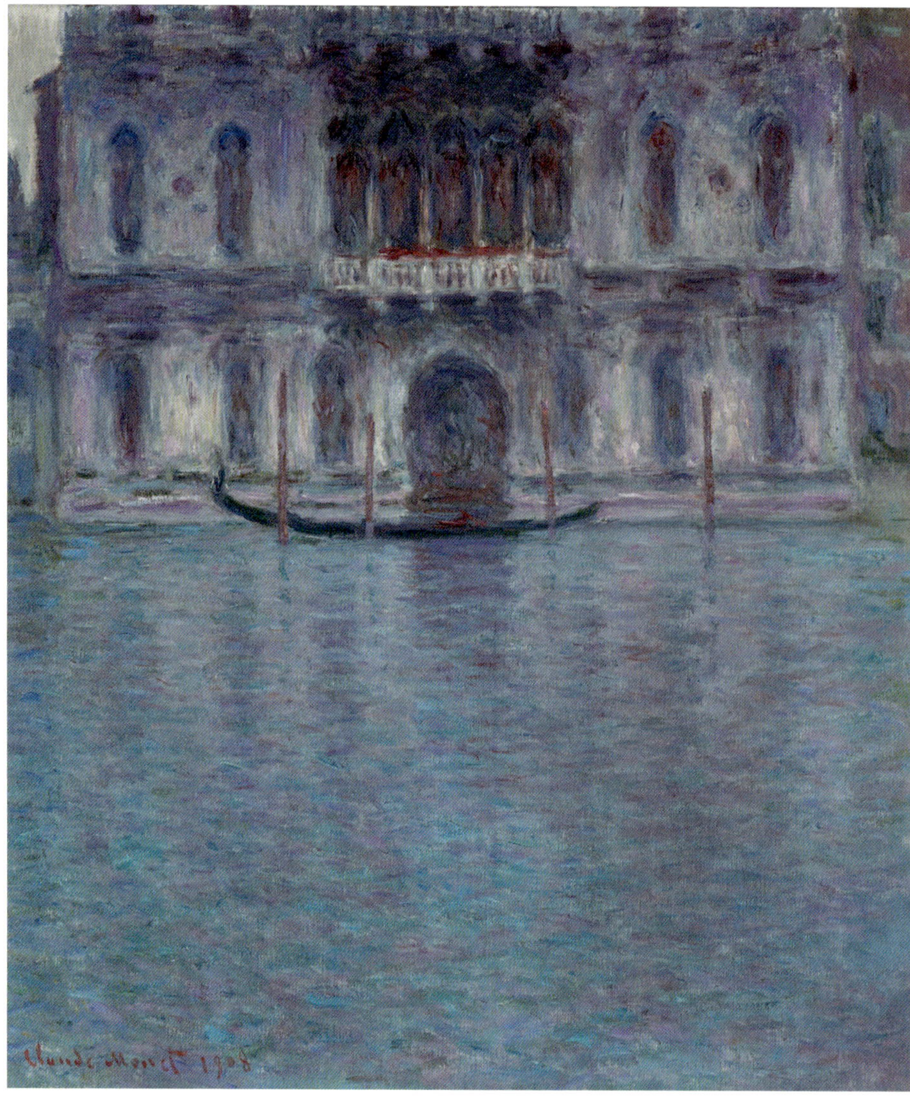

Fig. 81
CLAUDE MONET
Palazzo Contarini, 1908
Kunstmuseum St. Gallen

picture."[36] But he was very soon taken by the new technique. Autochrome gave an Impressionist feel to the photographs, the colors and rough grain highlighting the impression of softly shimmering luminosity and painterly effect. He was "[...] completely breathless and sick with Autochrome!" he admitted in a letter to Alfred Stieglitz.[37] He was particularly enthusiastic about the great contrast and the possibility of taking backlit photographs, because it enabled him to capture the same colored light in his photographs that distinguishes Monet even today.

Among the pictures that Kühn saw between 1900 and 1914 in Munich and in exhibitions in the Secession and various galleries were paintings like *Corner of the Garden at Montgeron (Coin du jardin à Montgeron)* (1876, W 418), *Under the Poplars, Sunlight Effect (Sous les peupliers, effet de soleil)* (1887, W 1135), and *Wheatstack, Thaw, Sunset (Meule, dégel, soleil couchant)* (1891, W 1284), which concentrate on light and on the way it changes color and contours.

The diffuser lenses and soft focus achieved with them were intended to mimic the luminosity and shimmer inherent to Monet's pictures. In *Wheatstack, Thaw, Sunset*, for example, the backlighting is obviously the theme, but the way in which Monet achieved it with blurred contours, the lightening of the edges, the reflected light in the shadows, the glare, was typical of the pictorial language that Kühn attempted to imitate with his Autochrome pictures. Even in his still lifes, Kühn was sensitive to the reverberation of light on things and of the magic it imbued objects with.

Kühn also borrowed many ideas from Monet's pictures and produced variations of compositions he had seen. His children and women sitting in the grass, the strollers and walkers through the fields speak a very clear language.

If one looks at the strollers in pictures like *Poppies at Argenteuil (Les coquelicots à Argenteuil)* (1873; W 274, fig. p. 64) or *Under the Poplars, Sunlight Effect*, or the seated figures in *Meadow at Bezons (Prairie à Bezons)* (1874, W 341) and *The Reader (La liseuse)* (1872, W 205), the structural similarities are more than evident. In Monet's *The Reader* (fig. p. 140), the light plays on the young woman's dress and the surrounding

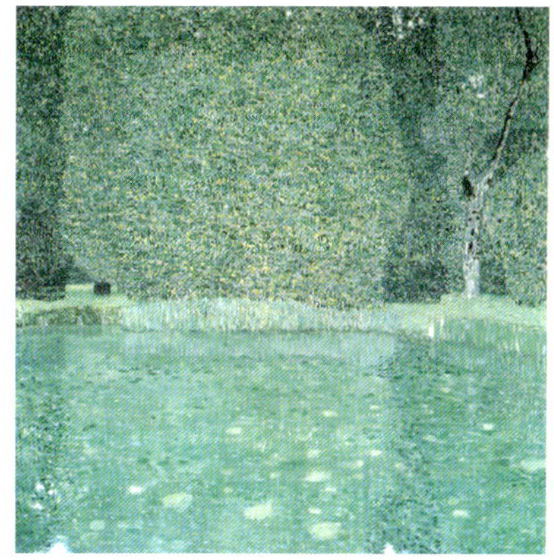

Fig. 83
GUSTAV KLIMT
Schloss Kammer on Lake Attersee III, 1909/10
Belvedere, Vienna

Fig. 82
GUSTAV KLIMT
Park at Kammer Castle, 1909/10
Neue Galerie, New York

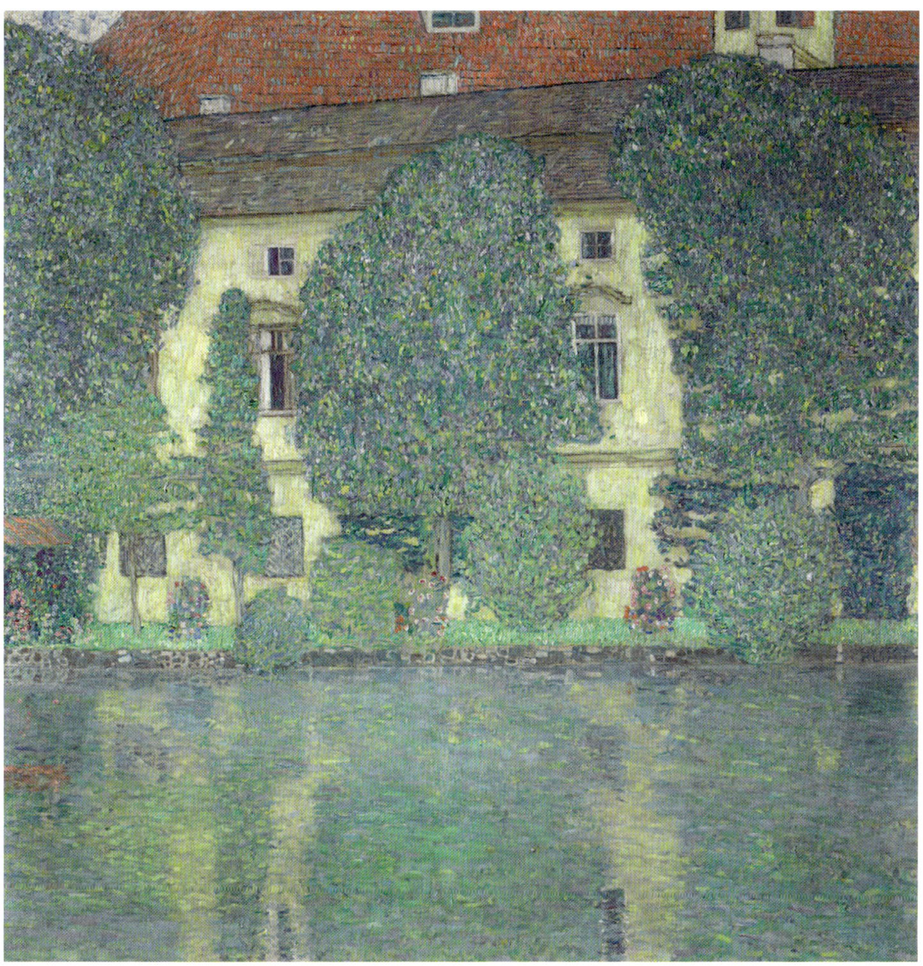

Fig. 84
GUSTAV KLIMT
Schloss Kammer on Lake Attersee IV, 1909/10
Private collection

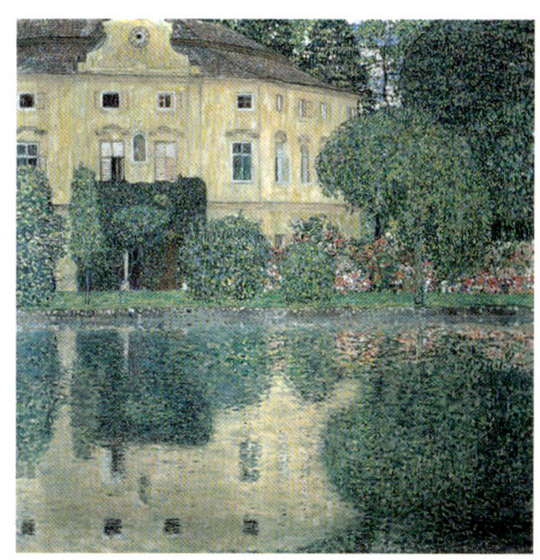

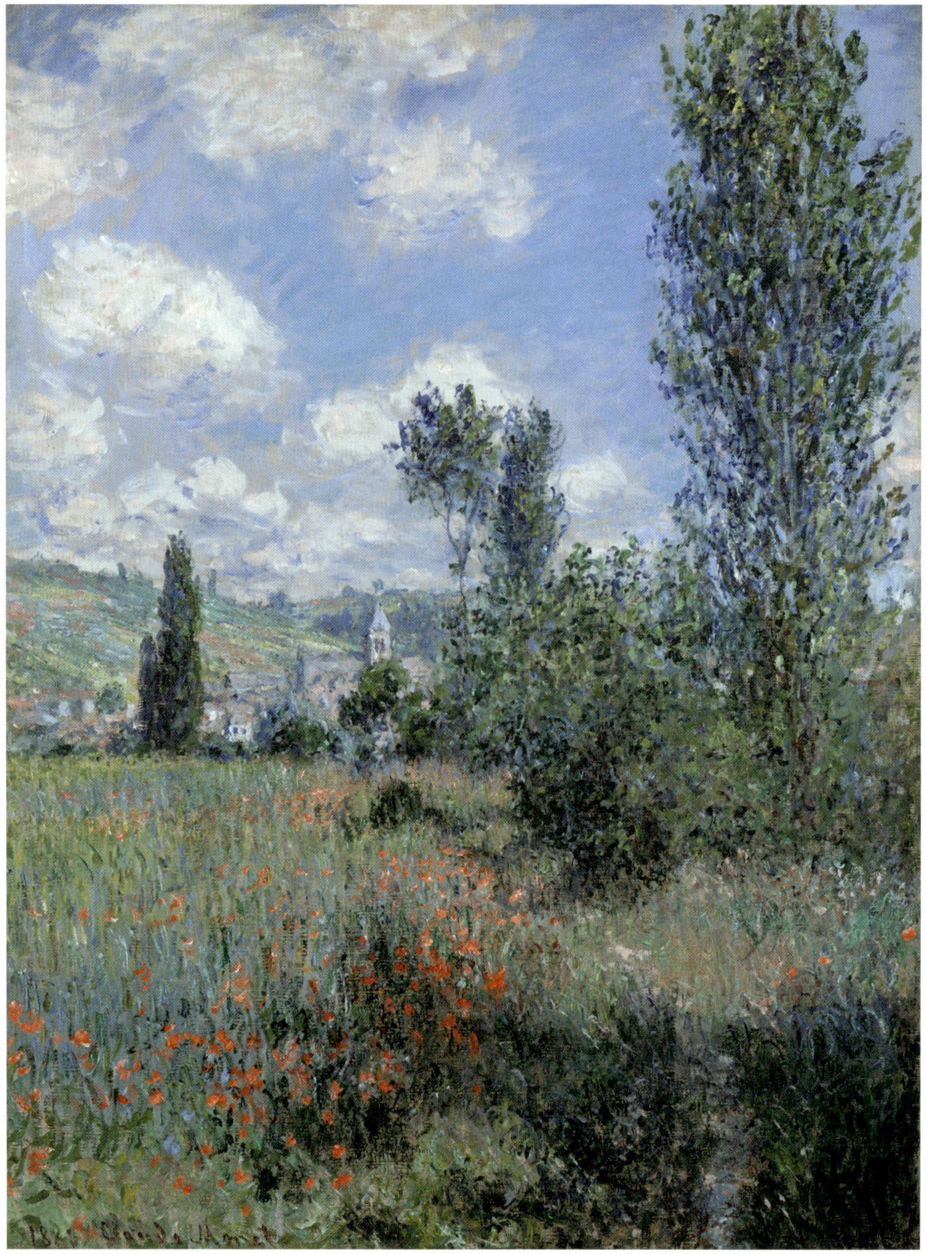

Fig. 85
CLAUDE MONET
View of Vétheuil, 1880
The Metropolitan Museum of Art, New York

Fig. 86
CLAUDE MONET
Poppy Field, 1881
Museum Boijmans Van Beuningen, Rotterdam

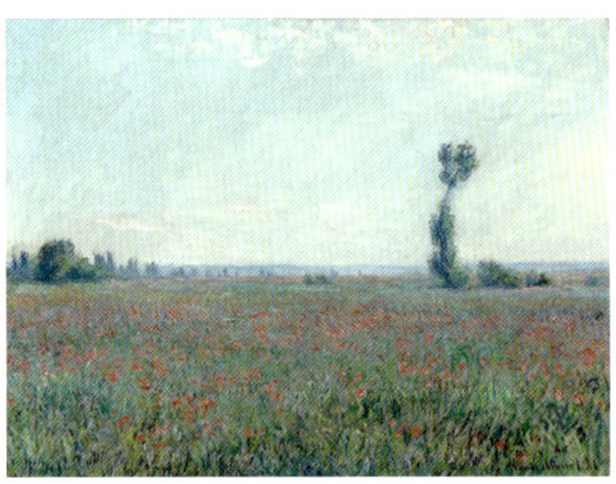

Fig. 87
HEINRICH KÜHN
Summerlandscape, 1897
Private collection

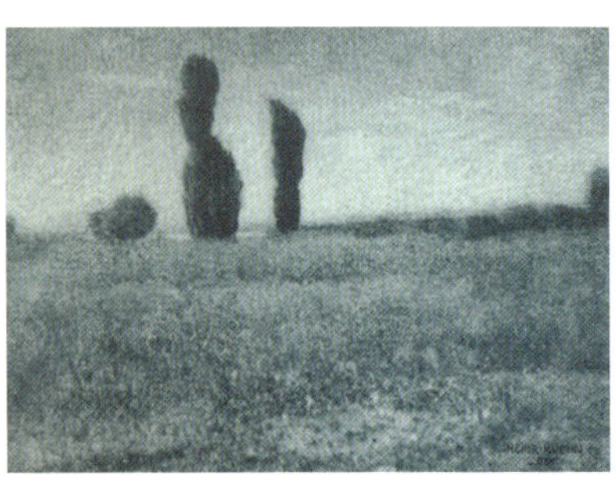

grass through dabs of light; in Kühn's Autochrome *Miss Mary and Lotte* (after 1907, fig. p. 140) bright flecks of sunlight dart over the two sisters.

The oblique view from below looking up embankments and slopes to be found in many of Kühn's photographs also appears to reference Monet's paintings. The backlit *Woman with a Parasol (La femme à l'ombrelle)* (1875, W 381), and some years later the twin pictures *Woman with a Parasol turned to the Right (Essai de figure en plein air, vers la droite)* (1886, W 1076) and *Woman with a Parasol turned to the Left (Essai de figure en plein air, vers la gauche)* (1886, W 1077), the latter also reproduced as a *gillotage* in 1891 in *L'Art dans les deux mondes*,[38] prefigure this type of view from below that we find in Kühn's works like *Miss Mary in a Blue Suit (Miss Mary im blauen Kostüm)* (after 1907), *The Gust of Wind (Der Windstoß)* (1905), or *Mary Warner and Edeltrude on a Hill Crest (Mary Warner und Edeltrude am Hügelkamm)* (1908).

Both Monet and Kühn attempted to make their pictures look spontaneous. Monet's paintings seem to have been completed directly under the impression of the moment—which was exactly what Monet wanted them to look like. In reality, however, they took several sessions, because the painter had to wait for the paint layers to dry so that the colors would not smudge.

Kühn's figurative pictures are also like snapshots, the walkers or strollers appearing to be captured spontaneously as they climb a hill or look into the distance. In reality, the photographs were the product of a sophisticated arrangement and choreography, and in inclement weather needed to be exposed for as much as half an hour. Kühn therefore preferred to work in sunlight or intensive artificial light. His children, who acted as dutiful and docile models, have described how hard and sometimes unpleasant it was to pose for such a long time for these pictures, which often turned into a genuine test of endurance.

To enhance the effect of his photographs as much as possible, Kühn radically simplified the landscape details, arranging less important figures in luminous colors and intensifying the effect even further by confining himself to a few large surfaces and selected articles of clothing adapted to the primary colors of the three photographic plates. His credo was "the simpler the means, the more intensive the effect."[39]

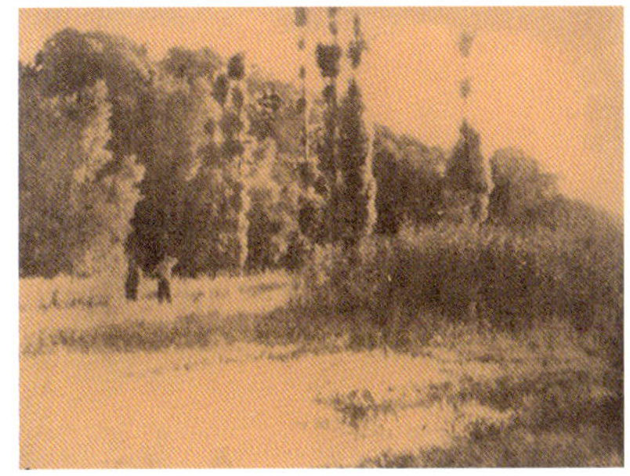

Fig. 88
HEINRICH KÜHN
Southern Landscape, 1897
ÖNB/Vienna

Fig. 89
HEINRICH KÜHN
Landscape in the South, 1897
ÖNB/Vienna

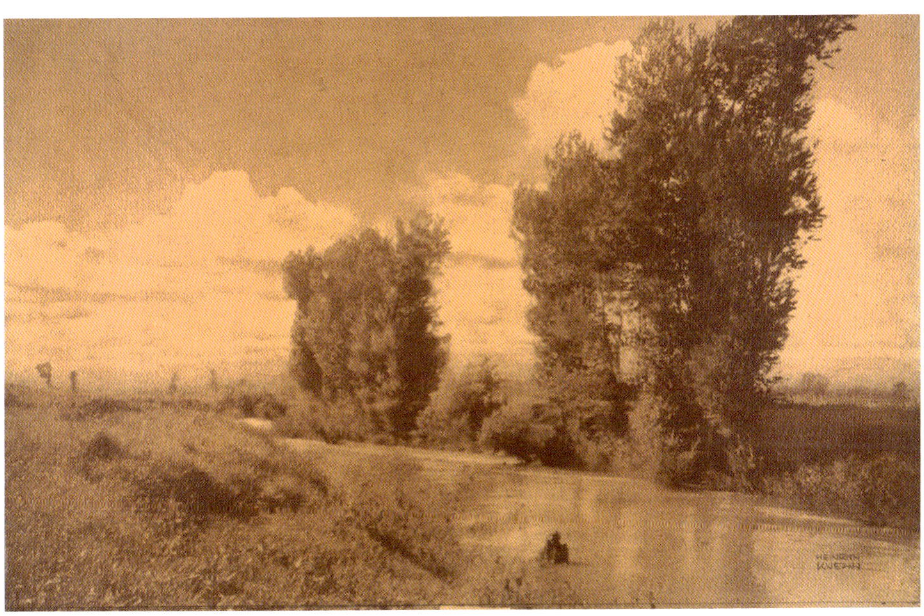

Fig. 91
HEINRICH KÜHN
Walther and Lotte Kühn in the Meadow, 1907-08
ÖNB/Vienna

Fig. 90
HEINRICH KÜHN
Edeltrude and Miss Mary in a white and blue dress, after 1907
ÖNB/Vienna

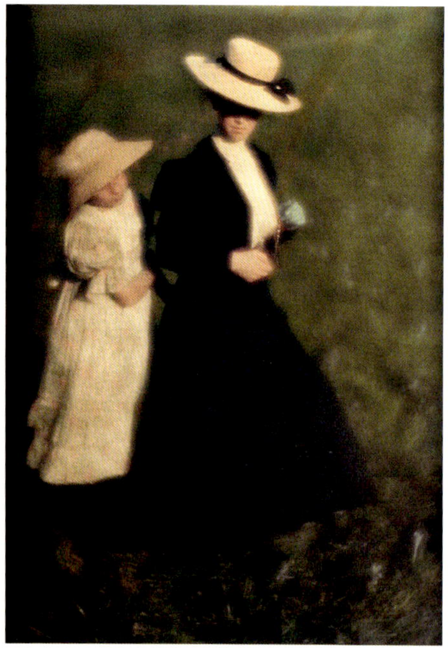

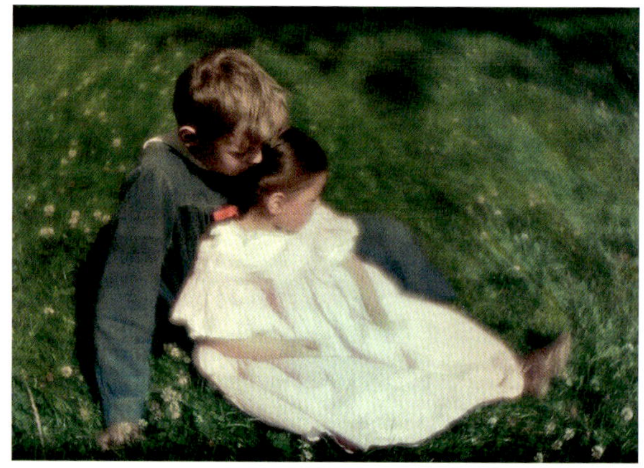

Fig. 93
HEINRICH KÜHN
Under the Trees at the River (In Summer), ca. 1917
ÖNB/Vienna

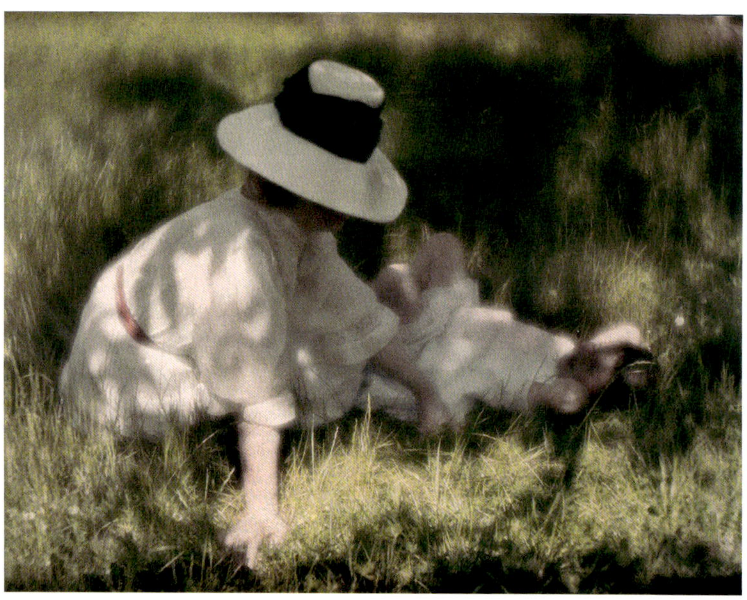

Fig. 92
HEINRICH KÜHN
Miss Mary and Lotte, after 1907
ÖNB/Vienna

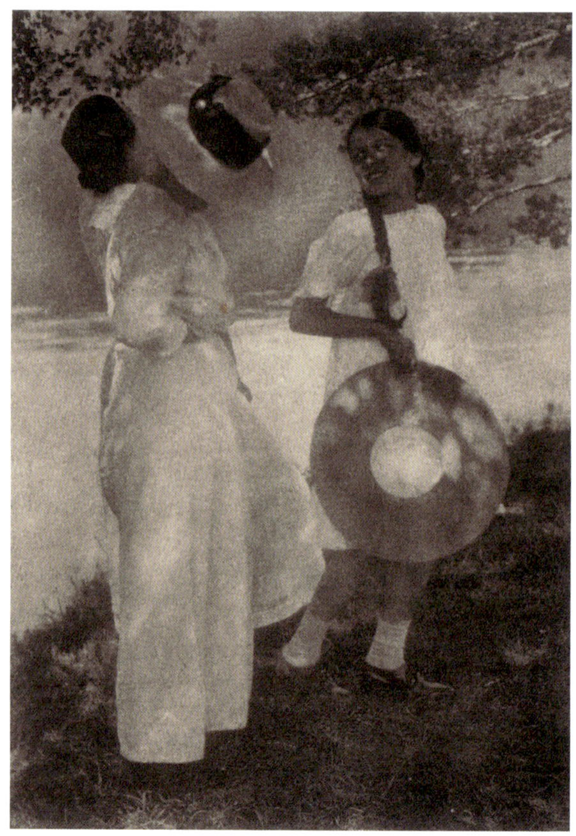

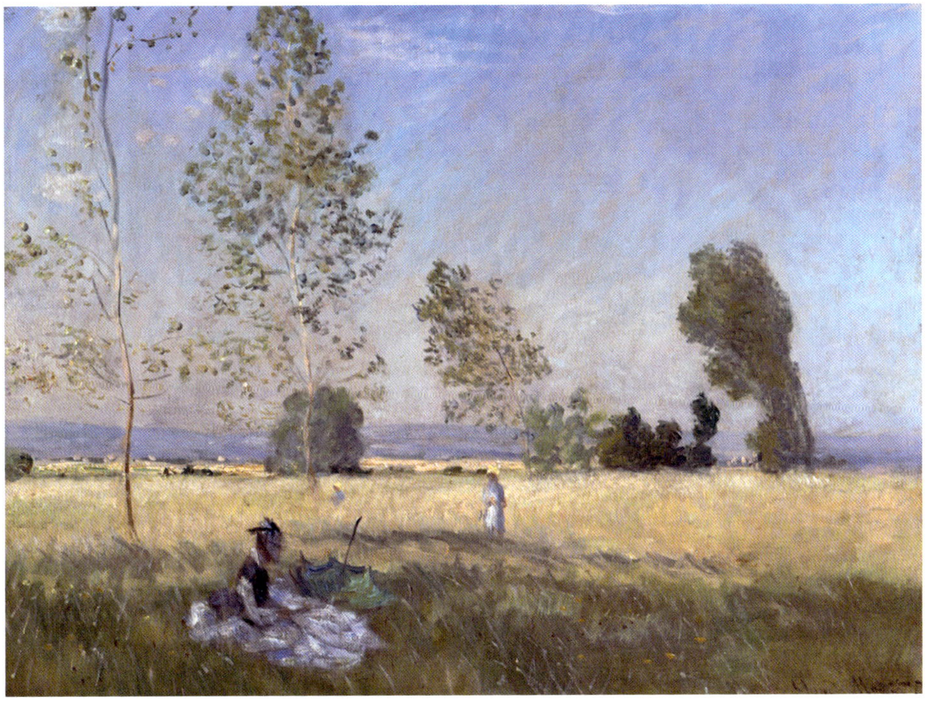

Fig. 94
CLAUDE MONET
Summer, 1874
Staatliche Museen zu Berlin, Nationalgalerie

Fig. 95
CLAUDE MONET
Sunlight Effect under the Poplars, 1887
Staatsgalerie Stuttgart

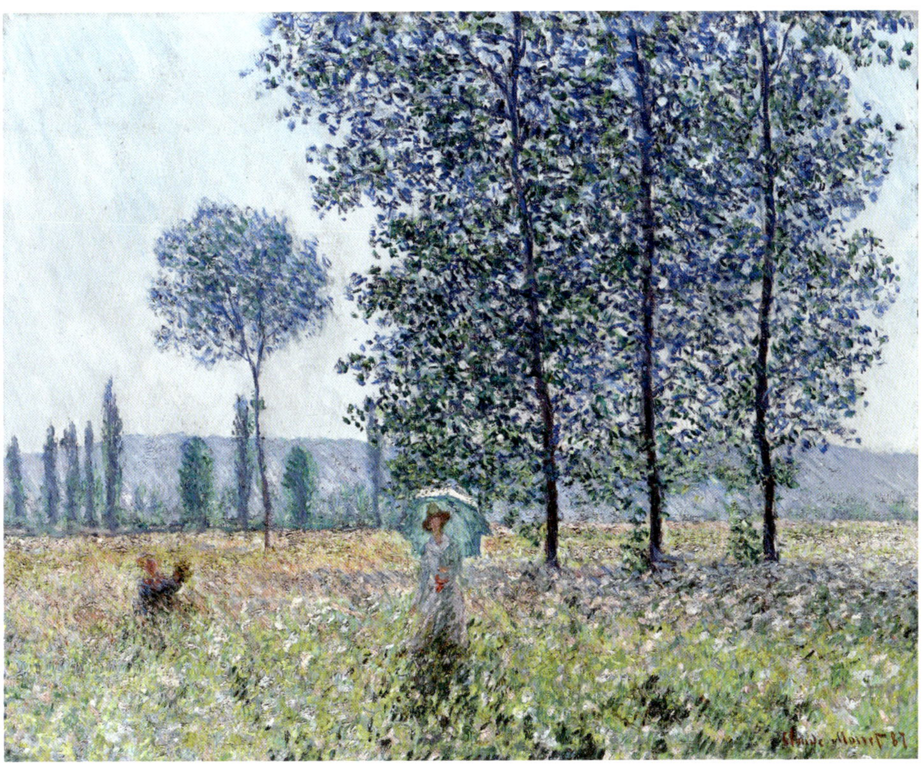

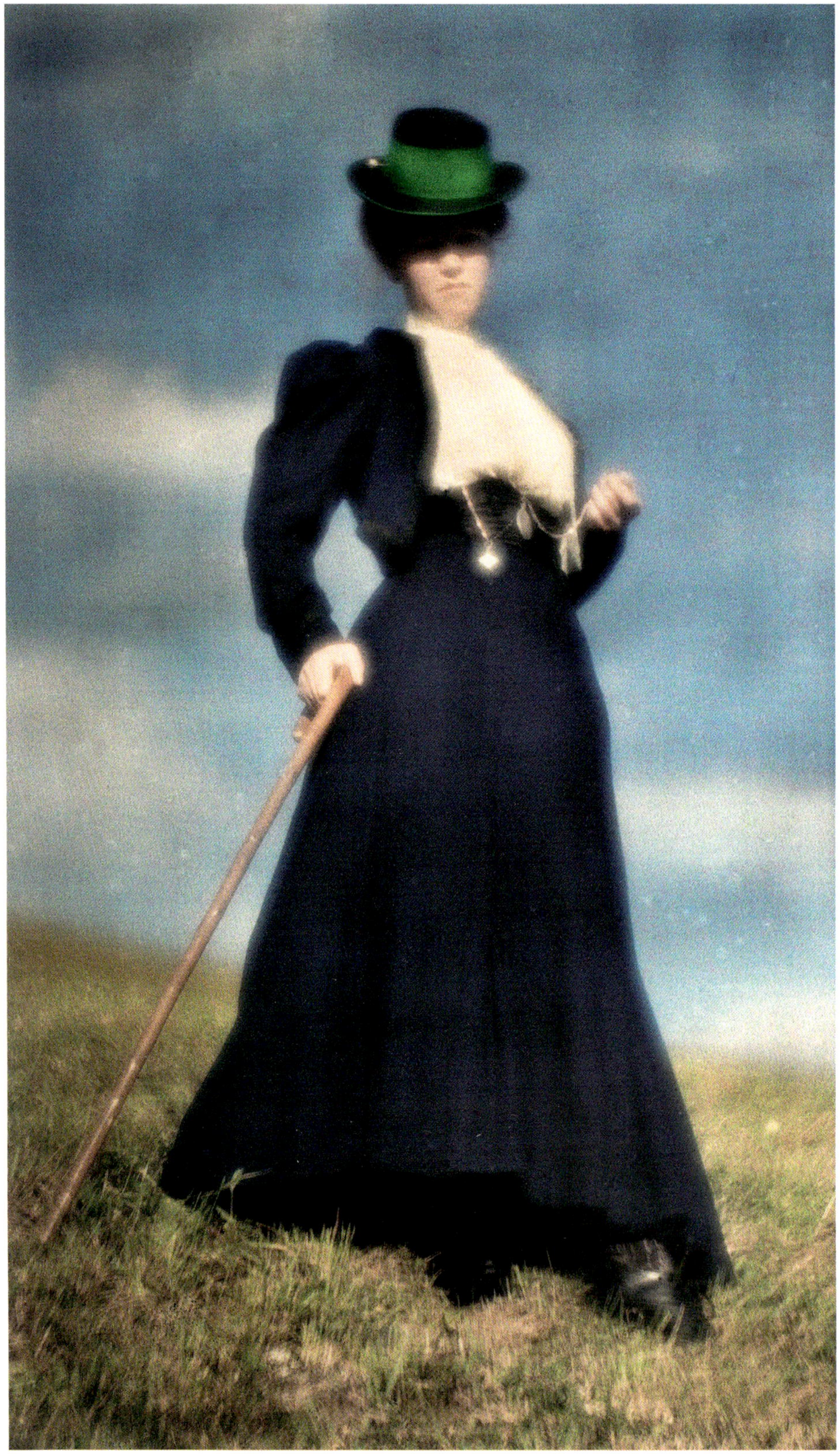

Fig. 96
HEINRICH KÜHN
Miss Mary in a blue dress, after 1907
ÖNB/Vienna

Fig. 97
Unpublished journal of M. CLAUDE MONET
in: *L'Art dans les deux mondes*, 1891

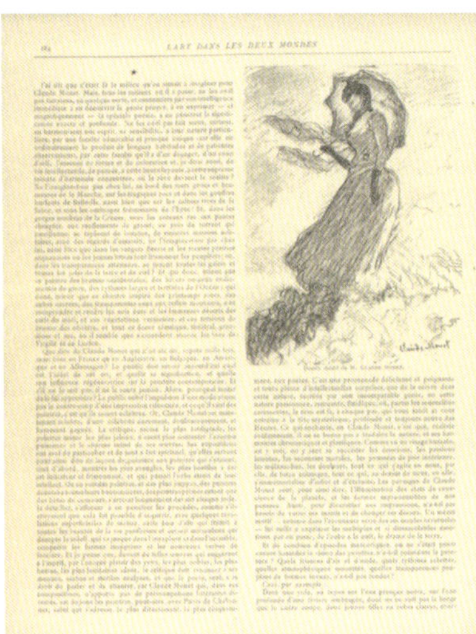

L'ART DANS LES DEUX MONDES

THE IDEA OF THE SERIES

The element of time, which made its way into art by way of photography, led to a new understanding of reality and played a significant role in Monet's search for *instantanéité*, for capturing the moment. However, his observations of atmospheric changes that became continuously more precise led, over time, to increasingly concentrated series of pictures stemming from his conviction that a single picture could not provide a complete description of a motif. In 1889, he further developed the groups of pictures of the early 1880s into the concept of the series that captured the colorist changes of the motif under the influence of the variations in the atmosphere of the light and weather as if these occurred in systematic steps. And soon, one canvas led to the next, the pictures reacted to each other and took on an increasingly independent existence from the motif of the painting.

This is what was so fundamentally new: the interrelationship between the works. The series were not concerned with repetitions but with the differences in similarities. The variation offered expanded insights into what was perceived but, in the modulation within the framework of the colored ensemble, created an even greater whole, a monumental work. This process made it possible for the object to recede further and further. And Monet increasingly simplified his motifs so that he could devote all of his attention to the colorist effects he wanted to create (see fig. pp. 84–86).

As early as in 1882, Emil Jakob Schindler developed the idea of making a cycle of scenes of the months the subject of a series of pictures depicting the changeability of nature under differing atmospheric conditions. He investigated the feeling of the different seasons and their predominant coloration in a series of works that could be united to form a sequence or series through the same format of the paintings and, above all, through the compositional repetition of a path leading diagonally into the depths of the picture and, in this way, already dealt with questions of the colorist equivalent of seasonal moods. For example, in *Road in a Forest in Rainy Weather. November Mood (Straße in einem Wald bei Regenwetter. Novemberstimmung)* (1884, fig. p. 143), the sophisticated grayish blue he used not only visualized the somberness of the day but provided a colorful interplay of reduced tones in the interaction between the blues, grays, and browns that reached its unexpected climax in the red umbrella of the women walking against the pouring rain. In *February Atmosphere – Early Spring in the Vienna Woods (Februarstimmung – Vorfrühling im Wienerwald*; ca. 1884), Schindler makes use of even cooler shades along with earthy tones and greatly increases the contrasts; on the other hand *March Atmosphere – Early Spring in the Vienna Woods (Märzstimmung – Vorfrühling im Wienerwald*; ca. 1884), alludes to the awakening of nature in its delicate harmony of brown, beige, and soft green hues (see fig. p. 150). It is unfortunately not known how far Schindler proceeded with this cycle—to date, we are only aware of four pictures belonging to it—however, it appears that here he already addresses concepts that were to make themselves felt in French Impressionism and especially in Monet's works—those of a growing autonomy of the visual means from the object of the picture and particularly an investigation of modulations of color in the repeated depiction of the same or similar motifs.

Schindler also dealt with different atmospheric conditions in a series of paintings of avenues of poplars as did Marie Egner in sequences of paintings of mills, poplars, and riparian landscapes.

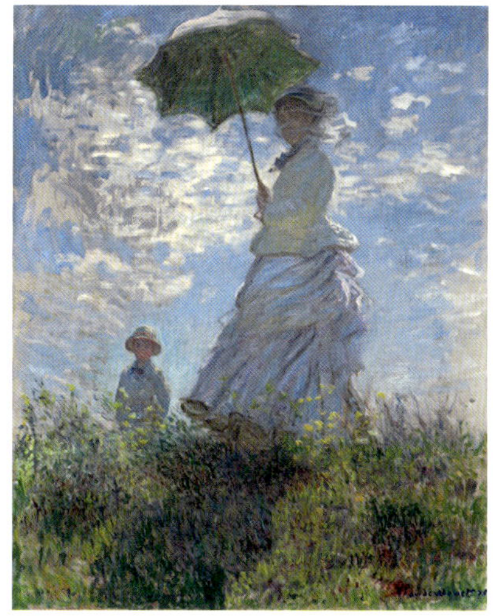

Fig. 98
CLAUDE MONET
The Walk, Woman with a Parasol, 1875
National Gallery of Art, Washington, D.C.

Fig. 99
CLAUDE MONET
Study of a Figure Outdoors (Facing Left), 1886
Musée d'Orsay, Paris

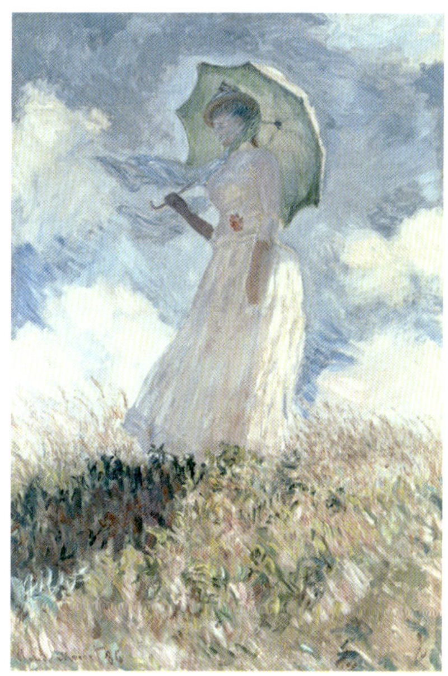

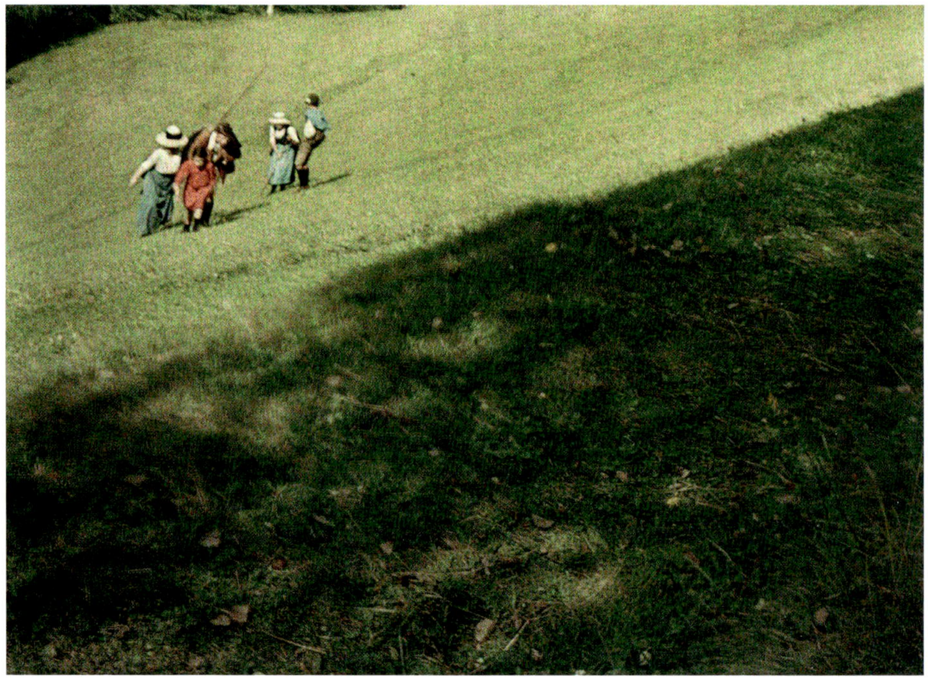

Fig. 100
HEINRICH KÜHN
Landscape with Hikers, 1912
ÖNB/Vienna

Fig. 101
HEINRICH KÜHN
Court garden in Innsbruck, after 1907
ÖNB/Vienna

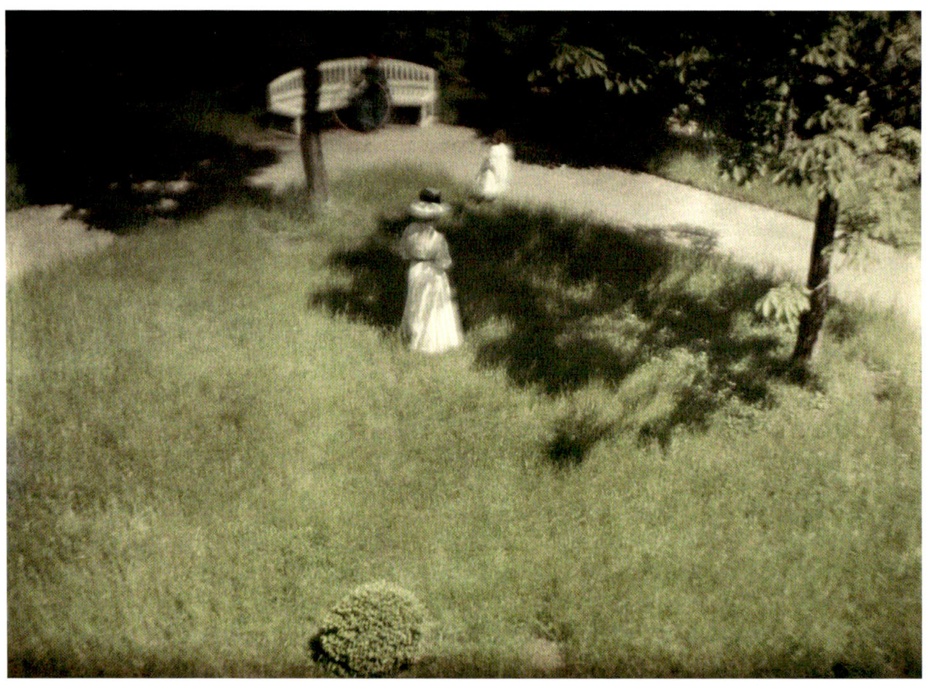

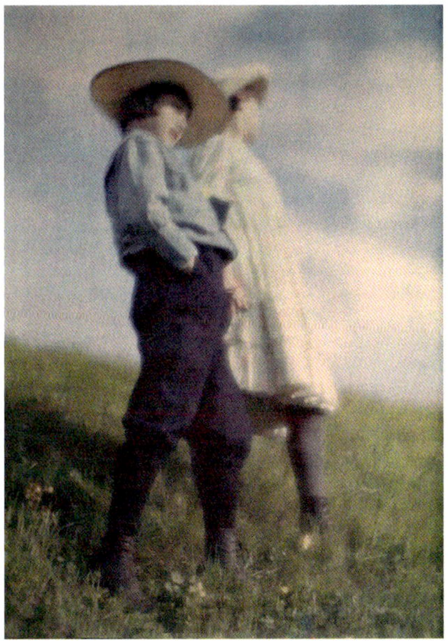

Fig. 102
HEINRICH KÜHN
Hans and Edeltrude Kühn, 1908
ÖNB/Vienna

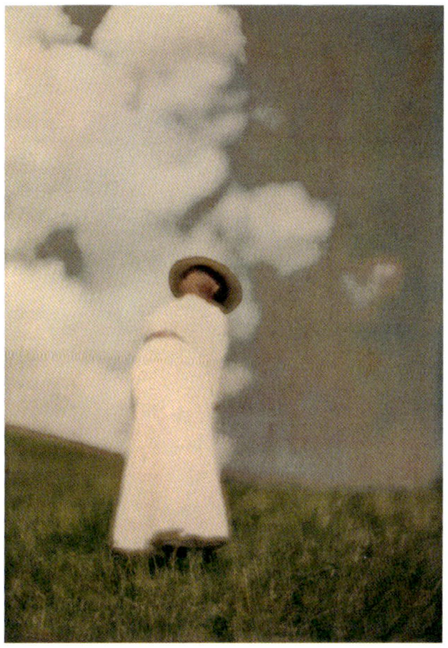

Fig. 103
HEINRICH KÜHN
Mary Warner in Landscape, 1907–08
ÖNB/Vienna

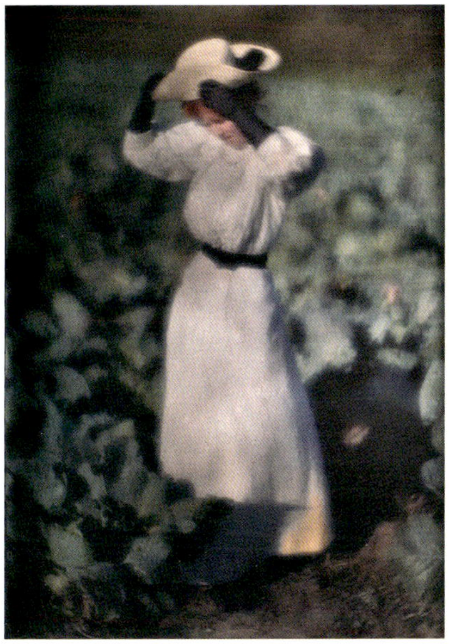

Fig. 104
HEINRICH KÜHN
Miss Mary in the Garden, after 1907
ÖNB/Vienna

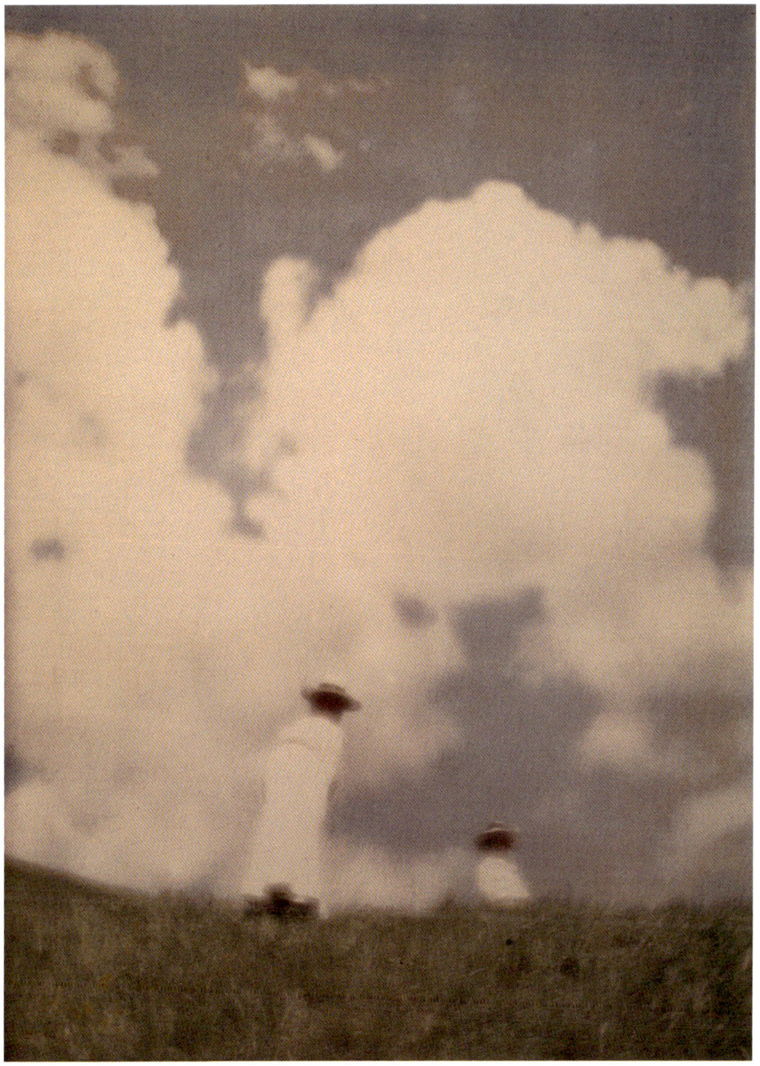

Fig. 105
HEINRICH KÜHN
Mary Warner and Edeltrude on the Brow of a Hill, ca. 1908
The Metropolitan Museum of Art, New York

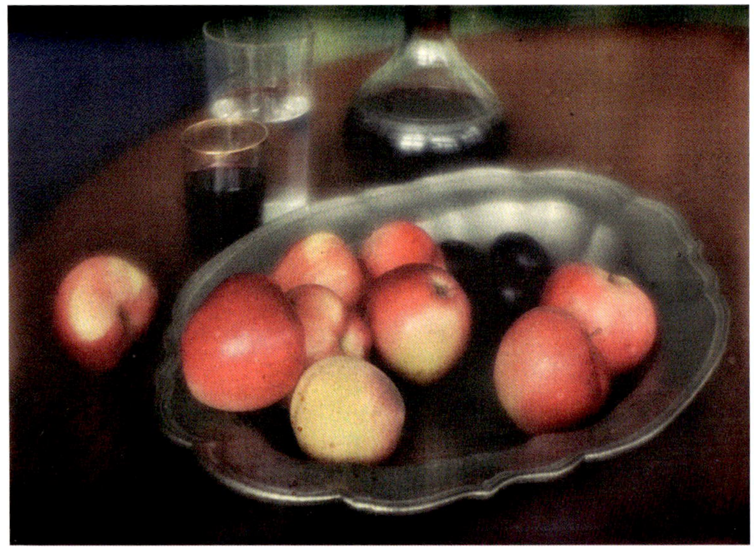

Fig. 106
HEINRICH KÜHN
Still life with apples, ca. 1907
ÖNB/Vienna

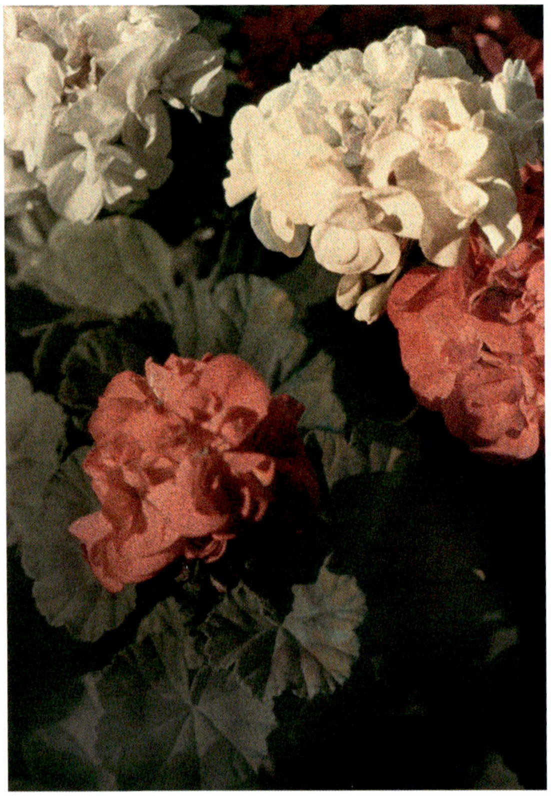

Fig. 107
HEINRICH KÜHN
Still life with geraniums, after 1907
ÖNB/Vienna

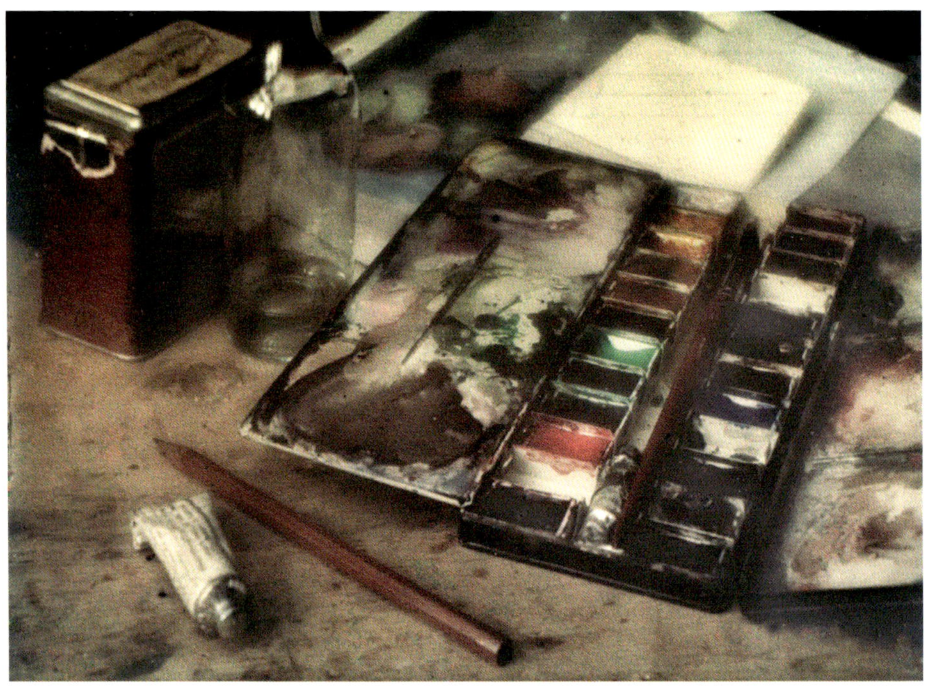

Fig. 108
HEINRICH KÜHN
The artist's table, ca. 1910
ÖNB/Vienna

As we have seen, Theodor von Hörmann had already absorbed Monet's thoughts more systematically and investigated the effects of various lighting conditions on one and the same motif when he painted his series of *Ice Floes on the Bank of the Thaya* in 1891. Emilie Mediz-Pelikan was just as methodical in her approach when she painted her pictures of Stein in winter around the same time and traced down the atmospheric changes while keeping the same detail (see fig. p. 219). Half a century later, Ludwig Heinrich Jungnickel captured the breakers crashing against a rocky formation on the Istrian coast in around 50 oil studies (see fig. p. 189).

However, the greatest impact was created by Monet's London series from 1899–1901. They were described journalistically immediately after their creation and in the following years. In July 1904, the *Gazette des beaux-arts* devoted a lengthy article, illustrated with two views of Waterloo Bridge, one of Charing Cross Bridge, and another one of the Houses of Parliament, to them.[40] In February of the same year, Theodore Duret's article "Claude Monet und der Impressionismus" was published in German in the *Kunst und Künstler* journal;[41] it dealt extensively with the series and also showed a painting of Charing Cross Bridge from 1899.[42] Meier-Graefe also made comments on the series in his essay "Über Impressionismus", which appeared in the journal *Die Kunst für alle* at the beginning of 1910 and reproduced (under the erroneous title of *Waterloo Bridge)* one of the depictions of *Charing Cross Bridge*[43]. Werner Weisbach's book *Impressionismus. Ein Problem der Malerei in der Antike und Neuzeit*, which also had an illustration of a *Waterloo Bridge* in a prominent position, was published in 1911.[44]

The motif of a city bridge seen from above was a popular contemporary subject that painters including Max Suppantschitsch had already tackled. However, the identical view of the motif at the same time of the day but in different seasons, such as Franz Jaschke showed in his pictures of the banks of the Danube Canal, indicates an adoption of Monet's idea of making the various atmospheric feelings created by the light more the subject of the work and creating an intensification of the effect by way of the decorative ensemble. Here, the great variety of the colors and the brushstrokes placed close to each other shows that the experience of late Impressionism had already left its mark on increasing the luminosity of the local colors.

Rudolf Junk was quite clearly inspired by Monet's paintings of the Houses of Parliament in which the buildings are dissolved into pure contours when he reduced the sections of his paintings of Lake Attersee into gently shimmering areas of color and only showed the trees on the lake's banks as silhouettes (fig. p. 200). In his paintings of *Steinbach in the Vienna Woods (Steinbach im Wienerwald)* (1906/07, fig. p. 83), that he depicted from the same observation point and showing the same section, the variations in coloration resulting from the changes in the seasons developed into the actual subject. Painted in his personal Pointillist style, their dazzling coloration informs us of Junk's enthusiasm for the new artistic style. The exhibitions in the Secession[45] and the confrontation with French art had led to his decision to become an artist and, as a result, also to his personal style. Their structure as an ornamental ensemble makes the four *Steinbach in the Vienna Woods* paintings correspond with Monet's concept of a decorative group of paintings connected to each other by the effect they produce.

Oskar Kokoschka probably also had Monet's London series in his mind's eye when he created his series of paintings of the New City in Dresden. Although landscapes had

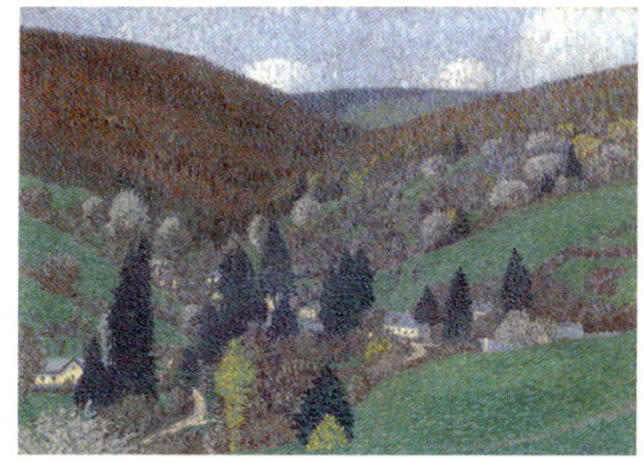

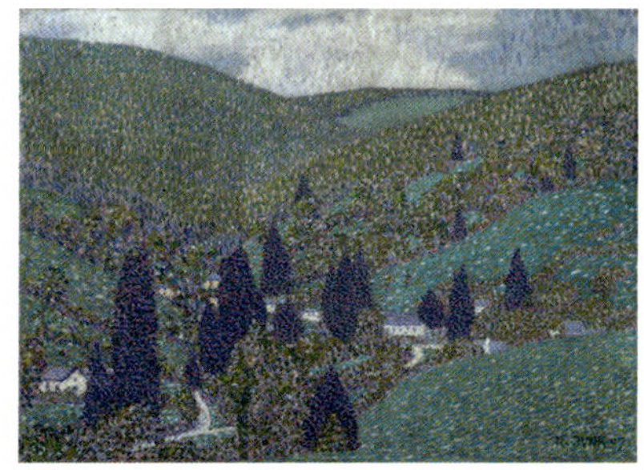

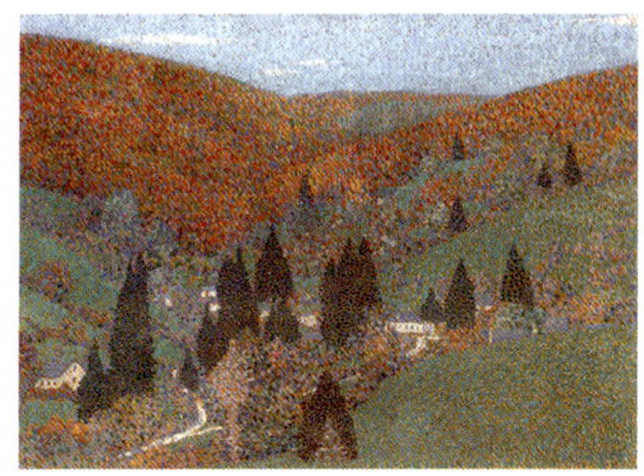

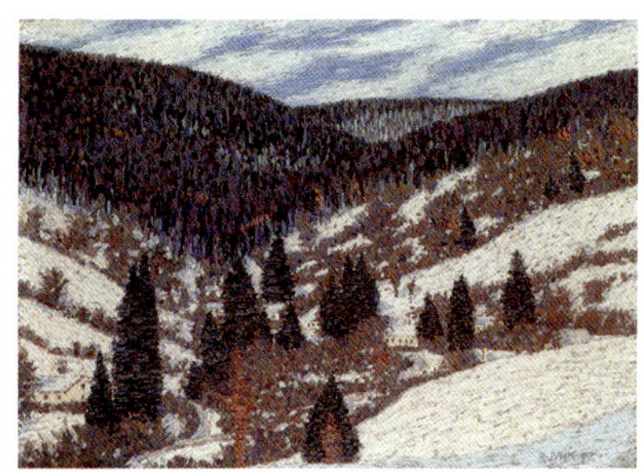

Fig. 109-112
RUDOLF JUNK
Spring in Steinbach in the Wienerwald, 1906
Private collection

Summer in Steinbach in the Wienerwald, 1907
Belvedere, Vienna

Autumn in Steinbach in the Wienerwald, 1906
Private collection

Winter in Steinbach in the Wienerwald, 1907
Private collection

Fig. 113
CLAUDE MONET
Waterloo Bridge, 1903
Worcester Art Museum, Worcester, Massachusetts

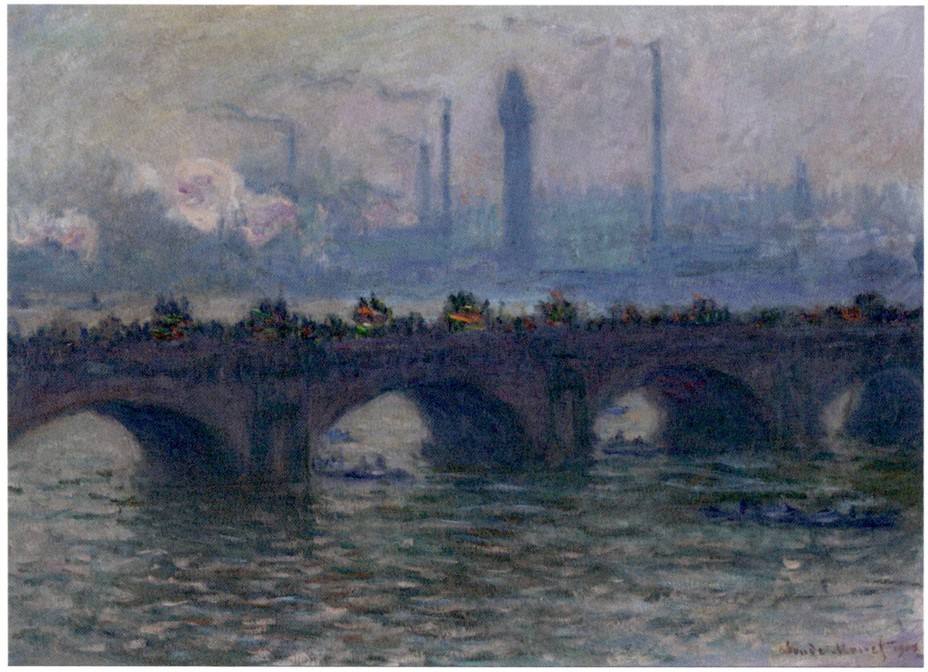

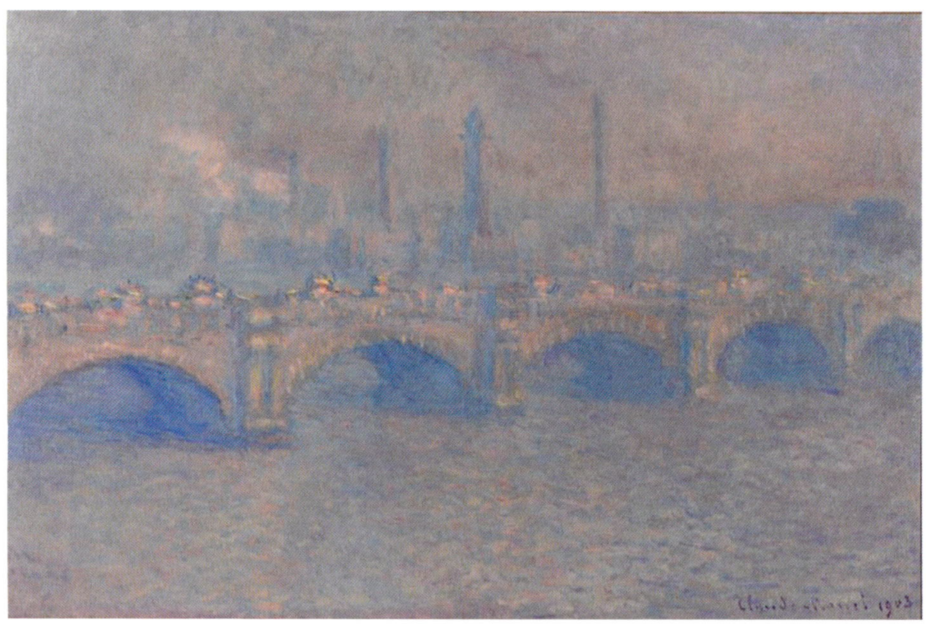

Fig. 114
CLAUDE MONET
Waterloo Bridge, Sunlight, 1903
McMaster Museum of Art, McMaster University, Hamilton, Ontario

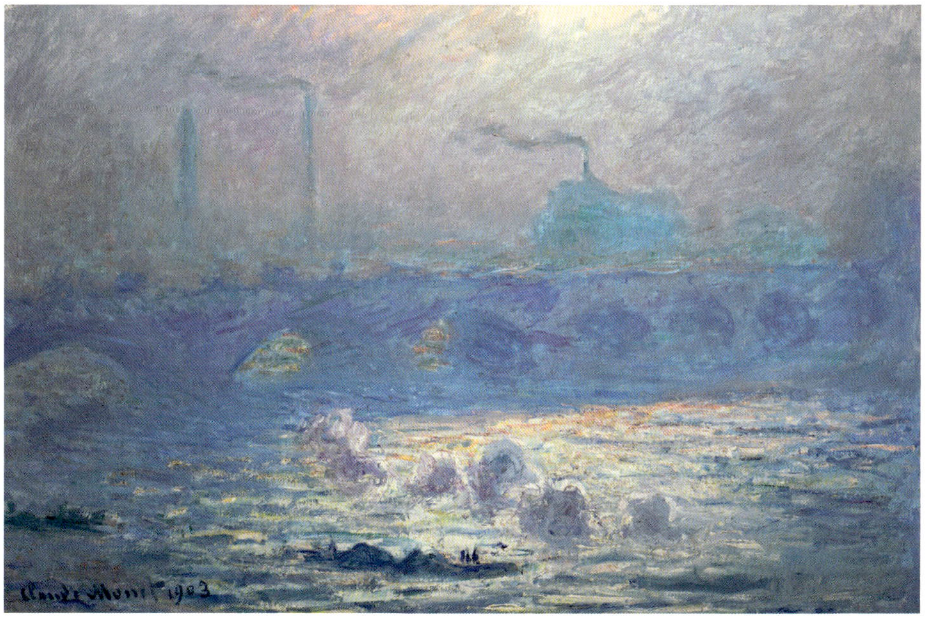

Fig. 115
CLAUDE MONET
Waterloo Bridge, Sunlight Effect, 1903
Denver Art Museum Collection

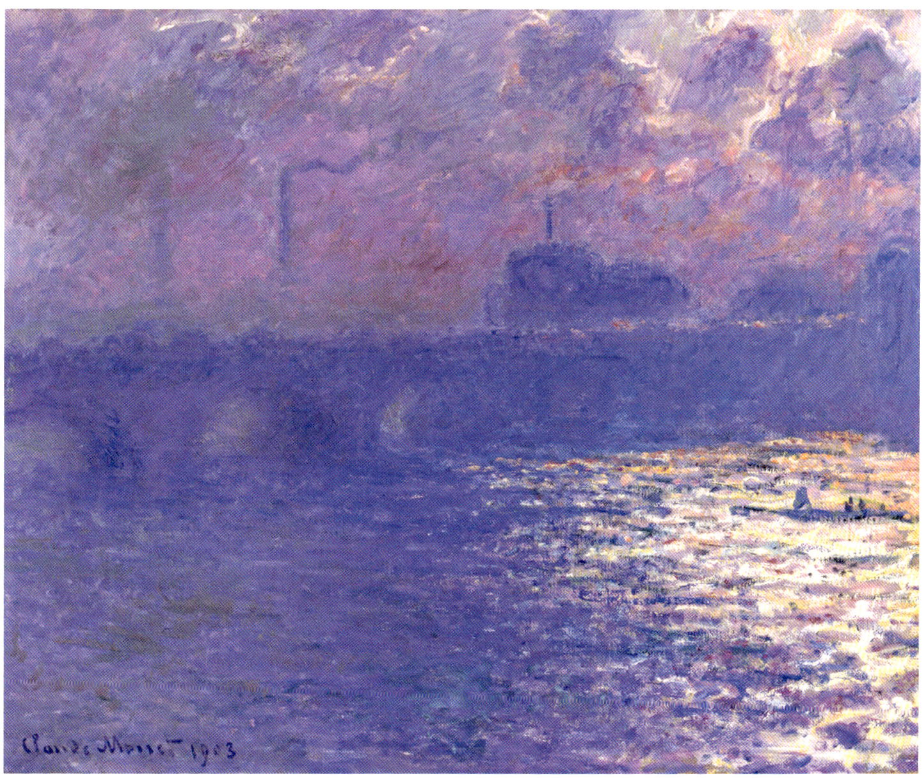

Fig. 116
CLAUDE MONET
Waterloo Bridge, Sunlight Effect, 1903
Milwaukee Art Museum

Fig. 117
CLAUDE MONET
Waterloo Bridge, 1902
Kunsthaus Zürich

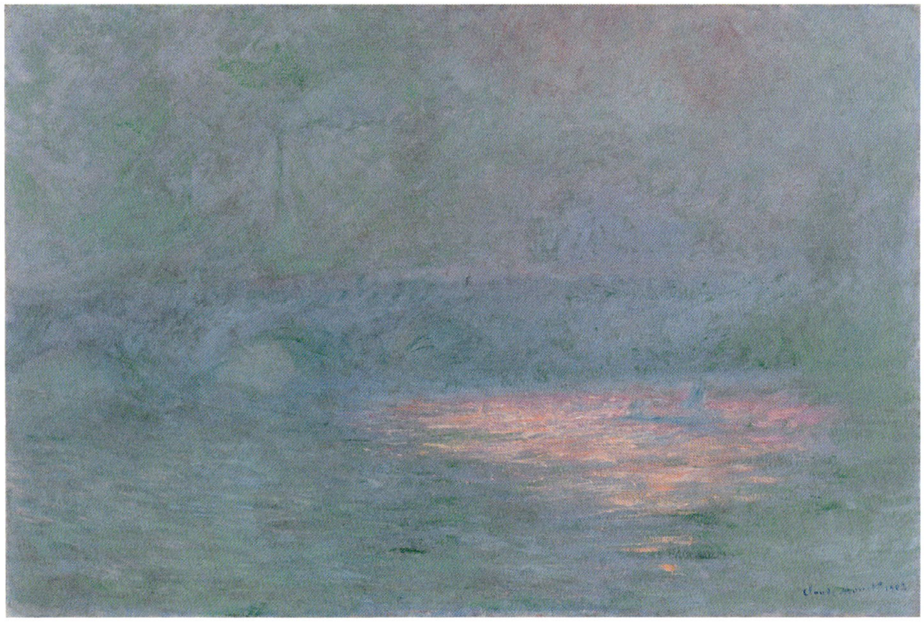

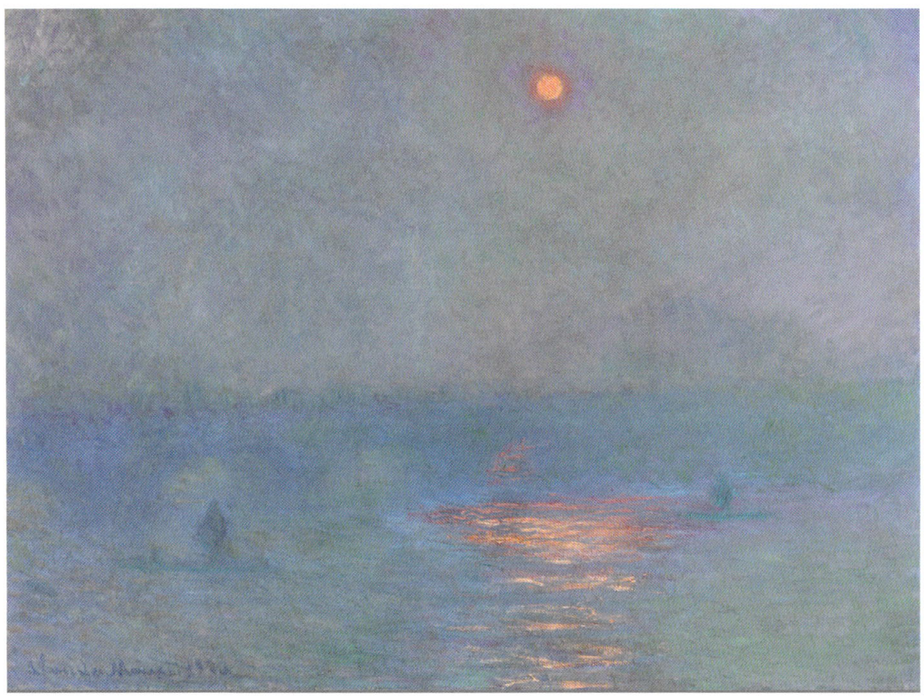

Fig. 118
CLAUDE MONET
Waterloo Bridge: the Sun in a Fog, 1903
National Gallery of Canada, Ottawa

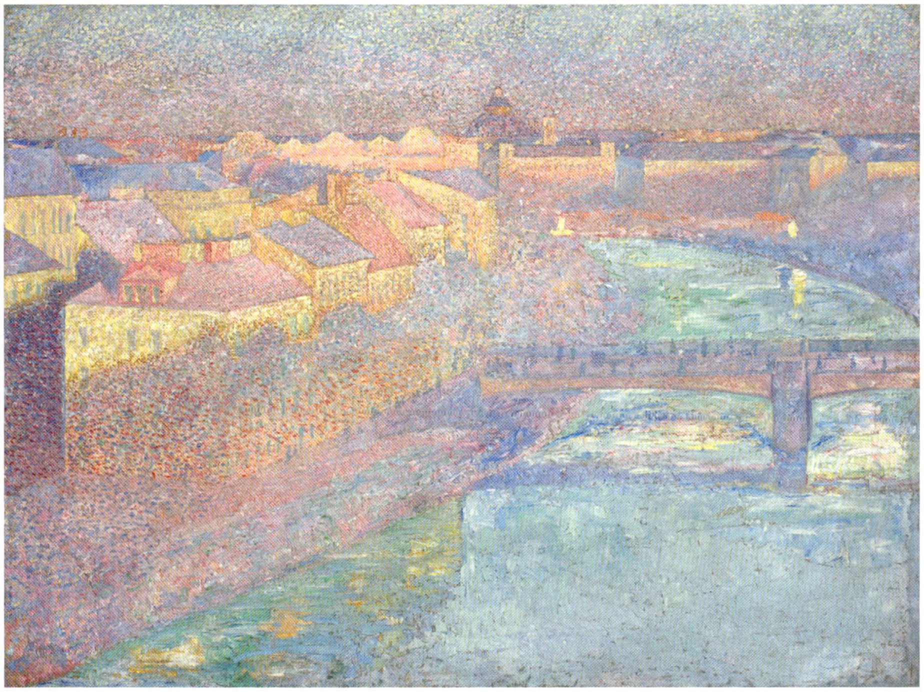

Fig. 119
FRANZ JASCHKE
Danube Canal in Summer, 1903
Belvedere, Vienna

Fig. 120
FRANZ JASCHKE
At the Danube Canal, 1903
Belvedere, Vienna

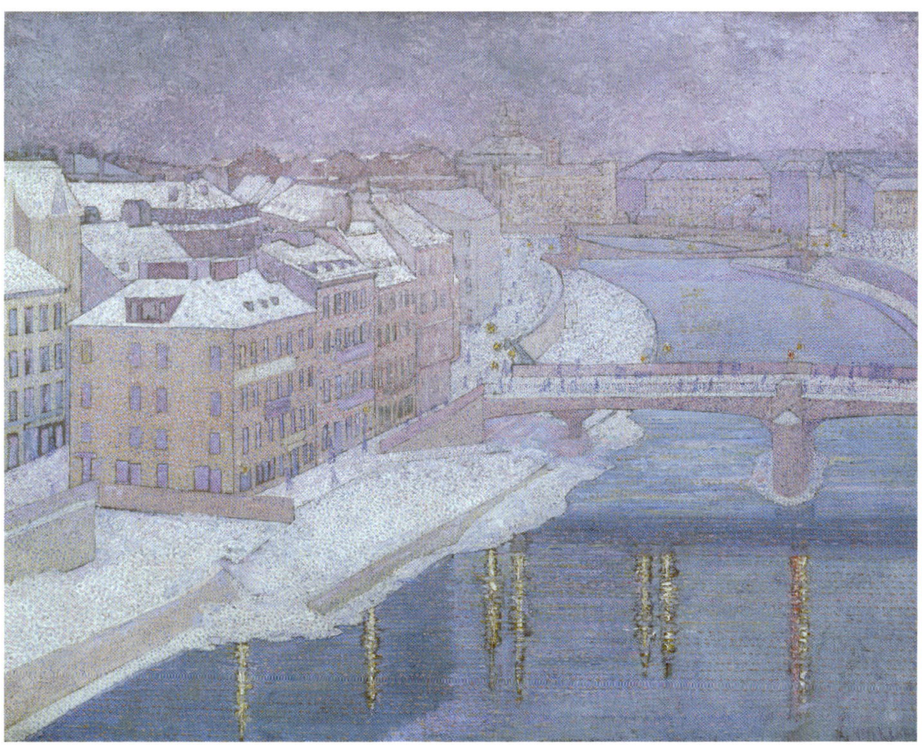

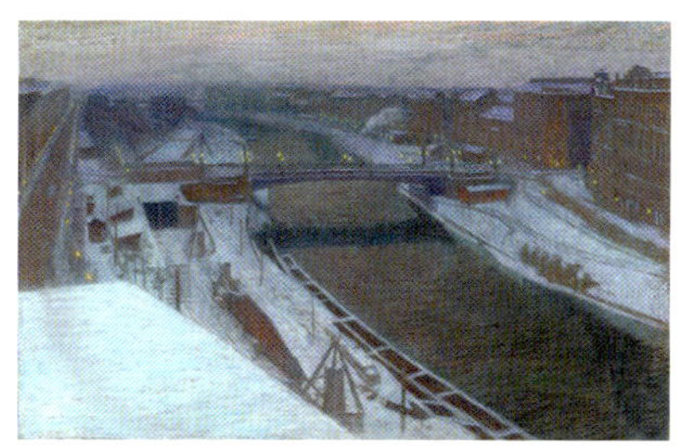

Fig. 121
MAX SUPPANTSCHITSCH
Stephanienbridge, 1901
Belvedere, Vienna

previously only played an insignificant role in his oeuvre, they now became the focus of his artistic activities. His Dresden period, which is commonly regarded as a phase of new orientation for Kokoschka, consummated a marked stylistic change in the artist's work—probably under the impression of the explosion of color in Emil Nolde's paintings that were displayed in Dresden at this time. The situation Kokoschka found himself in—he had to recover from severe war injuries as well as the traumatically experienced break up of his relationship to Alma Mahler on the one hand and his appointment as professor on the other—was the driving force behind this artistic new orientation. While dark tones had been predominant in the psychologizing portraits of his Viennese period in which the personalities he depicted stood out against full-toned colors and were often captured in agitated, restless brushstrokes, which were frequently gouged into the wet paint, and scratched lines and hatching, the colors used in the years from 1916 to 1918 developed in the direction of a chromatic bluish-violet overall atmosphere. Now, all of a sudden, his pictures were characterized by broadly applied areas of sonorous, brightly shining colors that invested them with a sumptuous splendor in the form of pulsating complementary contrasts. Shortly after his appointment as professor at the Akademie in Dresden (Dresden Academy), Kokoschka was able to move into his studio on Brühlsche Terrasse in the city in October 1919. In the spring of 1920, he painted the view across the River Elbe towards the New City in Dresden with the Augustus Bridge on the left and the tower of the Magi's Church on the right from this location; this was followed by nine additional paintings of the same motif in the period up to summer 1923.

Fig. 122
OSKAR KOKOSCHKA
Dresden, Neustadt I, 1919/20
Private collection

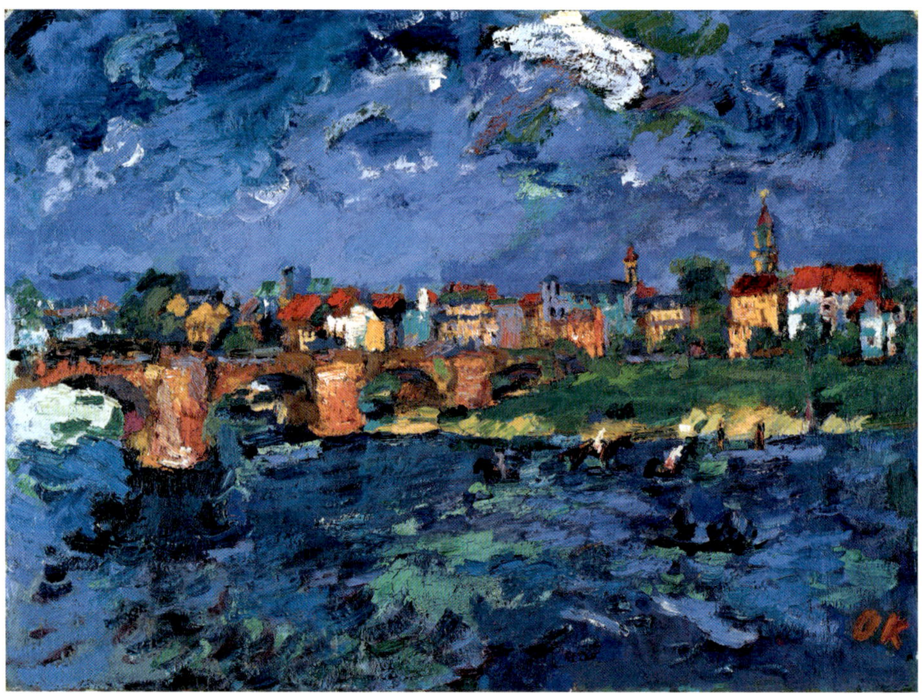

The views of the opposite bank of the Elbe in dazzling colors have something Impressionistic about them as they reflect the changing situation of the light and various times of the day and under differing weather constellations; in keeping with this, the light focuses on different sections of the picture in the individual works or makes them sink back in darker tones. The first painting in particular, with the dazzling sunshine shining on the facades and pillars of the bridge, the people washing their horses in the river, and the bright clouds driven across the dark blue sky by the wind, allows us to experience something of the festive cheerfulness of this day in springtime.
As the series of paintings progresses, the topographical details become increasingly unimportant and act much more as a motive for free artistic practice. The paint is applied alternately in thick and thin layers, the depiction becomes increasingly simplified and contracted into fields of color so that finally the depiction of spatiality in *Dresden New City VII (Dresden Neustadt VII)* dissolves into a fabric of full-toned areas of color.
The actual play had now become a drama of colors, their resonance, conflict, their ability to enhance each other. The eye frequently encounters the classical elementary contrasts of strong red, green, and blue tones in the broad expanses of color. This also makes it possible to interpret the views of the New City in Dresden as studies in colorist intensification, as experiments with color, made in order to acquire knowledge of the effect they produce. In these works, we see dazzlingly colorist fields of color spread out before us in a way that we never again encounter in Kokoschka's later works.
Kokoschka continued with his views across the Elbe in 1923; however, they were now painted from a glass annex on the roof of the exhibition hall next to his studio. In one of them—*Dresden, Augustus Bridge with Figure from the Back (Dresden, Augustusbrücke mit Rückenfigur)* (1923, fig. p. 208)—a putto, which—together with other statues—decorated the western annex of the art academy, is positioned in the foreground as a *repoussoir figure*. The view is now more upriver and the Augustus Bridge has become a much more dominant element and center of focus of the depiction creating an even closer connection with Monet's paintings of Waterloo Bridge. After the war, Kokoschka once again intensified his contacts with Herwarth Walden and Paul Cassirer and it appears possible that the latter motivated the artist to provide the bridge with a more dominant role. Cassirer had already shown 13 views of the Thames (along with four of the Houses of Parliament and nine of Waterloo Bridge) in his gallery in 1904 and was also able to offer a different version of Waterloo Bridge in both 1909 and 1911. Another picture from this series passed through his hands in 1914.[46]
The paintings with the space-defining element of the bridge now became invested with a more powerful structure that led the viewer's eyes from the foreground far into the depths of the picture and already show traces of Kokoschka's later works with their dynamically portrayed cityscapes. At the same time, the introduction of boats, walkers, and streetcars into the interplay of light and shadow and the reflections on the water added an Impressionist, momentary aspect to the paintings.
Kokoschka found one of the most dominant subjects for his work of the following decades in these views of a city.
Kokoschka was to paint three Thames landscapes that cannot deny his knowledge of

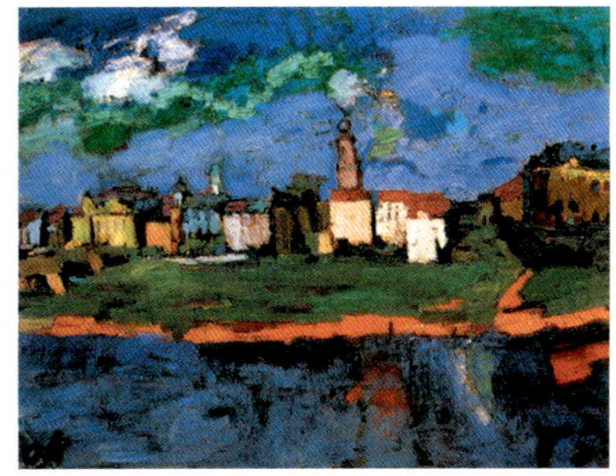

Fig. 123
OSKAR KOKOSCHKA
Dresden, Neustadt II, ca. 1921
The Detroit Institutes of Arts

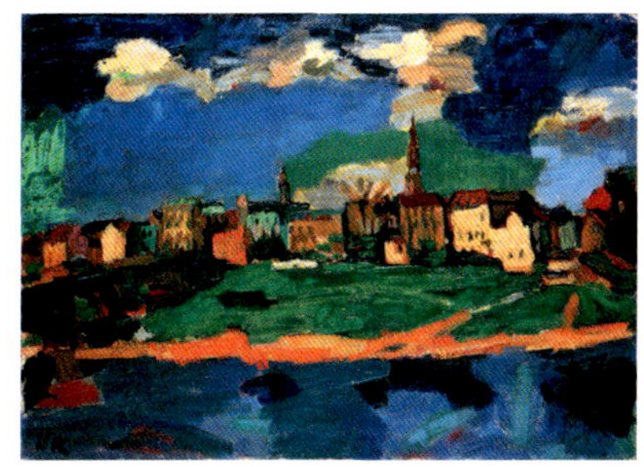

Fig. 124
OSKAR KOKOSCHKA
Dresden, Neustadt III, 1921
Museum Ludwig, Cologne

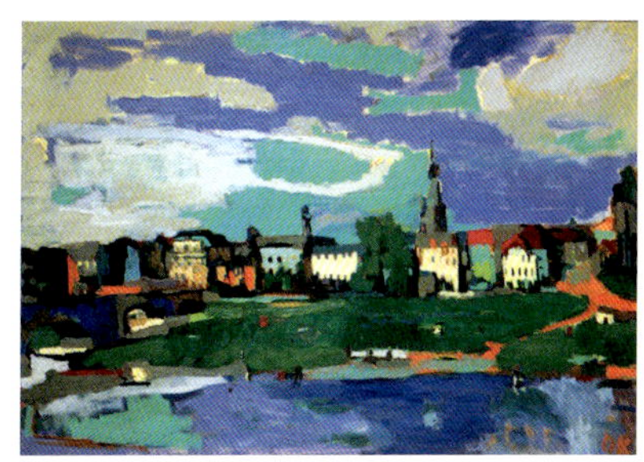

Fig. 125
OSKAR KOKOSCHKA
Dresden, Neustadt VI, 1921
Collection Arnold, New York

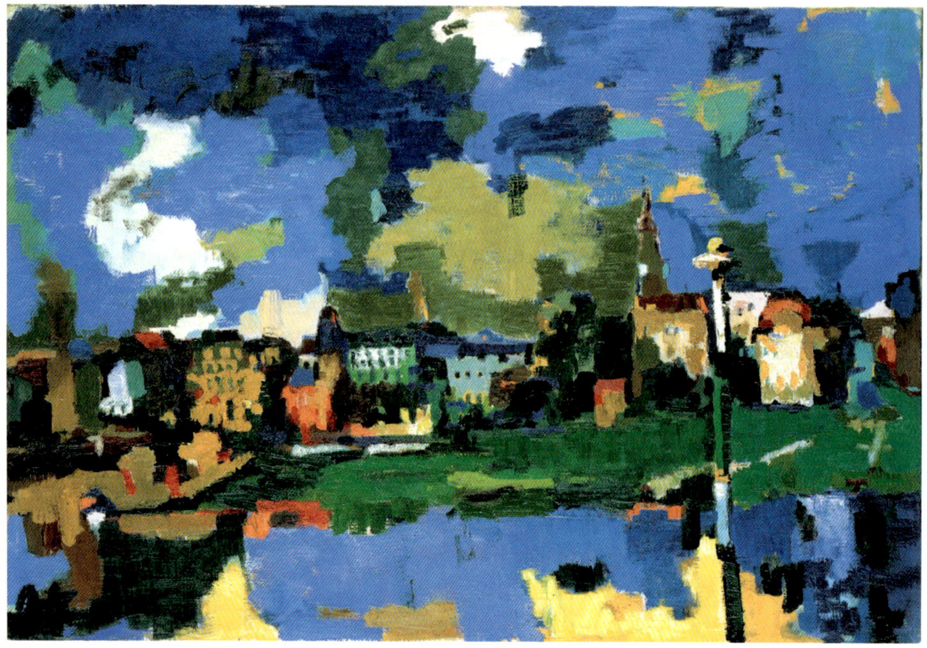

Fig. 126
OSKAR KOKOSCHKA
Dresden, Neustadt VII, 1922
Hamburger Kunsthalle

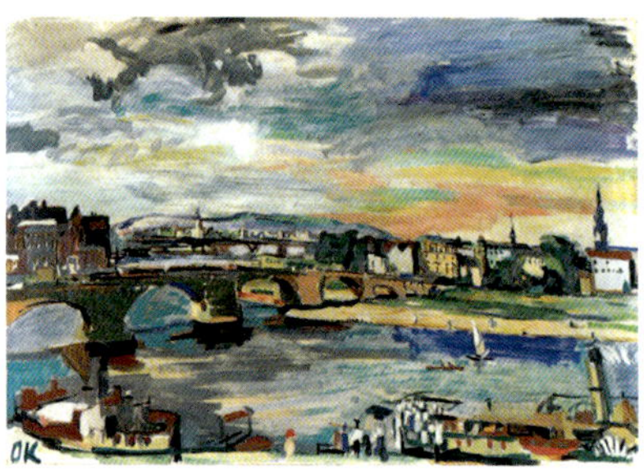

Fig. 127
OSKAR KOKOSCHKA
Dresden, Augustusbrücke with steamboat I , 1923
Private collection

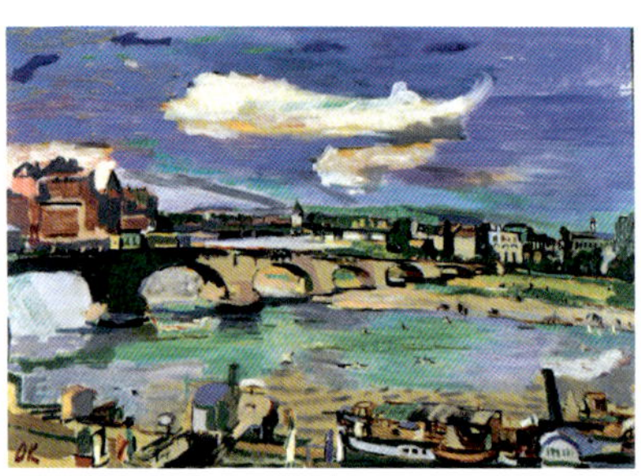

Fig. 128
OSKAR KOKOSCHKA
Dresden, Augustusbrücke with steamboat II , 1923
Stedelijk Van Abbemuseum, Eindhoven

Monet's famous series in the spring of 1926. He painted Waterloo Bridge and two scenes of Charing Cross Bridge with the Houses of Parliament in the background from the eighth floor of the Savoy Hotel—the same building where Monet also created his pictures.[47] In keeping with his nature, he chose a higher angle of view because, after his experiences in the trenches in the First World War, he had sworn that, in future, he would "[...] only observe what happens to the cities, what happens to the people vegetating in the cities, standing and looking from the highest buildings or the mountains, on the top, at the peak."[48] In particular, this applies to his two Thames landscapes in which Charing Cross Bridge dominates the scene and in which the interplay between the glowing yellow sky and the Houses of Parliament that have been dissolved into a silhouette not only have overtones of Turner's, but also of Monet's, visual creations.

The views of the Vltava River and across to Hradčany that he painted from his studio in Prague in the mid-1930s still partially follow the style of Monet's *Waterloo Bridge* paintings—one only has to consider *Charles Bridge (Karlsbrücke)* painted in 1934 (National Gallery, Prague) with a similar view down onto the water with the striking arches of the bridge on the left and the ship on the glittering water in the foreground. The construction of areas of color which we encountered in Kokoschka's views of the Dresden New City were to characterize Herbert Boeckl's *Erzberg* series painted more than two decades later—here, however, with a pronounced feeling of tectonics.

We frequently find series in Boeckl's works; they reach from the *Dominicans (Dominikaner)* (1948), over the *Flying Woodpecker (Fliegender Specht)* (1950), and the views of *Seville* (1952, fig. p. 184) to the series *In the Summerhouse (Im Gartenhaus)* (1962). However, none of these reaches an intensity or develops a heightening of the effect created by the juxtaposition of the individual paintings that can be compared with the eight-part *Erzberg* series in which the majority of the works show the same section from the same angle on the motif.

The changes in the lighting situation on the mountain prompted Boeckl to translate them into large areas of color. The motif complied with Boeckl's intentions in as much as he had always been fascinated by quarries. The painter, who had considered becoming an architect for a short while, always aimed at a tectonic construction, at firmly united structures, in his works. The terracing of this mountain, which was being stripped by the hand of man, already contained Cubist aspects. However, Boeckl monumentalized the forms even more by reducing them to a few, elementary sections of the painting.

This was augmented by Boeckl's lifelong study of the work of Paul Cézanne. After the First World War, while he was still a young artist, Boeckl became acquainted with his work through the Nötsch Circle and also had the opportunity to have a personal encounter with Cézanne's art during the period he spent in Paris in 1923. However, when Boeckl exhibited in the Jeu de Paume in Paris within the framework of the "Exposition d'art autrichien" in 1937, his study of the paintings by the master from Aix left an indelible impression on him. The paintings of the *Staatzer Kegel*[49] and the *Quarry in St. Margarethen*[50] that he created soon thereafter are a clear indication of this. One could even go so far as to say that the Erzberg was a kind of *Montagne Sainte Victoire* for Boeckl, a motif that lent itself to being treated as a *constructed* picture.

Fig. 129
HERBERT BOECKL
Erzberg II, 1947
Artothek des Bundes – On permanent loan to the Belvedere, Vienna

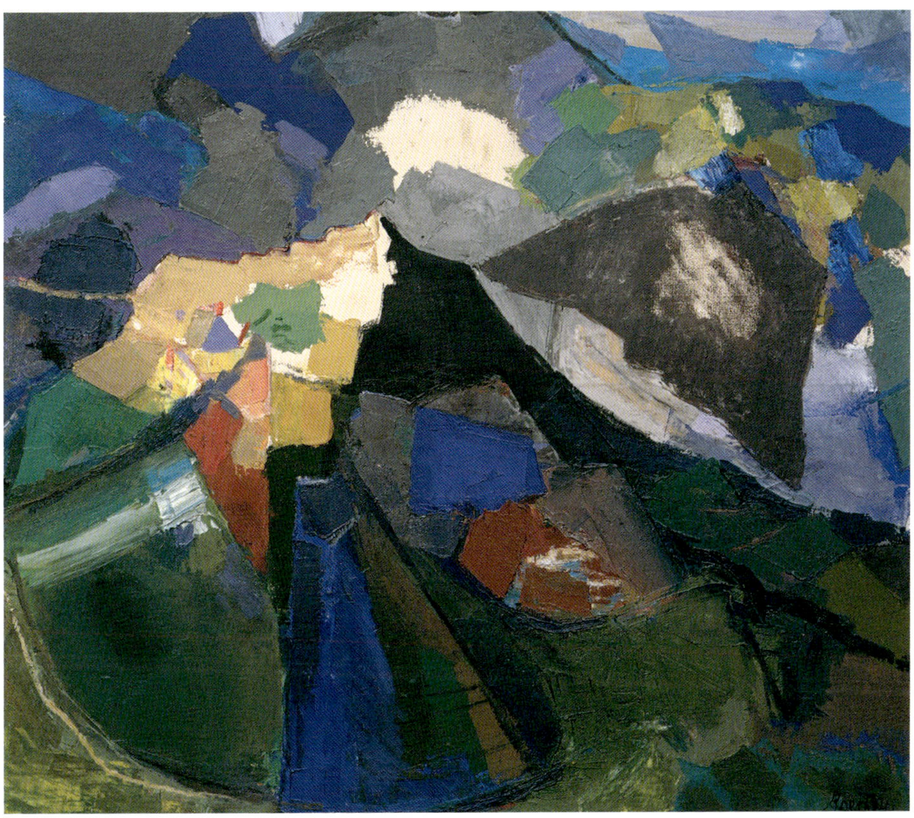

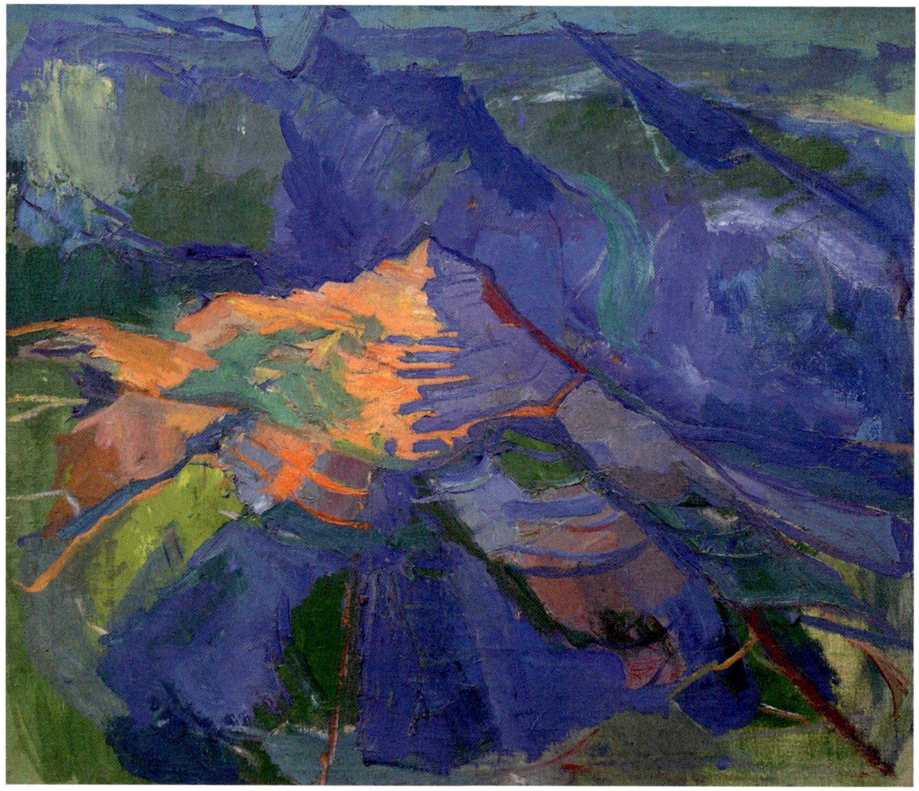

Fig. 130
HERBERT BOECKL
Erzberg V, 1948
Private collection

However, Boeckl does not resort to a fine fabric of colorful areas and strokes as Cézanne does but constructs a tower of heavy blocks of color. Not only the weight of the colors as a result of their tonal values, but also the material substance of their pastosity, plays a role here in creating an impression of solidity. When Boeckl concentrates the finely detailed terraces of the opencast mine (seen from afar) to create large sections of the picture, he is successful in heightening the impression of his, sometimes uninhibitedly dazzling, colors even further, introducing their sonority like the brass section of an orchestra and emphatically elevating the appearance of the mountain. The majestic mountain leaves an indelible impression on the viewer making the paintings of the *Erzberg* just as iconic as Monet's *Haystacks*.

When Meier-Graefe came to making a final characterization of Monet's series in his *Entwicklungsgeschichte der modernen Kunst*, he went as far as to claim that: "The naïveté of the young person who finds pleasure at looking at something and who, without any creative power but simply and with a sense of decency, relates it with his highly-developed sense of taste, has given way to the virtuosity of a doer who commits the non-economy and monstrous pretension of arranging seventeen immature thoughts instead of a single work."[51] He then concluded his chapter on Monet with a quotation from Octave Mirbeau to consolidate his argument: "Une attaque multiple ne crible pas la toile. On dirait que la main s'abandonne à suivre la lumière. Elle renonce à l'effort de la capter. Elle glisse sur la toile comme la lumière a glissé sur les choses. Le mouvement minutieux qui, pièce à pièce, bâtissait l'atmosphère cède au mouvement plus souple qui l'imite et lui obéit." And, Meier-Graefe's final sentence reads: "One can not pronounce anything more substantial against Monet's Impressionism than this."[52]

This not only makes clear Meier-Graefe's dismissive personal opinion on the importance of Monet, who he merely considered to be a transitional appearance on the path to final artistic positions such as those of Cézanne and van Gogh, but is also indicative of a general view that considered Monet's late work less important and a sign of artistic decline.

THE AUTONOMOUS PICTURE

With his *Nymphéas,* and especially his work on the *Grandes décorations* in the years from 1920 to 1926, Monet made decisive advances in the autonomy of the picture compared with its subject. The permanently increasing freedom in the application of color, the spontaneous painterly impetus, the limitation to the phenomena of light and color on the surface of the objects, developed into an increasing flatness of what was shown, to autonomous structures, to abstract painting. Of necessity, this restriction to the impressions of the eye resulted in the two-dimensionality of the picture. The fact that, although he had structured the individual ideas of his *Grandes décorations* in front of the motif, Monet then realized the monumental canvases in his studio entirely out of the coloristic demands of the overall work also played an important part. This was now painting from deep inside and out of the lifelong experience of his painter's hand.

But it was precisely this subordination of what was seen to an artistic will, the dissolution of the depiction in the colored surface, the stressed two-dimensionality, the suppression of the object, and finally the increasing autarchy of the brush style that a young generation of painters came to admire after the Second World War: the artists of American Expressionism and the French Tachists. And they were able to refer to this new liberation of the image from its mimetic function and the intrinsic qualities of gestural painting in their own artistic endeavors.

They also made use of large formats, let the colors speak for themselves, celebrated the audacity of their painting verve in expansive brushstrokes and, through pouring, dripping, and spraying, explored new methods of applying paint. They were fascinated by the "allover", by completely covering the surface of the picture with the artistic features that had been prefigured in Monet's paintings of water lilies.

After his frescoes and wall paintings in the post-war period, Max Weiler also arrived at large canvas formats in the 1960s. Standing on ladders and scaffolds over his gigantic canvases, he used meter-long brushes to be able to deal with their dimensions.

The large form also brought forth the wish to be surrounded on all sides by the color material, by his visual creations and, in such a way, achieve the greatest intensity possible. In several draft drawings for an exhibition house for his works, he designed a spacious, circular room in which the viewer would be surrounded, at body height, by pictures spanning the entire circle. This is no different than Monet's ideal concept of a round room for his *Nymphéas* where the viewer would be able to experience them from all sides almost as if he was standing in the center of a water lily pond. However, Monet's late work was fundamentally no longer concerned with recognizable objects, with water, clouds, trees, and flowers, but with the immersion

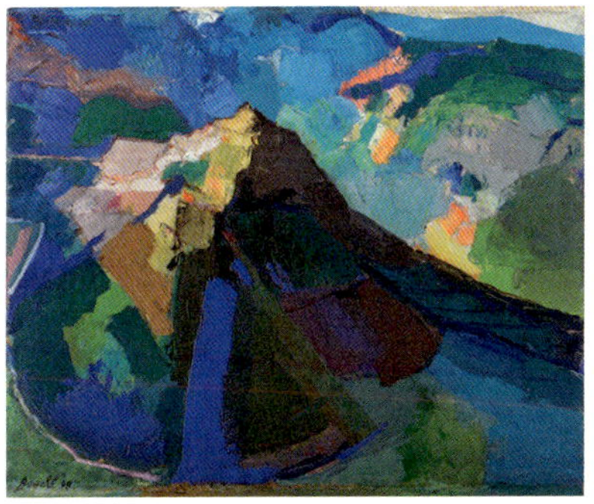

Fig. 131
HERBERT BOECKL
Erzberg III, 1948
Lent by WIENER STÄDTISCHE
VERSICHERUNG AG
Vienna Insurance Group

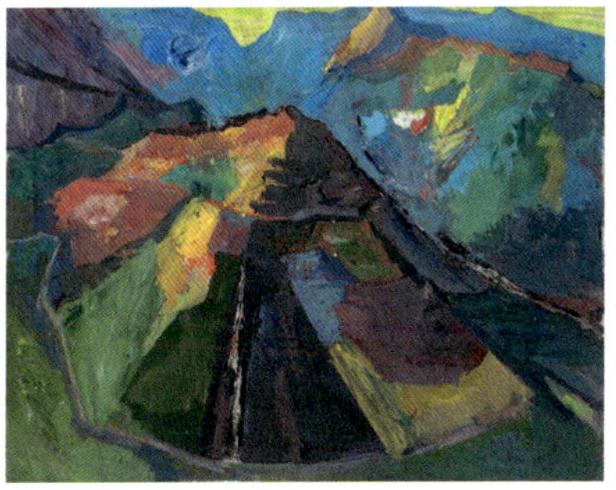

Fig. 132
HERBERT BOECKL
Erzberg IIIa, 1948
Collection Liaunig, Neuhaus

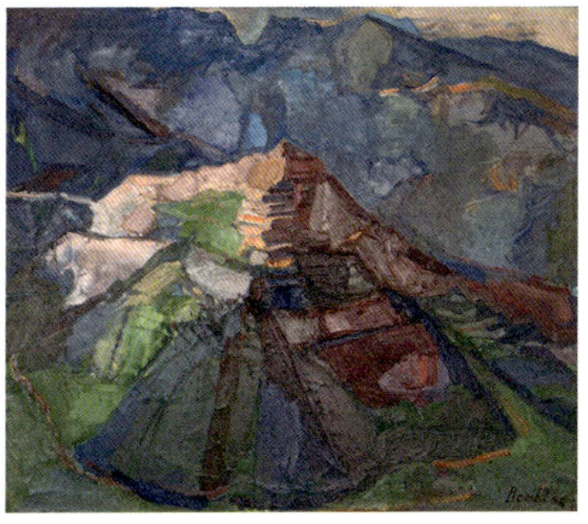

Fig. 133
HERBERT BOECKL
Erzberg IV, 1948
Private collection, Vienna

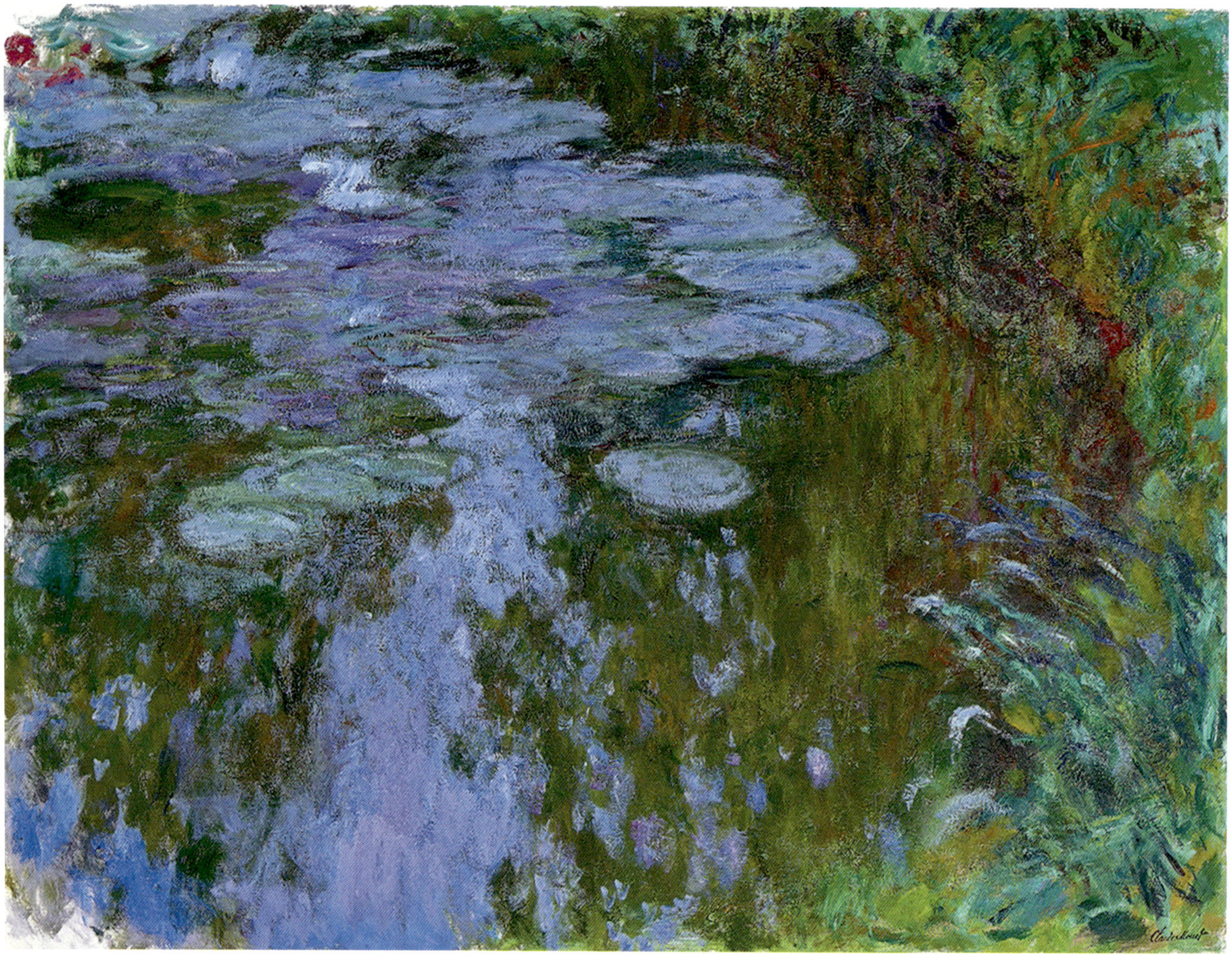

in pure painting, in that sea of color with its absolute harmony of richly orchestrated colorist tones. The splendor of these tones that intensified each other, that responded to each other in the most sophisticated polyphony, now laid claim to all attention and significance and spoke of the deeper understanding of another—an artistic—world. This is also the pictorial language of Max Weiler who developed a new level of artist expression for himself in years of experimentation and consolidation.

Both started out from nature. While Monet had concentrated on the permanent changes of nature in the different effects produced by the light during the day, Weiler understood it as a cosmos that he experienced spiritually and transformed into his personal visual images. Weiler did not reproduce nature; he created it anew on another, formal, level. With the help of his own technique of egg-tempera painting and, the previously mentioned, long brushes, Weiler now created symbols of nature and arranged the "natural" on his canvases and sheets of paper. "I want to create a type of nature that is as lively as the real one, full of coincidences but still organized. Arbitrariness and order—and completely developed out of artistic means. Out of my means, a fantastic, infinite nature."[53]

Fig. 134
CLAUDE MONET
Water Lilies, 1914–1917
Fondation Beyeler, Riehen/Basel

Fig. 135
CLAUDE MONET
Water Lilies, 1916/1919
Musée d'Orsay, Paris

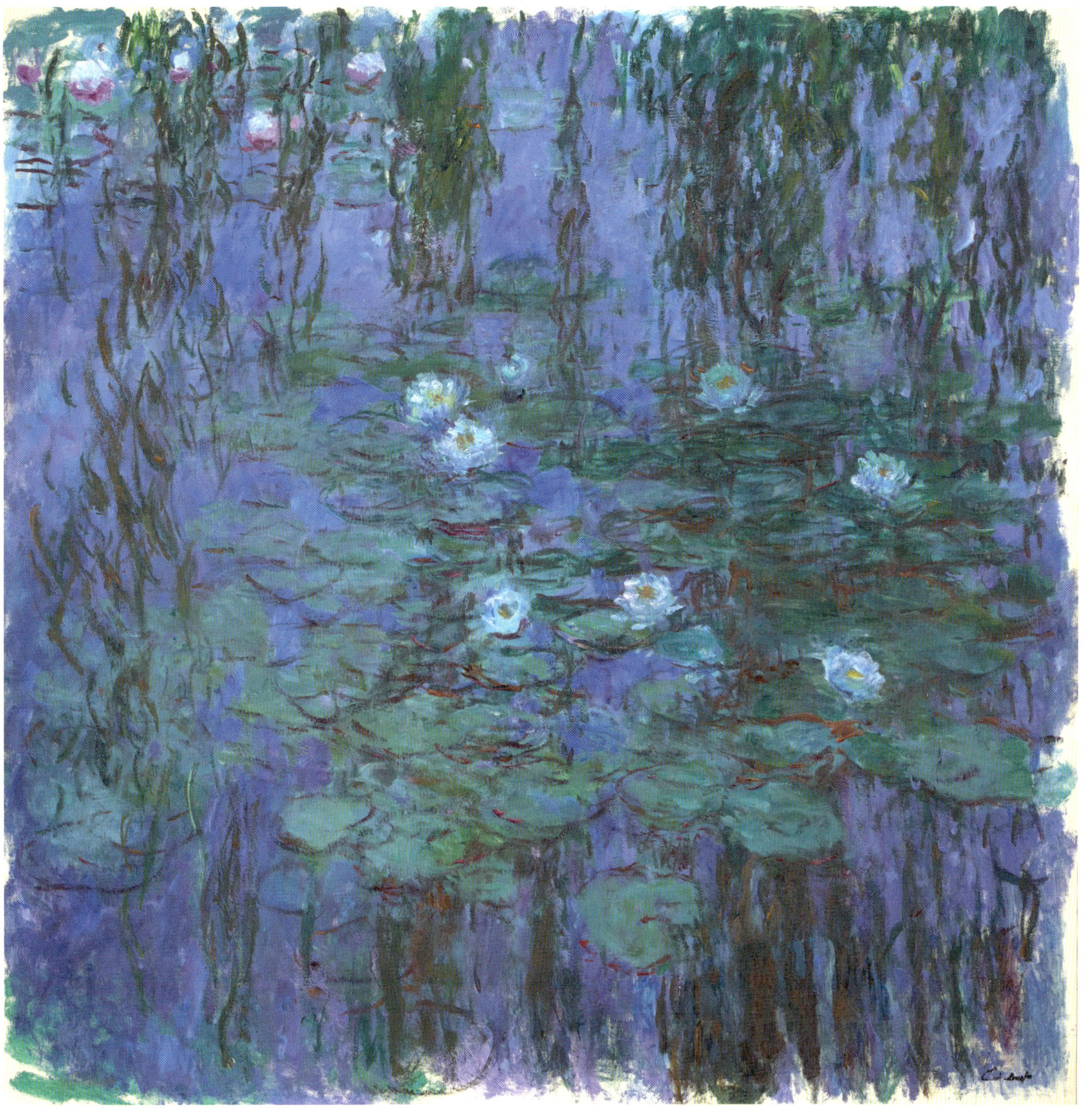

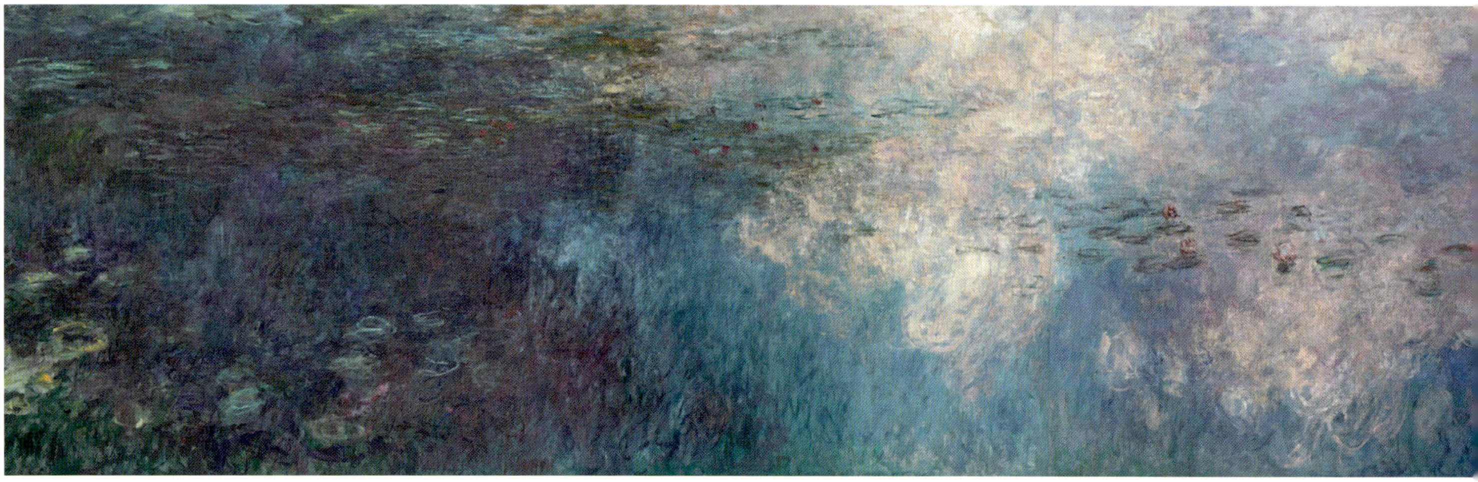

Fig. 136
CLAUDE MONET
The Clouds, 1920/26
Musée de l'Orangerie, Paris

Weiler was a lone wolf, both in his artistic vision and his lifestyle, and felt a close relationship to painters like Matthis Nitwald Grünewald, and Caspar David Friedrich. His life of seclusion allowed him to repeatedly create the condition of the inner collection that he needed to work. "These pictures in the studio develop on their own in a self-forgotten, almost unconscious way. There are no observers, everything is locked, the thoughts, the water, dryness, the forms, waiting, curiosity, everything develops. Brush and hand and all of the color powder and the large room and the picture being created."[54]

In Monet's *Grandes décorations*, feelings were no longer primarily addressed through the reproduction of objects but through the painting itself; the magnificent fabric of

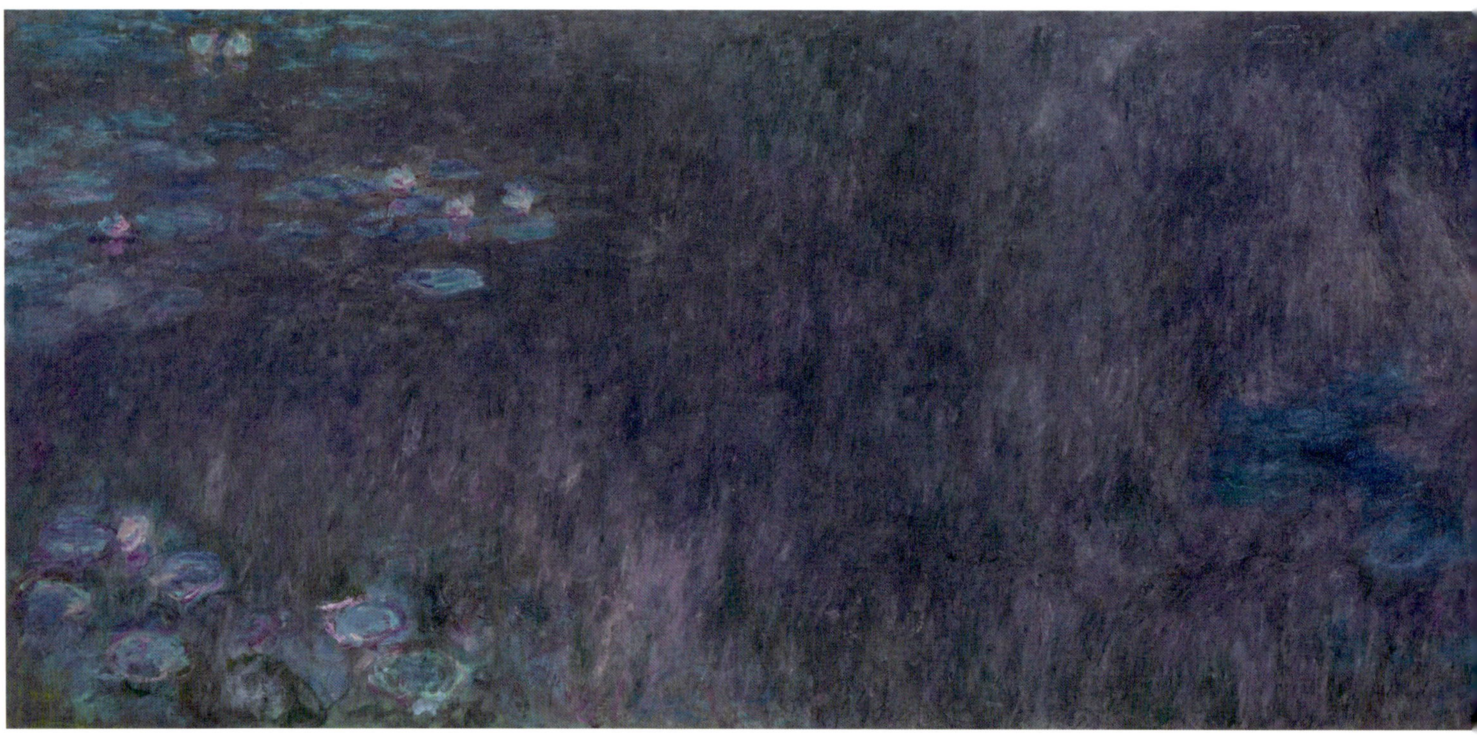

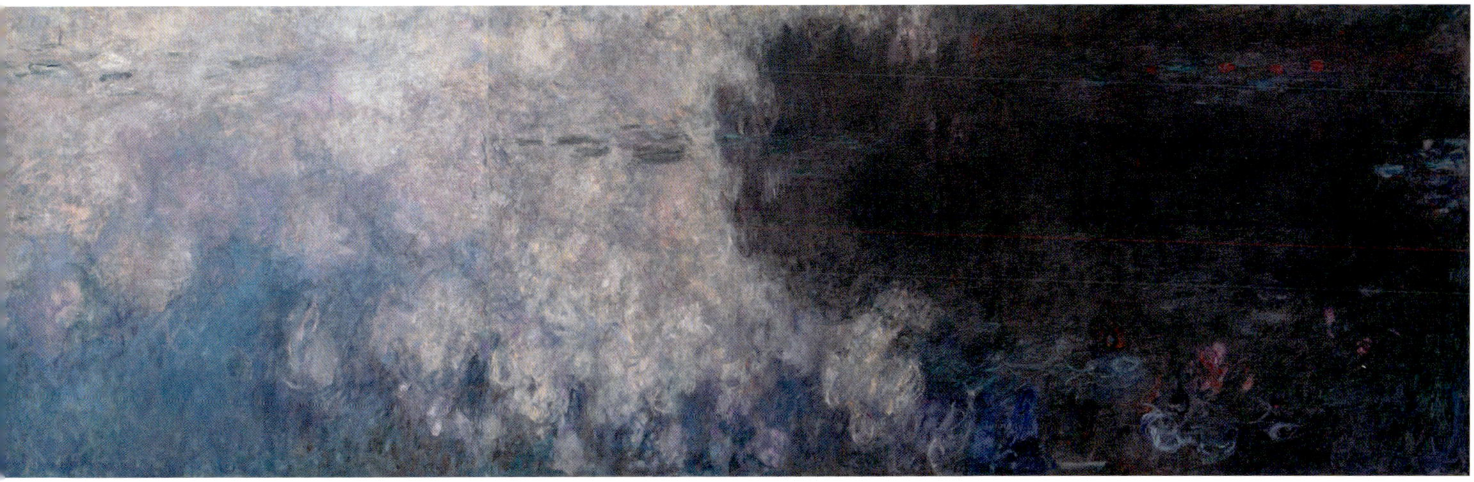

colors and shapes transmitted the experience of what was seen and evoked this in the viewer (see fig. pp. 30/31 and 96/97).

It is quite clear that Weiler could not have ignored the large paintings of water lilies in the Kunsthaus in Zurich and especially in the Orangerie in Paris. And, no painter of large formats could remain unmoved by rooms with the potency of those in the Orangerie. Also, on the back of one of Weiler's drawings for the round exhibition building for his art, we find a sketch that could be interpreted as a pond with water lilies and, therefore, makes it seem likely that he had studied Monet's large-format late work. In any case, the very title of the *Four walls (Vier Wände)* (1973–77)—the sketches previously mentioned were created in the same period—bears the idea of

Fig. 137
CLAUDE MONET
Reflection of Trees, 1920/26
Musée de l'Orangerie, Paris

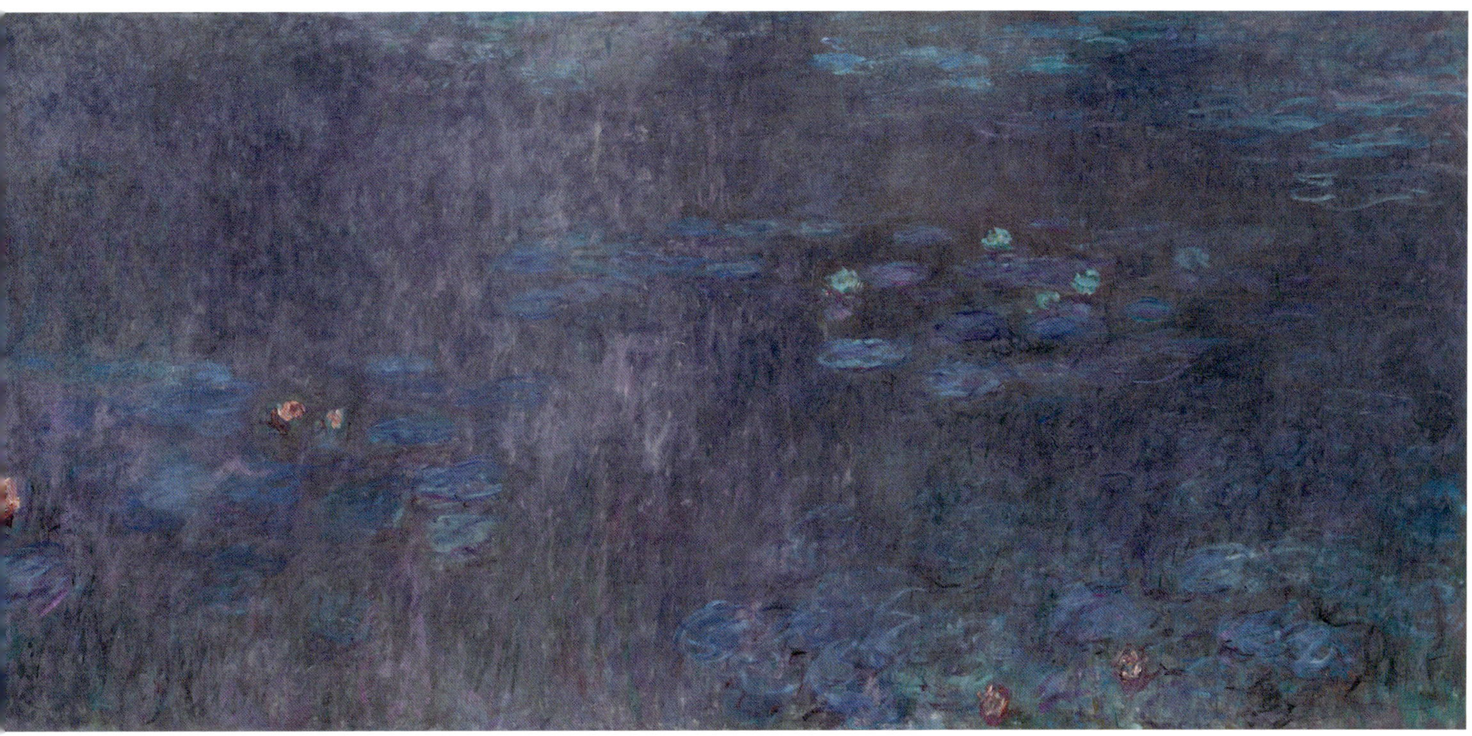

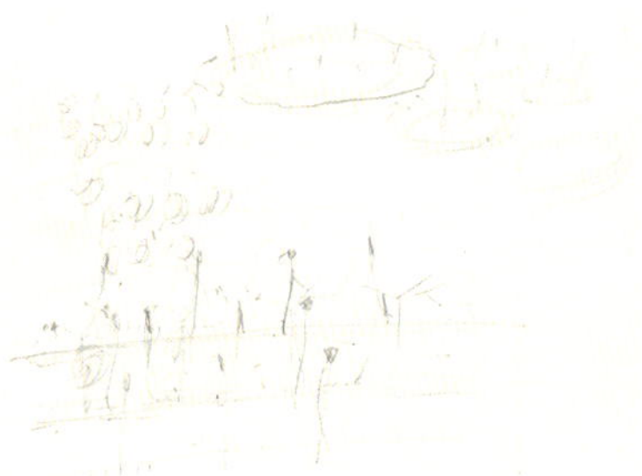

Fig. 138
MAX WEILER
without Title (Water-Lilies), ca. 1977
Private collection

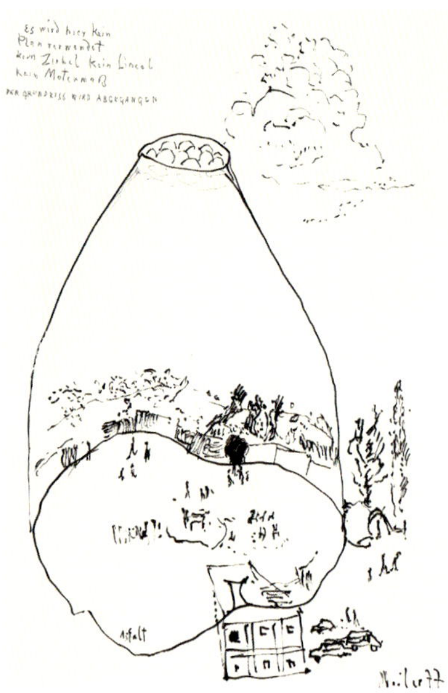

Fig. 139
MAX WEILER
without Title (design for a Max Weiler-House), 1977
Private collection

having the painting communicate with the viewer from all sides of the room—and making him a part of the art through the intensity of their effect, of transforming him, in a manner of speaking—in it. Recognizable natural forms are no longer represented but their fundamental elements or—as the very different character and various density of the works would suggest—the four cosmic elements. Weiler's monumental visual worlds, created without being commissioned, completely out of inner impulses, now overstep the borders of the gigantic canvases in all directions, show themselves as being tendentially infinite, and appear to be excerpts of a—much wider felt—whole. In his *Four Walls*, Weiler also came very close to Monet formally and created a, partially floating, partially hovering, impression of the elements and forms in the broad fields of the painting. Surrounded on all sides by color, the viewer can now immerse himself in the artistic universe of the ciphers that invite him to meditate over nature.

It is precisely this characteristic of Monet's late work—and especially the water lily pictures—that does away with all restrictions, reverses up and down, that allows reality and reflection, the surface and depth to flow together in the fabric of glorious colors, and create a new existence on a new level, of pure painting: that of the *picture*.

1 Albert Franz Seligmann, "Tina Blau. Ein letzter Besuch," in: *Neue Freie Presse*, no. 18759, November 10, 1916, p. 3.
2 Cf. Stephan Koja, "'The Invention was not Coincidental ...' Heinrich Schwarz and the 'Art in the Early Days of Photography 1840–1880' Exhibition in 1928," in Ulla Fischer-Westhauser/Miriam Halwani/Uwe Schögl (eds.), *PhotoResearcher* (*Looking at 175 Years of Photography*), no. 22, October 2014, pp. 30–47.
3 Letter from Bernatzik to Hörmann of March 18, 1891, Tiroler Landesmuseum Ferdinandeum, Innsbruck, FB 45.873.
4 Armand Silvestre, "Le monde des arts," in: *La Vie moderne*, March 17, 1883, p. 177f.
5 "Oeuvres de M. Claude Monet" in: *Gazette des beaux-arts*, vol. 27, August 1, 1883, p. 345.
6 Quoted in: Martin Suppan/Erich Tromayer, *Marie Egner. Eine Österreichische Stimmungsimpressionistin*, Vienna 1981, vol. 1, p. 70.
7 Carl Karger had already painted a frontal view into a station concourse in 1875 in *Arrival of a Train at Vienna Northwestern Station* (*Ankunft eines Zuges am Nordwestbahnhof in Wien*); two years before he had been on a study trip to France and possibly came across this subject matter while there.
8 Quoted in Theo Braunegger/Magdalena Hörmann-Weingartner, *Theodor von Hörmann*, Vienna 1979, p. 52.
9 Galerie Georges Petit, Paris, *Claude Monet—A. Rodin*, June/July 1889.
10 Galerie Georges Petit, Paris, *6e exposition internationale de peinture et de sculpture*, May 8–June 8, 1887.
11 *Cliffs on the Brittany Coast* (*Felsen an der bretonischen Küste*), c. 1887. – Cf. Marianne Hussl-Hörmann, *Theodor von Hörmann. Monographie mit Verzeichnis der Gemälde*, Vienna 2013, p. 214, cat. rais. no. I.238.
12 June/July 1887.
13 Cf. *View of Vétheuil, Ice Floes* (*Vue de Vétheuil, débâcle*), 1880 (W 559); *Ice Floes* (*Les glaçons*), 1880 (W 567), and *Ice Floes* (*Les glaçons*), 1880 (W 568).
14 Quoted in Braunegger/Hörmann-Weingartner 1979 (see note 8), p. 28.
15 Quoted in Ulla Weich, "Theodor von Hörmann (1840–1895)," in: Otmar Rychlik (ed.), *Natürlichere Natur. Österreichische Malerei des Stimmungsrealismus* (exh. cat., Kunsthaus Mürzzuschlag, Mürzzuschlag, summer exhibition 1994), Mürzzuschlag 1994, p. 208.
16 Letter from Hörmann to his cousin Robert Hörmann in Innsbruck, quoted in Braunegger/Hörmann-Weingartner 1979 (see note 8), p. 49.
17 Cf. Stephan Koja, "Hinausgehen über den Impressionismus. Carl Schuch und die Realität der Farbe," in: idem./Agnes Husslein-Arco (ed.), *Carl Schuch. Ein europäischer Maler* (exh. cat., Österreichische Galerie Belvedere, Vienna, June 26–October 14, 2012), Vienna/Weitra 2012, pp. 47–50.
18 Based on Claude Monet, *Le Côte Sauvage*, 1891, *gillotage*, 24.9 x 30.9 cm, in : *L'Art dans les deux mondes I*, March 7, 1891.
19 "Oeuvres de M. Claude Monet," in: *Gazette des beaux-arts* 27, August 1, 1883, p. 345.
20 Theodore Duret, "Claude Monet und der Impressionismus," in: *Kunst und Künstler: illustrierte Monatsschrift für bildende Kunst und Kunstgewerbe*, February 1904, p. 245.

Fig. 140
MAX WEILER
On the Far Right, Living Nature, 1973
Bundesimmobiliengesellschaft m.b.H., Vienna

Fig. 141
MAX WEILER
Above the Treeline, 1976
museum moderner kunst stiftung ludwig
Vienna

Fig. 142
MAX WEILER
Skyscape, 1977
museum moderner kunst stiftung ludwig
Vienna

21 Camille Mauclair, *L'impressionnisme. Son histoire, son estéthique, ses maitres*, Paris 1904, pp. 72–73.
22 See Martina Haja, "'Kraut und Rüben'—Beobachtungen zur österreichischen Freilicht-Malerei im späten 19. Jahrhundert," in: *Mitteilungen der Österreichischen Galerie* 30, no. 74, 1986, pp. 43–66.
23 Ludwig Hevesi, *Acht Jahre Secession*, Vienna 1906, p. 318.
24 Théodore Duret, *Les Peintres impressionistes. Claude Monet – Sisley – C. Pissarro – Renoir – Berthe Morisot*, Paris 1878, p. 19.
25 A. R., "Une collection de tableaux modernes," in: *Gazette des beaux-arts*, January 1, 1897, 475th issue, p. 79.
26 Cf. *Voiliers au large de l'aiguille*, 1885 (W 1032).
27 Cf. *Zaandam*, 1871 (W 183) or *The Bridge at Argenteuil (Le pont d'Argenteuil)*, 1874 (W 311).
28 Cf. *Antibes Seen from the Salis Gardens (Antibes vu de la salis)*, 1888 (W 1168), *Under the Pines, Evening (Sous les pins, soir)* (W 1191).

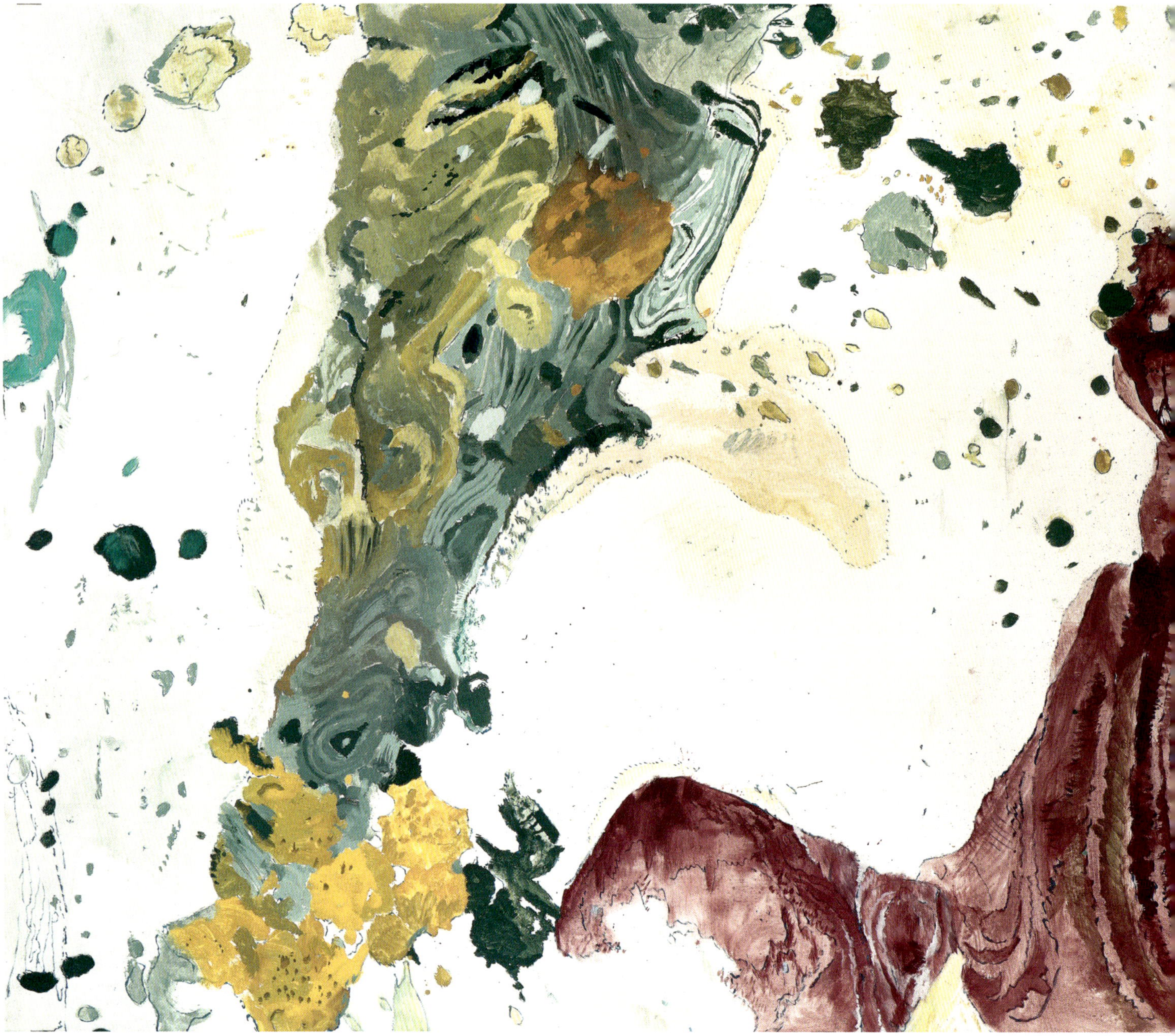

Fig. 143
MAX WEILER
Nature with Caput Mortuum, 1974
Bundesimmobiliengesellschaft m.b.H., Vienna

29 Cf. *Vétheuil in Summer (Vétheuil en été)*, 1879 (W 534).

30 Carl Karger and Egon Schiele might also have been inspired in their pictures of villages on the Danube by this type of village with predominant church tower depicted with pronounced frontality on the opposite bank of the river. See Maximilian Kahrer, *Dürnstein in the Evening Sun (Dürnstein in der Abendsonne)*, 1915; Egon Schiele, *Stein an der Donau*, 1913.

31 Theodore Duret, "Claude Monet und der Impressionismus," in: *Kunst und Künstler: illustrierte Monatsschrift für bildende Kunst und Kunstgewerbe*, February 1904, pp. 239 and 242.

32 Bernheim-Jeune & Cie, *Claude Monet, Venise*, Paris, May 28–June 8, 1912.

33 "I was particularly inspired by frequent visits to painting galleries, especially the first Secession exhibition in Munich. The new expression in fine arts had a decisive effect on my work." Quoted from Fritz Matthies-Maduren, "Heinrich Kühn," in: *Photographisches Centralblatt* 5, no. 9, 1899, p. 163.

34 Kühn was far superior to any of his contemporaries in his mastery of Autochrome photography. Unfortunately the Autochrome pictures by Alfred Stieglitz have been lost. Kühn's oeuvre using this technique comprises 350 pictures. Some are in international collections, but the majority are in the National Library in Vienna.

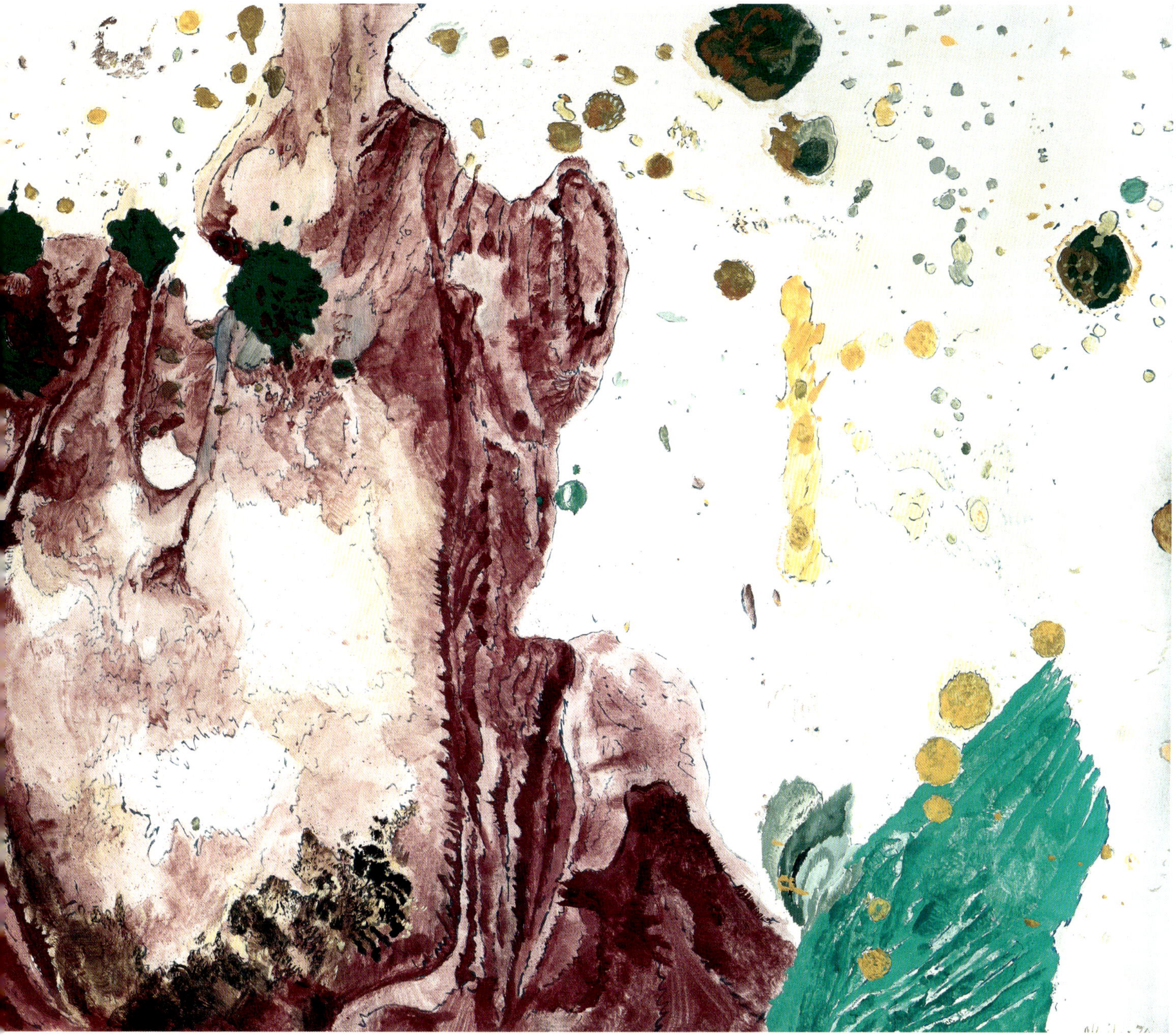

35 Heinrich Kühn, *Technik der Lichtbildnerei*, Halle a. d. Saale 1921, p. 224.

36 Ibid., p. 223.

37 Letter from Heinrich Kühn to Alfred Stieglitz on September 7, 1907. Yale Collection of American Literature, Beinecke Rare Book and Manuscript Library, Yale University, New Haven, Connecticut. Quoted from: Astrid Mahler, "Heinrich Kühn—Leben und Werk," in: Monika Faber and Astrid Mahler (eds.), *Heinrich Kühn. Die vollkommene Fotografie*, exh. cat., Albertina, Vienna 2010, p. 240.

38 Based on Claude Monet, *Woman with a Parasol*, 1891, *gillotage*, 14.3 x 10.8 cm, March 7, 1891, p. 184.

39 Heinrich Kühn 1921 (see note 35), p. 293.

40 Gustave Kahn, "L'exposition Claude Monet", in: *Gazette des beaux-arts*, 565th installment, July 1, 1904, pp. 82–88.

41 Theodore Duret's, "Claude Monet und der Impressionismus", in: *Kunst und Künstler: illustrierte Monatsschrift für bildende Kunst und Kunstgewerbe*, February 1904, pp. 233–245.

42 Ibid., p. 240.

43 Julius Meier-Graefe in: *Die Kunst für alle: Malerei, Plastik, Graphik, Architektur*, no. XXV, January 1, 1910, p. 161.

44 Werner Weisbach, *Impressionismus. Ein Problem der Malerei in der Antike und Neuzeit*, Berlin 1911, p. 141.
45 Above all, the VII. Exhibition (1900) with works by Paul Signac, as well as the XVI. Exhibition, *Die Entwicklung des Impressionismus in Malerei und Plastik*, in the year 1903 had a lasting influence on Junk.
46 Claude Monet, *Waterloo Bridge, Grey Weather (Waterloo Bridge, temps gris*, 1899/1901, W 1562). This painting, which was believed to have been lost, recently reappeared in the collection of Cornelius Gurlitt in Munich.
47 Oskar Kokoschka, *London. Waterloo Bridge, March/April 1926*, National Museum of Wales, Cardiff. *London, Large Thames View I*, March/April 1926, Albright-Knox Art Gallery, Buffalo, NY. *London, Small Thames View*, 1926, private collection, Liechtenstein.
48 Cited after: Heinz Spielmann, "Kokoschkas Bilder der europäischen Städte", in: exh. cat. *Oskar Kokoschka–Städteporträts* (Oswald Oberhuber, ed.?) Hochschule für angewandte Kunst, Vienna 1986, p. 8.
49 *Staatzer Kegel I*, 1940, Belvedere, Vienna; *Staatzer Kegel II*, 1940, Wien Museum.
50 *Der Steinbruch bei St. Margareten*, 1938, private collection; *Blauer Steinbruch bei St. Margareten*, 1938, Belvedere, Vienna; *Gelber Steinbruch bei Sankt Margareten*, 1938, Belvedere, Vienna; *Landschaft beim Steinbruch von St. Margareten*, 1938, private collection.
51 Julius Meier-Graefe, Entwicklungsgeschichte der modernen Kunst, 3rd ed., Munich 1920 (1st ed. 1904), vol. 2, p. 411.
52 Ibid., p. 414.
53 Max Weiler, *Tag- und Nachthefte*, entry from the year 1965, Estate of Max Weiler.
54 Max Weiler, "Meine Malerei – Nur von ihr kann ich reden", in: Wilfried Skreiner, *Max Weiler* (with a catalog of the works by Almut Krapf), Salzburg 1975, p. 42.
55 Hugo von Hofmannsthal, "Die Farben" (Aus den Briefen des Zurückgekehrten, May 26, Mai 1901) in: *Hugo von Hofmannsthal, Gesammelte Werke*, vol. 3, Berlin 1934, p. 225.

Fig. 144
CLAUDE MONET
Water Lilies and Willow Branches, 1916–1919
Lycée Claude Monet, Paris

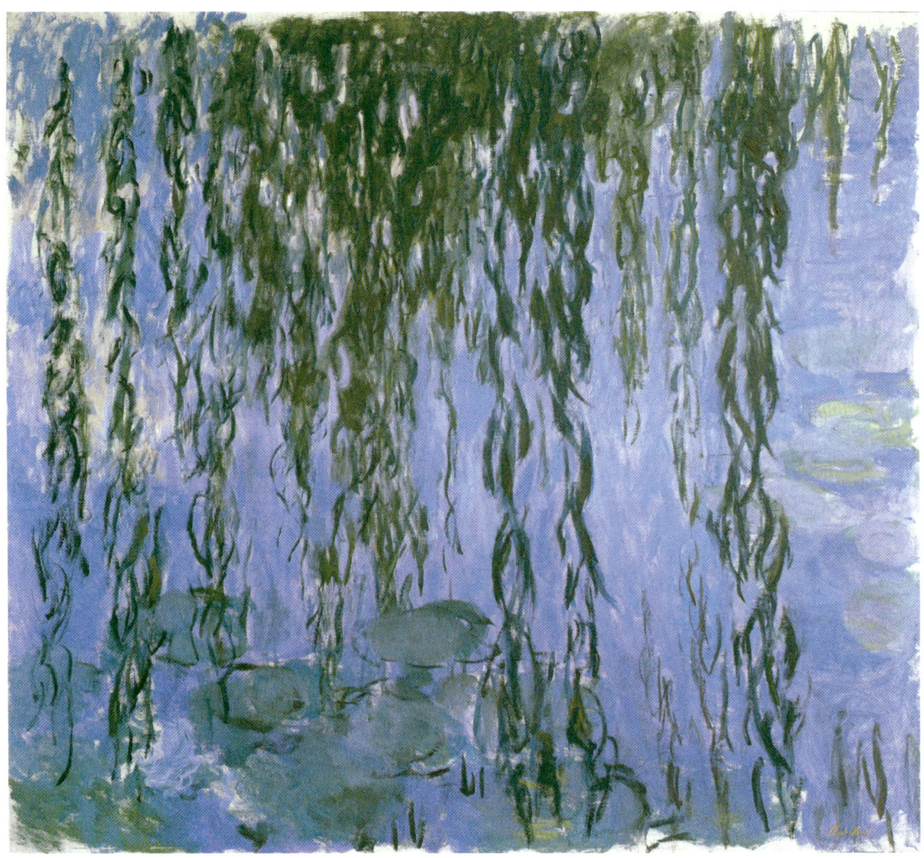

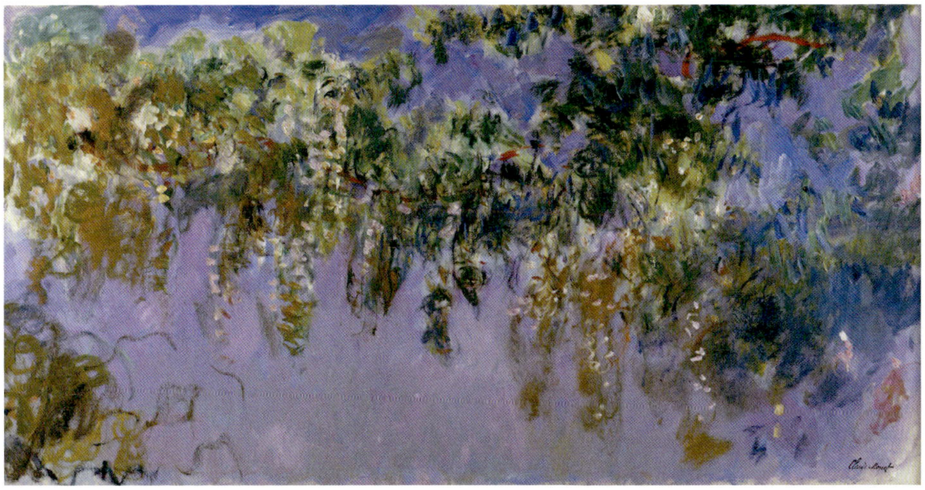

Fig. 145
CLAUDE MONET
Wisteria, 1917/20
Musée d'Art et d'Histoire Marcel-Dessal, Dreux

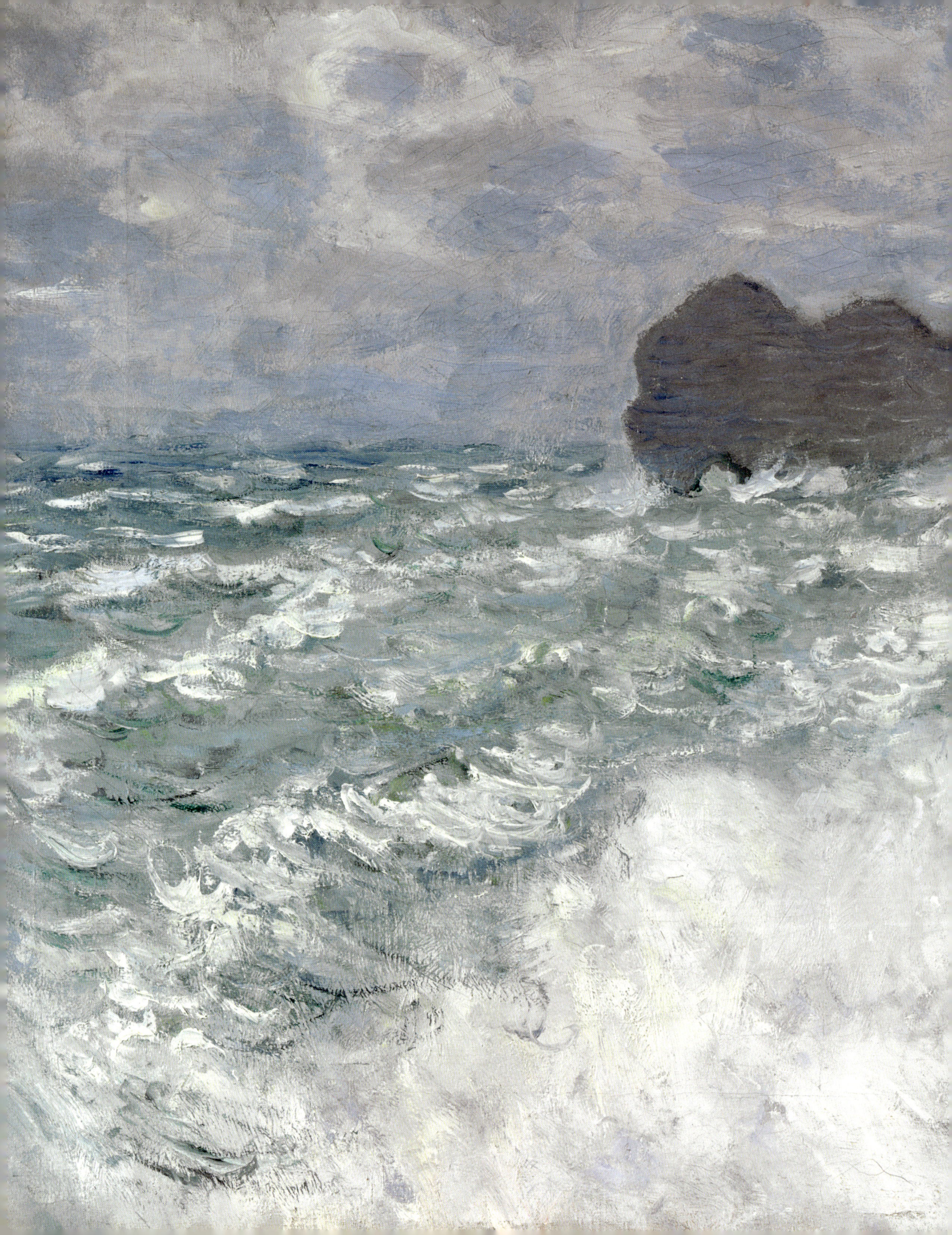

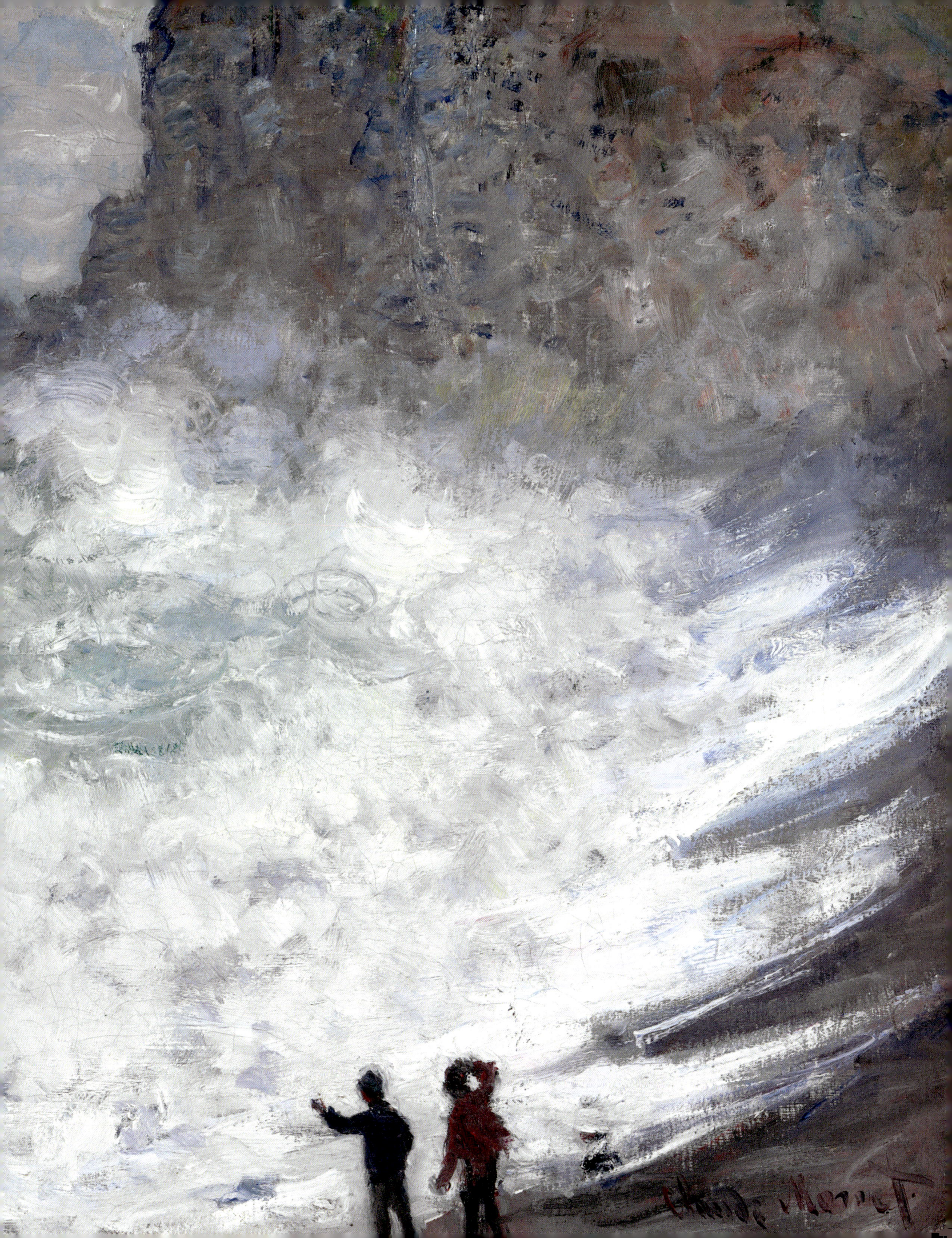
Claude Monet

„TODAY, IMPRESSIONISM IS TAKEN FOR GRANTED …“[1]

Paths of the Monet Reception: Exhibitions, Journeys, Reports

Bernadette Reinhold

The *Development of Impressionism in Painting and Sculpture* exhibition was held in the Vienna Secession from January 17 to March 1, 1903.[2] More than three years were required to take care of the complicated process of organizing the works to be loaned. Some members of the Secession who had lived in Paris for some time – including Wilhelm Bernatzik, Josef Engelhart, and Eugen Jettel—acted as intermediaries. The exhibition, which started with the "precursors" of Impressionism including Tintoretto, Velázquez, Rubens, Vermeer, Goya, Delacroix, and Corot,[3] had works by Manet, Monet, Sisley, Pissarro, and Degas as the center of attention. In keeping with art-historical continuity, they were followed by works by Whistler, Liebermann, Slevogt, the Neo-Impressionists Seurat and Rysselberghe, and the representatives of the "transitions to the style": van Gogh, Toulouse-Lautrec, Bonnard, Denis, Gauguin, and other artists. The developments in French art over a century had already been summed up in the *Expositions centennales* at the 1889 and 1900 World's Fairs in Paris where works by Monet were also shown.[4] However, it is noteworthy that, from an international perspective, the Secession exhibition of 1903 was the first to interpret Impressionism as a logical development within European painting, as a "bridge" to modern art.[5] This was due to the didactic concept of the German art historian Julius Meier-Graefe, who was living in Paris and had published his highly-regarded three-volume *Entwicklungsgeschichte der modernen Kunst (History of the Development of Modern Art)* at around the same time.[6] The catalog states, "Today, Impressionism is taken for granted—something historical. Wasn't that once a swearword? Each new feat of Impressionism gave rise to indignation and the greatest mirth." Not without taking a sideswipe at the then conservative response to modern art, he continued, "If one reads the reports from those days, one is quite touched with feelings of having been there before."[7] Around 100 articles were published locally and abroad and a marketing campaign led to it being possible to see the word "'Impressionism' […], black on red, on all omnibuses and street corners," so that the exhibition finally attracted 15,877 visitors.[8] In addition, it was accompanied by informational lectures given by Meier-Graefe and by Richard Muther, the no-less-eloquent professor of art history in Wroclaw and author of widely-discussed books on (French) painting of the 19th century.[9] The quality of the objects on display, the concept, the advertising and supporting program in this concentration was something completely new. Until that time, Impressionist works—and there, first and foremost, Monet—had only been shown sporadically. It therefore comes as no surprise that the exhibition created a great impact and, as will be shown, that local art history later regarded it as the anachronistic starting point for the reception of Impressionism. However, the mesh of Monet reception had begun to be woven considerably earlier so that the 1903 show fundamentally represented the culmination point of decades of artistic development.

The following investigation focuses on the possibilities that Austrian artists had to have come into contact with the "true Impressionist" (Hugo Othmar Miethke, 1910) Claude Monet, in the years between the 1870s and the eve of the First World War. Monet's motifs, his (shortened) detail, his specific use of color, and, not least, his distinctive artistic features and brush style set him so radically apart from painting as it had been before him that they evolved into a kind of trademark. In the case of this response to Monet, at least two cultural environments—the French and Austrian—came into contact with each other resulting in fields of encounter for a widescale cultural transfer, rather than merely affording points of contact.[10] This transfer took place by way of various media and intermediaries

Fig. 1
CLAUDE MONET
A Path (detail), 1873
Philadelphia Museum of Art

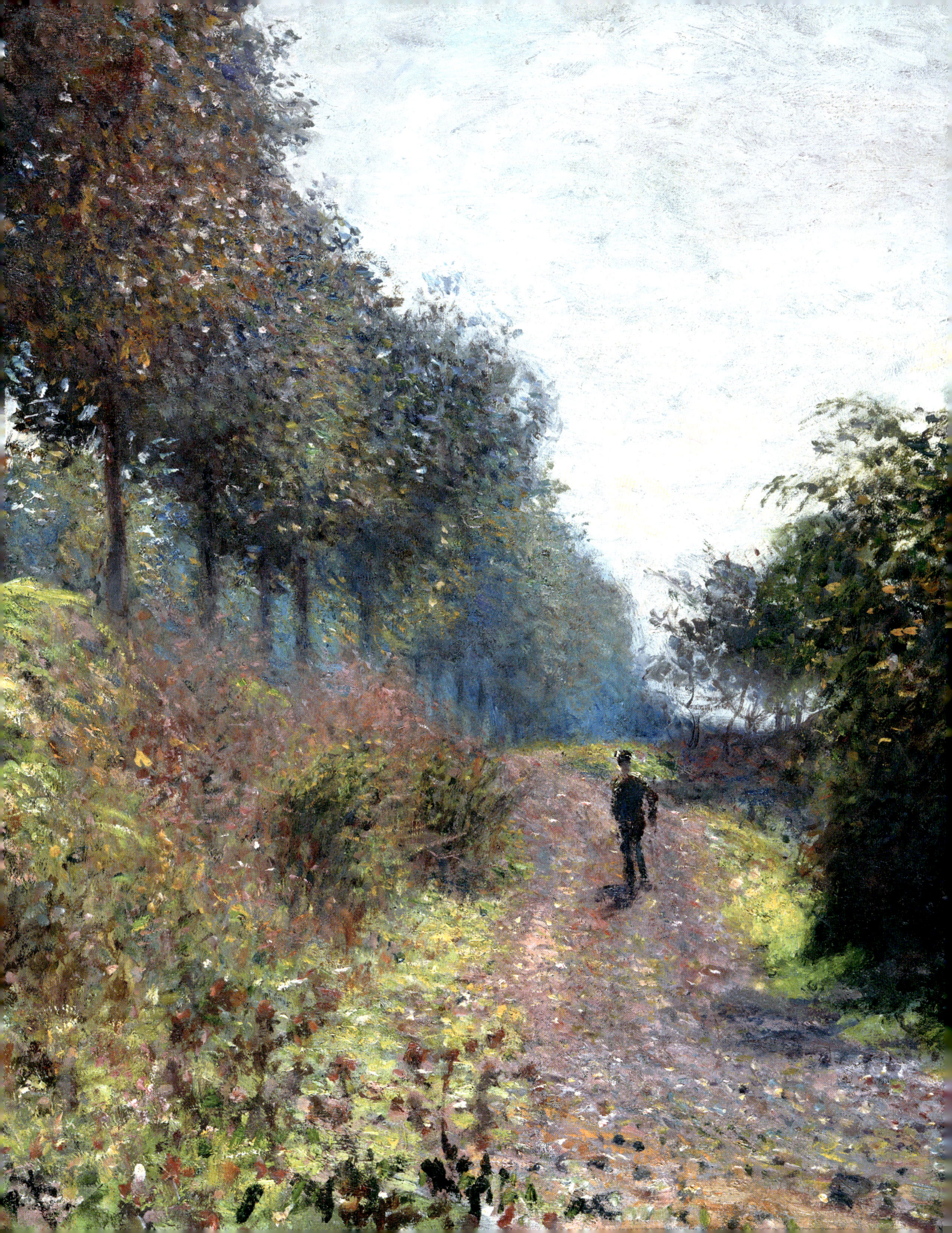

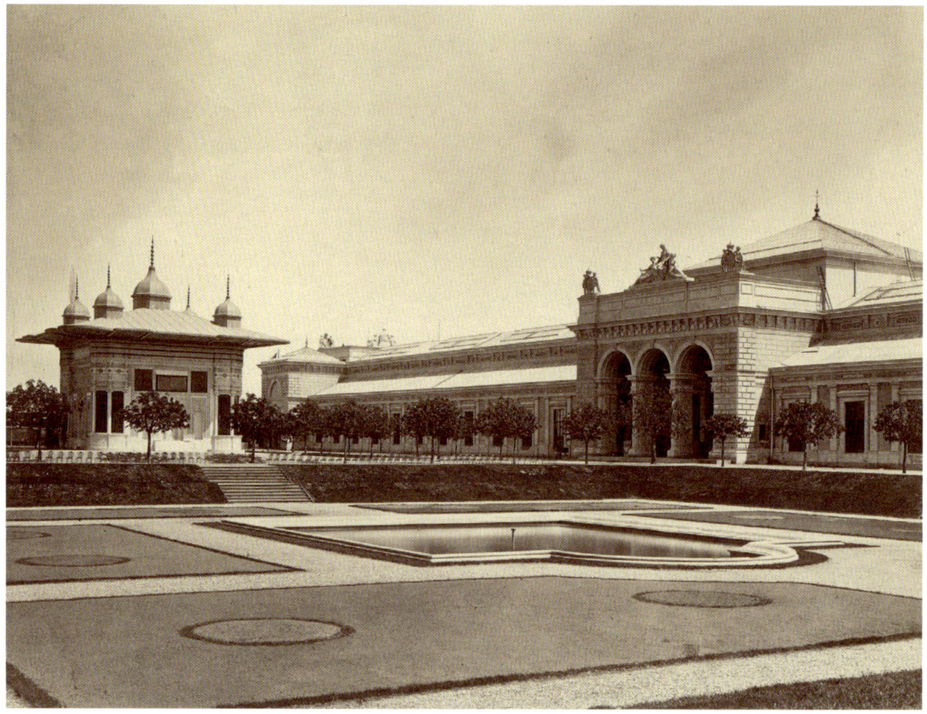

Fig. 2
The Art Pavilion at the World's Fair in Vienna, 1873
Wien Museum

including not only the artists themselves but also art critics and art historians, literati, politicians, society ladies, and, not least, art dealers and collectors – sometimes in both functions.

PARIS, THE PLACE OF DESIRE, AND OTHER VENUES FOR ENCOUNTERING MONET

In spite of the ongoing invectives against Monet, the paths these innovations took to the 1880s were manifold. Many of the "actors" lived and worked in Paris for a number of years. We are fundamentally dealing with two generations here; on the one hand, those born in the years around 1840/50, who were more or less of the same vintage as Monet (1840), and, on the other hand, many of the later representatives of the Secession, who saw the light of day around 1860/70. The painters Eugen Jettel, Carl Schuch, Karl Mediz, Theodor von Hörmann, Johann Victor Krämer and Josef Engelhart lived in Paris for several years. As Max Liebermann later reported, Eugen Jettel, as well as Josef Engelhart, acted as an intermediary for the newcomers and "the [Jettel] couple's charming little apartment on Montmartre was a meeting place for all German artists who lived either permanently or temporarily in Paris."[11] The Viennese art dealer Charles Sedelmeyer, who had established himself successfully in the metropolis on the Seine, offered Jettel a well-paid contract in 1873 and introduced him, as well as other Austro-Hungarian artists – here, first and foremost, Mihály Munkácsy – into the French market.[12]

Sedelmeyer initially guaranteed Jettel an annual fixed salary that – if an anecdote is to be believed – he reduced when the artist did not marry any one of the art dealer's five daughters.[13] Sedelmeyer wanted to perpetuate the position he had made for himself in Paris with suitable sons-in-law. In 1854, the 17-year-old Karl Sedelmeyer began working for the renowned Viennese art dealer Georg Plach and provided the wool wholesaler Gsell, as well as other clients, with advice on the development of one of the most famous collections of the Ringstraße era. Among the works Sedelmeyer acquired were paintings by artists of the Barbizon School who he had become acquainted with during his numerous sojourns in Paris; he took over the art business from Plach in 1860 but closed it already in 1866 and settled in Paris.[14] He soon developed into one of the most successful art dealers in the French capital and also arranged for artists from the Austro-Hungarian monarchy to move to Paris; along with Jettel and Munkácsy, they included Vacslav Brozik, August von Pettenkofen, Rudolf Ribarz, Eduard Charlemont and Julius Payer. He provided theatrical stagings for the paintings shown in his exhibition rooms: the most famous was certainly Munkácsy's "Christ before Pilate" that was prepared especially for him and subsequently sent on a three-year tour of Europe starting in 1881. This form of advertising helped him sell many smaller paintings and strengthen his connections to those American collectors who were playing an increasingly important role in the art market.

Jettel, who lived in Paris from 1873 to 1897, was extremely well informed about the latest artistic activities and completely integrated into the French capital. He was regularly represented in the Parisian *Salons* and his works were repeatedly reviewed in the Austrian and French press including the *Gazette des beaux-arts*.[15] He was also a member of the jury at the World's Fairs in Vienna in 1873 and Paris in 1889. Jettel was quite open to progressive movements, one of the "important members" of the Société Nationale des Beaux-Arts that had split from the official *Salon* in 1889 and, after his return to Vienna, also joined the Vienna Secession.[16]

Fig. 3
Exhibition hall in the Art Pavilion at the World's Fair in Vienna, 1873
Wien Museum

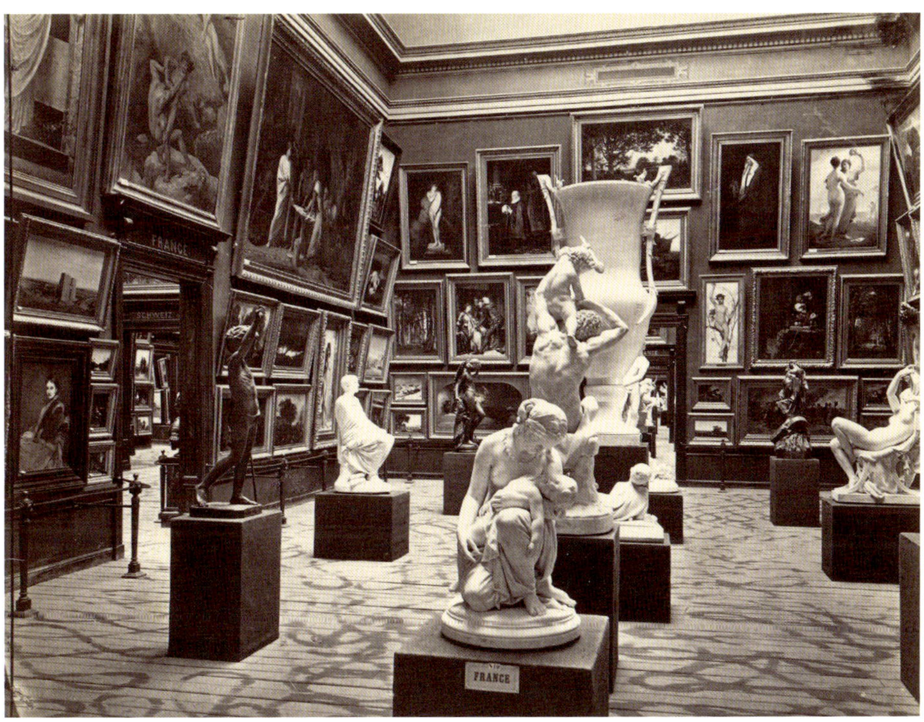

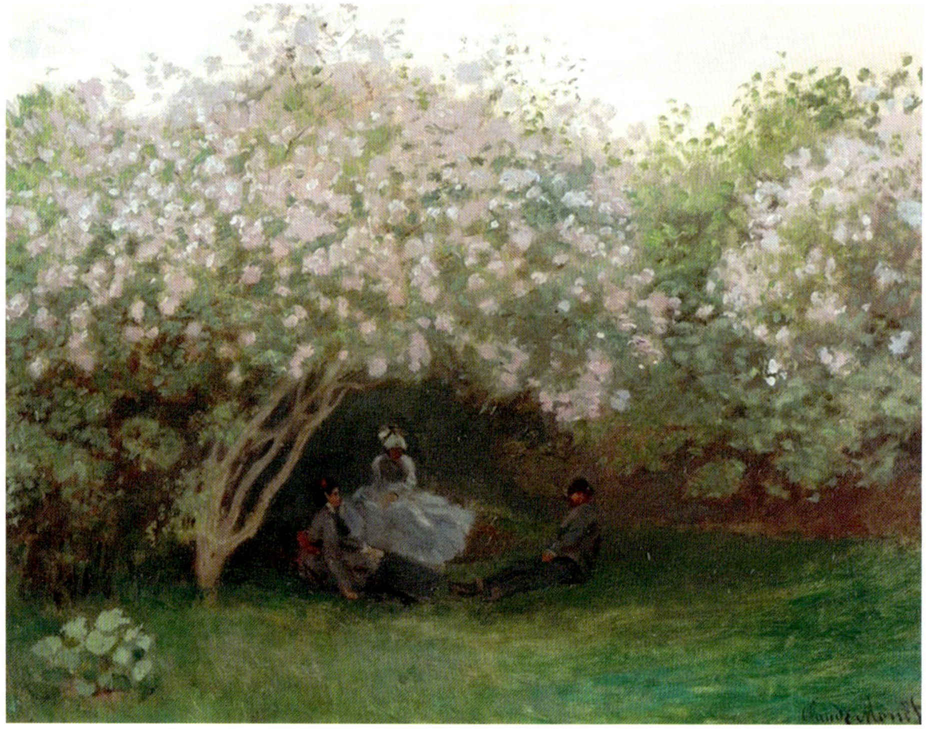

Fig. 4
CLAUDE MONET
Lilacs Grey Weather, 1872
The Pushkin State Museum of Fine Arts, Moscow

After studies and periods spent in Vienna and Munich, Carl Schuch spent a short time in Paris in 1871/72. In his painting *Parisian Houses* (*Pariser Häuser*, 1871/72), he anticipated characteristics of the Impressionists. In the ensuing years spent in Venice that were marked by great difficulties in connection with his painting, he placed great hopes in a move to Paris in 1882, and then lived in the city for 12 years, "Venice made me very ill – Paris is a climatic spa for the spirit."[17] He loved museums and was, therefore, naturally a frequent visitor to the Louvre, to galleries, and—as was the custom in those days—to private collections and artists' studios after making an appointment and also had excellent information about the Parisian art critics' scene.[18] He had studied Monet intensely and repeatedly commented on him with great esteem – but not uncritically.

In August/September 1889—the year of the Paris World's Fairs with the previously mentioned *Exposition centennale*—Emilie Mediz-Pelikan traveled to Paris for a few days and then on to Knokke. As Hevesi formulated, that resulted in a "play of Impressionism" in her work.[19] She made notes and sketched tiny studies of the impressions her visits to galleries and museums had made on her in her travel diary.[20] A second sojourn in Paris followed from mid-May to the end of October 1890, followed by weeks of work in Knokke. What she had seen in museums and galleries, as well as her interchange with, principally German, Impressionists like Paul Baum, left lasting traces on her oeuvre. Hardly any of her contemporaries surpassed the radicality of the pictorial means in her painting *Whitsun Service in Notre Dame/Paris (Pfingstandacht in Notre Dame/Paris,* 1890), which captures the flickering candlelight in the pitch-black church with patches of color applied in an almost gestural style. Many aspects of her painting *Sunrise over the Sea (Sonnenaufgang am Meer,* Duino, 1891)

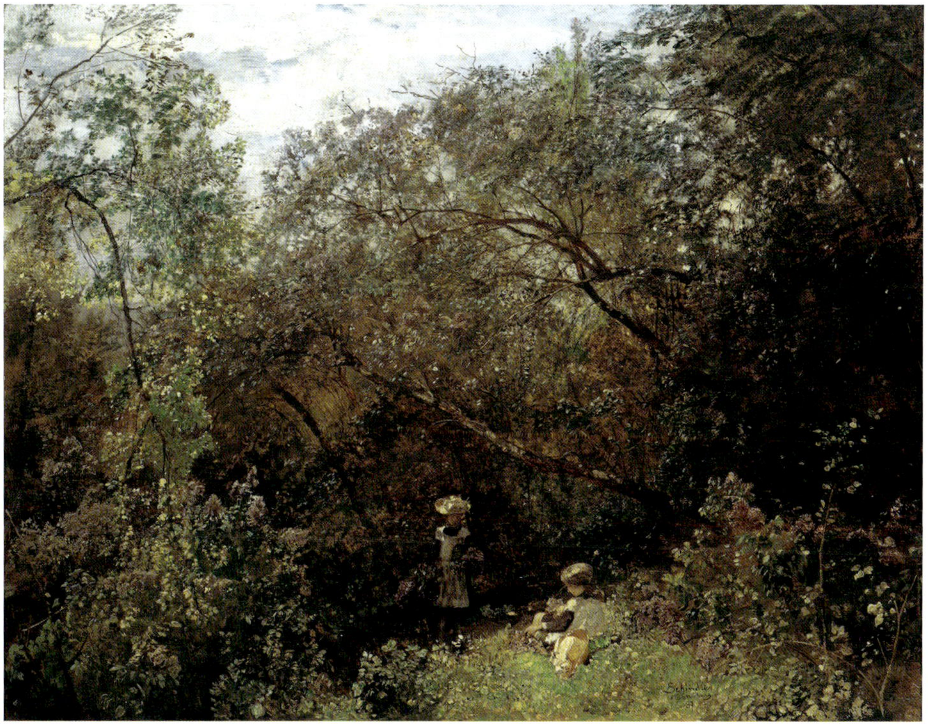

Fig. 5
EMIL JAKOB SCHINDLER
Park Landscape in Plankenberg (Lilac), 1887
Belvedere, Vienna

appear like a paraphrase of Monet's famous painting *Impression, Sunrise (Impression, soleil levant,* 1873).[21]

While Emilie Mediz-Pelikan and her husband Karl Mediz – who had studied at the Académie Julian, which was popular with foreigners, in Paris in 1888/89 – not only received substantial impulses from direct observation and, above all, from the network of German Impressionists, Theodor von Hörmann profited from his connection to the local Austrian group of artists during his period in Paris,[22] and he was obviously able to integrate himself easily: he exhibited at the *Salon des artistes français* in 1888. Two of his pictures were presented at the 1889 World's Fairs for which he received an honorable mention. He assimilated countless impressions; in particular, a series of motifs that were characteristic of Impressionism, such as the varied reflexes of modern, urban life, along with the fast style of painting. He possibly saw paintings by Monet at Georges Petit's always well-planned exhibitions or at the *5ᵉ* or *6ᵉ exposition international de peinture et de sculpture* in June/July1886 and May/June 1887 respectively. It is also conceivable that Hörmann visited the Galerie Boussod, Valadon & Cie when *Dix marines d'Antibes de M. Cl. Monet* was shown there in summer 1888. He definitely saw the three paintings by Monet that were exhibited at the 1889 World's Fair but the greatest impression must have been made by the gigantic *Monet-Rodin* exhibition organized by Georges Petit in June/July of the same year.[23] Rodin was represented with 36 objects and Monet with 145 paintings from all periods of his oeuvre. Although Monet research is divided on the broad response, the exhibition "attracted the public in droves."[24] There were dozens of reviews in almost all of the relevant newspapers and journals. In addition to his contribution to the catalog, Octave Mirbeau published an

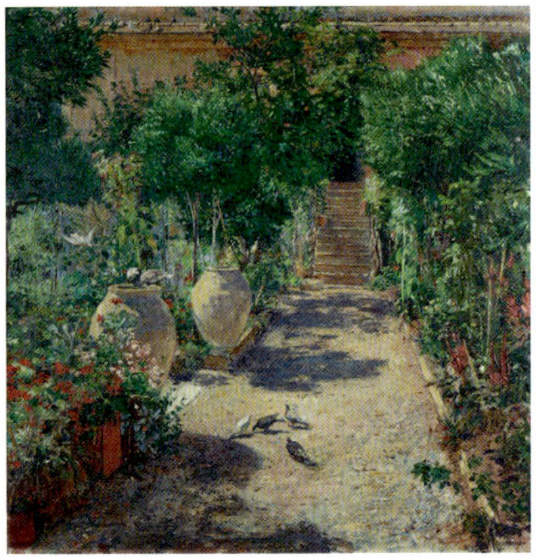

Fig. 6
JOHANN VICTOR KRÄMER
Taormina in the Sunshine, 1897
Belvedere, Vienna

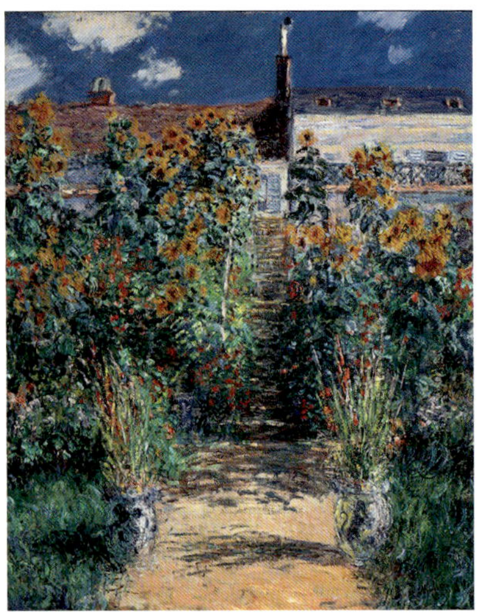

Fig. 7
CLAUDE MONET
The artist's Garden at Vétheuil (The Steps at Vétheuil), 1881
The Norton Simon Foundation, Pasadena

extensive text on Monet in advance of the exhibition in *Le Figaro* and later in *Gil Blas*.[25]
Tina Blau spent a few weeks in Paris in 1883.[26] She was invited to participate in the Paris Salon where she was awarded an honorable mention. It is not known whether she saw the major Monet exhibition in the Galerie Durand-Ruel. However, some of the works she created, including three pictures in the Tuileries that capture the changing moments of light and mood, inevitably remind one of Monet.

For a number of painters, the Monet reception was indirectly conveyed through exchanges with fellow artists who had spent lengthy periods in Paris. This shows that the impulses that emanated from Monet's work were not necessarily limited to the French capital. For example, the German academies (such as those in Munich, Düsseldorf, and Karlsruhe), private art schools, and one of the many artists' colonies that had become established at picturesque spots throughout Europe (Barbizon, Dachau, Knokke, etc.) also acted as forums.

The circle around Emil Jakob Schindler played a special role in this respect. Schindler himself had only spent two weeks in Paris in 1881—in a year for which there are no records of a Monet exhibition or of his participation in a group show—but subtle echoes of Monet's work make themselves felt in paintings such as *Park Landscape in Plankenberg* (*Parklandschaft in Plankenberg*, 1887) that shows his daughters Alma and Margarethe at play, and the series of variations on the *Poplar Avenue (Pappelallee)* in Plankenberg. However, an actual encounter remains in the sphere of speculation. There are several reasons for the paths of a possible Monet reception being hardly perceptible. Supported by Carl Moll's mythicizing biography,[27] local art history considered that Schindler was the central figure of an independent landscape school and the main representative of Austrian "Atmospheric Impressionism"—and it still does. This was more or less interpreted as a specifically Austrian concept vis-à-vis French Impressionism, first and foremost, Monet. In fact, Schindler was part of a well-linked network of internationally active art dealers, collectors, and artist friends. In this way, his pictures reached the renowned Galerie Goupil in Paris by way of the collector Dietrich W. Crone. And he also worked closely with the art dealer Georg Plach, the Parisian-by-choice Charles Sedelmeyer and Hugo Othmar Miethke in Vienna.[28] However, Miethke's gallery only became the top address for international modern art in Vienna through Carl Moll, Schindler's closest pupil. But, as can be seen by the artists mentioned so far, informal communication was often another possible reception channel. Martina Haja writes that, "Roughly speaking, the transfer of information could take place in two ways. On the one hand, through the conscious and unconscious exemplary function of the paintings [created by friends in Paris], who, for their part, had assimilated French stimuli and, on the other, or in addition, through verbal and written reports complemented by graphic works brought back with them. At the very best, Schindler only had second-hand contacts with Parisian artistic life in the 1880s […]."[29]

The 1889 World's Fairs in Paris marked a gradual change in the generations of the protagonists. A group of artists born around 1860/70 followed Monet's immediate contemporaries: this was the generation that was to produce the most important personalities of the Vienna Secession. In addition to the already mentioned Josef Engelhart, Johan Victor Krämer, whose painting *Taormina in the sunshine* (1897) displays startling analogies to Monet's garden paintings from Vétheuil (1881),[30] both in respect of motif and coloration, even though it remains uncertain as to where he received these stimuli, lived in Paris between 1888 and 1890. There is evidence that Wilhelm Bernatzik was able to choose from Paul

Durand-Ruel's private collection for the 1903 Impressionism exhibition.[31] The young Hugo von Hofmannsthal (1874–1929), who considered not only French literature, but also the country's art, a "remarkable treasure," had been to Paris as a tourist to visit the World's Fairs in 1900.[32] Intellectually he profited enormously from his friendship with art historians and connoisseurs including Eberhard von Bodenhausen and Harry Graf Kessler. Hofmannsthal made the tour of the galleries and museums that were on the Paris program of almost all painters from abroad and also visited Durand-Ruel's apartment, "In the early morning, I went to have a look at Durand-Ruel's private collection, which includes very beautiful works by Manet and Degas, with Hans [Schlesinger]."[33] Although Monet was not mentioned, it is likely that the young man from the Viennese world of literature saw some of his paintings and was also able to admire the numerous double doors the artist had decorated with still-lifes of flowers and fruits (1882–1885).[34] It can be assumed that experiences of this kind were not only mentioned in letters but were also discussed at length in diverse circles after his return to Vienna. In addition to Hermann Bahr, Emil Heilbut (Hermann Helferich), who wrote critiques for *Die Zeit* and other newspapers, also had family ties that led to him living frequently in Paris. He owned some paintings by Monet that he

Fig. 8
CARL MOLL
Anna Moll at the Desk, ca. 1903
Wien Museum

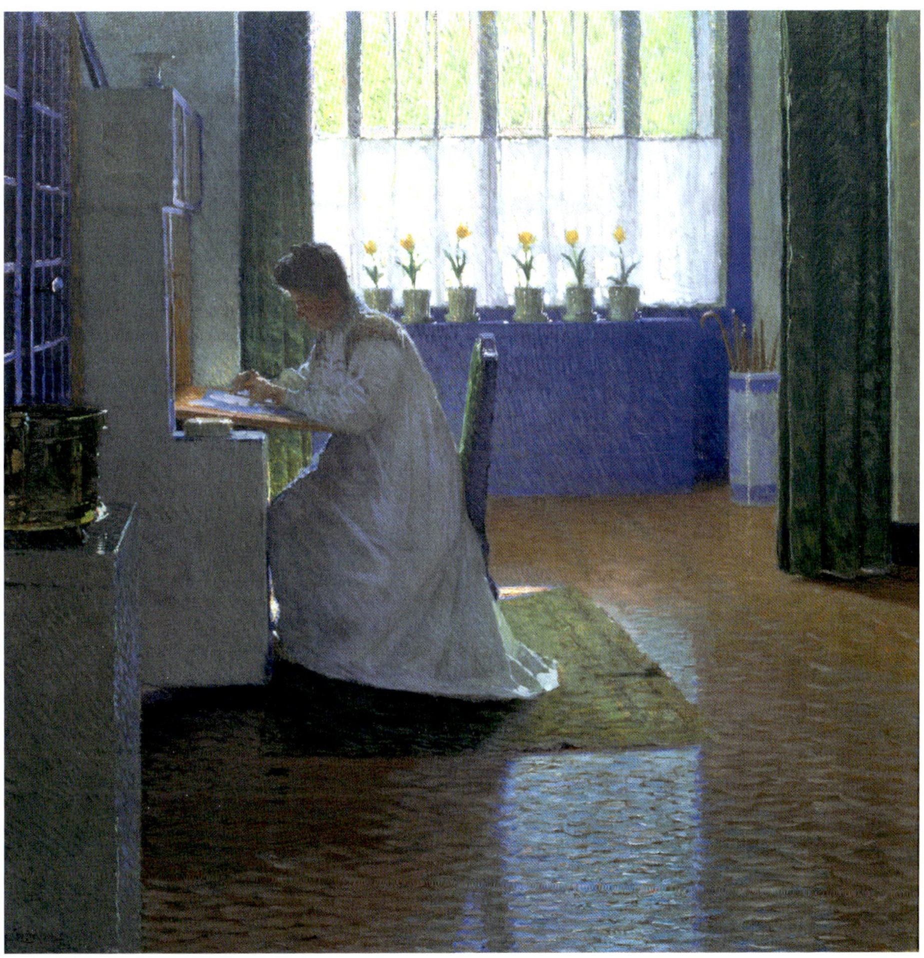

used in his lectures on French painting after 1889 and which met with an incredibly strong response. Heilbut wrote what is probably the first German-language monographic text on Monet.[35]

The well-known journalist and society lady Berta Zuckerkandl was also a member of this network. Her father, the newspaper publisher Moriz Szeps, had a close relationship with Crown Prince Rudolf and attempted to strengthen the French-Austrian political axis. Starting in 1883, contact with Georges Clemenceau, who published many newspapers alongside his political activity, was intensified in this connection. According to Zuckerkandl, he had been a youthful friend of Manet's and "experienced the heroic age of Impressionism" with him.[36] He had been acquainted with Monet since 1860 and purchased the first of a total of three paintings by the artist in 1890. Much later, in their twilight years, Clemenceau became something like the *alter ego* of the painter, whom he visited regularly in Giverny.[37] In any case, Berta Zuckerkandl's later brother-in-law Georges Clemenceau was the person who guided her in Paris when she visited the city for the first time in 1885. In retrospect, the prominent art critic and advocator of the Secession wrote, "I am grateful to Georges Clemenceau for introducing me to the wide field of art. Guided by him, at a time when the Impressionists were still being jeered at, he taught me to understand their magnificent revolution of seeing."[38] The seed for her commitment to contemporary art had been sown. In 1902, Zuckerkandl brought her friend, the famous sculptor Rodin, to Vienna as a guest at the Beethoven exhibition.[39] Personalities like Zuckerkandl were important factors in shaping public opinion on contemporary art.

ON THE ROLE OF THE ART BUSINESS

Naturally, exhibitions were the main avenue for spreading Claude Monet's art.[40] In this respect, artistic exchange profited not least from the technically accelerated means of transportation and communication. For example, exhibitions of French art were quite usual in the Künstlerhaus in Vienna but would have been inconceivable without the participation of the art business. Only in very rare cases did the artists themselves provide works. During the 19th century, modern, internationally focused, gallery and art-business activities became established in France—and particularly in Paris—parallel to the official Salon.[41] Here, it is necessary to draw particular attention to Paul Durand-Ruel, who must be considered as being *the* art dealer of the Impressionists. Monet and his comrades-in-arms found a congenial partner in him. He had become acquainted with Monet while he was in exile during the German-French War of 1870 through the Barbizon painter Charles-François Daubigny who stated, "This man is better than all of us… buy from him […]."[42] Durand-Ruel represented Monet in the long years of ignorance and ostracism and, after a gradual positive change in the mood of French art criticism started to be felt, risked taking his first extremely successful steps in the American market in March 1886.[43] On the occasion of the major Impressionism exhibition in the Viennese Secession in 1903, the *Neue Freie Presse* reported that, "A single art dealer has the entire movement in his hands, in a manner of speaking, and that is Mr Durand-Ruel in Paris. […] At a time when the entire world was laughing about the Impressionists, he was convinced—was it intuition or his feeling for art? —that it would ultimately be victorious and used his entire fortune to buy their pictures. He lost all his money on Impressionism and went bankrupt twice. Today, he is a millionaire many times over."[44] There are records that the first contacts between the dealer

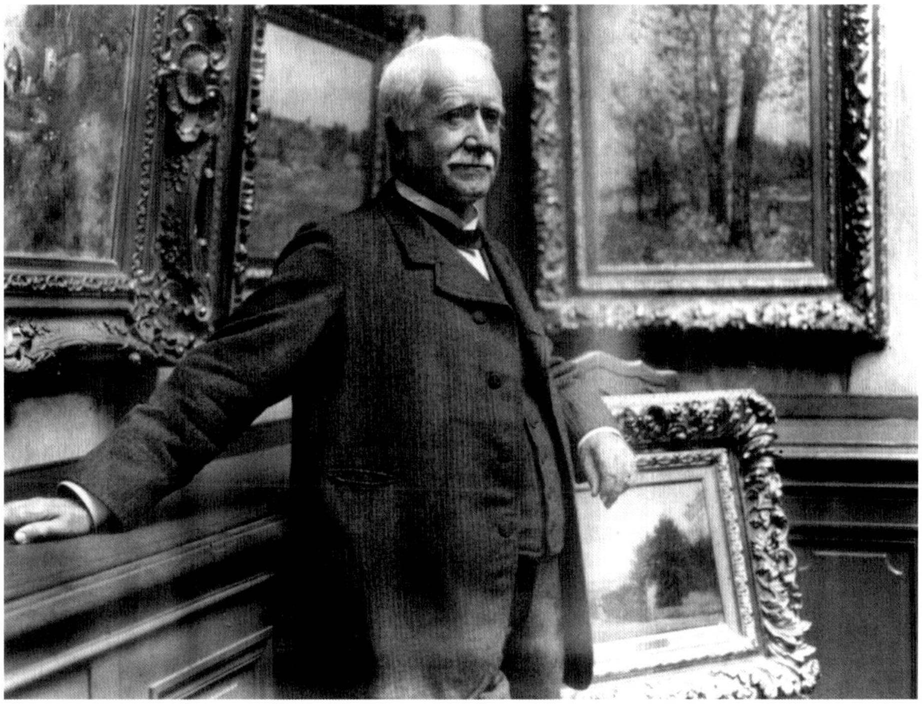

Fig. 9
PAUL FRANÇOIS ARNOLD CARDON (DORNAC)
Paul Durand-Ruel in his gallery
Paris, ca. 1910

and the Künstlerhaus in Vienna had taken place in the year 1870. Vienna was a promising market at the time, however not for Impressionist painting but for its forerunners, the painters of the Barbizon School. Their atmospheric plein-air painting had a great influence on the young Austrian landscape artists.[45] In 1873, the year of the Vienna World's Fairs, Durand-Ruel even rented business premises near the Künstlerhaus. (Gustave Courbet, who was also represented by Durand-Ruel, was so enthusiastic about Vienna in 1873 that he planned to settle permanently in the city.[46]) However, the outbreak of cholera and the stock market crash a few weeks later meant that all expectations remained unfulfilled and, as a result, the French dealer showed almost no interest in doing business in Vienna until the end of the century. He was also unsuccessful in selling two Monets when he presented them in the city in 1898. It was only through the good offices of his Berlin partner Paul Cassirer that Durand-Ruel, who was known to be easy to deal with, could be convinced to make major loans (some, from his private collection) to the Secession's 1903 Impressionism exhibition.[47] The Frenchman had experienced that it was only possible to sell the Impressionists in Europe if they were the focal point of an exhibition. And Vienna was not an ideal location for that.

Paul Cassirer was an important partner of Durand-Ruel and, subsequently, for the Secessionists and Galerie Miethke in Vienna. He was born into the assimilated entrepreneurial Cassirer family in 1871. The Cassirers had their roots in Silesia but had developed into one of the wealthiest and most influential families in Berlin by the end of the 19th century. After studying art history and years of apprenticeship in Paris, Paul also settled in Berlin and founded the "Bruno und Paul Cassirer Kunst- und Verlagsanstalt", together with his cousin Bruno, in 1898. They separated in 1901; Bruno took over the book publication activities and Paul the art business and related publishing.

Cassirer was completely familiar with Impressionism from his period in Paris and wanted to break open the inflexible structures of Wilhelmine Germany that also smothered artistic life and present the public with new movements – this triggered the following statement from Emperor Wilhelm II, "This Cassirer, who wants to bring French artistic rubbish to us!"[48]

Bruno and Paul were secretaries of the Berlin Secession and also played a decisive role in the selection of the pictures for exhibitions and the way they were hung. This provided an opportunity for introducing modern hanging concepts: casual hanging, exhibitions devoted to specific subjects, innovative use of lighting, and mobile walls, "If the Cassirers had a direct and sustainable impact, it was because they planned each exhibition as a unified whole and attempted to reveal the psychological and historical connections between the works of the various artists."[49]

The inaugural exhibition in 1899 with works by Max Liebermann, Edgar Degas and Constantin Meunier was followed by a show with Édouard Manet, Claude Monet, Giovanni Segantini, Vincent van Gogh, Paul Cézanne, and others, and, in 1908, there was even a Goya exhibition. Cassirer, who was married to the famous actress Tilla Durieux,[50] always followed his own feeling for quality and did not subject himself to the zeitgeist. It was said that he arrived at "money, by way of Monet over Manet".[51] Fifteen of the works shown at the Secession's major Impressionism exhibition, including four Monets, were provided by Cassirer, who regularly provided pictures for exhibitions in Central Europe.[52]

After the Plach art gallery ceased operating in Vienna in 1885, the Galerie Miethke assumed an important role in promoting French art. It had been founded by Hugo Othmar Miethke and Carl Josef Wawra in 1861.[53] During their partnership, but even more so while he was active as an art dealer who had to manage alone, Miethke forged international contacts throughout Europe. From the end of the 19th century, he worked in close collaboration with the Bernheim-Jeune Brothers, Ambroise Vollard, and Paul Durand-Ruel in Paris and Paul Cassirer in Berlin.

Miethke & Wawra commissioned Hans Makart with the monumental painting *Venice Pays Homage to Caterina Cornaro* (*Venedig huldigt Caterina Cornaro;* 1872/73), which was impressively staged and presented to the paying public on the occasion of the 1873 Vienna World's Fair. The audience was so large that the gallery managed to survive the collapse of the stock market a few days after the opening of the World's Fair more or less unscathed. The two men followed individual business paths after this crisis and Wawra became an important player in the copperplate engraving business. Miethke, on the other hand, specialized in painting.

In addition to dealing with old masters, Miethke also promoted Emil Jakob Schindler, Robert Russ, August Pettenkofen, and Arthur Strasser along with the already mentioned Hans Makart. Similar to Charles Sedelmeyer, Hans Miethke was not especially open to modern movements and this was probably the reason that he sold the gallery to Paul Bacher in 1904 but kept the palais as his personal residence. Bacher employed Carl Moll and Hugo Haberfeld as new directors; the latter became the sole manager in 1912 and the owner of the gallery in 1917.

This resulted in an important change in the reception of Impressionism, and especially Monet's work, in Austria: drawings by Monet had already been shown in 1903, followed in 1905 by paintings on which we have no precise information and finally by the great

"Manet-Monet" exhibition in 1910. This made it possible to compare *Paul Antoine Graff (Le Père Paul;* 1882; at the time, the only work by Monet in the collection of an Austrian museum) and the portrait *Eugénie Graff (La Mère Paul;* 1882), which was soon bought by Paul Wittgenstein.[54]

The Hungarian banker Baron Adolph Kohner purchased *Winter in Argenteuil/Thaw Period* (1873)[55] for his collection of contemporary French and Hungarian art. He had his original collection of old masters auctioned by Miethke to make it possible for him to finance his new passion. When his acquisitions had to be auctioned in 1934 as a consequence of unsuccessful banking deals, they included works by Pierre Bonnard, Gustave Courbet, Eugène Delacroix, Maurice Denis, Berthe Morisot, Auguste Renoir, Alfred Sisley and Édouard Vuillard.[56]

Galerie Miethke worked closely together with Paul Durand-Ruel in the field of presenting works by Claude Monet and, up to 1913, invested large sums to make purchases.[57]

However, Galerie Miethke saw itself confronted with strong competition from Galerie Arnot, which had been established by Guido Arnot in 1909. Branches in Paris and London made a program of exhibitions of works by English, Scottish, and French artists possible. In 1912, the Portal of *Rouen Cathedral at Midday (*1893), a milestone in Monet's oeuvre, was displayed in the *Exhibition of Works of Modern French Artists.*[58] The gallery also organized solo exhibitions of contemporary artists including Egon Schiele, Alfred Kubin, and Anton Faistauer. Writing in the *Neue Freie Presse,* Adalbert Franz Seligmann opined that, "the Arnot gallery [...] is advantageously conspicuous in that it manages to keep all of its presentations at a constant, decent level and manages to avoid kitsch, as well as any modish modern art that meets with cheap applause."[59]

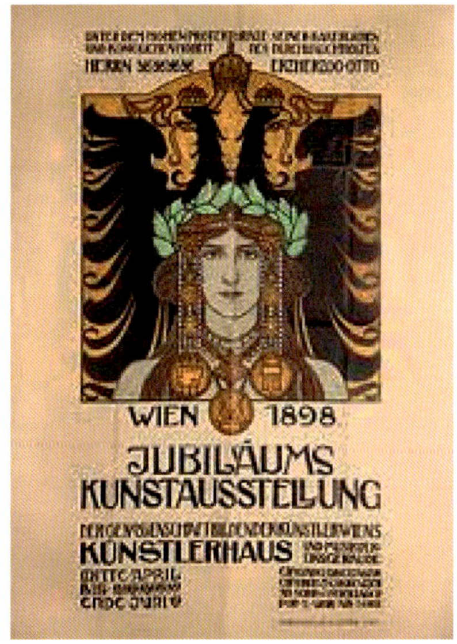

Fig. 10
Poster for the Jubilee Exhibition at the Vienna Künstlerhaus, 1898
Künstlerhaus archives, Vienna

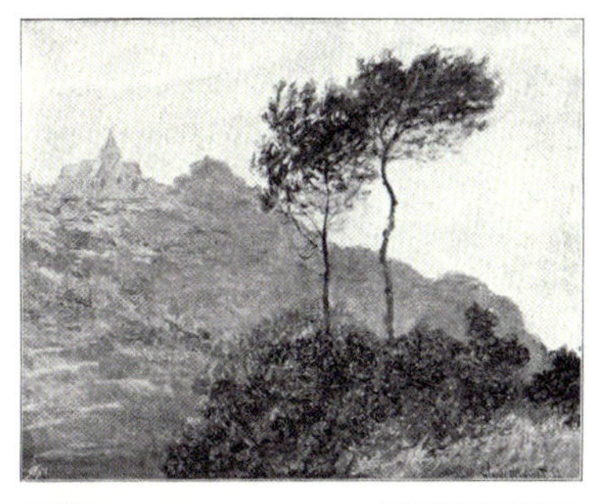

Fig. 11
Catalog of the Jubilee Exhibition at the Vienna Künstlerhaus, 1898

MONET EXHIBITIONS IN VIENNA

As mentioned at the start of this essay, Austrian art historiography only started to analyze the impact of Monet and French Impressionism on the Austrian artistic scene relatively late, after 1900. Here, the major Impressionism exhibition in the Vienna Secession in 1900 is seen as having provided the long overdue initiation into French premodern art to which Marian Bisanz-Prakken observes, "This [...] exhibition was – both in regard to the quality of the exhibits and unity of the concept—unquestionably one of the highlights in the early history of the Secession [...]. However, at the same time, it should not be overlooked that French Impressionism, which was already presented as a historical phenomenon in 1903, was ultimately never really accepted in Vienna."[60] Isolation from the rest of the world,[61] "animosity to Impressionism" and a "chronic lack of information,"[62] as well as—completely absurd as an argument—"traditionally" bad relationships with France, were given as reasons for this in the specialized literature.[63] In the art-historical narrative, these were compensated for in a way by the Austrian "separate path,"[64] so-called "Atmospheric Impressionism."[65] More recently, intensive critical studies of the sources, which have already been quoted several times, have disproved—or at least qualified—these arguments. As will be shown, the very presence of Monet's work in Viennese exhibitions is not the sole criterion for the extent of Monet's reception. But where and when could his works be seen in Vienna? There were, in fact, only a few possibilities to admire his works in Austria, respectively Vienna, before the first and only Monet retrospective in the year 1996.[66] Isolated sources verify that Monet participated in the 1873 World's Fairs in Vienna where his paint-

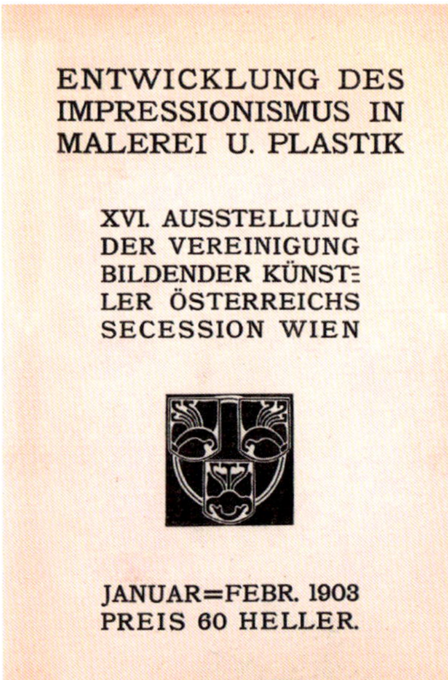

ENTWICKLUNG DES IMPRESSIONISMUS IN MALEREI U. PLASTIK

XVI. AUSSTELLUNG DER VEREINIGUNG BILDENDER KÜNSTLER ÖSTERREICHS SECESSION WIEN

JANUAR=FEBR. 1903
PREIS 60 HELLER.

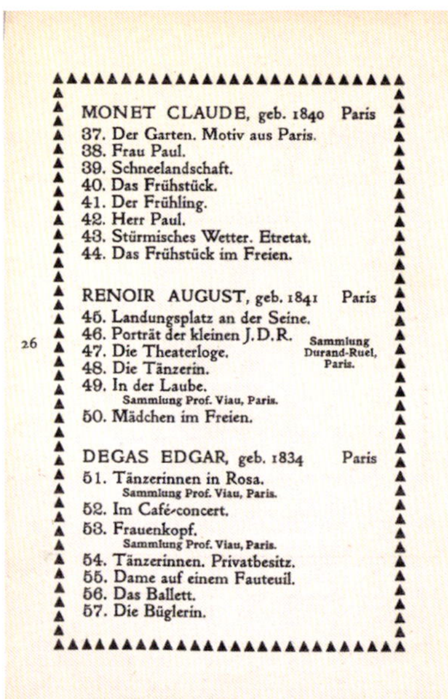

26

MONET CLAUDE, geb. 1840 Paris
37. Der Garten. Motiv aus Paris.
38. Frau Paul.
39. Schneelandschaft.
40. Das Frühstück.
41. Der Frühling.
42. Herr Paul.
43. Stürmisches Wetter. Etretat.
44. Das Frühstück im Freien.

RENOIR AUGUST, geb. 1841 Paris
45. Landungsplatz an der Seine.
46. Porträt der kleinen J.D.R.
47. Die Theaterloge.
48. Die Tänzerin.
Sammlung Durand-Ruel, Paris.
49. In der Laube.
Sammlung Prof. Viau, Paris.
50. Mädchen im Freien.

DEGAS EDGAR, geb. 1834 Paris
51. Tänzerinnen in Rosa.
Sammlung Prof. Viau, Paris.
52. Im Café-concert.
53. Frauenkopf.
Sammlung Prof. Viau, Paris.
54. Tänzerinnen. Privatbesitz.
55. Dame auf einem Fauteuil.
56. Das Ballett.
57. Die Büglerin.

Figs. 12 and 13
Catalog of the exhibition "Entwicklung des Impressionismus in Malerei und Plastik" at the Vienna Secession, 1903
Belvedere archives, Vienna

ing *The Goods Train (Le Convoi de chemin de fer,* 1872) was hung.[67] Two paintings—namely *Houses in Argenteuil (Maisons d'Argenteuil,* 1873; fig. p. 156) and *Church at Varengeville, Grey Weather (Église de Varengeville, temps gris,* 1882; see fig. p. 156)—were exhibited in the Künstlerhaus in Vienna at the international exhibition celebrating the 50th anniversary of Emperor Franz Joseph's reign in 1898.[68] The first picture was even awarded a small gold medal and the second shown as a full-page illustration in the catalog. Although Kolja Kramer feels that, "The paintings were shown isolated, and without a connection to the exhibition as a whole, in the middle of works of Salon art. That can only be understood against the background that the reception of French Impressionism, which had already made great progress internationally, was still in its infancy in the German-speaking world—and all the more so in Austria,"[69] it must be countered that the visitors were sufficiently used to the so-called Petersburg hanging and were able to "extract and view" individual works from the profusion of paintings just as is done in the Kunsthistorisches Museum in Vienna or the Palazzo Pitti in Florence. Even though Monet's pictures shown at the 1898 exhibition had classic, not oversized, art business formats, it would have been difficult not to notice the powerful effect made by the coloration of *Église de Varengeville, temp gris.* Here, I would like to quote two differing contemporary sources that give a clear impression of the increased perception of Monet's work. The formulation used by the painter Ernestine von Kirchsberg in her letter to Alfred Zoff is rather indirect, "To be honest, I find it [the exhibition] unsuccessful. Seeing that it was the intention of this exhibition to pay tribute to our Monarch, I do not consider it positive to have created this staging of a dazzling mass of works from abroad that completely crushes Austria."[70] There are no doubts in Wilhelm Schölermann's review in the *Kunstchronik,* "The French painters have shown up in full force: one name leads the way: *Claude Monet.* And just how dangerous the hand of the genius becomes to mere talents wherever it appears! There are only two small pictures there, but—for those who absorb them—they put everything around them completely in the shade."[71]

This was followed by the previously mentioned *XVI. Secession Exhibition* in January/February 1903, which was devoted to the *Development of Impressionism in Painting and Sculpture.* Monet was represented with eight – mainly earlier – works.[72] Works by younger artists such as Ludwig Heinrich Jungnickel, Franz Jaschke and Rudolf Junk make it possible to recognize that they had processed the methods of Monet or the Neo-Impressionists immediately after the exhibition.[73] However, not only the up-and-coming artists (some of whom are hardly known today) were fascinated by these works. Carl Moll, one of the most influential personalities in the Viennese artistic scene from the mid-1890s until well into the 1930s, also experienced important formal stylistic impulses. Moll, as the artistic director of the legendary Galerie Miethke, was also the person responsible for Monet's fourth stopover in Vienna in May 1910. This was the "Manet – Monet" exhibition that presented no fewer than 17 paintings by Monet and met with lively interest—at least in the circles of faithful artists and collectors.[74] It is amazing that, with all of his activities as organizer and curator at the Künstlerhaus, later the Secession and various state bodies, Moll could still find time for his own artistic work. In 1900, Moll spent four weeks in Paris as one of the Austrian administrators for the World's Fairs. He mainly deals with the famous, or infamous, nightlife in his memoirs but, in a postscript, mentions, "Later, when everything irrelevant [...] had been taken care of, I realized the outcome of my trip to Paris: an idea of French art, from its beginnings to the present—to Impressionism."[75] Among the people he had to thank for

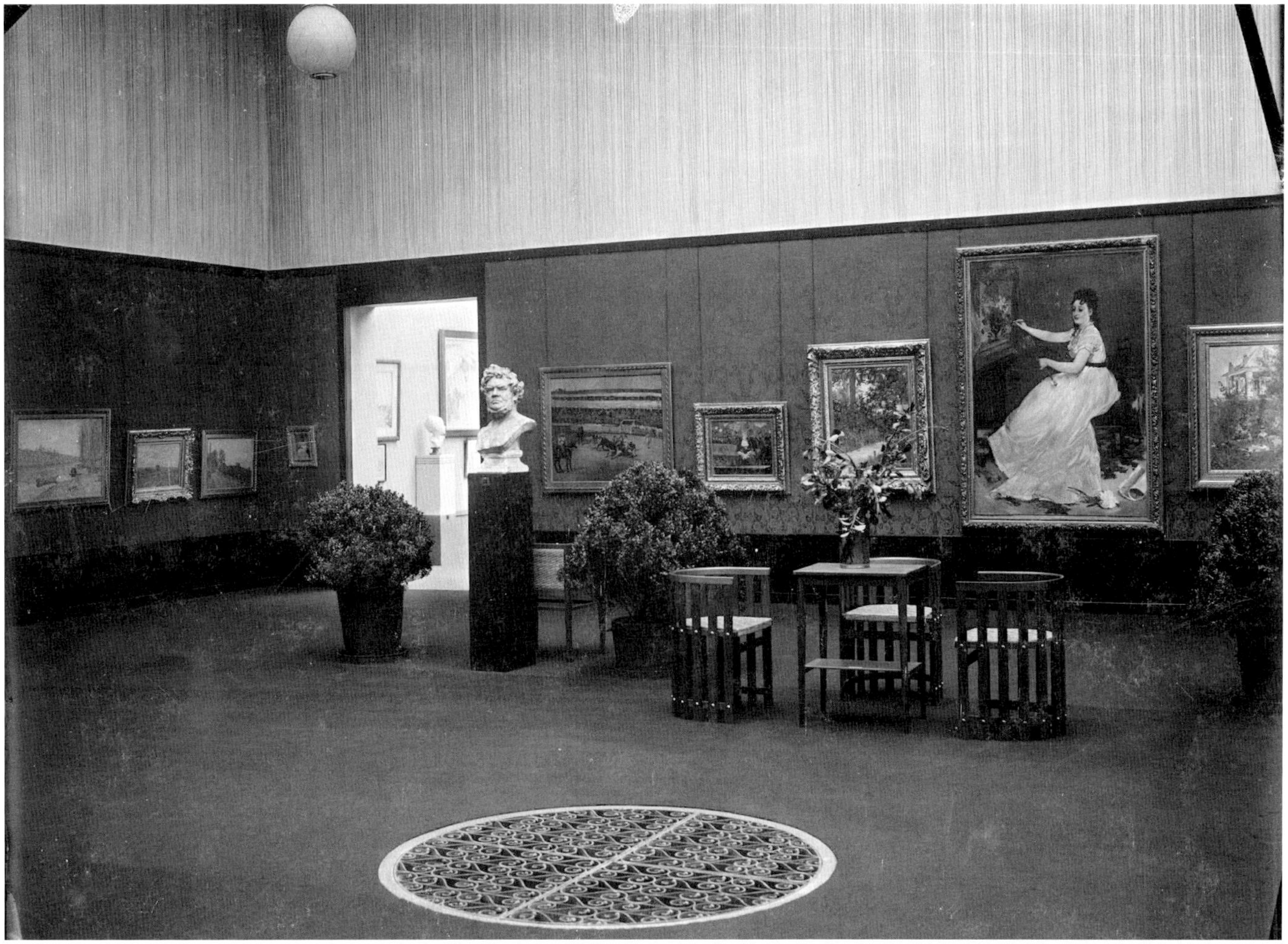

this was Julius Meier-Graefe, whom he met at the time and who was to become a close friend. Moll was an artist who was able to rapidly assimilate new impulses. His intensive study of Monet resulting from his inspection of the works at exhibitions is evident: there are immediate indications of this in the works he created after his trip to Paris in 1900, and following the Impressionism shows in 1903 and 1910 in the Galerie Miethke (fig. p. 113). In October/November 1911, eight paintings by Monet were shown at the "French Impressionists" exhibition organized by the Viennese Galerie Arnot, a new competitor to the Miethke Kunstsalon. So far, it has only been possible to identify five of them: *Flowering Plum Trees in Vétheuil* (1879), *Low Tide at Varengeville* (1882), *The 'Pyramids' at Port-Coton in the Sun* (1886), *Bridge in Monet's Garden* (1895–1896), and *Water Lilies* (1905).[76] Shortly thereafter, in January/February 1912, Miethke once again displayed *French Masters* with three paintings by Monet: *The Flowering Meadow (Dans la prairie*, 1876; see fig. p. 165) with its unsurpassable summery lightness, *La Seine près d'Argenteuil* (1874) and an unidentified still life.[77] In December 1912, *Rough Sea in Étretat* (1883) and the, previously mentioned, *Portal of Rouen Cathedral at Midday* (1894; see fig. p. 123) were displayed in the Galerie Arnot.[78] Miethke presented two works by Monet in March 1913 and one early painting at the turn of the year 1913/14: the still life with fish *Red Mullets* (1869), *Sheltered Path* (1873), and *Farm Courtyard in Normandy* (1879).[79] After the World War I, when Austria had become a

Fig. 14
View of the rooms for the exhibition "Entwicklung des Impressionismus in Malerei und Plastik" at the Vienna Secession, 1903
ÖNB/Vienna

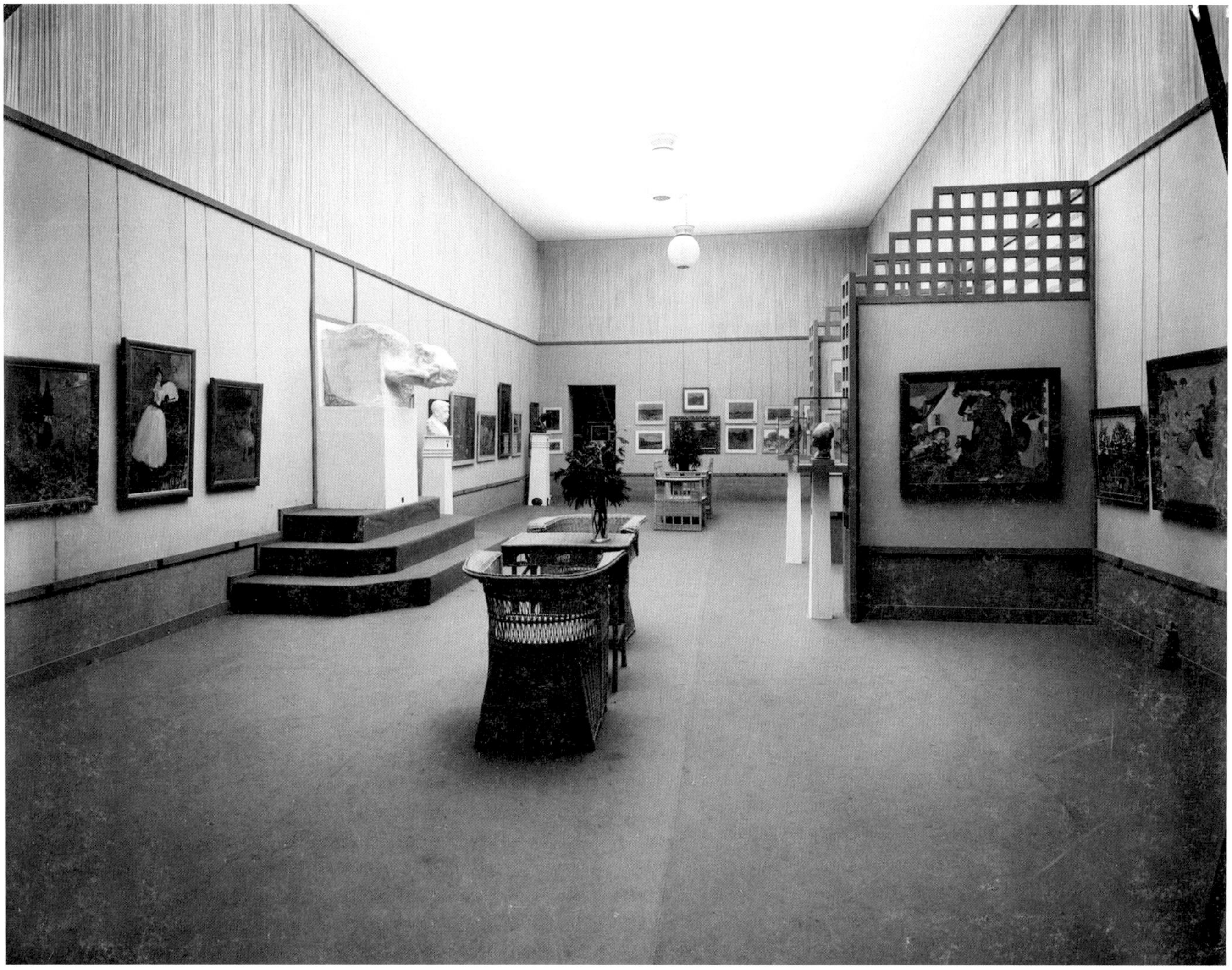

Fig. 15
View of the rooms for the exhibition "Entwicklung des Impressionismus in Malerei und Plastik" at the Vienna Secession, 1903
ÖNB, Vienna

loser vis-à-vis France, it took some time before the cultural relationship could be forged once again. The recess caused by the wartime economy made it impossible for Galerie Miethke to survive after 1918.

In 1925, three of Monet's works were once again shown in the 82nd Secession Exhibition *The Principal Masters of French Art in the XIX Century* organized under the aegis of Carl Moll: *Road to the Farm of Saint-Siméon* (1864), *Church at Vétheuil* (1878) and *Village of Lavacourt* (1878/79).[80]

As a talented curator, Moll was often able to emulsify the preoccupations of the artistic scene with the goals of the state's artistic authorities. This had led to concrete plans in 1899 for an *Imperial Travelling Museum,* which was intended to make the majority of the population aware of the developments of European art and, especially, create an understanding for contemporary artistic work.[81] In his role as one of the organizers, as well as the representative of the artistic community appointed by the responsible ministry, Moll was responsible for the didactic concept and selecting the artists to be shown. This mobile museum with —sometimes colored—reproductions toured the country accompanied by lectures given by art historians. French nineteenth-century painting was strongly represented and placed the Impressionists after the Barbizon painters in the line of development of modern art. In addition to two pictures by Manet, Monet's *Church in Vernon* (*L'église de Vernon*) could be seen in places in the monarchy like Innsbruck, Leoben, Görz (today, Gorizia or Gorica), Iglau (Jihlava), and Mährisch Ostrau (Ostrava) until 1918.

Until the Viennese Monet exhibition in 1996, the Österreichische Galerie Belvedere showed works from its own holdings—*Paul Antoine Graff (Le Père Paul)* (1882) and *Anglers on the Seine near Poissy* (1882),[82] which were acquired in 1903 and 1912 respectively and, after the Second World War, *Path in Monet's Garden in Giverny* (1902).[83] In 1947, in the early days of the Second Republic, Monet was also represented in the *Classique de la peinture française moderne exhibition* organized by the Haut-Commissariat de la République française en Autriche. [84]

It is evident that, with the simplification of the possibilities for travel, exhibitions would not only become important showcases for the works of Austrian artists in Vienna or Paris but also in the major cities in the monarchy and German-speaking countries. If one consults the listings of the Wildenstein Institute, one sees that, in the first half of the twentieth century, works by the painter were displayed in Budapest (1903, 1907, 1910, and 1913), in Prague (1902, 1907, 1914, 1923, and 1926) and in Posen/Poznań (1906),[85] and that there were exhibitions of his pictures in Berlin (starting 1882; especially as of 1900 until World War I on a yearly basis), in Dresden (1897, 1899, 1902, 1904, 1909, 1914 and 1926), in Munich (1891, 1900, 1901, 1907, 1909, 1910, 1911, 1913, 1914, and 1927) and – surprisingly late – in Zurich (1908, 1912, 1913, 1917, 1929, 1933, and 1943).[86]

In this connection, the Annual Munich Exhibition of Artworks from All Nations in the Royal Glass Palace ("Münchner Jahresausstellung von Kunstwerken aller Nationen im königlichen Glaspalaste") of 1891, in which "Auntie Olga"—as Olga Wisinger-Florian was lovingly nicknamed by Marie Egner from the Schindler circle—was represented with three works, alongside Alfred Zoff and Emil Jakob Schindler, has so far remained ignored. The show, which is not listed by Wildenstein, was the first major exhibition in Germany to display works by Manet, Monet, and Sisley.[87] The four Monet pictures—*By the Pond*, *Marine (Seascape)*, *Seascape* and *Landscape*—are not identified. However, the catalog reveals that three of them were hung in the large central hall immediately after the vestibule and definitely did not go unnoticed—neither by Olga Wisinger-Florian nor by Alfred Zoff who —as one sees from the title of the pictures alone— must have been inspired for his own "seascapes."

LITERATURE ON MONET

An additional field of encounter was provided by specialized publications, even though classical monographs on Monet did not appear until relatively late.[88] However, a consistently negative prevailing mood can be noticed with numerous French critics.[89] Starting in the 1860s, influential writers and critics, who were friends of each other, including Émile Zola, Théodore Duret, Octave Mirbeau, and Gustave Geffroy, placed important texts on Monet in the relevant newspapers, as well as in the art journals that were experiencing their heyday at the time. In a brilliant analysis, Christian Huemer recently investigated this "dealer-critic-system" (H. and C. White), the successful interaction between art criticism and the art business, in connection with the Austro-French art market.[90] These critiques were rarely illustrated: however, in general, reproductions were circulated that took advantage of the possibilities provided by highly developed artistic printing processes and, increasingly, the young media of photography. For example, in 1873, Durand-Ruel had a three-volume, lavishly illustrated sales catalog printed that included works by Monet.[91] It has not been established whether this was known in artists' circles but, in any case, Monet's name was "circulated" through many channels. Unfortunately, basic research into local art criticism in the 19th and early 20th centuries is still lacking. The spectrum of the daily newspapers alone was considerably broader than it is today and, both here and in France, art criticism sometimes even made its way onto the front page. The *Neue Freie Presse,*[92] with its two ultraconservative critics Adalbert F. Seligman and Max Nordau, as well as the open-minded Franz Servaes, must be mentioned here as one representative example, along with *Die Zeit* with its contributors Hermann Bahr, Richard Muther, Emil Heilbut (Hermann Helferich), Hugo von Hofmannsthal, and Berta Zuckerkandl—all critics with a close relationship to the Secession.[93] If one includes Émile Zola, Octave Mirbeau, and even Georges Clemenceau on the French side, it becomes clear that art criticism was not restricted to journalists working for the daily newspapers. It was not particularly difficult in Vienna to get hold of up-to-date French reports. To the extent that the information is still available, it was not only possible to read the important art journals in the Künstlerhaus and Secession, but naturally also in the Academy of Fine arts and School of Applied Arts and many coffee houses made international—and therefore French—newspapers available to their guests.[94] There was an out-and-out Francophile climate in the circle of the Secessionists, where numerous French journals were circulated.[95] The illustrations in them must have provided the first president Gustav Klimt, who had spent just under two weeks in Paris himself in 1909, with some inspiration for those of his works in which the motifs and painting style follow in the footsteps of Monet (see figs. pp. 65,68).

As examples of the many print media, we should mention the renowned *Gazette des beaux-arts* (from 1859) with its scientific concept, the *Gil Blas* magazine (from 1879), the daily newspapers *Le Figaro* and *Le Gaulois* and the numerous newspapers published by Clemenceau including *La Justice*. Of course, German criticism, such as that which appeared in the *Kunstchronik* (from 1866) or *Die Kunst für Alle* (from 1885), was also important. Art journals which were famous for their progressive attitudes, such as *Ver Sacrum* (from 1898), *The Studio* (from 1893), *Pan* (from 1895), etc., were not published until a time when engagement with Monet's work had already taken place for some of the artists discussed here.[96]

GERMAN-LANGUAGE ART CRITICISM AND ITS PREJUDICES AGAINST FRENCH ART

An in-depth investigation of the effect the 1889 World's Fairs had on the art world would far exceed the scope of this contribution. However, in the Austro-French context of the reception of Monet and his works, it is necessary to mention a few extra-artistic factors. The writer and art critic Hermann Bahr, who first lived in Paris for a lengthy period in 1889, wrote in his "Pariser Kunstbrief" at the time about the three art shows at the World's Fairs, the *Exposition décennale des artistes français*, which showed "the hopeless decay of the old school of convention," the already mentioned *Exposition centennale des artistes français*, and the *Exposition des artistes étrangers*.[97] Monet—who was only represented at the "Centennale"—was no stranger for Bahr, "And, finally one last word on the Impressionists;

Fig. 16
CLAUDE MONET
Rouen Cathedral, Sunlight Effect, 1893
Museum of Fine Arts, Boston

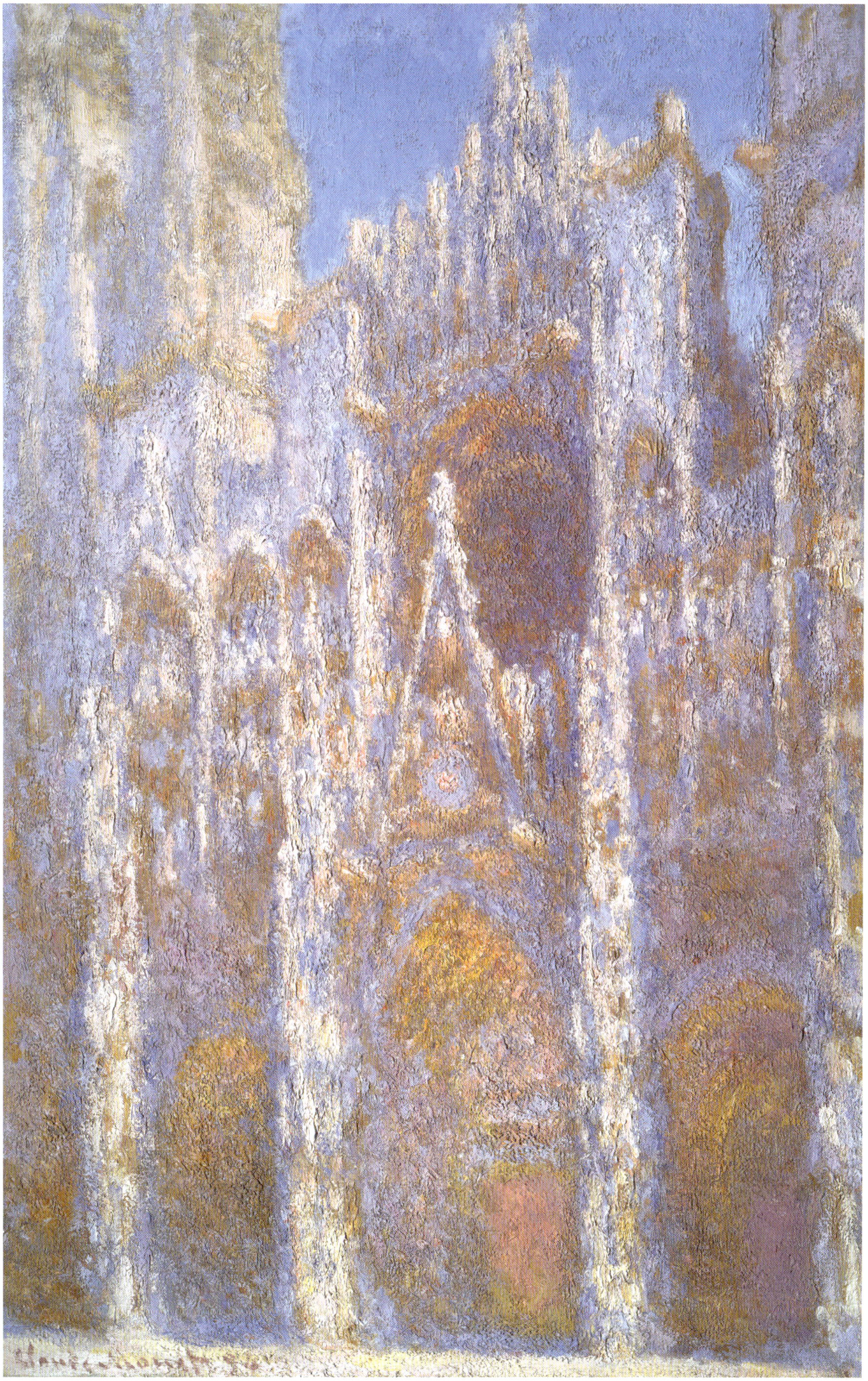

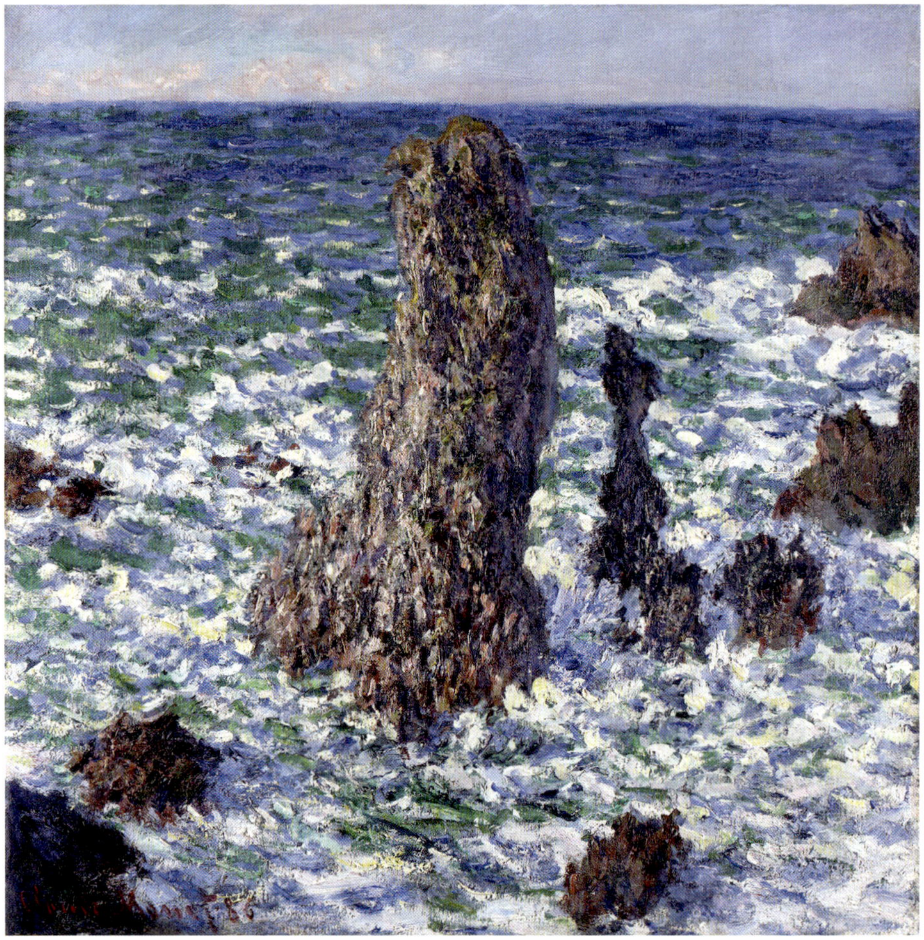

Fig. 17
CLAUDE MONET
The Pyramids at Port-Coton, Sunlight Effect, 1886
Private collection

I was only able to find two [sic] paintings by their current grand master, Claude Monet, with the crazy disciples and even crazier prices—both absolutely fabulous—here and the two landscapes are not particularly characteristic of his painting style."[98] Writing in the conservative *Kunstschrank*, Richard Gaul also praised the exhibitions in general and the "Centennale" in particular: it brings together "the most outstanding masters of our time" and gives "a clear impression of all movements of modern French painting." Gaul seems almost relieved to be able to add, "[…] even though certain extremes are missing, in Monet's work, for example."[99] Both reviews remain relatively close to the art on display and one hardly perceives any of those nationalistic feelings that could be found in the rest of the press—first and foremost in the German press. Although the 1989 Paris World's Fairs proved to be successful—not least due to the Eiffel Tower as its symbol—the run-up was politically controversial: most European countries were monarchies and harbored ill feelings toward republican France. The "Centennale", which was conceived as a jubilee show commemorating the 100th anniversary of the French Revolution, aroused additional suspicion. In addition, the psychological aftereffects of the German-French War could still be felt and were reflected in the German press. Austria, on the other hand, had lost a supporter of Austro-French relationships with the suicide of Crown Prince Rudolf in January 1889 and was more than ever caught between the poles of France and Germany. In spite of eloquent voices, including Bahr's, raised against them, factors of this kind became lasting hindrances to cultural exchange. German nationalist critics like Adolf Rosenberg, publisher of the *Kunstchronik,* Friedrich Pecht and others acted as spearheads in a battle against French modern art and found themselves in good company with Emperor Wilhelm II. His disdainful remarks about "purple pigs" and "gutter art" describing Impressionism became famous.[100] On the occasion of the Vienna World's Fairs in 1873, Pecht wrote about the "blasé nature" of French art, "that interesting mixture of the brothel and smell of blood" that it "needs to tickle the insensitive nerves of the elegant and low-class rabble."[101] French art, irrespective of whether it was Salon art, the plein-air painting of the School of Barbizon and, increasingly, Impressionist works were stereotyped as being "chic" and "stylish" in the sense of being technically virtuoso but superficial and without content. It was felt that the omnipresence of French art presented a danger to the nation's individual artistic character. For example, August Schaeffer von Wienwald, a prominent artist and Director of the Imperial Collection in Vienna, praised Charles Sedelmeyer's commitment to Austrian art in Paris but was worried that the artists who felt at home there might lose "their Austrian character, as well as the specific nature of their homeland."[102] The more French hegemony made itself felt within the artistic development of Europe (something in which German-speaking art historians and collectors were involved in no insignificant manner[103]) and could not be argued away, the stronger the argument of the economic upper hand of the French art business was advanced. One wanted to protect one's individual market – an argument which was to remain virulent until 1900.

The fact that the Monet reception took place over individual channels was also due to the long-lasting, preeminent position of the Künstlerhaus in Vienna and some influential conservative officials. Together with some critics—Adalbert Seligman has already been mentioned—they formed a tight network that—to put it positively—stressed traditional national values. Similar to the debate taking place in Germany, it was intended to show preference for exhibiting and championing Austrian artists. The younger generation, with the previously mentioned critics like Bahr, Zuckerkandl, and Hevesi on their side, never tired of branding this system of exclusion as antiquated. The attacks became personified in Eugen Felix, the portrait painter who was president of the Künstlerhaus for decades. Ludwig Hevesi got to the heart of the matter, "In those days in the Künstlerhaus, in the 'Felix era' as it is called today, there was a boycott against foreigners […] so as not to ruin the market for local artists."[104] Hermann Bahr characterized the situation more drastically, "[…] the period from 1880–1890, when our country was uncoupled from Europe in artistic matters."[105] And, elsewhere, "We were an Asian province; when people in Paris asked about Austria, the answer was simply: 'Là-bas? C'est en Roumanie? N'est-ce pas?'"[106]

Works by French artists were regularly exhibited in the Vienna Künstlerhaus—it was merely a question of which ones. In any case, the Impressionists, who had been relegated to an older generation by younger movements such as the Nabis or artists like van Gogh and Gauguin, were only marginally represented; if one neglects the single painting at the 1873 World's Fairs, Monet was not shown until the *Jubilee Exhibition* in 1898. Just how persistent the resentment was became obvious in 1911 with the so-called Vinnen conflict, named after a German painter who protested against the "excessive" import and purchase of French art by German museums. This protest was signed by numerous artists. As a result, Franz Marc called for a counter protest that was endorsed by Moll and Klimt, as well as the renowned art historian Hans Tietze, "We must not ignore the fact that, upon closer inspection, national advantages are often international shortcomings, that what is the German about an artist might not be appreciated by the whole world."[107]

The same Tietze could not help complaining about the failures of the recent past and put the role of the art dealers, who Vinnen had slandered as being "without scruples," into perspective, "The same Durand-Ruel [...] presented a large collection of works by French masters from Corot to Monet and Pissarro at the 1873 World's Fairs in Vienna and did not sell a single one of them: the pictures that cost a couple of hundred thousand francs at the time are now worth many millions and would form an unparalleled gallery."[108] The conservative perspective of the official art institutions (before 1897) and the fact that Durand-Ruel considered Vienna irrelevant as a market for Impressionists, resulted in their low presence—even though there were many other voices. It was probably only of little comfort for Tietze and his comrades-in-arms that the situation looked somewhat different in Germany and the Impressionism reception received a broader base through the individual initiatives of collectors, museum experts (Hugo von Tschudi, for example), and—last but not least—the Berlin Secession that was established in 1899.

At the same time, it should not be overlooked that, in the beginning, Monet was also not very successful in his home country. The first—now legendary—exhibition of those artists who were subsequently known as Impressionists was held in Paris in 1874. Monet was soon considered the leader of the group and was exposed to massive animosity in the press ("quand les enfants s'amusent avec du papier et des couleurs ils font mieux," "rien à faire avec l'art") and elsewhere.[109] For many years, he was accused of not being serious, of creating sketches (*ébauches*) in place of full-fledged paintings (*tableaux*) worthy of being exhibited. Paul Durand-Ruel's commitment and the already mentioned "art dealer-critic-system" of placing reviews by allied critics in the press slowly started to have an effect. In 1880, Monet had a solo exhibition in Galerie La Vie moderne. In spite of some positive press comments, Monet's friend and collector Théodore Duret later observed that many people simply came to the exhibition to have a laugh.[110] It was not until Monet participated in a group exhibition of the Impressionists with 40 paintings that he was able to convince some of his former skeptics and opponents: Armand Silvestre stressed Monet's special status and called him a "genuine contemporary poet of nature."[111] Even the ultraconservative critic Joris-Karl Huysmans, who was still speaking about Monet's "eye disease" in 1880, now admired his colors and considered him "cured."[112]

However, it should be borne in mind that Monet no longer exhibited with the Impressionists after 1882, and critics with a negative attitude could quite simply ignore him from then on.[113] The comprehensive analyses by David Wildenstein and Steven Z. Levine also do not provide us with a clear view of Monet's position in the opinion of the public in the 1880s.[114] It oscillated between flops, malicious critiques, and increasing recognition in expanding artistic circles. By 1889 at the latest, Monet had gained a fixed place not only in the local art scene but also in the history of French art—this was not least confirmed by the "Centennale". Apart from the reviews by German critics, the fact that he was still not exhibited very often in German-speaking countries was mainly due to sales to private collections being pushed as a result of the lack of interest of public bodies. In addition, Durand-Ruel, for one, only exhibited "his" artists where he thought there were possibilities of making sales. The "crazy" prices Bahr mentioned are put into perspective when compared with those of artists of the ilk of Mihály Munkácsy whose monumental staged pictures had attracted tens of thousands of paying visitors to Vienna until the mid-1880s. His painting *Christ before Pilate* (1881) was sold to an American collector for the incredible price of 600,000 francs while, for many years, Monet received only one thousandth of this amount for one of his works.[115]

However, after visiting the "Centennale" of French painting at the Paris World's Fairs in 1900 with Georges Clemenceau, Berta Zuckerkandl quoted him with the following words, "Those Impressionists who yesterday filled the *'Salon des Refusés'* have now become victorious, the most admirable works in the centennial exhibition."[116] The massive reception of French art, as well as Monet's painting, in Austria bears eloquent witness to this.

1 The "working committee" (Wilhelm Bernatzik, Leopold Bauer, Friedrich König, et al.), "Foreword", in: *Entwicklung des Impressionismus in Malerei u. Plastik. XVI. Ausstellung der Vereinigung bildender Künstler Österreichs Secession Wien* (exh. cat., Secession, Vienna, January/February 1903), Vienna 1903, p. 14.

2 On the background of this exhibition, see Kolja Kramer, *Die Ausstellungspräsenz des französischen Impressionismus im Wiener Künstlerhaus und in der Wiener Secession 1877–1903*, diss., Bern 2003.

3 As regretted in the catalog, the Englishmen, J.M.W. Turner and John Constable, who provided Monet with inspiration in 1870, were not represented, which led to the English "line of descent" remaining undocumented.

4 Cf. Hermann Bahr, "Die Kunst auf der Pariser Weltausstellung 1889," in: *Pariser Kunstbriefe*, cited after Claus Pias (ed.), *Hermann Bahr. Kritische Schriften in Einzelausgaben*, vol. I: *Zur Kritik der Moderne*, Weimar 2004, pp. 233–254, especially pp. 236–241 and pp. 241–245. Here, I would like to thank Dr Kurt Ifkovits, Theatermuseum Wien, for providing valuable information on Bahr.

5 Cf. Werner Hofmann, *Die Grundlagen der modernen Kunst. Eine Einführung in ihre symbolischen Formen*, 3rd ed., Stuttgart 1987, especially chapter, "Die Sattelstellung des 19. Jahrhunderts," pp. 166–190.

6 Julius Meier-Graefe, "Autobiographische Skizze," in: Catherina Krahmer (ed.), *Julius Meier-Graefe. Kunst ist nicht für Kunstgeschichte da. Briefe und Dokumente*, Göttingen 2001, pp. 11–17. – idem, *Entwicklungsgeschichte der modernen Kunst. Vergleichende Betrachtung der bildenden Künste, als Beitrag zu einer neuen Ästhetik*, 3 vols., Stuttgart 1904.

7 Working committee 1903 (as in note 1), p. 14.

8 Ludwig Abels, "Impressionismus," in: *Wiener Morgenzeitung*, January 17, 1903, p. 8, cited after Christian Huemer, *Paris–Vienna: Modern Art Markets and the Transmission of Culture, 1873–1937*, diss., New York 2013, p. 119. On the mentioned facts, cf. ibid., pp. 118–120. I take this opportunity to extend my most sincere thanks to Christian Huemer, Getty Research Institute, for generously providing information.

9 The well-attended lectures were held on February 7 and 14, 1903. Relevant lectures on Impressionism were not given in institutions such as the Volkshochschulen (adult education centers) until the 1920s. My gratitude goes to Mag. Thomas Dostal, Österreichisches Volkshochschularchiv. – On Muther: Rotraud Schleinitz, *Richard Muther – ein provokanter Kunstschriftsteller zur Zeit der Münchner Secession. Die "Geschichte der Malerei im XIX. Jahrhundert": Kunstgeschichte oder Kampfgeschichte?*, Hildesheim/Zürich/New York 1993. The prolific writer Muther was also active as an art critic in *Die Zeit* after Hermann Bahr's departure to the *Wiener Zeitung*.

10 Cf. Huemer 2013 (as in note 8), pp. 3–5.

11 Josef Engelhart, *Ein Wiener Maler erzählt. Mein Leben und meine Modelle*, Vienna 1943, p. 44. Engelhart was in Paris in 1891/92 and benevolently—if not without mythologizing the Bohemian aspects—devoted half of his report of his stay in the city to his older colleague. On the other hand, Liebermann lived in Paris from 1873 to 1878 and was also a friend of Jettel's. They both gave each other works of theirs. Cf. Tobias G. Natter, "'Ich war erstens Jude, zweitens reich und drittens hatte ich auch Talent.' Der Impressionismus Max Liebermanns zu Gast in Wien," in: idem/Julius H. Schoeps (eds.), *Max Liebermann und die französischen Impressionisten* (exh. cat., Jüdisches Museum, Vienna, November 7, 1997–January 18, 1998), Cologne 1997, p. 71.

12 There is no proof that Jettel actually suffered financial distress as a result of Sedelmeyer's supposed cuts. Cf. Engelhart 1943 (as in note 11), pp. 42–47.

13 Engelhart 1943 (as in note11), p. 43.

14 Christian Huemer, "Charles Sedelmeyer (1837–1925)", in: Stephan Koja (ed.), *Belvedere. Zeitschrift für bildende Kunst* vol. 2/1999, pp. 4–19, here p. 5.

15 Markéta Theinhardt, "'Auch in Österreich wird viel in Richtung Frankreich geschaut.' Österreichische Genre- und Landschaftsmalerei im Lichte der französischen Kunstkritik," in: Gerbert Frodl/Verena Traeger (eds.), *Stimmungsimpressionismus* (exh. cat., Österreichische Galerie Belvedere, Vienna, March 17–July 4, 2004), Vienna 2004, p. 55.

16 On the Société Nationale des Beaux-Arts, cf. Theinhardt 2004 (as in note 15), p. 58.

17 Carl Schuch, Venezianisches Notizheft I, fol. 43v, cited after Stephan Koja, "Hinausgehen über den Impressionismus. Carl Schuch und die Realität der Farbe," in: Agnes Husslein-Arco/Stephan Koja (eds.), *Carl Schuch. Ein europäischer Maler* (exh. cat., Österreichische Galerie Belvedere, Vienna, June 26–October 14, 2012), Vienna/Weitra 2012, p. 31.

18 Schuch's friend and later biographer Karl Hagemeister reports that he liked to translate interesting French critiques for him. Cf. Husslein-Arco/Koja 2012 (as in note 17), p. 33. Cf. also Isabelle Cahn, "Schuch in Paris", in: Brigitte Buberl (ed.), *Cézanne Manet Schuch. Drei Wege zur autonomen Kunst* (exh. cat., Museum für Kunst und Kulturgeschichte der Stadt Dortmund, May 30–July30, 2000), Munich 2000, pp. 71-85.

19 Ludwig Hevesi, "Karl Mediz – Emilie Pelikan," in: *Zeitschrift für bildende Kunst*, Leipzig 1903, cited after Oswald Oberhuber/Wilfried Seipel/Sophie Geretsegger, *Emilie Mediz-Pelikan 1861–1908. Karl Mediz 1868–1945* (exh. cat., Österreichisches Museum für angewandte Kunst, Vienna, April 24–May 25, 1986, Oberösterreichisches Landesmuseum, Landesgalerie, Linz, April 23–June 22, 1986), Vienna 1986, p. 10.

20 Cf. Mediz-Pelikan's travel journal, "Wien am Naschmarkt gekauft am 29. Jänner 1890." Notes on museum visits and travel experiences in Belgium and the Netherlands May–October 1890, complemented with sketches and description of works in museums, mostly old masters. Part of the estate of Emilie Mediz-Pelikan, Archiv des Belvedere, Vienna. I would like to take this opportunity to thank Katinka Gratzer-Baumgärtner and the team of the Belvedere Research Center for their support during my research.

21 Therese Backhausen, *Menage à trois. Emilie Mediz-Pelikan – Karl Mediz*, thesis, Salzburg 2008, p. 94.

22 The recently published, exemplarily researched, monograph complete with catalog of works makes the strengths of the oeuvre of this painter, who was previously often only mentioned in passing, apparent; Marianne Hussl-Hörmann (ed.), *Theodor von Hörmann. 1840–1895. Monographie mit Verzeichnis der Gemälde*, Vienna 2013.

23 The exhibtion was held from June 21 to August 1889 and has been thoroughly documented in: Jacques Vilain (ed.), *Claude Monet – Auguste Rodin: centenaire de l'exposition de 1889* (exh. cat., Musée Rodin, Paris), Paris 1989.

24 Cahn 2000 (as in note 18), p. 78.

25 Daniel Wildenstein, *Monet. Catalog Raisonné – Werkverzeichnis*, 4 vols., Cologne 1996, here vol. 1, pp. 256–257.

26 Tobias G. Natter, "Tina Blau. Ein Leben im Schatten des Doppeladlers," in: idem/Claus Jesina, *Tina Blau (1845–1916)*, Salzburg 1999, p. 126.

27 Carl Moll, *Emil Jakob Schindler. 1842–1892. Eine Bildnisstudie*, Vienna 1930.

28 Martina Haja, "Emil Jakob Schindler. Künstlerlegende versus Faktografie," in: Frodl/Traeger 2004 (as in note 15), especially p. 266.

29 Martina Haja, "Thema mit Variationen – Schindlers 'Pappelallee bei Plankenberg,'" in: Peter Weninger/Peter Müller (eds.), *Die Schule von Plankenberg. Emil Jakob Schindler und der österreichische Stimmungsimpressionismus* (exh. cat., Niederösterreichisches Landesmuseum, Vienna, May 16–October 13, 1991), Graz 1991, p. 36.

30 Wildenstein 1996 (as in note 25), vol. 2, pp. 256–257, W 682-685.

31 Kramer 2003 (as in note 2), p. 106.

32 Françoise Derré, "Hofmannsthal und die französische Malerei," in: *Hofmannsthal-Forschungen*, vol. 9: *Hofmannsthal und Frankreich*, Freiburg i. B. 1987, p. 27.

33 Derré 1987 (as in note 32).

34 Wildenstein 1996 (as in note 25), vol. 2, pp. 343–356, W 919–958.

35 Hendrik Ziegler, "Emil Heilbut, ein früher Apologet Claude Monets," in: Felix Billeter/Andrea Pophanken (eds.), *Die Moderne und ihre Sammler. Französische Kunst im deutschen Private collection vom Kaiserreich zur Weimarer Republik*, Berlin 2001, pp. 45–46.

36 Berta Szeps-Zuckerkandl, *Ich erlebte fünfzig Jahre Weltgeschichte*, Stockholm 1939, p. 171.

37 Sylvie Patin, "Clémenceau et Monet," in: Christophe Vital, *Manet, Monet, Rodin … Clemenceau et les artistes modernes* (exh. cat., Historial de la Vendée, Les Lucs-sur-Boulogne, December 8, 2013–March 2, 2014), Paris 2013, p. 166.

38 Szeps-Zuckerkandl 1939 (as in note 36), p. 80. Berta's sister Sophie married Paul Clemenceau, Georges' brother.

39 Dietrun Otten, "'Rodin schaut und schweigt'. Rodin in Wien," in: Agnes Husslein-Arco/Stephan Koja (eds.), *Rodin und Wien* (exh. cat., Österreichische Galerie Belvedere, Vienna, October 1, 2010–February 6, 2011), Vienna 2010, pp. 11–29, here p. 26.

40 Paul Rachler/Matthias Boeckl, "Das Medium als Botschaft. Ausstellungen als Verbreitungsmotor von Ideen der Moderne", in: Agnes Husslein-Arco (ed.), *Wien–Paris. Van Gogh, Cézanne und Österreichs Moderne 1880–1960* (exh. cat., Österreichische Galerie Belvedere, Vienna, October 3, 2007–January 13, 2008), Vienna 2007, pp. 11–21.

41 Cf. Huemer 2013 (as in note 8). – idem, *Charles Sedelmeyer (1837–1925). Kunst und Spekulation am Pariser Gemäldemarkt*, dipl. thesis, Vienna 2001.

42 Wildenstein 1996 (as in note 25), vol. 1, p. 86.

43 Wildenstein 1996 (as in note 25), vol. 1, p. 218.
44 Th. Thomas, "Impressionisten in Wien," in: *Neue Freie Presse*, January 11, 1903, p. 9.
45 Cf. the contribution by Peter Peer in this publication.
46 Cf. Huemer 2013 (as in note 8), pp. 24–30.
47 Cf. Kramer 2003 (as in note 2), pp. 90, 122–130.
48 Renate Möhrmann, *Tilla Durieux und Paul Cassirer. Bühnenglück und Liebestod*, Berlin 1997, p. 24.
49 Peter Paret, *Die Berliner Secession. Moderne Kunst und ihre Feinde im Kaiserlichen Deutschland*, Frankfurt/Main 1983, p. 47.
50 He married the actress Tilla Durieux in 1910. She was portrayed by several artists she was friendly with—including Lovis Corinth, Max Oppenheimer, Pierre-Auguste Renoir, and Oskar Kokoschka—during their turbulent marriage. Cf.: Verena Perlhefter, "'Andere halten sich Rennpferde…'. Tilla Durieux – Schauspielerin und meistportraitierte Frau ihrer Zeit", in: Stephan Koja (ed.), *Belvedere. Zeitschrift für bildende Kunst*, vol. 1/2006, pp. 32–45.
51 Tobias G. Natter, *Die Galerie Miethke. Eine Kunsthandlung im Zentrum der Moderne* (exh. cat., Jüdisches Museum der Stadt Wien, November 19, 2003–February 8, 2004), Vienna 2003, p. 118.
52 Cf. Kolja Kramer, "Eine Dreiecksbeziehung für den französischen Impressionismus. Die Impressionisten-Ausstellung 1903 in der Wiener Secession", in: *Belvedere. Zeitschrift für bildende Kunst*, vol. 2/2001, pp. 48–65, here especially pp. 53–56.
53 Cf. especially Werner J. Schweiger, "'Damit Wien einen ernsten Kunstsalon besitze'. Die Galerie Miethke unter besonderer Berücksichtigung von Carl Moll als Organisator", in: *Belvedere. Zeitschrift für bildende Kunst*, vol.2/1998, pp. 64–83 and Natter 2003 (as in note 51), pp. 16–44.
54 Natter 2003 (as in note 51), p. 117. Cf. Wildenstein 1996 (as in note 25), vol. 2, pp. 278–279: *Paul Antoine Graff (Le Père Paul*, W 744) and *Eugénie Graff* (*La Mère Paul*, W 745). The title *Der Koch (The Cook)* has become established at the Belvedere.
55 Wildenstein 1996 (as in note 25), vol. 2, pp. 110–111, W 255.
56 Natter 2003 (as in note 51), p. 117.
57 Natter 2003 (as in note 51), p. 118.
58 Kunstarchiv Werner J. Schweiger, http://www.schoenberg.at/library/index.php/attachments/single/2674 [last accessed on August 3, 2014].
59 Adalbert Franz Seligmann, "Kunstausstellungen," in: *Neue Freie Presse*, no. 16338, February 15, 1910, pp. 9–10. See Kunstarchiv Werner Schweiger, http://www.schoenberg.at/library/index.php/attachments/single/2674 [last accessed on August 3,2014].
60 Marian Bisanz-Prakken, *Heiliger Frühling. Gustav Klimt und die Anfänge der Secession 1895–1905*, Vienna/Munich 1999, p. 165.
61 Franz Ottmann, "Introduction," in: *Die führenden Meister der französischen Kunst im XIX. Jahrhundert. 82. Secessionsausstellung* (exh. cat., Secession, Vienna, March/April 1925), Vienna 1925, p. 5, cited after Kramer 2003 (as in note 2), p. 133. When Ottmann wistfully locates the Viennese artistic scene of 1925 in the European hinterland, he does this in the context of the image of Austria in the years between the wars that was marked by a climate of the (artistic) marginalization of a former empire that had radically shrunk to the size of a small state and its subcutaneous minority complex. This image of Austria also fools Kramer when dealing with the supposedly late reception of Impressionism in Austria; Kramer 2003 (as in note 2), p. 54.
62 In 1994, Winklbauer questioned both; Andrea Winklbauer, "Impressionismus contra Stimmung. Über das Verhältnis der Österreicher zur französischen Landschaftsauffassung – 1868 bis 1903," in: Otmar Rychlik (ed.), *Natürlichere Natur. Österreichische Malerei des Stimmungsrealismus* (exh. cat., Kunsthaus Mürzzuschlag, Mürzzuschlag, summer exhibition, 1994), Mürzzuschlag 1994, p. 19.
63 Gerbert Frodl, "Stimmungsimpressionismus – ein europäisches Phänomen," in: Frodl/Traeger 2004 (as in note 15), p. 9.
64 Natter 1997 (as in note 11), p. 72.
65 On the deconstruction of the term as a "patriotic construct" of the postwar generation, cf. Herbert Giese, "Der gemeinsame Nenner?" (ironically) in: Frodl/Traeger 2004 (as in note 15), pp. 29–30.
66 Stephan Koja, *Claude Monet* (exh. cat., Österreichische Galerie Belvedere, Vienna, March 14–June 16, 1996), Munich 1996.
67 The information on the paintings exhibited is provided by the Durand-Ruel archives (see catalog of exhibitions in Wildenstein 1996 [as in note 25], vol. 4, p. 1016, W 213) and by the Viennese art historian Hans Tietze 1911 (see Huemer 2013 [as in note 8], p.p 152–153.).
68 Wildenstein 1996 (as in note 25), vol. 2, pp. 118–119 and 270, W 277 and W 725.
69 Kramer 2003 (as in note 2), p. 54.
70 Letter from Ernestine von Kirchsberg to Alfred Zoff, 2 May, 1898, cited after Martin Suppan, *Alfred Zoff. Ein österreichischer Stimmungsimpressionist. Seestücke. Marinen*, Vienna 1991, p. 55.
71 Wilhelm Schölermann, "Die Jubiläumsausstellung der Genossenschaft bildender Künstler Wiens," in: *Kunstchronik*, Nr. 25, May 19, 1898, p. 403.
72 According to the catalog, the works were: *The Garden. Parisian Motif* (cat. no. 37); *Eugénie Graff* (*La Mère Paul*, 1882, WV 745); *Snow Landscape* (cat. no. 39); *Luncheon (Le Déjeuner*, 1868, WV 132); *Spring* (*Le printemps*, 1873, WV 273); *Paul Antonie Graff* (*Le Père Paul*, 1882, WV 744); *Rough Sea at Étretat* (*Gros temps à Étretat*, 1883, WV 826); *Luncheon on the Grass* (*Le déjeuner sur l'herbe*, 1865, WV 62). The WV numbers are those in the catalog of works; Cf. Wildenstein 1996 (as in note 25), vols. 2–4. Catalog numbers 37 and 39 are not included in the Wildenstein exhibition listing 1996 (as in note 25), vol. 4, page numbers not given.

73 Cf. the biographies in this volume.

74 *Manet – Monet* (exh. cat., Galerie Miethke, Vienna, May 1910), Vienna 1910, Österreichische Galerie Belvedere, Archive, Vienna, Kat.-Nr. 15–31. According to Wildenstein 1996 (note 25), vol. 4: WV 166, 255, 286, 373, 474, 533, 559, 650, 737, 744, 745, 748, 754, 819, 888, 1118, and 1403.

75 Carl Moll, *Mein Leben*, unpublished typescript, Vienna 1942, p. 136.

76 Cf. Wildenstein 1996 (as in note 25), vols. 2–4, W 520, 793, 1088, 1419a, and 1673. *Französische Impressionisten* (exh. cat., Galerie Arnot, October/November 1911), Vienna 1911, Archiv des Belvedere, Vienna, cat. nos. 5, 6, 4, 11, and 10 (in the order of the mentioned Wildenstein numbers). Catalog numbers 7 and 8, two views of *Vétheuil* and 9, the painting *The Orchard (Le verger)*, have not been identified to date.

77 *Französische Meister* (exh. cat., Galerie Miethke, Vienna, January/February 1912), Vienna 1912, Österreichische Galerie Belvedere, Archive, Vienna, cat. nos. 10, 14, 21. – Wildenstein only mentions two painting here: cf. Wildenstein 1996 (as in note 34), vol. 2, WV 405 and 327.

78 Cf. Wildenstein 1996 (as in note 25), vol. 2, W 826—was already shown in the Secession in1903—, and Wildenstein 1996 (as in note 25), vol. 3, W 1358. See *Ausstellung von Werken moderner Franzosen* (exh. cat., Galerie Arnot, December 1912), Vienna 1912, Bibliothek der Albertina, Vienna, cat. nos. 17 and 18.

79 *Französische Impressionisten* (exh. cat., Galerie Miethke, Vienna, March 1913), Vienna 1913, Österreichische Galerie Belvedere, Archive, Vienna, cat. nos. 23 and 26: the fish still life *Red Mullet/Rougets* (1869, WV 140), and *Country Lane (Chemin creux*, 1873, WV 288). – *Französische Meister* (exh. cat., Galerie Miethke, Vienna, December 1913/January 1914), Vienna 1913, Österreichische Galerie Belvedere, Archive, Vienna, cat. nos. 27: *Farm Courtyard* (*Cour de ferme,* 1878, WV 494).

80 Wildenstein 1996 (as in note 25), vol. 4, p. 1024: Wildenstein mentions *The Church in Vétheuil* (*L'Église de Vétheuil*, 1878, W 474) and *The Village of Lavacourt* (*Le village de Lavacourt*, 1878, W 501) with a question mark because they cannot be unambiguously identified. See *Die führenden Meister der französischen Kunst im Neunzehnten Jahrhundert* (exh. cat., Secession, March/April), Vienna 1915, Österreichische Galerie Belvedere, Archive, Vienna, cat. nos. 35, 41, and 70.

81 Jeroen V. van Heerde, "Das k. k. Wandermuseum: Ein sozial- und ethnischpolitisches Kunstunternehmen in Österreich um 1900," in: Péter Hanák/Waltraud Heindl/Stefan Malfèr/Éva Somogyi (eds.), *Kultur und Politik. Österreich und Ungarn*, Vienna/Cologne/Weimar 1994, pp. 92–117.

82 Wildenstein 1996 (as in note 25), vol. 2, p. 279, W 748

83 Wildenstein 1996 (as in note 25), vol. 4, pp. 742–743, W 1650.

84 Wildenstein 1996 (as in note 25), vol. 4, pp. 1025 and 1028. – Cf. also Günther Dankl, "'… über das Chaos des Augenblicks hinausführende Denkanstösse …' (Maurice Besset). Zur Rezeption der österreichischen Kunst in Österreich 1945 bis 1960," in: Patrick Werkner (ed.), *Kunst in Österreich 1945–1995. Symposion der Hochschule für angewandte Kunst in Wien*, Vienna 1996, pp. 64–83. – *Tirol – Frankreich. 1946–1960. Spurensicherung einer Begegnung* (exh. cat., Tiroler Landesmuseum Ferdinandeum, Innsbruck, September 12–October 6, 1991), Innsbruck 1991.

85 These were partially taken over from other exhibitions. It would be necessary to study Monet's impact on the Hungarian, Czech and Polish artistic world individually as they would make other, or at least wider, networks accessible than those analyzed here.

86 Wildenstein 1996 (as in note 25), vol. 4, pp. 1018–1022. Paintings by Monet were shown in Berlin in: 1882, 1883, 1896, 1900, 1901, 1902, 1903, 1904, 1905, 1906¸ 1907, 1908, 1909, 1910, 1911, 1912, 1913, 1914, 1916, 1924, 1925, 1927, 1928, 1930, in Dresden: 1897, 1899, 1901, 1902, 1904, 1909, 1914, 1926.

87 According to Wildenstein, on each of two previous occasions, only two paintings by Monet had been shown in Berlin (in 1882 and 1883). Cf. Wildenstein 1996 (as in note 34), vol. 4, pp. 1016–1017. – Ziegler 2001 (as in note 35), p. 47. – All of the catalogs of the Munich Glass Palace are available in digital form at: http://www.bayerische-landesbibliothek-online.de/glaspalast (last accessed on August 21, 2014).

88 Cf. Gustave Geffroy, *Claude Monet, sa vie, son temps, son oeuvre*, Paris 1922.

89 A fundamental analysis of the French press is provided in: Steven Z. Levine, *Monet and His Critics*, New York/London 1976.

90 Cf. Huemer 2013 (as in note 8), p. 7. – Harrison C. White/Cynthia A. White, *Canvases and Careers. Institutional Change in the French Painting World*, New York 1965.

91 *Galerie Durand-Ruel: recueil d'estampes gravées à l'eau-forte*, with a foreword by Armand Silvestre, Paris 1873.

92 The Belvedere Research Center is currently running the—unfortunately time-limited—project: *Die Rezeption des österreichischen und internationalen Kunstgeschehens in der österreichischen Tageszeitung* Neue Freie Presse *von 1901 bis 1910.*

93 Lucie Merhautová/Kurt Ifkovits (eds.), *Die Wiener Wochenschrift Die Zeit (1894–1904) und die zentraleuropäische Moderne. Studien – Dokumente*, Prague 2013.

94 Here, I would like to sincerely thank Paul Rachler, Künstlerhaus-Archiv Vienna, for his exceptional support and for providing information on the holdings of the libraries of the Künstlerhaus and Secession. It is difficult to reconstruct the history of the Künstlerhaus Library seeing that many old journals have been added as donations and are therefore not part of the "contemporary" stocks. After the first examination in the archives of the Künstlerhaus, the following media must be mentioned as being especially significant for the reception of Impressionism: *Gazette des beaux-arts* and, at least, *Pan*. However, it can be assumed that, at the time, the most important German, French, etc., journals were being purchased. The Secession suffered serious losses in the Second World War. In addition, its holdings only began in 1896/97. The following are available today: *Pan*, *Das Interieur*, *Die Zeit*, *The Studio*, *Kunst und Handwerk*, *Deutsche Kunst und Dekoration*, *Art et Decoration*, *The Artist*, *Dekorative Kunst*, *Die Insel*, *Jahrbuch der bildenden Kunst*, and individual numbers of *Mercure de France*, *L'art*

vivant, *La nouvelle revue française*. Without taking into account possible losses during wartime and for other reasons, as well as acquisition history, the libraries of the Vienna Academy and Applied Arts School (today. University of Applied Arts, Vienna) present a similar picture: along with other journals, their holdings also include *Gazette des beaux-arts*, the *Kunstchronik*, *Die Kunst für Alle*, *Pan*, *Das Interieur*, *Die Kunst* (= *Deutsche Kunst und Dekoration*).

95 Stephan Koja (ed.), *Gustav Klimt. Landschaften* (exh. cat., Österreichische Galerie Belvedere, Vienna, October 23, 2002–February 23, 2003), Munich [et al.], 2002, p. 38.

96 Cf. Maria Rennhofer, *Kunstzeitschriften der Jahrhundertwende in Deutschland und Österreich*, Vienna/Munich 1987.

97 Bahr 2004 (as in note 4), p. 233. The text was published in three installments in *Der Kunstwart*, nos. 20, 22 and 23, 1889.

98 Bahr 2004 (as in note 4), p. 244. A total of three paintings by Monet were shown at the 1889 World's Fair.

99 Richard Gaul, "Pariser Ausstellungen," in: *Kunstchronik*, no. 38, June 27, 1889, p. 596.

100 Felix Billeter/Andrea Pophanken, "Die französische Moderne und ihre deutschen Sammler," in: idem. 2001 (as in note 35), p. 15.

101 Friedrich Pecht, "Die deutsche und die französische Bauernmalerei," in: *Internationale Ausstellungs-Zeitung: Beilage der Neuen Freien Presse*, June 29, 1873, cited after Huemer 2013 (as in note 8), p. 22, note 42.

102 August Schaeffer, "Foreword," in: *Originalgemälde moderner Meister aus der Kollektion Ch. Sedelmeyer – Paris* [...], Vienna 1907, cited after Huemer 2013 (as in note 41), p. 38.

103 Cf. Billeter/Pophanken 2001 (as in note 35).

104 Cited after Huemer 2013 (as in note 8), p. 93, note 43.

105 Cited after Huemer 2013 (as in note 8), p. 92, note 42.

106 Cited after Huemer 2013 (as in note 8), p. 93, note 44.

107 Cited after Huemer 2013 (as in note 8), p. 152, note 54.

108 Cited after Huemer 2013 (as in note 8), p. 153, note 57.

109 Levine 1976 (as in note 89), pp. 27 and 32.

110 Levine 1976 (as in note 89), p. 43.

111 In 1873, Silvestre still wrote cautiously critically about Monet in an advertising catalog for Durand-Ruel. Cf. *Galerie Durand-Ruel* 1873 (as in note 91). – Levine 1976 (as in note 89), p. 47.

112 Levine 1976 (as in note 89), p. 48.

113 By analogy, mention should be made of a critique by Max Nordau, the conservative Paris correspondent of the *Neue Freie Presse*, whose theories on "degeneration" were the subject of heated discussion in artistic circles. It was written in reaction to an article by Carl Moll publicizing the coming Impressionism exhibition in 1903 in which he determined a change of position vis-à-vis the once disdained artists. Nordau replied taking Manet's *Olympia* as an example, "The truth is that the taste for Manet has not changed in the least. People still find the *Olympia* just as disgusting as they did thirty years ago but they no longer do it with raised voices and swollen vocal chords because they do not even stop to look at her moldy ugliness." See Carl Moll, "Die öffentliche Meinung über Werke der Kunst," in: *Neue Freie Presse*, March 31, 1901, p. 6. I would like to take this opportunity to thank Stefan Lehner, Belvedere Research Center, for his support in my press research. – Max Nordau, "Kunstwerke und Kunsturtheile,", in: *Neue Freie Presse*, April 13, 1901, pp. 1–4 – Cf. idem, *Entartung*, Berlin 1892/93.

114 Wildenstein 1996 (as in note 25), vol. 1, from p. 151. – Levine 1976 (as in note 89), especially Chapter II.

115 On the collaboration between Sedelmeyer and Munkácsy, see Huemer 2013 (as in note 8), pp. 44–60.

116 Huemer 2013 (as in note 8), p. 171. – On Zuckerkandl and Clemenceau: Armelle Weirich, "Berta Zuckerkandl-Szeps ou l'importance de l'amitié d'une femme et d'une critique d'art," in: Vital 2013 (as in note 37), pp. 44–47. – On Zuckerkandl in general: Michael Schulte, *Berta Zuckerkandl: Salonière, Journalistin, Geheimdiplomatin*, Zurich 2006. – Helga Peham, *Die Salonièren und die Salons in Wien. 200 Jahre Geschichte einer besonderen Institution*, Vienna/Graz/Klagenfurt 2014, pp. 191–225.

IN THE LIGHT OF IMPRESSIONISM

The Oeuvre of Austrian Pictorialist Photographers

Dominique de Font-Réaulx

In 1891, in his catalog preface for the art photography exhibition organised by the Vienna Amateur Photographers' Club in the Museum of Applied Arts, Vienna (Österreichisches Museum für Kunst und Gewerbe), Jacob von Falke underlined the parallels between the photographs and the work of Impressionist painters.[1] He focused on the similarities between how the human eye and the camera function, namely by picking out objects selected by talented photographers or painters in order to depict them in the light of their own vision. The 1891 International Exhibition, the second initiated by the club, following on from the initial show in 1888, aimed to present photography as a fully-fledged form of artistic expression; the initiative for the show came from a group of amateur photographers, whose patron was the Archduchess Maria Theresia. As Christian Joschke notes, the Viennese members of the Amateur Photographers Club, founded in 1886 by members of the Vienna Photographic Society, viewed their association's socialized framing of photography as a leisure-time activity as a means to ensure artistic recognition, in contrast to professional photographers working in commercial studios.[2]

THE RAPID DEVELOPMENT OF PHOTOGRAPHY IN VIENNA

Photography, a new invention, flourished and evolved rapidly in Vienna. Thanks to François Arago, news of Daguerre's work had spread from 1839 on, underpinned by daguerreotypes sent by the inventor to major figures in the Austro-Hungarian Empire in order to publicise his process. For example, he gave one of his beautiful daguerreotype still lives to Ambassador Antal Apponyi *(Still Life with Jupiter [Nature morte au Jupiter],* 1839, now in the National Museum of Science and Technology, Budapest*)*; it is also recorded that in May and June 1839 Apponyi had sent Klemens von Metternich, Austrian Minister of Foreign Affairs, two daguerreotypes, adding a further work to the gift from Daguerre, with Daguerre sending Metternich *Still Life with Jupiter Tonans (Nature morte avec Jupiter Tonans)* (now in the National Technical Museum, Prague). Metternich put these two photographs on display in Vienna from August 25, 1839; they were subsequently exhibited in the Imperial and Royal Academy of Fine Arts in the former St. Anna convent.[3] In late 1839, a number of prominent Viennese figures from artistic and scientific circles combined forces to found a club of photographic pioneers, the *Fürstenhofrunde*, selecting this name as a link to the venue for their meetings. The Photographische Gesellschaft was founded in Vienna in 1861. As demonstrated by the International Photographic Exhibitions held in the city in 1888 and 1891, Vienna subsequently became one of the most vibrant centers of Pictorialism, against the backdrop of the painting-driven Vienna Secession. From 1894 to 1898, the Camera Club published a prestigious journal, which presented works by photographers from its ranks, *Wiener Photographische Blätter.*[4] In 1897, three of the club's most talented members, Hugo Henneberg (1863-1918), Heinrich Kühn (1866-1944), and Hans Watzek (1848-1903) founded Das Kleeblatt (The Cloverleaf) with a view to experimenting with the new photographic printing techniques, in particular the gum bichromate method developed by French Pictorialist photographer, Robert Demachy.[5]

IMPRESSIONISM AS AN AESTHETIC REFERENCE

The preface to the catalog for the 16th Viennese Secession exhibition, "The Development of Impressionism in Painting and Sculpture (Entwicklung des Impressionismus in Malerei und Plastik)," picked up on and developed the comparison between Impres-

Fig. 1
HEINRICH KÜHN
The Kühn Siblings in the Meadow, 1912
ÖNB, Vienna

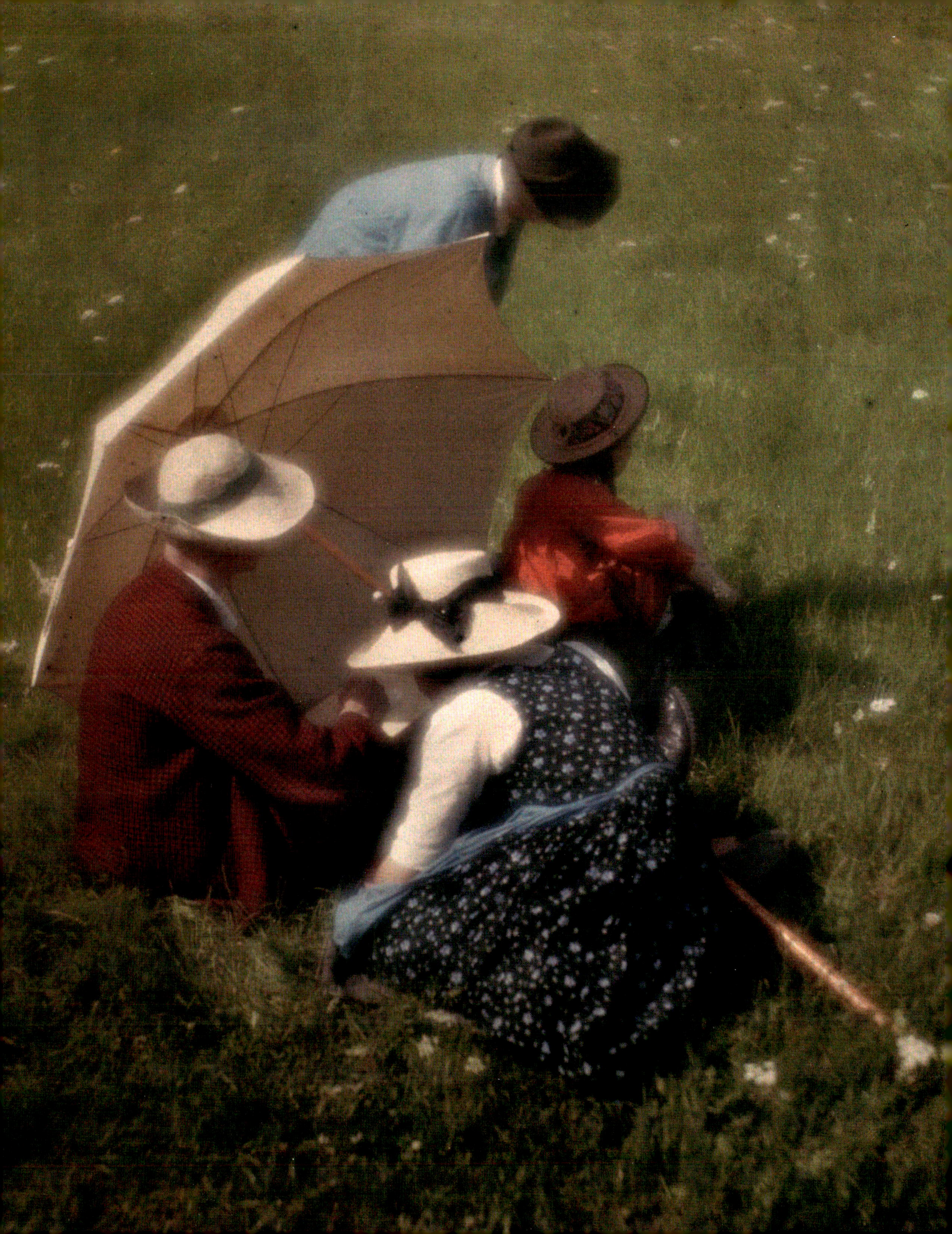

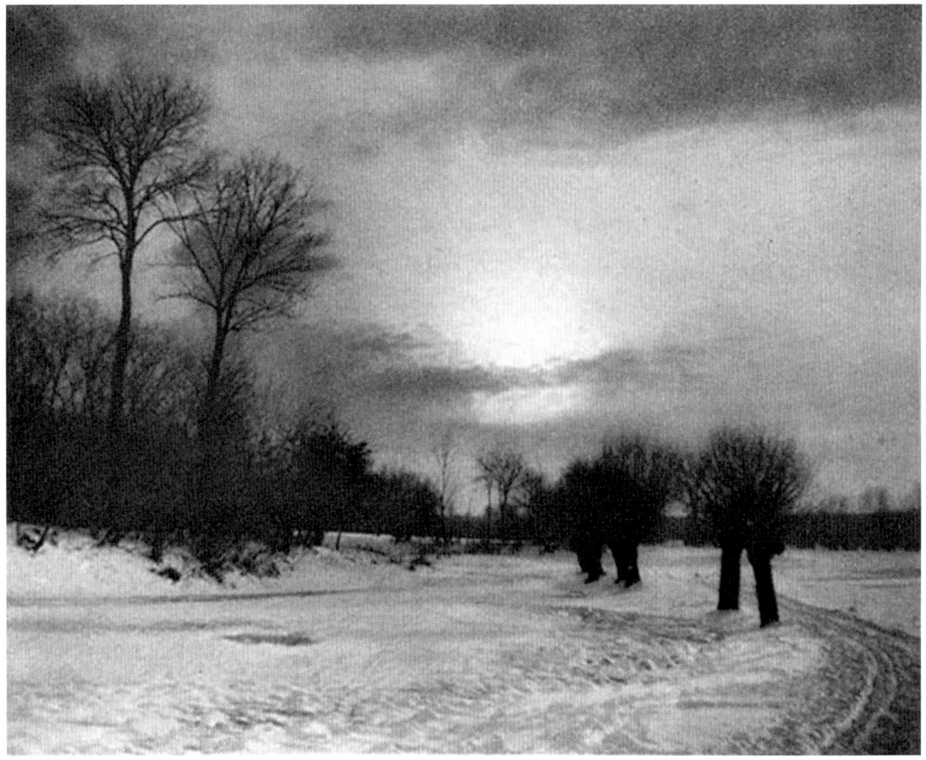

Fig. 3
JULIUS STRAKOSCH
End of the Day (Fin du jour), published in *Wiener Photographische Blätter*, 1895

Fig. 2
HEINRICH KÜHN
Outgoing Boat, 1898, published in *Camera Work*, January 1900

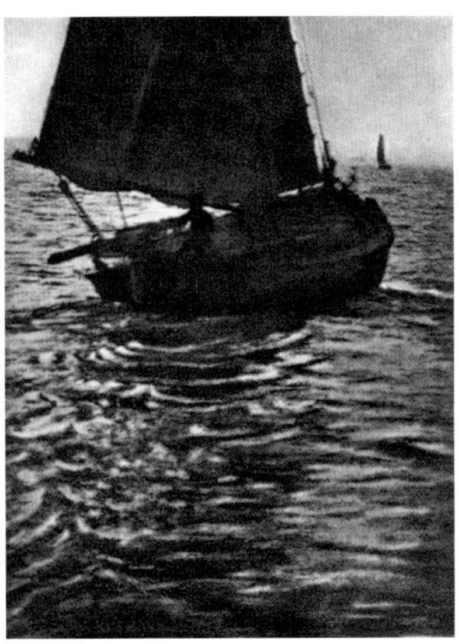

sionism and the art of photography.[6] It was a highly ambitious show; for the first time, art by Titian and El Greco was brought together in one space with works by artists who had taken part in the Impressionist exhibitions between 1874 and 1889 and by Neo-Impressionist artists, including the Nabis. "Impressionism aims to reproduce the appearance of things, the impression they produce upon the trained eye. The Impressionists therefore had above all to address the functioning of the human eye, how retinal images are generated. The construction of the human eye is based on principles akin to those used in a camera."[7] This carefully—chosen gaze provided an opportunity to produce the best effects by rendering only a portion of what was depicted in clear, sharp focus—"only one part of the image can and should be reproduced entirely in focus." The use of photographic vocabulary—"lens," "focus"—einforced the comparison. The authors of the preface—the organizers of the exhibition—produced a very interesting combination of the imperatives of realism—"the appearance of things"—and artistic subjectivity; Impressionism could not actually be based on some absolute impression but could draw only on relative impressions linked to the artist's own temperament—"not absolute but only relative impressions." Although no photographs were shown at this exhibition, the photographic paradigm of representation of the real underpinned the organizers' aesthetic reflections. By writing about "the appearance of things," the authors, perhaps unconsciously, evoked the terms Jacques-Louis-Mandé Daguerre used in his 1838 text, which sought to garner recognition for his invention—"the images form of their own accord in the camera obscura."[8]

A DISTINCTIVE AUSTRIAN VISION

On the cusp of the nineteenth and twentieth centuries, the Austrian photographers and painters most eager to obtain recognition for their creative output highlighted Impressionism as an aesthetic reference point. This kind of choice was unprecedented. As a matter of fact, during the same period Pictorialist photographers and French Symbolist painters distanced themselves from Impressionist works, viewing them as insufficiently faithful to reality. In 1899 Robert de la Sizeranne (1866–1932) published a work based on his visit to the 1896 Art Photography Exhibition in Paris, *La Photographie est-elle un art?*. Like the catalog of the 1891 International Art Photography Exhibition in Vienna, his work aimed to win recognition for photography as a form of artistic expression, on an equal footing with painting. La Sizeranne abhorred Impressionist paintings that lacked an idea, an artwork's principal quality in his view; he exhorted Pictorialist photographers to identify suitable models by looking at works by Italian, Flemish, or Dutch Old Masters, or by rediscovering the narrative symbolism of the British Pre-Raphaelites.[9] The singularity of the Austrian position stemmed from the way in which the Impressionist movement was presented in Vienna. In contrast, particularly to France, rather than underlining Impressionist painters' practice of painting directly from motifs in the open air, which, at least apparently, implied scrupulous study of the real world, Austrian artistic opinion underscored the originality of the Impressionist gaze and the subjectivity of impressions. The notion of a sensitive rendering of a particular atmosphere thus took center stage. The Impressionists' skill in deploying light and color, aiming not at an objective depiction of the landscape but instead portraying how the artists perceived and experienced nature, made them well-suited to

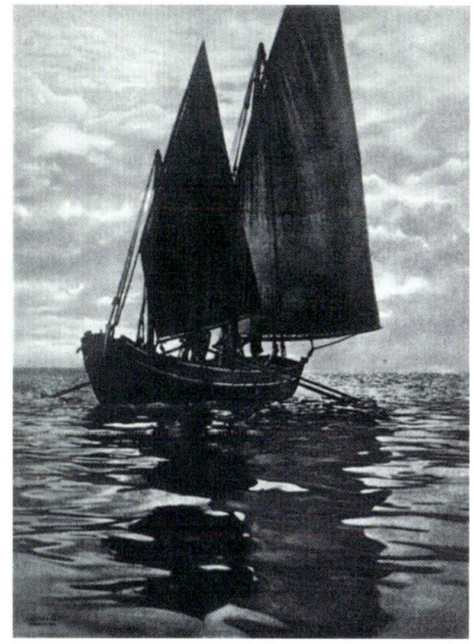

Fig. 4
HUGO HENNEBERG
Calm Sea, 1899
Private collection

Fig. 5
HUGO HENNEBERG
After Sunset, 1898
Private collection

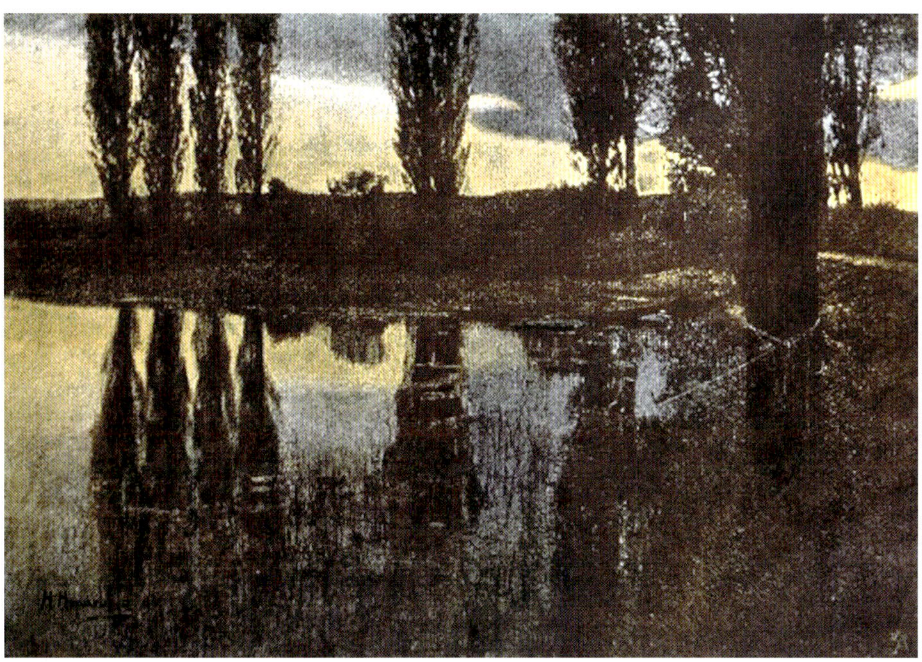

become models for painters looking to express themselves, and for photographers seeking artistic recognition.

Works by Claude Monet were given pride of place in the 1903 exhibition in which eight paintings were shown. These works made it possible to demonstrate the various facets of the French painter's art: bourgeois genre scenes, portraits, landscapes (see the list on pp. 157, 158). It also highlighted his talent, affording those who viewed his paintings an unambiguous impression of his personal vision. Monet's work was already well-known and appreciated in Vienna, thanks to the exhibitions organized by his dealers in Paris, London, and New York. His artistic universe, rooted in observation of nature and representation of contemporary bourgeois society, inevitably proved alluring for Austrian amateur photographers, with their backgrounds in Viennese high society.

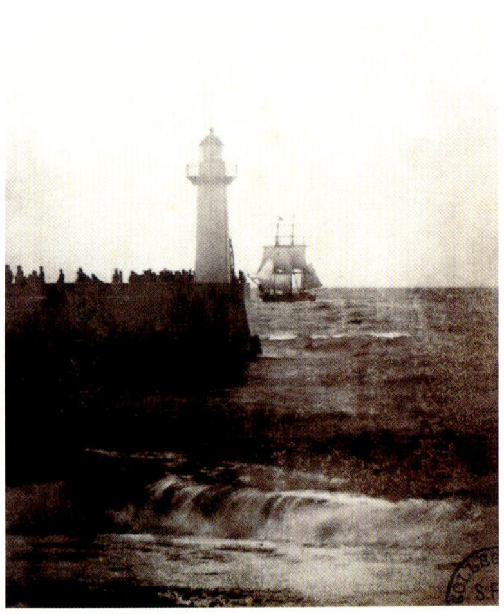

Fig. 6
AUGUSTE AUTIN
The Jetty in the Port of Le Havre, 1861
Société française de photographie, Paris

CLAUDE MONET AND PHOTOGRAPHIC IMAGES

The aesthetic reference was crucial. The Impressionist painter's interest in the shifting light, as well as in the changing look of the landscape due to the play of the weather and different times of day, proved highly attractive to photographers. Monet's paintings offered an opportunity for a renaissance in how the landscape was viewed and represented. Even before the first series, in the early 1880s, his attachment to the most subtle inflections of color and atmosphere revealed how much that things that seemed unchanging and identical—the landscape seen from his window or from his terrace—were in a constant process of renewal, allowing for as many distinct vistas as there are hours of the day or days of the year. Interestingly, it was doubtless also careful observation of photographs, from the 1860s on, that underpinned Monet's focus on how the landscape changed with the passage of time. The artist, born in 1840, belonged to the first generation to have grown up with photography; like his contemporaries, he therefore perceived it as being entirely self-evident, a well-established way of representing reality. Having spent his youth in Le Havre where, from 1854 on, photography had enjoyed artistic recognition alongside painting thanks to the influence of photographers Louis-Cyrus Macaire (1807–1871) and Jean-Victor Macaire-Warnod (1812–1892), Monet was certainly aware of the photographic experiments conducted by several photographers in Le Havre, including the Macaire brothers and Auguste Autin (1809–1889), who aimed to develop snapshots that would make it possible to take the most minute movements into account.[10] It was a utopian quest. The fixed image had no choice but to produce "freeze-frame" images. These frozen images afforded scope to create new forms and gave rise to the notion of the series by associating images with precise weather conditions and a specific time of day. Photography thus introduced a new relationship to time, linking duration and representation. The young Claude Monet, who, like Autin, was from Le Havre, probably saw the latter's prints. The fragile silhouettes tossed by the wind, which Monet painted, around 1866, in a work depicting the jetty in his birthplace, evoked the slightly blurred shadows of the strollers Autin photographed on the landing-stage at the same port.[11] A similar connection between a photograph by Macaire-Warnod and a painting by Monet has been pointed out by Stephan Koja (see fig. p. 26).

Similarly, the silhouettes of boats, simultaneously fragile and present, with their sails edged in black like butterflies, such as those found in photographic seascapes by Gustave

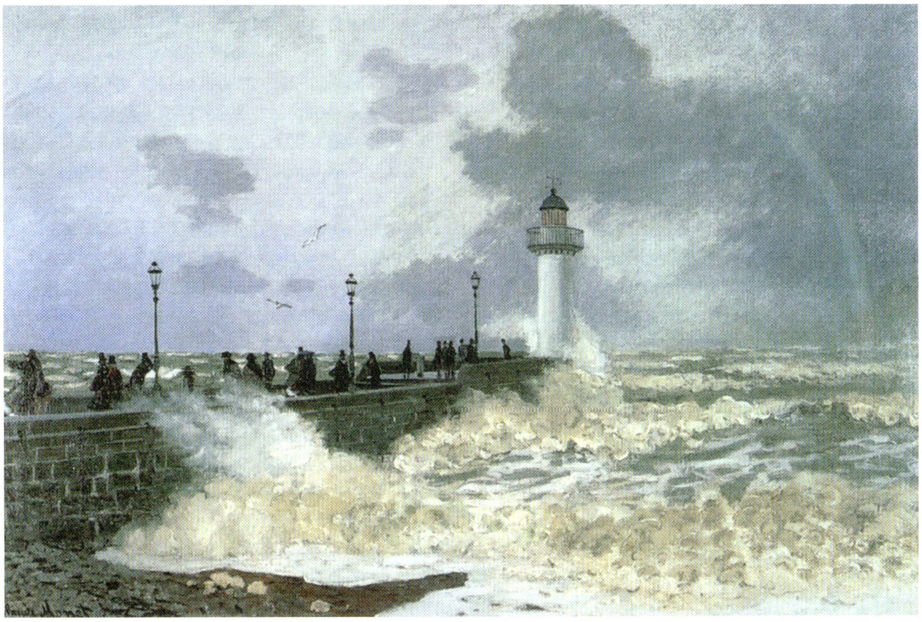

Fig. 7
CLAUDE MONET
The Jetty at Le Havre, 1868
Private collection

Le Gray (1820–1884) and Eugène Colliau (who worked in Paris between 1859 and 1864), certainly numbered among the artist's intellectual and visual points of reference. They fed into his own representations of Sainte-Adresse beach, which Le Gray had photographed around 1856. The photographic image thus offered a new model of representation, supplementing the young painter's pictorial references—Dutch painting, of course, the art of Corot, Courbet, and Delacroix, or the first Japanese images that had begun to circulate outside the country during the Meiji era. Kühn certainly did not know about these opportunities, which gave rise to Monet's sense of affinity with photography; however, Kühn, an acutely perceptive aficionado of artistic creation, did perhaps sense this link. He had a keen interest in all the painterly innovations of his era; the aesthetic references of his contemporaries fed into his photographic work.[12] Kühn's very beautiful 1898 print—*Das auslaufende Boot*—reveals the Austrian photographer's interest in Monet's seascapes, with their distinctive framing choices.

AUTOCHROME PRINTS, AN IMPRESSIONIST INVENTION?

Monet's vibrant brushwork was most certainly a source of inspiration for members of Das Kleeblatt who began to use gum bichromate. Applied by brush, it afforded scope to create effects similar to those produced by applying paint to canvas; in addition, it allowed photographic prints to acquire materiality, just like Impressionist paintings. Growing out of his subjective, masterful observation of reality, Monet's deft rendering of quivering light exerted a strong pull on Viennese photographers, Heinrich Kühn in particular. Initiated in 1907 by Alfred Stieglitz (1864–1946) into the art of the autochrome process, which was developed by the Lumière brothers in 1904 and patented in 1907, Kühn doubtless appreciated the scope this first commercialised color process offered to recreate the magical colors of Monet's canvases on photographic plates. As it called for long exposures, the autochrome print moved away from the brevity of the snapshot and its frozen movements. It meant that compositions once again had to be carefully prepared, picking up on a tradition that had shaped the first daguerreotypes, with compositional styles drawing on those found in painting. The subject therefore had to exist prior to the act of photographing; photographers had to choose and modulate the subject-matter, just as painters do.

In its very conception—a juxtaposition of starch grains of different colors, intimately related yet not merging together, the autochrome was an homage to the color theory of French chemist Eugène Chevreul (1786–1899) who attracted Delacroix's attention in the 1830s and by his work inspired Impressionist painters' studies on color and light. The Lumière brothers' invention thus referenced the luminosity of Impressionism.[13] Léon Gimpel (1878–1948), one of the photographers with the greatest mastery of this new technique, certainly had this parallel in mind when he wrote the following passage in his memoirs, "An artist who was a painter (even if he were a Pointillist!) would never be able to achieve what the autochrome has given me in this respect: the seventy million grains of colored starch covering the plates created an extraordinary effect (particularly when projected as slides), awaking the enthusiasm of a huge audience..." [14] For many photographers, the autochrome was thus the process that allowed virtuoso work inspired by painterly sources to come into its own, drawing on the most colorful subject matter possible. Representations of gardens thus became a topos of the art of the autochrome. Monet's garden in Giverny, a painter's garden and a garden for painting, was the most highly developed, subtle example. Etienne Clémentel (1864–1936), a French politician close to Georges Clémenceau and a friend of the painter, frequently photographed him on the paths and by the ponds of his garden, with their stunning color palette echoing his canvases. When Monet died, *L'Illustration* chose to supplement the artist's obituary with a reproduction of a striking autochrome print depicting the artist by the lily pond. Kühn gave an unusual interpretation of the art of the autochrome: he added the subtle effects of blurring to a sound mastery of pictorial composition. Consequently, for example in the very beautiful *Miss Mary and Lotte* (after 1907), the implicit reference to an Impressionist subject—two women in a garden—was mirrored in a visual effect, the sense of depth created by the starch layer seeming to be revealed, thanks to the blurred image, in a mode that echoed Monet's brushwork in his canvases.[15]

THE SOCIAL DIMENSION OF RECOGNITION

This aesthetic interest was paralleled by a social dimension; as Christian Joschke notes, most of the founders of the Vienna club—as was the case in other European clubs, but more consistently in the capital of the Austro-Hungarian Empire—belonged to a generation, born in the 1850s, that had assimilated scientific and technical references and shared a desire to see their principal cultural references escape from the aura of the illegitimacy that tainted technical knowledge, to which photography was assimilated. For them, the club, a public space rooted in civil society rather than in official institutions, seemed to be the most appropriate means to play an active role in constructing their own cultural references. Photography, straddling the border between the arts and the sciences, was the ideal medium to implement these shared reflections. It tapped into

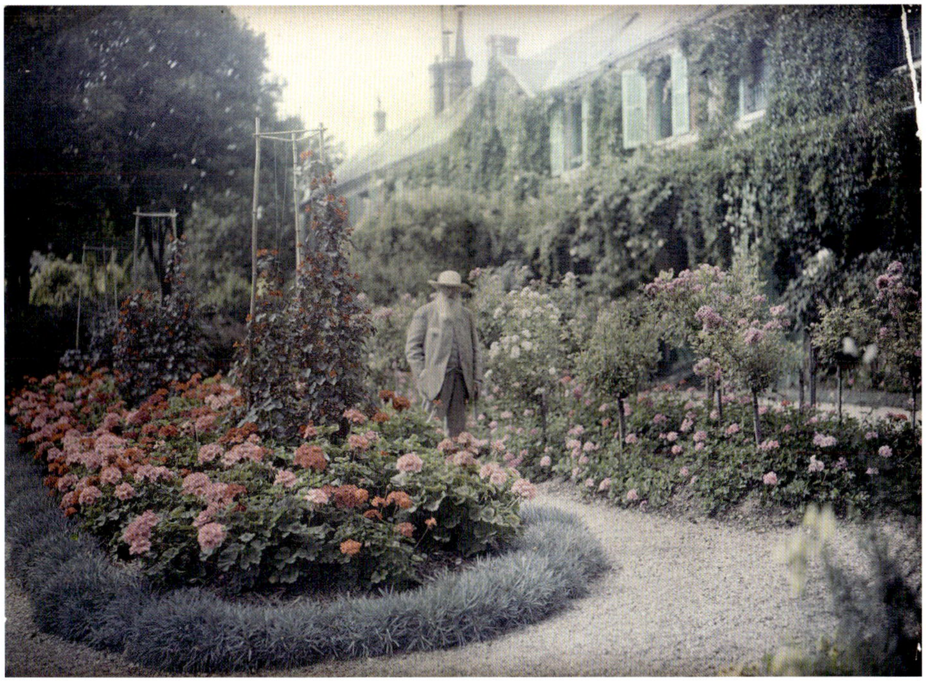

Fig. 8
ANONYMOUS OR LÉON GIMPEL
Claude Monet in his Garden in Giverny, 1921
Musée d'Orsay, Paris

practical know-how, giving these amateur photographers a sense of sharing a certain material knowledge and culture. It was also the most untainted medium, well-fitted to receive the iconographic, scientific, aesthetic, and philosophical symbols of modern culture, capable of freeing itself from old institutions, from academicism, from the traditional processes of cultural legitimacy. At the heart of these photography clubs, these societies of enlightened amateurs, these "enlightened" members of the bourgeoisie could discuss the scientific and aesthetic issues at stake in photography and thus subtly intertwine their social strategies and aesthetic discourses.[16]

This kind of attitude echoed the desire for recognition over and above the frame of institutional and commercial circles that motivated the young independent painters who showed their works in photographer Félix Nadar's former studio on Boulevard des Capucines in Paris in 1874. Adopting the term coined in Louis Leroy's acerbic critique, these painters became *Impressionists*. Despite their disagreements and despite their wide range of different talents, they succeeded in gaining recognition for a new form of painterly creation, which, more than a century later, still stands for the artistic and social expression of the late 19th century. The modern society painted by Monet and the other Impressionists was indeed a bourgeois middle-class, cultivated but without airs and graces; and urban society, in which nature—in its nearby, accessible manifestations, such as along the banks of the Seine, on the coasts of Normandy and Brittany, and indeed in the artists' gardens—afforded a wealth of motifs for their art. Impressionism also entailed painting that depicted particular subjects; the fact that the artists selected sub-

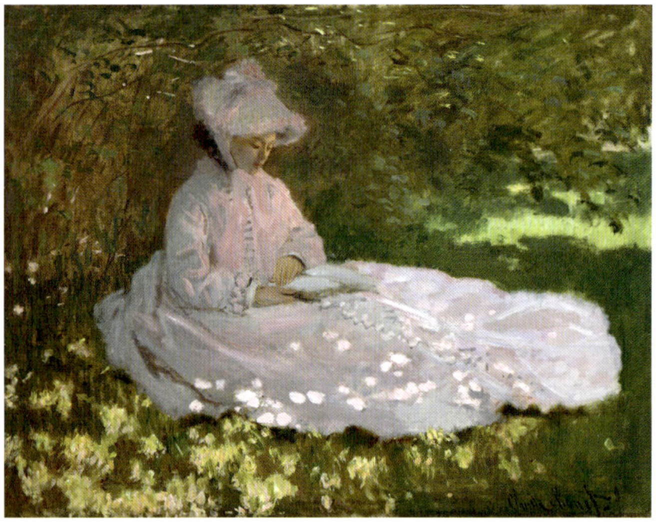

Fig. 9
CLAUDE MONET
The Reader (Camille reading), 1872
The Walters Art Museum, Baltimore

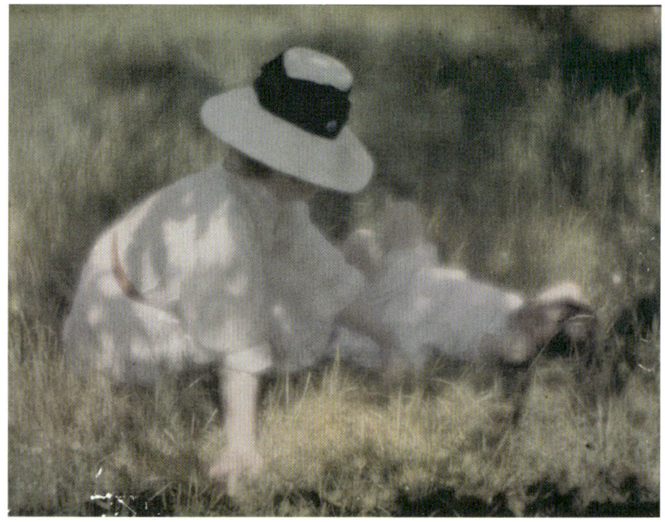

Fig. 10
HEINRICH KÜHN
Miss Mary and Lotte, after 1907
ÖNB, Vienna

ject matter that extended beyond mythological or religious traditions has sometimes, in the eyes of historiography with its rapid appraisals, meant that this aspect has been forgotten. Women in the garden, children playing, passers-by in Paris, transformations of the landscape as the winter ice melted: a plethora of references to the world in which they existed simultaneously as protagonists and as painters.[17] Allusions by Viennese Pictorialist photographers and the Secession artists to Impressionism constitute a twofold reference to the paintings' delicate beauty and to the social and cultural affirmation of an urban bourgeoisie seeking to make their mark aesthetically and socially.

1 The Vienna Amateur Photographers Club was founded on March 31, 1887; in 1893 it became the Camera Club of Vienna.

2 Christian Joschke, "Logiques de l'amateurisme et changement culture, la photographie en Allemagne et en Autriche," in: *La photographie pictorialiste en Europe, 1888-1918,* Cherbourg/Rennes, Le Point du jour/Musée des beaux-arts de Rennes, pp. 106–113. The exhibition was held in spring 1891; it showed works by Austrian, German, Belgian, British, American and Italian photographers. The catalog included thirty-seven photogravures. Cf. Christian Joschke, *Photographie amateur et société dans l'Allemagne de Guillaume II (1888–1914),* Dijon, Presses du réel, 2013.

3 Stephen Pinson, *Speculating Daguerre, Art and Enterprise in the Work of L.J.M. Daguerre,* Chicago, London, The University of Chicago Press, 2012, pp. 205–206. On the spread of the invention of daguerreotypes in Vienna, see Maren Gröning and Monika Faber, *Inkunabeln einer neuen Zeit, Pioniere der Daguerreotypie in Österreich, 1839–1860,* Vienna, Albertina, 2006.

4 See Christine Kühn, *Kunstfotografie um 1900. Die Sammlung Fritz Matthies-Masuren 1873-1938,* Berlin 2003; Astrid Lechner, *Der Wiener Camera-Club und die Kunstfotografie um 1900. Diss., Vienna 2005.*

5 Monika Faber, Andreas Gruber, Françoise Heilbrun, Astrid Mahler, Anne Tucker, *Heinrich Kühn, A la recherche de la photographie parfaite,* Paris, Vienne, Hatje Cantz/Musée d'Orsay, 2010. The art lover and collector Matthies-Masuren published, in folio, a very lovely ensemble bringing together experiments with the gum bichromate

method by the three Kleeblatt photographers: Frietz Matthies-Masuren, *Gummidrucke von Hugo Henneberg, Wien, Heinrich Kühn, Innsbruck, Hans Watzek, Wien*, 1902. Cf.: Christine Kühn, *Kunstphotographie um 1900: die Sammlung Fritz Matthies-Masuren, 1873–1938,* Berlin, Kunstbibliothek, 2003.

6 XVI. Ausstellung der Vereinigung Bildender Künstler Österreichs Secession, Vienna, January–February 1903.

7 Ibid., pp. 14–15.

8 See Quentin Bajac and Dominique de Font-Réaulx (eds.), *Le daguerréotype français, un objet photographique,* Paris, Réunion des musées nationaux, 2003. Daguerre's text is reproduced in its entirety in the anthology of texts at the end of the catalog.

9 Robert de La Sizeranne, *La Photographie est-elle un art?*, La Rochelle, Rumeurs des Âges, 2003. The work was first printed in *La Revue des deux mondes* in 1897, and was subsequently re-published by Hachette, with illustrations, in Paris in 1899.

10 Cf. Carole McNamara, *The Lens of Impressionism: photography and painting along the Normandy coast, 1850–1874,* Ann Arbor, University of Michigan of Art, 2009; Sylvain Amic (ed.), *Eblouissants reflets, cent chefs-d'oeuvre impressionnistes,* Rouen, Musée des beaux-arts, 2013.

11 Cf. Dominique de Font-Réaulx, "Les révolutions du paysage," in: *Peinture et photographie, les enjeux d'une rencontre,* Paris, Flammarion, 2012, p. 90.

12 Cf. Patrick Daum, "Unité et diversité du pictorialisme en Europe," in: *La photographie pictorialiste en Europe, 1888–1918*, ibid., pp. 14–18.

13 Antonin Personnaz (1855-1936), painter, friend of Monet and collector—part of his collection is now in the Musée d'Orsay—was a talented early 20th century autochromist; many of his works are now in the collection of the Cinémathèque de la Ville de Paris.

14 Léon Gimpel, *Quarante ans de souvenirs photographiques,* Collection of the Société française de photographie. Cf. on Gimpel: Thierry Gervais, Dominique de Font-Réaulx, *Léon Gimpel, les audaces d'un photographe,* Paris, Musée d'Orsay/Cinq Continents, 2008.

15 Cf. the article by Stephan Koja in this book, pp. 36–103, here p. 79.

16 Christian Joschke, p. 119. Joschke's analysis is remarkably perceptive.

17 The exhibition organized by Vincent Pomarède at the Musée des beaux-arts de Lyon in 2002, drawing a parallel between Impressionist painting and the emerging cinematograph of Auguste and Louis Lumière—who conceived the autochrome, which is no coincidence—clearly demonstrated the importance of this topic for Monet and his friends. Vincent Pomarède (ed.), *L'Impressionnisme et la naissance du cinéma*, Paris/Lyon, Réunion des musées nationaux/Musée des beaux-arts de Lyon, 2005.

"EVERYTHING IN NATURE IS MORE BEAUTIFUL AND POETIC THAN MAN."[1]

On Austrian Landscape Painting in the 19th Century

Peter Peer

Fig. 1
EMIL JAKOB SCHINDLER
Road by a Wood in Rainy Weather – November Atmosphere, 1884
Private collection

Rousseau was the first pure naturalist and also the greatest so far. He did not go out into nature to dominate it but to serve it. His technique was so perfect that it remained absolutely imperceptible and finally completely unfolded in the processes of nature. He searched for, and found, the structure of the clouds, of stones and of trees with his brush. He wanted to paint light, shining, brilliant, real daylight."[2]

The person who said these words was none other than Emil Jakob Schindler, the central figure in Austrian landscape painting in the late 19th century. And Schindler was not alone with his recognition. The admiration and receptiveness of Austrian art for the ideas of the painters of the Barbizon School and French Impressionism have their roots in a specifically Austrian characteristic—the orientation toward a narrowly defined detail of nature while observing contemporary life. There was traditionally a high level of esteem for simple nature pieces in Austrian landscape painting that can be traced back to Ferdinand Georg Waldmüller's studies of trees in the 1830s—works that he considered equal to, and placed alongside, his "finished" paintings in exhibitions at the Academy. The new feeling for realism in landscape pictures in the early 19th century overcame the compositional models of a Baroque-Classicistic tradition and made efforts to achieve the most objective approach to the object possible—occasionally, this even led to unmitigated, merciless realism. These were the prerequisites for the establishment of the reception of French visual ideas. However, this did not take place within the framework of a continuous line of development but, much more, as a reversion to the artistic intentions of the early 19th century. This was due to the fact that, in the years around the mid-century, landscape painting took another—in principle, contrary—direction and turned toward highly dramatic and monumental stylization, especially in mountain paintings. Here, intense lighting and weather situations, and oversized areas of the landscape that all topographic details were subordinated to, served as impacting elements. The spatial concepts of late-Baroque landscapes were absorbed in them as were the works of Flemish painting of the 17th century. Artists such as Anton Hansch, August Schaeffer von Wienwald, Ludwig Halauska and Albert Zimmermann reached a high level of mastery in this area and also stressed the aspirations of this form of painting through the monumental size of the works. Analogous to the painting of historical scenes showing "great" events from the past and corresponding stylistic reminiscences firmly anchored in the academic style of art that was officially predominant in Europe, an equally representative equivalent developed in landscape art. In addition, alpine painting in particular, where the motifs from the high mountain regions were impressively staged as "natural showplaces," reflected a generally increased national consciousness that also had its historical-philosophical foundations in the historicism of the 19th century. Andreas and Oswald Achenbach from Düsseldorf and the Munich painters around Carl Rottmann and in his succession were prominent representatives of this movement. For almost three decades—from the end of the 1840s until the mid-1870s—it formed a major branch of Central European landscape painting before being replaced in Austria by the *paysage intime*.

A return to simple, non-representative motifs and presenting them in nature that was increasingly perceived as being unstable began in the 1870s. It formed the point of departure for paintings in the so-called "atmospheric Impressionist" style.[3] As a reaction to the almighty doctrine of heroic alpine painting in the second third of the century, this school set standards by paying increased attention to purely emotionally experienced qualities

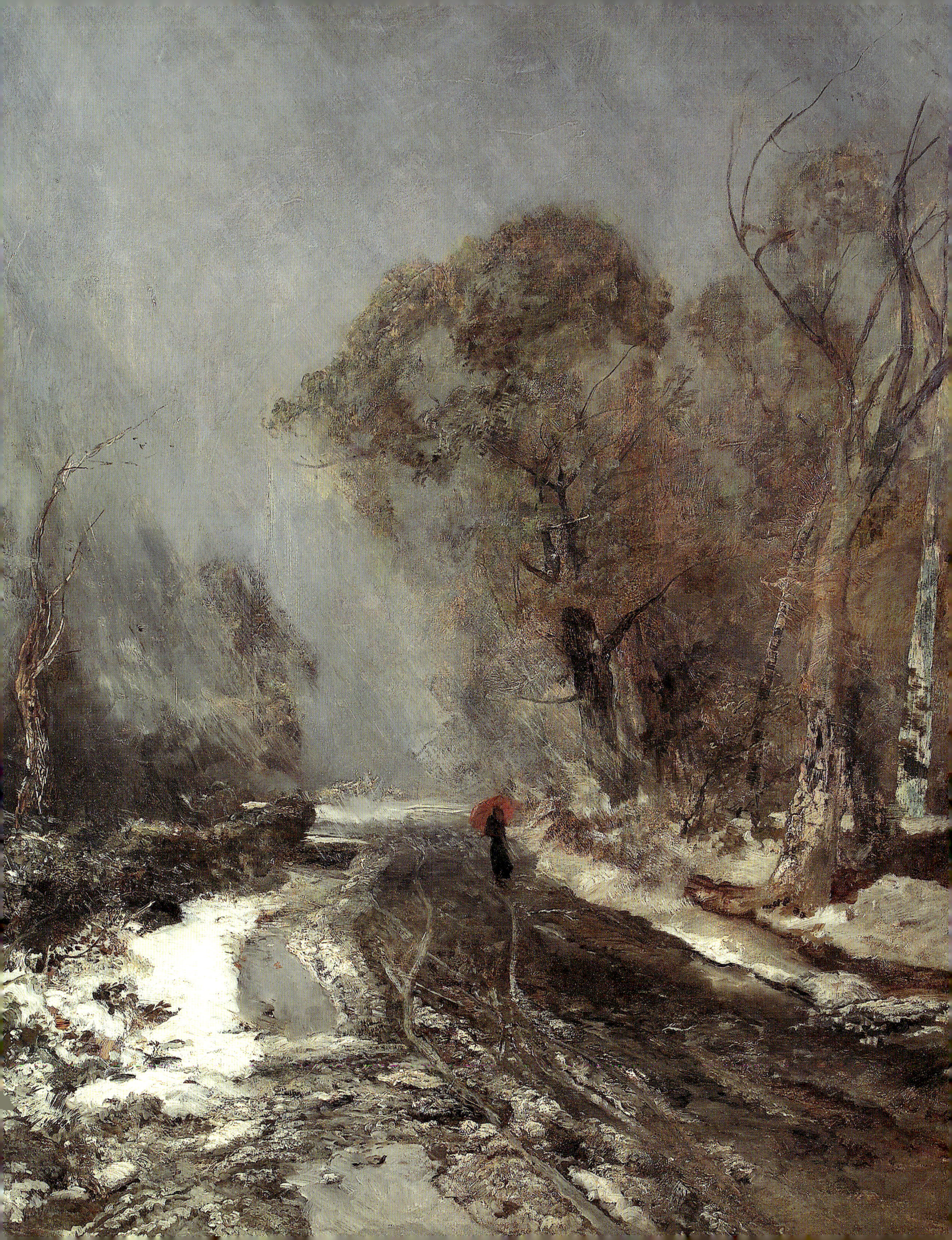

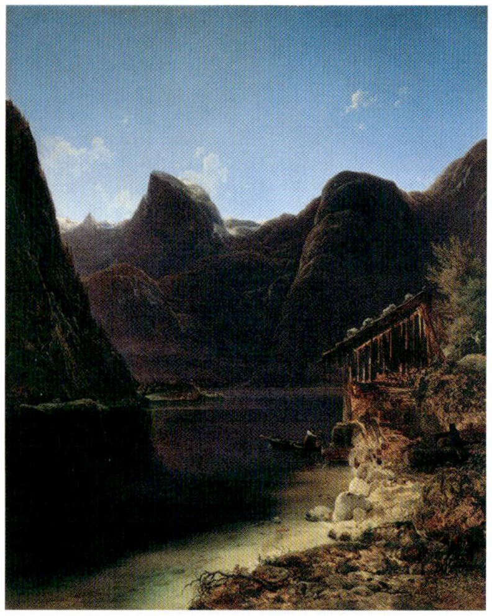

Fig. 2
FRANZ STEINFELD
The Lake at Hallstatt, 1834
Belvedere, Vienna

and the lyrical interpretation of the object while still objectively observing the model of nature. The Austrians found confirmation of this in the landscape painting of the Barbizon School.

The *paysage intime* united the sense of realism of the early 19th century with a romantically-colored interpretation of experiencing nature, as well as a new aesthetic of painting culture. The focus was placed on more or less simple motifs that Austrian painters had also discovered for themselves at the beginning of the 19th century with the exception that the French countryside partially differed from the local scenery and, therefore, possessed a specific regional character. As a result, Austrian—as well as countless other European—artists visited the scenes of French painting in Normandy, in the Fontainebleau Forest and in Holland in order to capture the specific atmosphere of the individual regions. Later, they searched for correspondingly "French" motifs in their own homeland. A canon of motifs began to be established, including river landscapes (with towering poplars), wide plains, heath landscapes, secluded forest paths and, frequently, sections of a meadow or blossoming field. One important aspect they had in common was the tendency to show rural regions far away from urban centers in keeping with the escapist longing for a distant pre-industrial age.

Emil Jakob Schindler, Eugen Jettel, and Rudolf Ribarz are considered the main representatives of atmospheric Impressionism. While Robert Russ only absorbed these tendencies hesitantly and vaguely, Tina Blau and Theodor von Hörmann developed a "naturalistic" or Impressionistic way of looking at things in which the atmosphere seemed to play a somewhat subordinate role. Although it originally met with violent objection and criticism, especially on account of its formal expressive values that were unusual in the Austrian artistic environment, atmospheric Impressionism gradually developed into the artistic archetype and model for several generations of Austrian landscape artists active until well into the 20th century.

A thematic change, which affected both atmospheric painting and the approach to the landscape in general, took place in the 19th century. The painterly quality of the motif of the picture took priority over the significance of its content.[4] The torrential mountain streams of the alpine painters were countered with tranquil landscapes of meadows and rivers; weathered green spruce bowed by the storms competed with unspectacular views of gardens, parks, and pastures; depictions of nature at peace with itself, which stimulated contemplation through their atmosphere and lack of drama, were preferred to the spectacular scenes of the world of mountains and glaciers in a state of turmoil, which led to the artists being accused of "intentionally looking for uninteresting motifs."[5] The academicians were particularly skeptical about the contents of contemporary landscape painting. August Schaeffer saw it as "empty objective painting [...] that harbors the superstition that everything in nature, just the way it is, is also an object of art." In contrast, he still preferred the "meaningful" mountain pictures painted by Albert Zimmermann.[6]

Fig. 3
IGNAZ RAFFALT
Landscape with Rising Mist, ca. 1850
Neue Galerie am Universalmuseum Joanneum, Graz

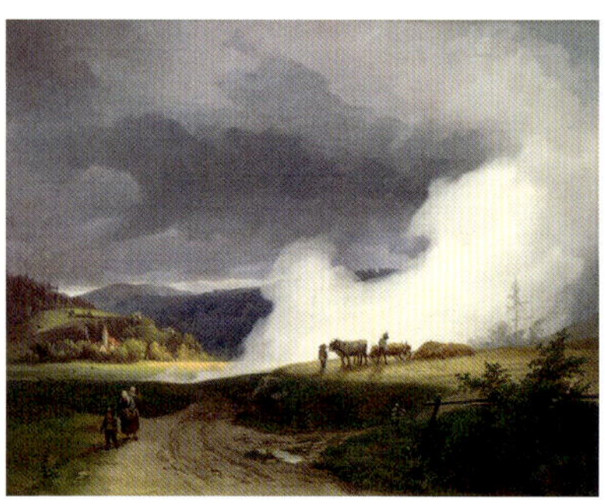

"ATMOSPHERE" AS THE CONTENT OF MODERN ART

"Discovering beauty in truth"[7] and capturing it in the recording of simple landscape motifs was the actual driving force behind Austrian landscape painting in the late 19th century—"atmosphere" was the keyword of the period. Franz Wickhoff and Alois Riegl considered striving for artistic effect and conveying atmosphere as the characteristic feature and actual mission of contemporary painting and, as such, a reaction to the growing cultural pessimism of the age that was spreading in the epoch's consciousness as a result of the far-reaching economic and social changes taking place and the resulting value shifts.[8]

Riegl in particular attempted to define the character and significance of the phenomenon of "atmosphere" out of its context in cultural history. The findings of the natural sciences had led to traditional concepts based on a religious view of the world becoming shaky and losing ground but, in return, they had also opened the eyes of man to an objective, rational view of the relationships in nature. Modern art, atmospheric art, was essentially founded on this harmony based on the knowledge of the laws of nature. In the final analysis, "atmosphere" as the goal of all modern art was nothing more that the comforting assurance of the "unshakeable workings of the laws of causality"[9] and Riegl therefore demanded absolute "truth to nature" from artists because the strict observation of the laws of causality formed the core of modern aesthetics. For Riegl, the artist coping with the continuous changes of nature while simultaneously taking its inherent laws into consideration elevated the landscape to the highest position in contemporary art.[10] According to Riegl, the artistic realization of the atmosphere was achieved through "peace" and "being seen from a distance" while "movement" and "a close-up view" destroyed—or even prevented—atmosphere. In keeping with the differentiation between the visual and haptic qualities of a work of art, he considered that the fulfillment of these factors (in contrast to sculpture) could only be guaranteed by painting which was "innately far-sighted."[11]

Fig. 4
ALBERT ZIMMERMANN
Sunset in the High Mountains, 1858
Private collection

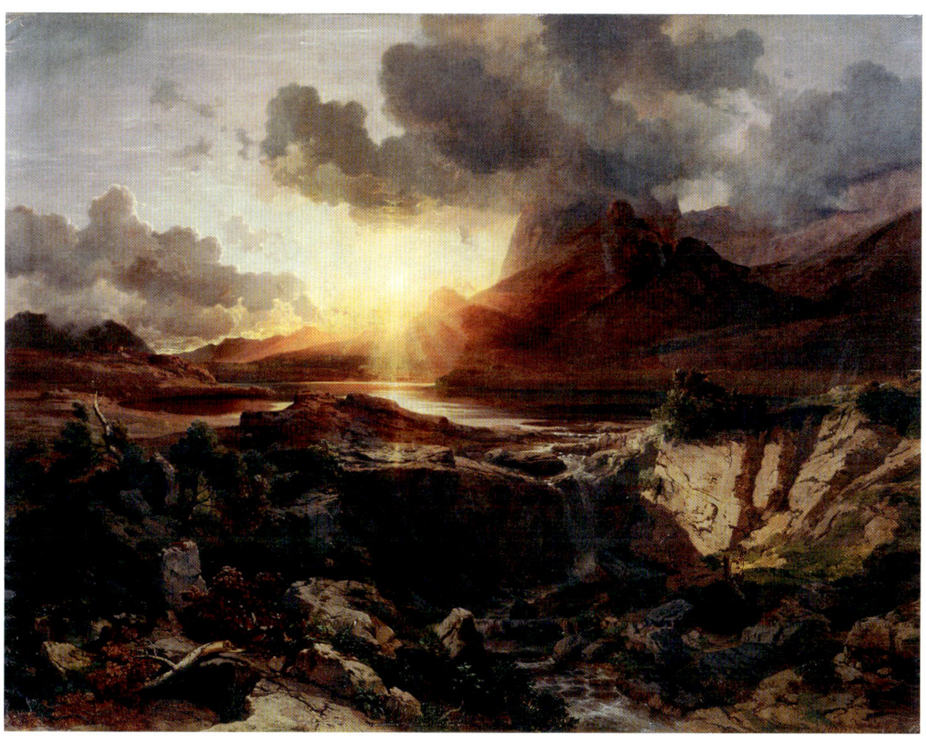

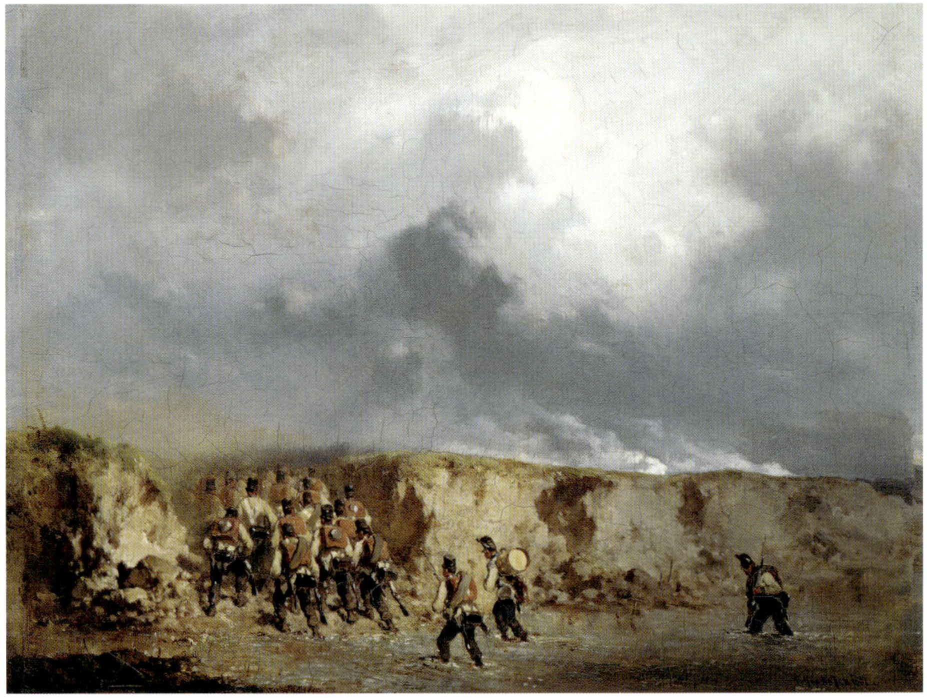

Fig. 5
AUGUST VON PETTENKOFEN
Austrian Soldiers Crossing a Ford, 1851
Belvedere, Vienna

In Austria, the concept of the atmospheric landscape is mainly connected with the art of Emil Jakob Schindler. The artist had already drawn attention to the significance of atmosphere for contemporary art, "Where the heck do those certain vedutisti who whip up souvenir pictures of the drinking hall at the spas peopled with the obligatory horsemen hundreds of times live? I don't know of any and would like to inform the charming deprecator that, since the invention of photography, things of the kind are hardly understood. The scholars who have become blind to art should know that today artists paint and awaken atmosphere in a way never achieved before and that—since they are no longer involved in it—wherever he happens to be, and that it is rather unimportant where he was as long as he kept his eyes open and really saw what was in front of him."[12] Ludwig Hevesi felt that the "progress of the Viennese landscape" was, first and foremost, linked with Schindler and called him the "master of the Viennese atmospheric landscape [...], the most purely lyrical personality in recent Austrian art."[13] As Hartwig Fischel summarizes, "Irrespective of the many directions Schindler moved in [...], he always led us into an atmospheric world full of poetic charm."[14] Schindler anticipated the "truth to nature" called for by Riegl by considering each artwork an independent creation that was, however, dependent on nature to the extent that it was impossible for the artist to transcend the form and appearance of nature.[15] It was necessary "to start out from nature and, through it, arrive at the work of art and to crystallize the artistic act out of the elements of nature."[16]

It comes as no surprise that Schindler was critical of the new medium of photography that he was prepared to accept as an aid for painters although "the hand, eye, and spirit are completely inactive." However, in his opinion, its products "do not come into contact with our soul but merely appeal to our eye and are then dismissed forever after a quick glance. It appears that these pictures are far superior to anything art has so far achieved when it comes to the absolute accuracy of the shapes, the shadows; but, in terms of inner edification, their possibility to create an impression, their artistic language, in give-and-take, they are abysmally below the worst works of any artistic period so far."[17]

Correspondingly, Wickhoff felt that the spread of photography had simultaneously liberated painting from the constraints of mimetically depicting objects and made it possible for it once again to devote itself to purely artistic activities.[18] While photography actually provided stimuli for French Impressionism (perspective, snapshots), the medium's artistic expressiveness and inspirational effect were hardly recognized in Austrian landscape painting circles until the beginning of the 1890s.[19] This once again points out the differences between French Impressionism and Austrian atmospheric painting.[20] Wickhoff explains, "The French always look for technical problems" and that Impressionism and *plein-air* painting, "extremely important transitional stages in the development of modern art," were created and championed in France.[21] However, for him, the pinnacle of modern art was reached in English painting that, from the early 19th century and later, had aimed at "creating and asserting atmosphere in the painting that has finally now become the common heritage of all civilized peoples." For him, this development reached its peak in the work of James Abbott McNeill Whistler.[22]

Wickhoff also felt that the depiction of atmosphere in modern painting was a function that had previously only been successfully accomplished by music and poetry.[23] In this way, he created a link between the individual artistic disciplines based on their specific capabilities. Whistler transported this associative way of thinking in paintings to which he gave titles such as *Nocturne* or *Symphony*; this was actually not different to Hartwig Fischel who described individual works by Schindler as a "symphony in green" or "symphony in gray".[24] And Schindler himself spanned an arc over the various areas of art, "Poetry condenses and forms the being, music the sounds, the fine arts the 'appearance'."[25]

Fig. 6
EMIL JAKOB SCHINDLER
At the Thaya River near Lundenburg I, 1877
Belvedere, Vienna

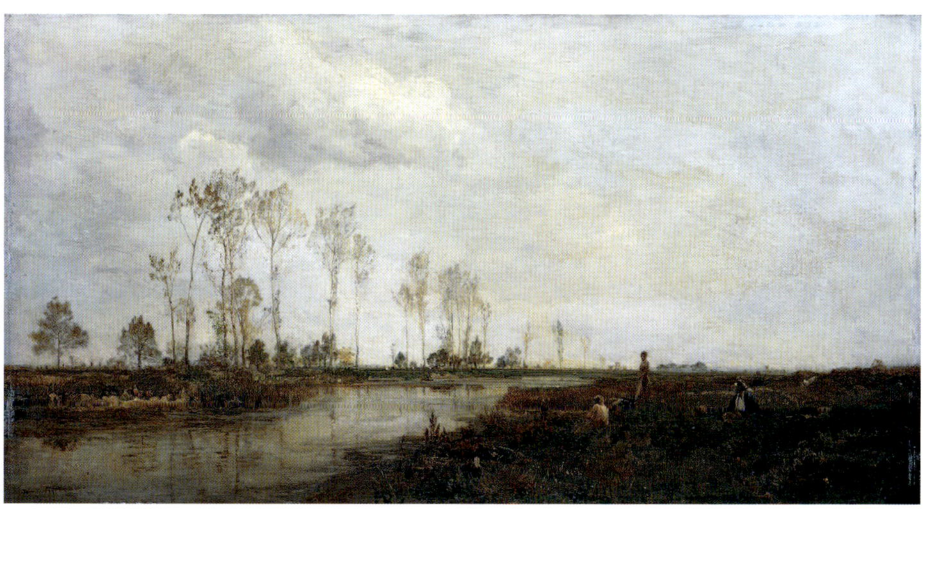

FORMAL AND COMPOSITIONAL ASPECTS

However, the manner in which many Austrian artists approached the motifs of their pictures was frequently markedly different to that of their European contemporaries. A compositional style, which selected sections in which the foreground takes up the largest part of the surface of the painting while the view toward the background plays a less significant role as a result of the horizon being raised high up, developed in Austrian painting. Tendencies of this kind started to be recognized in the late 1860s.[26] Depictions of nature of this kind were subsequently cultivated by Eugen Jettel and Rudolf Ribarz in particular, as well as Schindler's pupils Marie Egner and Olga Wisinger-Florian, but they can also be found in works by Rudolf von Alt. The foundation for the motif was mainly formed by field and meadow landscapes as well as rustic garden views with vegetable patches and fruit trees, which led to the term "cabbage and turnip pictures".[27] Olga Wisinger-Florian's painting *Flowering Poppies (Blühender Mohn)* from 1895/1900 is an outstanding example of this style. One has the feeling that one is looking through a wide-angle lens, that the landscape becomes flatter as it recedes toward the background, and that its individual features amalgamate into a conglomeration of light and color. This contrast creates a feeling of far and near without awakening the impression of spatial depth in the sense of a perspective constructed using classical methods. This genre more or less led to Gustav Klimt's introduction to landscape painting. Here, attention should be drawn to the first of four paintings of fruit orchards and a farmhouse—these, still in upright format—as well as two views of ponds and the *Farmhouse with Birch Trees (Bauernhaus mit Birken)* (1900). The first painting for which Klimt chose a broad view of the landscape was the *Large Poplar I (Große Pappel I)* from 1900, but he frequently returned to motifs shown with a concentrated view from close up. In addition to the selected motif and sectional view, the relationship between the more distant sections and foreground, which appears to be folded down, creates a link with the works of atmospheric Impressionism.

In this connection, the formal and compositional influence of Japanese art is unmistakable. Painters such as August von Pettenkofen, Rudolf Ribarz, and Eugen Jettel visited France frequently—or spent several decades in the country—where Japanese woodcuts had started to enjoy great popularity in the early 1860s. The World's Fairs, such as the one held in Vienna in 1873, also offered the general public the possibility of becoming familiar with Japanese art. These tendencies become increasingly apparent from the late 1870s, especially in the works of Jettel and Ribarz. The segmentation of elements of the landscape, the decorative arrangement of views of the landscape with grass or flowers positioned close-up in the foreground and the broad landscape behind, are clear indications of these stimuli in the two artists' work.

CAPTURING THE CHANGEABLE

The new style of painting and the casual application of paint in combination with the earthen coloring not only fulfilled the formal-aesthetic demands placed on the landscape picture but was also principally intended to do justice to the depiction of what was changeable through fluctuations in the light, the atmosphere and the movement of objects in the natural environment-phenomena that were invested with a hitherto unknown importance.

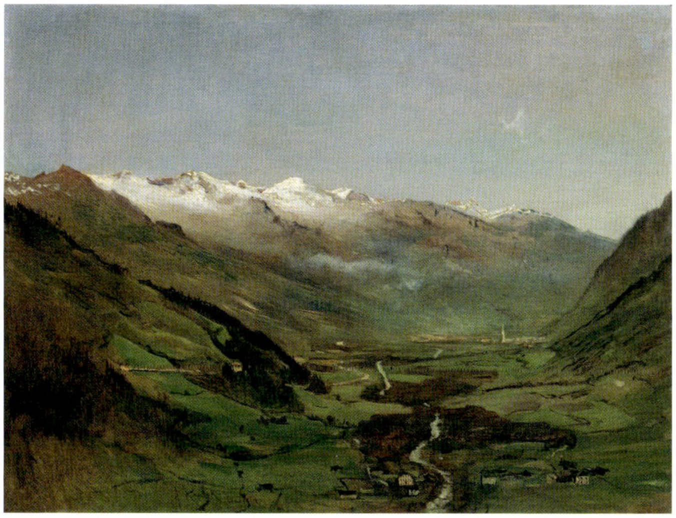

Fig. 7
ANTON ROMAKO
Gastein Valley I, 1877
Belvedere, Vienna

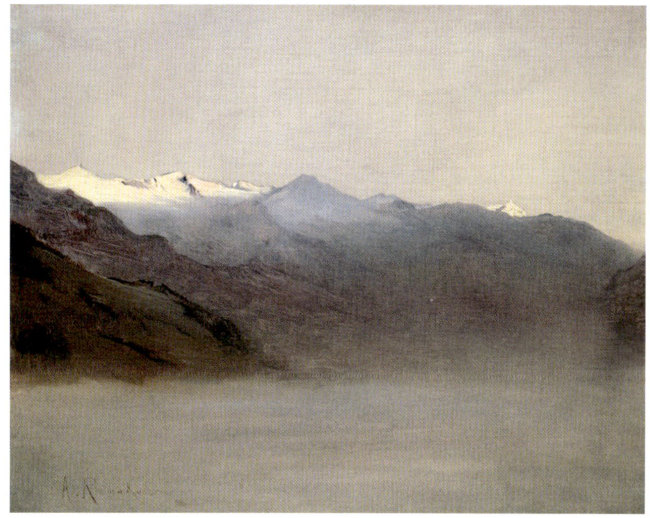

Fig. 8
ANTON ROMAKO
Gastein Valley in the Fog, 1877
Belvedere, Vienna

Series and cycles also provided the possibility for illustrating what was changeable in nature. Anton Romako's views of the Gastein Valley that have the autumnal atmosphere of the situation at various times of the day as their theme are among the earliest—and most important—testimonies to this kind of nature study in Austrian art. Although the formats of the three paintings vary slightly, Romako always chose almost identical sections. Emil Jakob Schindler also created similar series of works. He was not as much concerned with the depiction of the changeable as a visual phenomenon as with the overall experience of nature. To achieve this, he planned a cycle of *The Months (Die Monate)*, which remained unfinished, in which he made the various atmospheres at different times of the year his subject (fig. p. 150).[28] Only four paintings from this group of works are known; all of them were created around 1884 and are of almost the same size. One particular characteristic of the pictures is that–in spite of the differing motifs—they have a relatively large number of compositional similarities. Each painting shows a path or brook running diagonally into the background. It appears that this acts as a link between the individual works.

Cycles of this kind definitely show connections with the considerations of contemporary natural sciences. "Law" and "series" were fundamental concepts in modern science. Hermann von Helmholtz thought that the observation of individual circumstances was only of value if they made it possible to identify the "law of a series of recurrent phenomena." In this case, the individual was considered a link in a chain that was either already known or waiting to be discovered.[29] And Ernst Mach made a series of optical experiments that demonstrated that the aligned orientation of various marks left a pleasant impression on the viewer. Riegl also used similar arguments when he placed the knowledge of causal connections in nature ("far sight") above the observation of the individual ("near sight") and recognized it as a fundamental basis for atmosphere.[30] Riegl saw analogies between the intrinsic laws of nature and art.[31] Instead of copying natural things, art should work this law of nature appropriately in order to make its symmetry and proportions visible.

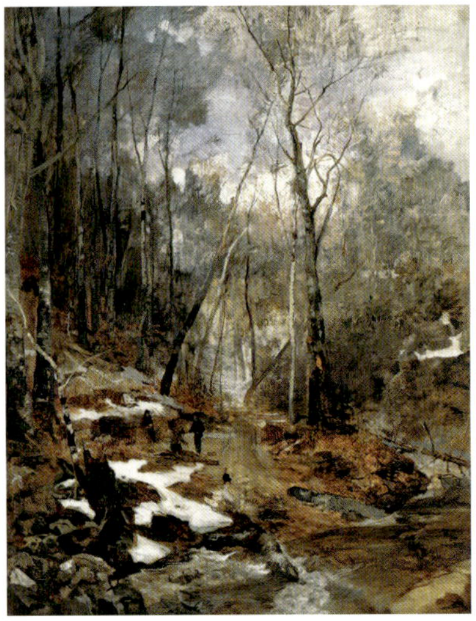

Fig. 9
EMIL JAKOB SCHINDLER
February Atmosphere – Early Spring in the Vienna Woods, 1884
Belvedere, Vienna

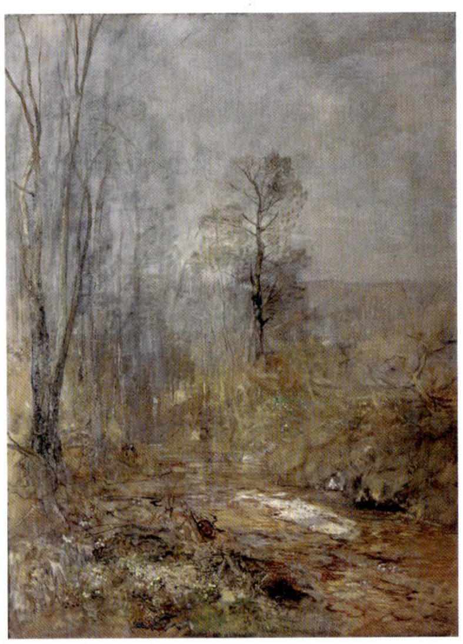

Fig. 10
EMIL JAKOB SCHINDLER
March Atmosphere – Early Spring in the Vienna Woods, ca. 1884
Belvedere, Vienna

THE RELATIONSHIP TO IMPRESSIONISM IN AUSTRIA

In contrast to the *paysage intime*, Impressionism was initially only hesitantly assimilated in Austria; it was only one of several artistic movements and even had to struggle for a long time to be recognized in France. Precisely the concept of atmosphere, which had helped the Barbizon painters become accepted in this country, was a hindrance to the acceptance of Impressionism. And this, although fundamental thoughts on an "Impressionist" theory were being developed at the same time in Austria—namely, on the scientific level. Ernst Mach's famous book *The Analysis of Sensations* (1886) saw reality dissolved in a sea of elements of sensations and described experiencing this reality as a permanently changing stream of elements of sensation. Impressionist painting was received in a similar fashion. Hermann Bahr noted that he had always had works by Manet, Degas, and Renoir in his mind's eye when he was reading Mach. He considered that the skepticism toward Impressionism was founded on a social and cultural mentality that rejected the notion that everything was in a permanent state of movement and change and that all perceptions were phenomena and, consequently, could not understand a style of painting that transmitted impressions of the moment that were ultimately illusions.[32]

Of course, Impressionism did not simply depict visual phenomena. One was well aware of the difference between "impressions" and "sensations."[33] Impressionism had also cultivated a characteristic aesthetic through its culture of color and painting technique. However, the concern was not as much the "nature" of the objects as experiencing the moment, the magic of the point in time. That also had something to do with poetry and atmosphere, albeit in a different manner from the way it was understood in Austria. Impressionism was in no way an art of metaphysical observation. The fleetingness of the experience, which the French artists translated into pulsating images of the moment, was seen as a metaphor for transience in Central Europe. The aestheticism of the Viennese intelligentsia, with its countless metaphysical references and distanced view of the world, in the years around 1900 much preferred the sophisticated style of painting and subdued coloration of symbolists like James Abbott McNeill Whistler, Fernand Khnopff, and Giovanni Segantini. They were not to remain without influence on Austrian painting of the fin-de-siècle, especially Gustave Klimt. This resulted in Impressionism being more received by way of intermediaries such as the divisionism of Segantini and not being presented in exhibitions in Vienna until relatively late—around the turn of the century.

IMPRESSIONIST TENDENCIES IN AUSTRIAN PAINTING

If nothing else, this was also due to a problem of different generations. Those artists who had so enthusiastically taken up the *paysage intime* in the years around 1870 now found it difficult to cope with Impressionism. This means that, with a few exceptions, young artists were those who started to process Impressionist tendencies around 1890. They took up typical motifs and subjects such as life in the metropolis and the technical achievements of the age and made them the subjects of their pictures. In parallel, their palettes became brighter, unmixed colors were increasingly used, and the earthy tones of the atmospheric artists left behind.

One of the few older artists to deal intensively with Impressionism was Theodor von Hörmann. He spent the years from 1887 to 1891 in Paris and created paintings completely imbued with the Impressionist feeling of the time during this period. He painted scenes of moments of everyday urban life and also documented the contemporary aspects of living in the big city (fig. p. 190).

The fundamental concern of Impressionism–perceiving the object as a sensation of light–also became widely accepted in Austrian painting. The younger artists no longer had many reservations about Impressionism and, from the turn of the century, the references become quite obvious. The works of Claude Monet, as well as the Pointillist further development of Impressionism–in more or less strong formulations–now found their way into Austrian painting.

"OVERCOMING NATURALISM" AND THE LEGACY OF THE ATMOSPHERIC LANDSCAPE

The aesthetic interpretation of Impressionism became the starting point for art in the Secessionist style *("Stilkunst")*, which continued with the intellectual legacy of atmospheric painting but also included symbolist elements, in Vienna in the years around 1900. Hermann Bahr proclaimed the "overcoming of naturalism" (and, in this connection, also referred to Impressionism as its visual medium) to the benefit of a style of art that aimed to act as the expression of psychological feelings. [34] It searched for the "secret behind the physical appearance, the more profound backgrounds behind the visible world"[35] to counterbalance the positivism and artistic naturalism that were dominant at the time. This way of thinking resulted in Expressionism in which the picture was understood as the bearer of a "spiritual message"[36] and also manifested itself in the "New Objectivity" school from the 1920s.[37]

In parallel, Impressionist tendencies still played a role in Austria until well into the 20th century; here however, less in Vienna and more in the cities in the provinces. Historicism was still a force to be reckoned with at the Vienna Academy of Fine Arts and the landscape field was still devoted to dramatically effective alpine paintings to a large degree. Possibly due to these rather conservative educational methods, quite a few talented young artists moved to Germany where they were able to absorb the latest developments in landscape painting. Munich, Karlsruhe, and Düsseldorf started to play an important role, and an independent school developed out of these cities' involvement with Impressionism. After their years of schooling abroad, many artists did not return to Vienna, but if they came back to Austria at all it was to the provinces where regional centers of artistic expression developed. A synthesis of Expressionist and Impressionist characteristics, as can be seen in the late works of Alfred Zoff and later in paintings by Herbert Boeckl and Anton Mahringer, was typical of the works of landscape painting in the decades that followed. Most likely as a result of ongoing, violent change in the political circumstances, a specific relationship to nature, marked by feeling and sensitivity, as had already been formulated by atmospheric Impressionism, was a significant aspect of them.

This movement remained effective as a contemporary response to the Naturalism of the French and their sense of *réalité moderne.*

Fig. 11
OLGA WISINGER-FLORIAN
Pergola near Mentone, 1900
Neue Galerie am Universalmuseum Joanneum, Graz

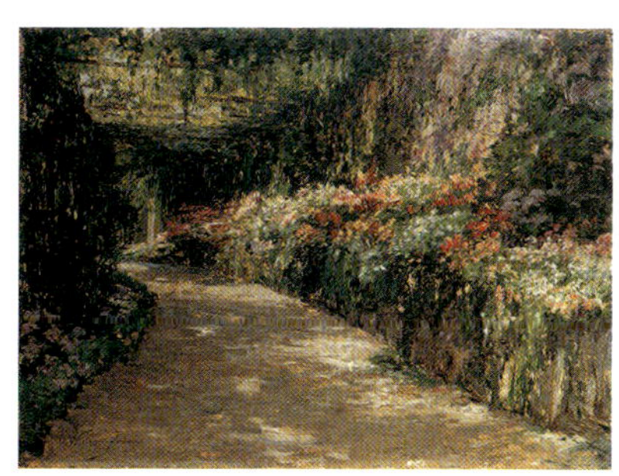

1 Diary entry by Emil Jakob Schindler from the year 1864, cited after A. Spier, "Jakob Emil Schindler (1842–1892) österreichischer Landschaftsmaler," in: *Die Kunst unserer Zeit. Eine Chronik des modernen Kunstlebens*, Munich 1893, pp. 1–21, here p. 2.

2 Emil Jakob Schindler, cited after Hartwig Fischel, "J. E. Schindler über Landschaftsmalerei," in: *Ausserordentliche Beilage zu den Monatsblättern des wissenschaftlichen Club in Wien*, IV for no. 6, 14th vol., 1893, p. 102.

3 Fritz Novotny used the—later disputed—concept of "atmospheric Impressionism" for the first time in his work *Hundert Jahre österreichischer Landschaftsmalerei* (Vienna 1948). Seeing that Impressionism of the French kind had never actually developed in Austria, he added the word "atmosphere." Klaus Demus continues with this des-ignation in an essay in, "Emil Jakob Schindlers Zyklus 'Die Monate' und der Stimmungsimpressionismus," in: *Mitteilungen der Österreichischen Galerie*, 3rd vol., no. 34–36, October–December 1959, pp. 35–38. Martina Haja first expressed doubts about the use of this term in her catalog contribution "Der österreichische Stimmungsimpressionismus" in: *Landschaft im Licht. Impressionistische Malerei in Europa und Nordamerika 1860–1910* (Götz Czymmek (ed.), exh. cat., Wallraf-Richartz-Museum, Cologne, April 6–July 1, 1990, Kunsthaus Zurich, Zurich, August 3–October 21, 1990, Cologne1990) but continued to use it without offering an alternative. In the exhibition catalog *Natürlichere Natur. Österreichische Malerei des Stimmungsrealismus* (Mürzzuschlag 1994), Otmar Rychlik finally replaced the term "atmospheric Impressionism" with "atmospheric realism" because–by definition–"atmosphere" and "Impressionism" represented different approaches to the object depicted. According to this, Impressionism was devoted to the strict depiction of only what could be seen while, when portraying the atmosphere created by the weather, the time of day and seasons, the Austrians pursued a completely different variant of *plein-airism*. First of all, equating "atmosphere" with the "special feeling and awareness for weather conditions" when dealing with specific situations in nature is problematic. In no way does Impressionism preclude depicting this phenomenon. Monet's series of paintings can be cited as absolutely exemplary in this regard as they live from the fine nuances in the turbulent processes of nature. In addition, this is actually an international phenomenon and can definitely not be seen as a specifically Austrian characteristic in the field of *plein-air* painting. Going further, the declaration that the Impressionists only showed visible reality can be traced back to the starting point of naturalism. In practice, however, one discovers specific formal and color features, such as can be found in art in general, which subject these paintings to a distinctive aesthetic. And some contemporaries were well aware of these facts. For example, Peter Behrens vehemently rejected the "idiotic accusation of naturalism"; quite the opposite, it was a matter of "individual, absolutely artistic works that remain unforgettable" (Peter Behrens, "Walter Leistikow," in: *Dekorative Kunst*, vol. 3, 1899, p. 233.) As a rule, in art history, general terms do not serve to completely describe the complex phenomena behind them but the position within a stylistic and thematic historical overall context. That is the reason that, here, the term "atmospheric Impressionism," following the example of the comprehensive descriptions by Novotny and Demus, is used. A good summary of the problems surrounding this controversial term is provided by Bärbel Holaus, *Studien zu Emil Jakob Schindler*, dipl. thesis, Vienna 1994, vol. I, pp. 157–173.

4 Cf. Götz Pochat, *Geschichte der Ästhetik und Kunsttheorie. Von der Antike bis zum 19. Jahrhundert*, Cologne 1986, p. 555.

5 *Kunst-Chronik*, supplement to *Zeitschrift für bildende Kunst*, 9th vol., issue 25, 2.4.1874, p. 405.

6 August Schaeffer, *Die kaiserl. Gemälde-Galerie in Wien. Moderne Meister*, Vienna 1903, p. 202.

7 Carl Schuch, cited after Gottfried Boehm (ed.), *Carl Schuch 1846–1903* (exh. cat., Städtische Kunsthalle Mannheim, Mannheim, March 8–May 19, 1986, Städtische Galerie im Lenbachhaus, Munich, June 11–August 11, 1986), Munich 1986, p. 103.

8 Franz Wickhoff, "Über moderne Malerei" (1897), in: idem, *Abhandlungen, Vorträge und Anzeigen*, Max Dvořak (ed.), Berlin 1913, vol. 2, pp. 21–44. – Alois Riegl, "Die Stimmung als Inhalt der modernen Kunst" (1899), in: idem, *Gesammelte Aufsätze*, Karl M. Swoboda (ed.), Augsburg 1928, p. 28–39.

9 Riegl 1928 (as in note 8), pp. 34–35

10 Riegl 1928 (as in note 8), p. 36.

11 Riegl 1928 (as in note 8), p. 34.

12 Cited after Hartwig Fischel, "Emil Jakob Schindler," in: *Die graphischen Künste*, 16th vol., 1893, p. 57.

13 Ludwig Hevesi, *Österreichische Kunst im 19. Jahrhundert*, Leipzig 1903, vol. 2, p. 254.

14 Hartwig Fischel, "Jakob Schindler," in: *Zeitschrift für bildende Kunst*, N. F., 1897/98, p. 102.

15 Fischel 1893 (as in note 12), p. 56. A similar passage in the text in which Riegl speaks of the assimilation of natural impressions that art "cannot surpass, but recreate with its unique means" leads to the assumption that Riegl must have orientated himself strongly on statements on the atmospheric landscape made by Schindler. Cf. Riegl 1928 (as in note 8), p. 34.

16 Cited after Heinrich Fuchs, *Emil Jakob Schindler*, Vienna 1970, p. 24.

17 Fischel 1897/98 (as in note 14), p. 108.

18 Wickhoff 1913 (as in note 8), p. 33.

19 The Austrians active in France, such as Eugen Jettel, were isolated exceptions. The motifs of some of the works he created at the beginning of the 1890s show clear parallels to the works of French landscape photographers; their formal realization demonstrates a naturalistic approach similar to photographs. Of course, attention must be drawn to Vienna Secession's later intensive examination of photography. However, as a whole, research into the history of photography in Austria and the way artists dealt with it is in an extremely rudimentary state that must be lamented and makes it necessary to exercise great caution when making judgments.

20 Cf. Andrea Winklbauer, "Impressionismus contra Stimmung. Über das Verhältnis der Österreicher zur französischen Landschaftsauffassung – 1868 bis 1903," in: *Natürlichere Natur. Österreichische Malerei des Stimmungsrealismus* (exh. cat., Kunsthaus Mürzzuschlag, Mürzzuschlag, summer exhibition 1994), Mürzzuschlag 1994,

Fig. 12
CARL MOLL
View from Heiligenstadt at the Nussberg, ca. 1905
Belvedere, Vienna

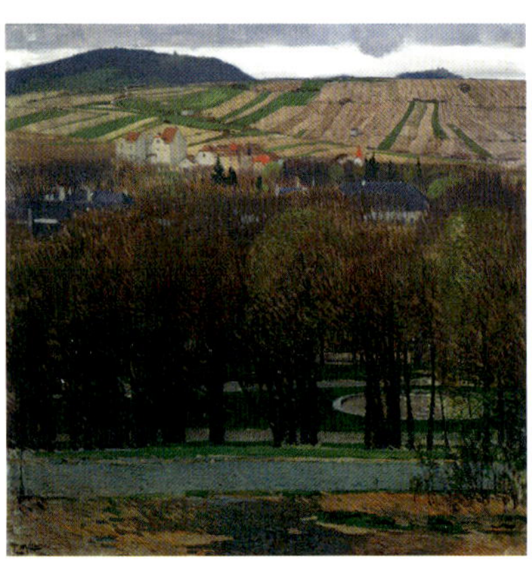

pp. 14–21. – Michael Kausch, "Impressionismus und Stimmungsimpressionismus. Wechselwirkungen, Gemeinsamkeiten und Unterschiede der französischen und österreichischen Landschaftsmalerei des 19. Jahrhunderts," in: *Faszination Landschaft. Österreichische Landschaftsmaler des 19. Jahrhunderts auf Reisen* (exh. cat., Residenzgalerie Salzburg, Salzburg, July 23–September 24, 1995), Salzburg 1995, pp. 27–47.

21 Wickhoff 1913 (as in note 8), p. 36.

22 Wickhoff 1913 (as in note 8), p. 36.

23 Wickhoff 1913 (as in note 8), p. 33.

24 Fischel 1893 (as in note 12), pp. 59–60

25 Fischel 1893 (as in note 12), p. 57.

26 The earliest picture to which these characteristics apply is probably a study of pumpkins by August von Pettenkofen; cf. Martina Haja, "'Kraut und Rüben' – Beobachtungen zur österreichischen Freilicht-Malerei im späten 19. Jahrhundert," in *Mitteilungen der Österreichischen Galerie*, 30th vol., no. 74, 1986, p. 44.

27 Going back to a quotation made by the painter Rudolf Ribarz, who speaks about "cabbage and turnips painting," Martina Haja introduced the term to stress the depiction of a detail in addition to the main motif of the paintings; cf. Haja 1986 (as in note 26), p. 43, note 1.

28 H. O. Miethke, *Katalog des künstlerischen Nachlasses Emil Jakob Schindlers. Versteigerung 5. Dezember 1892, Künstlerhaus Wien, Ausstellung im Künsterhause vom 26. November bis zum Auctionsbeginn*, Vienna 1892, nos. 14–17. – cf. Demus 1959 (as in note 3), p. 35.

29 Oskar Bätschmann, *Entfernung der Natur. Landschaftsmalerei 1750–1920*, Cologne 1989, p. 187, note 133.

30 Riegl 1928 (as in note 8), p. 34.

31 Bätschmann 1989 (note 29), p. 193.

32 Hermann Bahr, "Impressionismus," in: idem, *Dialog vom Tragischen*, Berlin 1904, taken from: Hermann Bahr, *Zur Überwindung des Naturalismus. Theoretische Schriften 1887–1904*, Gotthart Wunberg (ed.), Stuttgart 1968, pp. 196–197.

33 Albert Schug, "Über den Gegenstand der impressionistischen Landschaftsmalerei," in: Czymmek 1990 (as in note 3), p. 74.

34 Hermann Bahr, "Die Überwindung des Naturalismus" (1891), in: idem, *Die Überwindung des Naturalismus*, Dresden/Leipzig 1891, taken from: Bahr 1968 (as in note 32), p. 86.

35 Stephan Koja, "Jenes völlige Verschlungensein in der Schönheit des Scheins …," in: idem (ed.), *Gustav Klimt. Landschaften* (exh. cat., Belvedere, Vienna, October 23, 2002–February 23, 2003), Munich 2002, p. 32.

36 Patrick Werkner, *Physis und Psyche. Der österreichische Frühexpressionismus*, Vienna 1986, p. 274.

37 Klaus Albrecht Schröder, "Malerei aus der Distanz. Zur Geschichte und Phänomenologie der Neuen Sachlichkeit in Österreich", in: *Neue Sachlichkeit. Österreich 1918–1938* (exh. cat., Kunstforum Bank Austria, Vienna, April 1–July 2, 1995), Vienna 1995, p. 61.

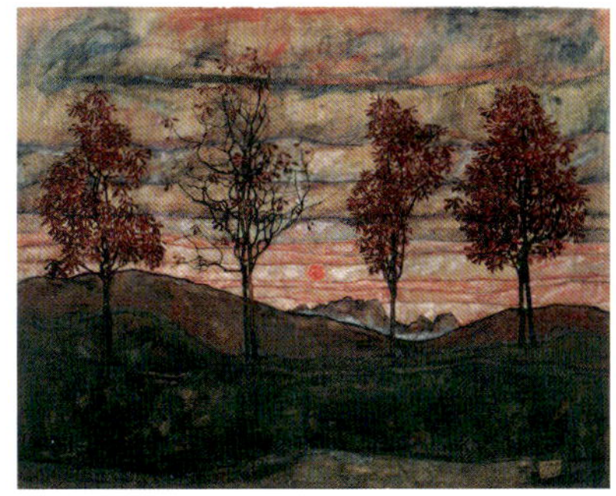

Fig. 13
EGON SCHIELE
Four Trees, 1917
Belvedere, Vienna

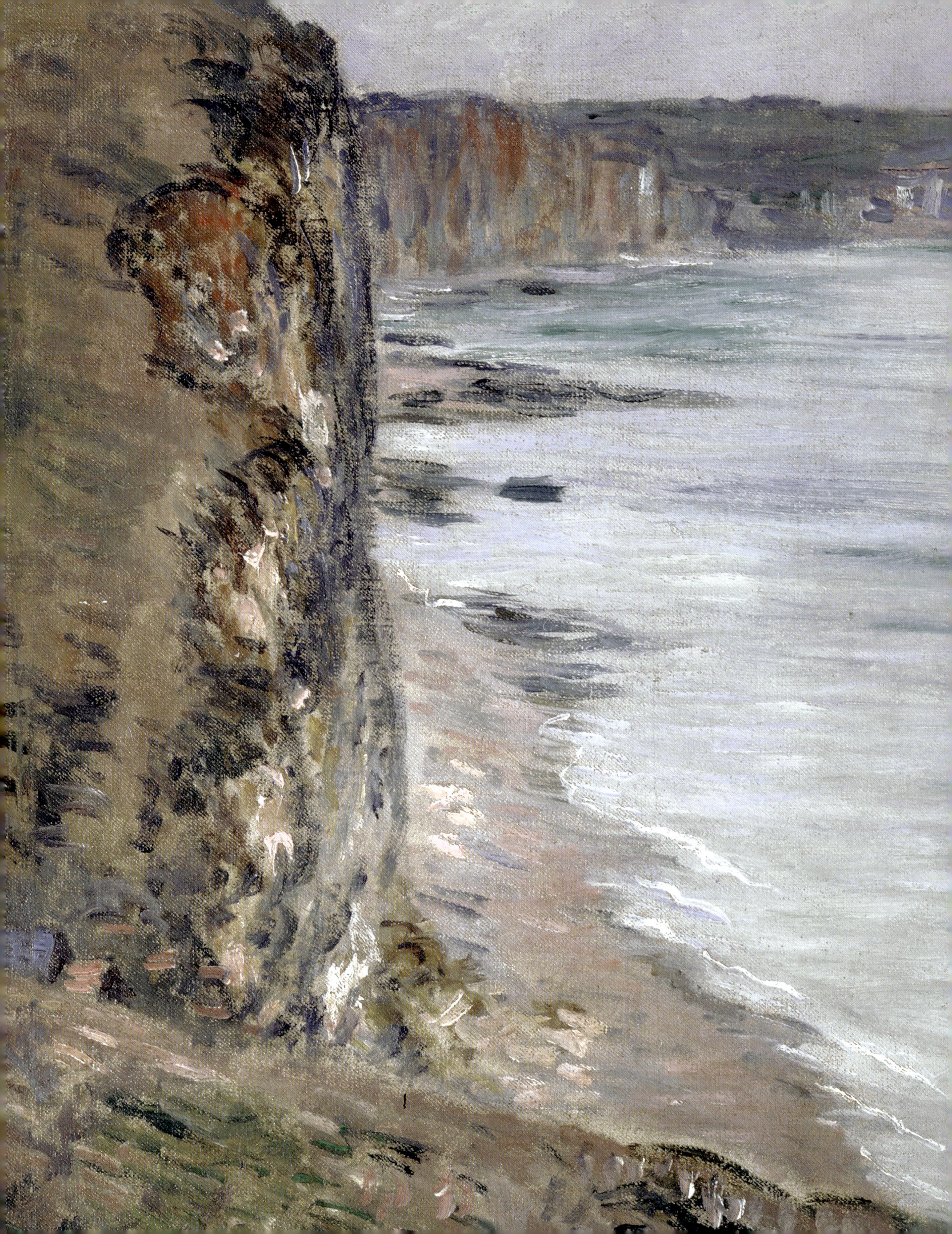

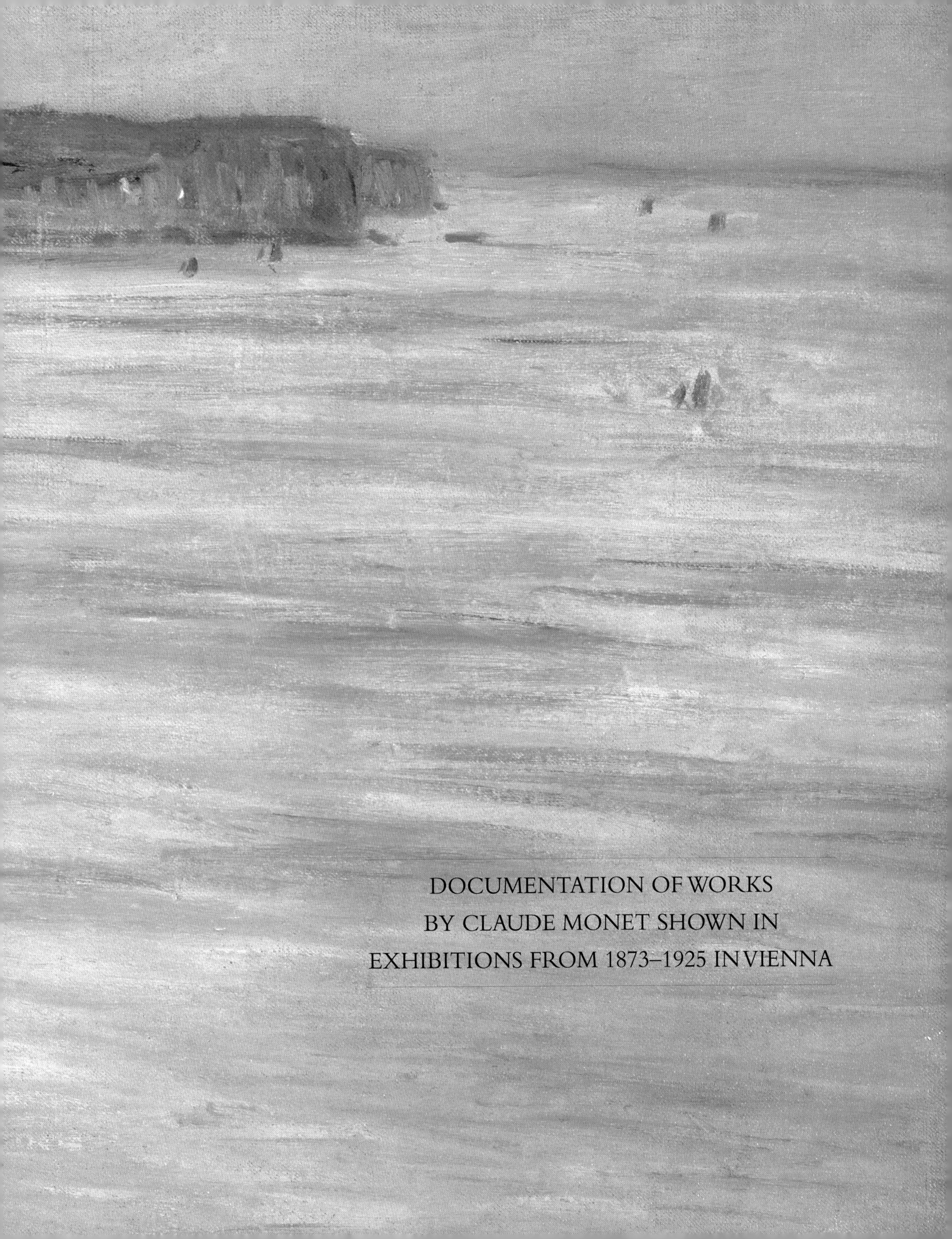

DOCUMENTATION OF WORKS BY CLAUDE MONET SHOWN IN EXHIBITIONS FROM 1873–1925 IN VIENNA

THE GOODS TRAIN
(*LE CONVOI DE CHEMIN DE FER*), 1872
Oil on canvas, 48.1 x 75 cm
Pola Museum of Art, Hakone
W 213

Wiener Weltausstellung (World Exposition in Vienna), 1873

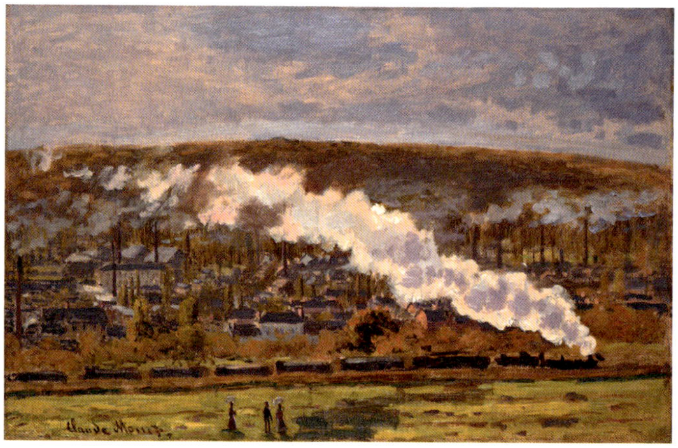

HOUSES AT ARGENTEUIL
(*MAISONS D'ARGENTEUIL*), 1873
Oil on canvas, 54 x 73 cm
Staatliche Museen zu Berlin, Nationalgalerie
W 277

Künstlerhaus, *Jubiläumsausstellung (Jubilee Exhibition)*, 1898

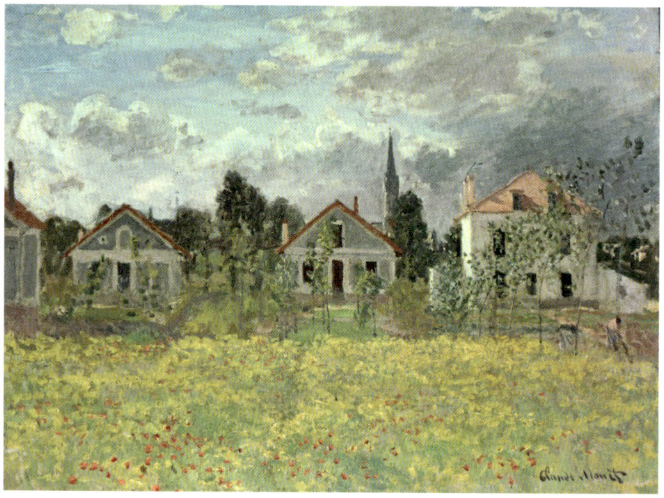

THE CHURCH AT VARENGEVILLE, GREY WEATHER
(*ÉGLISE DE VARENGEVILLE, TEMPS GRIS*), 1882
Oil on canvas, 65.1 x 81.3 cm
Collection of the Speed Art Museum, Louisville, Kentucky
W 725

Künstlerhaus, *Jubiläumsausstellung (Jubilee Exhibition)*, 1898

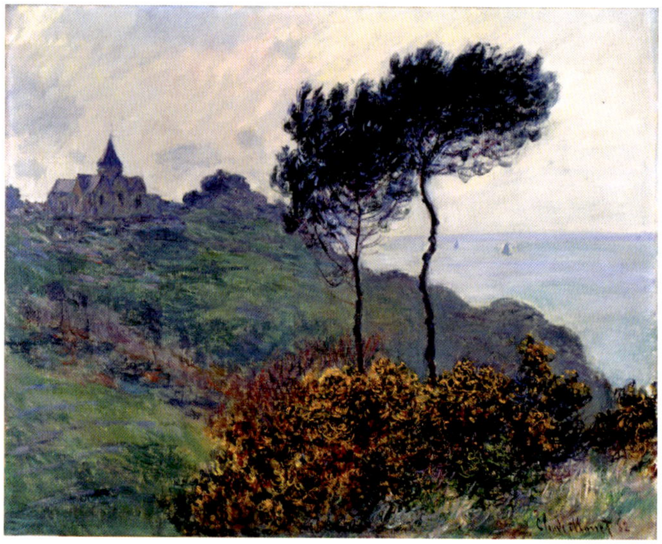

LUNCHEON ON THE GRASS
(*LE DÉJEUNER SUR L'HERBE*), 1865
Oil on canvas, 130 x 181 cm
The Pushkin State Museum of Fine Arts, Moscow
W 62

Secession, *Entwicklung des Impressionismus in Malerei und Plastik*, 1903, Cat. No. 44

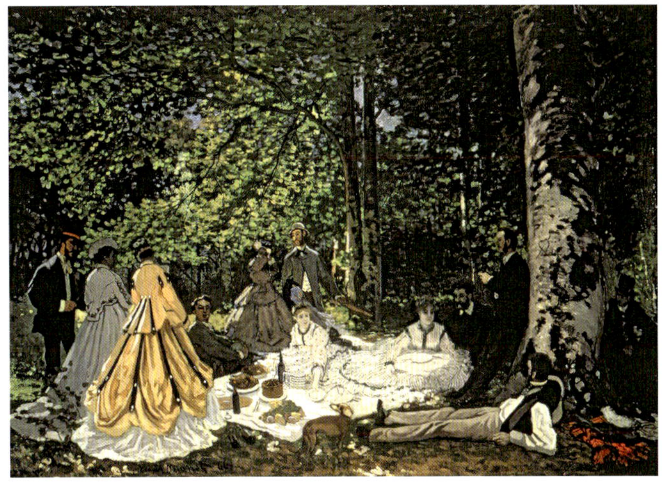

THE LUNCHEON
(*LE DÉJEUNER*), 1868
Oil on canvas, 230 x 150 cm
Städel Museum, Frankfurt am Main
W 132

Secession, *Entwicklung des Impressionismus in Malerei und Plastik*, 1903, Cat. No. 40

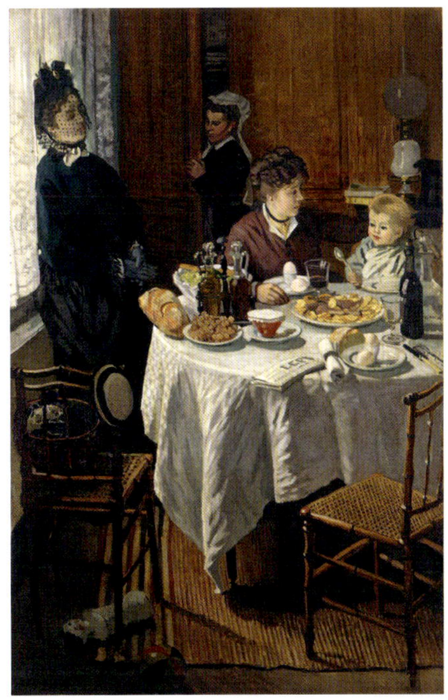

DER FRÜHLING
(*LE PRINTEMPS*), 1873
Oil on canvas, 58 x 78.5 cm
Johannesburg Art Gallery
W 273

Secession, *Entwicklung des Impressionismus in Malerei und Plastik*, 1903, Cat. No. 41

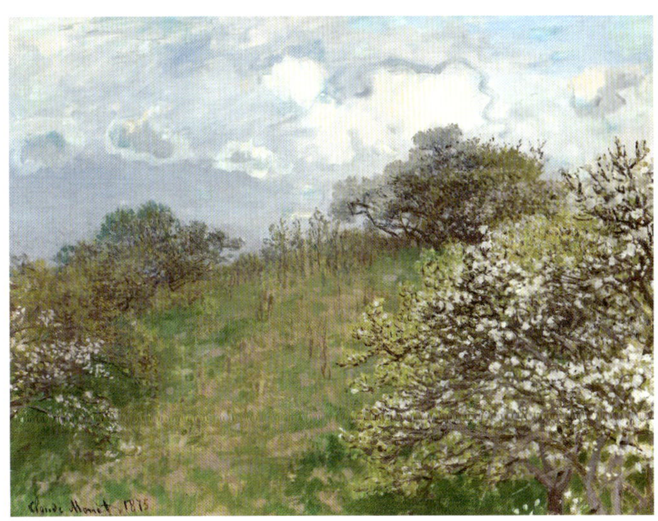

EUGÉNIE GRAFF
(*LA MÈRE PAUL*), 1882
Oil on canvas, 65 x 54.5 cm
Harvard Art Museums/Fogg Museum, Cambridge, Massachusetts
W 745

PAUL ANTOINE GRAFF
(*LE PÈRE PAUL*), 1882
Oil on canvas, 64.5 x 52.1 cm
Belvedere, Vienna
W 744

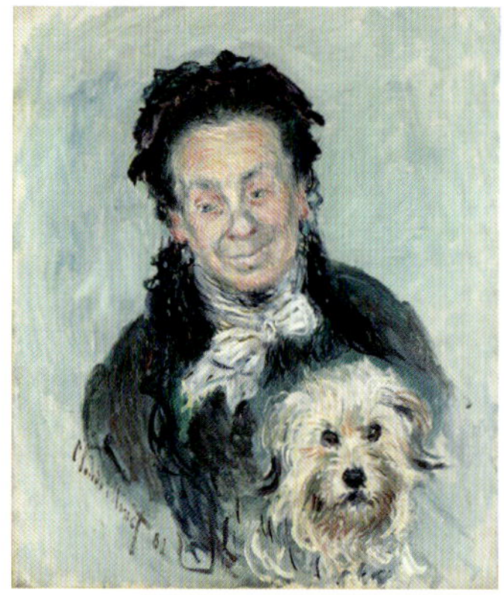

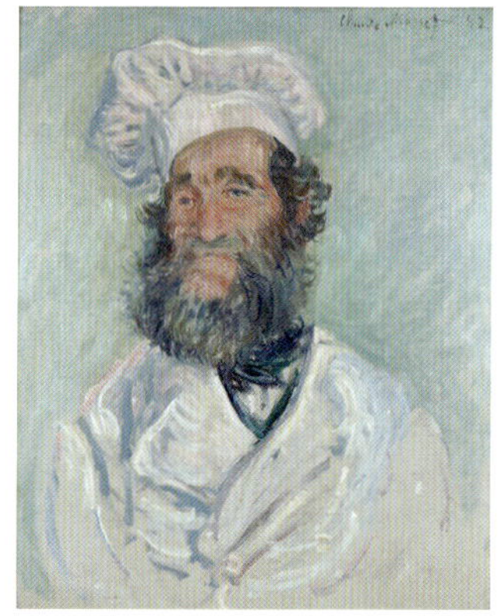

Secession, *Entwicklung des Impressionismus in Malerei und Plastik*, 1903, Cat. No. 38 respectively No. 42
Galerie Miethke, *Manet – Monet*, 1910, Cat. No. 20 respectively No. 26

STORMY WEATHER AT ÉTRETAT
(*GROS TEMPS À ÉTRETAT*), 1883
Oil on canvas, 65 x 81 cm
National Gallery of Victoria, Melbourne
W 826

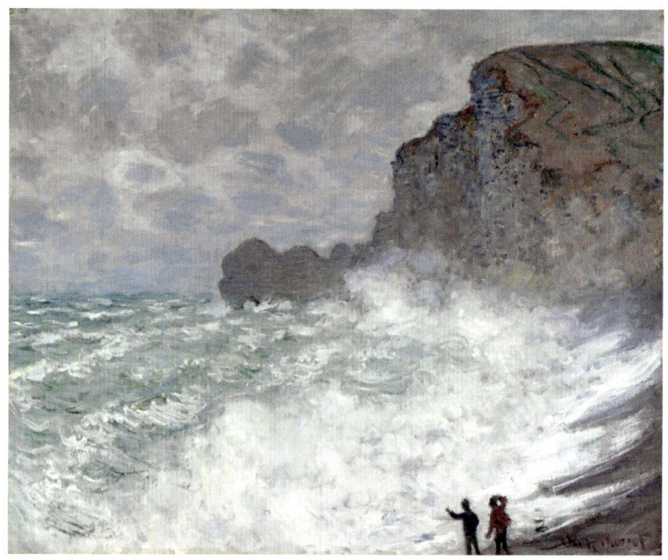

Secession, *Entwicklung des Impressionismus in Malerei und Plastik*, 1903, Cat. No. 43
Galerie Arnot, *Ausstellung von Werken moderner Franzosen*, 1912, Cat. No. 17

THE THAMES BELOW WESTMINSTER
(LA TAMISE ET LE PARLAMENT), 1871
Oil on canvas, 47 x 73 cm
The National Gallery, London
W 166

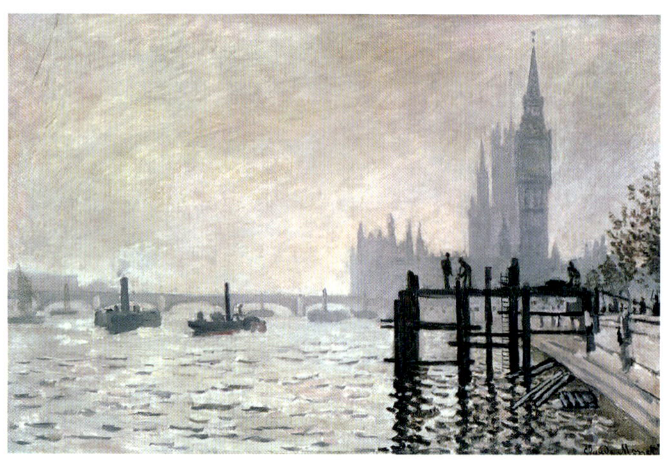

Galerie Miethke, *Manet – Monet*, 1910, Cat. No. 19

THAW IN ARGENTEUIL
(*LE DÉGEL*), 1873
Oil on canvas, 55 x 73 cm
Private collection
W 255

Galerie Miethke, *Manet – Monet*, 1910, Cat. No. 16

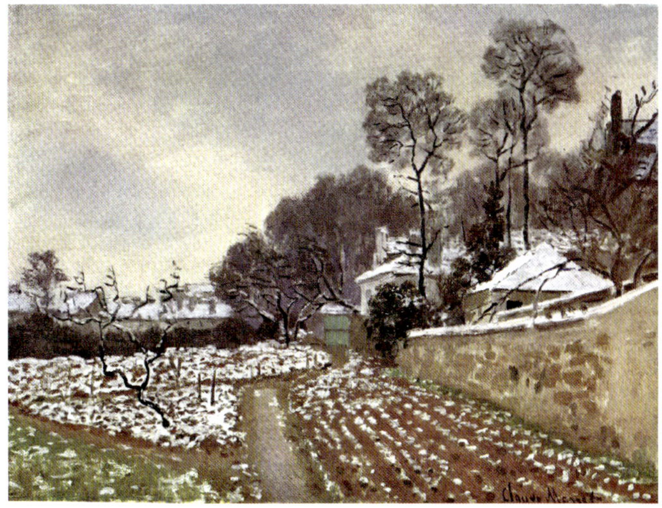

MONET'S GARDEN AT ARGENTEUIL (THE DAHLIAS)
(*LE JARDIN DE MONET À ARGENTEUIL, LES DAHLIAS*),
1873
Oil on canvas, 61 x 82.5 cm
National Gallery of Art, Washington, D.C.
W 286

Galerie Miethke, *Manet – Monet*, 1910, Cat. No. 29

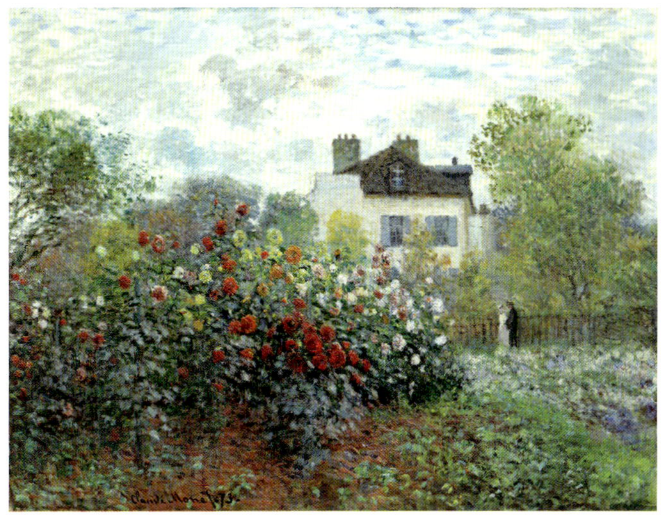

THE SEINE AT ARGENTEUIL
(*LA SEINE À ARGENTEUIL*), 1875
Oil on canvas, 60 x 80 cm
Private collection
W 373
Galerie Miethke, *Manet – Monet*, 1910, Cat. No. 30

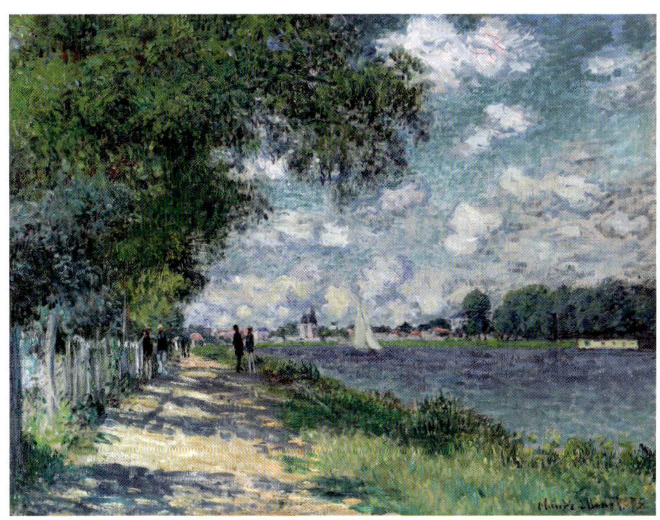

THE CHURCH AT VÉTHEUIL
(*L'ÉGLISE DE VÉTHEUIL*), 1878
Oil on canvas, 65 x 55 cm
Scottish National Gallery, Edinburgh
W 474

Galerie Miethke, Manet – Monet, 1910, Cat. No. 24
Secession, *Die führenden Meister der französischen Kunst im neunzehnten Jahrhundert*, 1925, Cat. No. 41

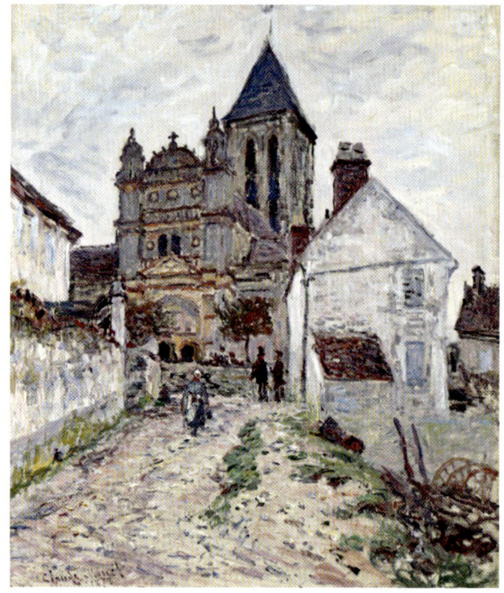

VÉTHEUIL, 1879
Oil on canvas, 60 x 81 cm
National Gallery of Victoria, Melbourne
W 533

Galerie Miethke, *Manet – Monet*, 1910, Cat. No. 15

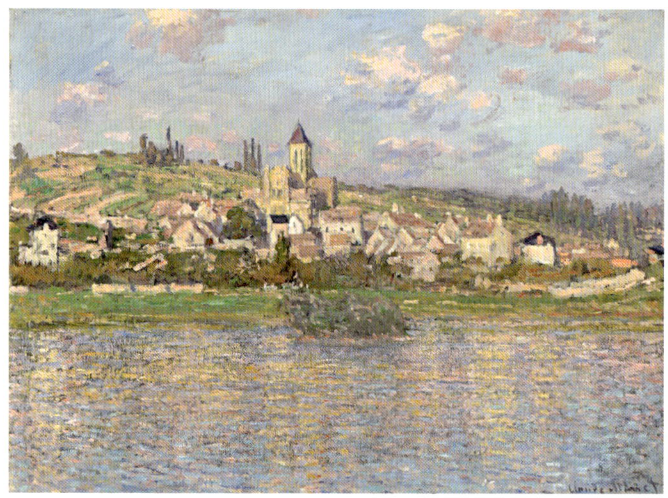

VIEW OF VÉTHEUIL, BREAKUP OF ICE
(*VUE DE VÉTHEUIL, DÉBÂCLE*), 1880
Oil on canvas, 71 x 100 cm
Private collection
W 559

Galerie Miethke, *Manet – Monet*, 1910, Cat. No. 27

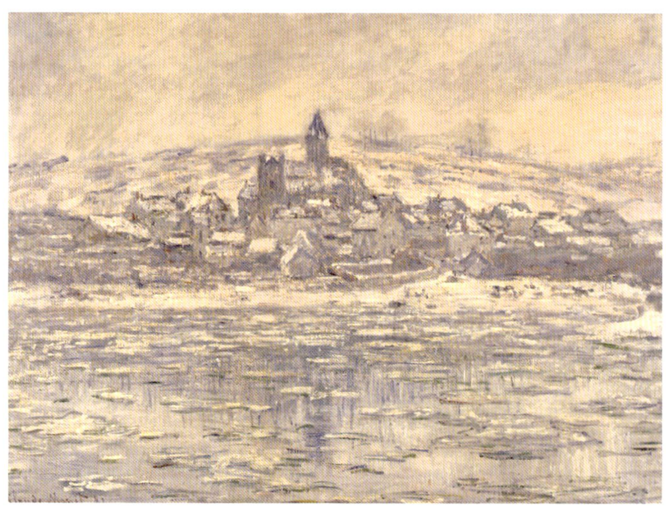

CALM WEATHER, FÉCAMP
(*TEMPS CALME, FÉCAMP*), 1881
Oil on canvas, 60 x 73.5 cm
Sammlung Rudolf Staechelin, Deposit im Kunstmuseum Basel
2002
W 650

Galerie Miethke, *Manet – Monet* 1910, Cat. No. 31

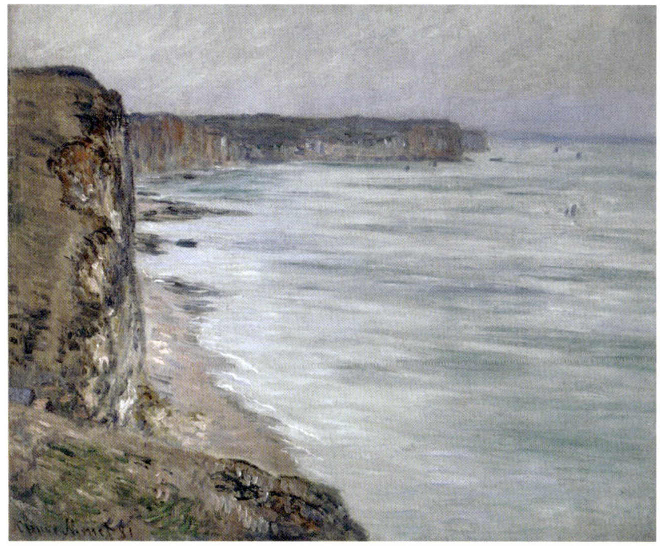

THE CUSTOMS HOUSE, AFTERNOON EFFECT
(*CABANE DE DOUANIERS, EFFET D'APRÈS-MIDI*),
1882
Oil on canvas, 58 x 81 cm
Musée national des douanes, Bordeaux, Dépôt du Musée
d'Orsay, Paris
W 737

Galerie Miethke, *Manet – Monet*, 1910, Cat. No. 23

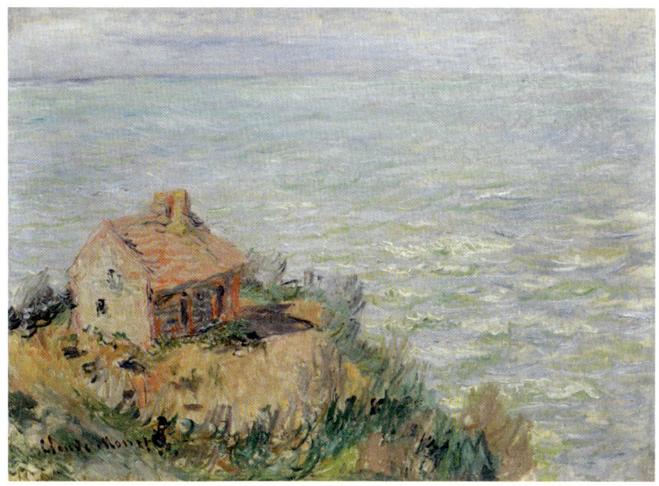

ANGLERS ON THE SEINE AT POISSY
(*PÊCHEURS À LA LIGNE SUR LA SEINE À POISSY*),
1882
Oil on canvas, 59.8 x 81.7 cm
Belvedere, Vienna
W 748

Galerie Miethke, *Manet – Monet*, 1910, Cat. No. 21

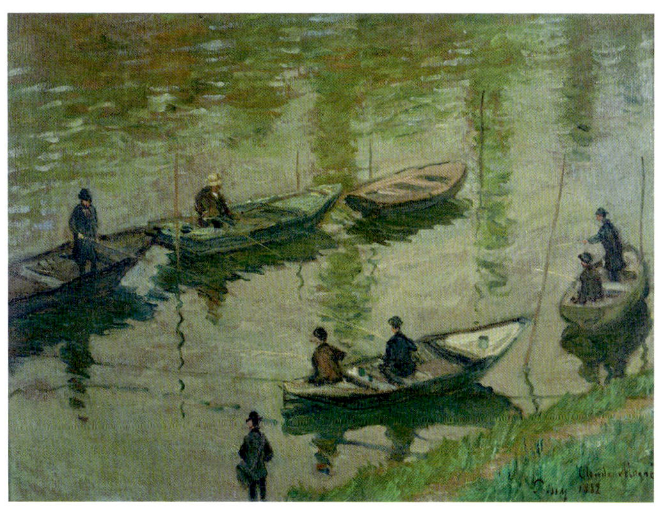

ON THE CLIFF AT DIEPPE
(*SUR LA FALAISE À DIEPPE*), 1882
Oil on canvas, 60 x 100 cm
National Gallery of Art Washington, D.C.
W 754

Galerie Miethke, *Manet – Monet*, 1910, Cat. No. 28

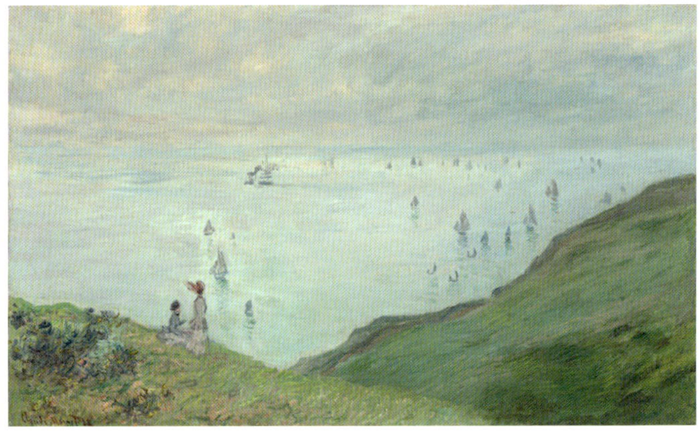

THE NEEDLE ROCK AND THE PORT D'AVAL
(*LA FALAISE ET LA PORTE D'AVAL*), 1883
Oil on canvas, 60 x 81 cm
Private collection
W 819

Galerie Miethke, *Manet – Monet,* 1910, Cat. No. 17

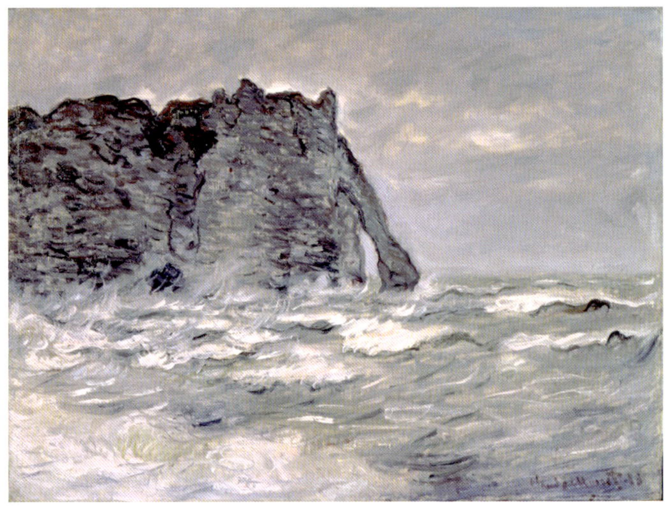

LEMONS ON A BRANCH
(*CITRONS SUR UNE BRANCHE*), 1884
Oil on canvas, 65 x 54 cm
Private collection
W 888

Galerie Miethke, *Manet – Monet*, 1910, Cat. No. 18

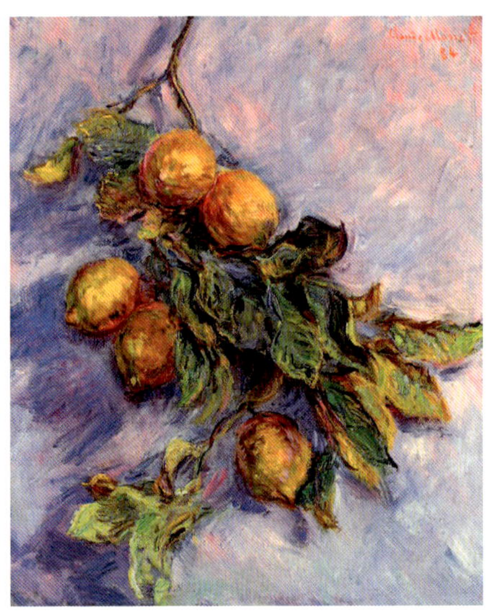

THE RAGING SEE
(*MER DÉMONTÉE*), 1886
Oil on canvas, 65 x 81 cm
Musée national des Beaux-Arts d'Alger, Algeria
W 1118
Galerie Miethke, *Manet – Monet*, 1910, Cat. No. 22

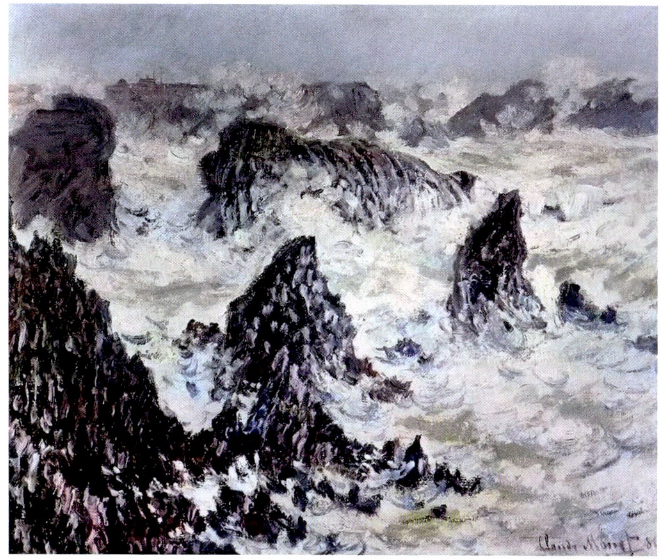

ON THE BANKS OF THE FJORD NEAR CHRISTIANIA
(*AU BORD DU FJORD, PRÈS CHRISTIANIA*), 1895
Oil on canvas, 65 x 100 cm
Private collection
W 1403

Galerie Miethke, *Manet – Monet* 1910, Cat. No. 25

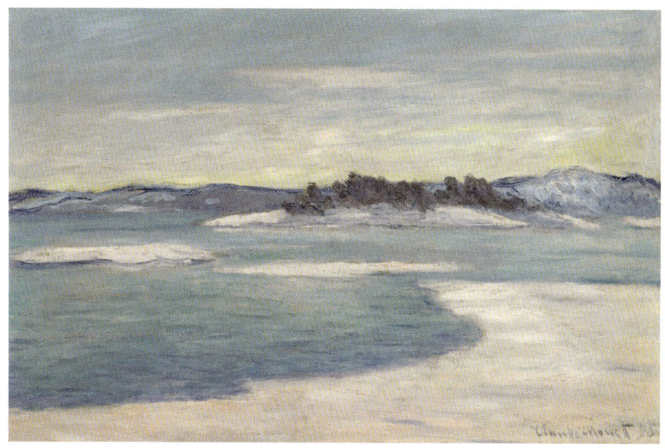

PLUM TREES IN BLOSSOM AT VÉTHEUIL
(*LES PRUNIERS EN FLEURS À VÉTHEUIL*), 1879
Oil on canvas, 64.5 x 81 cm
Museum of Fine Arts, Budapest
W 520
Galerie Arnot, *Französische Impressionisten*, 1911, Cat. No. 5

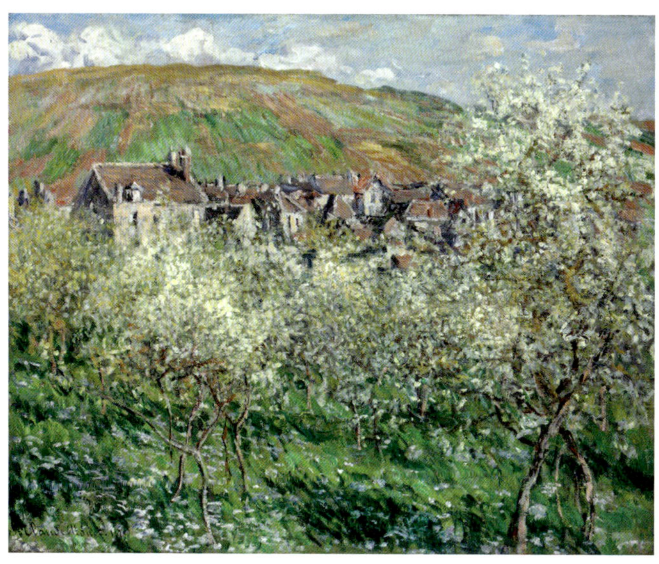

LOW TIDE AT VARENGEVILLE
(*MARÉE BASSE À VARENGEVILLE*), 1882
Oil on canvas, 60 x 81 cm
Private collection
W 793

Galerie Arnot, *Französische Impressionisten*, 1911, Cat. No. 6

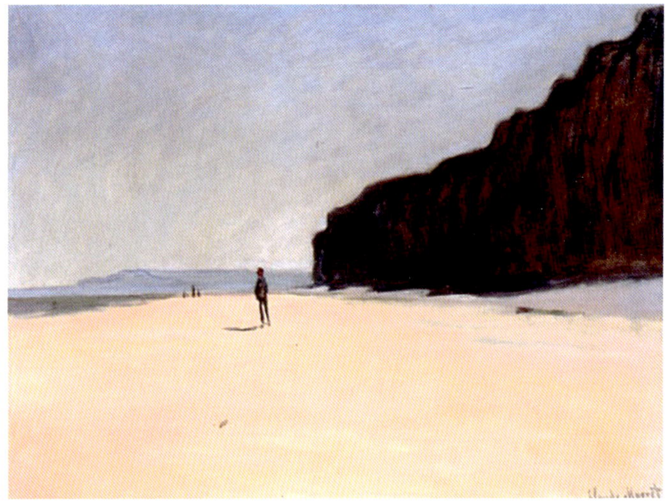

THE PYRAMIDS AT PORT-COTON,
SUNLIGHT EFFECT
(*LES PYRAMIDES DE PORT-COTON,*
EFFET DE SOLEIL), 1886
Oil on canvas, 64 x 64 cm
Private collection
W 1088

Galerie Arnot, *Französische Impressionisten*, 1911, Cat. No. 4

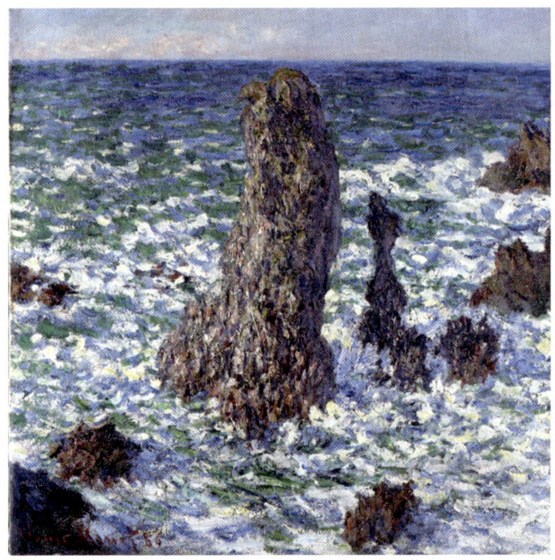

THE BRIDGE IN MONET'S GARDEN
(*PONT DANS LE JARDIN DE MONET*), 1895/96
Oil on canvas, 89 x 92 cm
Private collection
W 1419 a

Galerie Arnot, *Französische Impressionisten*, 1911, Cat. No. 11

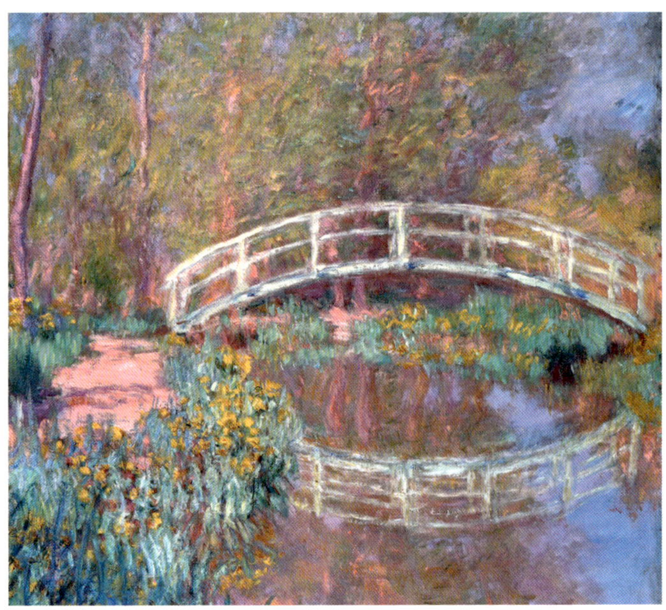

WATER-LILIES
(*NYMPHÉAS*), 1905
Oil on canvas, 90 x 100 cm
Private collection
W 1673

Galerie Arnot, *Französische Impressionisten*, 1911, Cat. No. 10

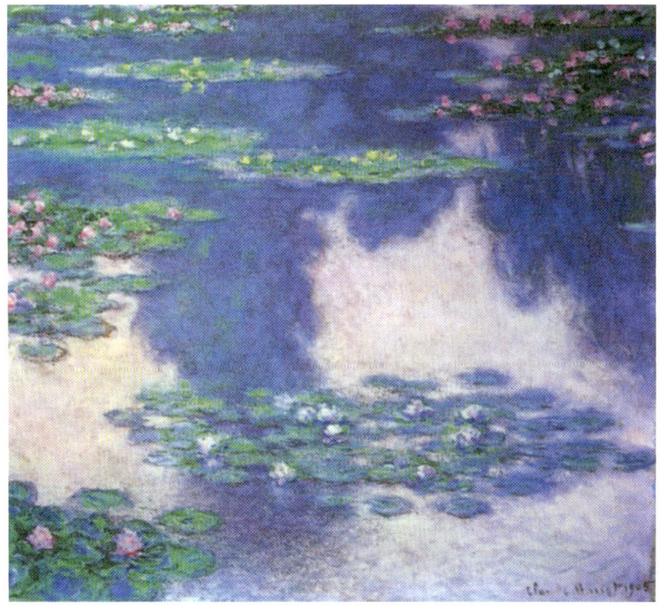

IN THE MEADOW
(*DANS LA PRAIRIE*), 1876
Oil on canvas, 60 x 82 cm
Private collection
W 405

Galerie Miethke, *Französische Meister*, 1912, Cat. No. 10

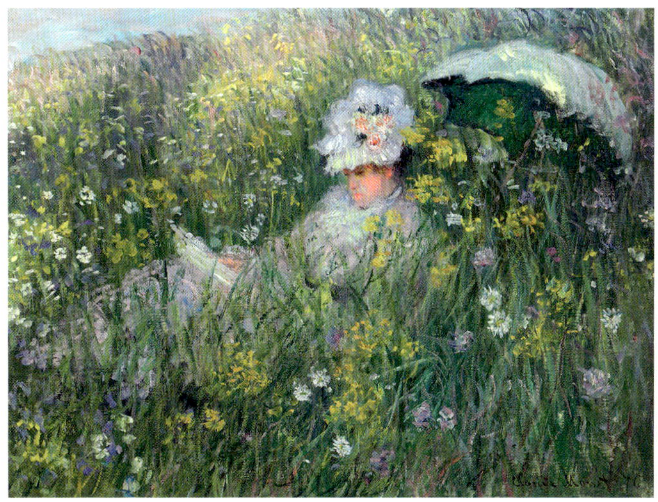

THE SEINE NEAR ARGENTEUIL
(LA SEINE PRÈS D'ARGENTEUIL), 1874
Oil on canvas, 55 x 65.2 cm
Kunstmuseum Bern
W 327

Galerie Miethke, *Französische Meister*, 1912, Cat. No. 14

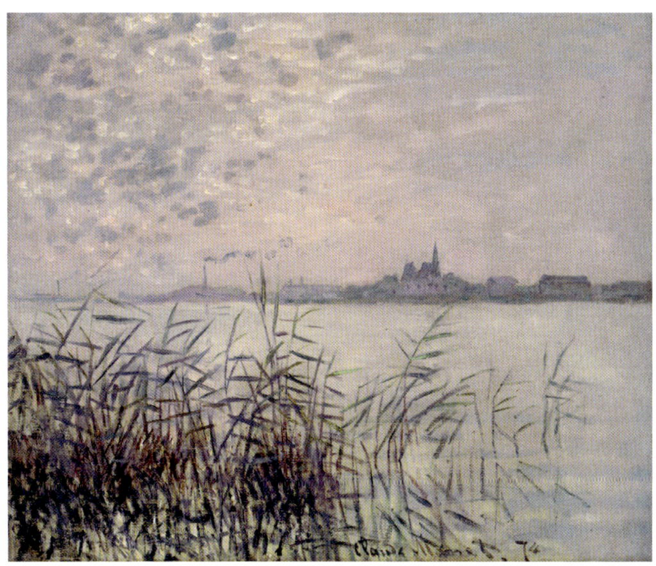

THE PORTAL OF ROUEN CATHEDRALE AT MIDDAY
(*CATHÉDRALE DE ROUEN, PORTAIL PLEIN MIDI*),
1894
Oil on canvas, 106.7 x 73.7 cm
Sterling and Francine Clark Art Institute, Williamstown
W 1358

Galerie Arnot, *Ausstellung von Werken moderner Franzosen*, 1912,
Cat. No. 18

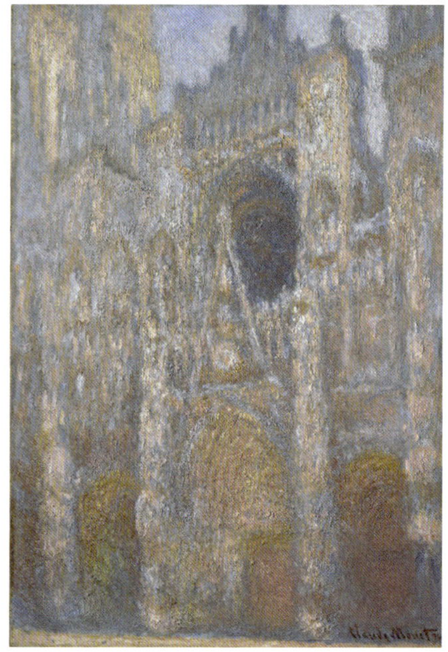

RED MULLETS
(*ROUGETS*), um 1870
Oil on canvas, 31.1 x 46 cm
Harvard Art Museums/Fogg Museum, Cambridge,
Massachusetts
W 140
Galerie Miethke, *Französische Impressionisten*, 1913,
Cat. No. 23

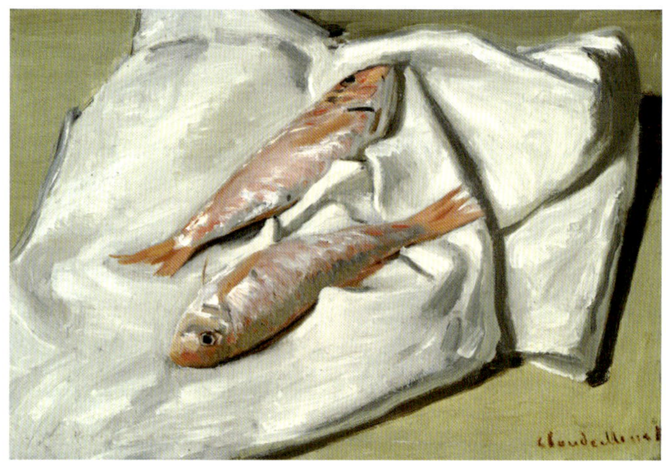

A PATH
(*CHEMIN CREUX*), 1873
Oil on canvas, 54.1 x 65.7 cm
Philadelphia Museum of Art
W 288

Galerie Miethke, *Französische Impressionisten*, 1913,
Cat. No. 26

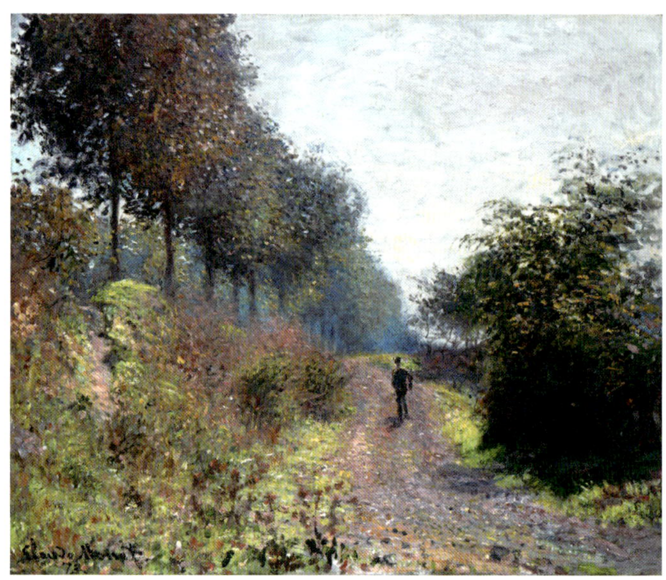

FARMYARD
(*COUR DE FERME*), 1878
Oil on canvas, 65 x 50 cm
Antoun Nabil Sehnaoui
W 494

Galerie Miethke, *Französische Meister*, 1913/14

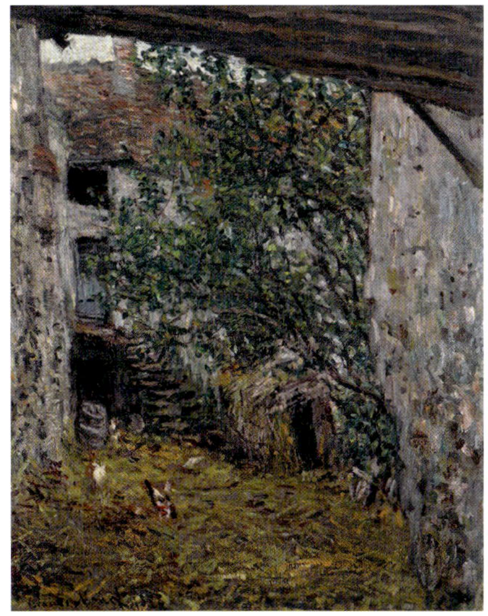

ROAD BY SAINT-SIMÉON FARM
(*LA ROUTE DE LA FERME SAINT-SIMÉON*), 1864
Oil on canvas, 81.6 x 46.4 cm
The National Museum of Western Art, Tokyo
W 29

Secession, *Die führenden Meister der französischen Kunst im neunzehnten Jahrhundert*, 1925, Cat. No. 35

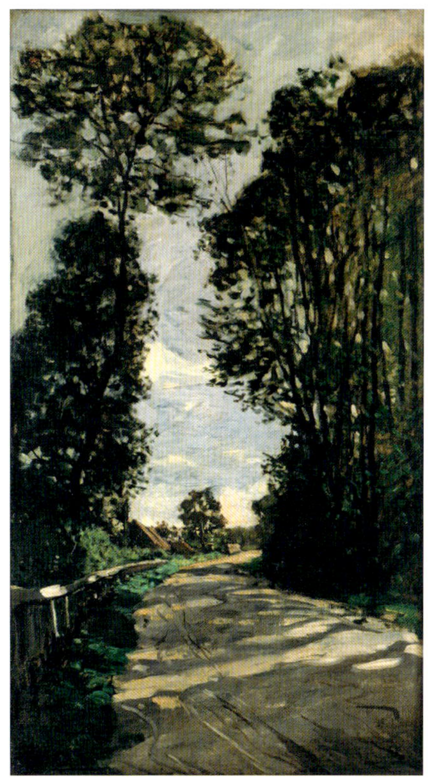

THE VILLAGE OF LAVACOURT
(*LE VILLAGE DE LAVACOURT*), 1878
Oil on canvas, 35.5 x 73 cm
Private collection
W 501

Secession, *Die führenden Meister der französischen Kunst im neunzehnten Jahrhundert*, 1925, Cat. No. 70

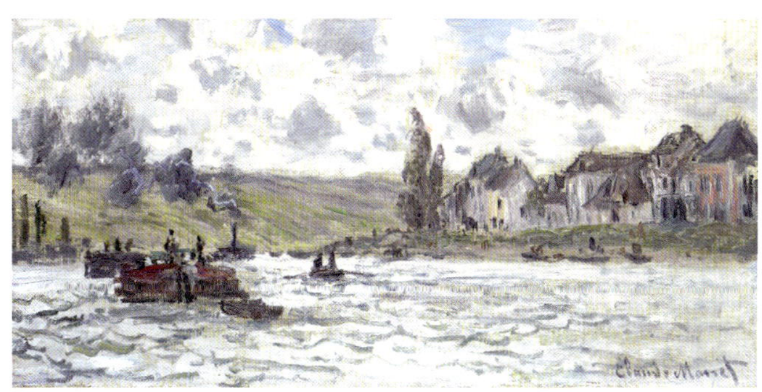

THE ARTISTS

CLAUDE MONET
(1840 Paris – 1926 Giverny)

"Painting is such a torment! I am really useless."[1]

Stephan Koja

Oscar-Claude Monet was born in Paris on November 14, 1840, as the second child of Claude Adolphe Monet and Louise Justine Aubrée. In 1845, the family moved to Ingouville near Le Havre, where Monet went to school. Eugène Boudin discovered him after seeing his caricatures in an art supplies store. He recognized Monet's talent and persuaded him to accompany him on outdoor painting excursions. Monet claimed later that it was through Boudin that he learnt how to see and understand.[2]

After the death of his mother, her role was taken over by Monet's aunt Marie-Jeanne Lecadre, who also painted and had artist friends.

Monet's attempts to obtain a scholarship to study art in Paris were unsuccessful and he therefore moved into a studio of his own in Paris in 1857. He discovered the landscape painters Charles-François Daubigny, Camille Corot, and Théodore Rousseau in the Paris Salon and enrolled in the Académie Suisse in the French capital.

He was conscripted for military service in 1861 and stationed in Algeria. He later stated that the light and landscape there prepared him for Impressionism. He was posted back to France due to a severe illness in 1862 and was exempted from further military service following a payment by his aunt. Once again in Paris, he was admitted to the painting school of the history painter Charles Gleyre, in whose studio he met Piere-Auguste Renoir, Frédéric Bazille, and Alfred Sisley. He also made the acquaintance of James McNeill Whistler at this time. With Bazille, Monet rented a studio to complete the planned monumental work *Luncheon on the Grass (Le déjeuner sur l'herbe)*, with which he hoped to impress the Salon. However, time constraints forced him to submit two other pictures. One of them, *The Woman in the Green Dress (La femme à la robe verte)*, showing his lover and future wife Camille Doncieux, was well received and marked Monet's first success in the Salon.

Plagued by money worries, he lived at various addresses in Paris over the next few years and spent long periods on the Normandy coast, where he painted seascapes and winter landscapes. Monet's first son, Jean-Armand-Claude, was born in 1867.

In 1870, during the Franco-Prussian War, Monet and his family fled to London, where Daubigny arranged for him to meet the art dealer Paul Durand-Ruel, who in turn introduced him to Camille Pissarro. Durand-Ruel was to become Monet's most important dealer. The pictures by John Constable and J.M.W. Turner that Monet and Pissarro saw during their visits to London museums and galleries made a lasting impression on the two artists.

After returning to France, Monet moved to Argenteuil, just fifteen minutes from Paris by train, at the end of 1871 and worked there with Sisley in early 1872. Monet had not only a garden, where he could pursue his love of flowers, and a studio, but also a studio boat on the Seine, which he had had specially made in emulation of Daubigny. It was here that he painted many of his pictures in 1872. The sale of these pictures by Durand-Ruel now enabled him to live a comfortable life.

The first exhibition of the Société anonyme des artistes peintres, sculpteurs, graveurs, etc. (Society of painters, sculptors, engravers, etc.)

ETIENNE CLÉMENTEL
Claude Monet in his Garden in Giverny, ca. 1920
Musée d'Orsay, Paris

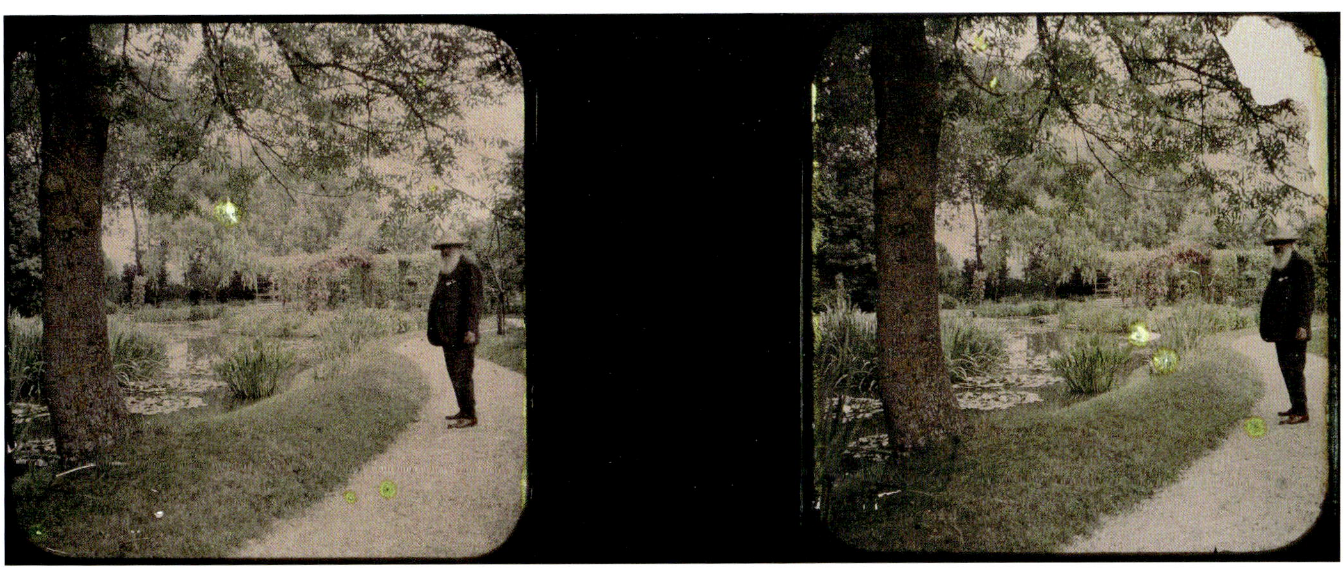

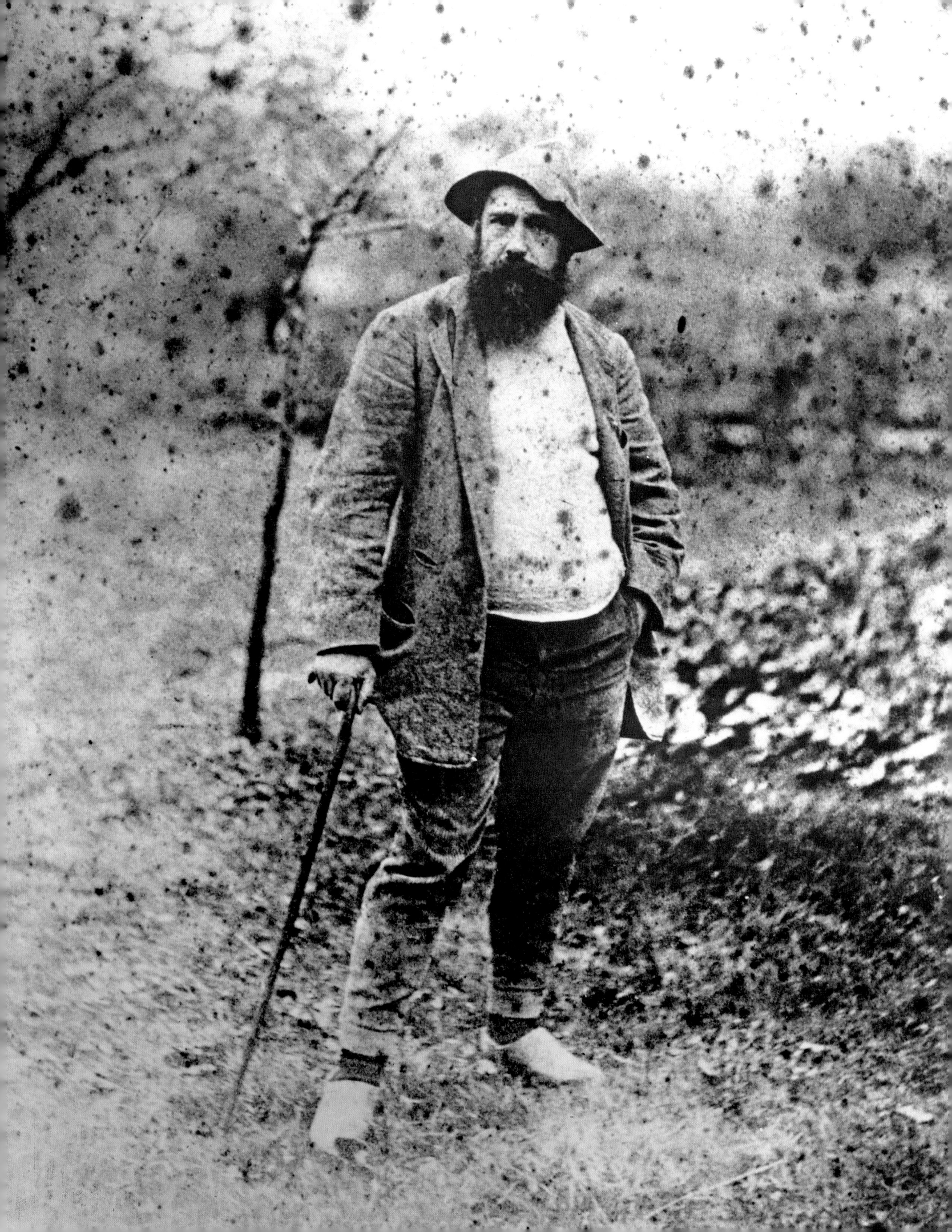

took place in the studio of the photographer Nadar (Gaspard Félix Tournachon) on Boulevard des Capucines in 1874. It was later to be regarded as the first Impressionist exhibition. Monet showed a view of the port of Le Havre entitled *Impression Sunrise* (*Impression, soleil levant*, 1873). The title inspired the art critic Louis Leroy to coin the term "Impressionists"—in this case meant disparagingly—for the satirical magazine *Le Charivari*.

When lack of business forced Durand-Ruel to close his London gallery in 1875, Monet was once again faced with difficult years of financial worry. With the support of Gustave Caillebotte, whom he had met in 1873, he rented a small studio near Saint-Lazare Train Station as a salesroom for his customers in Paris in 1877. He was also given permission to paint in the station itself, producing his legendary views of steaming locomotives and the hustle and bustle of a railway station.

In his 1878 brochure in support of Impressionism *Les peintres impressionnistes*, Théodore Duret described Monet as the "Impressionist par excellence." That year, the Monet family moved with Ernest and Alice Hoschedé and their six children to Vétheuil, where the seriously ill Camille gave birth to a second son, Michel. To raise money to look after his wife, Monet desperately painted still lifes, as these were the easiest to sell. Camille died, however, on September 5, 1879.

In 1880, Monet's first solo exhibition was shown at the gallery of the magazine *La vie moderne* in Paris with eighteen pictures, some of which he was able to sell on the spot. His economic situation gradually improved thanks to positive articles in various magazines; his pictures were well received and found buyers. In addition, Monet began to exhibit, much to Durand-Ruel's displeasure, in the Galerie Georges Petit, with Bernheim-Jeune, and in Goupil & Cie (later Boussod, Valadon & Co), an art gallery managed by Theo van Gogh, thus creating even greater opportunities for selling his pictures.

Visits to Normandy in the following summers inspired Monet to paint dramatic views of the steep cliffs. He insisted on having identical conditions when he continued with a painting he had started. Every change in the subject caused him great difficulties and could lead him to abandon pictures; he sometimes needed as many as sixty sittings and daily observation to capture the same mood for half an hour. In early 1897, for example, he stopped people burning grass on the cliffs of Pourville while he was painting a picture[3] and he had the leaves cut off a blossoming tree in spring when he took up a work again after a long pause.[4]

No effort was too great for Monet when he wanted to capture a particular mood. When painting on the Normandy coast, he fought continuously against the wind, battening down his easel and canvases with rope and pegs hammered into the ground. To find a subject, he would also clamber to the remotest of beaches. In his struggle to create a picture he once lost all his painting materials in the sea after being caught by a wave and thrown against the cliffs;[5] while painting in Fresselines in the Creuse valley, he caught rheumatism in his right hand because of the cold, forcing him to wear glycerin gloves day and night;[6] and in Antibes he got sunstroke while working relentlessly in the bright sunlight.[7]

THEODORE ROBINSON
Claude Monet in his Garden in Giverny, 1887
Musée Marmottan, Paris

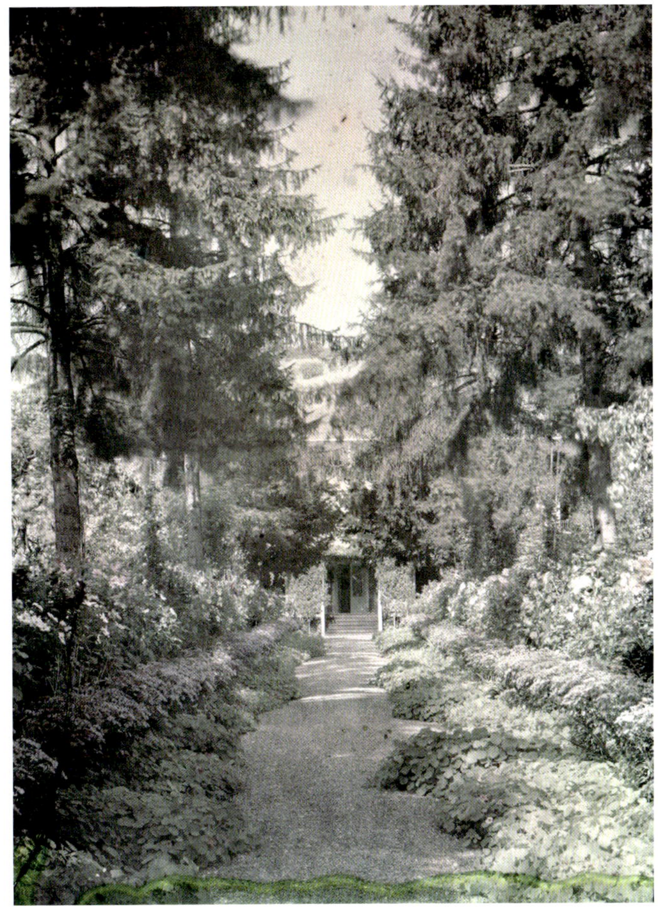

ANONYMOUS
The Alley in Monet's Garden in Giverny, after 1920
Musée Marmottan, Paris

Monet moved to Poissy in December 1881 but he never really felt comfortable there. In 1883, however, he found a large farmhouse with an extensive garden in Giverny near Vernon, which he rented and later bought. He began to design the garden with paths, flowerbeds, channels, a pond, and bridges, and was to build three studio buildings for his requirements.

Trips to Bordighera on the Mediterranean in 1883 and to Étretat on the rugged Atlantic coast in 1885 offered enormous visual challenges and once again brought about developments in his colorism and picture composition.

An Impressionism exhibition organized by Durand-Ruel in New York in 1886 with around three hundred pictures from his own collection was praised to the skies by the media and established Monet's reputation in the United States. Thereafter, American buyers, who were will-

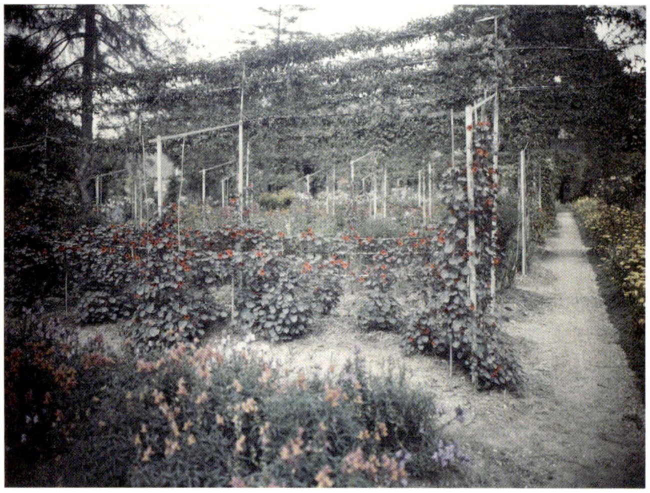

ANONYMOUS
The Rose Garden in Giverny, 1921
Musee d'Orsay, Paris

ing to pay high prices, were to be amongst the most important collectors of his works.

The artist never ceased to seek creative stimulation by exploring new landscapes, and he frequently underestimated the difficulties involved. In 1886, for example, he had to extend a planned one-week visit to the harsh Belle-Île island off the Atlantic coast of Brittany to three months in order to come to terms with the subjects and weather.

Two major exhibitions in 1889 were resounding successes. Theo van Gogh organized a solo exhibition with Boussod,Valadon & Cie, which was subsequently shown in London, and Georges Petit presented the exhibition "Claude Mone – Auguste Rodin" featuring thirty-six sculptures by Rodin and 145 paintings by Monet at his gallery during the World's Fair in Paris. Good reviews and essays by Octave Mirbeau and Gustave Geffroy had already won over the moneyed clientele.

Following trips to Italy and the South of France in 1890, Monet began painting the grainstacks near Giverny and the poplars on the banks of the Epte, his first real series. In 1892, a visit to Rouen inspired him to paint a series of pictures of the cathedral. In the same year he married the widow Alice Hoschedé.

Monet was fascinated by the light on a trip to Norway in 1895. It was in that year as well that he painted his first picture of a Japanese bridge over a lily pond, following on from his first efforts to paint his garden in Giverny in 1887. During a visit to London in 1899 the weather drove him initially to despair—he started several canvases that he was unable to complete—but he soon recognized the potential for a series and returned to the Thames in the next two years to capture the light and fog of Waterloo Bridge, Charing Cross Bridge, and the Houses of Parliament in a hitherto unknown intensity of color reminiscent of Turner.

In 1896, France was shaken by the Dreyfus affair. Monet supported Émile Zola, who had asserted Dreyfus's innocence in his article "J'accuse," published in Georges Clemenceau's newspaper *Aurore*. Monet's fame continued to rise at a breathtaking pace and his pictures were also purchased by private collectors and museums in Germany, Japan, and Russia. In 1902, Durand-Ruel organized Monet's first solo exhibition in the USA and, in 1909, the presentation of Monet's *Water Lilies* series *(Les Nymphéas: series de paysages d'eau)*, on which he had worked intensively from summer 1906 onwards, caused a sensation with critics and the general public alike.

More and more people streamed to Giverny to see the master and his garden. The visitors who were admitted found not only a garage but also guest rooms and a sales studio.

As a young man, Monet had already been described as a dandy capable of making an immediate impression on account of his self-assured manner. Now he was known as a bon vivant who, after his early years as a struggling artist, was finally able to lead a pleasant bourgeois existence, enjoying the comfortable life of a wealthy garden owner with servants, indulging in his love of flowers and ceaselessly perfecting his water garden, having expensive clothes made for him, cultivating a taste for fine food and choice ingredients, and owning cars and attending motor races—so much so that his love of speed earned him a fine, whereupon, interestingly, he recorded his strong opposition to speeding.[8]

For all this indulgence, it is easy to forget that Monet was notoriously dissatisfied and self-critical. Reports by Monet in letters and conversations about the difficulties of his work are legion. There is hardly a letter in which he does not complain about the vagaries of the weather, distractions by other hotel guests, or the difficulty of capturing new moods and their nuanced colors.

Monet was an eternal doubter, extreme when it came to quality demands, incredibly demanding of himself, always trying to challenge himself with even more difficult subjects and tasks. Never were the results satisfactory. "I do my utmost but am not really satisfied. The further I come, the more I look for the impossible, the unattainable, and sometimes I fear that I am fooling myself. In the end it's a never-ending struggle."[9]

Exhilarating moments could be succeeded directly by phases of deep despondency. "For a month I haven't managed to do anything good. I have scratched off or torn practically everything I have done, and I loathe myself: a wonderful summer wasted. Painting is such a torment! I am really useless."[10] In his relentless self-criticism, Monet did not stop at destroying pictures, probably several hundred over the course of his life.

This might have been because Monet was thinking of posterity ("[...] as long as I can, I need to think about my artistic reputation [...]"[11]) or because of attacks of rage at his inability. He once kicked a hole in a painting in disappointment at what he had produced, and another time he threw all his painting materials into the water from a boat.[12] Even *The Washington Post* found the painter's rigor worthy of an article, reporting that he had probably thrown away 100,000 dollars through the destruction of his pictures.[13]

There were years in which Monet was plagued almost continuously by doubts and depression, closing himself in and often ignoring his wife's calls to the dinner table. For years, he refused to take part in exhibitions, continuously revised his pictures or simply cut them up by the score. "Yesterday was bad for him; he destroyed three pictures, unfortunately a frequent experience," wrote his troubled wife.[14]

The lily pond in his garden exerted an increasing fascination for him, and he invested practically all of his money in enlarging the property and in the cultivation of rare lilies and other flowers. A heated greenhouse and a team of gardeners ensured that plants were always in flower or ready for inclusion in this colorful *Gesamtkunstwerk*.

Monet felt less and less cause to leave his home and his years in Giverny were interrupted only by occasional trips to Spain, Venice, and Switzerland.

The garden and the lilies had become his favorite subjects for painting. Monet had a rigid work routine. He got up very early, often before sunrise, and then worked in a steady rhythm: he painted his lilies from 7 to 11 a.m., again from 1 to 3 p.m. and finally from 5 p.m. to sunset. In the afternoon he received visitors and showed them his garden. In Venice he worked for two hours on each of four subjects, from 8 to 10 a.m., 10 a.m. to noon, 2 to 4 p.m., and 4 to 6 p.m. In London he worked on his Thames bridge paintings in the morning and on the Parliament in the afternoon. He always attempted to make the best use of the time and did everything not to waste it. If this happened nevertheless—on account of bad weather, for example—he would become restless. That was also one of the reasons he began to plant flowers right after moving to Giverny in 1883—to have subjects to paint even when the weather was bad, as he mentioned in a letter to Durand-Ruel.[15]

In 1908 Monet's eyesight began to fail, sometimes making it impossible for him to paint. In 1912, his ophthalmologist Dr Vallude diagnosed cataracts. Because of his defective sight, he often had to arrange the colors on his palette from memory. Clemenceau assured him that he would not lose his sight, but Monet kept postponing the operation and it was not until 1923 that his full sight was restored.

The death of his second wife Alice in 1911, the painful passing of his

ANONYMOUS
The Water Lily Pond in Giverny, 1921
Musee d'Orsay, Paris

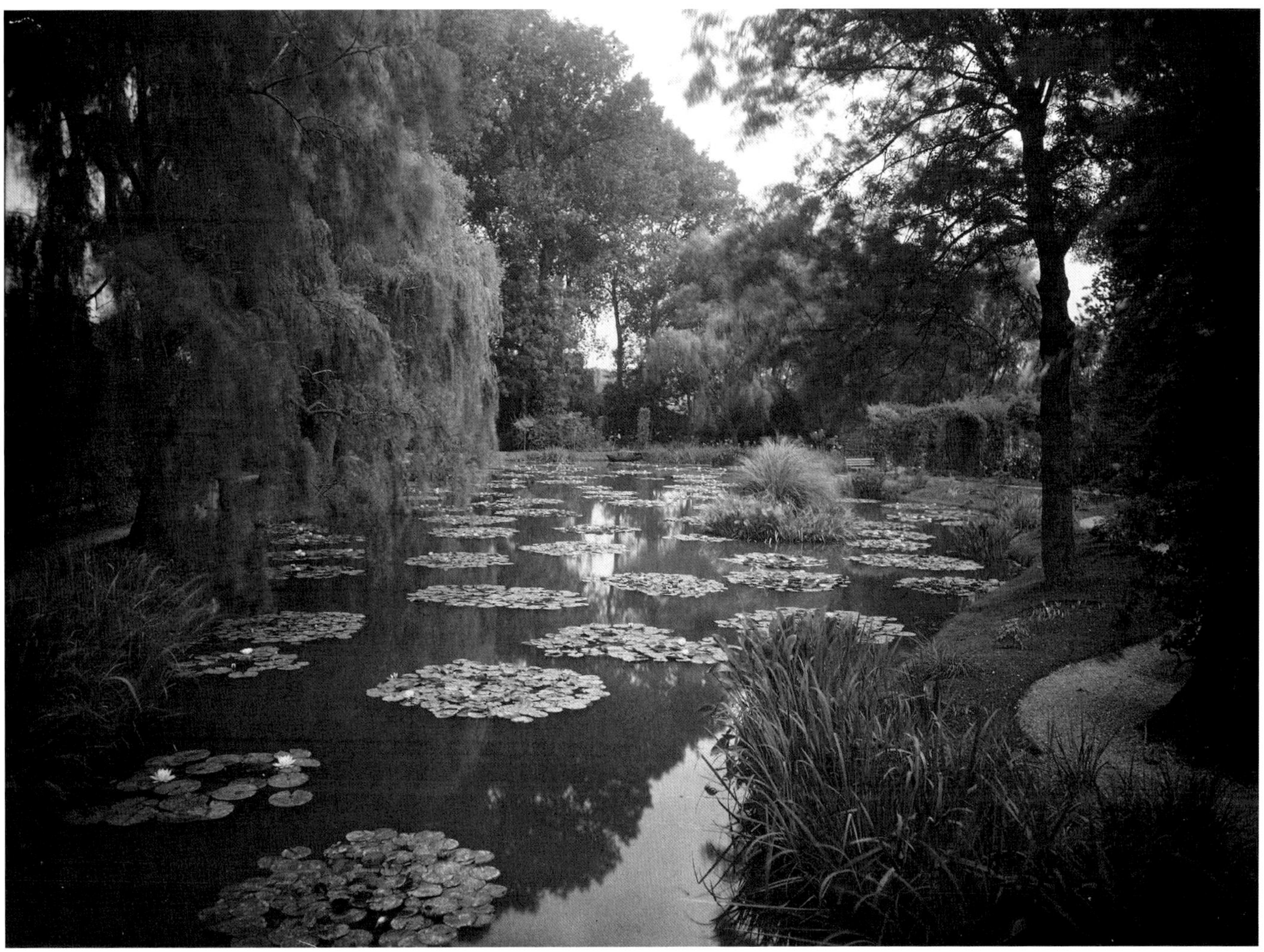

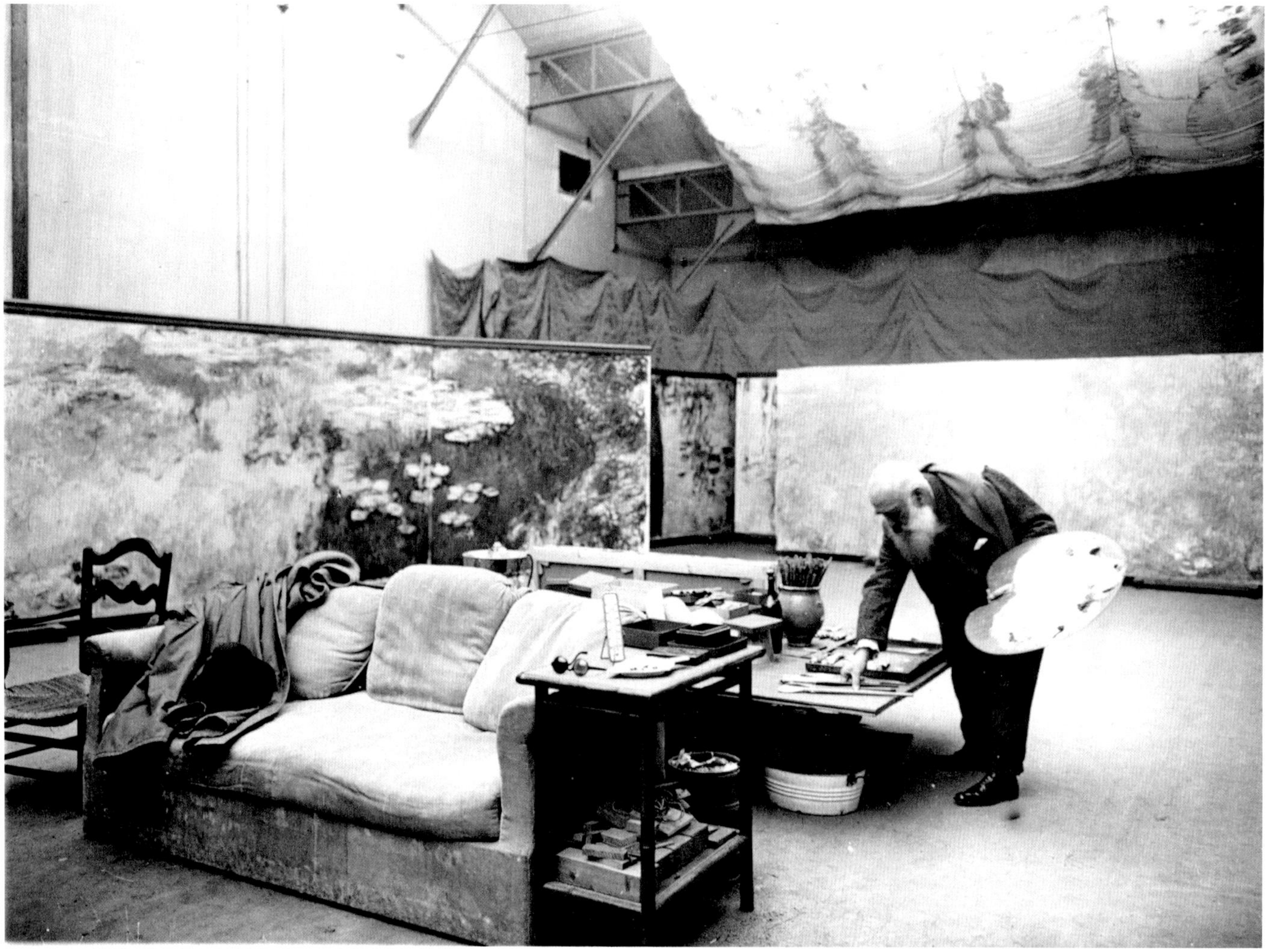

HENRI MANUEL
Claude Monet in his studio in Giverny, ca. 1920
Collection Harlingue/Roger-Viollet

son Jean in 1914, and the conscription of his younger son Michel into the army on the outbreak of World War I overshadowed the coming years, despite the commercial success they brought.

In 1914, Monet started work on large-scale wall decorations with pictures of his lily pond. The painter, who preferred to work in the studio after 1900, had a 23 x 12 meter hall with overhead lighting, in which he worked on and matched up the huge canvases, specially constructed. During these years, Monet frequently gave pictures to charity. After the armistice in 1918, he decided to donate *Grandes Décorations* to the state. After considering a round building in the grounds of Hôtel Biron (today, Musée Rodin) in Paris, it was finally agreed to install them in the Orangery in the Tuileries Garden, where the paintings were to be displayed in two purpose-built oval rooms. It was not until after Monet's death, however, that the presentation was finally completed. Prior to that, the painter had been too busy endlessly improving and refining the pictures, unable to part with them.

Monet's friend Georges Clemenceau was at his bedside when the artist died of a lung tumor on December 5, 1926. Monet was buried in Giverny village cemetery.

1 Letter from Monet to Gustave Caillebotte, Giverny, September 4, 1887, quoted in Daniel Wildenstein, *Claude Monet. Biographie et catalog raisonné*, 5 vols., Lausanne/Paris 1974–1991, vol. III, p. 298, letter 1424.
2 Letter from Monet to Eugène Boudin, Giverny, August 22, 1892, ibid., p. 268, letter 1162.
3 See letters from Monet to Alice Hoschedé, Pourville, February 21, 1897, ibid., p. 294, letter 1373.
4 See letter from Monet to Alice Hoschedé, Fresselines, May 8 and 9, 1889, ibid., p. 248, letters 975 and 976.
5 See letter from Monet to Alice Hoschedé, Étretat, November11, 1885, ibid., vol. II, p. 268, letter 631.
6 See letter from Monet to Alice Hoschedé, Fresselines, April 7, 1889, ibid., vol. III, p. 243, letter 840.
7 See letter from Monet to Alice Hoschedé, Cap d'Antibes, February 9, 1888, ibid., p. 229, letter 832.

8 See John House, *Monet. Nature into Art*, New Haven/London 1986, p. 12.

9 Letter from Monet to Gustave Geffroy, Château de la Pinède (near Antibes), February 25, 1888, quoted in Wildenstein (see note 1), vol. V, p. 191, letter 2732.

10 Letter from Monet to Gustave Caillebotte (see note 1).

11 Quoted in Lilla Cabot Perry, "Reminiscences of Claude Monet from 1889 to 1909," in: *The American Magazine of Art* XVIII, no. 3, March 1927, p. 119, quoted in Charles F. Stuckey (ed.), *Claude Monet 1840–1926*, Cologne 1994, p. 181.

12 See Cabot Perry 1927 (see note 11).

13 Anon., "Destroys his Paintings," in: *The Washington Post*, May 16, 1908, printed in Charles F. Stuckey (ed.), *Monet – A Retrospective*, New York 1985, p. 250.

14 Letter from Alice Hoschedé to her daughter Germaine, married name Salerou, April 15, 1908, quoted in *Claude Monet au temps de Giverny* (exh. cat., Centre Culturel du Marais, Paris, April 6–July 17, 1983), Paris 1983, p. 271.

15 Letter from Monet to Paul Durand-Ruel, Giverny, June 5, 1883, see Lionello Venturi, "Lettres à Paul Durand-Ruel, 1876–1926," in: ibid., *Les Archives de l'impressionnisme*, New York/Paris 1939, vol. I, p. 255.

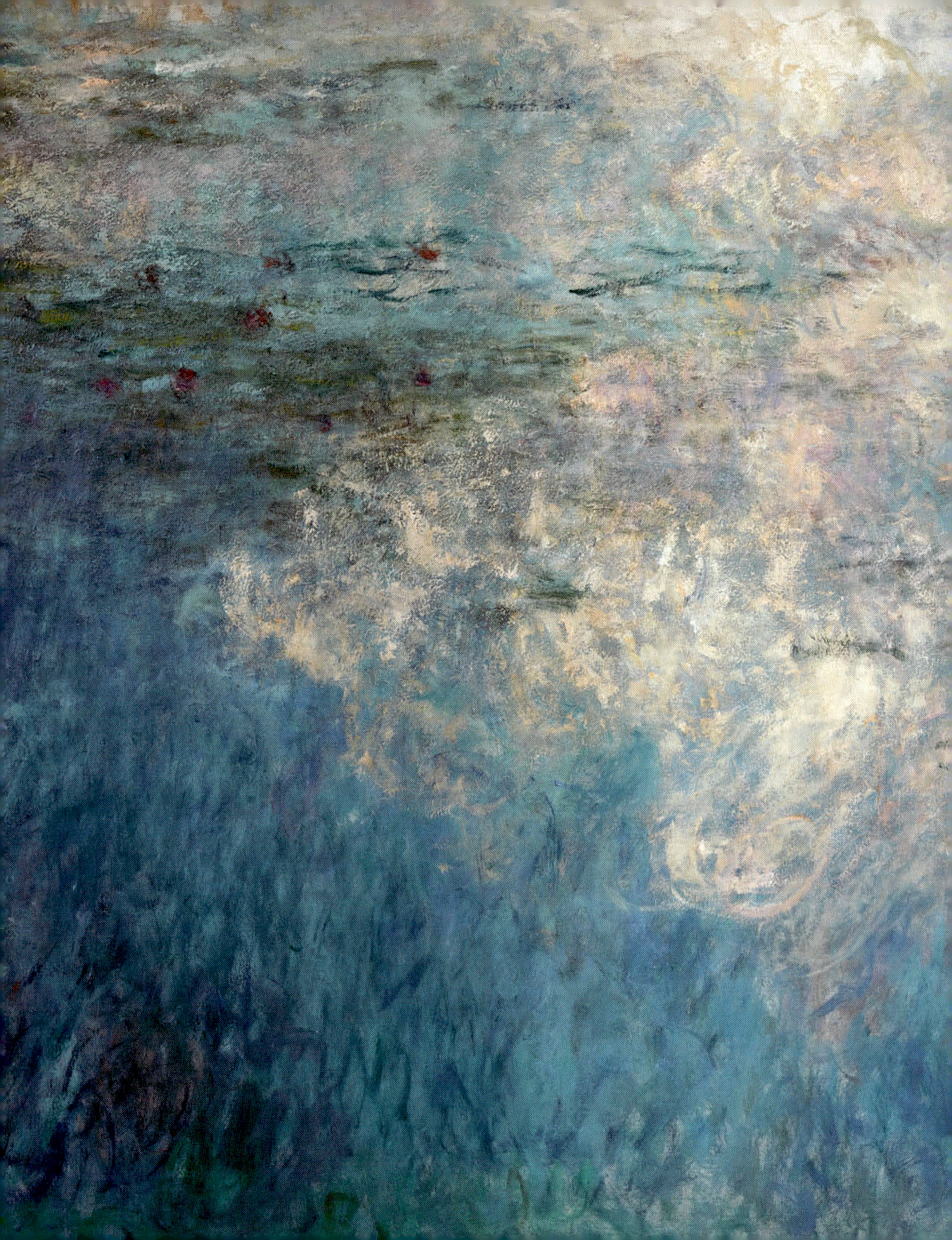

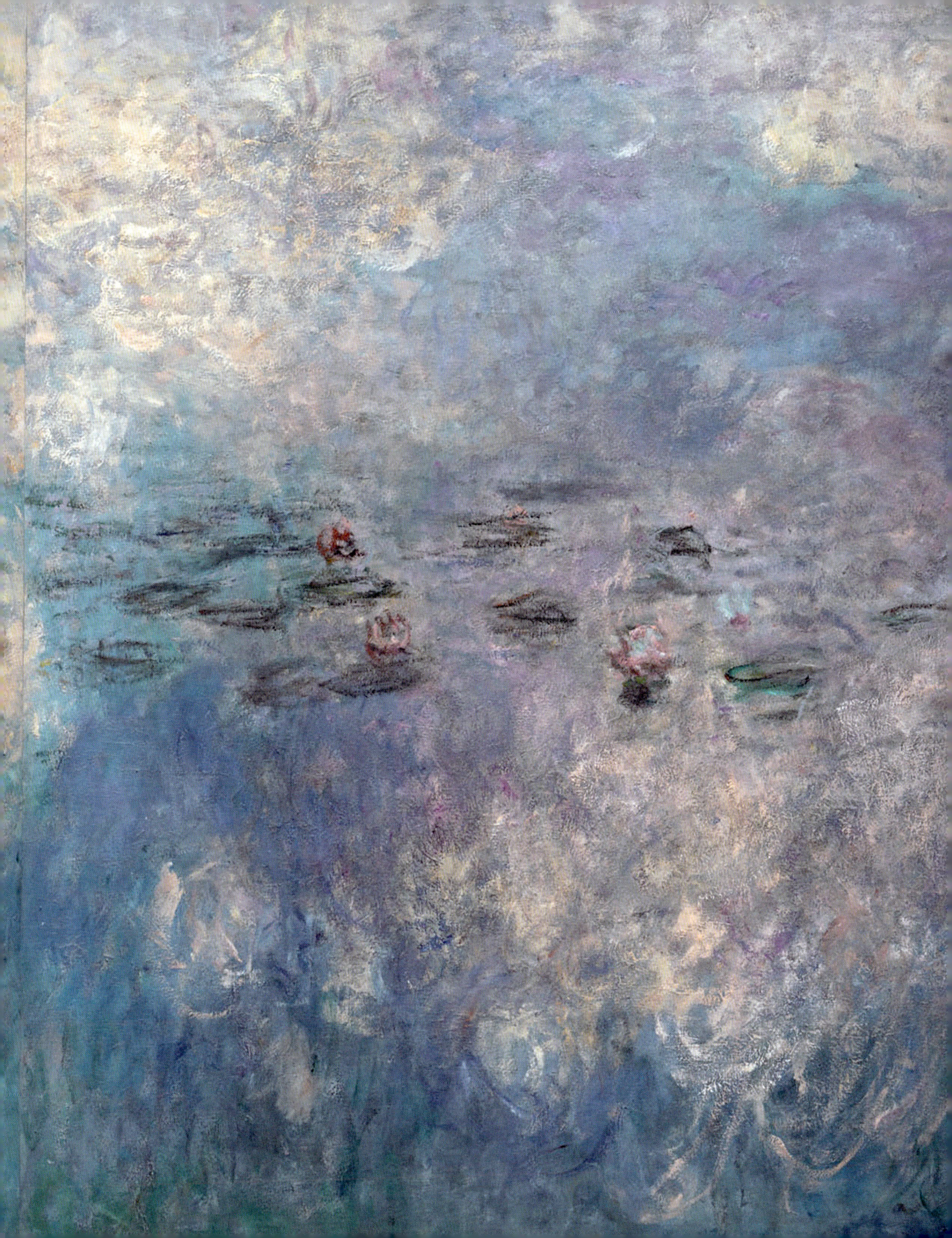

TINA BLAU
(1845 Vienna – 1916 Vienna)

A Picture "whose stark natural realism is almost frightening"[1]

Claus Jesina

Tina Blau was born in Vienna on November 15, 1845, the second of three children of Simon and Theresia Blau. She felt attracted to art from an early age. Her father supported her interest, and when she was fourteen Tina had drawing lessons with Antal Hanély, a student of Waldmüller. From the winter of 1860/61 August Schaeffer von Wienwald, one of the main representatives of the late Biedermeier heroizing landscape painting taught at the time at the Akademie der bildenden Künste (Academy of Fine Arts) in Vienna, became one of her most important teachers and supporters. In his smaller works, Schaeffer mainly followed the ideas of Ferdinand Georg Waldmüller and his demand for the transfer of artistic creativity from the studio to the outdoors. His works in these formats were surprisingly modern. He not only recognized Tina Blau's talent but also advised her from the outset to study nature on the spot, a method taught at the Akademie by Albert Zimmermann and Eduard Peithner von Lichtenfels and practiced by them.

Schaeffer ultimately advised Blau not to base herself on his opinion alone but to seek the judgment and criticism of other artists. She followed this advice when she met the painter Josef Matthias Aigner during a summer vacation in Nasswald, Lower Austria, and attended his painting school the following fall. During this time, she also painted works with a more open painterly style and execution, in which her mastery of carefully observed lighting situations is evident.

The sale of a painting in the Österreichischer Kunstverein (Austrian Art Association) in 1869 enabled Tina Blau to travel to the major International Art Exhibition in Munich that year. With a letter of recommendation from Aigner, the young artist had an introduction to Munich artists' circles. After the sale of a picture in the Munich Kunstverein (Art Association), she was able to extend her stay in the Munich area. Blau took the opportunity to consign herself to the care of Wilhelm Lienschmit the Younger, who was admired at the time throughout Germany.

The situation in Germany—and particularly Munich—was quite different to Vienna. Several artists had already shown an interest in the innovations in landscape painting from France since the mid-nineteenth century, an interest that encouraged artists to experiment with *plein air* painting. Tina Blau's great success and the friends and acquaintances she had made prompted her to prolong her stay in the Munich area until winter 1873/74.

In Munich she familiarized herself not only with German painting but also with the international trends of the time, particularly from France, which was soon reflected in her work. A number of paintings were completed that would not have been conceivable without the influence of Munich painters like Eduard Schleich the Elder. Blau's brushwork became more open and her interest in light phenomena grew.

NEW LIGHT EXPERIENCES

During summer 1872, which Tina Blau spent in Vienna, she sought subjects for painting in Fischamend to the east of the city. Here she met Emil Jakob Schindler and also made the acquaintance of Eugen Jettel, Franz Rumpler, and Hugo Charlemont. It was only at this point that Blau began to experiment with the Austrian version of *plein air* painting that was evolving.

At this time and in subsequent years she produced a series of works with the regulation of the Danube to the east of Vienna as their subject. She painted these pictures outdoors in strong sunlight, concentrating particularly on the effect of this specific light on different surfaces. This interest in the effect of the glaring light and the brown loam soil presaged the works completed in Szolnok, where Tina Blau sought to paint not only the authentic and exotic-seeming life of the local inhabitants but also the new light experience created by the intense sunshine and dust-filled atmosphere. After 1873 the artist frequently visited Szolnok on the Tisza, which had been discovered by August von Pettenkofen and was to attract a whole generation of *plein air* artists.

NETHERLANDS—IN SEARCH OF DULL WEATHER

A few months after moving from Munich to Vienna, Schindler and Blau traveled in 1875 via Nuremberg, Cologne, and Düsseldorf to the Netherlands. The seventeenth-century Dutch painting they saw there on their visits to museums left a deep impression.

From 1905 to 1908, Tina Blau traveled every year to the Netherlands, which she appreciated, like other painters of her generation, for its subtle changing light and the subjects there, preferring it, particularly as she got older, to the bright and unsubtle light of the south. In fact, in her landscape painting she appears always to have had more of a penchant for dull weather. She wrote in 1875, "The enduring blue weather is as tiring as persistent rain."[2]

ITALY—THE LIGHT OF THE SOUTH

Once again the sale of a picture enabled Blau to travel. It was the sale of a Dutch subject at the World's Fair in Paris that provided the funds to travel to Italy, where the artist spent the summer and fall of 1876. This first trip, and even more so the second in 1879, which took Blau via Rome to Naples, led to a marked brightening of her palette and a greater interest in subjects in strong sunlight. Between 1884 and 1894, Blau spent the winter months in Munich before returning to Vienna for good. She undertook a further trip to Rome in 1885.

Although there are no records of major exhibitions by the Macchiaioli group of landscape painters at the time of Blau's visits to Italy, it may be assumed that Blau was aware of the work of these painters.

In common with the Macchiaioli, Blau had a certain fascination for the light colors of Italian fresco painting of the Quattrocento, which had an influence on her colors and also gave

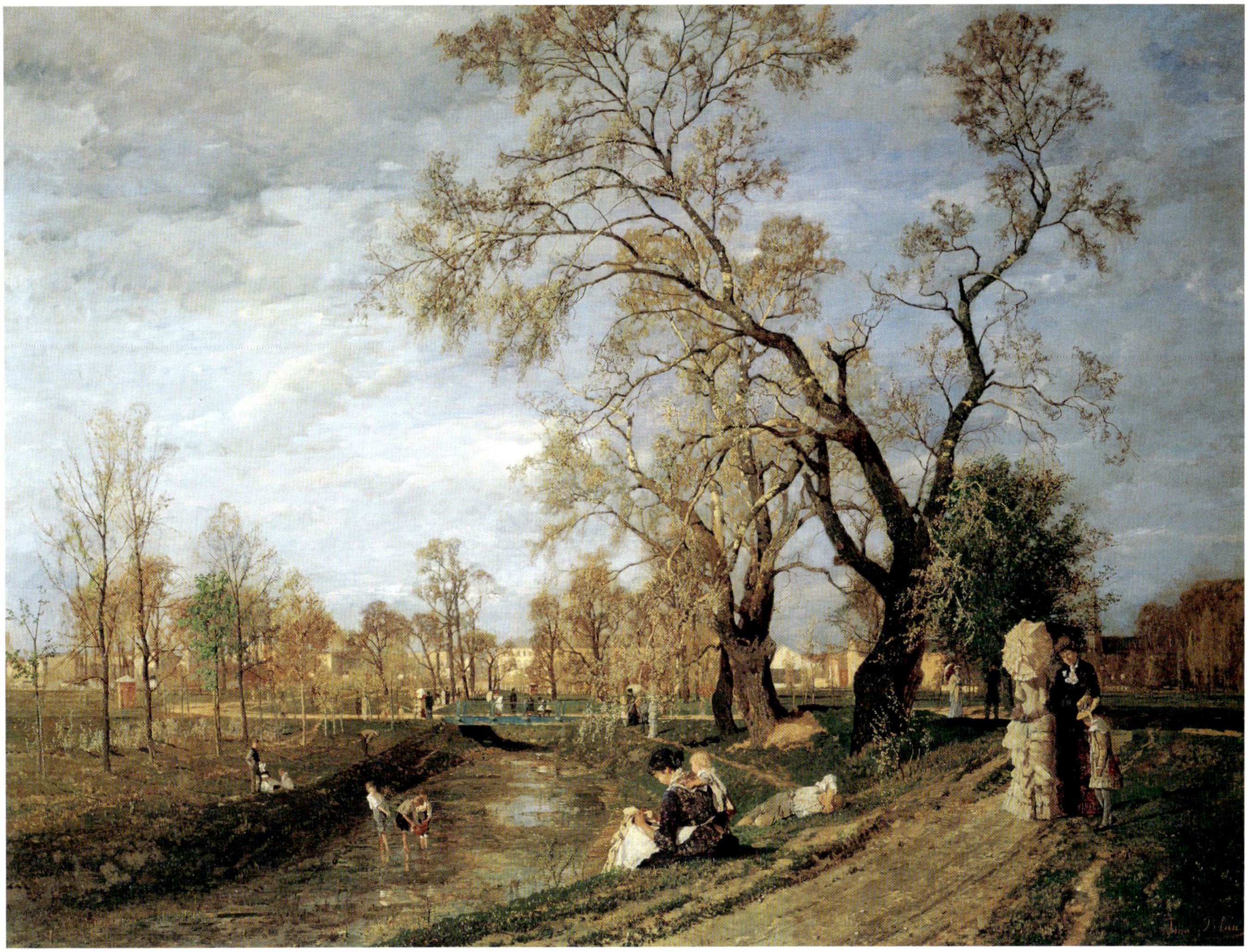

TINA BLAU
Spring in the Prater, 1882
Belvedere, Vienna

her the idea of using unprimed wooden panels for her pictures.

THE PRATER—A FAVORITE SUBJECT

While still a student, Tina Blau had been repeatedly drawn to the landscape of the Prater, a preference reinforced by Schindler, who, like a number of other *plein air* painters, had discovered the Prater as a place to work. After studying in Munich, Blau sometimes worked with Schindler in his studio in the Prater, which had been given to him by the state around 1876/77. This cooperation lasted only a short while, however, because from 1879 at the latest Blau rented the premises for herself. Blau's Prater subjects give the clearest indication of her ability to vary the composition and brushwork. These variations were due to weather and light, but also to the format requirements and the demands these made on the artist herself.

The confrontation with this landscape, popular with artists since the Biedermeier era, ultimately led Tina Blau to attempt a monumental format painting, which is regarded as her most important work. This 214 x 291 cm painting set new standards for *plein air* painting in Austria. The challenges that it presented were huge, so much so that this was the only occasion on which the artist attempted to paint such a large picture. It is puzzling today that the jury of the First International Art Ex-

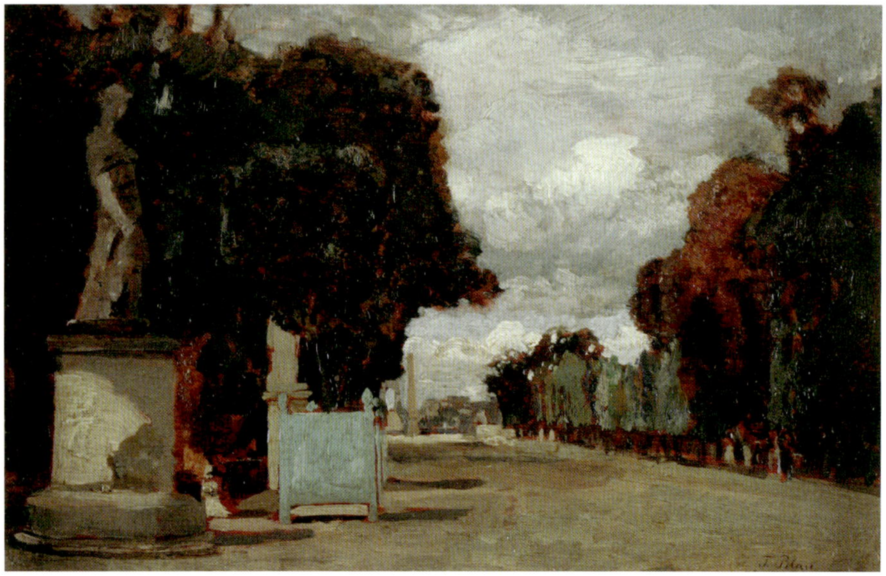

TINA BLAU
From the Tuileries, 1883
Oberösterreichisches Landesmuseum, Linz

hibition in 1882 at the Künstlerhaus should have had so many objections to the work. They attempted to dismiss it by saying that it would be difficult to hang because it was so bright and would "make a hole in the wall" wherever it was.[3] It was only through the intervention of Hans Makart, who was a member of the jury, that the work was admitted at all. Its success proved Makart to have been right. When the French Minister of Art Antonin Proust visited the exhibition, which also featured numerous French artists, he chose this painting for the Paris Salon in 1883, where it received an honorable mention.

In this painting, completed in 1881/82, Blau made an important step forward in her observation of bright sunlight, which would probably not have been possible without the first two trips to Italy and the lightening of her palette produced by them. In spite of the detailed observation of the sunlight and a shimmering surface, the deliberate and sometimes construed lighting reflected the situation in nature but was further enhanced in the studio for the sake of the composition as a whole. The individual natural elements are precisely observed and portrayed with subtle brushstrokes. The artist was also interested in representing different surfaces in the light. The bright and often dappled palette reveals extreme nuances. Great importance was attached to the reproduction of genre-like

TINA BLAU
From the Tuileries – Sunny Day, 1882
Belvedere, Vienna

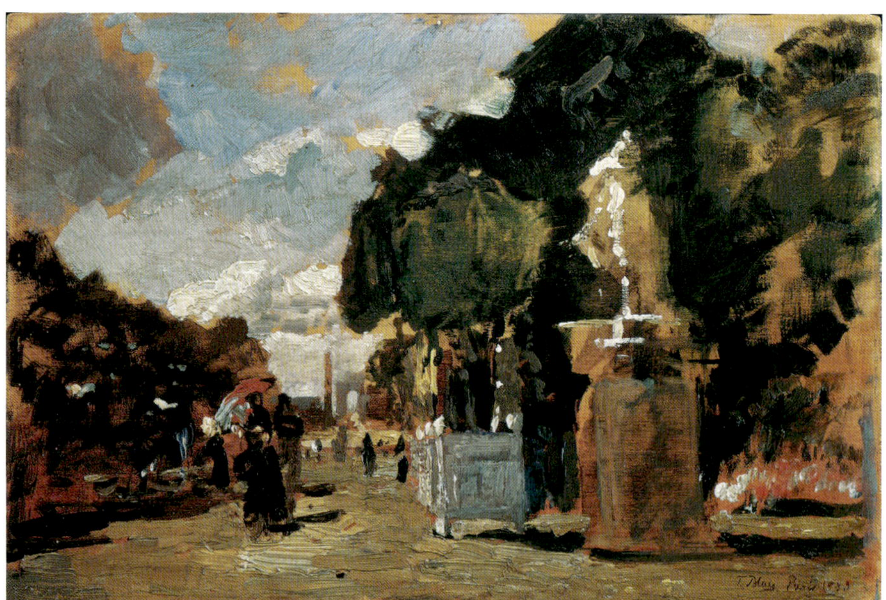

scenes, and the figures are of a remarkable quality for Blau. In his obituary of the artist, the painter and writer Adalbert F. Seligmann points to the modernity of the picture, which he had seen years before during a visit to the studio, "An early spring landscape in glaring white sunlight, with rich green grass, light blue shadows, and thickly applied cold lights. I had never seen anything like it before, which is in fact quite understandable. Only in Paris were there a few painters who saw nature in a similar way, but they were unknown elsewhere, and even in France they were seen at best as fanciful revolutionaries, derisively nicknamed 'Impressionists,' a designation they later assumed, like 'Les Gueux,' as an honorary title. It should be pointed out that Tina Blau knew nothing of these artists at the time. [...] As an artist in her early thirties, she had without a doubt made the most progress toward an 'unconditional' representation of outdoor light, quite different from the tradition and prevailing taste. It is hardly surprising that little was understood of this art, which was quite new."[4] In fact, the artist traveled for the first time to Paris in 1883 for the exhibition of her picture in the Salon.

VISIT TO PARIS

The Tuileries Garden series was completed while Blau was in Paris in 1883. All three of the works shown here are small and painted on wooden panels. In each case, this backing has a very different influence on the overall impression. Diverse weather and light situations are observed, and once again they are reflected in the differing brushwork and impasto effect. The serial nature of these pictures is interesting, something that at the time played an important role among the French Impressionists and was completely in line with the artistic mood of the 1880s, at the end of which Monet's major series were painted.
After 1900, Tina Blau traveled not only to different parts of Austria, Germany, and the Netherlands, but also to Copenhagen, Paris, London, Trieste, Wengen, Venice, Pirano, and Lago di Garda.
Shortly before 1900, she visited the Wachau and joined the rediscovery by artists of this landscape that had been so highly appreciated in the Biedermeier era.
The financial freedom that the artist enjoyed, not only thanks to her family but also and above all to the sale of her paintings, meant that she was relatively free of money worries and could lead a life that may be regarded as highly emancipated by the standards of the social conventions of the time. Tina Blau taught still life and landscape classes in Munich in 1889 at the Damenakademie des Künstlerinnenvereins (Ladies' Academy of the Association of Female Artists).
The Kunstschule für Frauen und Mädchen (Art School for Women and Girls) was not founded in Vienna until 1897. In 1898, the co-founder Adalbert Franz Seligmann managed to recruit Tina Blau to teach a course on landscape and still life, which she continued until 1915. It is within this context that most of her still lifes, primarily flowers, can be seen. By the time Tina Blau died in Vienna on October 31, 1916, a large number of female artists had attended her course. As her great-nephew later reported, she had "always emphasized that she wanted to be judged as an artist and not as a woman who paints."[5]

1 A. F. S. [Adalbert F. Seligmann], "Tina Blau. Ein letzter Besuch," in: *Neue Freie Presse*, November 10, 1916, pp. 1–3, here p. 3.
2 Letter from Tina Blau to her parents, September 21, 1875, copy in T. Blau archive, Vienna.
3 Alexandra Ankwicz-Kleehoven, "T. Blau – Eine österreichische Malerin," in: *Frauenbilder aus Österreich. Eine Sammlung von zwölf Essays*, Vienna 1955, p. 255.
4 Seligmann 1916 (see note 1), p. 2.
5 Walter Taussig, in: Tobias G. Natter/Claus Jesina, *Tina Blau*, Salzburg 1999, p. 134.

HERBERT BOECKL
(1894 Klagenfurt – 1966 Vienna)

"[...] the painter's real concern is transformation"[1]

Kerstin Jesse

Herbert Boeckl, who was born on June 3, 1894, in Klagenfurt, saw his art as the moment of metamorphosis. His oeuvre, which has an important place in Austrian Modernism, shows numerous stylistic changes over the years, which characterize him as a contemplative and restless artist with enormous potential for change and an undeviating curiosity for new things. In his works the painterly strength and materiality of his paintings contrast with the sensitive and spirited lightness of his work on paper.
After his application to the Akademie der bildenden Künste (Vienna Academy of Fine Arts) had been rejected in 1912, Boeckl enrolled the same year to study architecture at the Technische Hochschule (now University of Technology).[2] His artistic talent was already evident during his studies. In 1913, three of his works were exhibited at Salon Pisko in Vienna. Following initial attempts based on the works of nineteenth-century Austrian painters, Boeckl soon incorporated symbolist and Post-Impressionist influences. His rapid development was interrupted by the outbreak of World War I. In 1915 he was stationed in Malborghetto in Val Canale where, in spite of the difficult conditions, he still found time to paint and draw. On the Italian front he also met the art historian Bruno Grimschitz (from 1919 employee of the Österreichische Galerie, 1939 to 1945 its director), who was later to become one of his most important supporters. As a self-taught artist, Boeckl was free of any academic conservatism and approached his work with great autonomy. Expressionist influences were already to be seen in 1915. His greatest inspiration apart from Egon Schiele and Oskar Kokoschka was Paul Cézanne. In 1918 he concluded a sale-on-commission

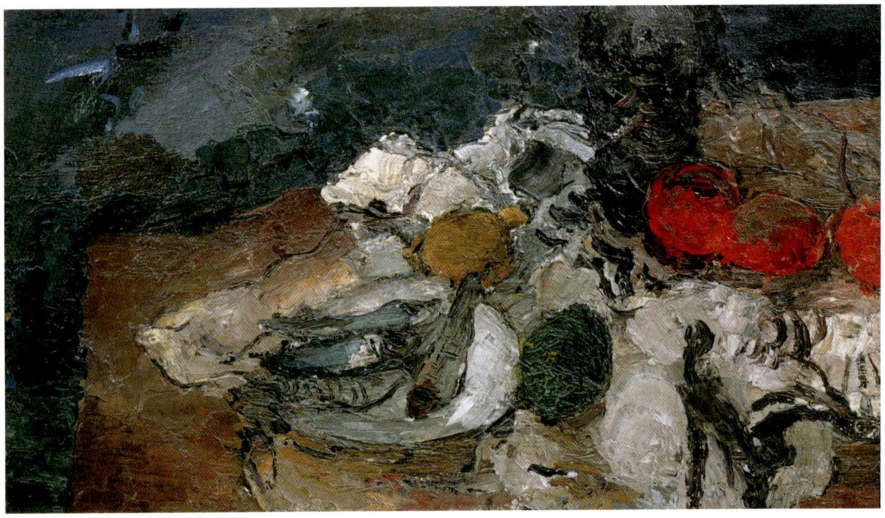

HERBERT BOECKL
Still Life with Fish, 1922
Belvedere, Vienna

agreement with the Viennese art dealer Gustav Nebehay, which lasted until 1931. In 1919 he married Maria Plahna, daughter of a drugstore owner, and moved into a studio in Klagenfurt, which he used until 1923. The first monographic presentation of the artist's work took place in 1927 as part of the Vienna Secession fall exhibition. A year later Boeckl moved to his studio in the 4th district of Vienna, which still survives today. For some of the time he also lived there, before the entire family settled in 1930 near Vienna, finally moving to the capital in 1937.

Around 1920, Boeckl had started to develop a kind of thickly pastose dappled style in a highly idiosyncratic form of Expressionism. With reduced and mostly dark coloring, he constructed a landscape with thick, pastose, almost three-dimensional paint application, sometimes directly from the tube. The materiality of the color gives it an autonomous character. Toward the end of the decade this "walled"[3] painting style was less to the fore, and lines, surfaces, and contours became more important again. The artist also devoted considerable energies to graphic art and completed countless watercolors, charcoal, and pencil drawings of high quality. The heaviness of his oil paintings contrasts unusually with the minimalistic lightness of his works on paper. Boeckl remained an expressionist painter with a distinctive style, while his later works showed cubist and abstract influences. His oeuvre remained wide-ranging. Apart from landscapes and still lifes he also painted portraits and nudes. Among his most important works today are *The Engaged Couple (Die Verlobten)* (1918), *Reclining Female Nude (Liegender Frauenakt)* (1919), *Group at the Edge of the Wood (Gruppe am Waldrand)* (1920), *Blue Jay (Eichelhäher)* (1922), *Anatomy (Die Anatomie)* (1931), the *Erzberg* series (from 1942; see figs. pp. 91–93), *The World and Man (Die Welt und der Mensch)* (1956–58; tapestry), and the frescos for the Engelkapelle in Seckau Abbey (1952–60).

Throughout his life, trips to countries in Europe and North Africa were very important for Boeckl's artistic development and inspiration.[4]

In spite of difficult financial circumstances and a family with nine children, he worked consistently on his art. Through the numerous exhibitions in Austria and other countries, participation in the Biennale in Venice in 1932, 1934, 1936, 1950, and 1964, his position as rector of the Akademie in Vienna from 1945 to 1946 and again from 1962 to 1964, and the evening life drawing class[5] (called "Abendakt") held by him from 1939 to 1964, Boeckl was an established figure in inter-war and post-war Austria.[6]

In 1964, the Museum des 20. Jahrhunderts in Vienna mounted an extensive retrospective exhibition. In the same year Boeckl suffered a stroke and was no longer able to work. He died on January 20, 1966, in Vienna and was buried in an honorary grave of the city of Vienna.

BOECKL, IMPRESSIONISM, AND MONET

There can be no doubt that French art of the late nineteenth century provided the inspiration for early twentieth-century European Modernists. Many artists were attracted to Paris; Boeckl also stayed in the French capital several times and visited the Louvre.[7] Apart from his enthusiasm for Velázquez, Goya, and Rembrandt, he showed a great interest in particular in the (Post-)Impressionists. From the start of the twentieth century, the possibilities for studying contemporary French art in the German-speaking world had begun to multiply. The newly founded Secessionist societies in Munich, Vienna, and Berlin were a "vital forum for the dissemination of French Modernism."[8] In 1903, the Vienna Secession put on the exhibition "The Development of Impressionism in Painting and Sculpture," and a

HERBERT BOECKL
The Engaged Couple, 1918
Private collection

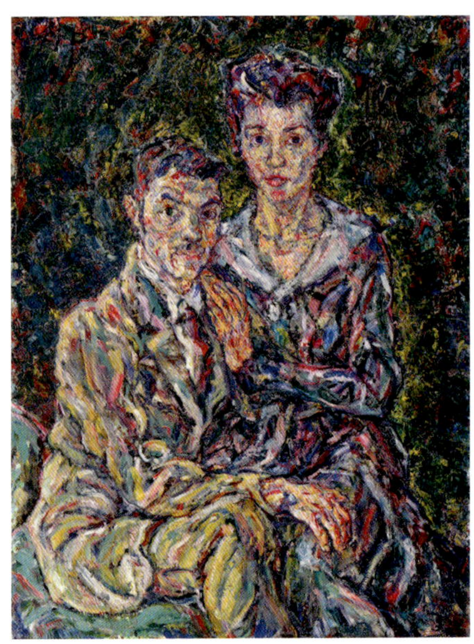

few years later, Galerie Miethke presented "Manet – Monet" (May 1910), "French Masters" (1912), and "French Impressionists" (1913). The rival Galerie Arnot in Vienna had shown an exhibition of French Impressionists in 1911 and a year later an exhibition with works by French Modernists. More than a decade later, in early 1925, the Vienna Secession once again organized a major exhibition entitled "Leading Masters of French Art in the Nineteenth Century." In all of these exhibitions—and in the Österreichische Galerie collection—the young Boeckl would also have encountered works by Monet.[9] In addition, newspaper reviews and, in particular, art magazines, which were generally illustrated, provided information about exhibitions, artists, and new trends. For example, the art historian Julius Meier-Graefe wrote a long article in 1910 on Impressionism with numerous illustrations, including a picture from the *Waterloo Bridge* series by Monet.[10]

Following trips to Berlin in 1921 and 1922 and to Paris in 1923, Boeckl gradually began to feel more drawn to the French than the German Expressionists.[11] It is highly likely that he visited the Cézanne exhibition in Paul Cassirer's gallery in November 1921.[12] Years later, Boeckl took part in the "Exhibition of Austrian Art from 1700 to 1928" in Berlin in January and February 1928.[13] At the same time, ninety-six works by Manet were put on show at Galerie Matthiesen in Berlin in February. The exhibition catalog was in Boeckl's private library, as was the art book *Edouard Manet* published in 1923 by Verlag Paul Cassirer.[14]

Although Boeckl's pictorial style throughout his life revealed expressionist traits, the influence of the French is evident in his oeuvre and in the works of the Modernists in general. In early works such as *The Engaged Couple* or *Portrait of Kurt Plahna (Bildnis Kurt Plahna)* (both 1918), which were certainly inspired by Schiele and Kokoschka, there are coloristic touches similar to those found in Impressionist paintings and in particular in the works of Monet with almost expressionist brushwork. Monet favored direct and seemingly spontaneous brushwork, forming his pictures with an array of colors applied with clearly evident brush strokes. In this way, and by turning his back on a detailed portrayal advocated by the realists of the previous generation, the painter, and the Impressionists in general, potently emphasized the moment of transformation of the subject. This transformation was also important for Boeckl, albeit in a different way. He was interested in "separating the perishable from the imperishable, the mortal from the immortal, the abiding from the lost."[15] The "volatility" of the impressionist brushwork is barely to be found in Boeckl's paintings, however, although it is certainly present in his watercolors.[16]

It was also this confrontation with Impressionist and Post-Impressionist painting that motivated Boeckl during the 1920s to move toward a less pastose painting style and an increasingly brighter color palette. The "light of the South" during a visit to Sicily in 1923–24 would also have had an influence on his subsequent choice of color.[17] "He was drawn by the hot sun that made all colors glow. The fiery light aroused Boeckl's strong colorist instincts with a powerful brush that was always in a great hurry to chase after what he saw."[18]

A characteristic feature of Boeckl's later work is the recurrent treatment of the same subject, producing small "groups" like *Still Life with Cloth, Vase, and Oranges I–III (Stillleben mit Tuch, Vase und Orangen I–III)* (1937), *Dead Mountains (Rotgeschirr) I–III (Totes Gebirge [Rotgeschirr] I–III)* (1950), *Flying Woodpecker I–VI (Fliegender Specht I–VI)* (1950), or *Seville I–V (Sevilla I–V)* (1952), and the more extensive *Erzberg* series (1942–48) and *Dominican (Dominikaner)* (1948),[19] reminiscent perhaps of Monet's famous series.

Around 1890, Monet began to paint series of pictures which went beyond the conventional work groups. The artist was interested above all in capturing his subject in different lights,

HERBERT BOECKL
The Engaged Couple (detail), 1918
Private collection

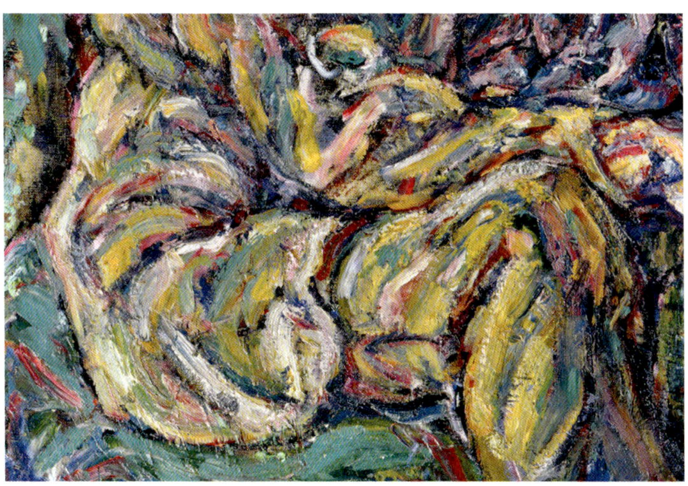

CLAUDE MONET
The Church at Varengeville, Morning Effect, 1882
Private collection

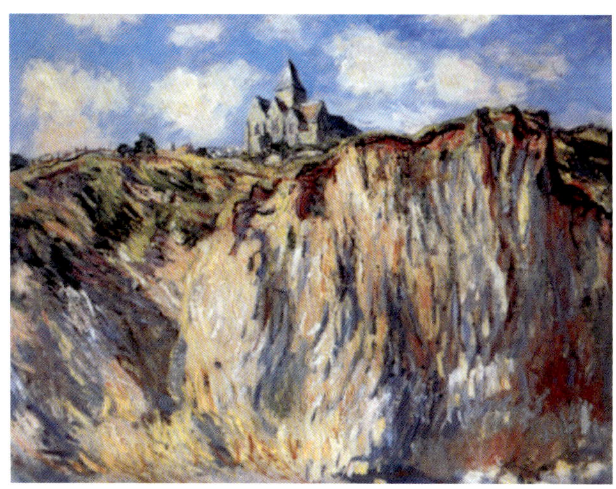

making the series look increasingly like a scientific study.[20] The subject became less important than the way in which it was portrayed, just as the separate works lost their individuality. Influenced by J.M.W. Turner, Monet increasingly pushed his series in the direction of color and objective abstraction. The subject is barely recognizable and the coloring removed from a realistic context.[21]

In Boeckl's works as well, the contours are lost in the "randomly" colored shapes and distort the subject being portrayed.[22] The artist was always concerned with capturing the essence in the relationship between color, form, and contour. His individual works are more autonomous than those of Monet, not least because there are fewer variations in the observer's viewpoint.

On closer inspection and comparison of the works within a particular group, it is nevertheless possible to distinguish different times of day and changes in the coloring: *Seville I* shows the Spanish cathedral in sunlight, *Seville IV* at night, and *Seville V* with approaching thunderclouds. The different light is also evident in the *Erzberg* series: In *Erzberg V* the summit appears to be sunlit, while *Erzberg IV* conveys a cool evening mood (fig. p. 93).

These brief remarks about Boeckl's work show that the artist's stylistic development was also able to profit from the accomplishments of the Impressionists and Post-Impressionists and in particular from Claude Monet.

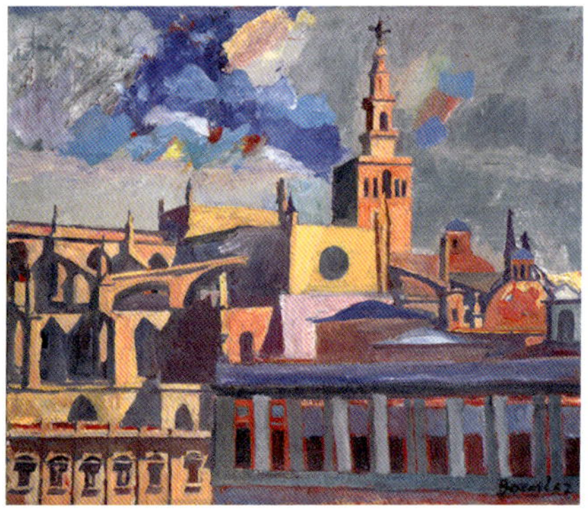

HERBERT BOECKL
Seville I, 1952
Private collection, Washington, D.C.

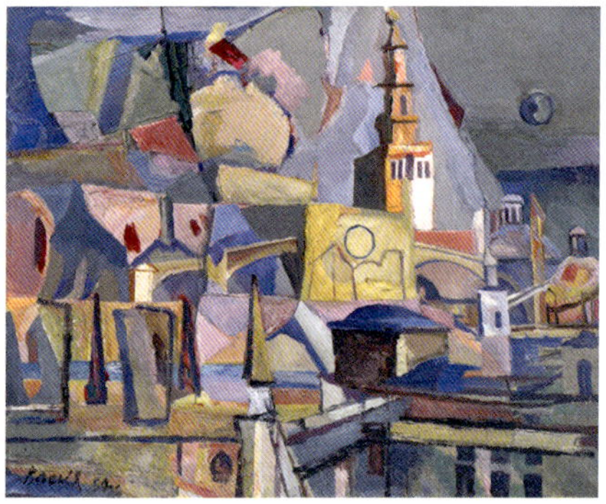

HERBERT BOECKL
Seville IV, 1952
Private collection

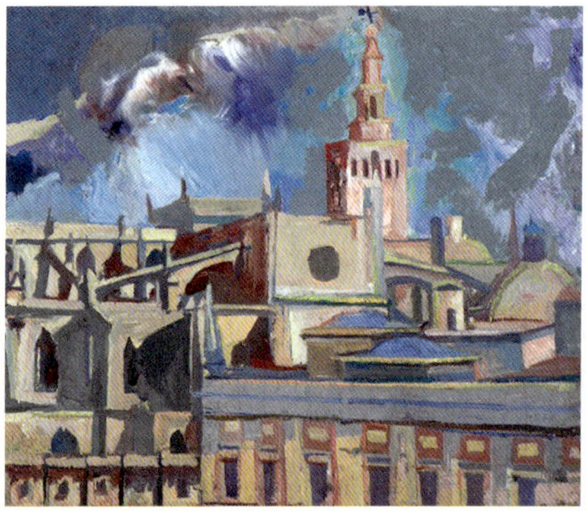

HERBERT BOECKL
Seville V, 1952
Private collection

1 Herbert Boeckl, "Verwandlung und Wandlung. Rede anlässlich der Inauguration zum Rektor der Akademie," in: *Forum* 10, no. 109, 1963, p. 54.
2 He sat the First State Examination in 1918. Current monograph with detailed biography and list of exhibitions: Agnes Husslein-Arco (ed.), *Herbert Boeckl* (exh. cat., Österreichische Galerie Belvedere, Vienna, October 21, 2009–January 1, 2010), Vienna 2009.
3 Cf. Michael Guttenbrunner, "Herbert Boeckl," in: *Herbert Boeckl zum 100. Geburtstag* (exh. cat., Galerie Maier, Innsbruck, June 3–July 5, 1994), Innsbruck 1994.
4 He traveled to Berlin (spring and November 1921; February to April 1922; winter 1942), Paris (February 1923; May 1937; May 1949; July 1956), Venice and Rome (fall 1938), Sicily (Palermo, November 1923 to May 1924), London (winter 1935), Spain (Seville, Barcelona, Madrid, from September 1951), Greece (September to October 1955), and Egypt (March to April 1959). He maintained a friendship and contact with the Nötsch Circle: Carl Moll, Otto Nirenstein, Franz. M. Haberditzl, Otto Benesch, Arnulf Rainer, Otto Mauer, Fritz Wotruba, Karl Hofer, Erich Heckel, Max Pechstein, Clemens Holzmeister, and Alfred Kubin.
5 A compulsory course for art students at the Akademie in Vienna.
6 Boeckl was awarded the Grand Austrian State Prize in 1934 and 1954 and the Ring of Honor of the City of Vienna in 1964.
7 He exhibited twice at the "Exposition d'art autrichien" in the Musée du Jeu de Paume des Tuileries in Paris (1937, 1957).
8 Jill Lloyd, "International Trends in Austrian Art and the Case of Herbert Boeckl," in: Husslein-Arco 2009 (see note 2), p. 21.
9 The Belvedere acquired two paintings by Monet, in 1903 and 1912. See the explanation by the then director Friedrich Dörnhöffer on the desired purchase of *Anglers on the Seine at Poissy (Les Pêcheurs de Poissy)* (1882), 1912: Österreichisches Staatsarchiv, AVA, CuU, 13752/1912, letter of March 10, 1912, to the Ministry of Education.
10 Julius Meier-Graefe, "Über Impressionismus," in: *Die Kunst für Alle* 25, no. 7, January 1, 1910, pp. 145–62. *Olympia* by Édouard Manet was probably an inspiration for Boeckl's *Reclining Female Nude with Bunch of Violets (Liegender weiblicher Akt mit Veilchenbouquet)* (1932).
11 Cf. Edith Schlocker, "Schöpferische Impulse aus der Peripherie. Positionen österreichischer Malerei zwischen den beiden großen Kriegen," in: *Parnass* 21, no. 18, 2001, p. 76.
12 *Cézanne-Ausstellung. Cézannes Werke in deutschem Private collection* (exh. cat., Galerie Paul Cassirer, Berlin, November/December 1921), Munich 1921. See Curt Glaser, "Eröffnungsausstellung des Kunstsalons Paul Cassirer, Berlin," in: *Die Kunst für Alle* 28, no. 8, January 15, 1913, pp. 169–74.
13 *Ausstellung österreichischer Kunst 1700–1928. Zeichnungen, Aquarelle, Graphik* (exh. cat., Preussische Akademie der Künste zu Berlin, Berlin, January/February 1928), Berlin 1928.
14 *Edouard Manet 1832–1883. Gemälde, Pastelle, Aquarelle, Zeichnungen* (exh. cat., Galerie Matthiesen, Berlin, February 6–March 18, 1928), Berlin 1928. Boeckl either traveled himself to Berlin in 1928 or obtained the catalog through Alfred Stix or Otto Benesch, who organized the exhibition. Bruno E. Werner, "Die Manet-Ausstellung in der Galerie Matthiesen, Berlin," in: *Die Kunst für Alle* 43, 1927/28, pp. 264–69. Emil Waldmann, Edouard Manet, Berlin 1923.
15 Boeckl 1963 (see note 1).
16 Cf. Husslein-Arco 2009 (see note 2), pp. 109, 115, 118, 129, 260, and 262.

17 "[...] Monet must be regarded as one of the first to recognize the new glory of the sun [...] He broke down the sunray by welding together every tone from an enormous number of very fine chromatically scaled color particles." E. H. "Vorwort," in: *Sonderausstellung französischer Impressionisten* (exh. cat., Kunstsalon Emil Richter, Dresden), Dresden 1904, pp. 8–9.

18 F., "Professor Herbert Böckl," in: *Neues Wiener Abendblatt*, no. 320, November 19, 1935, p. 4.

19 See Agnes Husslein-Arco 2009 (see note 2), Catalog, pp. 334–96. On series by Boeckl: Burghart Schmidt, "Boeckl oder das Kunst-Gesetz der Serie," in: Ingried Brugger/Klaus Albrecht Schröder (eds.), *Herbert Boeckl* (exh. cat., Kunstforum Bank Austria, Vienna, September 7–November 27, 1994), Munich/New York 1994, pp. 214–22.

20 Some series comprised over thirty individual works. On the concept of series, see Katharina Sykora, *Das Phänomen des Seriellen in der Kunst. Aspekte einer künstlerischen Methode von Monet bis zur amerikanischen Pop Art*, Würzburg 1983.

21 Cf. Herbert Boeckl's *Tower Bridge* (1935), in which blue predominates as the basic color. Apart from the light in London, Boeckl, like Monet, was inspired by Turner *(Charing Cross Bridge* [1899, WV 1531], Collection Carmen Thyssen-Bornemisza*)*. Compare Herbert Boeckl, *Trees in the Mist (Bäume im Nebel)* (1914; WV 9) with Claude Monet, *Ice Floes (Les Glaçons)* (1893; WV 1338).

22 Compare *Flying Woodpecker II* with *Flying Woodpecker III* or *Nappersdorf I* with *Nappersdorf II* (1951).

MARIE EGNER
(1850 Radkersburg – 1940 Vienna)

The Tranquility of Nature

Peter Peer

Marie Egner's decision to pursue a career as an artist did not fit conventional gender roles, as indeed was the case with Tina Blau, Olga Wisinger-Florian, and other women painters.[1] Even in the late nineteenth century, there was complete denial of women's creative potential, sometimes backed up by pseudo-scientific arguments. Until 1918, women were not allowed to study at the Vienna Akademie der bildenden Künste (Academy of Fine Arts), as the outmoded moral code barred female participation in the (compulsory) life-drawing classes of male nudes. Marie Egner's decision, as an unmarried woman, to focus both her professional and personal life on painting, had fundamentally different consequences for her than for many of her male colleagues. And it was a decision that the artist did not arrive at easily, as her diaries disclose. For above all, she believed family life was incompatible with her aspirations to become an artist. "If I devote myself to art entirely, I will become increasingly ill-suited—not for my noble view of marriage, but for men as they are in general. Then there is an important point—whether I have enough talent to make the pursuit of such a life worthwhile," the twenty-two-year-old artist confided in her diary.[2] Yet in spite of sacrifices, in spite of times of loneliness, she continued to cherish her independence right up to a great age.

ACADEMIES IN GRAZ AND DÜSSELDORF

Between 1867 and 1872, Marie Egner was taught by Hermann von Königsbrunn in the landscape class at the Graz Ständische Zeichnungsakademie (Styria's art academy). It was a happy time for the budding painter. Königsbrun, who took his students on many excursions in Styria, fostered Egner's deep sensitivity to nature. "I was so completely preoccu-

MARIE EGNER
Forest Water with Bridge, undated
Belvedere, Vienna

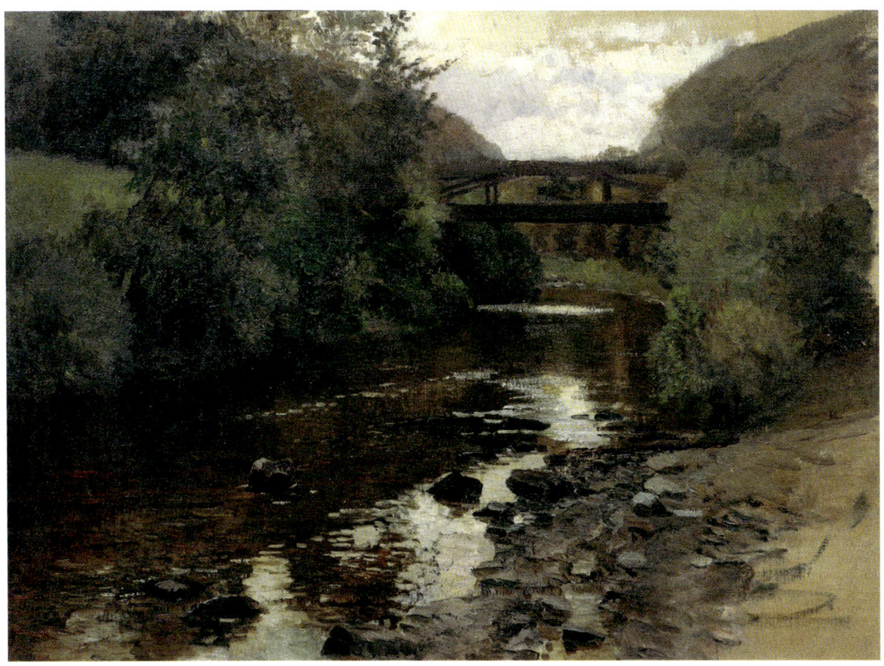

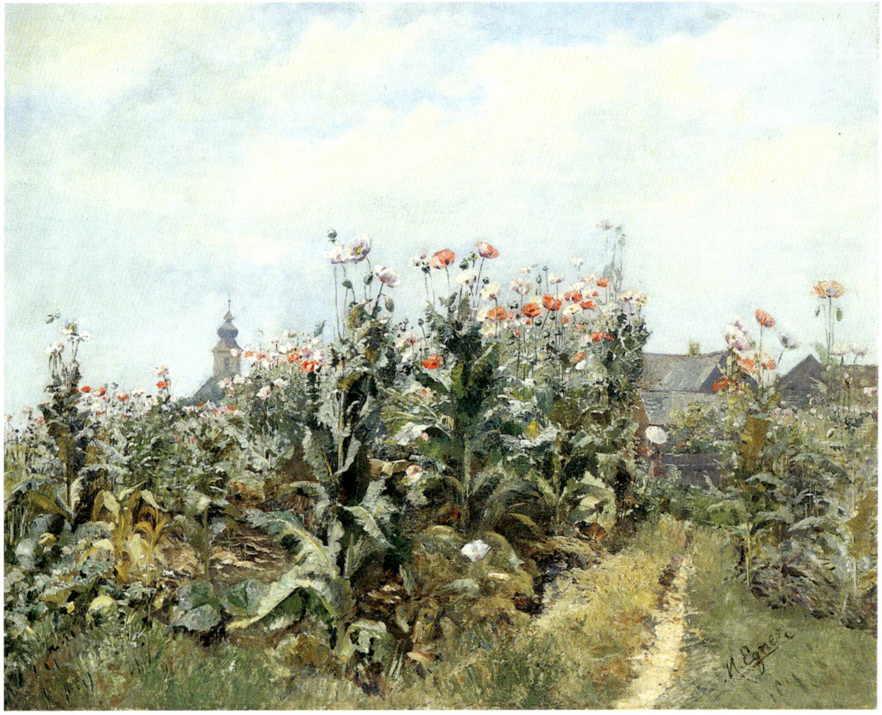

MARIE EGNER
Blooming poppy field in Styria, ca. 1896
Neue Galerie am Universalmuseum Joanneum, Graz

pied with drawing from nature as I could spend hours looking through and correcting my sketches [...]"[3] At this time she also became increasingly interested in landscape painting, stating, "He [Königsbrunn] has already turned me into a bit of a landscape fanatic."[4] Furthermore, her preference for those familiar motifs materialized, subjects that were at the heart of the emerging style of *Stimmungsrealismus* (atmospheric realism) that would occupy her for decades to come. To deepen her knowledge of oil painting, she switched in 1872 to the Düsseldorf Academy, where she was taught by Carl Jungheim. The Düsseldorf School itself, however, with its dramatic compositions, did not have any impact on her work. In 1875 Egner moved to Vienna where she had a studio and gave lessons in oil painting.

WITH EMIL JAKOB SCHINDLER

Meeting Emil Jakob Schindler in 1880 was of crucial importance in Marie Egner's life. Schindler had attracted a cluster of young painters, including Carl Moll and Olga Wisinger-Florian, who were taking private lessons with him. Since 1885 the master, his family, and his students had been living at Schloss Plankenberg near Tulln in Lower Austria. Egner's style changed at this time, moving toward the *paysage intime* Schindler had adopted, and her work started to closely resemble that of her teacher. At the same time, however, she harbored amorous feelings for the artist she so admired, "But what do I want from him really?! I could never be his lover, after all; to continue on the margins of this half-concealed, half-confessed passion, half humble, half haughty—that indeed is a sad purpose in life."[5] It was presumably personal reasons that prompted her to leave Schindler and his circle in 1887 and accept a job teaching drawing at a boarding school for young ladies near London.

TIME IN ENGLAND AND RETURN TO VIENNA

In England two experiences had a profound influence on Marie Egner's future art. Through the influence of contemporary British landscape painting, she first discovered watercolor. She had hardly ever painted in this medium up until that time, "[...] the master did not love this technique," she recalled about Schindler.[6] In the British painter Robert Weir Allan, she found a teacher who was expert in this field. His "swift, fluid English technique" prompted her to abandon "Viennese (*Pimpelhuber*) watercolor painting."[7] Egner would stay true to this technique right through to the latter years of her life. And she transferred some of watercolor's spontaneity into her oil paintings as well. Seeing the seventeenth-century Dutch landscape paintings in London collections also had a brief impact on her work. Their influence can be clearly detected in some of her paintings from this period.

In 1888 Marie Egner left Britain and returned to Austria. She made regular and successful contributions to exhibitions, including the annual shows at the Vienna Künstlerhaus. One of her paintings, *Harvest in Lower Austria (Ernte in Niederösterreich)*, was bought by Emperor Franz Joseph from the Künstlerhaus exhibition in 1894. Egner became a member of the Verein der Schriftstellerinnen und Künstlerinnen (Association of Women Writers and Artists, to which Olga Wisinger-Florian also belonged) as well as the group Acht Künstlerinnen (Eight Women Artists), founded in 1901. She also taught art, a job she found arduous, to judge by her diary entries (she referred to it as "the training of pupils"). It would seem this was just a means of making a living rather than motivated by any sense of artistic mission.[8]

In the subsequent two decades she traveled widely to countries including Hungary, Italy, Dalmatia, France, Holland, and Greece. Her many stays in France between 1905 and 1914 prompted her to explore French Impressionism. In 1918 she started having problems with her eyes, leading to two cataract operations in 1920 and 1931. Egner's first solo exhibition featured over 180 pictures and was held at the Vienna Künstlerhaus in 1926. Not only did this lead to recognition but it was also a financial success. Marie Egner spent the last years of her life in a retirement home at Maria Anzbach in Lower Austria.

HER WORK

Looking back on her work, Egner summed it up in true self-critical fashion, "I frittered away the first ten years (20–30) (including Düsseldorf). Then came the Schindler era (30–40) with love, new faith, and exploration, and after the master's death the first successes (40–50). I should have left for Munich or Paris at that time. Since 1900 (50–60), the searching and doubting has set in. A bit late—like everything with me!"[9]

Broadly considered, Marie Egner's work essentially evolved in three phases (even if the different traits also pervaded her work of later years). In her first years as an artist, when she was still with Königsbrunn, she cultivated a detailed realism, with echoes of early nineteenth-century styles, for instance so-called "Biedermeier painting." But even then her preference for familiar subject matter, for a section of a landscape or an architectural motif, clearly emerged.

The second phase reflected the influence of Emil Jakob Schindler. Egner developed an extremely painterly approach to color and adopted Schindler's greenish to grayish-blue palette, sometimes even painting the same subjects as her master. (The latter led to confusions on the art market even decades later.[10]) In addition, Egner explored a series of motifs in studies of changing light and atmospheres. A certain pathos also made itself felt in her works during these years. Light and weather situations were no longer tackled for their own sake, but conveyed a view of nature with a numinous tinge in the manner of the Romantics. Similarly, Egner used wide, focused distant views, as vehicles of mood and atmosphere in a comparable way to Schindler.

The third phase emerged in the late 1880s, when Egner was in England and gradually started detaching herself from Schindler's brand of atmospheric realism. Influenced by watercolor painting and experiencing the Impressionists a few years later, her palette became lighter, her brushwork more dynamic. She attempted to adopt the stylistic devices of the French artists without—as she herself concluded—ever achieving the same quality of her models. In doing so, she could clearly appreciate the difference between her sketches and finished works.

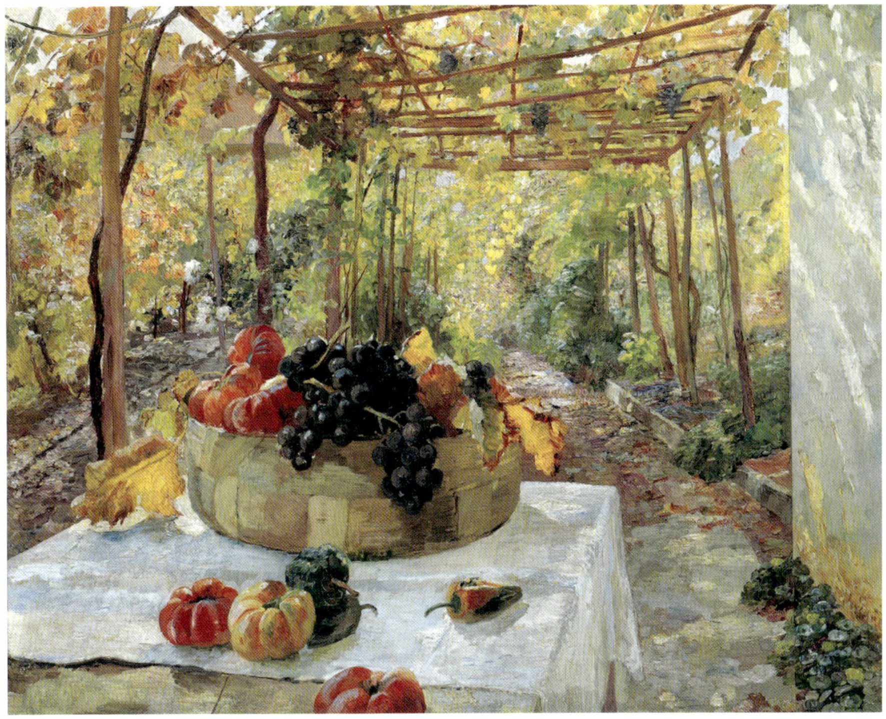

MARIE EGNER
Under the Pergola, ca. 1910
Belvedere, Vienna

Some of the typical motifs in Austrian landscape painting feature in Marie Egner's oeuvre almost like textbook examples. Egner was not a painter of "modern" life. Like Schindler, she favored tranquil, secluded nature in which people are merely incidental. Yet she did appreciate nature cultivated by humanity, such as gardens or fields. In this she was adopting a characteristic pictorial type in Austrian landscape painting from the late nineteenth century, known as the *"Kraut-und-Rüben-Stück"* (literally "cabbage and turnip piece").[11] These were extremely close-up views of the immediate foreground, depicting, with tremendous painterly skill, dense grasses and flowers or an opulent array of vegetables—cabbage, pumpkins, or kale for example—to produce a veritable feast for the eyes. The appeal of these views is enhanced through the contrast between extreme closeness and distance in which our gaze drifts from the immediate foreground to the distant, high horizon.

Another frequent subject in Egner's oeuvre are scenes in which she consciously focused on the idyllic. These include country gardens, courtyards as well as pergolas with a profusion of vegetation. She only represented cropped sections of the architecture. The idyll is defined by the seclusion, often suggested by representing just a small slice of the scene. The close ties between humanity and nature also play a part, inasmuch as people do not only foster an aesthetic relationship with nature, but are also beneficiaries of nature's bounty, as demonstrated by baskets brimming with fruit and vegetables. The picturesque view is a fundamental factor. Meticulous depiction of material qualities—weathered walls, rotten wood, overgrown paths and the like—heightens the viewer's sensory experience. Gardens were also Schindler's domain. Marie Egner recalled the overhaul of the park at Plankenberg, which was full "of stinging nettles, wild undergrowth, acacia bushes, and tall grass. Schindler and Carl [Moll] cleared and worked and turned it into a painter's Eldorado."[12]

Marie Egner also explored other topical motifs in landscape painting, such as forest interiors, tranquil streams, and solitary paths that disappear into the broad expanse of landscape. She followed the developments in contemporary art with a certain interest, yet went her own way, always true, in both style and subject, to the atmospheric realism of her day. She continued working as an artist until a great age. Her last known painting dated from the year 1937, when she could look back on a career spanning almost seven decades. "In creating all these paintings and sketches I really lived, was happy, sometimes 'on top of the world' like lovers, and then 'in the depths of despair'; there was much, very much that was genuine in this life of mine."[13]

1 Edith Futscher, "Professioneller Dilettantismus? Zur Akzeptanz weiblichen Kunstschaffens im ausgehenden 19. Jahrhundert," in: Otmar Rychlik (ed.), *Natürlichere Natur. Österreichische Malerei des Stimmungsrealismus* (exh. cat., Kunsthaus Mürzzuschlag, Mürzzuschlag, summer exhibition 1994), Mürzzuschlag 1994, pp. 28–34.
2 From the artist's diary, May 22, 1872, quoted from Martin Suppan/Erich Tromayer, *Marie Egner. Eine österreichische Stimmungsimpressionistin*, vol. 1, Vienna 1981, p. 29.
3 From the artist's diary, July 20, 1869, quoted from Suppan/Tromayer 1981 (see note 2), p. 22.
4 From the artist's diary, September 12, 1869, quoted from Suppan/Tromayer 1981 (see note 2), p. 22.
5 From the artist's diary, December 13, 1882, quoted from Suppan/Tromayer 1981 (see note 2), p. 45.
6 From the artist's diary, in retrospect, 1937, quoted from Suppan/Tromayer 1981 (see note 2), p. 51.
7 From the artist's diary, in retrospect, 1937, quoted from Suppan/Tromayer 1981 (see note 2), p. 51. *Pimpelhuber* is a colloquial term meaning not particularly good and overly tentative.
8 From the artist's diary, June 2, 1905, quoted from Suppan/Tromayer 1981 (see note 2), p. 65.
9 From the artist's diary, February 28, 1910, quoted from Suppan/Tromayer 1981 (see note 2), p. 75.
10 From the artist's diary, in retrospect, 1937, quoted from Suppan/Tromayer 1981 (see note 2), p. 45.
11 Based on a quote by Rudolf Ribarz that referred to *"Kraut-und-Rüben-Malerei"* ("cabbage and turnip painting"), Martina Haja introduced the term *"Kraut-und-Rüben-Stück"* ("cabbage and turnip piece") to emphasize not only the main subject but also the closely cropped depictions. Cf. Martina Haja, "'Kraut und Rüben.' Beobachtungen zur österreichischen Freilicht-Malerei im späten 19. Jahrhundert," in: *Mitteilungen der Österreichischen Galerie* 30, no. 74, Vienna 1986, p. 43.
12 From the artist's diary, in retrospect, 1937, quoted from Suppan/Tromayer 1981 (see note 2), p. 46f.
13 From the artist's diary, March 12, 1935, quoted from Suppan/Tromayer 1981 (see note 2), p. 88.

MARIE EGNER
Poppies, ca. 1890
Private collection

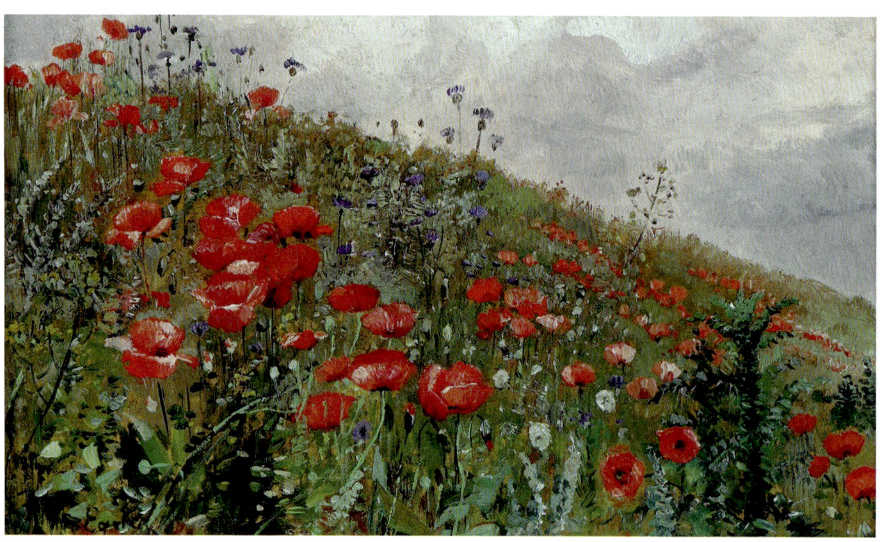

THEODOR VON HÖRMANN
(1840 Imst – 1895 Graz)

"Open-air painting means not painting by heart"[1]

The "Accurate" Interpretation of Reality

Kathrin Wolf

Theodor von Hörmann's arrival in Paris in 1886 was the logical conclusion of a consequent artistic development. At this time Eugen Jettel, Rudolf Ribarz, Václav von Brožik, and Otto von Thoren were all working there, represented by the Viennese art dealer Charles Sedelmeyer, in whose gallery they often met. August von Pettenkofen and Carl Schuch had already been living in Paris for several years, and Tina Blau had also become acquainted with the city during a study visit.

During his artistic career up to that time, Hörmann's radical commitment to *plein air* painting and his years of untiring efforts to capture light had led the artist to a form of expression that gave absolute priority to direct visual experience. He must have felt all the more reassured that this was the right approach by the work of the French Impressionists. In a studio in Montparnasse, he began to absorb the plethora of new impressions with an almost fanatical energy. "Paris was like a revelation for him," wrote Hermann Bahr. "From that day he foreswore all leisure activities, worked without rest, and devoted himself exclusively to art."[2]

Born in 1840 in Imst and brought up in Tyrol, the young Hörmann started military training in Krems in 1855 and embarked on a career as an army officer. His real passion, however, was painting and drawing, and he gave lessons in freehand drawing at the officer training schools in Brünn [today Brno] and later in Vienna.

Hörmann made his first independent attempts at painting in 1869. Three years later,

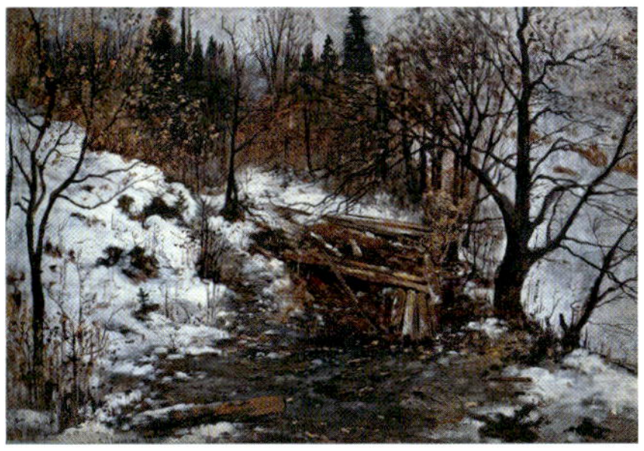

THEODOR VON HÖRMANN
Forest Stream near Lilienfeld in Winter, 1878
Landesmuseum Niederösterreich, St. Pölten

with the permission of the military authorities, he began his studies at the Akademie der bildenden Künste (Academy of Fine Arts) in Vienna under Eduard Peithner von Lichtenfels and Anselm Feuerbach, remaining there until September 1875. Although he saw little value in his academic training, he had an experience of incisive importance while he was there: the encounter with the art of the Barbizon School, on show at the 1873 World's Fair in Vienna in an exhibition hall specially built by Karl von Hagenauer, as well as the exhibition in two *pavillons des amateurs* with pictures by Corot, Daubigny, Díaz de la Peña, Dupré, Rousseau, Troyon, and others. The natural authenticity of these pictures fascinated him. Inspired by them, he immediately sought to obtain a scholarship to study in Paris, albeit unsuccessfully.

Two years later Hörmann met Emil Jakob Schindler; the painter, who understood his burning commitment to *plein air* painting, his striving for authenticity and painterly "accuracy," encouraged him and became Hörmann's most important teacher. Very early works like *Forest Stream near Lilienfeld in Winter* (*Waldbach bei Lilienfeld im Winter;* 1878) had already revealed the artist's precise observation of nature, his attempts to achieve tonal accuracy and his vigorous and bold painting style.

In March 1884 Hörmann, by now a captain, left the army at his own request. In the same year, he married Laura Bertuch and moved with her to Vienna where he became a member of the Genossenschaft bildender Künstler (Vienna Artists' Cooperative). The art scene in Vienna was by no means ready for the new interpretation of art. Hörmann met with great rejection, which, in his almost missionary zeal, he refused at first to recognize.

He had frequently visited the Lake Balaton region in 1873 and 1874 and began to travel regularly to Hungary starting in 1882 where he probably came into contact with the Szolnok group of artists, including August von Pettenkofen, Tina Blau, Carl Leopold Müller, and Gualbert Raffalt. At least, there is some evidence of their influence in the pictures painted there. Through Mihály Munkácsy in particular, the artist colony was in direct communication with the Barbizon School of painters, which no doubt reinforced Hörmann's desire to go to France. He painted the vastness of the landscape, the pig and cattle herdsmen, harvesting, women steeping straw for thatched roofs (ca. 1884), and soaking hemp (ca. 1884/85).

Whereas his previous works had been conventionally constructed and were mostly notable for their simple realism, Hörmann moved toward a freer and more spontaneous depiction of nature in Hungary. Through his experience of very bright light, he abandoned the brown tonality of his earlier work and developed the style of the Barbizon School in the direction of a more realistic use of color. At the same time, he attempted to increase the immediacy of the way he showed nature through a seemingly random selection of the scene (*On the Ligeti Puszta* [*Auf der Ligeti Puszta*], 1884).

PARIS YEARS

Hörmann had already experimented with a number of painting techniques and developed his own artistic identity by the time he could finally afford to go to Paris. The French capital, with its scandals, discussions, and radical advances and developments, was without a doubt the center of European art at the time. Hörmann eagerly soaked up all the stimuli that this fascinating metropolis

THEODOR VON HÖRMANN
On the Ligeti Puszta, 1884
Belvedere, Vienna

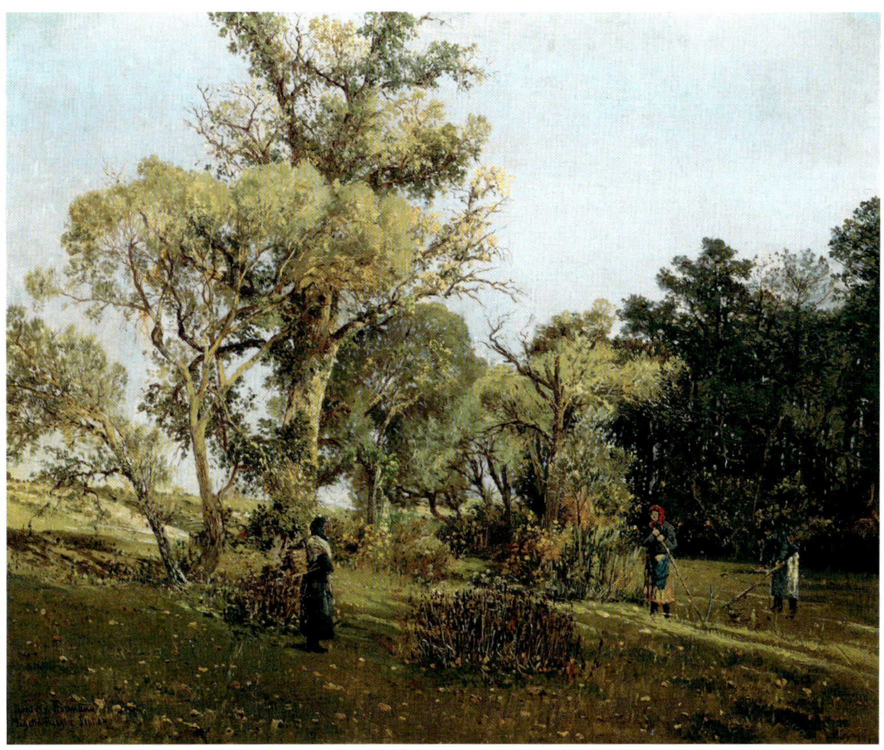

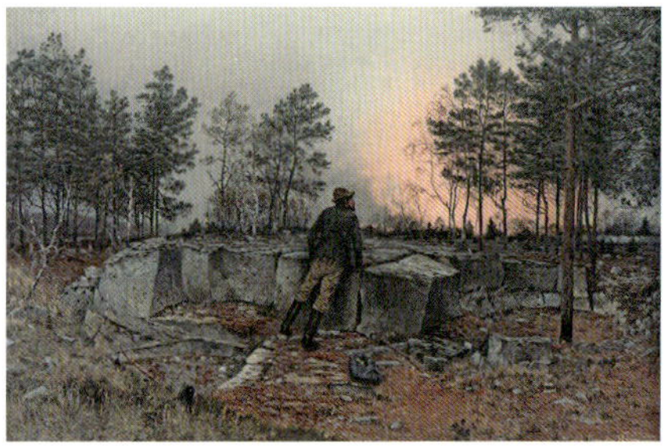

THEODOR VON HÖRMANN
The Arsonist, 1888/91
Private collection

had to offer. Although he enrolled in Louis-Joseph-Raphaël Collin's private art school, his greatest passion, *plein air* painting, was of necessity self-taught. "I know one thing: this work is so gripping," he later wrote, "that I can think of nothing else and that on the way to and from home and at night, when there is no longer any light, there is only this vision of nature, without a thought for observers, the public, or critics."[3]

At the start of his stay in Paris, Hörmann continued to paint mostly landscapes, traveling in the footsteps of the Barbizon painters and Impressionists to the Forest of Fontainebleau, to Saint-Malo, and to Saint-Servan in Brittany, to the islands of Jersey and Guernsey in the English Channel, and finally to Samois-sur-Seine, where he rented a villa.

Hörmann's works at this time clearly reveal his ardent fervor to achieve "accuracy" in his portrayals; a fervor which also led him to make great sacrifices. In Samois-sur-Seine, for example, he sometimes spent half the night sitting motionless at a corner of the house observing the light for his picture *Moonlit Night in the Village* (*Mondnacht im Dorfe*). He risked his life painting a picture of the cliffs on the French coast as the tide came in. Later he was to paint *Znojmo in the Snow* (*Znaim im Schnee*) with frozen fingers in order to lose nothing of the immediacy of the color.

THEODOR VON HÖRMANN
Construction of the Eiffel Tower, 1887
Neue Galerie am Universalmuseum Joanneum, Graz

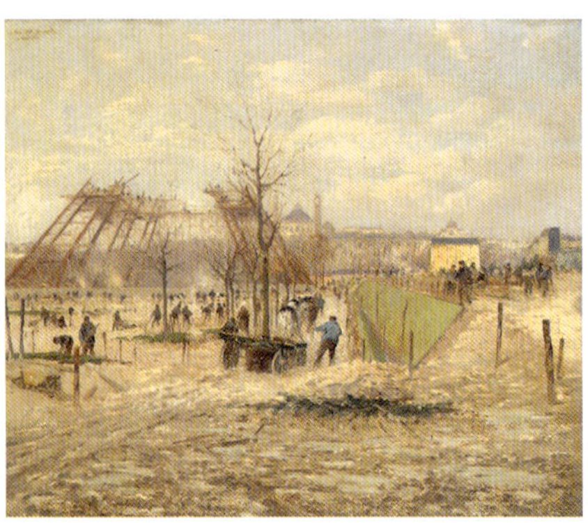

Following the example of the Impressionists and of Monet in particular, Hörmann soon began to study modern city life on the Seine, as can be seen in *Construction of the Eiffel Tower* (*Bau des Eiffelturms*) in 1887 and particularly *In the Tuileries Garden* (*In den Tuilerien*; ca. 1888), in which Hörmann's style, subject, and sensitivity bear a particularly close resemblance to the contemporary French art. Dynamic dabs and short strokes captured the diverse color impressions of a mild, late summer day. The neglect of detail underlines the sense of immediacy. Even the sketchy portrayal of the faces such as those that can be seen in *Anglers on the Seine* from 1882 is modeled on works by Monet.

All Hörmann's subsequent pictures were painted *en plein air*. They included more conventional and very detailed works like *Place Sulpice* (1889) and pictures full of experimentation. *Nighttime Paris with the Eiffel Tower* (*Paris bei Nacht mit Eiffelturm; see fig. p. 52*), painted the same year, is a momentary record of a nocturnal mood. Reduced to a few colors, the artist endeavors to reproduce the enchanting effect of the illuminated Eiffel Tower, glowing red wisps of cloud, and glittering lights. It was painted from the same studio window as *View of Paris* (*Blick auf Paris*; fig. p. 51) completed the following year. Hörmann, who had evidently visited Georges Petit's exhibition "Monet – Rodin" in 1889, adopted a number of Monet's subjects and was also inspired by his pictorial structures and brushwork. He sought an even more spontaneous approach, employing an almost stenographic style to make the pictures appear to have been painted hurriedly and hence evoke an impression of immediacy. The composition of *Field of Sainfoin near Znojmo* (*Großes Esparsettenfeld*; ca. 1893), with its strongly colored fields tapering into the depth of the painting, is clearly influenced by Monet's *Field of Tulips in Holland* (*Champ de tulipes, Hollande*) (1886). The series *Ice Floes on the Banks of the Thaya* (*Eisschollen am Ufer der Thaya*) (1891) was also probably inspired by Monet's *Ice Floes on the Seine* painted in 1880, two versions of which were on show at Georges Petit's exhibition. Hörmann will also have seen Monet's famous *Boulevard des Capucines* (1873) and *Rue Montorgueil: Festival of June 30, 1878* (*La Rue Montorgueil, fête du 30 juin 1878*) (1878), whose sketchy depiction of people is adopted in his *View from the Paris Studio* (*Blick aus dem Pariser Atelier*) from

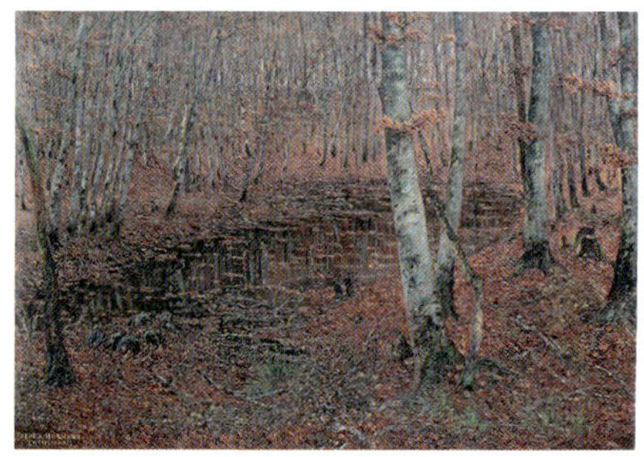

THEODOR VON HÖRMANN
Pond in a Beech Forest, 1892
Tiroler Landesmuseum Ferdinandeum, Innsbruck

1890.

Altogether, Hörmann's Paris years are informed by his constant fluctuation between sketchy momentary depictions and meticulous observation of nature on the one hand, and anecdotal or figurative compositions on the other, a phenomenon that can be explained not only by taking a glance at public taste and the preferences of the time but also by Hörmann's own personal conviction of what a complete picture should be.

He will no doubt have been encouraged by the award of an honorable mention for *Moonlit Night in the Village of Samois* (*Mondnacht im Dorfe Samois*) (ca. 1888) at the 1889

World's Fair in Paris and the critical acclaim accorded to *The Arsonist* (*Der Brandleger*) (1888/91), acknowledging the great realism of the figure scouting in the foreground and the dramatic scene with the clouds of smoke in the background.

In early 1890, the Hörmanns had to return to Austria for personal reasons. The couple stopped in Vienna and moved to Znojmo three months later.

REFORM OF THE KÜNSTLERHAUS AND FOUNDING OF THE MODERNE GALERIE

Hörmann was initially excluded from exhibitions at the Künstlerhaus in Vienna—a rejection that he vehemently protested against. He was regarded as an "energetic and ultramodern talent with fanatical natural authenticity."[4] In spite of the efforts of Albert Zimmermann, Eduard Peithner von Lichtenfels and Anton Hansch to increase the general appreciation of landscape painting, Makart-style history painting remained the only yardstick for public recognition in Vienna. A landscape without figures or heroic emphasis was suspicious enough, and its modern interpretation with open brushstrokes or unconventional colors even more so.

Thus, Hörmann's *Pond in a Beech Forest* (*Tümpel im Buchenwald*) (1892) was slated by the public and art critics alike. Hörmann was disappointed at the complacency of the Vienna art scene and its favoritism, "They are a miserable bunch," he wrote in a letter in 1891.[5]

In 1892, the year Schindler died, Hörmann reacted with a polemic attacking the prevailing forces in the Künstlerhaus and the Viennese art critics, which only made him further enemies, although at the same time he was seen as a beacon of hope, particularly by younger artists.

By contrast, the exhibition of twenty-five pictures in the Munich Kunstverein in 1892 was a great success, as he joyfully reported in his letters, "I received very good reviews, which pleased me all the more as I am completely unknown there."[6]

In 1893, Hörmann joined the school of artists around his former student friend Adolf Hoelzel. Hoelzel had developed the so-called New Dachau style together with Ludwig Dill and Arthur Langhammer in Dachau, a style that concentrated on the essentials and sought increasing simplification. Whether under the influence of the New Dachau painters or with consideration for the public, Hörmann's painting now underwent a remarkable transformation toward more density and small-scale detail, with noticeably lighter colors as can be seen in *Znojmo in the Snow* (ca. 1891/92), *October Day in Dachau* (*Oktobertag in Dachau*) (1892), *The Artist in the Flower Garden* (*Der Maler im Blumengarten*) (ca. 1892), *Beer Garden in Dachau* (*Biergarten in Dachau*) (ca. 1892), and *Lederertal near Znojmo* (*Das Lederertal bei Znaim*) (ca. 1893), for example.

Hörmann returned to Vienna in the fall of 1894. After trying for a long time to have a solo exhibition at the Künstlerhaus, he was ultimately granted a show with thirty-eight pictures. The reaction was not euphoric, but for the first time there was a modicum of recognition, no doubt because Hörmann was once again painting in a naturalistic style more in line with public taste, while his innovative boldness and artistic curiosity were confined to his sketches. In 1894, in spite of diminishing health, he undertook a trip to Italy with Josef Engelhart, Johann Victor Krämer and his wife. However, it failed to provide new artistic inspiration or to improve his condition and Hörmann died a year later on July 1, 1895, at the age of fifty-five, in Graz.

In his last years, Hörmann had been committed to bringing about a reform of the rules of procedure of the Genossenschaft der bildenden Künstler in Vienna and the founding of a museum of modern art that would set off contemporary Austrian art against the best achievements of international Modernists. He was not to live to see this become reality, but the Secessionists took up his idea (honoring him as the "first Secessionist") and pursued it until the Moderne Galerie was founded in 1903 in its own premises in the Lower Belvedere.

In his approach to art, Hörmann, who was occasionally dubbed the "most important Austrian Impressionist," was driven by the claim for truth, captured in spontaneous visual experiences. His importance is therefore to be found in his uncompromising use

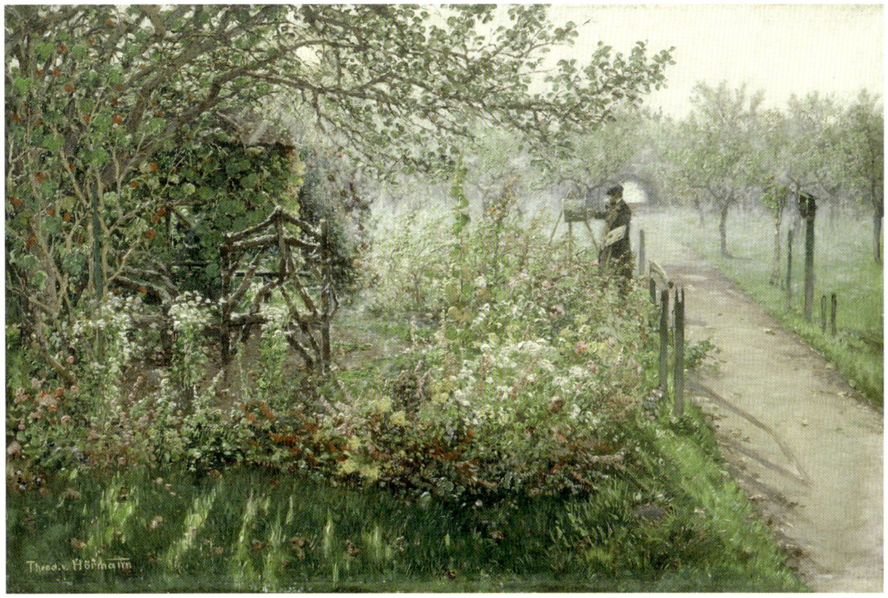

THEODOR VON HÖRMANN
The Artist in the Flower Garden, ca. 1892
Tiroler Landesmuseum Ferdinandeum, Innsbruck

of *plein air* painting and his commitment to the momentary impression as the only valid yardstick. In his emphasis on pure and often uninhibited color, and particularly the subjective brushwork of his studies, he went beyond Impressionism, pointing the way to an art form that emphasized even more the artist's subjective experience.

1 Hermann Bahr based on Theodor von Hörmann, quoted from Martina Haja, "Der österreichische Stimmungsimpressionismus," in: Götz Czymmek (ed.), *Landschaft im Licht. Impressionistische Malerei in Europa und Nordamerika 1860–1910* (exh. cat., Wallraf-Richartz-Museum, Cologne, April 6–July 1, 1990, Kunsthaus Zürich, Zürich, August 3–October 10, 1990), Cologne 1990, p. 162.
2 Hermann Bahr, "Der erste Secessionist," in: *Die Zeit*, no. 230, February 2,1899, quoted from Theo Braunegger/Magdalena Hörmann-Weingartner, *Theodor von Hörmann*, Vienna 1979, pp. 27f.
3 Quoted from Braunegger/Hörmann-Weingartner 1979 (see note 2), p. 28.
4 Review text, quoted from Peter Müller, "Theodor von Hörmann," in: *Die Schule von Plankenberg. Emil Jakob Schindler und der österreichische Stimmungsimpressionismus* (exh. cat., Niederösterreichisches Landesmuseum, Vienna, May 5–October 3, 1992), Graz 1992, p. 61.
5 Letter by Hörmann of March 18, 1891, Tiroler Landesmusem Ferdinandeum, Innsbruck, FB 45.873, quoted from Marianne Hussl-Hörmann, *Theodor von Hörmann 1840–1895. Monographie mit Verzeichnis der Gemälde*, Vienna 2013, p. 60.
6 Letter by Hörmann of December 31,1892, from Znaim to his cousin Robert von Hörmann in Vienna, Landesmuseum Ferdinandeum, Innsbruck, FB 45.873, quoted from Braunegger/Hörmann-Weingartner 1979 (see note 2), p. 101.

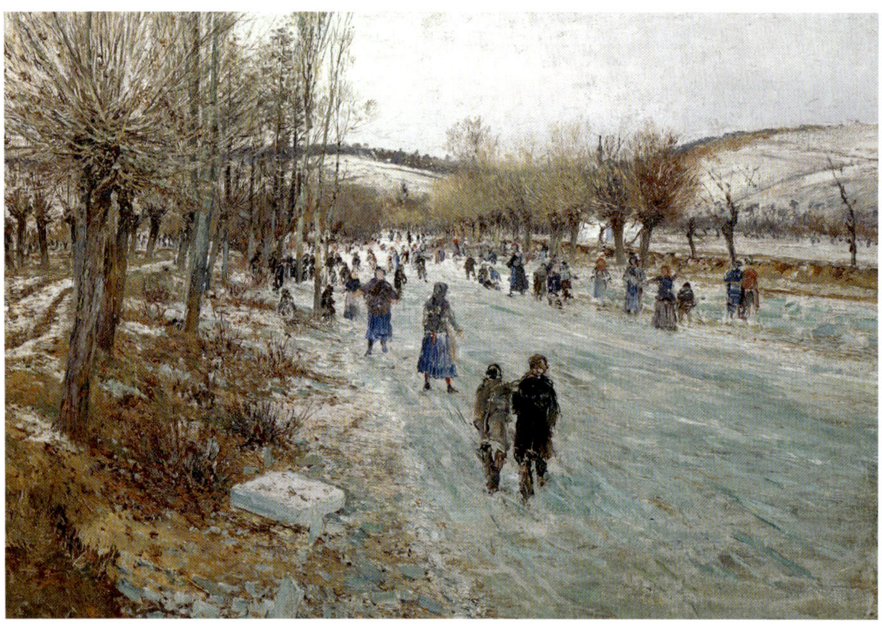

THEODOR VON HÖRMANN
Ice Skaters on the Thaya near Lundenburg, 1893
Belvedere, Vienna

FRANZ JASCHKE
(1862 Vienna – 1910 Vienna)

"Franz Jaschke, born in Vienna and never left"[1]

Kathrin Wolf

Following four years' training at Vienna's Kunstgewerbeschule (School of Applied Arts), Franz Jaschke,[2] the son of a construction metalworker, started studying at Vienna's Akademie der bildenden Künste (Academy of Fine Arts) with August Eisenmenger and Joseph Matthias Trenkwald, both traditional history painters from the Ringstraße period. Jaschke's major early works included an altarpiece, *The Lamentation of Christ (Beweinung Christi)*, painted around 1891 for the parish church at Balzers in Liechtenstein, which had been commissioned by Prince Johann II von und zu Liechtenstein. In addition, the Bulgarian court ordered a series of paintings on the history of Bulgaria, comprising thirty-six scenes that are now lost.

Around the turn of the century, when Jaschke became a member of the Hagenbund artist association and then, in March 1901, of the Vienna Secession, his style changed radically. Pointillist paintings by Théo van Rysselberghe, Georges Seurat, and Paul Signac, shown at the Secession as of 1899,[3] made such a deep impression on him that Jaschke abandoned his "academic tonal" style in favor of a light, vibrant palette and brushwork in the manner of both Impressionism and Post-Impressionism. Along with Rudolf Junk, he was one of the few Austrian artists to explore Pointillism. Josef Engelhart, who had studied the latest art trends in Paris in 1891/92, was one of his closest friends.

Jaschke ran his own private painting school, where his students included Hans Böhler. In addition to history paintings, he mainly painted children's portraits, much esteemed by his contemporaries, landscapes, and modern cityscapes. His companion pieces show-

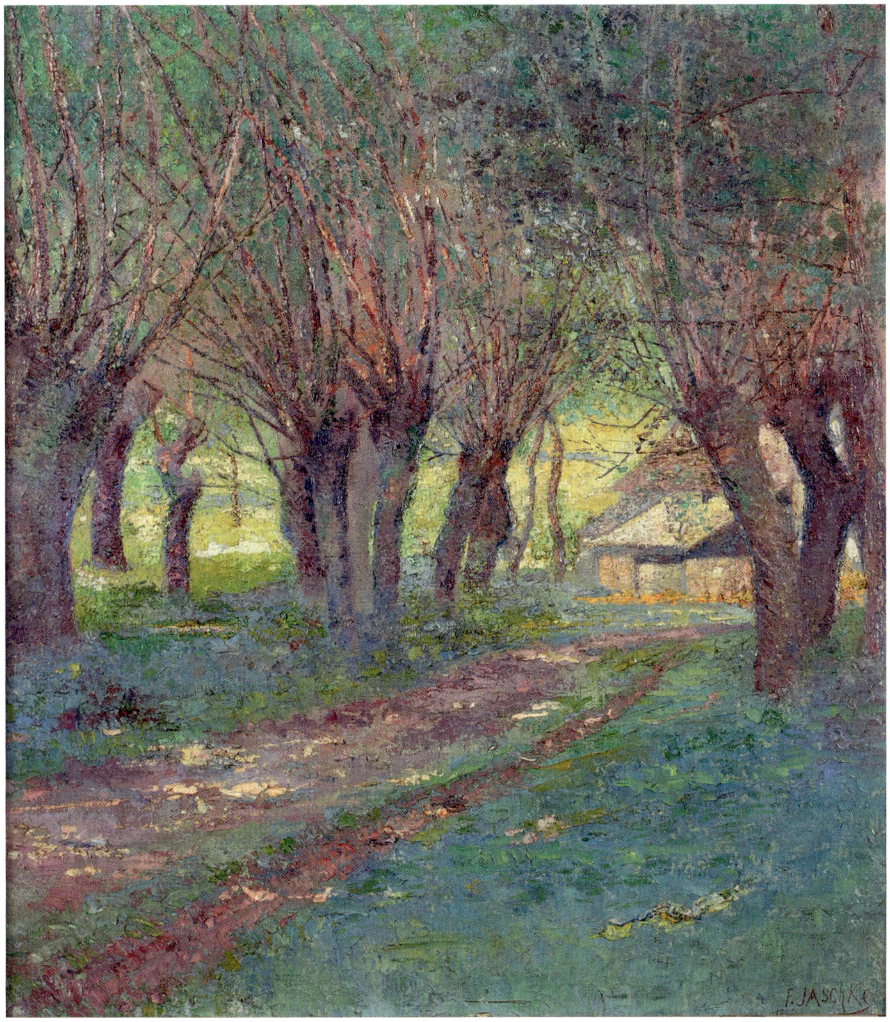

FRANZ JASCHKE
Pollard Willow Trees in Weyer, 1909
Belvedere, Vienna

ing the Danube Canal (figs. p. 87) adopt Monet's concept of the series by representing the same view in different seasons. Although Jaschke did not separate his colors into the pure hues of the spectrum with scientific rigor, his small dabs of paint still make his canvases vibrate with color. The winter scene was shown at the major art exhibition in Dresden in 1904.

When Jaschke died on December 1, 1910, after a serious illness, the Vienna Secession organized a memorial exhibition the following year. With the exception of a small selection of pictures in the Belvedere's collection, the majority of Jaschke's oeuvre was lost in the wars or is today in private collections.

1 *XXXVIII. Ausstellung der Vereinigung bildender Künstler Österreichs Secession. Gedächtnisausstellung Franz Jaschke*, Vienna 1911, n.p.

2 To date, no monograph has been compiled about Franz Jaschke's work. Relevant encyclopedia entries provide some basic information about the artist's life. In the estates of Marianne Gerstenberger and Rudolf Schmidt at the *Österreichische* Galerie Belvedere, Vienna, there are some folders with photographs and notes.

3 The Secession's third exhibition in January 1899 featured thirty-two works by Theó van Rysselberghe including etchings and paintings. In Vienna, van Rysselberghe was regarded as the star of Pointillism, while the true founders of this new painting style, Georges Seurat and Paul Signac, who are today much more famous than van Rysselberghe, were very much on the sidelines in Vienna at that time. The Viennese only had the opportunity to see six paintings and seven watercolors by Signac at the Secession's seventh exhibition in 1900. Georges Seurat was first shown in 1903 at the Secession's major Impressionism exhibition that included three of his works. Van Rysselberghe presented seven works at the same show.

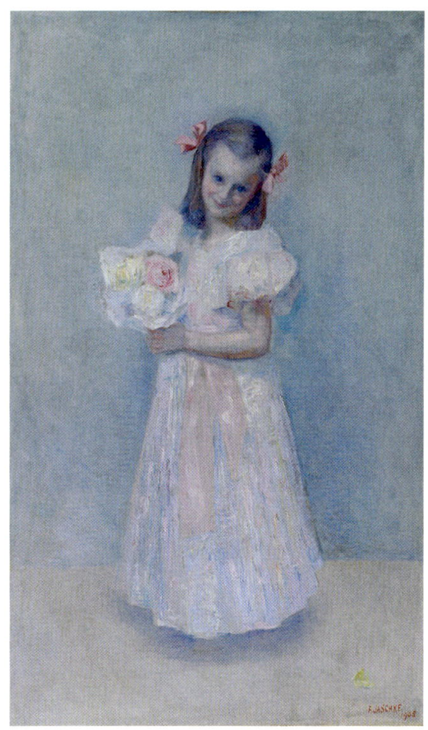

FRANZ JASCHKE
The Well-Wisher (Anna, the artist's daughter), 1905
Belvedere, Vienna

EUGEN JETTEL
(1845 Johnsdorf, Moravia – 1901 Lussingrande, Croatia)

He loved "[...] especially the soft dusky moods of the waning evening hours [...]"[1]

Kathrin Wolf

Eugen Jettel[2] was born on March 20, 1845, in Johnsdorf near Römerstadt in Moravia, the son of an ironworks administrator. After his mother's premature death, his family moved to Vienna when he was five. In 1860 he began his studies at the Vienna Akademie der bildenden Künste (Academy of Fine Arts), where he was a student of Albert August Zimmermann. Zimmermann, who had succeeded Franz Steinfeld as head of the landscape painting class in 1859, specialized in heroic mountain scenes and, having introduced *plein-air* studies to the curriculum as Waldmüller had previously demanded, took Jettel and his classmates—Rudolf Ribarz, Robert Russ, and Emil Jakob Schindler, among others—on study trips to the mountains in Bavaria, Salzburg, and Tyrol. Jettel was soon recognized for his work. In 1864 his painting *Lake Hintersee near Berchtesgaden* (*Der Hintersee bei Berchtesgaden*) was purchased by Emperor Franz Joseph, and in subsequent years he received a number of awards for other pictures at exhibitions in Austria and sometimes abroad. Yet the young artist soon turned his back on his successful mountain scenes painted in a naturalistic style. Shortly after completing his studies at the academy in 1868 and being accepted as a full member of the Vienna Künstlerhaus, art critics at its annual exhibition referred to this graduate from Zimmermann's class as a "true disciple of the French *paysage intime*."[3] On the one hand, from 1868 young artists had the opportunity to see works from the Barbizon School at exhibitions in Vienna (Stadtbaumeister Bösch collection; F. J. Gsell collection) and Munich ("I. Internationale Kunst-Ausstellung"), and on the other a preference for unspectacular but highly atmospheric scenes of nature painted *en plein air* had already emerged in Jettel's work in the mid-1860s. Diary entries by his like-minded friend Emil Jakob Schindler, revering the beauty and poetry of nature, bear witness to an intimate relationship to the "experienced" landscape.[4]

MEETING PETTENKOFEN

In 1869/70 Jettel met the acclaimed August von Pettenkofen through the art dealer Georg Plach, who acquired Jettel's first pictures. Pettenkofen would prove not only to be a good friend (he created the staffage in several of Jettel's paintings), but also a second teacher, encouraging trips to Holland (1870) and Hungary (1871). In 1870 Jettel first traveled to northern France (Normandy and Picardy, especially Dieppe). These trips abroad were a crucial influence on Jettel's later artistic development. The artist, who had already seen works by the Hague School at exhibitions in Vienna and Munich prior to his travels, sparked off a veritable Holland craze on his return. In the words of Carl von Lützow, commenting on the Künstlerhaus annual exhibition in 1874, "Although Jettel does not feature this time, it is riddled with his imitators [...] Namely 'landscapes from Holland' in Jettelesque style now seem to be all the rage."[5] Only the 1872/73 tour of Naples and Sicily with Leopold Carl Müller left no lasting impact on Jettel's work.

YEARS IN PARIS

Around 1873[6] Jettel accepted an offer from the Paris-based Austrian art dealer Charles Sedelmeyer to give him all his new paintings in return for a fixed salary. The painter then moved to the metropolis on the Seine where he married Cäcilie Mailer from Vienna, and where he was to remain over the next twenty years. His apartment in Montmartre became a place where many German-speaking artists gathered, including Josef Engelhart, Franz von Lenbach, Max Liebermann, Mihály Múnkacsy, his friend August von Pettenkofen, and Rudolf Ribarz. Yet he was also in touch with French artists—Pierre Puvis de Chavannes, Emile Auguste Carolus-Duran, Jean-Léon Gérôme, and Ernest Meissonier, among others. At that time the artist started signing his work "Eugène Jettel" and was often mistaken for a French artist as a result. In 1875 he first

EUGEN JETTEL
Moonlit Landscape in Holland, 1884
Oblastni Galerie v Liberci

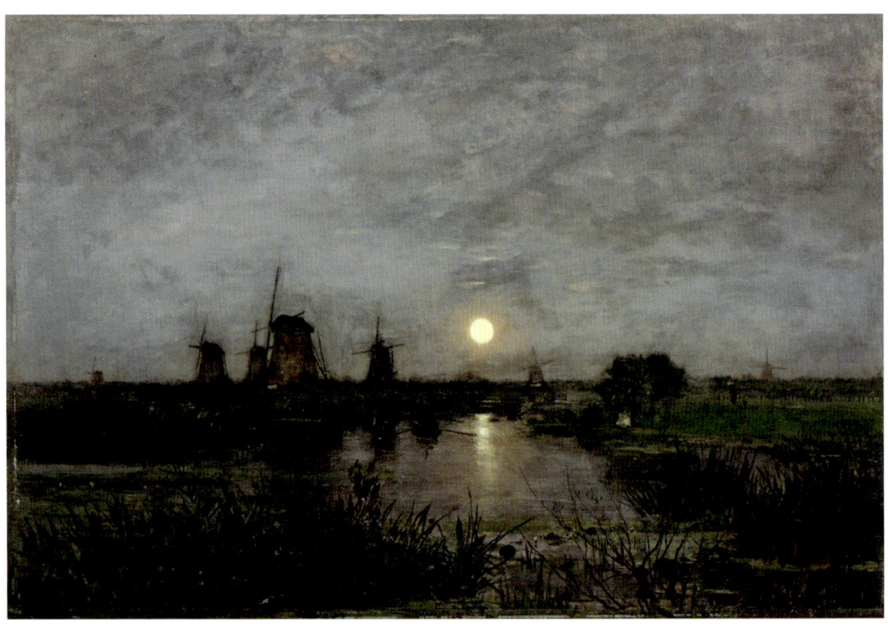

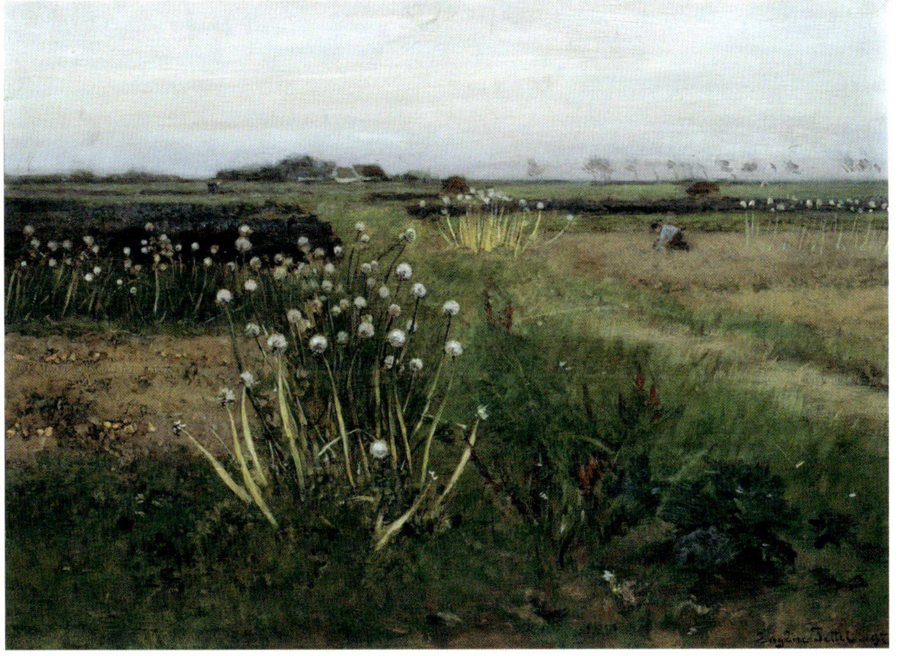

EUGEN JETTEL
Flowering Onion Field, 1897
Belvedere, Vienna

went to Barbizon. By that time one no longer encountered the first generation of painters there, including the artists Jettel so admired, like Charles-François Daubigny, Théodore Rousseau, and Constant Troyon, but the Impressionists. In subsequent years he frequently painted in Picardy (Cayeux-sur-Mer), Normandy, and in Holland. From 1887 Jettel went on painting tours to Auvers-sur-Oise and Pont-Aven. As of 1877 he exhibited regularly at the Salon des Champs-Elysées and later at the new Salon du Champ-de-Mars, but continued to send his work to the Vienna Künstlerhaus. His work enjoyed great acclaim in Paris, and in 1889 he was made a Knight of the French Legion of Honor for his contribution to the Paris World's Fair. Back in 1873, his work had featured at the World's Fair in Vienna; in 1893 and 1894 he took part in the fairs in Chicago and Antwerp, where he was awarded a gold medal on both occasions.

RETURN TO VIENNA

In 1897 Jettel returned to Vienna after a twenty-four year absence with the express purpose of contributing to the Secession's first exhibition. He became a member of the Secession after leaving the Künstlerhaus that same year. The positive reception of his works, combined with the financial difficulties he had recently been facing in Paris, Sedelmeyer having reduced his salary, prompted the painter to move back to Vienna. Jettel used his good contacts in Paris to promote the interests of the Secession, mainly contributing scenes from the Karst landscape in Istria to its exhibitions. In the latter years of his life he traveled both to Istria and to Staatz in Lower Austria on frequent occasions. Jettel died at the age of fifty-six on August 27, 1901, following a heart attack in Lussingrande. He had been waiting there for his patron Archduke Carl Stephan before setting out on a trip to southern Italy.

JETTEL'S DEVELOPMENT AS AN ARTIST

Influenced by the Barbizon and Hague schools, Jettel had made a radical break from the academic paintings of mountains by his teacher Albert August Zimmermann back in the mid-1860s. *Moonlit Landscape in Holland (Mondlandschaft in Holland)* is an extremely atmospheric nocturnal scene and a classic example of Jettel's predilection for horizontal, tranquil flat landscapes beneath a wide expanse of sky. Hermann Voss sees Jettel as "a lyrically inclined nature," who loved "especially the soft dusky moods of the waning evening hours," "when the setting sun and rising moon greet one another, and the misty, damp atmosphere swathes the Dutch and Normandy lowlands like a veil. The delicate dual accord of a very light, pale blue and a silvery dove gray is characteristic of his pictures."[7] Dusk was Jettel's favorite time of day, as the optical phenomena of the dim atmosphere conveyed a varied spectrum of colors and he had brilliantly mastered rendering this special mood in painting, using delicately nuanced shades and subtle light effects. The artist very often painted on the banks of a river or canal, as here he could find the ideal backdrop for the interplay between landscape motifs and their silhouetted reflections in water. Windmills, haystacks, and farmhouses with thatched roofs are among his most frequently recurring architectonic motifs. A staffage of people tends to play only a subordinate role in these depictions, and in the main one sees rural animals such as cows and sheep, grazing in lush meadows or gathering around ponds that reflect the colors of the landscape in their waters. This tendency to a dark palette and flat, panoramic landscapes arose from studying seventeenth-century Dutch painters in Zimmermann's class.

Austrian critics of the time were all too willing to accuse Jettel of "the deliberate quest for uninteresting motifs"[8] and criticized a "certain virtuoso flinging."[9] One even advised him to return to Austria, "Jettel is becoming increasingly restless, quivering, unrestrained in his handling. Foreign lands are obviously not doing him any good—he should come home."[10] In the mid-1880s, the painter started raising his horizon line and focusing attention on the foreground. He painted works such as *Onion Field in Flower (Blühendes Zwiebelfeld)* in the Austrian tradition known as ("cabbage and turnip painting"),[11] in which the focus was on the foreground flora, at the painter's feet, and the main subject was vegetables, ren-

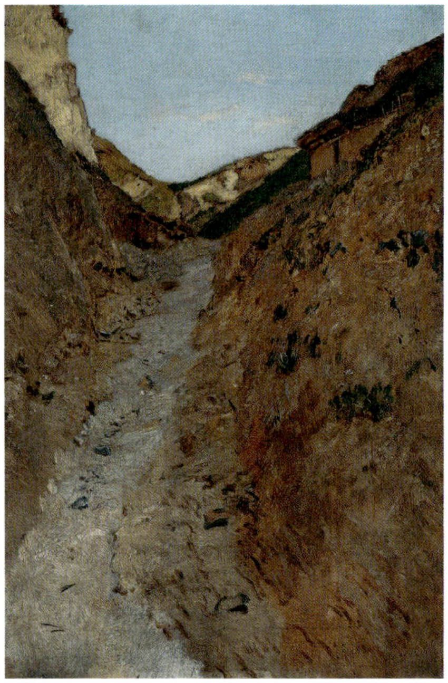

EUGEN JETTEL
The Path through the Quarry, ca. 1895
Belvedere, Vienna

dered close-up with meticulous precision. As a result of the high horizon, the close-up representation of the foreground, and abandoning techniques of linear perspective, Jettel conceals the effect of depth and conjures up a planarity akin to a wall hanging, revealing the obvious influence of Japanese woodcuts. This tendency culminated in the painting *Path in a Quarry (Weg im Steinbruch)* of approximately 1895, in which an unspectacular track, viewed from a bold perspective, becomes a motif that takes over the picture space. The extremely foreshortened path guides the eye into the picture space, yet this sense of depth is significantly diminished by the closely cropped view and paint evenly applied to all areas, which has the effect of pushing the subject back onto the picture plane. This is further emphasized by the gently undulating lines indicating the stones and conveying a planar-decorative effect.

Jettel spent over two decades in the art metropolis of Paris and it is highly probable that he would have seen works by Monet at the Durand-Ruel gallery or the Impressionists' exhibitions.[12] That being said, he had different artistic aims in painting, never took the step to solely represent optical phenomena in the manner of Impressionism, by which the object was purely a vehicle of colors and light and often receded entirely. In the course of his artistic career, Jettel's colors became cooler and lighter, and from 1890 he also worked in pastels. His style of painting became more fluid and rapid, his brushstrokes more restless, shorter and denser, yet his paintings never reveal the pure, vibrant, luminous hues and bold color contrasts so typical of the Impressionists. His *View of Auvers-sur-Oise (Ansicht von Auvers-sur-Oise)* is a characteristic example of Jettel's late work in terms of color, painting technique, and composition and has distinctly impressionist traits. However, the artist still favored describing the landscape with its specific charms as opposed to capturing the purely optical effect of the motif. (see also fig. p. 39). At the Paris Salon du Champ-de-Mars in 1893, a critic made an apt comparison between modern French painting and Jettel's work, "The landscape of French artists is always approached with greater objectivity than the Germans. It does not wish to move the personal feelings of the viewer, but rather exists outside of him and for itself. Thus the landscapes by the Austrian artist Jettel, who has lived for many years in Paris, stand out from all the others on account of their German characteristics of mood and a certain type of tone."[13]

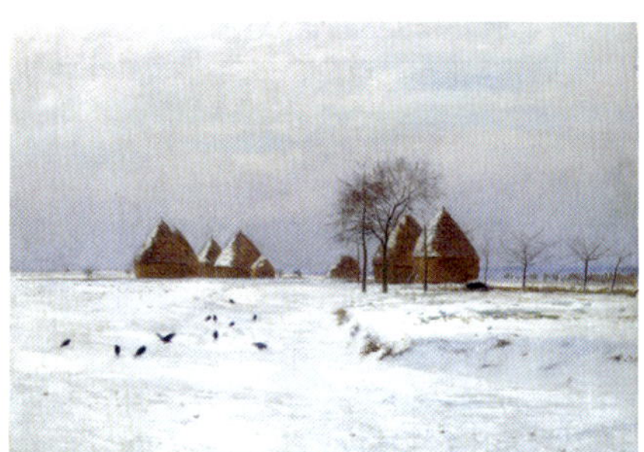

EUGEN JETTEL
View of Auvers-sur-Oise in Winter, 1895
Private collection

1 H. V. [Hans Vollmer], entry about Eugen Jettel, in: *Thieme-Becker XVIII,* Leipzig 1925, p. 542f., here p. 542.

2 There is one published monograph about the artist to date: Heinrich Fuchs, *Eugen Jettel,* Vienna 1975. In addition, Jettel's oeuvre has been explored in many exhibition catalogs about Austrian and European landscape painting. The author would like to draw particular attention to the articles by Martina Haja and Andrea Winklbauer: Martina Haja, Der österreichische Stimmungsimpressionismus," in: Götz Czymmek (ed.), *Landschaft im Licht. Impressionistische Malerei in Europa und Nordamerika* (exh. cat., Wallraf-Richartz-Museum, Cologne, April 4–July 1, 1990; Kunsthaus Zürich, August 3–October 21, 1990), pp. 156–163. – Martina Haja, "Eugen Jettel," in: Gerbert Frodl/Verena Traeger (eds.), *Stimmungsimpressionismus* (exh. cat. Belvedere, Vienna, March 17–July 4, 2004), Vienna 2004, pp. 134–135. – Andrea Winklbauer, "Eugen Jettel," in: Otmar Rychlik (ed.), *Natürlichere Natur. Österreichische Malerei des Stimmungsrealismus* (exh. cat. Kunsthaus Mürzzuschlag, Mürzzuschlag, summer exhibition 1994), Mürzzuschlag 1994, pp. 223–226. – Andrea Winklbauer, "Impressionismus contra Stimmung. Über das Verhältnis der Österreicher zur französischen Landschaftsauffassung – 1868 bis 1903," in: Rychlik 1994, pp. 14–21. – Andrea Winklbauer, "Eugen Jettel," in: Roland Dorn/Klaus Albrecht Schröder/John

Sillevis (eds.), *Van Gogh und die Haager Schule* (exh. cat., Bank Austria Kunstforum, Vienna, February 28–May 27, 1996), Vienna 1996, pp. 345–347. The articles cited here were valuable sources for the author.

3 *Zeitschrift für bildende Kunst*, vol. 4, 1869, p. 259.

4 Diary entry by Emil Jakob Schindler, 1864, quoted in Fuchs 1975 (see note 2), pp. 8–9.

5 *Kunst-Chronik*, supplement to *Zeitschrift für Bildende Kunst* 9, no. 37, June 26, 1874, p. 585.

6 In the catalog of Eugen Jettel's estate for the auction at Ca. J. Wawra, Vienna 1902, p. 6, August Schaeffer states that Jettel moved to Paris in 1873. In *Thieme-Becker* the same year is cited. Other authors, however, give the date as 1874 or 1875.

7 Vollmer 1925 (see note 1), p. 542.

8 *Kunst-Chronik*, supplement to *Zeitschrift für Bildende Kunst* 9, no. 25, April 2, 1874, p. 405.

9 *Kunst-Chronik*, supplement to *Zeitschrift für Bildende Kunst* 10, no. 8, December 4, 1874, p. 123.

10 *Kunst-Chronik*, supplement to *Zeitschrift für Bildende Kunst* 14, no. 16, January 30, 1879, pp. 253–254.

11 Martina Haja, "'Kraut und Rüben.' Beobachtungen zur österreichischen Freilicht-Malerei im späten 19. Jahrhundert," in: *Mitteilungen der* Österreichischen *Galerie* 30, no. 74, Vienna 1986, pp. 43–66.

12 In 1874, when the first of the Impressionists' exhibitions was held at the photographer Nadar's studio (the exhibition that gave the group its name), Jettel was already living in Paris.

13 *Zeitschrift für Bildende Kunst*, N. F. 4, 1893, p. 295.

LUDWIG HEINRICH JUNGNICKEL

(1881 Wunsiedel, Fichtelgebirge – 1964 Vienna)

"It is not sufficient for a work of art to be fashionable; it must come from the heart. Then it will remain forever beautiful, modern, and very precious."[1]

Claus Jesina

Ludwig Heinrich Jungnickel was born on July 22, 1881, the son of a railway worker, in Wunsiedel in the Fichtelgebirge. He spent his youth and school years in Munich. His artistic training was initially somewhat irregular: in 1896, at the age of fifteen, he enrolled at the Kunstgewerbeschule (Academy of Applied Arts) in Munich, were he remained until 1897, while at the same time attending the Gewerbliche Fortbildungsschule (Higher Technical School) for six months. Jungnickel's childhood and youth were spent in depressing circumstances at home, as described in detail in his brother's memoirs. When his mother died in 1897, there was nothing to keep him at home any longer. Having suffered considerably from the family circumstances, he felt an urgent need to seek something new and better, which he hoped to find in the world and in art. Thus he decided finally to set off and seek his fortune. With his brother he walked to the Grossglockner in 1897 and then continued to Italy. In the artists' circles in Rome, he met an archeologist who gave him access to the Vatican collections. Jungnickel earned a living copying paintings and also doing portrait drawings.

NEW START IN VIENNA

Jungnickel arrived in Vienna in 1899, where he enrolled in the Akademie der bildenden Künste (Academy of Fine Arts) and Christian Griepenkerl's general painting class, which he abandoned, however, the same year.

In 1902, he attended the k. k. Kunstgewerbeschule (Imperial and Royal Academy of Applied Arts), where the progressive teaching in Alfred Roller's preparatory figurative classes were to have a decisive influence on the young artist. In interminable exercises Roller made his students draw the different phases of movement. At this time Jungnickel also made the acquaintance of Gustav Klimt and his circle. In 1903, he began to work for the newly founded Wiener Werkstätte.

In 1905, he went to Munich and studied under Carl Marr at the Akademie der bildenden Künste before returning after a few months to Vienna, where he continued his studies at the Akademie in William Unger's graphic arts class. During his studies he worked freelance, not only earning a living but also attracting increasing attention in Austria and elsewhere through his work.

In 1904, Jungnickel started drawing illustrations for magazines. His first works using the stencil spray technique were completed in

LUDWIG HEINRICH JUNGNICKEL
The Animals' Paradise (draft for the Palais Stoclet, Brussels), 1908/09
Private collection, Vienna

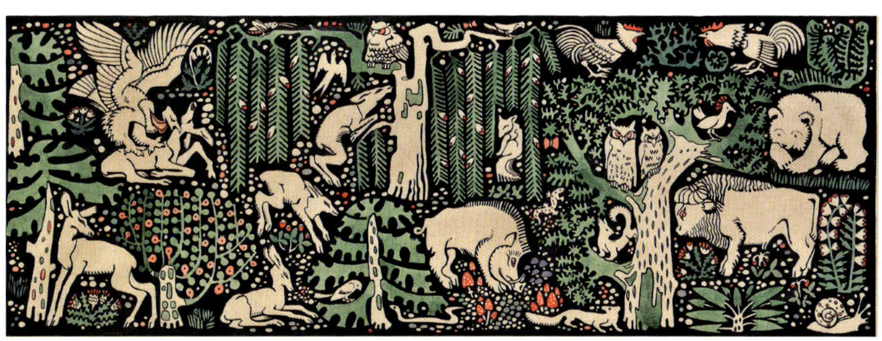

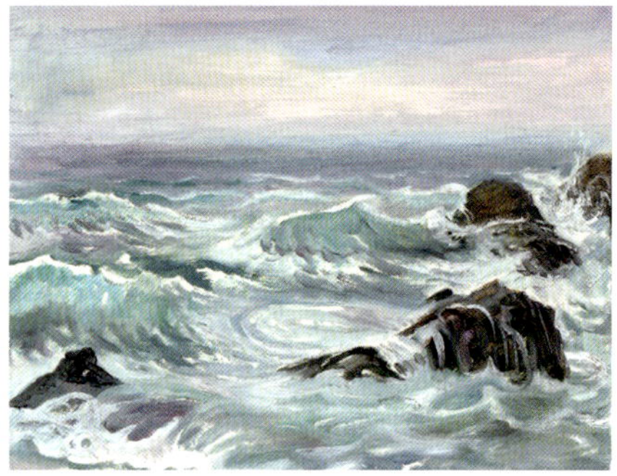

LUDWIG HEINRICH JUNGNICKEL
Atmosphere in the Morning at the Adria, ca. 1940
Private collection

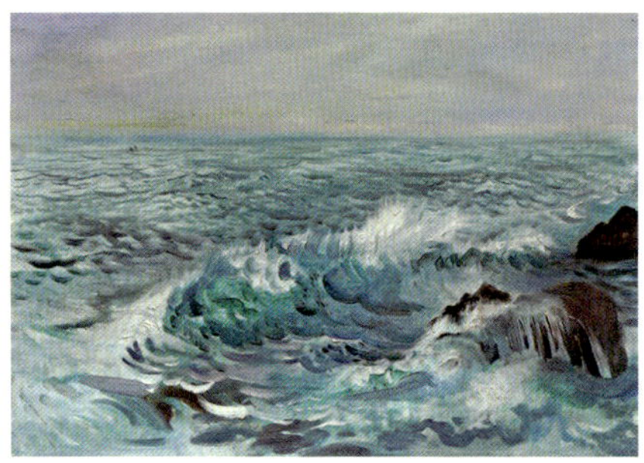

LUDWIG HEINRICH JUNGNICKEL
Heaving Sea, ca. 1940
Private collection

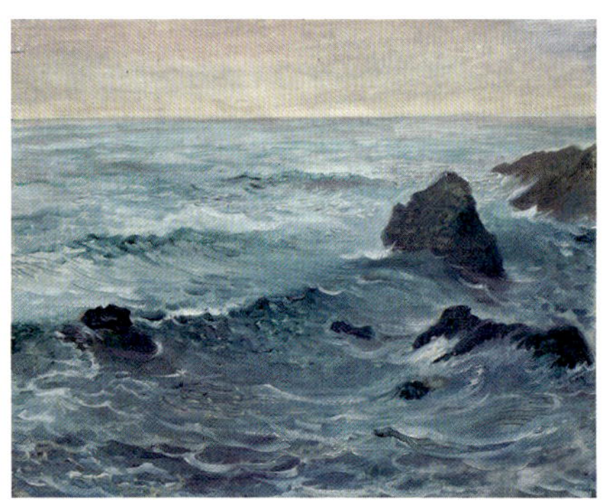

LUDWIG HEINRICH JUNGNICKEL
Atmosphere in the Evening at the Adria, ca. 1940
Private collection

1905. From 1903 to 1910 he worked as a designer for the Wiener Werkstätte. In 1907 he was given an annual pass offering him free admission to paint at Schönbrunn Zoo. In 1909 he received an imperial subsidy to make colored woodcuts of the various animals in the zoo. In 1911, he was invited to the Kunstgewerbeschule (Academy of Applied Arts) in Frankfurt am Main and he also took part in a major international art exhibition in Rome. In the winter semester 1912, however, Jungnickel dropped out and returned finally to Vienna. Thereafter, he undertook a number of trips, including a visit with Egon Schiele to Krumau.

ISTRIA AS A REFUGE WITH CONSEQUENCES

The political climate prompted the artist to flee in 1939 to what was still the free world, to Istria, which he had traveled to frequently hitherto. His relationship to the Nazi rulers after 1939 was very tense, resulting in the confiscation of his Vienna studio in 1942 and a charge of "activities against the state." Jungnickel used delaying tactics and the excuse of his health to remain in Abbazia [now Opatija], where he was obliged to stay, not completely voluntarily, until 1952, before finally being able to return to Austria.

He spent his last years in Carinthia and above all Vienna, where he died on February 14, 1964. These years were also filled with travel, exhibitions, awards, and prizes.

THE ANIMAL AS METAPHOR FOR NATURE

"A person without a relationship to animals is not a whole person, because he is missing the organic foundation; this person feels unsure, errs, and withers. People need a relationship to animals more than ever today. The many technical achievements confuse human nature, and people become estranged from themselves and can only come to their senses by observing the harmonious life of animals and their connection to nature.

Animals can never be bad, tasteless, inharmonious, unless they have been made so by man. Man deprives domestic pets of their divinity, for while man strives, he errs.

Animals teach harmony, socialism, elegance, technique, goodness, health. Every animal that lives like one is a secret divinity for us."[2]

Jungnickel's great love of nature led him to concentrate increasingly on the animal world, but this natural attraction was also rooted in his character and solitary existence. He never married or had a partner and lived frugally and withdrawn. His vegetarianism, particularly in his later years, is an almost inevitable consequence of this strong love of animals.

Pictures of animals account for more than three quarters of the artist's oeuvre. Apart from animals, landscapes were also important for him. Depictions of people, including portraits, are less prominent, which does not mean that his rare ventures into this world were not masterly. Until the 1920s, Jungnickel also worked intensively on the portrayal of people as nudes, portraits, and also within pictures, but this interest was to dwindle in later years.

Through animals, he tried to divine the secrets of life and of nature. In his work he captured the character, mood, and condition of the species and of the individual. The artist appears to have wanted to create some kind of portrait. Like an expressionist painter, he often circled around the core of what makes up the individual, namely his history and through it his psyche and momentary mood. There is also a strong narrative element in Jungnickel's work, not only in his early works, such as those for Palais Stoclet, or in his illustrations, but also in his expressionist paintings. This aspect also played a major role in his pictures of animals.

While other artists used animals only as occasional figures in landscapes and were more interested in their effect, Jungnickel tended to omit everything extraneous so as to concentrate on the creature he was depicting.

SURF PICTURES—NEW ASPECTS IN THE ARTIST'S OEUVRE

Although landscapes were not the main focus of the artist's oeuvre, he also completed several hundred works of this kind with all kinds of media. Initially his landscapes were influenced by the Vienna Jugendstil, which left a considerable mark on Jungnickel. With the spray technique used for the field in *The Reapers* (*Schnitter*) this influence is evident in the rhythmic and ornamental dissolution of the forms. His expressionist landscapes are notable for the exaggerated coloring and in particular the dynamic brushstrokes and paint application. The color effects included very strong light-dark contrasts but also intensive coloring. This expressionist style is found again in his later landscapes.

The move in 1939 to Istria and to Optija, his favorite place there, was a decisive turning point in the life of the artist, which was also reflected in his choice of subject. The coastal and maritime landscape around Kvarner Gulf and the view of the island of Cres fascinated Jungnickel to such an extent that he completed whole series of pictures of the surf, coastline, and sea, with much fewer pictures of animals. Between 1939 and 1952 he created 200 to 300 works on these subjects in a variety of media and formats. These pictures maybe subsumed under the heading of seascapes. They include a number of series featuring subjects observed with little change in the point of view but at different times of day and in different lights and weather conditions. This prolonged concentration on specific subjects and their reproduction under different circumstances suggests parallels with Monet. In Jungnickel's case, the analysis of the experience of nature often extended to the difference in wave shapes under various meteorological conditions. Apart from sensitive observations there are also works in which the form and color are dynamically emphasized. All of these works will also have been influenced by the artist's mood and situation.

1 Ludwig Heinrich Jungnickel, quoted from Ilse Spielvogel-Bodo, *Ludwig Heinrich Jungnickel. Ein Leben für die Kunst*, Klagenfurt 2000, p. 97.
2 Letter by the artist, Vienna, January 22, 1926, from the estate.

RUDOLF JUNK
(1880 Vienna – 1943 Rekawinkel)

"As an oil painter, Junk is a pointillist ..."

Kathrin Wolf

As an oil painter, Junk is a pointillist," wrote Karl Michael Kuzmany in 1908, "not on account of theoretical considerations, but because he merely finds a satisfactory means with this painting style of reproducing his visual impressions. For all the boldness with which he abandons himself to an incessant frenzy of color, his palette and application with woodcuts is all the more restrained."[1] Rudolf Junk was mainly involved in painting between 1903 and 1907,[2] after which he devoted himself almost exclusively to graphic art. In contrast to the large number of graphic prints, he completed a maximum of 120 oil paintings and watercolors.[3] His predilection for handicrafts goes back to

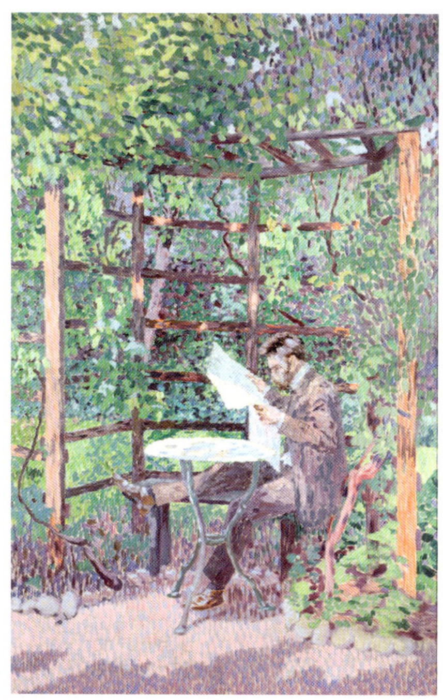

RUDOLF JUNK
Man Reading in an Arbor, 1905
Belvedere, Vienna

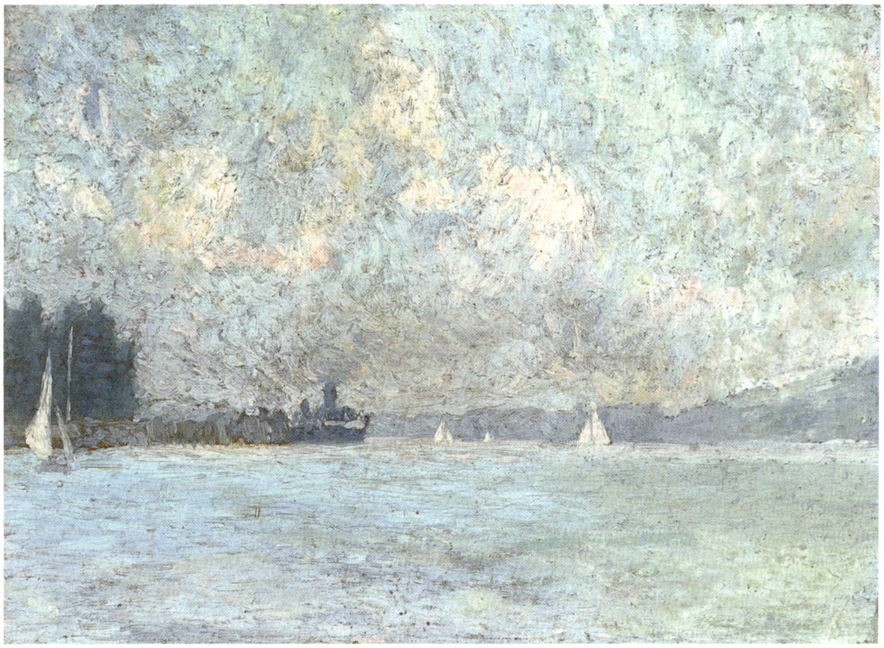

RUDOLF JUNK
Steamboat on the Attersee, 1904
Private collection

his childhood and youth. The son of an architect and engineer, his visits to his grandparents in Niederheidisch [now Dolní Hede] in Bohemia introduced him to the age-old tradition of *Herrgottschnitzerei*, the carving of religious subjects, and even allowed him to try his hand at carving and gilding crucifixes and manger figures. He was later impressed by the old books in the library of Melk Abbey, in whose venerable walls he spent his school years. His art teacher, the academic painter Benedikt Hager, took him and his fellow pupils, including the future painter Leopold Blauensteiner, on Sunday excursions to the Wachau, where they made sketches of their natural surroundings.[4]

For Blauensteiner and Junk, the visit to the third Secession exhibition in 1899, which presented the art of Pointillism to the people of Vienna, was something of an epiphany, "[…] the pictures by Seurat from Paris and Rysselberghe from Belgium in particular [made] an extremely deep impression on the Melk pupil Junk and his young eyes, receptive to everything to do with painting, and were to have a lasting impact especially on his landscape painting."[5] After completing his studies at the University of Vienna and his doctorate in philosophy in 1903, Junk went first to Professor Heinrich Lefler at the Akademie der bildenden Künste (Academy of Fine Arts). "The summer between graduating from the university and enrolling in the Akademie was used for all-out painting, the last selfexamination before changing careers."[6] Even as a student at the university, he had enthusiastically followed the activities of the Vienna Secession. The major Impressionism exhibition in 1903 finally prompted him to devote his life to art. In 1904 for the first time he exhibited oil and watercolor landscapes in the Hagenbund that were clearly influenced by the Impressionists. His pointillist painting *Man Reading in an Arbor* (*Lesender Mann in einer Laube*) (1905) was completed while he was studying at the Akademie. Junk was never an advocate of strict divisionism, in which pure colors were dotted separately on the canvas, but mixed his colors on the palette. Pointillism inspired him to make his pointed brush strokes, which created a vibrant tension on the canvas, and to a color palette diverging from the natural colors of objects.

In summer 1904, he painted a series of pictures in silver-blue tones on Lake Attersee. They are reduced landscape impressions, in which Junk experimented with the possibilities of abstracting nature.[7] Some paintings were marked with the date and time. Following on from his exhibition debut, Junk was a frequent contributor to the Hagenbund exhibitions. In 1907, the state purchased the painting *Summer in Steinbach in the Wienerwald* (*Sommer in Steinbach im Wienerwald*, 1907; see fig. p. 83) for the Moderne Galerie, the present-day Belvedere—a major recognition for a young artist. This picture is part of a series showing the seasons (see fig. p. 83), which Junk, emulating Monet, painted from the same position and with the same composition. Only the colors changed to reflect the seasons. Although some critics described Junk's pictures as "soulless dots,"[8] his paintings reflected the fashion of the times. Leopold Blauensteiner, Franz Jaschke, Gustav Klimt, Broncia Koller-Pinell, and Carl Moll were also attracted to Pointillism, at least for a time. Ludwig Hevesi wrote enthusiastically about Théo van Rysselberghe's pictures at the third Secession exhibition, "Approaching the canvas, one is gripped by a feeling of amazement and admiration. All one can see is a system of points, individual dabs by the brushes. Swarms of colored dots that in the blink of an eye become alive and confused; every area a Milky Way of colored stars that merge into a blaze of light."[9]

In 1906, Junk presented colored woodcuts in the Hagenbund for the first time. Shortly afterwards, he was persuaded by colleagues to

RUDOLF JUNK
Attersee- Light Sun after Rain & Fog, 1904
Private collection

design the society's exhibition catalogs. For that reason, his painting gradually took a back seat. In 1908, on conclusion of his studies, he was made an ordinary member of the Hagenbund, and in 1911 he was elected its president. He started working for the Österreichische Staatsdruckerei (Austrian State Stationery Office) in 1909, designing securities, tax and postage stamps, and banknotes. He also reformed artistic typography, designing his own "Junk-Fraktur" Gothic type. In 1909, at the age of just twenty-nine, he was nominated for the Ministry of Education Art Commission. He fought to support young artists like Anton Faistauer, Egon Schiele, and Oskar Kokoschka. Many artistic book designs are attributable to the "master calligrapher"[10] Rudolf Junk. His style is highly ornamental, often embellished with arabesques, leaves, and rosettes, recalling lace patterns. In 1924, Junk was appointed director of the Graphische Lehr- und Versuchsanstalt (Graphic Teaching and Research Institute) and in the same year he became a member of the Künstlerhaus in Vienna.

As a painter, Rudolf Junk is known today only to initiates, although he is well-known for his activities in the Hagenbund and for his graphic art. In view of his outstanding painting oeuvre, situated somewhere between Secessionism, decorative planar art, Impressionism, Pointillism, and, in some paintings, also Symbolism, he nevertheless occupies an important place in Austrian art and deserves to be recognized for his distinctive style.

1 Karl Michael Kuzmany, "Jüngere Österreichische Graphiker," in: *Die graphischen Künste* 31, 1908, p. 86.
2 Alice Proché, "Das malerische Werk von Rudolf Junk," diss., Vienna 2008.
3 *Herbstausstellung Bel Etage* (exh. cat., Galerie Bel Etage, Vienna, September 27–November 30, 2002), Vienna 2002, p. 62; http://www.beletage.com/herbst02/BE_2.PDF (last visited September 26, 2014).
4 Richard Kurt Donin, "Dem Andenken an Hofrat Dr. Rudolf Junk," in: Photographische Gesellschaft in Wien (ed.), *Jahrbuch der Photographischen Gesellschaft in Wien 1943–1944–1945*, special reprint, Vienna n.d. (1945), p. 1.
5 Ibid., p. 2. In fact, works by Georges Seurat were first seen at the Secession Impressionism exhibition in 1903.
6 Kuzmany 1908 (see note 1), p. 86.
7 Rudolf Minichbauer (ed.), *Rudolf Junk. Bilder von 1903–1907* (exh. cat., Galerie Walfischgasse, Vienna 2000), Vienna 2000. This catalog and the dissertation by Alice Proché are the only monographic works on the artist to have appeared to date.
8 Gustav Er., "Vom Hagenbund," in: *Arbeiter-Zeitung*, Vienna, October 16. 1907, quoted from Minichbauer 2000 (see note 7).
9 Ludwig Hevesi, *Acht Jahre Sezession*, Vienna 1906, reprint Klagenfurt 1984, p. 103.
10 This epithet was coined by Ludwig Hevesi; see Minichbauer 2000 (see note 7).

GUSTAV KLIMT

(1862 Vienna – 1918 Vienna)

"Whoever wants to know something about me … ought to look carefully at my pictures …"[1]

Stephan Koja

Gustav Klimt was born on July 14, 1862, in Vienna, the second of seven children, to the engraver Ernst Klimt and his wife Anna. He attended the Kunstgewerbeschule (School of Applied Arts) at the k. k. Österreichisches Museum für Kunst und Industrie in Vienna from 1876 to 1883, where he studied under Michael Rieser, Ludwig Minnigerode, Ferdinand Laufberger, and Julius Victor Berger; his brothers Ernst and Georg were also students there. To help his family make ends meet, the Klimt brothers produced watercolor portraits from photographs or did technical drawings.

Influenced by the Historicism of the time, Klimt enjoyed success early on in the "Maler Compagnie" (Painters' Company), which he founded in 1883, together with his brother Ernst and Franz Matsch. Their commissions included decorative schemes for the theaters at Reichenberg (Liberec), Karlsbad (Karlovy Vary), Fiume (Rijeka), and Bucharest, and even the ceiling paintings in the staircases at Vienna's Burgtheater, thus casting Gustav Klimt as the legitimate successor of the "painter prince" Hans Makart.

In 1890, Klimt was awarded the "Kaiserpreis" for his watercolor *Auditorium in the Old Burgtheater (Der Zuschauerraum des alten Burgtheaters)* (featuring 200 people from Vienna's high society, who had clamored to be portrayed in the picture); his friend Franz Matsch had depicted the opposite view toward the stage.

Klimt's brother Ernst died in 1892. He had been married to Helene Flöge and Gustav became the guardian of their daughter, also named Helene. Emilie Flöge, sister of Ernst's widow, would become his lifelong partner.

A change in Klimt's style, already hinted at in his paintings for the spandrels in the Kunsthistorisches Museum's stairway, clearly emerged in works like *Portrait of the Pianist Joseph Pembauer (Porträt des Pianisten Joseph Pembauer)* (1890) or *Pallas Athene* (1898). Klimt began turning his back on Historicism and developing his own style of painting in which he combined delicately modeled, sculptural passages with stylized planes. It was a style that would have a decisive impact on Viennese Jugendstil.

This new artistic approach was first presented to a wider public in his three ceiling paintings for the University of Vienna's Great Hall. In 1894, Klimt had been awarded a commission to represent the faculties of Philosophy, Medicine, and Jurisprudence on ceiling paintings. When *Philosophy (Philosophie)* was shown in 1900, it met with vehement opposition (although it was awarded a gold medal at the Paris World's Fair that same year), while the depictions of nudes in *Medicine (Medizin,* exhibited in 1901), and *Jurisprudence (Jurisprudenz,* 1903) even caused public scandals. Klimt confronted an art tradition that had always been somewhat reserved toward Symbolism with his own interpretation of the world. Instead of honoring the academic disciplines for their accomplishments and dependability, he placed an emphasis on the dark, unexplored sides of humanity, hidden dormant below the surface, on instinctual drives, and ultimately the forces of destiny that govern human existence. He thus raised issues that would be important to the younger generation.

GUSTAV KLIMT
Philosophy, 1900/07
Destroyed in a fire

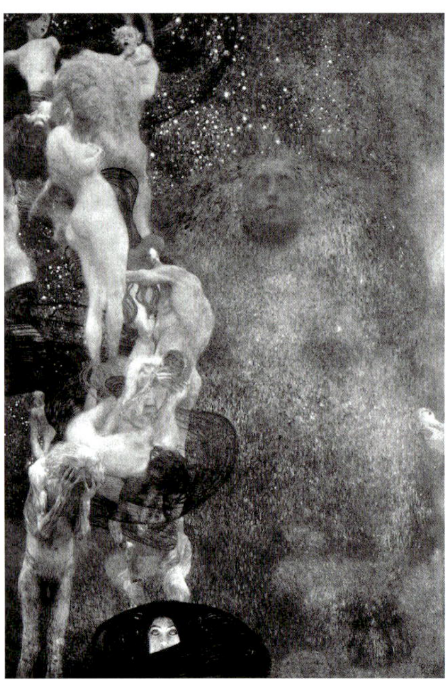

All of a sudden, Klimt had become the "villain of the piece," the target of all cultural reactionaries, so that his fight for freedom of artistic expression assumed a far deeper dimension. Klimt paid back his fee for the three pictures and, to prove his independence, completed them for himself.

By emphasizing the hidden inclinations and instincts that influence people, in the faculty paintings Klimt tried to draw awareness to the all-determining power of Eros, and to break down traditional patterns of thought. The artwork thus assumed the role of providing insight into the essence of things, and, ahead of all the science, all the tenacious, petty quest for detail, opening the beholder's eyes to something greater, more intangible, and more unpredictable.

In April 1897, Klimt and a group of colleagues, including Rudolf von Alt, Josef Hoffmann, and Carl Moll, left the Künstlerhaus—the "Genossenschaft bildender Künstler Wiens" (Vienna Artists' Cooperative)—where he had been a member since 1891. Following the example of Munich and Berlin the new association called themselves "Secession," and their aims were to reform the art and exhibition scene, bringing Austrian art up to the international standard. In 1898 the first issue of the Secession's magazine *Ver Sacrum* (Sacred Spring) was published; Klimt would contribute numerous illustrations to this publication up until 1903. Klimt, who was also the first president of the association, thus became a pivotal figure in Vienna's artistic renewal during these years.

For the fourteenth Secession exhibition in 1902, centered around the Beethoven sculpture by Max Klinger, Klimt created the twenty-four-meter-long *Beethoven Frieze.*

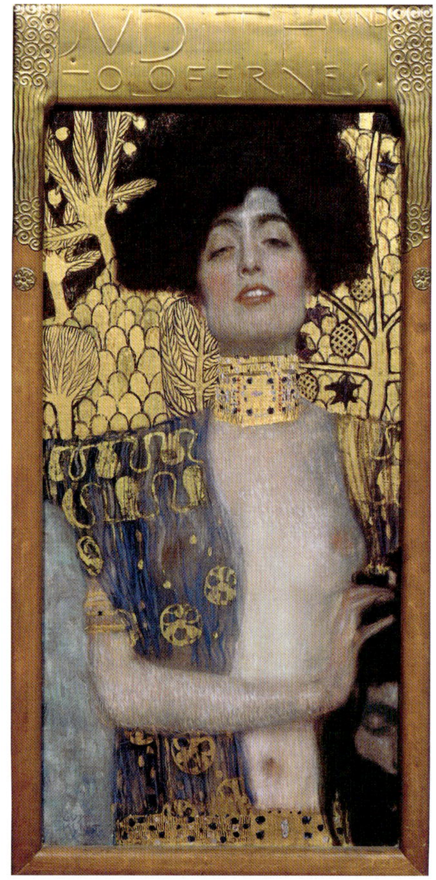

GUSTAV KLIMT
Judith, 1901
Belvedere, Vienna

Here the artist provided an escapist answer. In keeping with the Secession's ethos of alleviating the difficulties of modern existence by transforming life into art, in the *Beethoven Frieze* Klimt offered the viewer a Utopian haven of perfect happiness. In 1903, Hermann Bahr, a longtime friend and defender of Klimt, compiled all the debate and polemic unleashed in the press by the *Beethoven Frieze* in the book *Gegen Klimt* (Against Klimt).

Klimt and the other Secessionists pursued an ideal of art that sought to embrace all areas of life and to place its stamp on every manifestation of human existence. One of the fruits of this attitude was the foundation of the Wiener Werkstätte by Fritz Waerndorfer, Josef Hoffmann, and Kolo Moser in 1903. Each handcrafted object, created in close collaboration between producer and consumer, would contribute to realizing this all-encompassing idea of harmony.

In 1905, the "Klimt Gruppe" (Klimt Group) left the Secession. Besides Klimt himself, this group included the architects Josef Hoffman and Otto Wagner, the painter Carl Moll, and the applied artist Kolo Moser. In other words, these were the "Stylists" who were splitting from the "Naturalists" in the Secession. The main problem for the seceding group was now that they no longer had a venue for their exhibitions. In 1908, after finding an empty plot of land, later the site of the Konzerthaus, Josef Hoffmann created with lightning speed a venue for an exhibition of recent Austrian art: the "Kunstschau" (where Klimt's recently completed *Kiss [Kuss]* was acquired for the Moderne Galerie). As the site was still available, the "Internationale Kunstschau" was staged one year later, an exhibition showcasing paintings by foreign artists of the day.

erything—even postures, gestures, feelings—was stylized. These had to be aesthetic. While the art of the Wiener Werkstätte, with its emphasis on craftsmanship and rejection of mass production, was in reality an art for the elite, far removed from the average person, the quest for beauty became a type of substitute religion. By aspiring to merge art and life, life became both idealized and mythologized. The *Kiss* represented both the pinnacle of the quest for happiness within the world and an elusive ideal. Even the picture *The Three Ages of Woman (Die drei Lebensalter der Frau)* (1905) reveals the ugliness of age from an aesthetic point of view—the lucid, perfect, and still stylized painting casts a mantle of artistry across the distressing truths of reality.

For a young generation of artists this was tantamount to provocation. Whereas the artistic approach of Klimt and the Secessionists ultimately aimed to bring art and life

Yet, despite some conflicting views, Klimt was always a generous supporter of young artists. Whether Oskar Kokoschka or Egon Schiele, he always tried to facilitate their participation in exhibitions and to draw their works to the attention of a wider public.

Klimt had been deeply shaken by the opposition to the faculty paintings and the *Beethoven Frieze* and felt let down by politicians who suddenly distanced themselves. Added to this, in 1905 a professorship at Vienna's Akademie der bildenden Künste (Academy of Fine Arts) was turned down once and for all, after an academic chair had already been declined in 1901. The lack of understanding for his art, indeed the blatant polemic, plunged him, an artist so accustomed to success, into a veritable crisis. After always having seen himself as a public figure and reformer of art, all of a sudden he felt inclined to step down from the public stage.

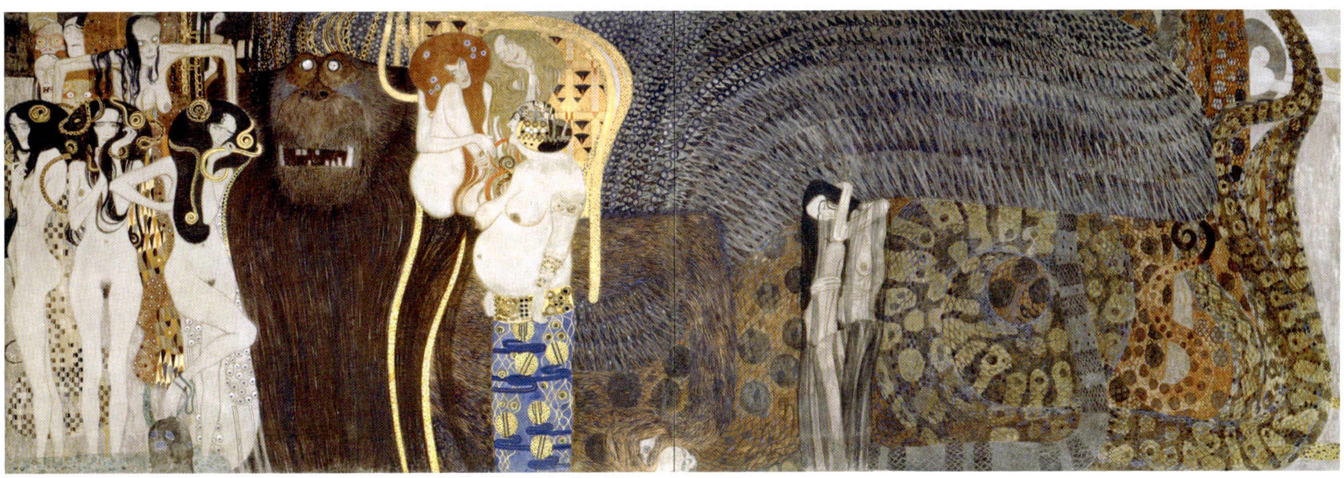

GUSTAV KLIMT
The Hostile Forces (detail from the *Beethoven Frieze*), 1902
Belvedere, Vienna

The "Kunstschau" in 1908 was again a presentation of the "Stylists" program and their aim to permeate every area of life with contemporary art and design of the highest quality. However, this stylization could also stifle the expressive power of Klimt's work, leaving him trapped in an art in which ev-

into harmony in a way that was both world-affirming and did not challenge the social system, the young Expressionists were diametrically opposed to this attitude. They regarded the world as threatening, hostile, false or superficial, and the lone artist as one of the few upholders of truth.

He struggled to reshuffle his role as a modern artist and wavered between rebellion and hurt withdrawal. The outcome was that although works like *Goldfish (Goldfische)* (1901/02), which he originally intended to name *To My Critics (An meine Kritiker)*, or *Jurisprudence* (1903/07) were still obvious attacks on his critics, he otherwise redefined his self-conception as an artist.

He withdrew completely from public roles and shifted the focus of his art to the private sphere: portraits from high society, predominantly of ladies (the majority from the wealthy Jewish bourgeoisie), a commission to decorate the dining room at Palais Stoclet in Brussels and, making up a considerable proportion of his art in the last fifteen years, landscapes.

In life Klimt had intimate relationships with some of his patrons (so apparently with Sonja Knips and Adele Bloch-Bauer) as well as with some of his models (Marie [Mizzi] Zimmermann, for instance, with whom he had a son Gustav [Ucicky]). In art he explored the fascination of woman but also the threat she posed using a stream of new metaphors. He devoted thousands of drawings to her beauty and enticing unfathomable depths, to her eternally elusive nature. In his female portraits he captured her in a precious, bejeweled world. "They have a great longing to rise above the everyday world [...] like princesses and madonnas [...] in a beauty that can never be ravaged and devastated by the greedy hands of life."[2] However, in addition to the general debate concerning the nature of woman and the relationship between the sexes, Klimt used these symbolic images to include and give valid form to his own experiences.

In a multitude of plays, Arthur Schnitzler captured the frivolity, hypocrisy, and unacknowledged lustful desires of Viennese society with fascinating, piercing clarity.[3] Klimt made this visible. He often depicted his women as if in a dream, be this a pleasurable daydream (in the erotic works like *Danae* [1907/08] or the drawings), or a dream of longing (*The Virgin [Die Jungfrau]*, 1912/13, *The Bride [Die Braut]*, 1917/18). These works come alive through the art of gesture, poses painstakingly prepared in hundreds of studies, in which the cast of his thoughts was paraded.

In a series of pictures, Klimt also addressed basic situations in human lives, ranging from birth (*Hope I [Hoffnung I]*, 1903/04, *Hope II [Hoffnung II]*, 1907/08), to childhood (*Baby*, 1917) and adolescence (*The Virgin [Die Jungfrau]*, 1913), maturity (*The Bride [Die Braut]*, 1917/18, *Adam and Eve [Adam und Eva]*, 1917/18) and motherhood (*Family [Mother and Children] [Familie (Mutter mit Kindern)]*, 1909/10), up to old age (*The Three Ages of Woman*, 1905) and death (*Death and Life [Tod und Leben]*, 1910/11, revised 1916).

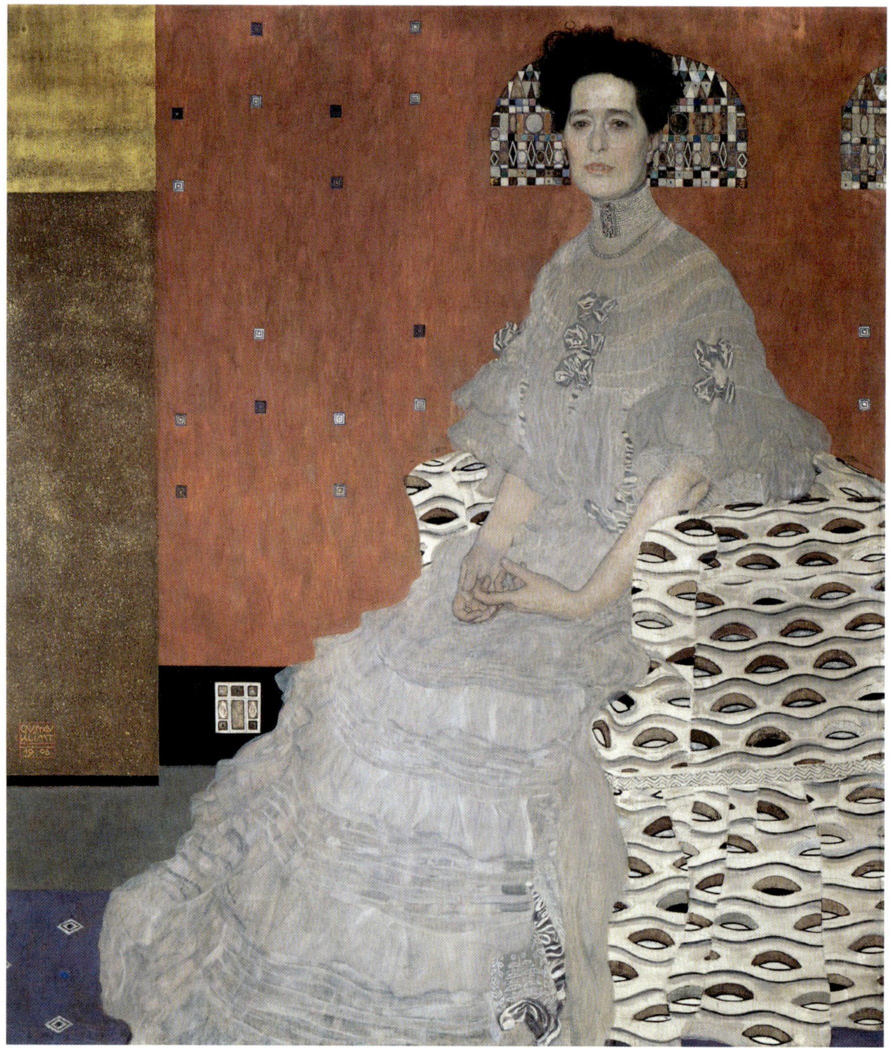

GUSTAV KLIMT
Fritza Riedler, 1906
Belvedere, Vienna

Klimt had responded to the criticism of his public work through withdrawal. It was this element of "aesthetic retreat"[4] that would make a fundamental contribution to shaping Klimt's new identity and style as an artist—a retreat from the public and from art connoisseurs, and also a retreat from his subject, as would emerge in his landscapes in particular. Engagement was replaced by contemplative observation, using nature's inspiration to create an exquisite work of art.

From 1900 through 1916, Klimt spent almost every summer with the Flöge family at Lake Attersee, with a trip to Lake Garda in 1913 being an exception. In summer 1917 the painter also took a cure at Bad Gastein. In the relaxed atmosphere of these sojourns, Klimt created his landscapes.

Klimt's explorations of French Impressionism and Post-Impressionism and its consequences were of decisive importance in his landscapes. Initially his choice of subject matter was guided by the Austrian tradition of *Stimmungsimpressionismus* (Atmospheric Impressionism) and included orchards, ponds, and forest interiors. Yet paintings like *A Morning by the Pond (Ein Morgen am Teiche)* (1899, fig. p. 67) or *Attersee I (Am Attersee)* (1900, fig. p. 68) clearly demonstrate that Klimt had examined Monet's art. This is reflected both in the composition, with the seemingly frameless cropped scene and the radical absence of foreground, as well as in the brushstrokes representing the ruffled water. In later years, Klimt continued to draw inspiration from Monet, as displayed in his paintings of Schloss Kammer, the villages on the opposite shores of Lake Attersee and Lake Garda, and his depictions of ponds.

Klimt was also influenced by the paintings of van Gogh, Pointillism (that Klimt freely interpreted as a "painted mosaic," covering the canvas like a densely woven tapestry of shapes), the Nabis (whose vibrant, two-dimensional patterned surfaces mirrored Klimt's efforts toward a planar, ornamental composition), and later the Fauves. In his paintings, Klimt's colors constantly grew in brightness and luminosity, his brushwork became looser, freer, and softer in its transitions.

There had been ample opportunity for Klimt to explore French art, both contemporary and from the previous generation; the Künstlerhaus and the Galerie Miethke had provided plenty of possibilities. In addition, Klimt was partially responsible for the subjects and objects at the Secession's exhibitions. The Secession's sixteenth exhibition entitled "The Development of Impressionism in Painting and Sculpture," for instance, featured six works by Monet as well as paintings by Bonnard, Corot, Degas, Delacroix, Denis, Gauguin, van Gogh, Manet, Pissarro, Seurat, Sisley, and Toulouse-Lautrec. Later, the "Internationale Kunstschau" in 1909, showcased works by Bonnard, Denis, Gauguin, van Gogh, Matisse, Vlaminck, and Vuillard, among others. In addition, there were the reports about contemporary art in international newspapers and art magazines of the day. Published with growing regularity and increasingly well illustrated, these were avidly read in Secessionist circles.

Many of Klimt's landscapes are characterized by a framework of orthogonal lines or planes, lending the scenes an air of great tranquility. This impression of a stringently ordered composition was enhanced in no small measure by the square format Klimt used for all his landscapes from 1899.[5] Through its equal sides and its lack of direction, the square conveys a sense of both equilibrium and stability, channels attention to the order within the picture, heightens the exquisite effect of the colors.

Klimt outlined his pictures in front of the subject, painting directly onto the canvas without preliminary drawings, and defining the colors of the various objects using a few further brushstrokes. This was enough for him to then complete a work back in his studio in Vienna. In his sketchbook he always carried a square "viewfinder," which he would use to select his subject and identify a possible composition. He also frequently used a telescope with a ten-fold magnification, as a way of compacting his depiction of the scene, transforming it into a spectacle of colored planes. This device compressed the layers of space and Klimt used it to observe distant subjects, usually on the opposite shore of the lake. Klimt worked slowly and was always modifying his pictures at his Vienna studio. He had to part fairly quickly with many of his landscapes, however, as these would be virtually snatched out of his hands.

Klimt's fame steadily grew; his works were shown at international exhibitions in Bohemia, Germany, Italy, Sweden, and Switzer-

GUSTAV KLIMT
The Church in Unterach at the Attersee, 1915/16
Private collection

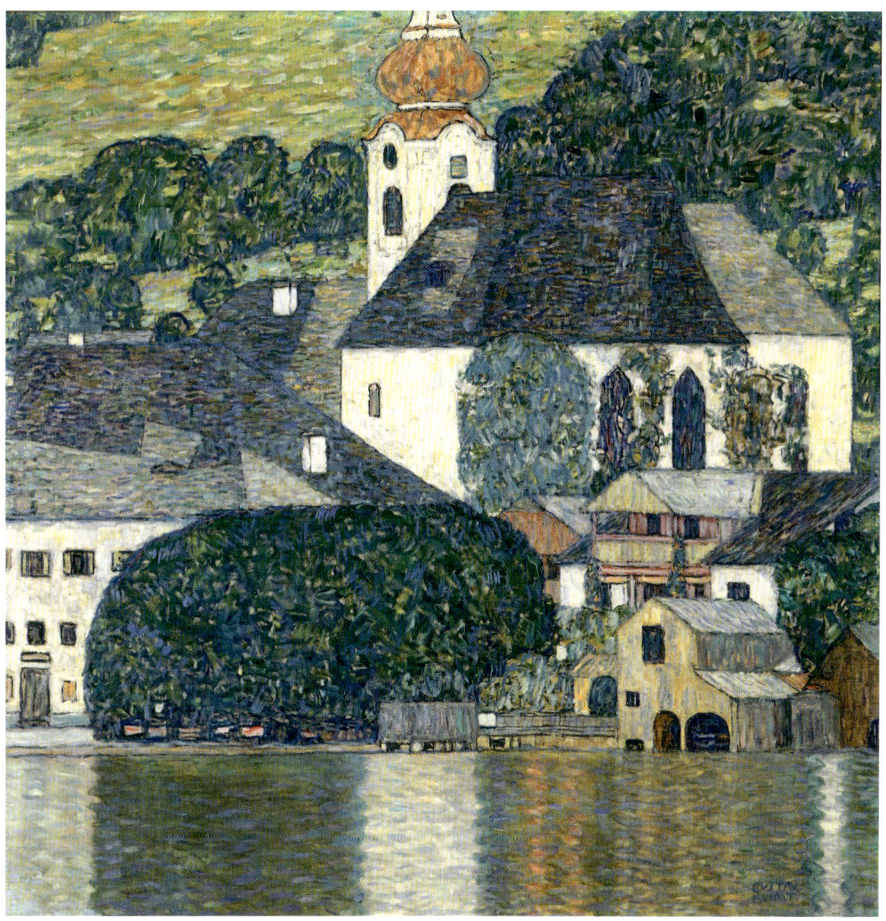

land. In 1906 he was elected an honorary member of Munich's Königlich Bayerische Akademie der bildenden Künste (Royal Bavarian Academy of Fine Arts). For Vienna's Moderne Galerie, the Austrian state bought *Attersee I* (1900) in 1905, his masterpiece *The Kiss (Lovers) (Der Kuss [Liebespaar])* in 1908 and, on Klimt's fiftieth birthday in 1912, *Upper Austrian Farmhouse (Oberösterreichisches Bauernhaus)*. In 1911 Klimt won first prize for his painting *Death and Life* at the "International Art Exhibition" in Rome; in 1916 he became a member of Dresden's Sächsische Akademie der bildenden Künste (Saxon Academy of Fine Arts). His work was acquired by museums in Venice, Rome, Dresden, and Prague even during his lifetime.

After suffering a stroke in January, on February 6, 1918, the painter died at Vienna's general hospital. Egon Schiele, who held Klimt in great esteem and also drew him on his deathbed, tried to preserve his studio for posterity, but his efforts were in vain.

1 "I have the gift of neither the spoken nor the written word, especially if I have to say something about myself or my work. Even when I have a simple letter to write, I am filled with fear and trembling as though on the verge of being sea-sick. For this reason people must do without an artistic or literary self-portrait. And this should not be regretted. Whoever wants to know something about me—as an artist, the only notable thing—ought to look carefully at my pictures and try to see in them what I am and what I want to do." Gustav Klimt manuscript in the Wienbibliothek im Rathaus, quoted in Otto Breicha (ed.), *Gustav Klimt. Die Goldene Pforte. Bilder und Schriften zu Leben und Werk*, Salzburg 1978, p. 33. English translation quoted in Frank Whitford, *Klimt*, London 1990, p. 18.

2 Josef A. Lux, in: *Deutsche Kunst und Dekoration*, vol. XXIII, 1908/09, p. 46.

3 After visiting Klimt at his studio in 1915, Schnitzler stated that he felt a deep sense of kindredship with the artist. Arthur Schnitzler, *Tagebuch 1913–16*, Vienna 1983, p. 198.

4 Carl E. Schorske, *Fin-de-Siècle Vienna. Politics and Culture*, New York 1980, p. 273.

5 Concerning the significance of the square in the art of the Secessionists cf. Marian Bisanz-Prakken, "Das Quadrat in der Flächenkunst der Wiener Secession," in: *Alte und moderne Kunst* 27, no. 180/181, 1982, pp. 40–46.

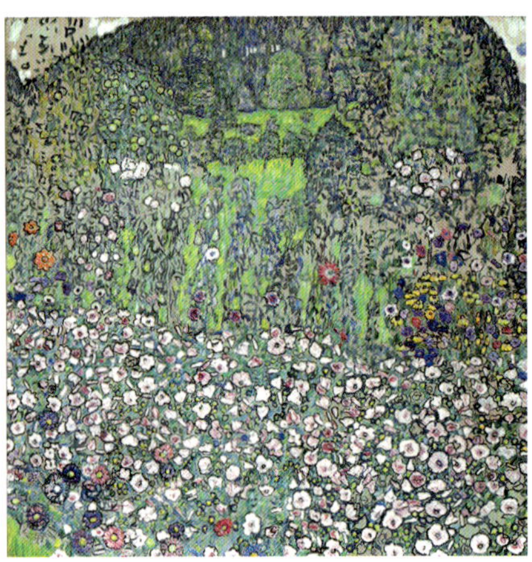

GUSTAV KLIMT
Flower Field with Schoberstein, 1916
Kunsthaus Zug, Stiftung Sammlung Kamm

OSKAR KOKOSCHKA
(1886 Pöchlarn, Lower Austria – 1980 Montreux)

"The 'Oberwildling' [chief savage] is called Kokoschka ..."[1]

Beatrice von Bormann

Oskar Kokoschka lived for ninety-four years and worked as an artist for seventy of them. He lived in Vienna, Berlin, Dresden, Paris, Prague, London, and Villeneuve, and traveled throughout Europe, North Africa, and parts of North America. His life covers practically the whole of the twentieth century, from the Vienna of Klimt and Freud, through two world wars, to post-war England and Switzerland, from the Jugendstil era to the era of abstraction and Neo-Expressionism. Kokoschka's art—oil paintings, posters, postcard designs, drawings, lithographs, sculptures, talks, and essays, not to mention seven theater plays, which, like the early paintings, are among the major examples of Austrian Expressionism—bear witness to these turbulent times.

A few months after Kokoschka's birth, his parents—his father came from a respected family of goldsmiths in Prague—moved from Pöchlarn to Vienna, where a younger sister and brother were born. After graduating from high school, at the instigation of his art teacher Johann Schober he applied for admission to the Kunstgewerbeschule (Academy of Applied Art) and was one of three out of 153 candidates to be accepted.

He began initially to study to be an art teacher, switching to fine art after a year. He was a student of Carl Otto Czeschka, who encouraged him, and in 1907 and 1908 obtained commissions for him from the Wiener Werkstätte to design postcards, book covers, illustrated broadsheets, and fans. His first plays were performed at Cabaret Fledermaus, which had been founded by the Werkstätte, and one of his major works of this time, the illustrated book of poetry *The Dreaming Youths*

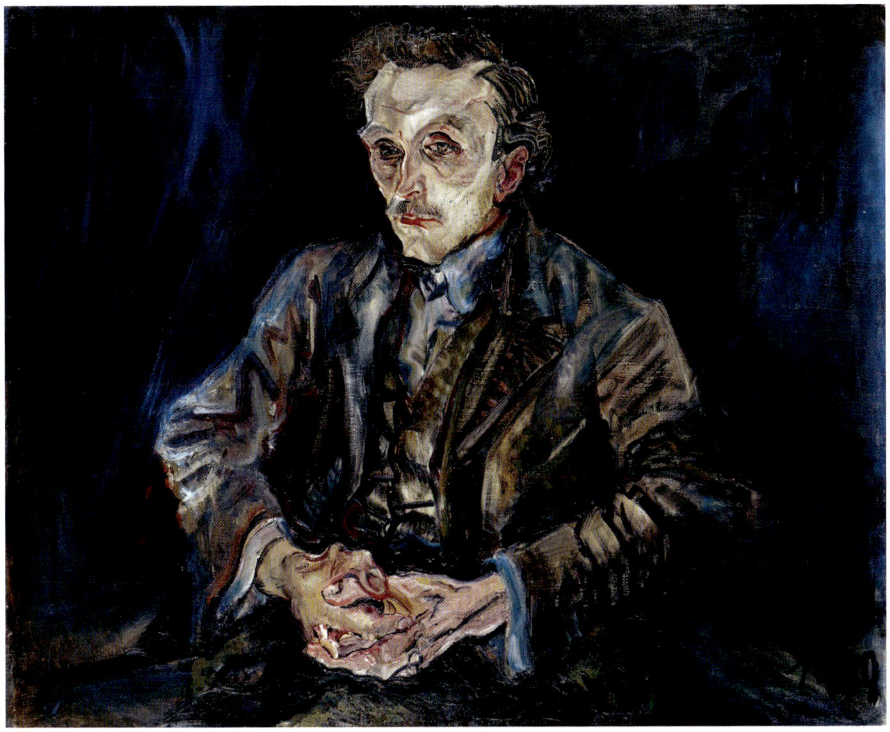

OSKAR KOKOSCHKA
Adolf Loos, 1909
Staatliche Museen Preußischer Kulturbesitz, Neue Nationalgalerie, Berlin

(*Die träumenden Knaben*) (1908), inspired by a youthful flame Lilith Lang, was commissioned and published by it.

At Gustav Klimt's suggestion, Kokoschka was given the opportunity in 1908 for the first time to exhibit works at the Kunstschau, the most important exhibition of contemporary art in Austria at the time. His tapestry designs *The Bearers of Dreams* (*Die Traumtragenden*), which subsequently disappeared, caused a stir. The Viennese critics were disdainful; Ludwig Hevesi, for example, wrote of a "wildes Kabinett" (wild room) and described Kokoschka as the "Oberwildling" (chief savage).[2] There were also, however, authors who recognized the young artist's talent, "I shall have to note the name Kokoschka," wrote one.[3] Kokoschka's nude drawings, which were also on display, sold out on the first day. The artist took part in the International Art Exhibition staged the following year, where his plays *Murderer, the Hope of Women* (*Mörder, Hoffnung der Frauen*) and *Sphinx and Strawman* (*Sphinx und Strohmann*) were performed for the first time. The architect Adolf Loos was in the audience and, recognizing the young artist's talent, encouraged him to leave the Wiener Werkstätte. "I couldn't understand how Loos saw my pictures as works of art and was flattered by it."[4] Loos persuaded many of his friends to pose for Kokoschka, and some seventy portraits were painted in this way between 1909 and 1914. Through Loos, Kokoschka met authors like Karl Kraus and Peter Altenberg, and musicians like Arnold Schönberg and Anton von Webern. In his portraits he experimented with expression, incorporated ideas from contemporaries, but concentrated in the main axis on the facial and hand expression, attempting to capture "the aura of the person in space."[5]

These early portraits are notable for their strong psychological interpretation of the subjects. In his "painting of the soul," Kokoschka attempted to record psychological tensions using a combination of glazed and impasto paint application and the drawing-like scratching of the paint surface, often with his fingernails or the brush stick. Asked why he didn't "use a brush like other people," he answered, "Look, the path from the brain through the arm and then through the brush is much too long. I would paint with my nose if I could."[6]

In early 1910, Kokoschka designed a legendary poster for the magazine *Der Sturm*, a "manifesto for modern art," which had been founded that year by Herwarth Walden. To justify his reputation as an *enfant terrible*, Kokoschka shaved his head and portrayed himself on the poster as a bald modern martyr pointing with his finger to an open wound on his chest. This gesture was meant to be understood as a "criticism of the Viennese."[7] A short while afterwards, Kokoschka moved to Berlin, where he collaborated with Walden on the publication of the magazine. He remained there for nine months but continued thereafter to travel regularly from Vienna to Berlin, contributing numerous drawings to *Der Sturm* until 1916. Galerie Cassirer in Berlin exhibited works by Kokoschka for the first time in 1910; the art collector Karl Ernst Osthaus visited the exhibition and arranged for Kokoschka to have his first solo exhibition at Museum Folkwang in Hagen that August. In 1912, Walden opened his Sturm gallery with an exhibition by Kokoschka and the artists of the Blauer Reiter school. A year earlier, in February 1911, twenty-five paintings by Kokoschka had been shown at the Hagenbund exhibition in Vienna. The reviews were so scathing that Kokoschka decided not to show his works again in Vienna for the time being. At this time, however, he also found collectors like the Viennese doctor Oskar Reichel, and Franz Hauer, owner of the Griechenbeisl restaurant in Vienna and collector of contemporary Austrian art. Until 1914, Loos possessed the largest collection of Kokoschka's pictures, since he purchased the portraits if their subjects didn't like them—which was often the case.

Through Carl Moll, one of the artists who had left the Secession in 1905 and was then director of the progressive Galerie Miethke, in April 1912 Kokoschka met Alma Mahler, widow of the composer Gustav Mahler and Moll's stepdaughter. A passionate three-year affair ensued. It ended because of Kokoschka's jealousy and Alma's reluctance to commit

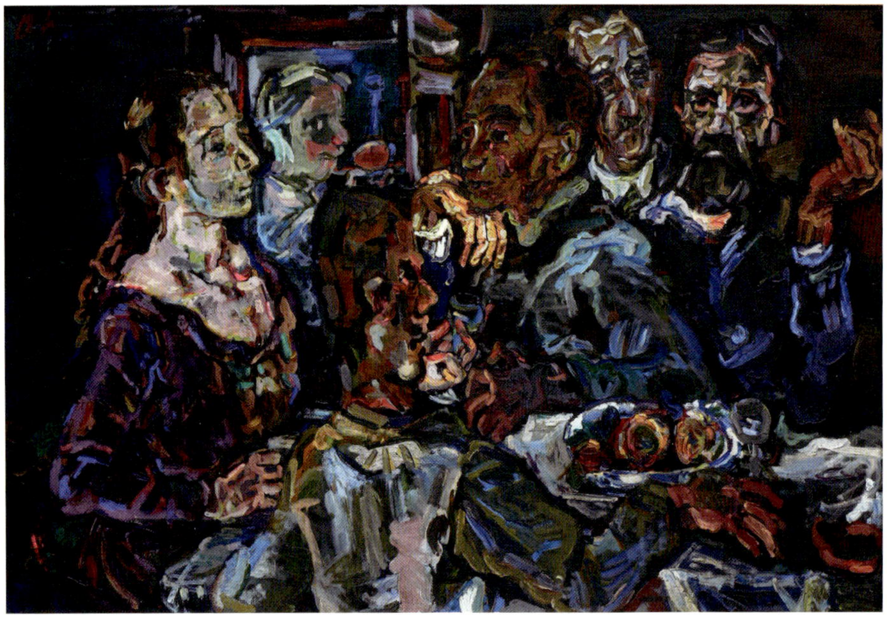

OSKAR KOKOSCHKA
The Friends, 1917
Lentos Kunstmuseum Linz

herself to the younger and still unknown painter. Some four hundred love letters to Alma have survived, as well as numerous drawings and graphics, seven fans painted for Alma, and three double portraits, including *The Bride of the Wind* (*Die Windsbraut*), inspired by a storm in Naples during a trip there by the couple. In 1913, Alma aborted their child, which Kokoschka had great difficulty coming to terms with. At the end of 1914, Kokoschka enlisted voluntarily into the army and thanks to Adolf Loos's intervention was conscripted to the Dragoons, the élite cavalry regiment.

Kokoschka was badly wounded several times during the war, convalescing in Vienna, and later in Berlin and Dresden. He was declared unfit for service and began again to work on his art. At this time he learned that Alma Mahler had married the architect Walter Gropius in 1915. He sought closure for the failed love affair in the drama *Orpheus and Eurydice* (*Orpheus und Eurydike*) (1918), and then in 1918 by commissioning the Munich doll maker Hermine Moos to make a life-size fetish doll based on his former lover. He was greatly disappointed by the result but used the doll as a model before destroying it, probably in a drunken fit.

In 1916, Kokoschka concluded a very favorable contract with the Berlin gallery owner Paul Cassirer, which remained in force until 1931 and for the first time freed the artist of financial concerns. At the same time he sought a post at the Akademie in Dresden. He was treated in Dresden from 1916 to 1918 at Dr. Heinrich Teuscher's sanatorium in the Weißer Hirsch district of the city. Through Dr Fritz Neuberger he was able to make many new friends, including actors and writers. The painting *The Friends* (*Die Freunde*), completed in 1917–18, shows this illustrious group, in which Kokoschka embodies the lost son, a lonely figure among strangers, homeless and uprooted.[8]

While the Austro-Hungarian Monarchy disintegrated, Kokoschka finally achieved recognition as an artist. His plays were performed at this time at Cabaret Voltaire, a Dada stronghold in Zurich, in Dresden under Kokoschka's own direction, in Berlin under the direction of Max Reinhardt, and in Frankfurt with Heinrich Georges as director. In 1917, Paul Westheim's monograph was published, and a year later Galerie Cassirer presented Kokoschka's works in a solo exhibition. Dresden's flourishing cultural life and the new, happier phase in the artist's life brought fresh inspiration. In Dresden he completed the transformation from an Expressionist portrait painter to a landscape artist. The views of Dresden

OSKAR KOKOSCHKA
Dresden, Augustus Bridge with Figure from the Back (*Dresden, Augustusbrücke mit Rückenfigur*), 1923
Museum Folkwang, Essen

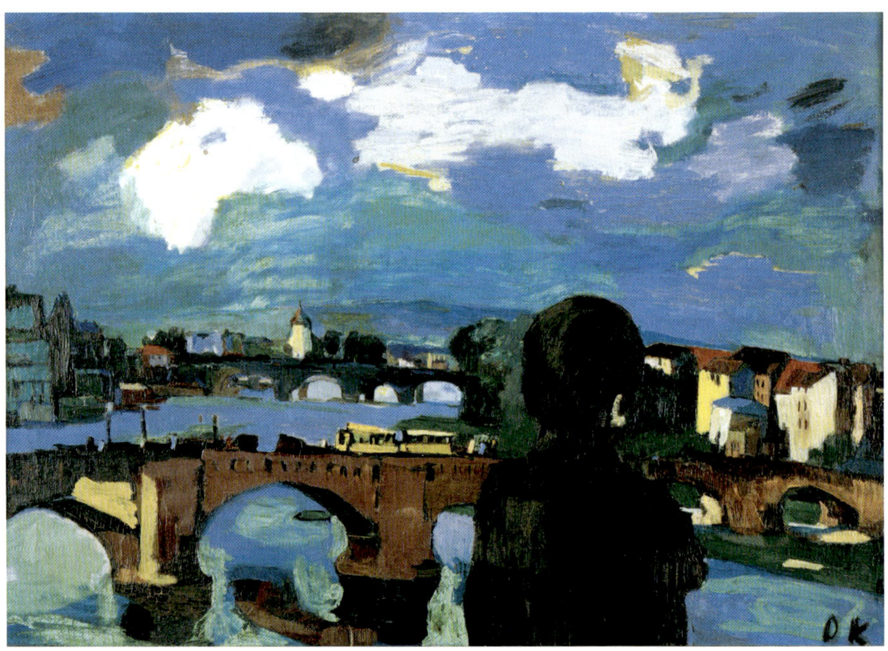

(see figs. pp. 88–90) mark the start of his impressive landscape series, which combine tradition and twentieth-century painting in singular fashion. Kokoschka brought Bernardo Bellotto's eighteenth-century views of Dresden into the twentieth century, employing expressive colors and impulsive brush strokes to produce panorama-like views of the Elbe, showing a particular interest in the "rhythmic tension of the bridge arches over the expansive and agitated surface of the water."[9] Kokoschka left Dresden in September 1923 after being given two years' leave of absence from the Akademie. He was not to return.

Kokoschka spent the years 1923 to 1930 traveling extensively through Europe and North Africa. Galerie Cassirer paid for the travel in return for exclusive rights to the works completed on the way. It proved worthwhile: the landscape views of the cities fetched high prices. In 1927, Kunsthaus Zürich organized a solo exhibition of Kokoschka's works. In 1930, the artist rented a studio in Paris, where he met the writer James Joyce and the photographer Brassaï. In November of that year for the first time works by Kokoschka, in Schlossmuseum Weimar, were confiscated by the Nazis. Paul Schultze-Naumburg compared Kokoschka's works in *Kunst und Rasse* with those of a mentally deranged person. A year later, Kunsthalle Mannheim put on a major retrospective. Kokoschka canceled his agreement with Galerie Cassirer, which wanted to reduce his fee because of the economic crisis. The painter endeavored in vain to reclaim his position at the Akademie in Dresden. Adolf Hitler was appointed Reich Chancellor on January 30, 1933, and Adolf Loos died the same year. Kokoschka returned temporarily to Vienna. With the death of his mother in 1934 and the increasing political tensions, however, he decided to leave Austria. He went first to Prague with the intention of continuing via Moscow to Shanghai. In Prague, however, he met his future wife Olda Palkovská (1915–2004) and completed a portrait of President Tomáš Masaryk, who awarded him Czech nationality. Kokoschka painted sixteen large cityscapes during this time. Apart from London, no other city was so often a subject of his paintings. In *Prague Harbor* (*Der Prager Hafen*), he looks down on the bridge over the Vltava in a manner reminiscent of his harbor paintings of Monte Carlo, Marseilles (both 1925), Hamburg, and London (both 1926). The dynamic brushwork evokes a powerful, swirling, turbulent atmosphere. According to Kokoschka himself, he chose to paint cityscapes from a high vantage point because of his traumatic experiences during World War I and his desire to compensate for the confined space in the trenches by portraying the vast expanse of the landscape.

In response to the bombing of Guernica in April 1937, Kokoschka designed a poster with an appeal to support Basque children. More than four hundred of his paintings had been confiscated at that time in Germany; sixteen or seventeen were shown at the 1937 exhibition "Degenerate Art" in Munich. Kokoschka reacted by painting *Self-Portrait as a Degenerate Artist* (*Selbstbildnis als entarteter Künstler*) (1937) and writing a critical essay entitled "Entartete Kunst" (Degenerate Art). At Olda's insistence they both fled to London on October 18, 1938, shortly after the annexation by Germany of the Sudetenland.

Great Britain declared war on Germany on September 3, 1939. Some 125 works by Kokoschka confiscated from German museums were sold by the notorious Auktionshaus Fischer in Lucerne. From 1939 to 1940, Oskar and Olda lived in Polperro, Cornwall. It was here that Kokoschka painted his first political allegories by way of criticism of the British attitude of appeasement. He fought for the release of refugees from British internment camps and joined the Freier Künstlerbund (Free Association of Artists) in Paris and the Free German League of Culture in London. In 1940, Otto Kallir, former director of the Neue Galerie in Vienna, organized a successful Kokoschka exhibition in his Galerie St. Etienne in New York, founded in 1939; other exhibitions in the United States were to follow. Kokoschka and Olda Palkovská married on May 15, 1941, in an air raid shelter in London.

Germany surrendered on May 7, 1945. That

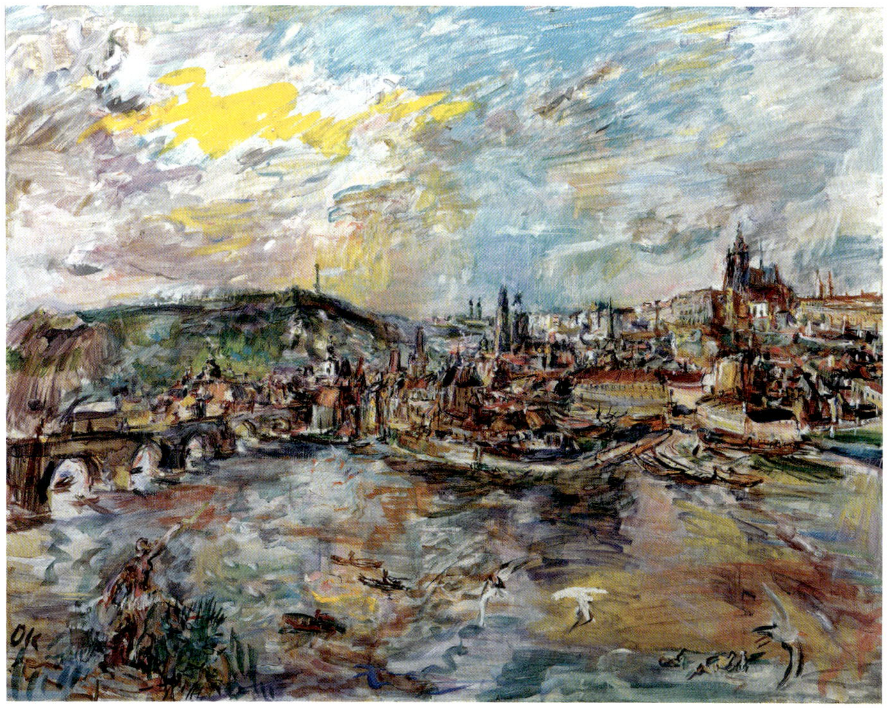

OSKAR KOKOSCHKA
Prague Harbor, 1936
Belvedere, Vienna

winter, Kokoschka's poster *Christ Helping the Starving Children* (*Christus hilft den hungernden Kindern*) appealing for hunger aid for European children was displayed in the London Underground.

In 1946, Kokoschka received congratulations and honors from Austria to mark his sixtieth birthday, but attempts by his homeland to welcome back the artist, who was now famous and successful, fell on deaf ears. He and Olda obtained British citizenship a year later. Edith Hoffmann's monograph of Kokoschka appeared in 1947, followed by major exhibitions in Europe and the USA. Kokoschka painted a portrait of the Austrian President Theodor Körner in 1949 and the German President Theodor Heuss a year later. George Grosz said mockingly of these official portraits in 1954, "Oschka Kokoschka has become the semi-official painter of the Federal Republic. He was represented in Haus der Kunst with several oil paintings; he also painted President Heuss. In terms of style he is the complete 'Impressionist.'"[10] Kokoschka had the ambition to paint the great personalities of the time and for that reason sought to make contact with Churchill, Gandhi, and the Pope. In 1966, he was commissioned to paint the portrait of the former Federal Chancellor Konrad Adenauer; as often before, he gave the fee to charity.

In November 1951, Kokoschka acquired a piece of land in Villeneuve on Lake Geneva and built a house, Villa Delphin, there; in 1953, he and Olda moved definitively to Switzerland. In the summer of that year the International Summer Academy was held for the first time in Salzburg, where Kokoschka was to give an annual course entitled "Schule des Sehens" (School of Seeing). In 1958, the Künstlerhaus in Vienna mounted an exhibition containing 682 works by Kokoschka, the largest show to date, and four years later the Tate Gallery organized a Kokoschka retrospective. The artist continued to travel extensively and wrote his autobiography *Mein Leben* (*My Life*) (1971).

Kokoschka's later works are notable for their mythological themes. His enthusiasm for Greece dated back to his early childhood, when his father had given him an illustrated book of Greek mythology, and was subsequently nourished by countless trips to the centers of antiquity, from which he brought back twenty-three sketchbooks of antique monuments, a collection of antique coins and small archeological finds, and an extensive library on classical antiquity. In 1972, his last self-portrait, *Time, Gentlemen Please* (as the last round in British pubs is announced before closing time) also marked the end of Kokoschka's artistic career. It is painted in a free, expressive style, seeming to anticipate the painting of the "Neue Wilden" of the 1980s. Kokoschka hardly produced any paintings in the following years, although he completed many drawings and graphic works. After the Belvedere had paid tribute to Kokoschka in 1971 with a major retrospective to mark his eighty-fifth birthday, the painter reclaimed his Austrian nationality in 1975 at the request of the Austrian Federal Chancellor Bruno Kreisky. Kokoschka died on February 22, 1980, in a hospital in Montreux following a stroke; his widow Olda survived him by twenty-four years.

OSKAR KOKOSCHKA
Herodotus (*Herodot*), 1963
Belvedere, Vienna

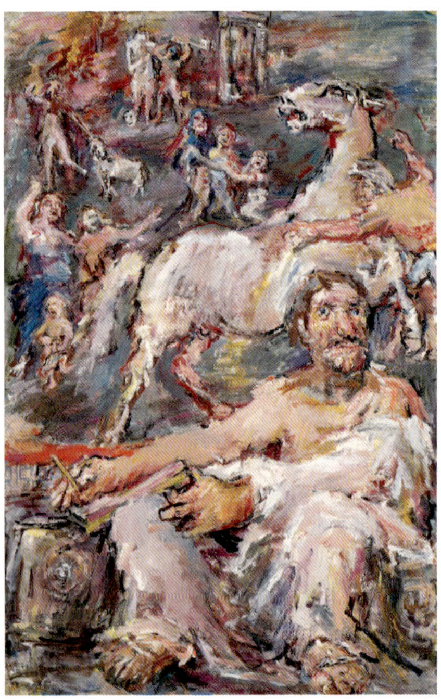

1 Ludwig Hevesi, "Kunstschau 1908, 31. Mai 1908," in: ibid., *Altkunst – Neukunst. Wien 1894–1908*, Vienna 1909, p. 313.
2 Ibid.
3 Richard Muther, "Die Kunstschau," in: *Die Zeit. Morgenblatt*, no. 2049, June 6, 1908, p. 1.
4 Oskar Kokoschka, *Mein Leben*, Munich 1971, p. 75.
5 *Kokoschka – Ein Selbstporträt*, director: Hannes Reinhardt, NDR 1966, 53 min.
6 Quoted from Jens H. Friedrich, *Ein Vagabundenleben. Erinnerungen von Jens H. Friedrich*, unpublished typescript, New York 1994, p. 122.
7 Kokoschka 1971 (see note 4), pp. 114–115.
8 Johann Winkler/Katharina Erling, *Oskar Kokoschka. Die Gemälde 1906–1929*, Salzburg 1995, p. 78.
9 Ludwig Goldscheider, *Kokoschka*, Cologne 1963, p. 76, no. 22.
10 Letter from George Grosz to Herbert Fiedler, August 8, 1954, quoted from Herbert Knust (ed.), *George Grosz. Briefe 1913–1959*, Reinbek bei Hamburg 1979, p. 483.

JOHANN VICTOR KRÄMER
(1861 Adamsthal, Moravia – 1949 Vienna)

"Krämer is an artist who seeks light, and he is most certain of finding it at the source—in the Orient."[1]

Kathrin Wolf

Johann Victor Krämer was one of the most traveled artists of his day. His study tours led him through Europe, North Africa, and the Middle East, and he drew on this inexhaustible trove of impressions in his paintings for the rest of his life.

Krämer's father worked as an engineer at the factory of Prince Johann II von Liechtenstein in Adamsthal near Brno, and it was the prince who gave the aspiring young artist a scholarship so he could study at the Kunstgewerbeschule (School of Applied Arts) in Vienna. Between 1878 and 1881, he was in the class of Ferdinand Laufberger, where his classmates included Franz Matsch and the brothers Gustav and Ernst Klimt. From 1881 to 1888, Krämer studied at the Vienna Akademie der bildenden Künste (Academy of Fine Arts), first in the General School of Painting with Christian Griepenkerl, Carl Wurzinger, and August Eisenmenger and, from 1883, with the famous Orientalist painter Leopold Carl Müller at the Special School for History Painting. Even as a student he was showered with important awards: the Gundel Prize (1883), the Special School Prize (1884), the Reichel Prize (1888[2]) for his painting *Deposition from the Cross (Kreuzabnahme)*[3] at the Künstlerhaus jubilee exhibition, and finally, in 1888, the sought-after Austrian state's Rome Prize for his painting *Judgment of Paris* (*Urteil des Paris*).

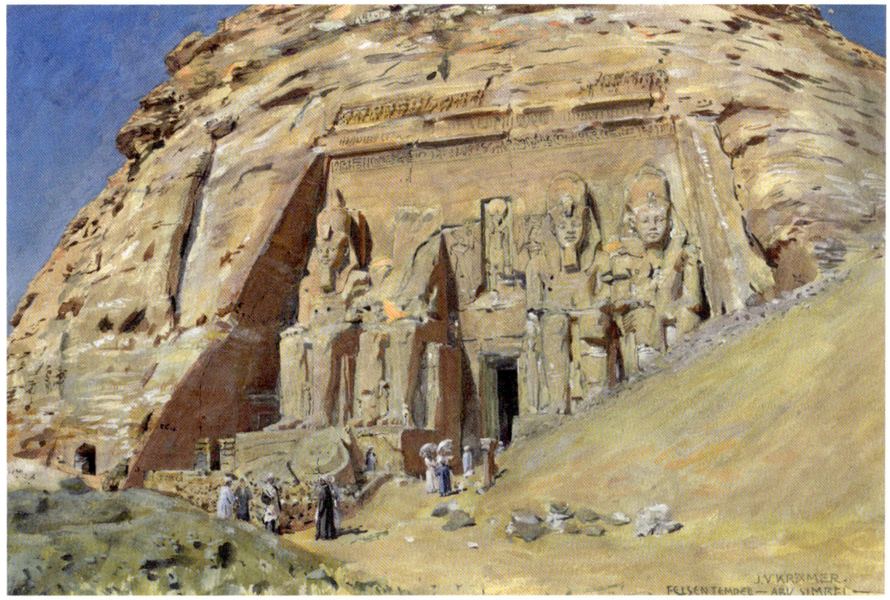

JOHANN VICTOR KRÄMER
Abu Simbel Rock Temple
(Felsentempel von Abu Simbel), 1899
Wien Museum

FIRST STOP: PARIS

The travel bursary that came with the prize led Krämer to the metropolis on the Seine in late 1888, where he would stay for quite some time.[4] "Paris doesn't seem so foreign to me. It is as if I have been here before,"[5] is how he described his first impressions of the city. Initially he lived in a hotel in the ninth arrondissement and mentioned that he would soon take an apartment in a hotel by the Jardin du Luxembourg and later rent a studio. He intended to improve his French by engaging a teacher upon arrival. The letter concludes by announcing that he would now go to the Palais du Luxembourg and visit the gallery of living artists. His initial enthusiasm soon vanished, however. In his next letter to his parents, Krämer complained about the incredibly cold weather, the fact that there was not much to see, and that the low temperatures even prevented him from taking a walk. "The lifestyle is different here, too—without work or studying you couldn't bear it. The whole of Paris gives the impression of the Hof or the Freiung in Vienna during the Christmas market season—the bustle and spectacle go on well into the night [...] I get nothing from this kind of life. I'm looking forward to moving on, but I have to stay here until spring or summer. The pictures and things don't impress me much, but you have to go along with it all."[6] At the end of February he first mentions his own painting, "I would once like to see what I can achieve in representing nature. I've felt the compulsion to try this out for a long time. Speaking for myself, I want to see if I can't match up to the best. You can know this, but others would think me arrogant. There's nothing to delay me; I've also abandoned all unnecessary visits—for example to Herr Sedelmeier and the sculptor Beer [...]"[7] Unfortunately Krämer does not go into any detail about his studies of nature. Apart from a self-portrait with a cigarette and a portrait of a colleague, his letters make no further mention of any works from Paris. By February he had already decided to wait out the start of the Salon and then leave for London in May or June. He had not been particularly keen on going to Paris, but he had to see it.[8] And yet he regretted not having exhibited there, musing, "I could have had success."[9] In the middle of May, after waiting for the beginning of the World's Fair, he traveled to London. He described the city as being much lovelier than Paris and, with its wealth of collections, more interesting.[10] His art dealer Thomas Wallis,[11] manager of the French Gallery to whom he had been introduced in Vienna by Leopold Carl Müller, helped him to find an apartment. Yet Krämer only stayed in the British capital for a month, for on June 19, 1889, he wrote to his parents from Paris once again.[12]

SPAIN AND NORTH AFRICA

In October 1889, Krämer journeyed from Paris, via Biarritz, to Madrid, where he met the art critic Hermann Bahr and traveled with him to southern Spain. On January 1, 1890, they crossed to Tangier and were joined by Hungarian Orientalist painter Gyula Tornai. Krämer and Tornai went on painting excursions in the surrounding area of Tangier, where they worked on the same motifs.[13] Krämer's studio painting *Motif from Tangier (Motiv aus Tanger)* can be traced back to studies from this time.[14] This painting captures rotting animal carcasses in a barren and bleak desert with blatant realism, detailed brushwork, and a pared-down palette. The bold contrast between the yellowish-brown sand and the pale blue sky and jet black shadows, convincingly conveys the sense of oppressive heat and dazzling sunlight. In March 1890, the painters returned to Spain and Krämer stayed on in Granada for almost seven weeks. Here, like many Orientalist painters before him, it was the Alhambra that fascinated him most.[15] To translate into painting this masterpiece of Moorish architecture, with its awe-inspiring stalactite vaulting and intricate, all-encompassing decoration, Krämer used watercolor with delicate glazes, but did not lose himself in detail. Brushwork, very sketchy in places, captures the shimmering impression of the architecture.

His journey continued via Málaga to Algiers and Tunis, where Krämer visited the ruins of Carthage, on to Naples, and then finally to his actual destination: Rome. He stayed there until fall and painted Madonnas as well as a large-scale mythological painting.[16]

SETTLING IN VIENNA

In early 1891, Krämer took over the studio of Orientalist painter Hans Ludwig Fischer in Vienna, where he would stay until he died. Over the next seven years he worked for Karl Wittgenstein as an art tutor for his children, as well as completing a commission at his ironworks in Bohemia in 1892/93. In 1893 Krämer became a member of the Künstlerhaus. In 1894 he spent half a year in Sicily with Josef Engelhart and Theodor von Hörmann, and traveled there again in 1897, returning with a wealth of resources for his art. The loosely painted, vibrant scene *Taormina in the Sunshine (Taormina im Sonnenschein;* fig. p. 112*)* is based on sketches and drawings from this trip. On the one hand, the path motif and the dappled brushstrokes recall Monet—Krämer could have seen his views of Vétheuil in Paris. However, the square format and decorative effect have echoes of Secessionist works, particularly of Klimt.[17] Krämer was a founding member of the Secession,[18] which presented a solo show[19] of his work at its eleventh exhibition in 1901.[20] It was here that he showed his art from his great Oriental journey through Palestine and Egypt from 1898 to 1900.[21] Krämer had traveled up the Nile to Abu Simbel, capturing his impressions not only in pencil or paint but also with a small Kodak camera.[22] He often used these photographs as resources for his paintings, as in the watercolor *Abu Simbel Rock Temple (Felsentempel von Abu Simbel)*, in which Krämer was one of the few Orientalist painters not to hide the presence of European tourists. By traveling to the original sites of the New Testament and producing studies of local models, Krämer aimed to add authenticity to his religious history paintings—his favorite genre beside Orientalist pictures—as had been encouraged by Leopold Carl Müller.[23]

After 1900 his skill as a portraitist attracted ample commissions from public figures.[24] In 1904, a solo exhibition was opened at Galerie Miethke comprising 145 works by Krämer, who "renders in particular his coloristic adventure in southern Spain, North Africa, Sicily, and Palestine with delightful gusto."[25] In his exhibition critique, Friedrich Stern referred to the "impressionist power" in Krämer's landscapes.[26]

Further trips followed after the turn of the century: Corfu and the Ionian Islands (1903[27]), Bosnia and Herzegovina (1907), and Dalmatia (1914). Of his many awards and honors, his title of professor (1917) deserves special mention. In 1941 Krämer, by this time eighty, contributed to his last major exhibition, a collective show at Vienna's Künstlerhaus. The artist continued to paint until a great age, concentrating on Orientalist painting—although by this time out of fashion—and religious subjects. He devoted his twilight years to completing a project begun in 1900: an eight-volume illustrated travel memoir of his trip to Egypt and Palestine titled *Das Reisewerk—Reiseerinnerungen aus Ägypten und Palästina 1898–1900*.[28]

JOHANN VICTOR KRÄMER
Motif from Tangiers (Motiv aus Tanger), 1890
Belvedere, Vienna

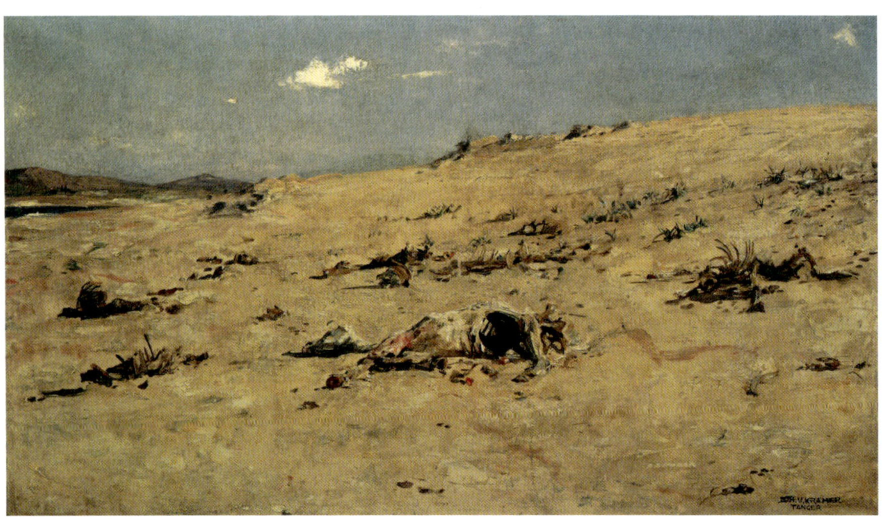

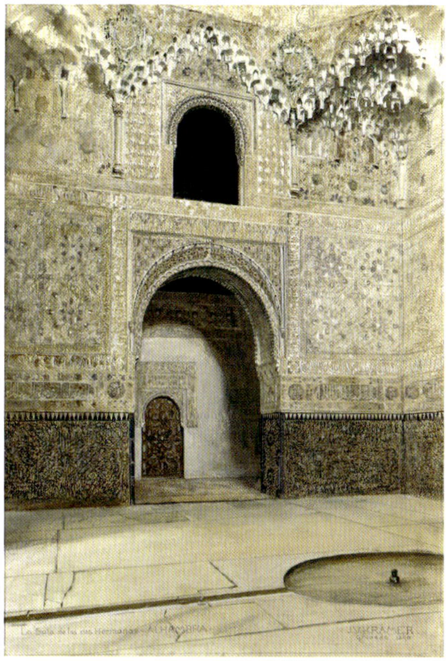

JOHANN VICTOR KRÄMER
Hall of the Two Sisters in the Alhambra, Granada (Saal der beiden Schwestern in der Alhambra, Granada), 1890
Wien Museum

1 Balduin Groller, "Secession. J. V. Krämer," in: *Neues Wiener Journal*, no. 2719, May 21, 1901, p. 9.

2 Thieme/Becker and the Österreichische Biographische Lexikon cite 1887, but Krämer was in fact given the award in 1888. See *Kunstchronik* 26, April 5, 1888, p. 419, and Johann Victor Krämer estate (cf. note 4), document 17.11.: Academy, letter to Krämer with signature of C. Zumbusch h.c., award of the Reichel Prize, Vienna, March 21, 1888.

3 For more detailed information and a photograph of the painting see the Österreichische Galerie Belvedere Archive, Vienna, estate of Hans Ankwicz-Kleehoven, documentation about producing a replica of the painting *Deposition from the Cross (Kreuzabnahme)* by Johann Victor Krämer (Gustav Krämer, June 20, 1990).

4 At the Vienna City Library in City Hall (estate of Johann Victor Krämer, manuscript collection, ZPH 1393, http://share.obvsg.at/wbr02/LQH0237519-1201.pdf [accessed September 2, 2014]) there are seven archival boxes storing the artist's letters and documents. These include letters Krämer wrote from Paris to his parents and Leopold Carl Müller, among others, between December 28, 1888, and May 9, 1889, as well as June 19 and October 13, 1889.

5 Johann Victor Krämer estate (see note 4), file 4.1., letter of December 30, 1888.

6 Johann Victor Krämer estate (see note 4), file 4.1., letter of January 8, 1889.

7 Johann Victor Krämer estate (see note 4), file 4.8., letter of February 27, 1889.

8 Johann Victor Krämer estate (see note 4), file 4.8., letter of February 27, 1889.

9 Johann Victor Krämer estate (see note 4), file 4.8., letter of May 9, 1889.

10 Johann Victor Krämer estate (see note 4), file 4.8., letter of May 17, 1889.

11 Johann Victor Krämer estate (see note 4), files 2.25., 2.26., 2.29., 2.47., 2.48., 4.7., 4.9., 5.6., 5.11., 5.26. Thomas Wallis purchased Krämer's painting *Deposition from the Cross (Kreuzabnahme)*. He exhibited it in London and other British cities before later selling it to an American collection. After that it is supposed to have appeared at the National Gallery in Sydney. In 1990 it was in Adelaide. Wallis also organized a large art print of the original in a limited edition (cf. note 3).

12 Johann Victor Krämer estate (see note 4), file 4.8., letter of June 19, 1889.

13 Martina Haja, "Johann Victor Krämer," in: idem./Günther Wimmer, *Les orientalistes des écoles allemande et autrichienne*, Paris 2000, p. 282.

14 Erika Mayr-Oehring/Elke Doppler, *Orientalische Reise. Malerei und Exotik im späten 19. Jahrhundert* (exh. cat., Wien Museum, Hermesvilla, Vienna, October 16, 2003–April 12, 2004), Vienna 2003, pp. 152–155.

15 Mayr-Oehring/Doppler 2003 (see note 14), pp. 156–157.

16 Haja 2000 (see note 13), p. 282.

17 Agnes Husslein-Arco, *Gartenlust. Der Garten in der Kunst* (exh. cat., Österreichische Galerie Belvedere, Vienna, March 22–June 4, 2007), Vienna 2007, p. 161.

18 Krämer was expelled from the Vienna Künstlerhaus on May 28, 1897, for "ill-considered comments relating to the founding of the Secession" and was not readmitted as a full member until February 26, 1942. See Künstlerhaus Archive, Vienna, file on Johann Victor Krämer.

19 This honor, which diverged from the usual group exhibitions, was later given only to Gustav Klimt and Josef Engelhart.

20 *Katalog der XI. Kunstausstellung der Vereinigung bildender Künstler Österreichs Secession. Werke von Johann Victor Krämer* OM, Vienna 1901.

21 The journey was funded by Leopoldine Wittgenstein, to whom the artist dedicated the first two volumes of his work about his travels (see note 28).

22 Elisabeth Mariel-Seeböck researched Johann Victor Krämer's photographic estate in the photograph collection at the Albertina, Vienna, for her master's thesis. Elisabeth Mariel-Seeböck, *Johann Victor Krämers Fotografien einer Studienreise in den Orient der Jahre 1898 bis 1900*, Vienna 2013. The text can be found on the internet at http://othes.univie.ac.at/25796/1/2013-01-08_0047357.pdf (accessed August 8, 2014).

23 Erika Oehring, "Der Orient als Bildmotiv. Leopold Carl Müller und die österreichische Orientmalerei nach 1870," in: Agnes Husslein-Arco/Sabine Grabner, *Orient & Okzident. Österreichische Maler des 19. Jahrhunderts auf Reisen* (exh. cat., Österreichische Galerie Belvedere, Vienna, June 29–October 14, 2012), Vienna 2012, pp. 29–49, here p. 47.

24 Krämer portrayed the mayor, Karl Lueger, among others.

25 Ludwig Hevesi, "Wiener Brief," in: *Kunstchronik. Wochenschrift für Kunst und Kunstgewerbe*, N. F. 15, no. 23, April 29, 1904, p. 374.

26 Friedrich Stern, "Sezessionisten. In der Wienzeile – Johann Victor Krämer bei Miethke," in: *Neues Wiener Tagblatt* 38, no. 95, April 5, 1904, pp. 1–3.

27 Regarding the date of this trip see Mariel-Seeböck 2013 (see note 22), p. 53, note.

28 For more about this account of the artist's travels see Erika Mayr-Oehring (ed.), *Orient. Österreichische Malerei zwischen 1848 und 1914* (exh. cat., Residenzgalerie Salzburg, Salzburg, July 20–September 24, 1997), Salzburg 1997, pp. 250–253. The book project has never been published; the original is today in a private collection.

HEINRICH KÜHN

(1866 Dresden – 1944 Birgitz, Tyrol)

"The mechanical device has the same importance for the photographer as the brush does for the artist."[1]

Stephan Koja

Heinrich Kühn, probably one of the most important Pictorialist photographers, was convinced throughout his life that photography deserved recognition as an art form on an equal footing with painting. He endeavored consistently and methodically to achieve complete mastery of the technical and chemical aspects of the picture so as to present his artistic vision in as pure a form as possible.

He was born on February 25, 1866, in Dresden as the son of the wealthy wholesale trader Carl Christian Heinrich Kühn and his wife Anne Sophie Conradi.[2] He already developed an interest in photography as a young man. After graduating from Zum Heiligen Kreuz High School in 1885 and having done voluntary service in the army for one year in Lindau on Lake Constance, he began studying medicine, which took him from Leipzig to Freiburg im Breisgau and Berlin, and ultimately to Innsbruck in 1888.

HEINRICH KÜHN

Tonal value Study III (Mary Warner), 1908

Private collection

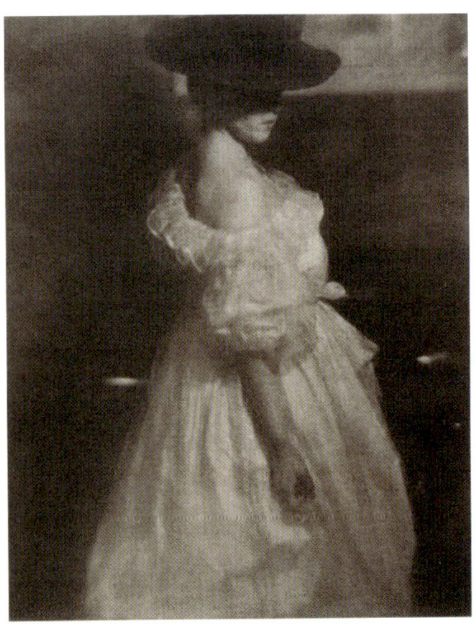

Here, Kühn was able to combine two of his main interests: mountaineering and photography. In 1899/1900 he published several articles on photographing in the mountains in the magazine *Der Tourist* and also gave a number of talks at meetings of the Alpenverein, of which he was a member.

By 1891, Kühn had completed his military service and was discharged as unfit, which did not prevent him from undertaking strenuous journeys and mountain tours in subsequent years. For example, he accompanied the Africanist Robert Hans Schmitt on a trip through Dalmatia and Herzegovina as far as Ragusa [now Dubrovnik]. Here he met Giuseppe Pizzighelli, who was stationed as an officer there and was also a member of the Vienna Camera Club. Founded in Vienna in 1887 to foster artistic photography by amateurs who took pictures because they enjoyed doing so and not for any commercial interests, the club neither intended to be a forum for professional photography nor for inept holiday snapshots. This was also the sense in which Alfred Lichtwark, the legendary director of the Kunsthalle in Hamburg, expected fresh artistic stimuli to come not from photographs by professional studios but from amateurs and encouraged them to take a greater interest in photography as an art form. One topic that gave rise to considerable discussion in the Vienna Camera Club was the work of the two English photographers Peter Henry Emerson and Henry Peach Robinson, who raised the question of the importance of sharp and soft focus and their effect on different paper qualities.

Heinrich Kühn's father died in 1893, leaving the family fortune to his son, thereby ensuring his financial independence and allowing him to devote his entire attention to photography. This made it possible for him to abandon his studies in 1900 in order to work full-time as a photographer.

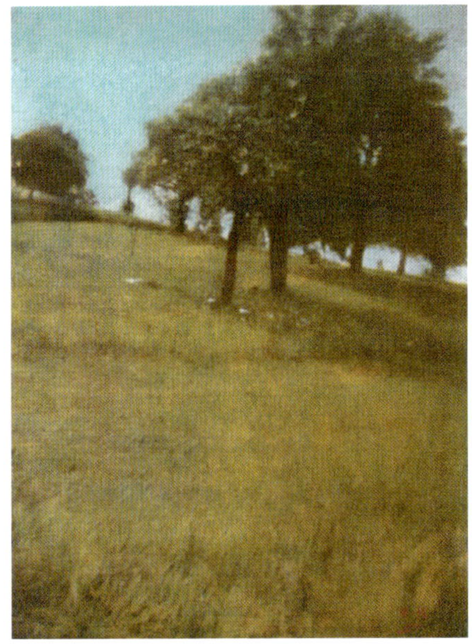

HEINRICH KÜHN

Meadow with Trees, 1897

Private collection

He was also able to start a family and settle permanently in Innsbruck. He married Emma Rosa Katzung in 1894 and purchased a villa, the "Dreimäderlhaus," in the city. During their honeymoon, which also took them to Vienna, Kühn met Hugo Henneberg and Hans Watzek at the Camera Club, encounters that were to play an important role in his subsequent development. In the same year he submitted some photographs for the Camera Club's Christmas Exhibition; one year later he became a member of the Club and a corresponding member of the Gesellschaft zur Förderung der Amateur-Photographie (Society for the Promotion of Amateur Photography) in Hamburg. In 1895 he was invited to join the celebrated British amateur society known as The Brotherhood of the Linked Ring.

When Kühn saw five gum bichromate prints by the French photographer Robert Demachy at the Camera Club Christmas Exhibition that year, he was fascinated by the new expressive possibilities of this type of printing. Demachy's pictures looked more like drawings or graphic prints than photographs, since the choice of paper, the pigment dosage, and the print size offered new flexibility in the pictorial language.

Kühn, Henneberg, and Watzek immediately started experimenting with the new technique and were able to develop the pictorial possibilities even further. By overlaying pictures that had been exposed for different lengths of time, they managed to achieve a larger spectrum of gray tones, enabling them to control the tonal values and hence dramatize the photographs as they desired. Moreover, by using colored gum printing they were also able to introduce the element of color into the images. The lively interaction between the three photographers mutually inspired them and they were able to refine the results even further. In 1896, they presented their gum prints for the first time in the German-speaking world at the *International Exhibition for Amateur Photography* in Berlin. In contrast to Demachy's single-layer Impressionist prints, they were able to achieve a wide range of tonal values through the combination of several printing processes.

These works had an enormous impact on the photography scene in Berlin, "In the peaceful atmosphere of our exhibition, in the relatively tame discussion on new objectives for artistic photography, Kühn's submission, the first attempts at gum printing, exploded like a bomb—there is no other way to describe it," recalls a photographer who was present at the time.[3] The possibility of enlarging the prints was completely in line with Kühn's artistic idea of processing the pictures to enhance their effect (cf.fig. p. 75).

At the same time, he was always at pains to arrive at the desired painterly effect through purely technical means without any manipulation. To achieve this aim, he would sometimes take as many as 100 pictures of a subject, usually landscapes.[4]

In 1897, the three photographers began to call their group the "Kleeblatt" (clover leaf) or "Trifolium" (the Latin term) and to sign their works with a stylized clover leaf. That

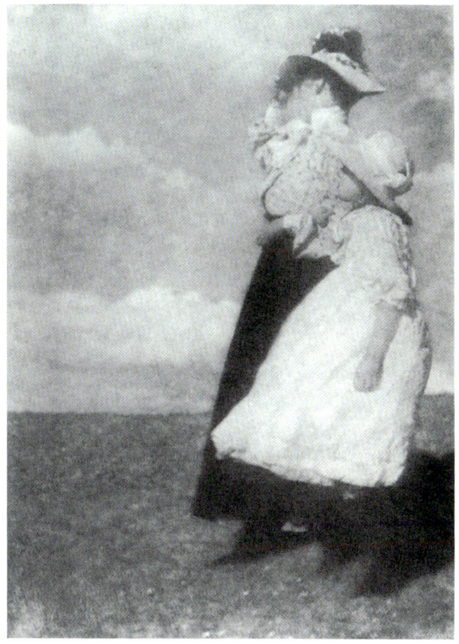

HEINRICH KÜHN
Blast, 1905
Private collection

year they traveled together to Hamburg, Venice, Lago di Garda, and Lake Constance, and on an extended trip along the Danube. Kühn was also able to present a three-color gum print for the first time in Hamburg in the same year.

Through his numerous visits to Vienna, Kühn made the acquaintance of the families of Carl Moll and Gustav Klimt. He often traveled to Munich, where he was in contact with the Munich Secession Artists' Association. It was during this time that his children Walther Karl Heinrich (1895) and Edeltrude "Grete" Margarethe (1897) were born.

When Hans Watzek died unexpectedly in 1903 and Hugo Henneberg turned his attention to graphic prints, Kühn lost two important sources of inspiration. As a result, he changed his status at the Vienna Camera Club from ordinary to corresponding member.

In the meantime, Kühn's own interest had also shifted, focusing more on his children following the birth of his son Hans Hugo Heinrich (named after the three members of the Kleeblatt group) in 1900. Moreover, he concentrated with scientific precision on the spectrum of light and dark tones—which he called "tonal values"—in photographs and the most effective means of reproducing them. In 1902, he wrote an article on the subject for a book of photogravures by Henneberg, Kühn, and Watzek, published by Fritz Matthies-Masuren.[5] The catalyst for these new experiments on tonal values was an encounter with North American photographs, which were increasingly to be found in international magazines and at exhibitions in Germany and Austria—such as the Camera Club presentations at Galerie Miethke in Vienna in 1902 and 1905 with works by Alfred Stieglitz, Edward Steichen, and Gertrude Käsebier. The platinum prints that Kühn saw there were to exert a sustained fascination on him. He had previously concentrated on marked surface contrasts and a "strong separation of tones,"[6] in his large-format prints but now saw that much finer distinctions were possible. He wrote to Stieglitz and expressed his admiration, "[…] since I have seen the outstanding American pictures, my own prints are no longer sufficient for me."[7]

The correspondence rapidly led to mutual admiration and was the start of a friendship that lasted more than thirty years. Stieglitz came to Europe in 1904, and the two met for the first time that summer in Igls in Tyrol, continuing their dialog thereafter by letter. Stieglitz gave his friend a subscription to his magazine *Camera Work*, which enabled Kühn to keep up to date with the latest international trends in photography.

HEINRICH KÜHN
Fishermen on the Canal, 1908,
published in *Camera Work*, 1911

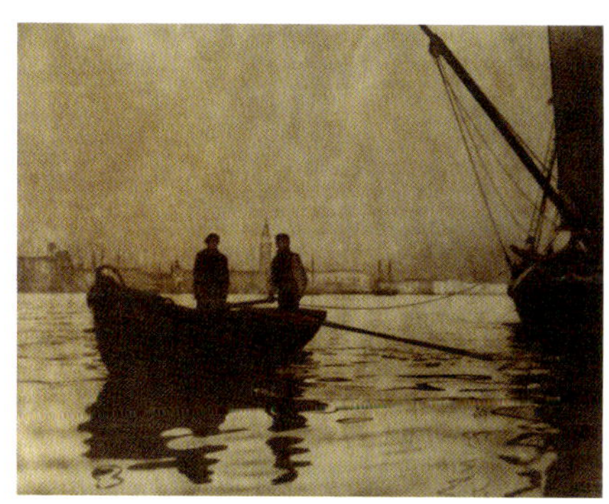

Kühn's fourth child, Charlotte "Lotte" Anneluise Rosemary, was born in 1904, but his wife Emma died of tuberculosis the same year. Her place at Kühn's side and in the family was taken by the English nanny Mary "May" Hannah Warner, who moved into the Jugendstil house designed by Kühn in the Saggen district of Innsbruck and became a favorite subject of Kühn's photographers, which were often taken on excursions to Igls or Lake Lans.

From 1905, Kühn began increasingly to photograph portraits commercially to cover the enormous expense of building the house. In these works as well, he endeavored to heighten the intensity of the pictures by reducing them to their simplest forms. Here he was obviously influenced by the work of two of the founding fathers of photography, David Octavius Hill and Robert Adamson. Kühn set up two large studios in his house to take these pictures, one with dark and the other with light paneling. Depending on the background, he could influence the statement made by the pictures—having the subjects merge with their surroundings or stand out against them. The white and black clothing used in

HEINRICH KÜHN
Glass of Water, ca. 1911
Private collection

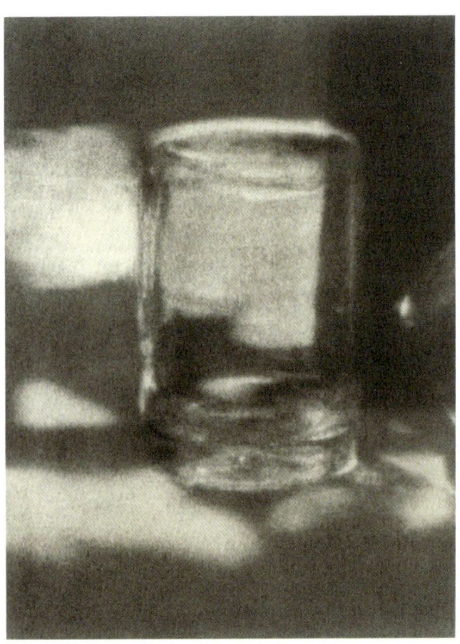

the portraits had the same effect. By adjusting the focus, he could emphasize elements of the picture or suppress unimportant details.

In 1905, Kühn was a member of the jury at the Camera Club International Exhibition of Selected Artistic Photographs at Galerie Miethke, which featured a representative selection of national schools. He curated the Austrian contributions, while Matthies-Masuren was in charge of the German, and Stieglitz of the American works. Emil Orlík and Kolo Moser were responsible for the presentation.

In 1906, Kühn visited the United States on the occasion of the exhibition organized by Stieglitz in New York entitled "Austrian and German Work: Heinrich Kühn, Hugo Henneberg, Hans Watzek, Theodor and Oscar Hofmeister," which was also shown in Philadelphia. In the same year, Kühn had his first solo exhibition at Galerie Schulte in Berlin, which helped considerably to heighten his fame and reputation.

He was not so successful in his applications for an academic post—as head of the new Department of Photography at the Dresden Technische Hochschule (University of Technology) in 1907 and at the k. k. Graphische Lehr- und Versuchsanstalt (Imperial and Royal Graphic Training and Research Institute) in Vienna in 1909.

Kühn and Matthies-Masuren helped to organize one of the pavilions at the 1909 International Photography Exhibition in Dresden, which highlighted major achievements in international art photography. The collaboration was marked by disputes with the organizers and other photographers, however, as not everyone satisfied the demanding standards set by Kühn, who envisaged an elite exhibition of artistic photography and strongly disapproved of some photographers, including Stieglitz, also wanting to participate in other sections devoted to applied photography.

At this time, Kühn had begun to experiment with different pigmentation combinations and to start photographing more outdoors, where he was particularly fascinated by sunlight effects. He had met Frank Eugene and Edward Steichen in summer 1907 together with Stieglitz in Tutzing, Bavaria. On that occasion, Steichen had shown the friends the Lumière brothers' new color technique with Autochrome plates. Everyone, especially Kühn, was excited by the first attempts with this new additive technique. In his thorough and methodical way, he conducted extensive tests during the following two years and published a number of articles on the technique.

Kühn was to remain captivated by this photographic process until the end of World War I. He appreciated the Autochrome plates' capability to deal with high contrasts and their exposure range that opened the way to completely new areas of experimentation such as backlit photography. In addition, the nature of the colors and the coarse graining produced a "painterly" effect that was further enhanced by Kühn's deliberately unfocused style (see figs. pp. 76–82).

As the exposure time was very long, there was a need for sunlight or intensive artificial light, as well as precise preparations and composition. Kühn often took his inspiration for this from contemporary painting, especially atmospheric painting and Impressionism, which he was able to study at exhibitions in Munich and Vienna. Many of his Autochrome pictures—for which members of his family, wearing clothing designed specially by him in red, blue, and green (the three color layers of the Autochrome plate), stood patiently as models—were reminiscent of the works of Monet and the French Impressionists.

This also applied to the arrangement of the figures outdoors and under trees, the play of light on their clothes, the radical low-angle shots in the pictures of Mary Warner or the children, recalling Monet's *The Walk, Woman with a Parasol* (*La promenade, la femme à l'ombrelle*) (1875; National Gallery of Art, Washington) and his garden paintings. It applies in general to the luminosity and bright colors, which even in the still lifes made the light one of the most important factors. Kühn's ability to make the pictures look

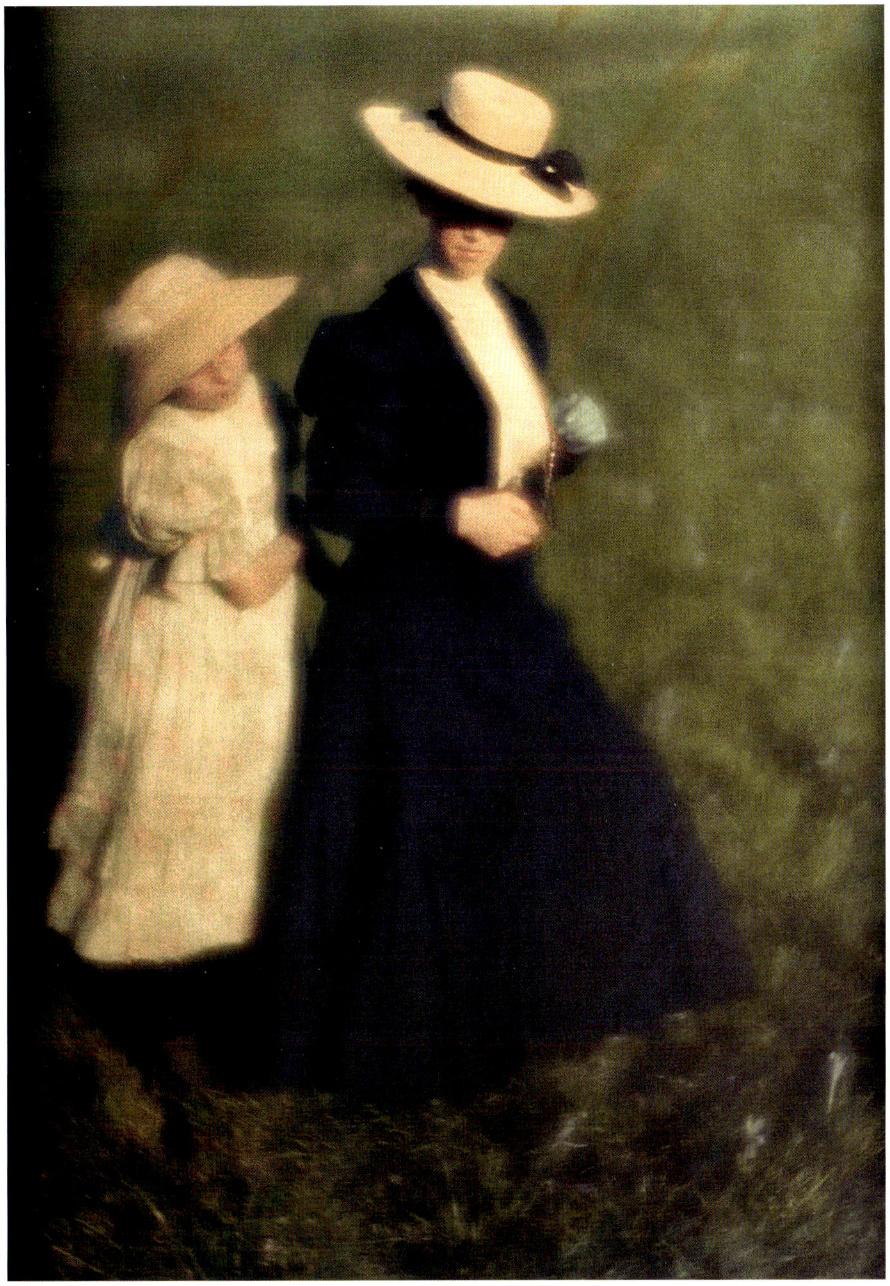

HEINRICH KÜHN
The Kühn Siblings in the Meadow, 1912
ÖNB/Vienna

spontaneous is due to the clever arrangements, because the long exposure times made instant pictures impossible.

Kühn was to become unarguably the most consummate master of this technique, not least as he increased the luminosity of the colors even further through deliberate simplification and concentration on a few elements and large surfaces. As he himself said, he had to "renounce anything multifaceted or complex"[8] and "compose with account taken of the color."[9]

Kühn was at the highpoint of his international fame when *Camera Work* devoted a monographic presentation to his work in 1911, with Stieglitz giving him complete freedom regarding the choice of pictures shown.

At this time, he was in intensive contact with the major photographers of the time: not only Stieglitz, but also James Craig Annan, Alvin Langdon Coburn, Reginald W. Craigie, George Davison, Robert Demachy, Frank Eugene, Gertrude Käsebier, and Adolf de Meyer.

His finances, by contrast, had taken a turn for the worse. In 1910, his brother-in-law had lost most of the family fortune through unwise investments, leaving Kühn with just a small income from properties in Dresden. He was unsuccessful in obtaining a professorship in photography at the University of Innsbruck, and the Lichtbildnerschule (Photography School), founded in 1914, had to close in 1915 after just two semesters following the outbreak of the First World War and the conscription of his assistant Peter Paul Atzwanger. During the war, Kühn attempted to improve his income through the publication of articles and expert opinions on industrial products.

The family once again became the dominant subject in his photography. The pictures were almost abstract, with reflections on the relationship between space and depth and unusual angles. Kühn experimented tirelessly with refinements of the tonal values and color pigments.

It was not until 1921 that Kühn's first book, *Technik der Lichtbildnerei*, appeared. The year before he had been obliged to sell the villa in Innsbruck that he had constructed with so much dedication and financial outlay and he moved with his family to Rietz in Oberinntal. In 1921, he bought a house in the village of Birgitz near Innsbruck, where he lived until his death. Shortly after the move to Rietz, however, Kühn was once again on the verge of bankruptcy and in 1923 had to seek new ways of earning money. He attempted to have various patents registered in other countries, continued to publish articles, and his second book, *Zur photographischen Technik*, was issued in 1926.

Production of the Kühn-Stegemann Studien-Kamera C, a bellows camera mounted on a triangular rail, which allowed it to be tilted in all directions and was a forerunner of the monorail camera, commenced in

1927. It was the belated fruit of extensive experiments performed jointly with Hans Watzek.

During these years Kühn also developed a lens together with Franz Staeble, the founder of the Staeble-Werk, with interchangeable filters permitting an adjustable circle of confusion to be superimposed on the sharply focused core so as to achieve the desired "softness without sweetness,"[10] while taking the photograph. This lens was sold by the name "Anachromat Kühn" and was later developed into the Rodenstock Imagon, which was available until the 1990s.

In 1924, after an interruption of several years, Kühn once again took part in exhibitions. From 1926 to 1929 he coedited the *Photographische Rundschau und Mitteilungen* with Matthies-Masuren.

The last part of Kühn's life was overshadowed by the loss in 1933 of his loyal housekeeper and support Mary Warner, which affected him deeply. Kühn's own health deteriorated rapidly from 1940 and he died of intestinal complications and circulatory failure on September 14, 1944.

During these latter years, people began to recognize Kühn's contribution to the development of artistic photography. In 1929 he was made an honorary member of the Verband Österreichischer Amateurphotographen-Vereine (Association of Austrian Amateur Photography Societies), and subsequently an honorary member of the Photographische Gesellschaft (Photography Society) in Vienna and a member of the Vereinigung Bildender Künstler (Artists' Association) in Innsbruck. He was finally awarded an honorary doctorate by the University of Innsbruck in 1937.

1 Heinrich Kühn, *Technik der Lichtbildnerei*, Halle a. d. S. 1921, p. 415.
2 For biographical details, see the detailed biography of Kühn by Astrid Mahler, "Heinrich Kühn – Leben und Werk," in ibid./Monika Faber (ed.), *Heinrich Kühn. Die vollkommene Fotografie* (exh. cat., Albertina, Vienna, June 11–September 12, 2010, Musée de l'Orangerie, Paris, October 19, 2010–January 23, 2011, Museum of Fine Arts, Houston, March 6–May 30, 2011), Vienna 2010, pp. 225–255.
3 Fritz Matthies-Masuren quoted here "einige Worte aus Dr. Stettiners Bericht," in: Fritz Matthies-Masuren, *Künstlerische Photographie. Entwicklung und Einfluß in Deutschland* (part of the series *Die Kunst. Sammlung illustrierter Monographien*, ed. by Richard Muther, vols. 59 and 60), Berlin 1907, p. 45.
4 Wolfgang Baier, *Quellendarstellungen zur Geschichte der Fotografie*, 2nd edition, Munich 1980, pp. 537-539.
5 Heinrich Kühn, "Studie zu Tonwerten," in: Fritz Matthies-Masuren (ed.), *Gummidrucke von Hugo Henneberg, Wien, Heinrich Kühn, Innsbruck, und Hans Watzek, Wien*, Halle a. d. S. 1902.
6 Kühn 1921 (see note 1), p. 288.
7 Letter from Heinrich Kühn to Alfred Stieglitz of February 2, 1905. Yale Collection of American Literature, Beinecke Rare Book and Manuscript Library, Yale University, New Haven, CT. Quoted from Mahler 2010 (see note 2), p. 234.
8 Kühn 1921 (see note 1), p. 408.
9 Ibid., p. 223.
10 Quoted from Baier 1980 (see note 4), p. 536.

EMILIE MEDIZ-PELIKAN

(1861 Vöcklabruck – 1908 Dresden)

Awakening of Light and Color

Therese Backhausen

The paintings were ugly, daubings, and the execution was too superficial, a prospective buyer informed the artist.[1] Another advised her to abandon painting because he feared for her, as this type of painting had no future.[2]

Comments like this must have hurt the sensitive Emilie Mediz-Pelikan, a painter whose work was situated somewhere between Realism, Impressionism, and Symbolism, and who was notable for her early integration of new stylistic tendencies.[3]

In spite of all the criticism, Mediz-Pelikan appears to have been confident about the Impressionistic painting style that was regarded so dismissively and that she developed around 1890 in the bright light of the Belgian coast.

The young and gifted Emilie Pelikan from Vöcklabruck felt the desire to be an artist from an early age and was also permitted to become one. This was unusual for a young

EMILIE MEDIZ-PELIKAN

Suburb in the Snow, 1888

Private collection

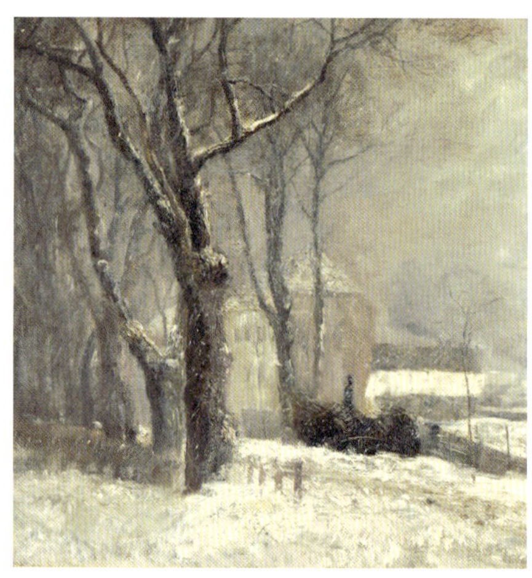

girl from a bourgeois household, expected traditionally to become a housewife and mother. Her parents enabled her to obtain a solid basis as a painter through private tuition[4] with the landscape painter Albert August Zimmermann.[5] His influence is clearly evident in her early work.

She sought more decisive changes from 1885 in the artists' colony at Dachau near Munich, where she created delightfully intimate landscape scenes that captured the mood of the Barbizon School's *paysage intime*. She also benefited there from the teaching of Adolf Hölzel and the sympathetic advice of Fritz von Uhde.

At this time she met her future husband, the painter Karl Mediz, whom she visited while he was studying in Paris and with whom she spent two seasons in Knokke on the Belgian coast, a site also sought out by French Impressionists. It was there that she completed her transformation to a fleeting, sketch-like style. Mediz was an important partner, adviser, and critic, and he was instrumental in her artistic development. Their years together until Emilie's untimely death were marked by a symbiotic relationship of equals, and by parallel and mutually enriching creative development.

Painting trips to Italy, Hungary, and Bohemia, and the birth of a daughter followed. In 1894, Mediz-Pelikan turned her back on Munich for the artists' colony in Goppeln near Dresden, which had been formed as a counter-movement to the rigid Salon painting. Although Goppeln was the artistic home of the Impressionists, she had already abandoned this style in favor of emphatic contours, graphic linearity, and a more detailed pictorial language. Her landscapes were increasingly characterized by mystical moods and symbolic parameters. Her success at exhibitions such as the first Secession exhibition in 1898 and the Hagenbund exhibitions in 1902 and 1903 marked the zenith of her artistic career. At the high point of Jugendstil, her stylized pictures fell on fertile ground in Vienna—in contrast to Dresden. The enthusiasm for her paintings even made her consider moving to Vienna, a plan that after much hesitation was ultimately abandoned. She was too brittle and reserved for the social life sometimes necessary for an artist of her significance. She remained in Dresden with Karl Mediz until her premature death, mentally and physically battered—no doubt also as a result of her constant battle for acceptance as a painter.

Impressionist influences can be seen as early as 1885, in pictures like the marsh studies. Here for the first time she was able to capture fleeting natural phenomena with generous and rapid brushstrokes. In *Lake Starnberg (Starnberger See)* the surface of the water is depicted with short, arching parallel strokes. These pictures are notable for their intensive play of light and shadow effects.

The winter scene *Suburb in the Snow* (*Vorort im Schnee*) (1888) also bears witness to her experimentation with atmospheric light effects. Mediz-Pelikan begins to dissolve contours and makes the white snow shimmer with a network of short and rapidly juxtaposed and unordered brushstrokes in pastel shades like pink and blue.

She wrote in her diaries that she came across Impressionist paintings in Paris at exhibitions in 1889 and particularly 1890, and that these fascinated her more than any other works that she saw.[6] On the Belgian coast where, according to Ludwig Hevesi, "impression appeared to lie on the street,"[7] she experimented intensively with these new ways of seeing. She distanced herself from the Barbizon tonal painting, and her style came closer to that of the French, with pictures showing a predominant Impressionist influence. In view of her earlier *plein air* experiences on Dachau Moor, it was not difficult for her to adapt to the French influences, such as working outdoors with a loose and rapid brush texture, and the spontaneity and randomness of *alla prima* painting, the lighter palette, and the objective representation.

She caused a furor in Munich with a picture painted during her first stay in Knokke in 1889, which has unfortunately disappeared. Hevesi speaks of a yellow field of gorse

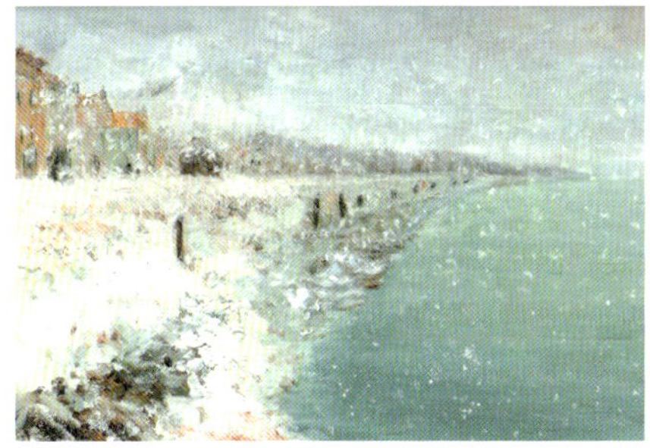

EMILIE MEDIZ-PELIKAN
Winter in Stein on the Danube, 1893
Private collection

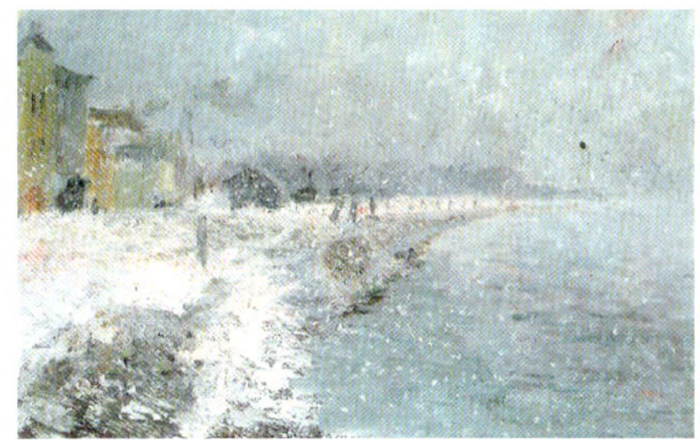

EMILIE MEDIZ-PELIKAN
Winter in Stein on the Danube, 1893
Private collection

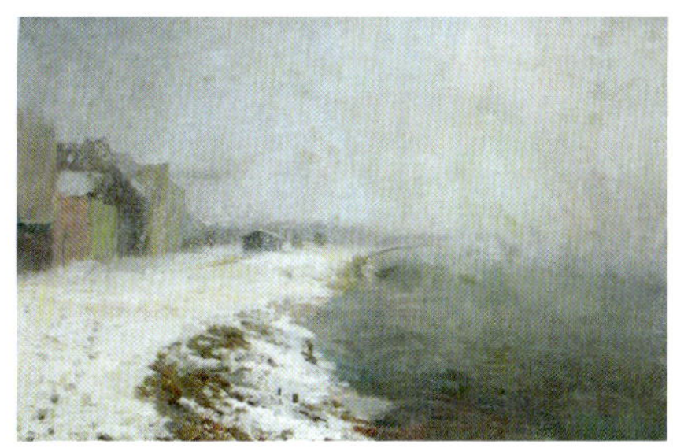

EMILIE MEDIZ-PELIKAN
Winter in Stein on the Danube, 1893
Private collection

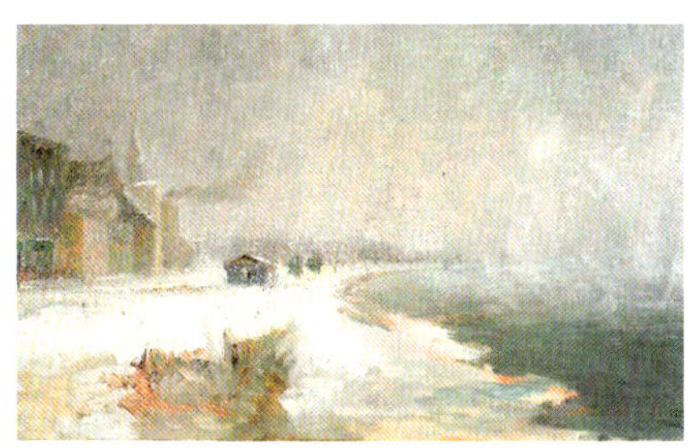

EMILIE MEDIZ-PELIKAN
Winter in Stein on the Danube, 1893
Private collection

painted in an Impressionistic style hitherto unseen in the Bavarian capital.[8] This is interesting, considering that Impressionism as a style concept was not really acknowledged in Munich[9] and only a few artists were regarded as innovative, but at the same time the Secessionists there were calling for new artistic approaches.[10] Mediz-Pelikan was more than willing to take this step, and as such she may be compared with Lovis Corinth, Wilhelm Trübner, or Fritz von Uhde. The situation in Vienna was similar: here, too, occasional pictures by the Impressionists were to be seen at exhibitions,[11] but a comprehensive overview of the modern French tendencies was not seen until the Impressionism exhibition in the Secession organized by Carl Moll in early 1903.

Water, sand, rocks, and leisure were the subjects that she now painted, making the most of the effects of changes in the atmosphere. It would seem from a number of Mediz-Pelikan's paintings that she had seen pictures by Claude Monet early on, perhaps while she was in Paris. The pictures completed in Knokke, Duino, and Krems give an indication of the possible influence of his works.

Like Monet's seascapes, the absence of borders in *Sea in the Midday Heat* (*Meer in Mittagsglut*) (1890; fig. p. 49) conveys an impression of distance and endlessness. Sky, water, sand—everything merges in an atmosphere of bright color and light that appears to absorb objects as matter coming from the outside.

In *Afternoon in the Dunes* (*Nachmittag in den Dünen*) Mediz-Pelikan interprets the subject in a way reminiscent of Monet's *Poppy Fields Near Argenteuil* (*Les coquelicots à Argenteuil*) (1873; fig. p. 69), notably with full- and half-length figures wandering across the picture. She captures a moment with women walking in the dunes. The sand, reflecting the sun and portrayed with thick brushstrokes, offers a wide spectrum of color nuances, with a shimmering effect achieved through the use of pink, blue, and yellow tones.

Between 1883 and 1886, Monet painted countless series of views of the rocks at Étretat. In 1891, Mediz-Pelikan painted at least two versions of the steep cliffs at Duino (fig. p. 57) with powerful, unusually luminescent colors. The emphasis is not on the trivial rocks in their local colors but the effects of light. The depiction of the purely superficial stimuli, the blurring of internal structures, even their dematerialization, are elements in which Mediz Pelikan's painting resembles the French.

In the sketch-like *Outskirts of Krems* (*Stadtrand von Krems*; 1891) the houses that structure the picture disappear blurringly in the background mist. The work is painted two dimensionally with powerful brushstrokes. In the foreground a woman with a red umbrella crosses the picture diagonally. The distinctive red fleck in the gleaming snow shows how important visual impressions were for Mediz-Pelikan.

Snapshots of urban life such as busy city boulevards were popular with the Impressionists, including Monet. Similarly, in *Torchlight Procession* (*Fackelzug*) (1892) Mediz-Pelikan takes up this theme. With rapid strokes, the painter recorded the anonymity of the city dweller as she saw it: the movements of people who here at night become dark lines with shadows, the torches a sea of light and reflections, and the fiery building façades disappearing into the dappled structure of the dark sky.

And like Monet with his hayricks or the cathedral in Rouen, she also recorded the various lights and moods of the same subject at different times of day. In 1893 she painted a series of four views of *Winter in Stein*, which show the same almost endless riverbank with only slight variations between the pictures. Two pictures depict a snowfall, one a hazy sunny atmosphere, and one a gloomy misty view. The riverbank is in the center but appears to change in the diverse lighting of the individual pictures.

It is sometimes claimed that Emilie Mediz-Pelikan was uninfluenced by French Impressionism, but the evidence does not bear this out.[12] Long before the Impressionism exhibition in Vienna in 1903 she had studied these innovations and met all formal criteria, such as subject, light, and color, even if she failed to consistently abide by the concept of breaking down the picture scientifically into spectral colors.

She should therefore be counted among the Austrian Impressionists alongside Theodor von Hörmann, Tina Blau, Rudolf Quittner, Otto von Thoren, and Olga Wisinger-Florian, who also incorporated the new theories as autonomous artistic means.[13]

In her lyrical interpretation and more tonal

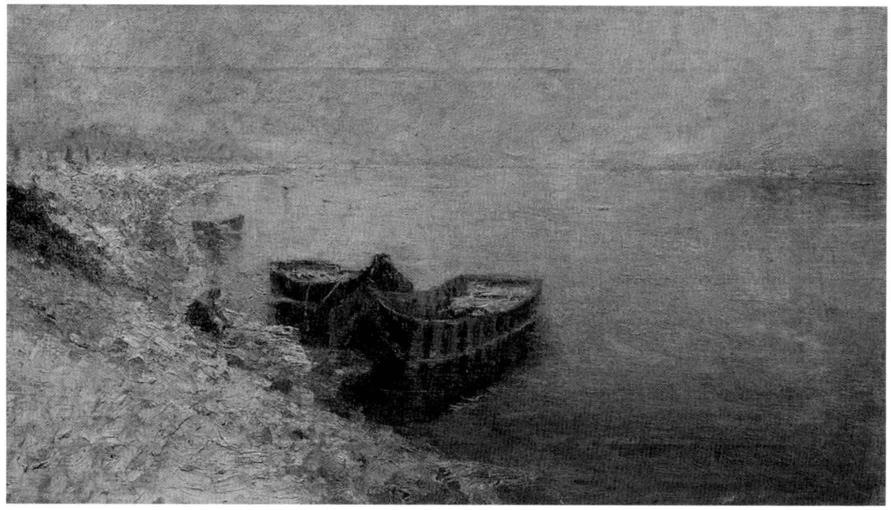

EMILIE MEDIZ-PELIKAN
Fishing boats on the Donaushore, 1890
Belvedere, Vienna

chromaticism, her work is closer to the Impressionism developed in Germany under the French influence or in Austria under the influence of the *Stimmungsimpressionisten* (Atmospheric Impressionists).

1 Letter from Emilie to Karl Mediz of April 19, 1890, Archiv der Österreichischen Galerie Belvedere, Vienna, Emilie Mediz-Pelikan and Karl Mediz estate.
2 Letter from Emilie to Karl Mediz of January 12, 1890, ibid.
3 Therese Backhausen, *Menage à trois. Emilie Mediz-Pelikan – Karl Mediz. Ein Leben für die Kunst*, diss., Salzburg 2008.
4 And not as often incorrectly claimed at the Akademie.
5 Women were not allowed to study at the Akademie at this time, not least because of the morality issue surrounding nude studies.
6 Travel diary, vol. 19, Archiv der Österreichischen Galerie Belvedere, Vienna, Emilie Mediz-Pelikan and Karl Mediz estate.
7 Ludwig Hevesi, "Karl Mediz – Emilie Pelikan," in: *Zeitschrift für bildende Kunst*, Leipzig 1903, quoted from Sophie Geretsegger/Oswald Oberhuber/Wilfried Seipel, *Emilie Mediz-Pelikan 1861–1908. Karl Mediz 1868–1945* (exh. cat., Österreichisches Museum für angewandte Kunst, Vienna, April 24–May 25, 1986, Oberösterreichisches Landesmuseum, Landesgalerie, Linz, April 23–June 22, 1986), Vienna 1986, p. 10.
8 Hevesi (see note 7).
9 Cf. Andreas Strobl, "Aufstieg und Fall der Kunststadt München. Zu den Bildern der Zeitgenossen Fritz von Uhdes in der Neuen Pinakothek," in: *Fritz von Uhde. Vom Realismus zum Impressionismus* (exh. cat., Neue Pinakothek, Munich, June 25–September 19, 1999), Munich 1999, p. 97.
10 Cf. Jürgen Kastl, *Die Anfänge der Münchener und der Wiener Secession und ihre kunst- und kulturpolitischen sowie künstlerischen Austauschprozesse im Zeitraum von 1894 bis 1905*, diss., Graz 2003, p. 69.
11 Marian Bisanz-Prakken, *Heiliger Frühling. Gustav Klimt und die Anfänge der Wiener Secession 1895–1905*, Vienna/Munich 1999, p. 21.
12 Gerbert Frodl, "Landschaftsmalerei," in: *Geschichte der bildenden Kunst in Österreich Band 5: 19. Jahrhundert*, Vienna 2002, p. 313.
13 For the Austrian Impressionists, see Agnes Husslein-Arco (ed.), *Wien–Paris. Van Gogh, Cézanne und Österreichs Moderne 1880–1960* (exh. cat., Österreichische Galerie Belvedere, Vienna, October 3, 2007–January 13, 2008), Vienna 2007, p. 68.

CARL MOLL
(1861 Vienna – 1945 Vienna)

Eternal Student, Brilliant Organizer, and Ardent Supporter of Modern Art

Kathrin Wolf

"I was not allowed to have lessons, but should keep myself occupied, so I was given a pencil and watercolors to play with. The first coincidence that influenced my life's path,"[1] Carl Moll recounted his first attempts at painting and drawing many years later. Born on April 23, 1861, into a middle-class family in Vienna, he suffered from anemia as a child and frequently had to miss school. In 1876, during a summer vacation to Salzburg, Munich, and the Großglockner region, he filled his first sketchbook with many studies of nature. His father Julius Moll, a merchant and margarine manufacturer, died in 1877, aged just forty-nine, leaving his family a fairly large fortune, which allowed sixteen-year-old Carl to pursue his artistic

CARL MOLL
The Roman Ruins in Schönbrunn, 1891
Belvedere, Vienna

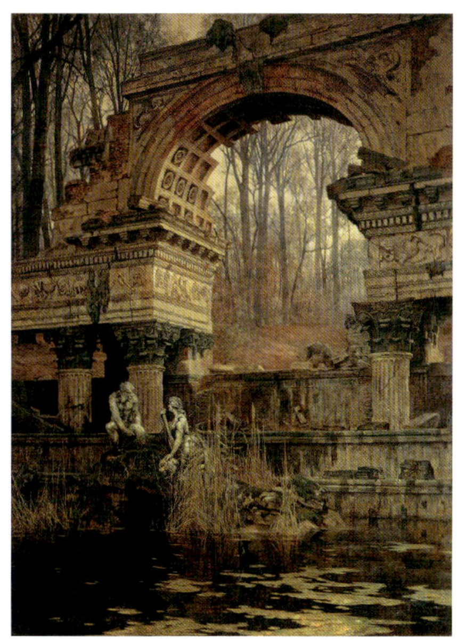

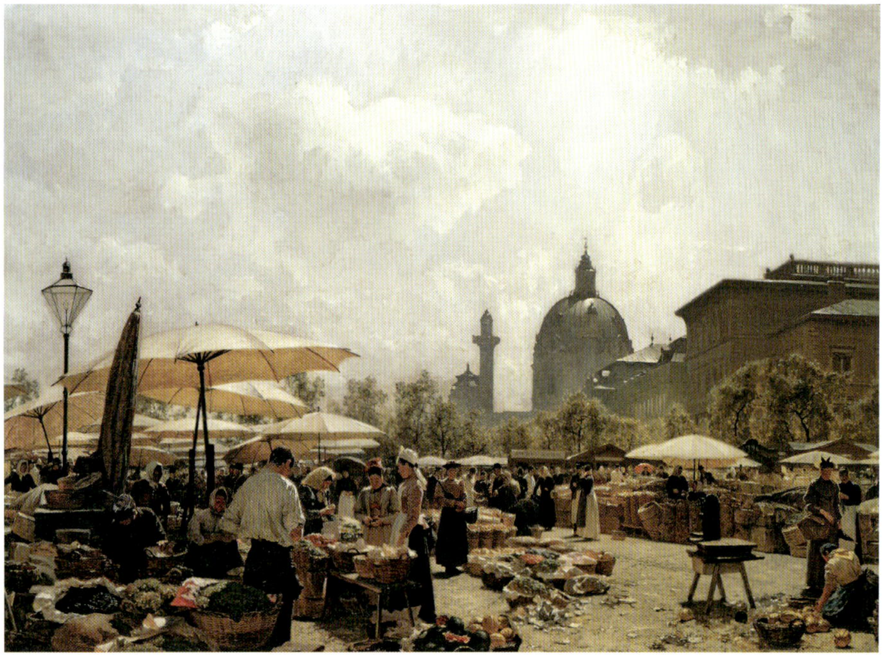

CARL MOLL
Naschmarkt in Vienna , 1894
Belvedere, Vienna

inclinations. With the support of his mother, he first took private tuition with the landscape painter Carl Haunold. Moll was unimpressed by traditional painting studies, involving hours spent drawing plaster casts, which he began in 1879 at the Vienna Akademie der bildenden Künste (Academy of Fine Arts) under the tutelage of Christian Griepenkerl. A severe attack of meningitis, however, forced him to abandon his studies and left him suffering from deafness for the rest of his life.

"I SEE MEETING MY MASTER AS MY SECOND, MY SPIRITUAL BIRTH"[2]

In 1881 Moll saw the painting *Backwater of the Traun River near Goisern (Altwasser an der Traun bei Goisern)*[3] by Emil Jakob Schindler at the Künstlerhaus and was deeply impressed. Not long afterward, he became his private student. Schindler, whom Moll admired as his "master" all through his life, became his closest friend and mentor. Previously concentrating on still life, it was probably Schindler who inspired Moll to paint landscapes. He admitted that it was Schindler who had taught him to really see nature, and especially to absorb the different atmospheres and capture them in paintings, "He [Schindler] did not teach his students to paint, but to feel."[4] Moll accompanied Schindler on his travels to the Salzkammergut, to Lundenburg an der Thaya, Dalmatia, Corfu, and Berlin, painting the same subjects at his teacher's side. His style at that time so resembles Schindler's that some of his works verge on imitations or copies. In 1885 Schindler and his family, as well as his students Olga Wisinger-Florian, Marie Egner, and Carl Moll, moved to Schloss Plankenberg near Neulengbach, a mansion that Schindler rented. Dubbed by art history the Schindler circle or Plankenberg School, the group used the mansion's idyllic surroundings as a source of subject matter and a place where they could paint together.

On a walk through Schönbrunn in 1884,[5] Schindler urged Moll to tackle a larger work. *The Roman Ruins in Schönbrunn (Die Römische Ruine in Schönbrunn)*, a colossal painting with polished perspective, was to occupy Moll for many years. Although purchased in 1891 by Emperor Franz Joseph for the department of modern art at the Hofmuseum, it was slated by the critics, "[...] echoing his master's palette entirely, colorlessly gray, almost without light, with a gloomy autumnal atmosphere. Ultimately this fits the underlying mood of the subject, but why so much canvas?"[6]

A TIME OF REORIENTATION

Following the sudden death of his teacher on the island of Sylt in 1892, Moll organized a memorial exhibition at the Künstlerhaus and an auction of the estate at Galerie Miethke. Bereft of his confidant and artistic mainstay, Moll traveled north for several summers where he looked for new subject matter in Lüneburg, Lübeck, and Danzig. Here he came across Impressionist painter Gotthardt Kuehl, who had returned from Paris, and who gave Moll new ideas about subject matter and painting technique. Influenced by Kuehl, Moll started exploring cityscapes and especially interiors, which characterized his oeuvre for a good decade thereafter. It was with his painting *Naschmarkt in Vienna (Der Naschmarkt in Wien)*, bought by the Ministry of Culture in 1894, that Moll finally managed to step out of Schindler's shadow. "I am all too aware that my lack of imagination and poor memory means that I have to adhere strictly to nature; so I finally install myself with my canvas in the midst of the market [...],"[7] was how Moll described his working

CARL MOLL
Twilight, before 1900
Belvedere, Vienna

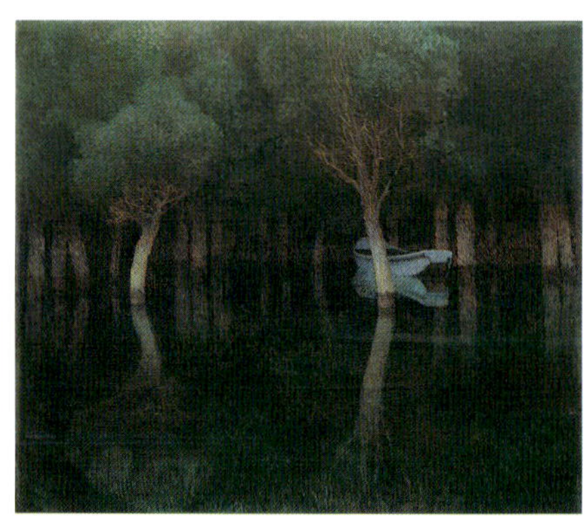

method. Starting out *en plein air* and completing the painting in his studio, this is an impressive example of the reception of French modern art. Moll captured the bustling market in a composition of pale colors, saturated with light, and although earthy shades predominate, he included some highly charged complementary color contrasts. In addition to drawing on the subject matter of "modern life," such as bustling city squares, passersby in urban park, and factory chimneys (fig. p. 44), in some paintings he adopted Claude Monet's signature brushwork and cropping of the picture space (cf. figs. p. 41).

MOLL—THE GIFTED ORGANIZER

In 1895 Moll married Schindler's widow and thus became the stepfather of Margarete and the sixteen-year-old Alma, later Mahler-Werfel.[8] At roughly the same time he joined the Vienna Künstlerhaus and his activities as an exhibition organizer and promoter of art began. In 1897 he was one of the founding members of the Vienna Secession and its first vice president. In 1900 he was sent as an Austrian delegate to the World's Fair in Paris, where he was awarded a silver medal for his painting *Before the Dinner* (*Vor dem Diner*).[9] Four weeks in the French capital provided him with ample opportunity to explore French modern art. The highly acclaimed and successful Impressionism exhibition at the Secession in 1903 was largely the result of his efforts. It was from here that important paintings were purchased for the newly founded Moderne Galerie (today's Belvedere). In 1900/01 Moll was president of the Secession. He cofounded the Wiener Werkstätte in 1903. Between 1904 and 1912 he was artistic director of Galerie Miethke and organized important exhibitions about Gauguin, van Gogh, Hodler, Manet, Monet, Schiele, and other avant-garde artists. With Moll at its helm, the gallery advanced to become a center of modern art. His commercial activities with the gallery caused a conflict of interest within the Secession, however, and in 1905 the Klimt Gruppe (Klimt Group) left the organization.

RETURN TO PAINTING

In Moll's works of around 1900 the influence of Symbolism is clearly apparent. The painting *Twilight (Dämmerung)* reflects the influence of Belgian artist Fernand Khnopff, who was so esteemed by the Secessionists. This glassy pond is bathed in a mysterious, almost foreboding atmosphere, and trees grow from its optically impenetrable depths, their dense leaves blocking out the sky. Although the brushwork with its brief, comma-like strokes recalls Neo-Impressionism, the shapes are still clearly defined.

After this symbolist interlude, Moll's Secessionist phase began, in which the interior came to the fore in his work. Moll hoped "to be able to fashion Ver Meer-esque [sic] masterpieces out of Hoffmann's cool interiors,"[10] and was referring to his *Self-Portrait in the Studio (Selbstbildnis im Atelier)*.[11] On a trip to Holland in 1903, works by the Dutch masters had left a lasting impression on him. The black-and-white checkered floor, heavy dark furniture, and the curtains of his study in the villa designed by Josef Hoffmann at Hohe Warte were perfect props for his tribute to Vermeer, complete with its skilled perspective. Moll has combined the old master's typical slant of light from the left with the Impressionists' densely juxtaposed brushstrokes, and the Secessionists' characteristic square format. He also explored his home's surrounding area in a series of woodcuts, as this technique was very well suited to the planar-decorative style of the Secession.

The Klimt Gruppe's secessionist endeavors culminated in the famous art exhibition *Kunstschau 1908* that was co-organized by Moll. In 1912 he was also involved in founding the Österreichischer Werkbund (Austrian Association of Craftsmen). During the following decades he worked intensively to promote young talents, such as Oskar Kokoschka, Anton Kolig, Egon Schiele, and Franz Wiegele, he advised Austrian museums and continued to organize successful exhibitions, including shows on behalf of the Verein der Museumsfreunde, the association of museum friends in Vienna.

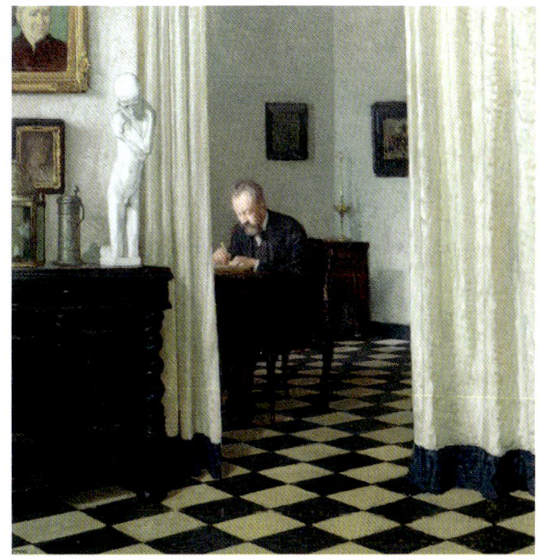

CARL MOLL
Self-Portrait in the Studio, ca. 1906
Gemäldegalerie der Akademie der bildenden Künste, Vienna

After a number of years when his art had taken a backseat to his various organizational commitments, he left Galerie Miethke in 1912 and thereafter was able to devote more time to landscape painting. On his travels to Rapallo, Algeria, and the South of France, he painted sun-drenched images such as *View of Cagnes (Ansicht von Cagnes)*, in which Moll harked back to Schindler in subject matter, but with his broad, expressive brushwork and intensive colors adopted a completely different artistic language. In 1930, when he was approaching seventy, Moll, who had a low opinion of his own artistic talent, took lessons in still-life painting from the much younger Robin Christian Andersen.

That same year he published an important monograph about his teacher Emil Jakob Schindler and organized a retrospective exhibition to mark his hundredth birthday in 1942. When Russian soldiers burst into his house in the night of April 12, 1945, Carl Moll, his daughter Maria, and son-in-law all committed suicide.[12]

1 Carl Moll, *Mein Leben*, typed manuscript, Vienna 1943, p. 20. A photocopy of the unpublished typescript can be found at the Österreichische Galerie Belvedere library. In addition to Moll's autobiography, two monographs have been published about the artist's

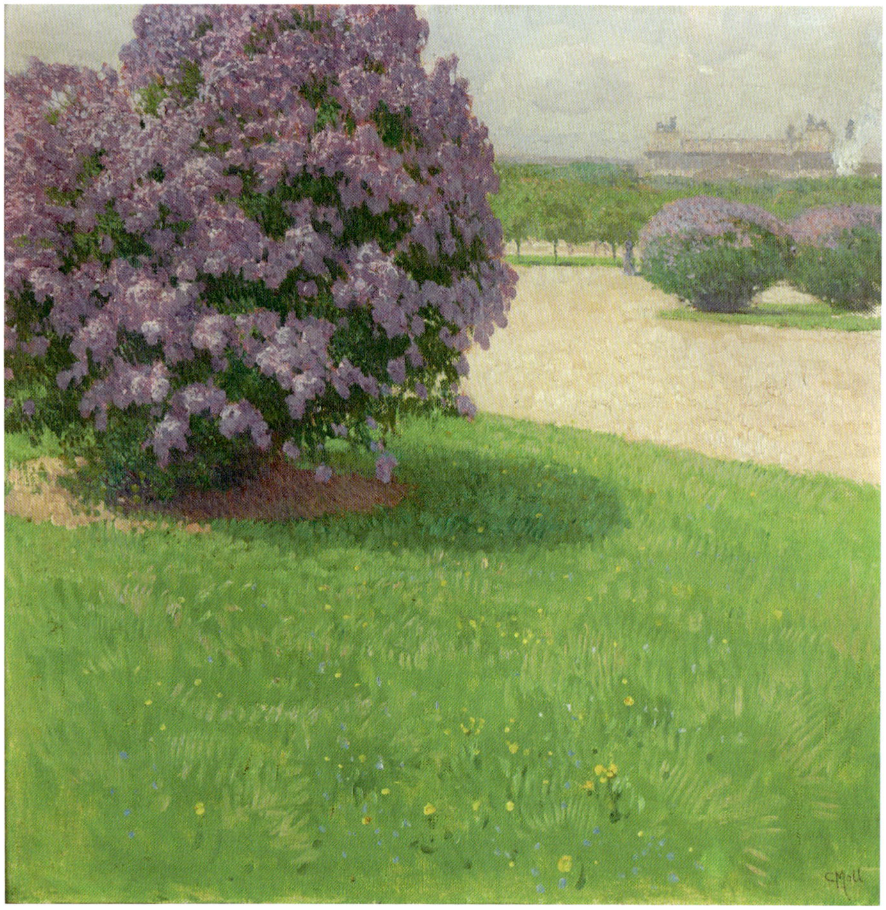

CARL MOLL
Heldenplatz with Lilac (Heldenplatz mit Flieder), ca. 1900/05
Belvedere, Vienna

RUDOLF QUITTNER
(1872 Troppau, Austrian Silesia – 1910 Neuilly-sur-Seine, France)

An Austrian Impressionist

Kathrin Wolf

When in January 1910, at the age of just thirty-seven, Rudolf Quittner[1] died of cancer in Neuilly-sur-Seine near Paris, where he had lived most of the time, one could read in his obituary that with his death "the most wonderful hopes had been taken to the grave."[2] Quittner, was "a talent that blossomed unusually quickly, had the greatest artistic prospects,"[3] another review stated.

Born in Troppau in 1873, Quittner completed his studies at the polytechnic, and then worked as a technical drawer and later as an authorized officer for his father's cloth mill. Even as a student he had enjoyed painting, so he eventually abandoned his career in the family business in order to devote himself to art. He studied at the Vienna Akademie der bildenden

life and work: Hans Dichand (ed.), *Carl Moll. Seine Freunde. Sein Leben. Sein Werk*, Salzburg 1985. – Tobias G. Natter/Gerbert Frodl (eds.), *Carl Moll (1861–1945)* (exh. cat., Österreichische Galerie Belvedere, Vienna, September 10–November 22, 1998), Vienna 1998.

2 Moll 1943 (see note 1), pp. 244–245.

3 Heinrich Fuchs, *Emil Jakob Schindler. Zeugnisse eines ungewöhnlichen Künstlerlebens. Werkkatalog*, Vienna 1970, cat. no. 343, fig. 51.

4 Carl Moll, *Emil Jakob Schindler. Eine Bildnisstudie*, Vienna 1930, p. 9.

5 Peter Weninger, "Carl Moll 1861–1945," in: idem/Peter Müller, *Die Schule von Plankenberg. Emil Jakob Schindler und der österreichische Stimmungsimpressionismus* (exh. cat., Nieder-österreichisches Landesmuseum, St. Pölten, May 16–October 13, 1991), Graz 1991, pp. 38–44, here p. 39.

6 J. Langl, "Die Jahresausstellung im Wiener Künstlerhause," in: Carl von Lützow (ed.), *Kunstchronik*, supplement to *Zeitschrift für Bildende Kunst* III, 1891/92, no. 28 (June 16, 1892), column 486; quoted from Ulla Weich, "Carl Moll (1862–1945)," in: Otmar Rychlik (ed.), *Natürlichere Natur. Österreichische Malerei des Stimmungsrealismus* (exh. cat., Kunsthaus Mürzzuschlag, Mürzzuschlag, summer exhibition 1994), Mürzzuschlag 1994, pp. 246–250, here p. 247.

7 Moll 1943 (see note 1), p. 103.

8 Gustav Mahler married Moll's stepdaughter in March 1902. Moll deeply admired the composer, "If my 'Schindler' experience had become my destiny, my second experience of equal magnitude, both in terms of art and as a person, was to be Gustav Mahler." Cf. Moll 1943 (see note 1), p. 138.

9 1899, oil on canvas, 84 x 106 cm, Staatliche Kunstsammlungen Dresden.

10 Moll 1943 (see note 1), p. 130.

11 Gerbert Frodl, "Der Maler Carl Moll. '... mein Pflänzchen Talent'," in: Natter/Frodl 1998 (see note 1), p. 13.

12 There are conflicting reports and eyewitness accounts about the circumstances surrounding the suicide.

RUDOLF QUITTNER
Saint Michel, ca. 1900
Private collection

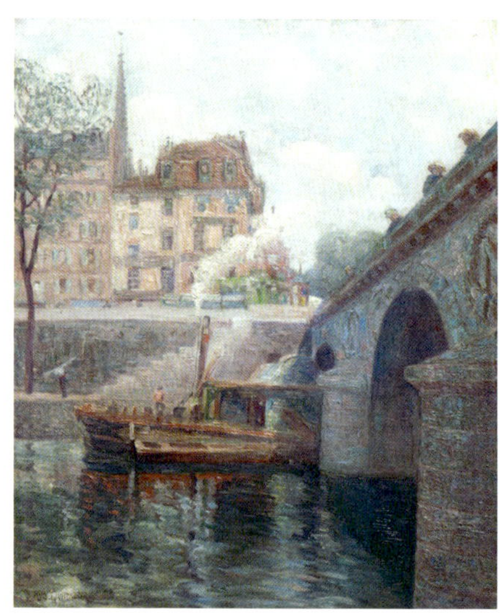

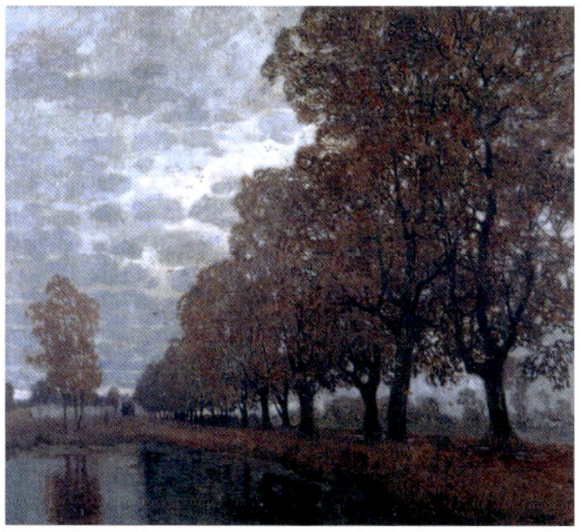

RUDOLF QUITTNER
Falling Leaves, ca. 1908
Private collection

Künste (Academy of Fine Arts),[4] before finally moving to Paris, where he enrolled at the acclaimed Académie Julian. Quittner himself claimed that he had learned landscape painting from Camille Pissarro, and he traveled for his artistic studies through Europe, North Africa, the Middle East, as well as North America and Canada. He returned intermittently to Paris where he found "support and valuable artistic advice"[5] from the Norwegian painter Fritz Thaulow and from Claude Monet (see fig. p. 47). The influence of Monet and Pissarro, as well as Henri Le Sidaner and Paul Signac, can indeed be detected in Quittner's oeuvre. Atmospheric effects of air and light and (Post-)Impressionistic brushwork are defining features of his landscapes. His choice of subject matter was similar to his French colleagues: views of Paris, crowded boulevards, boats and bridges on the Seine, and atmospheric rural scenes in France, Bohemia, Moravia, and Austria. Often his cropped views seem to have been randomly selected—a typically impressionist compositional device. Sometimes Quittner adopted a palette tending to pastel shades and used generous brushwork; in other paintings, however, his colors are muted, although his striking, densely juxtaposed mass of brushstrokes conveys a shimmering, pointillist overall effect.

As of 1901, Quittner started spending more time in Vienna; in 1905 he became a member of its Genossenschaft der bildenden Künstler (Vienna Artists' Cooperative) and his work featured at almost every Künstlerhaus exhibition thereafter.[6] In 1906 he was awarded the Golden State Medal, and in 1908 he received the Archduke Karl Ludwig Medal for his painting *Falling Leaves (Fallende Blätter).*

Quittner also contributed to exhibitions in Berlin, Dresden, Düsseldorf, Munich, and Venice, where, in 1908, King Victor Emmanuel bought his painting *Railway Train (Der Eisenbahnzug)* and gave it to the modern art museum there. Furthermore, the artist often exhibited at the Salon des Artistes Français in Paris, where he was given an honorable mention in 1907 and nominated *officier de l'académie.*

Shortly after Quittner died, the Künstlerhaus organized an exhibition of his estate in 1910.[7] In the following year, Galerie Georges Petit showed paintings by Quittner in Paris.[8] After this exhibition, French painter Julien Bucas sued the deceased Austrian artist, accusing him of plagiarism. Bucas made allegations that Quittner, claiming to be a collector, had frequently bought his paintings, scratched Bucas's

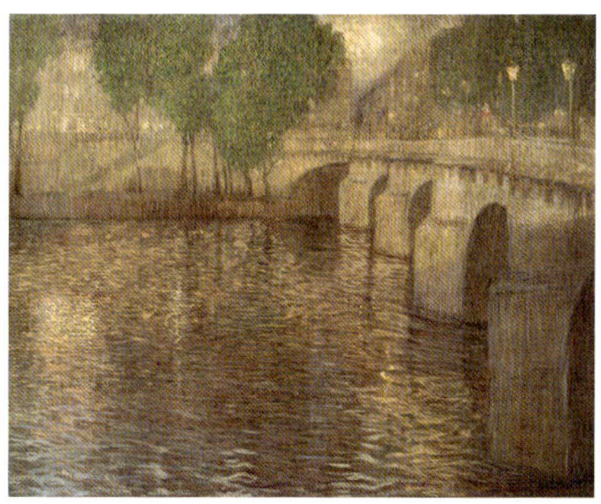

RUDOLF QUITTNER
Pont Neuf, ca. 1900
Private collection

signature from the canvas replacing it with his own, and submitted these to the Salon as his own work.[9] House searches and statements from acquaintances, colleagues, and Quittner's wife followed.[10] Verdict was passed in Paris in 1914, judging Quittner to be a plagiarist.[11] However, it is quite conceivable that Bucas, previously an unknown artist, was using this scandal to attract public attention to his work (especially in light of the fact that he raised these allegations after Quittner's death). The French press vehemently backed Bucas, while, as is only to be expected, the Austrian media took Quittner's side.

1 In addition to the newspaper articles cited below, documents in the following archives provided sources for this essay: Österreichische Galerie Belvedere Archive, Vienna, estate of Hans Ankwicz-Kleehoven. – Österreichische Galerie Belvedere Archive, Vienna, estate of Rudolf Schmidt. – Künstlerhaus Archive, Vienna.

2 Adalbert Franz Seligmann, "Künstlerhaus," in: *Neue Freie Presse*, no. 16610, November 18, 1910.

3 Ludwig Hevesi, in: *Kunstchronik. Wochenschrift für Kunst und Kunstgewerbe*, N. F., 21, 1910, p. 229.

4 Hevesi 1910 (see note 3). In his own résumé, Quittner does not mention that he studied at the Vienna Academy (see note 5).

5 Quittner's application to the Genossenschaft der bildenden Künstler Wiens of January 10, 1905, Künstlerhaus Archive, Vienna, Rudolf Quittner file. In his accompanying letter, Quittner described his career. However, his claims have yet to be verified by other sources. Bénézit mentions that Quittner was a student of Thaulow and Sisley; Thieme-Becker, on the other hand, cites Thaulow and Pissarro as his teachers.

6 The Künstlerhaus is the building where the organization held its exhibitions and was often used as the name of the association itself.

7 *Herbstausstellung und Gedächtnisausstellung Carl Freiherr v. Merode und Rudolf Quittner* (exh. cat., Künstlerhaus, Vienna, November 13, 1910), Vienna 1910, pp. 38–39.

8 Cf. review in *L'art et les artistes*, vol. 14, 1911/12, pp. 133–34.

9 Cf. e.g. *Neue Freie Presse*, no. 16965, November 13, 1911, p. 7. – *Le Figaro*, no. 316, November 12, 1911, p. 3.

10 Cf. *Neues Wiener Journal*, no. 6489, November 14, 1911, p. 3. – *Neue Freie Presse*, no. 16966, November 14, 1911, p. 10. – *Le Figaro*, no. 329, November 25, 1911, p. 4.

11 Cf. the entry in Wladimir Aichelburg, "Mitglieder-Gesamtverzeichnis des Wiener Künstlerhauses," in: idem, *150 Jahre Künstlerhaus Wien 1861–2011*, 2011, http://www.wladimir-aichelburg.at/kuenstlerhaus/mitglieder/verzeichnisse/mitglieder-gesamtverzeichnis/ (accessed June 20, 2014). Here the following comment was added "Mysterious; August Schaeffer von Wienwald believed he was innocent."

RUDOLF RIBARZ
(1848 Vienna – 1904 Vienna)

"[...] a ray of sunlight from Monet [...]" "

The Artist Who Brought a Taste of France to Austria

Irina Katnik

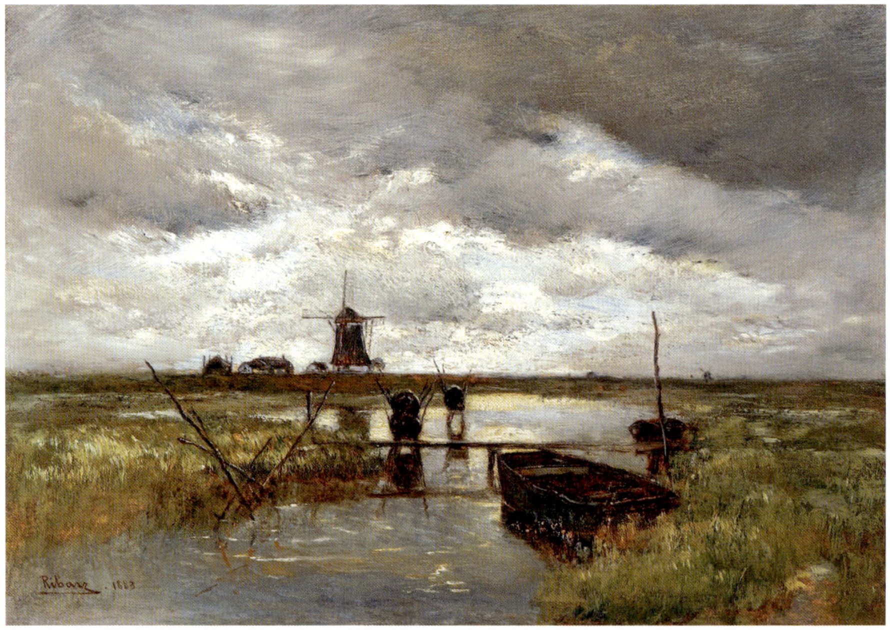

RUDOLF RIBARZ
Dutch Canal with Windmill, 1883
Private collection

In his obituary of Rudolf Ribarz on November 14, 1904, the *Neue Freie Presse* critic Adalbert Franz Seligmann described him as one of "the few Viennese artists in whose studio a ray of sunlight from Monet fell."[1] This was a remarkable appraisal and a great compliment. What was behind it?

Ribarz, "an amiable artist, an honest man, a good colleague," was extremely popular with artist friends and acquaintances, and contemporaries described him as a "highly respected, diligent man, who loved practically nothing more than his profession."[2] He was born on May 30 in the revolutionary year of 1848 on what is now Kohlmarkt in Vienna, the son of a successful wholesaler. He was expected to follow in his forebears' footsteps and take over the family business,[3] and after completing his schooling in 1861, he did indeed enroll in the Handelsakademie (commercial college), but he quickly discovered that his real passion was art. He is thought to have studied as a twelve-year-old with Josef Holzer, a traditional Biedermeier Viennese painter, and therefore, after completing the Handelsakademie, decided on a completely different career. From 1864 until the end of his studies in 1869, he was also enrolled as an ordinary student at the Akademie der bildenden Künste (Academy of Fine Arts) in Vienna, rubbing shoulders with the likes of Emil Jakob Schindler, Eugen Jettel, Robert Russ, and Adolf Ditscheiner.[4] Their teacher was regarded as modern and progressive, with a preference for *plein air* or outdoor painting. Albert August Zimmermann traveled every year with his students to the Berchtesgaden region, where between 1864 and 1869 Ribarz completed countless nature studies, drawings, and oil paintings of the changing mountain landscape. During this time he developed his predilection for powerful dark and light contrasts and the interaction of blue and green. Apart from nature studies, the courses at the Akademie also involved analyses of the school's own collection of seventeenth-century Dutch painting.

INITIAL SUCCESS

In September 1868, Rudolf Ribarz exhibited a work for the first time at the third "Allgemeine Wiener Kunstausstellung" (General Viennese Art Exhibition) to mark the opening of the newly built Künstlerhaus. That same year he joined the Genossenschaft bildender Künstler (Vienna Artists' Cooperative), to which he remained loyal until his death, refusing to switch to the Secession, as many of his contemporaries did. The following year, along with Jettel, Russ, and Schindler, he exhibited three works at the first *International Art Exhibition* in Munich, where a number of French *plein air* artists were also to be seen, including Gustave Courbet, Camille Corot, and Constant Troyon, whose modern interpretation of nature caused a furor. Ribarz was already being seen as a representative of *paysage intime*, a painting style that concentrated on simple and intimate views of nature and, with its *plein air* painting, was a forerunner of Impressionism. A discourse to mark the opening of the Künstlerhaus in Vienna in 1869 stated, "(Albert August Zimmermann's) talented students Jettel, Russ, Schindler, and Ribarz prove to be great supporters of atmospheric landscapes in the French *paysage intime* style."[5] Impressed by the French painting style, Ribarz wanted to visit Paris, but out of moral principles his father refused to support him.

In the following years Ribarz therefore spent his time in Austria and Ramsau near Berchtesgaden. Later he went as far as Venice, where he obtained inspiration for the Italian subjects presented at the 1873 World's Fair in Vienna.[6] In 1875 he went with a recommendation from the Dutch painter Remi van Haanen to the sculptor

Charles van der Stappen in Brussels. There he met the painters of the Hague School, exhibiting two works the same year at the exhibition "Tentoonstelling van Kunstwerken van levende Meister" (Exhibition of Works by Living Masters) in The Hague.[7]

THE PARIS YEARS

After his father's death and settling of business matters, Ribarz was finally able in 1876 to fulfill his dream and move to Paris, where he stayed until 1892 and met up again with his student friend Eugen Jettel, who had been in Paris since 1873. With Jettel's help he was able to meet the Austrian and German artists in Paris, represented at this time by the Austrian art dealer Charles Sedelmeyer. Tina Blau and Theodor von Hörmann were also living in Paris. Later Charles Daubigny and Jules Dupré joined Ribarz's circle of acquaintances and introduced him to the Barbizon School. Daubigny is supposed to have said to him, "My dear man, you draw very well but you try too hard to capture the object itself rather than what you see with your eyes."[8] Ribarz first started showing works at international exhibitions in 1877. At the Paris Salon his first picture was *View of Dordrecht* (*Ansicht von Dordrecht*). Showings in Munich, Vienna, Berlin, and Venice, and at the World's Fairs in Paris (1889), Chicago (1893), and Antwerp (1894) were to follow. He joined the Paris artists' association Société nationale des beaux-arts in the mid-1880s and turned, as he put it, to "*Kraut- und Rüben-Malerei*" ("cabbage and turnip painting"), still-life flower and fruit pictures inspired by the Japonism of the time.[9] The Austrian portrait and genre painter Eduard Charlemont invited him to collaborate in painting the ceiling of the Burgtheater in Vienna, a work that was very well received. In March 1891, Ribarz married Marie-Louise Schorer from Switzerland, seven years his junior; the marriage was childless.

LAST YEARS IN VIENNA

In spite of his long absence, Ribarz was offered a professorship in flower painting at the Kunstgewerbeschule (School of Applied Arts) in 1892, a position he held until 1899. In 1896 he was curator of the Austrian section of the applied arts exhibition in Brussels and was a member of the art council of the Austrian Ministry of Education, to which his close friend Robert Russ also belonged. In 1897 an extensive collective exhibition of his works was staged by the Künstlerhaus for the first time since his return.

Following further trips and awards, including the Gold Medal at the World's Fair in Paris, Ribarz withdrew from the art scene on account of a degenerative nervous disorder. Partly for health reasons and partly because of the new fashions and changes in art following the founding of the Secession in 1897, he retired from teaching in 1899. His successor at the Kunstgewerbeschule was Koloman Moser.

Ribarz remained loyal to the Artists' Cooperative and declined to identify with the aims of the Secession and Hagenbund. Around 1900 he was awarded the Knight's Cross of the Order of Franz Joseph for his services as a teacher.

RUDOLF RIBARZ
French Town with a Bridge over the River,
undated
Private collection

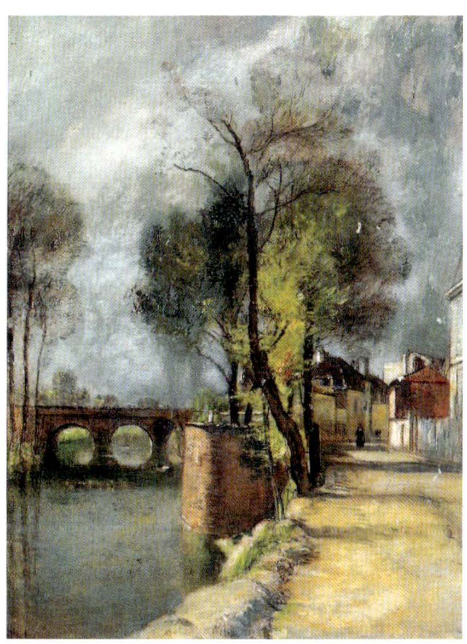

In his last years he painted with flagging energy primarily in the area surrounding Vienna, in the Waldviertel, and on the Chiemsee. He died after a long illness on November 12, 1904. The following year his estate was auctioned at Galerie Miethke in Vienna. In accordance with Ribarz's own wish, a commemorative exhibition devoted to him and curated by Karl Karger and Carl Moll was held in 1906 at the Künstlerhaus in Vienna, bringing together pictures that were dispersed throughout Austria and other countries.

WORKS

In the mid-1860s, when Rudolf Ribarz entered the Akademie in Vienna, artists throughout Europe were beginning to concentrate on depictions of nature and the light and weather conditions found in it. In this way, landscape painting became one of the main themes of the late nineteenth century.

Through the exhibitions in the Künstlerhaus and the 1873 World's Fair, Austrian artists were able to obtain a good idea of French painting and the *paysage intime* style. "Rudolf Ribarz handles the brush completely in the style of Courbet; in his *Fish Market in Chioggia* (*Fischmarkt in Chioggia*), however, his realism reaches the limits of what is acceptable," was the comment at the World's Fair in Vienna.[10]

The years in Paris must have been particularly important for Ribarz, because he was able there to study French painting on the spot and in direct contact with French artist colleagues. He was actively involved in the Paris art scene and exhibited in the official Salon.

Influenced initially by the fine painting of the Biedermeier era, Ribarz managed with time to acquire a freer and partly impressionistic style. The cropping of nature that already marked many works by Claude Monet also dominated in his pictures.[11]

Clear parallels to Monet can be seen particularly in *Dutch Canal with Windmill* (*Holländischer Kanal mit Windmühle*) and *Ships in the Harbor* (*Schiffe im Hafen*; fig. p. 43), not

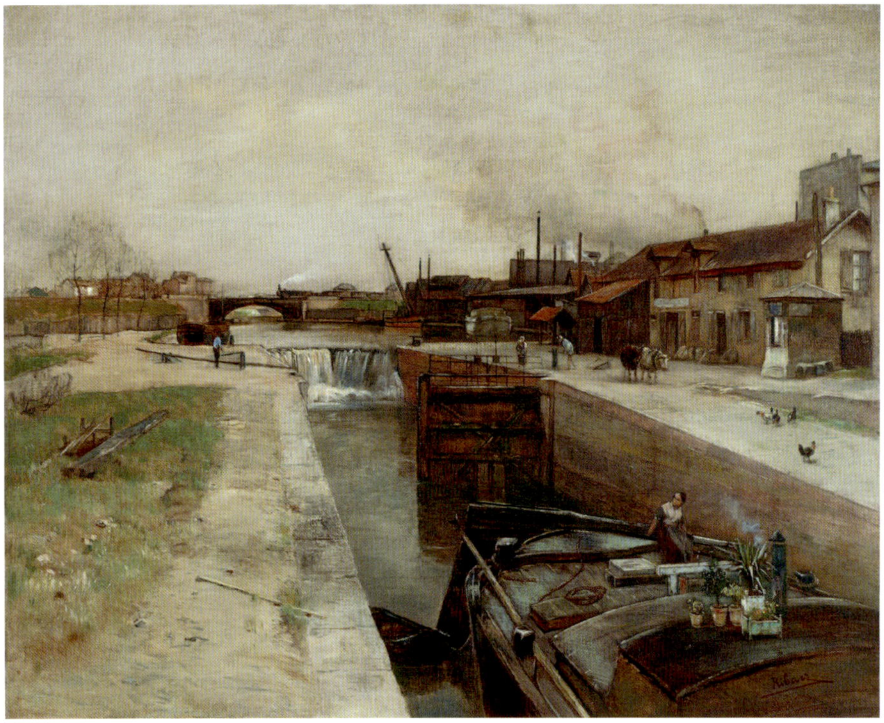

RUDOLF RIBARZ
Lock on Canal Saint-Denis (Schleuse am Kanal von St. Denis), 1883
Belvedere, Vienna

only in terms of the subjects but also in the representation of light and shadow. The pictures make it seem as if Ribarz had attempted to capture his first direct impression of nature. He also chose subjects from the *vie moderne*, as in *Lock on Canal Saint-Denis* (Schleuse am *Kanal von St. Denis*), whose bold scene selection shows not only the lock, sailors and lockkeepers, but also the smoking chimneys in the background and a railway bridge in the distance, on which a steam train is crossing the canal.

Ribarz learned to focus on atmosphere and mood using a subtle modeling brushstroke. His impasto painting style was loose and sought to capture the slightest light reflections. The subjects of Ribarz's pictures are also similar to the French painters': in the 1870s in particular he painted landscapes of the northern French coast and the Netherlands, windmills, boats, and bridges. His second creative period starting toward the end of the 1880s produced masterly depictions of plants, while "in the background," as Ludwig Hevesi formulated it in his inimitable way, "something landscape-like evaporates."[12] The result was a number of pictures that reflected the specifically Austrian version of a nearsighted view of nature and ultimately established Ribarz as a genuine Viennese painter.

1 Adalbert Franz Seligmann, "Maler Rudolf Ribarz," in: *Neue Freie Presse*, November 14, 1904, p. 8.
2 Ibid.
3 All biographical details in this essay were taken from the following publication: Martina Haja, *Rudolf Ribarz 1848–1904. Ein Maler des österreichischen Stimmungsimpressionismus* (exh. cat., Österreichische Galerie Belvedere, Vienna, August 29–October 29, 1978), Vienna 1978.
4 Akademie der bildenden Künste Wien, archive of former students, lists of students in landscape class from 1860 to 1869.
5 *Zeitschrift für bildende Kunst* IV, Leipzig 1869, p. 259.
6 *Officieller Kunst-Catalog der Welt-Ausstellung 1873 in Wien*, 3rd ed., Vienna 1873.
7 Andrea Winklbauer, "Rudolf Ribarz (1848–1904)," in: Roland Dorn/Klaus Albrecht Schröder/John Sillevis (ed.), *Van Gogh und die Haager Schule* (exh. cat., Bank Austria Kunstforum, Vienna, February 28–May 27, 1996), Vienna 1996, p. 349.
8 Quoted from Andrea Winklbauer, "Rudolf Ribarz (1848–1904)," in: Otmar Rychlik (ed.), *Natürlichere Natur. Österreichische Malerei des Stimmungsrealismus* (exh. cat., Kunsthaus Mürzzuschlag, Mürzzuschlag, summer exhibition 1994), Mürzzuschlag 1994, pp. 232–235.
9 Martina Haja, "'Kraut und Rüben'. Beobachtungen zur österreichischen Freilicht-Malerei im späten 19. Jahrhundert," in: *Mitteilungen der Österreichischen Galerie* 30, no. 74, Vienna 1986, pp. 43–66.
10 *Kunstchronik* 9, 1874, p. 44, quoted from Andrea Winklbauer, "Impressionismus contra Stimmung" (see note 8), pp. 14–21, here p. 16.
11 Elke Doppler, *Zur künstlerischen Rezeption Ferdinand Georg Waldmüllers*, diss., Vienna 2007, p. 186.
12 Ludwig Hevesi, *Österreichische Kunst im 19. Jahrhundert, zweiter Teil: 1848–1900*, Leipzig 1903, p. 260.

EMIL JAKOB SCHINDLER
(1842 Vienna – 1892 Sylt)

A Painter of Poetic Realism

Peter Peer

In a period spanning just over two decades, Emil Jakob Schindler produced an extensive oeuvre that is regarded as the epitome of the style known in late-nineteenth-century Austrian landscape painting as *Stimmungsimpressionismus* (Atmospheric Impressionism).[1] Schindler studied with an artist who worked in a completely different style: Albert August Zimmermann, who was a major exponent of Alpine painting. Zimmermann—from the circle of Carl Rottmann in Munich—had succeeded Franz Steinfeld as head of the landscape class at the Vienna Akademie der bildenden Künste (Academy of Fine Arts) in 1859, a post he would hold until 1871. Schindler studied in Zimmermann's class from 1860 to 1868 together with other artists who would later become important exponents of atmospheric painting, such as Eugen Jettel, Rudolf Ribarz, and Robert Russ. Zimmermann had taken the progressive step of introducing open-air painting as part of the curriculum and took his students on excursions in the summer months to paint in Salzburg and Berchtesgaden. These walks resulted in paintings of forest streams and mills, as well as panoramic landscapes of the Alpine foothills, reminiscent of works by Rottmann. Schindler would tackle all of these motifs later on, too, although with an entirely different approach.

At the end of the 1860s, the younger painters turned away from Alpine painting. Schindler criticized the genre because, on the one hand, he rejected the theatrical choreography and, on the other, he considered the atmospheric conditions of the high mountains as incompatible with his aesthetic ideals of tonal painting. He was particularly critical of the intense local colors on account of the clear air.[2] "The mountainscape appears in exhibition rooms or fairly well-lit homes rather like traditional mountain costumes at a city station: untruthful, ridiculously and self-importantly isolated, and more,"[3] Schindler noted in his theoretical writings.

Alpine painting, however, had two characteristics that suited Schindler's artistic nature and the romantic aspect of the *paysage intime* in general. On the one hand, it captured nature unspoilt by man and, on the other, it represented an unfathomable expanse of space, often supported by a focus toward a distant view on a low horizon. The former reflected a generally prevalent escapism, a yearning for a bygone, preindustrial age. The latter was a symbol for the infinity of the Creation, a romantic reflex in reaction to the sociocultural crisis of identity in the nineteenth century. Moreover, Schindler was a great admirer of Andreas Achenbach, who, with his brother Oswald, was one of the leading masters from the Düsseldorf School, widely famed for its highly dramatic and monumental scenes of nature.

Schindler belonged to the circle of young artists who transformed Austrian landscape painting as part of the style known as *Stimmungsimpressionismus*. A major influence behind this trend came from the French *paysage intime*, which had become well known outside of France in the 1860s. Schindler greatly admired French painters, "Of the modern painters it is Rousseau who combined all good qualities, all great art, all periods [...] He did not seek out nature in order to rule but to serve. His technique was so perfect that it became completely invisible until finally dissolving into the process of nature entirely [...] He is the first landscape painter ever to have lived who was superior to nature itself."[4] He described Corot as the unrivaled "master of linear beauty," a "painter of the greatest of joys, beauty itself," and saw in his hues a "silver sonorous poetry of colors."[5] Schindler had probably seen only a few works by Corot, and yet one feels there are some of the French artist's traits in his work. In Schindler's paintings, too, muted shades of blue and gray tend to dominate the overall color scheme, and he indicated leaves blowing in the treetops using similar, delicate brushstrokes.

It was not only the characteristic painting styles of French artists that were influential; their subject matter became fashionable as well (fig. 2). Broad expanses of flat panoramic

EMIL JAKOB SCHINDLER
The Steamer Station on the Danube opposite Kaisermühlen, ca. 1871/72
Belvedere, Vienna

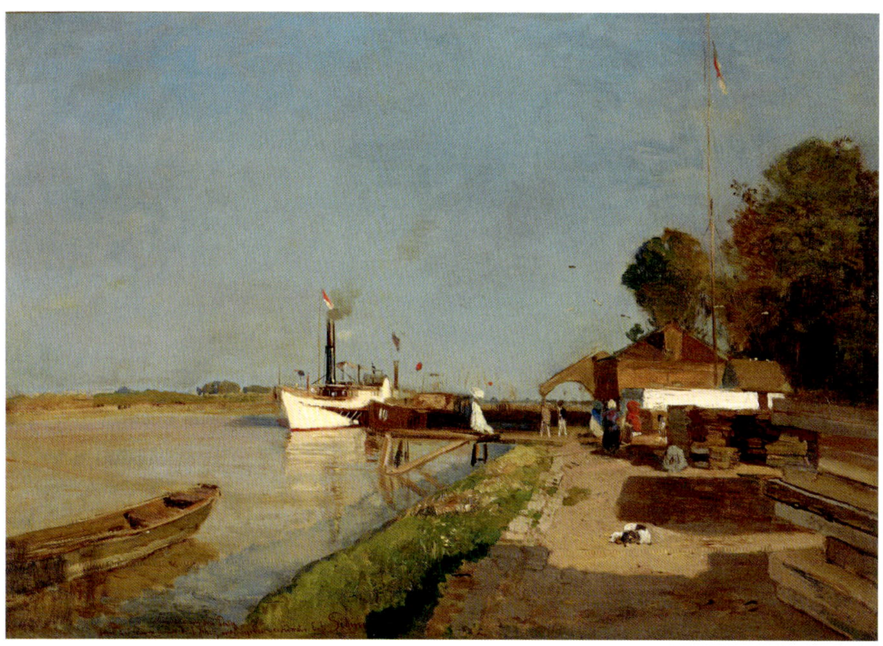

landscapes, rivers and meadows, and typically "Dutch" landscapes with windmills on the horizon occur, as do relatively secluded scenes—glimpses into forests with deserted paths or clearings in riverside woods with glassy ponds. Water as the vehicle of atmosphere also plays an important role in Schindler's landscapes. One of the painter's specialities was the depiction of mills—a motif he had started tackling in his student days and now developed using the new expressive means of the *paysage intime* (fig. 3).

During the 1870s, Schindler traveled abroad on a number of occasions—to Holland in 1875 (with Tina Blau), to Paris in 1881, among other destinations—seeking, like many other artists, suitably "poetic" subject matter. Yet apart from these years, Schindler spent the majority of his life in Austria. To find subjects for his paintings he mainly explored the Danube water meadows near Vienna at Fischamend, Haslau, and in the Prater, where in 1874 he took on a studio in one of the pavilions previously used for the World's Fair. In the early 1880s, he spent several summers in Lundenburg an der Thaya (today Břeclav, Czech Republic; see fig. p. 147) and at Bad Goisern in Upper Austria. As of 1885 he lived with his family[6] and a small circle of students (including Carl Moll, Marie Egner, and Olga Wisinger-Florian) at Schloss Plankenberg near Tulln in Lower Austria. Contemporaries described Schindler as sociable, although he was often plagued with doubts about his art and beset with existential fears. The years between 1878 and 1880 were overshadowed by worries about providing for his family. In his diary he repeatedly lamented his dire financial straits, "At last the letter with 50 Gulden arrived. That doesn't help me at all; it's not enough to live or die from—as usual."[7] By the early 1880s, however, there was a marked shift toward greater stability in his life. Recent research has conclusively revealed that Schindler enjoyed a successful career as an artist with all the triumphs and appropriate income this entailed.[8] His working methods were geared toward the market, as was the case with most painters.[9] When requested he would paint replicas of particularly successful subjects. He also created variations of the same motif in different weathers or times of day to cater for the special wishes of his clientele. Appealing motifs that had proven popular on the market could thus be sold many a time in slightly adapted versions. In spite of this, he wrestled with his situation, as his repeated complaints demonstrate. This could be explained by the fact that he was in the shadow of his celebrated friend Hans Makart, an artist who earned princely sums.[10] After Schindler's sudden death on the island of Sylt in 1892, he was given a grave of honor at Vienna's central cemetery, and a monument in the city's Stadtpark commemorates his life.

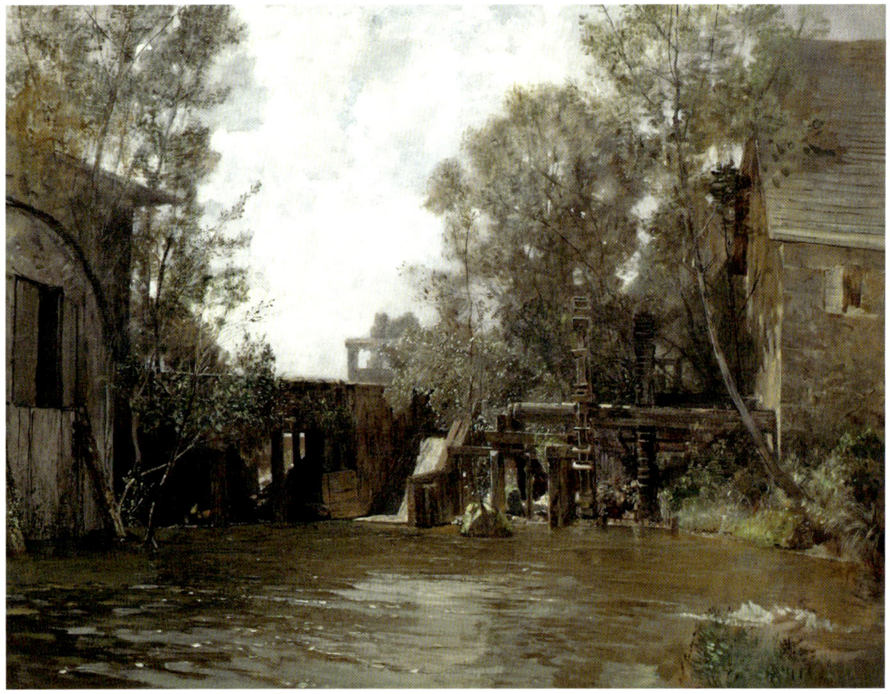

EMIL JAKOB SCHINDLER
Mill in Plankenberg, 1890
Wien Museum

SCHINDLER'S ARTISTIC APPROACH "NATURE GAVE US LOOKING—BUT ART TEACHES US TO SEE"[11]

Just how Emil Jakob Schindler went about expressing his inner vision in his pictures was recounted years later by his student and friend Carl Moll, "Again I observed Schindler's painting-before-nature—so very different from Waldmüller's way of working, whom he accuses of copying the scene piece by piece. He is painting the 'bridge,' the silvery water with bridge and willow bush. In the background the mass of the Saarstein mountain weighs heavily on the light tones of the foreground. Schindler paints, and the bush becomes trees, the Saarstein clouds. He sees his picture from within, taking from the outside world only what fits the painting."[12]

Schindler was undoubtedly the preeminent figure in Austrian atmospheric painting. Ludwig Hevesi saw the "progress of the Viennese landscape" as being connected primarily with his name and regarded him as the "master of the Viennese atmospheric landscape."[13] Schindler himself described his artistic approach as "poetic realism," borrowing a term from contemporary literature.[14] This maintained that an artwork should not simply illustrate external reality but should compellingly capture its essential characteristics. "But the closer art pushes toward nature, the more it loses itself and only with difficulty can it then find itself again,"[15] Schindler warned, adding, "From the first lines in pencil to the first picture, I presumed a period of ten years to be normal. If by then it has become clear to the student how to probe nature, after reading it in great depth, and thus create an artwork, it has become clear to him that art's truth is not real but parallel, it has become clear that a picture is not a mirror image but […] a noble dream image, and then he can enter the temple of art."

From a poetic point of view, the world occupies a central position somewhere between the objective truth of things and the "law our spirit compels us to impose […] 'Naturalists' are more concerned with diversity, 'idealists' more with unity. These two directions are one-sided, 'artistic realism' unifies them in one artistic center,"[16] Otto Ludwig, a proponent of this concept in literature, noted. This, in essence, outlines Schindler's approach, too. It was his concern, "to arrive at the work of art through nature and beyond," and to extract "the artistic act out of natural elements."[17] It is worth noting that, at roughly the same time, Friedrich Theodor and Robert Vischer were exploring this way of observing nature in their theories about the aesthetics of empathy.[18]

Schindler's diaries and his fragmentary writings about landscape painting also offer glimpses of his view of nature and the world. Experiencing nature held deep metaphysical significance at a time when age-old convictions about the world and the role of humanity were being questioned in light of groundbreaking scientific discoveries. Schindler explained that "an awareness of the wish for a God […]," must surely stem from "the unconscious feeling of our planet oscillating and floating through space." It is the "wish for a nail to which it is perhaps somehow secured."[19] Landscape painting also acts as a symbolic vehicle of a spiritual awareness of nature, which at the same time corresponds with the yearning for traditional certainties.

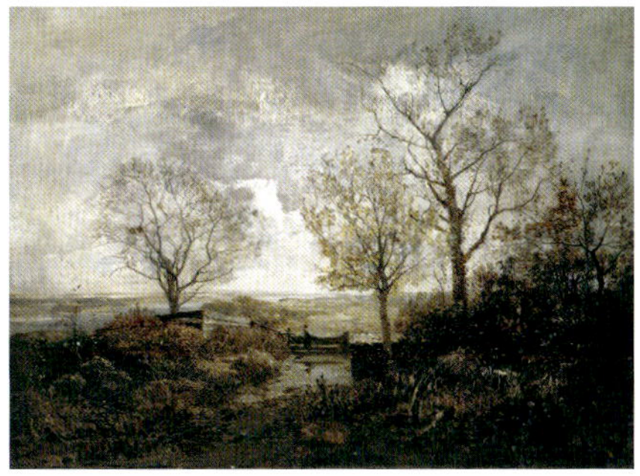

EMIL JAKOB SCHINDLER
Autumnal Landscape by a River, ca. 1887/88
Belvedere, Vienna

1 A biography by Martina Haja, with many details about Emil Jakob Schindler's life, can be found in Gerbert Frodl/Verena Traeger (eds.), *Stimmungsimpressionismus* (exh. cat., Belvedere, Vienna, March 17–July 4, 2004), Vienna 2004, pp. 196–198.
2 Heinrich Fuchs, *Emil Jakob Schindler. Zeugnisse eines ungewöhnlichen Künstlerlebens. Werkkatalog*, Vienna 1970, p. 23.
3 Elisabeth Edith Kamenicek, *Emil Jakob Schindler (1842–1892). Sein schriftliches Werk im Kontext von Kunsthandel, Mäzenatentum und Kunstkritik seiner Zeit*, diss., Salzburg 2002, vol. II, p. 297.
4 Kamenicek 2002 (see note 3), pp. 325–326.
5 Carl Moll, *Emil Jakob Schindler 1842–1892. Eine Bildnisstudie*, Vienna 1930, pp. 48, 53.
6 Schindler married the Hamburg-born singer Anna Bergen in 1879. They had two daughters: Alma (1879–1964), later wife of Gustav Mahler and Franz Werfel, and Grete (1880–1912).
7 Moll 1930 (see note 5), pp. 21–22.
8 Martina Haja, "Emil Jakob Schindler. Künstlerlegende versus Faktografie," in: Frodl/Traeger 2004 (see note 1), pp. 263–267.
9 Kamenicek 2002 (see note 3), p. 273.
10 Haja 2004 (see note 8), p. 267.
11 Emil Jakob Schindler, quoted from Kamenicek 2002 (see note 3), p. 232.
12 Moll 1930 (see note 5), p. 39.
13 Ludwig Hevesi, *Österreichische Kunst des 19. Jahrhunderts*, 2 vols., Leipzig 1903, p. 254.
14 Harald Fischel, "Emil Jakob Schindler," in: *Zeitschrift für bildende Kunst*, N. F., no. 9, p. 102. Cf. also Alexander Klee, "Paysage intime – Stimmung – Poetischer Realismus," in: Agnes Husslein-Arco/Alexander Klee (eds.), *Emil Jakob Schindler. Poetischer Realismus* (exh. cat., Belvedere, Vienna, September 27, 2012–January 13, 2013), Munich 2012, pp. 9–24.
15 Kamenicek 2002 (see note 3), p. 288.
16 Otto Ludwig, "Der Poetische Realismus," in: idem., *Werke*, ed. by Arthur Eloesser, part 4: *Dramatische Studien*, Berlin 1908, pp. 319–320, quoted from Andreas Huyssen (ed.), *Bürgerlicher Realismus* (= Die deutsche Literatur. Ein Abriß in Text und Darstellung, ed. by Otto F. Best and Hans-Jürgen Schmitt, vol. 11), 2nd ed., Stuttgart 1999, pp. 45–46.
17 Quoted from Fuchs 1970 (see note 2), p. 25.
18 Markus Fellinger, "Naturanschauung bei Adalbert Stifter und Emil Jakob Schindler," in: Husslein-Arco/Klee 2012 (see note 14), p. 47.
19 Fuchs 1970 (see note 2), p. 27.

MAX SUPPANTSCHITSCH
(1865 Vienna –
1953 Krems an der Donau)

"[He] had a special reputation as a painter of idyllic regions"[1]

Kathrin Wolf

Vienna-born artist Maximilian Suppantschitsch studied at the Vienna Akademie der bildenden Künste (Academy of Fine Arts) under Eduard Peithner von Lichtenfels from 1884 to 1891. It was in his class that he first visited Weißenkirchen in the Wachau in 1886.[2] This section of the Danube between Krems and Melk, with its southern, almost Mediterranean light and colors, was a true El Dorado for a multitude of painters in the nineteenth century. Starting with the *vedute* painters Laurenz Janscha, Rudolf von Alt and his father Jakob Alt, then British artist J.M.W. Turner, Orientalist Leopold Carl Müller, and later the atmospheric painters Emil Jakob Schindler, Tina Blau, and Marie Egner, artists came to this picturesque region of the Danube in quest of tranquil, atmospheric scenes of nature, seeking an alternative to the heroic mountains and urban cityscapes.[3] "[...] Close to the metropolis, not such a long way to meander upstream, the Wachau offers landscapists an abundance of motifs; the romantic Danube valley, rich in legends and still unspoilt with all its natural beauties, holds the same significance for Vienna as the Forest of Fontainebleau for Paris and Dachau for Munich."[4]

In the summer of 1888, Suppantschitsch joined the "legendary" Dürnstein excursion of the Lichtenfels School.[5] The writer Hermine Cloeter,[6] who made a lifelong study of the Wachau and its painters, recounted the following about this study trip, "[There] were a lot of young people gathered around the master with earnest ambition and the frivolity of youthful joy and madness. All sorts of yarns are told here about the harebrained activities of boisterous young artists, to whom, back then, the whole world, or at least the whole of the Wachau, belonged."[7] Hans Wilt, Johann Nepomuk Geller, and Heinrich Tomek were among the artists on this trip with Suppantschitsch.[8] In 1889/90 and 1892, this was followed by further sojourns in Dürnstein. Often choosing the same motifs as his teacher Lichtenfels, Suppantschitsch's work moved toward the poetic realism of Emil Jakob Schindler, who wanted to take him on as a student, a plan that was thwarted by Schindler's sudden death in 1892.[9]

Most of Lichtenfels's students remained attached to the Wachau all through their lives; some even moved there permanently. The majority of these Wachau painters were originally from Vienna's art scene, and, around 1900, a high proportion of them were members of the artists' association, the Hagenbund.[10] "The Wachau painters are a body of their own, exponents of a late Romantic, discerning style of painting, placing an emphasis on atmospheric, Impressionist effects while maintaining truth to nature. In some ways they represent similar tendencies to the young Hagenbund, but they are, above all, a group of painters who surrendered themselves completely to the unique magic and beauty of the Wachau landscape."[11] Suppantschitsch belonged to the Hagenbund from 1900 to 1905, too, and he was a member of the Vienna Künstlerhaus both before and after. There can be no doubt that he was the most important of the Wachau painters. Always drawn to paint in this region as a young man, later on he moved there permanently. From 1897 he lived in Rossatzbach, and later at the former Poor Clare's convent in Dürnstein, where he was made an honorary citizen in 1935. In old age he finally withdrew in the summer months to Dürnstein's Augustinian monastery (from 1944).[12] In winter he would move to the inn "Zum Richard Löwenherz," where the Thiery family treated him as one of their own.

His masterpiece *At the Weißenkirchner Gate*

MAXIMILIAN SUPPANTSCHITSCH
At the Weißenkirchner Gate in Dürnstein, 1890
Landesmuseum Niederösterreich, St. Pölten

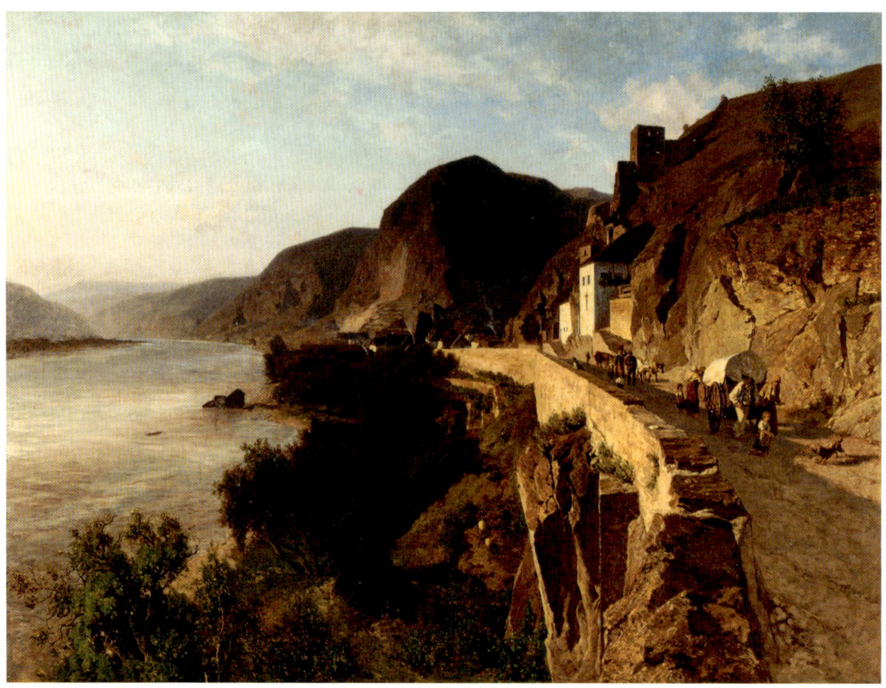

in Dürnstein (Beim Weißenkirchnertor in Dürnstein) was probably based on an assignment Lichtenfels set during an excursion in 1890. Its subtle use of light and color already suggests the influence of Emil Jakob Schindler. In 1908 this painting, then titled *In the Romantic Land (Im Lande der Romantik)*, was awarded the Small Golden State Medal at the Emperor's jubilee exhibition.[13]

By the time he had completed his studies at the academy, Suppantschitsch had already gained a reputation as an excellent painter and graphic artist. Study trips took him to Italy (Venice and Rome) and Germany (Nuremberg). During the course of his career he was awarded many prizes and medals and a large number of his paintings were purchased by the imperial family. In 1900 he contributed to the World's Fair in Paris and received an honorable mention. Unfortunately, there is no record of whether Suppantschitsch traveled to Paris for the exhibition. He was chairman of the Watercolorists' Club from 1913 to 1915; in 1919 he was a founding member of the Wachau artist group, Wachauer Künstlerbund. In 1933 he received the title of professor.

In addition to many large-scale landscape paintings (see p. 87), he produced a multitude of pencil sketches and studies of architectural details such as wayside shrines, oriels, roofs, and so on. Today these are housed at the Niederösterreichisches Landesmuseum and are of special relevance for heritage conservation work. Suppantschitsch sought "nature in its various forms, both large and small" and aspired "to sharpen his eye more and more to its intimate charms." He traced "the miniature life of the plant world that exists in the cottage garden, by the wayside, on the wall's edge, or in the overgrown flowerbeds of a rural terrace."[14]

1 *Die Graphischen Künste* 30, 1907, p. 87.
2 Martin Suppan, *Paradies Wachau. Gemaltes Weltkulturerbe*, Vienna 2004, p. 275.
3 Cornelia Cabuk, "Wachau—Bilderfluss und Malerwinkel," in: Suppan 2004 (see note 2), pp. 12–25, here pp. 13–17.
4 *Die Graphischen Künste* 1907 (see note 1), p. 87f.
5 Wolfgang Krug, *Wachau. Bilder aus dem Land der Romantik*, Vienna 2003, p. 170.
6 Hermine Cloeter's essay "Die Wachau und ihre Maler" of 1922 is printed in Krug 2003 (see note 5), pp. 42–49.
7 Hermine Cloeter, "Max Suppantschitsch," in: *Der getreue Eckart* 2, 1924/25, vol. 2, no. 13, pp. 519–532, here p. 524.
8 Cloeter 1922 (see note 6), p. 46.
9 Suppan 2004 (see note 2), p. 275.
10 Krug 2003 (see note 5), p. 34.
11 Hanna Egger, "Wachau als Künstlerlandschaft," in: Géza Hajos (ed.), *Denkmal—Ensemble—Kulturlandschaft am Beispiel der Wachau*, Horn 1999, pp. 182–186; quoted from Cabuk 2004 (see note 3), p. 18.
12 Suppan 2004 (see note 2), pp. 275–276.
13 Wolfgang Krug, *Waldmüller bis Schiele. Meisterwerke aus dem Niederösterreichischen Landesmuseum*, St. Pölten 2002, p. 132.
14 Josef Folnesics, "Max Suppantschitsch," in: *Die Graphischen Künste* 23, 1900, pp. 113–116, here p. 113.

MAX WEILER

(1910 Absam bei Hall in Tirol – 2001 Vienna)

The Inner Figure

Regina Doppelbauer

In terms of its individuality, diversity, and scope, Max Weiler's was amongst the most important in twentieth-century Austrian and European art. The ideas expressed in the large public works, paintings, and drawings had to do, to a greater or lesser extent, with nature and existential processes. Starting from an objective basis, Weiler's art over the decades abandoned all representationality and evolved into pure form, sheer painting. His work may be studied from two fundamental perspectives: that of the artist influenced by a transcendental experience of nature, and that of the analyzing formalist, who continuously reconsidered his own need for permanent development and reflected on his place in the national and international art scene. Weiler was always at pains to retain his autonomy and never felt part of the groups of Austrian artists that emerged after 1950. He was born in Tyrol, where he spent the first half of his life, until he was appointed to teach a master class for painting at the Akademie der bildenden Künste (Academy of Fine Arts) in Vienna. After his retirement as a lecturer there in 1981, he remained in Vienna, where he died in 2001.

Max Weiler's life covers practically the entire century. His artistic career began in the late 1920s and continued until a few days before his death. For decades he was a witness of and participant in all of the main Modernist movements, which started out with abstract art and came together after 1950 in the universal language of informal art before fragmenting in the 1960s into diverse directions, thus redefining the traditional concept of art. Within this period, Weiler settled in 1963 on his highly distinctive form of abstract art—a turning point in his artistic life and one that was to inform all of his later works and hence the contents of *Four Walls* (*Vier Wände*), which he completed between 1973 and 1977.

Weiler always enjoyed experimenting and was driven by a desire to find the "inner figure," which was to come to him in 1963. Inspired by this, his subsequent work went through diverse and very different phases. Processes extending sometimes over several years culminated in his large-scale public works. These different work phases are mirrored in a wide range of techniques: he used frescos, oil, and later egg tempera paint and, increasingly after 1960, drawing in equal measure to express his artistic ideas.

Weiler was born in 1910 and raised in a middle-class background. In the 1920s in Tyrol he encountered the reformist Catholic ideas of Bund Neuland and developed his close association with nature. While studying at the Akademie in Vienna from 1930 to 1937 the spirituality and forms of ancient Chinese landscape painting of the Sung epoch (960–1279 AD) left a deep impression. These early substrates are fundamental to Weiler's art, even if their contribution changed over the years and gave way sometimes to other stylistic and formal approaches.

MAX WEILER
Thrust of a Lance, 1947 (fresco on the east wall of the Theresienchurch on the Hungerburg, Innsbruck)

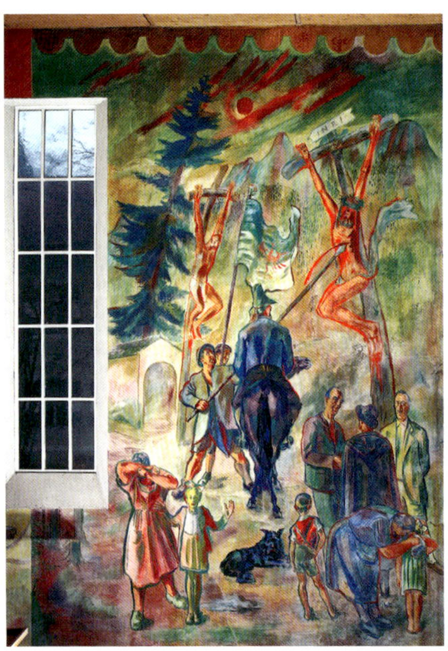

In 1945 he returned from the war, and in his first and highly controversial fresco for the Theresienkirche in Innsbruck immediately presented himself as a figurative painter and ardent colorist. He soon embraced international Modernism, inspired by exhibitions at the Institut français in Innsbruck and a visit to Paris. Abstract tendencies and planarity characterize his next public works, the apse fresco in Friedens-kirche in Linz-Urfahr (1951) and the murals at Innsbruck main railway station (1954/55). In his canvas painting he developed an icongraphically charged cipher language,[1] whose narrative elements gradually receded to make way for an interpretation in the form of a colored abstract structures. The 1960 Biennale in Venice marked a caesura, followed by a short and intensive involvement with informal painting, as expressed in his 29-part cycle *While All Things …* (*Als alle Dinge …*).[2]

The categorical turning point in Weiler's artistic development came in 1963, when he discovered the creative force of chance: in the unintentional splashes of paint and shapes on his scrap paper—throwaway items on which he wiped his brushes and mixed paint—he found an inexhaustible abstract reservoir of shapes. He carefully outlined the interesting bits with a pencil and transferred them to monumental paintings. Tiny structures created by paint drips and dried egg tempera, brushstrokes, even oil diffused on the paper, all had potential. The paintings *Like a Landscape* (*Wie eine Landschaft*), which followed this discovery, are landscapes without an equivalent elsewhere, events created through the forms and colors occurring during the painting process. The theme of nature, which had evolved decades previously from a spiritual experience, was now interpreted quite differently as the "nature of painting" itself.[3]

This wipe-off paper technique has only recently been identified. Its relevance to the work and within an international context was described for the first time in 2010.[4] According to the description, this progression by the artist may be seen as a contribution to the renewal of painting through the process itself.

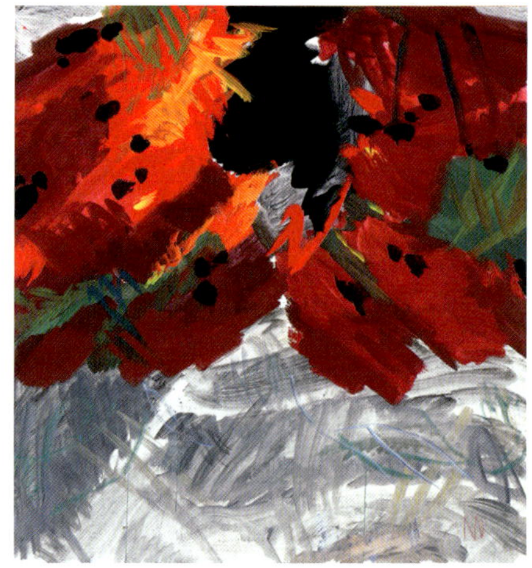

MAX WEILER
Things II, 1960
(from the series *While All Things …*)
Essl Museum Klosterneuburg/Vienna

Weiler's discovery, tried out first in painting and then also in drawing, infused all his subsequent works. In 1967 he summarized this language on a surface of around 10 x 10 meters in the highly expressive iron safety curtain at Landestheater Innsbruck. This phase in the artist's work, which was to prove to be merely transitional, was followed by the experimental group of twelve projecting *Wing Paintings* (*Flügelbilder*) and then the intensely colored *Landscapes on Resonant Grounds* (*Landschaften auf tönenden Gründen*).

In 1973 he reverted to earlier formal concepts. In the center of the luminous but mutedly colored *New Landscapes* (*Neue Landschaften*) are the *Four Walls* (*Vier Wände*), which he worked on from 1973 to 1977. Nature, earth, emptiness, and sky—Weiler "sublimated" these major themes from his studio waste into *Four Walls* (see figs. p. 235 below and pp. 99, 100)).[5] This ensemble, hitherto unseen in Austrian art, was a culmination of his years of experience with large formats, coupled with a confidence regarding the painting method and, not least, since his first public works, the desire for an intensive interaction between space, picture, and viewer. Added to this was the inspiration[6] from a postcard of the large fresco mural from Akrotiri in the National Museum in Athens. Even all of this, however, cannot explain why Weiler ultimately undertook this project without an outside commission. He created it for himself, for a virtual space that did not yet exist when the work was completed. When it was presented for the first time in 1978 in the Akademie der bildenden Künste in Vienna, it was spread out over several rooms, but in 2004 the four canvases were temporarily brought together in the Museumsquartier.[7] For several reasons,[8] this was a more suitable presentation, one intended by Weiler, as his drawings indicate. Two ideas in 1977 for an exhibition house—*Four Walls* had just been completed—show an organically round central room, at the edges of which the pictures are joined in a connected chain (fig. p. 98). In the sketch the pictures cannot be identified individually, but Weiler seems to have had combined his abstract works, whether from the 1960s or his recent *New Landscapes* with *Four Walls*, into a continuum. The nature of art, the nature of the artist—a pendant to real nature that Weiler has sprouting outside the walls of the building he has drawn. It is quite conceivable that Claude Monet's *Grand Decorations* (*Grandes décorations*) were an inspiration.[9] In one of the drafts—after spiritual connotations had been pushed into the background for years—a decidedly religious understanding is evident. Weiler entitles it *The Train of His Robe* (*Der Saum seines Kleides*). This, according to the prophet Isaiah, is the form in which God will reveal himself.

MAX WEILER
Wipe-off Paper for „Natur with Caput mortuum“, 1974
Private collection

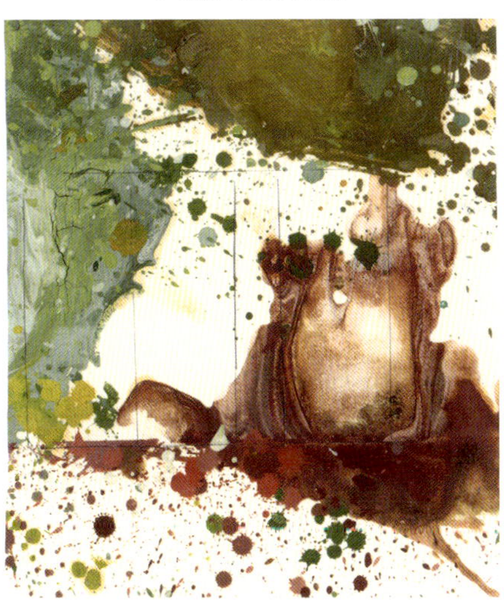

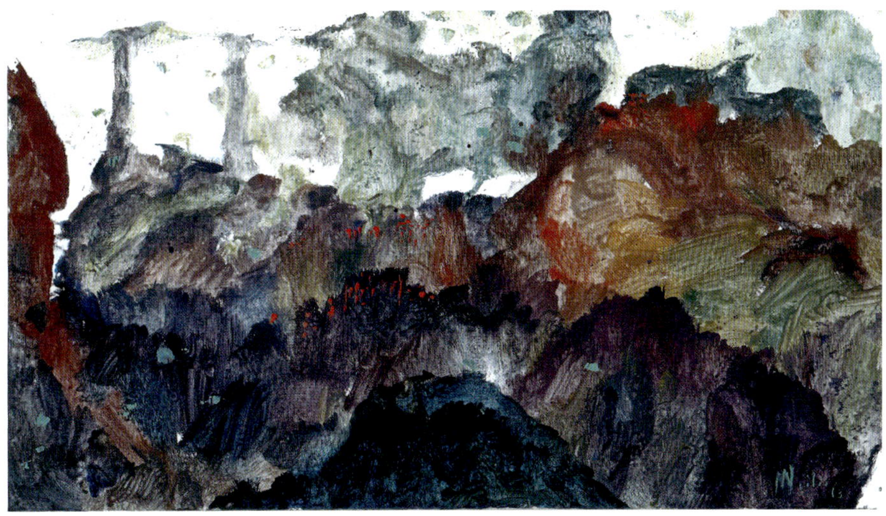

MAX WEILER
Like a Landscape, Primary Formation, Two Columns, 1963
Private collection

After *Four Walls*, Weiler's painting activities declined. At this time he believed he had said everything that could be said with paint and painting.[10] He now turned his large-scale technique to drawing. Between 1978 and 1980 he completed eighteen drawings of up to 3 meters in length, in which with the sparsest of means the artist depicted his ideas of the forces of nature, landscapes and the plant world, lightness and drama. He limited himself to charcoal, with which he extracted all black and gray shades and every linear and painterly effect. In 1985 he completed *Natural Form* (*Naturgebild*), a 10-meter long drawing, whose inherent rhythms invited the observer to walk up and down and also to enter into the picture: an open composition that could be conceived ad infinitum, reminiscent of his invitation to the public of *Four Walls*.

In 1986 Weiler took up painting again and by 1995 had completed several hundred works, most of them a celebration of color and vitality. There were a number of major commissions, *Like a Symphony* (*Wie eine Symphonie*) 1990, today in the Salzburg Festspielhaus,[11] and in 1992/93 the monumental canvases for Casino Innsbruck. This new painterly development also included works on paper, and it was on the lively surface of handmade paper that he was able to reinterpret his established fami-liar artistic language. In 1995, Weiler, then eighty-five years old, abandoned the large format and concentrated until his death in 2001 on small and medium-sized works using wax crayon on paper.

Max Weiler completed around 1,600 paintings, 3,500 drawings,[12] and 40 large-format works in public, with over 1,000 sketches, rough copies, and full-scale versions on board.[13] Added to this were his *Day and Night Notebooks* (*Tag- und Nachthefte*), which he kept for over thirty years, with its jottings about his daily life and reflections on the work of an artist. The trenchant aphorisms and profound philosophical thoughts feature repeatedly in publications and exhibition catalogs. For almost twenty years, from 1964 to 1981, Weiler taught at the

Akademie der bildenden Künste in Vienna, an obligation that had to be reconciled with his artistic activities. His students included Hubert Scheibl and Felix Waske, and he was assisted by Thomas Stimm and Peter Pongratz.

Most of Max Weiler's oeuvre has been shown in the last twenty-five years in exhibitions[14] and publications.[15] It is unlikely that new discoveries as profound as his wipe-off paper, which offered a new way of seeing his work, will occur so quickly. Now that so many of his works have been published, the next step might be to obtain an overall picture of their relationship to one another, considering his public works, paintings, and drawings as equal and interrelated aspects of an overall oeuvre.

1 Gottfried Boehm, in: *Der Maler Max Weiler. Das Geistige in der Natur*, 2nd edition, Vienna 2010, pp. 171–172.
2 Cf. Wolfram Morath-Vogel (ed.), *"Als alle Dinge ...." Der Meister-Eckhart-Zyklus von Max Weiler* (exh. cat., Angermuseum Erfurt, Erfurt, May 4–August 3, 2003), Erfurt 2003.
3 This is the title of the Max Weiler exhibition curated by Edelbert Köb at Sammlung Essl, Klosterneuburg, 2010 (see note 4).
4 The discovery is attributed to Margret Boehm; cf. Margret Boehm, "Von mir entdeckt und doch Natur – Max Weilers 'Probierpapiere,'" in: *Max Weiler. Die Natur der Malerei* (exh. cat., Essl Museum, Klosterneuburg, March 19–August 29, 2010), 2nd revised edition, Munich 2010, pp. 32–39. For the historical context, see Edelbert Köb, "Die Natur der Malerei," in: ibid., pp. 8–29.

MAX WEILER
Like a Symphony, 1990
Private collection

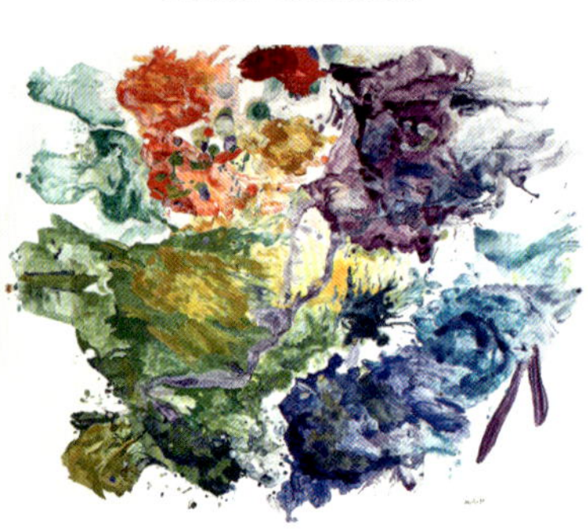

5 Weiler used this term in 1971 referring to another picture (*Day and Night Notebooks* [*Tag- und Nachthefte*]), June 18, 1971).
6 Entry in *Day and Night Notebooks*, August 30, 1973, in: *Max Weiler. Wie die Natur* (exh. cat., Akademie der bildenden Künste Wien, Vienna March 7–April 30, 1978), Vienna 1978.
7 *Max Weiler – Vier Wände* (exh. cat., Museum moderner Kunst Stiftung Ludwig Wien, Vienna, January 21 – May 2, 2004), Vienna 2008.
8 See the essay by Stephan Koja in this catalog on pp. 93–98.
9 Ibid.
10 *Day and Night Notebooks*, October 4, 1980, on the exhibition of large-scale drawings at Galerie nächst St. Stephan, Vienna 1980.
11 Originally painted for a lecture theater at the Salzburger Landesausstellung "Mozart – Bilder und Klänge" 1991 in Schloss Klessheim.
12 Klaus Albrecht Schröder (ed.), *Max Weiler. Der Zeichner* (exh. cat., Albertina, Vienna, June 10–October 16, 2011), Ostfildern 2011. An online list of Max Weiler's works on paper is currently being prepared in the Albertina.
13 *Max Weiler. Die großen Werke* (exh. cat., Tiroler Landesmuseum Ferdinandeum, Innsbruck, June 18–October 31, 2010), Innsbruck 2010.
14 In addition: Edelbert Köb (ed.), *Max Weiler. Im Jahrhundert der Moderne. Malerei seit 1927* (exh. cat., Künstlerhaus Wien, Vienna, October 16, 1999–February 6, 2000), Vienna 1999.
15 A general discussion can be found in: Boehm 2010 (see note 1) – Wieland Schmied, *Max Weiler. Ein anderes Bild der Natur. Der Weg zum Spätwerk*, Salzburg 1998.

OLGA WISINGER-FLORIAN
(1844 Vienna – 1926 Grafenegg)

"[...] until I proposed drinking beer [...]"

Verena Perlhefter

When Olga Wisinger-Florian entered the United States in 1893, the following occurred at the customs, "She had a small sketch showing a chicken run, which she had packed at the bottom of her suitcase as a gift for friends. The importation of works of art into the USA is subject to very high customs duty, and luggage is thoroughly searched. The customs officer discovered the sketch and studied it for a long time without being able to make much of it, because he was holding it upside down. Asked what the picture was worth, the artist replied that it was just a sketch of no value. He summoned a colleague for advice, and the two of them studied the upside-down picture without hitting on the idea of turning it round. Finally, Olga Wisinger-Florian said: 'It has no value because I made it myself.' 'Oh, OK,' said the customs officers dismissively, returning the sketch without charging any duty on it."[1]

At this time, the artist was so well-known that she had even been mentioned in a comedy by Arthur Schnitzler. In *Countess Mizzi*, written in 1909, a young woman who is encouraged by her teacher to exhibit her works, has "no reason to hide her head alongside Wisinger-Florian."[2] A disparaging comment about the countess elsewhere in the play, that just because "someone paints roses and violets, it doesn't mean they are overwrought,"[3] gives an indication of the way women were seen in nineteenth-century society.

Middle-class women of the time were expected to transfer smoothly from the tutelage of the father to that of the husband. Girls should aspire to become wives and mothers. If they failed to do so and had to earn a living as a governess or lady's companion, they were to be pitied. This situation offered material for countless novels, usually with a happy ending and the marriage, after various obstacles had been overcome, of the heroine and the master of the house. Without a clear aim or a liberal father or husband, it was very difficult for young women to escape this material and social dependence.

Activities and skills that made the home more decorative and welcoming (pretty floral pictures, music-making in the home) were encouraged as long as they remained within bounds.[4] As far as male society was concerned, a contented woman had no need of artistic expression, as her situation in the home gave her no reason to complain and hence no grounds for writing a novel or painting a picture.[5]

Olga Wisinger-Florian was born on November 1, 1844, the daughter of a high-ranking civil servant, Franz Florian, and his wife Minna, née List. Her parents encouraged her interests and allowed her to take art and music lessons. She studied under Professor Julius Epstein at the Konservatorium (Conservatory) in Vienna to become a concert pianist and performed successfully in Austria and Germany. In 1874 she married Franz Wisinger, owner of the pharmacy on Schwarzenbergplatz (today Internationale Apotheke), and their only child, Oskar, was born a year later.

Wisinger-Florian had to abandon her musical career after injuring her hand and thus at the age of thirty began to paint. Her marriage to the wealthy pharmacist and the income from the letting of the pharmacy after his death gave her the necessary material base to establish herself as a painter, to demonstrate her seriousness through her constant painting and drawing and frequent visits to galleries, and to set herself apart from the typical well-bred young women who dabbled in art.[6] As a woman of independent means she was also able to participate fully in social life.

She had private lessons initially with Melchior Fritsch and August Schaeffer von Wienwald, and then from 1880 with Emil Jakob Schindler, who had attracted a group of young female artists including Marie Egner and Tina Blau. Wisinger-Florian herself reckoned that this was the real start of her artistic education, because Schindler not only encouraged her talents but also set up contacts and urged her to participate in exhibitions.[7]

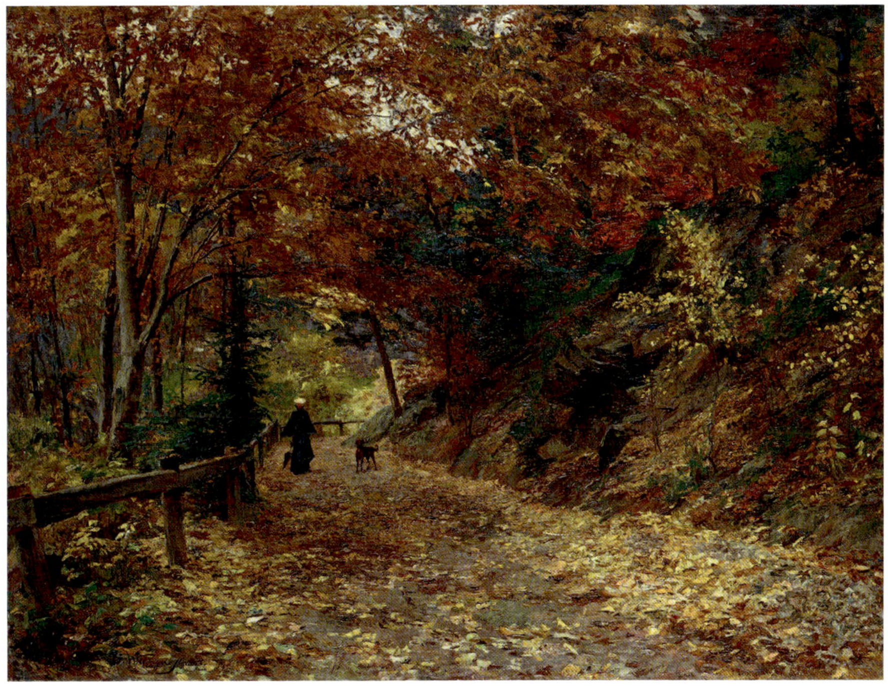

OLGA WISINGER-FLORIAN
Falling leaves, 1899
Belvedere, Vienna

From the establishment of the Akademie der bildenden Künste (Academy of Fine Arts) in Vienna in 1692 until 1918, women were not allowed to study there. Apart from the k. k. Österreichisches Museum für Kunst und Industrie (Imperial and Royal Austrian Museum of Art and Industry), the only option open to women in the second half of the nineteenth century was private tuition, "Dilettantism was seen as [...] the synthesis of 'femininity' and art. The female artist as a person with the same scope for action as was granted to male artists did not exist; there were either complaisant, 'agreeable artists,' ambitious hermaphrodites or, at best, professional dilettantes."[8] A woman artist did not need to be taken seriously, and the prevailing image of women among the wealthy and propertied classes of someone who devoted herself entirely to the home and raising children was not questioned.

The main problem with women's education was the study of anatomy. It was inconceivable for young women to draw naked men. An attempt was made to solve the problem at the Kunstgewerbeschule (School of Applied Arts) in Vienna by providing male models with a "pole and bathing costume."[9] The predilection of many women painters for flowers and landscapes rather than the far more respected history painting might not only have been an inclination but also a necessity because of the training available to them.

Olga Wisinger-Florian's perception of herself as an artist, however, was based on male role models and was far from the prevailing image of women painters as dilettantes;[10] nor did she, like Marie Egner or Tina Blau, "identify with the lonely artist type who lived only for his work, but rather saw herself more as a female version of the 'artist prince.'"[11] Because of her success as a pianist, she was probably not used to withdrawing modestly. When she heard in 1897 that Tina Blau had also been awarded the State Medal, she said, "Stupid! I would have preferred to be the only one."[12] She taught several female students, including members of the imperial family who also dabbled in painting.

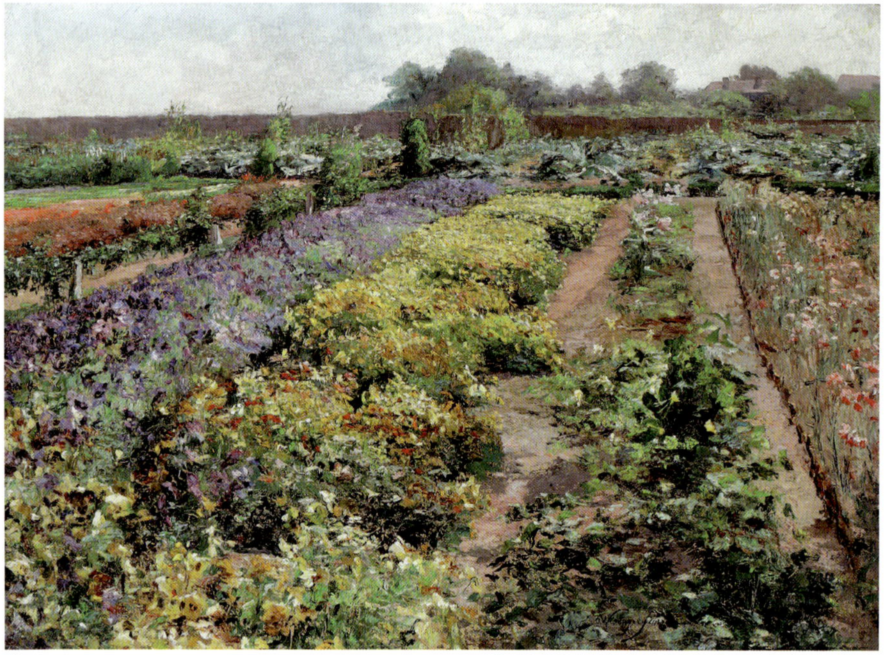

OLGA WISINGER-FLORIAN
Flower beds in the Park in Grafenegg, ca. 1904
Private collection

Just a few years after she started training, Wisinger-Florian was already the recipient of the first of numerous medals and awards for her works, in Austria, Germany, France, and the United States of America. The Emperor himself heard of her, which was regarded as the highest acclaim possible.[13] *Kronprinzenwerk*, a representation of the *Österreichisch-Ungarische Monarchie in Wort und Bild* (Austro-Hungarian Monarchy in Words and Pictures) in twenty-three volumes, contained three of her landscapes (*Acanthus Group in Ragusa* [*Akanthusgruppe in Ragusa*], *Easter Roses in Semmering* [*Schneerosen am Semmering*], *Nymphaea thermalis at the Thermal Springs in Großwardein* [*Nymphaea thermalis in den Thermen von Großwardein*]), and a small tailpiece in the second volume. By contrast, there were no works at all by Tina Blau.[14] One reviewer at the International Anniversary Exhibition in Vienna in 1888 considered that her work *Stall in a Lower Austrian Farm* (*Stable eines niederösterreichischen Bauernhofes*) was not free of gender-specific roles, referring to the "tasteful breadth and masculine edge to her rendering"[15] but adding "how much more artistic merit does a manure heap and still life with piglet, however well it might be painted, have than any badly painted Battle of the Teutoburg Forest?"[16]

Wisinger-Florian was a founding member of the Verein der Schriftstellerinnen und Künstlerinnen (Association of Women Writers and Artists), established in Vienna in 1885, and was its president from 1900 to 1917. She reports on one of the first meetings that it only got off the ground through her intervention and reshaping like a men's gathering, "First meeting this evening in the Silbersaal, strained at first, until I proposed drinking beer; great acclaim, as we women began to quaff!"[17]

The association was founded to make women artists known to a wider public and to offer them an old-age pension.[18] A library was established containing works above all by women writers; readings were organized and a pension fund set up with voluntary contributions from members. In 1897 the first pension was paid out to a member.[19]

Olga Wisinger-Florian organized exhibitions for the association with "women's art" and for the "8 Künstlerinnen" (Eight Women Artists) group founded in 1900, which offered a platform for women artists through exhibitions in Salon Pisko.[20] In the same year the Ministry of Culture and Education purchased *Falling Leaves* (*Fallendes Laub*) for the Mo-derne Galerie, and in 1904 the Kaiserliche Gemäldegalerie (Imperial Painting Gallery) acquired *Praterallee in the Fall* (*Praterallee im Herbst*). Finally, in 1906, *Bunch of Wild Flowers* (*Feldblumenstrauß*) was acquired for the Moderne Galerie. All three can be found today in the Österreichische Galerie Belvedere.

In the 1890s, the artist increasingly distanced herself from Schindler's influence and—apparently after a visit to Paris in the late 1880s—experimented with impressionistic *plein air* painting, evident in particular in the park, avenue, and garden landscapes in the years 1890 to 1910, as mentioned above.[21] The light and its different reflections on foliage and leaves on the ground and the sunlight on the water became signature features. Wisinger-Florian used dappled flecks of paint with markedly luminescent, strident coloring, achieving a plasticity in the piles of leaves through the impasto paint application. Her paintings were often notable for a shimmer that gave an impression of bright sunlight.

Like Monet, Wisinger-Florian was at pains to make her painting seem spontaneous and brisk, an effect she achieved with her energetic brushstrokes. In *Flowering Poppies* (*Blühender Mohn*), one of her masterpieces, painted in 1895–1900 (see fig. p. 64), the field of view is narrow and appears to have been chosen at random, the high horizon making viewers feel as if they had been placed in the midst of a sea of flowers. The composition of works like *Pergola at Mentone* (*Pergola bei Mentone*) in 1906 also shows similarities with Monet (fig. p. 62).

Moreover, the artist did not hesitate to include subjects from the *vie moderne* in her pictures, like telegraph poles or passing trains, as in the painting *Landscape with Railway* (*Landschaft mit Eisenbahn*; fig. p. 46).

August Schaeffer, however, felt compelled to comment derisively on the efforts of his former female students and to put down their efforts, "Our lady painters bestir themselves, their efforts are more spirited than those of men, they are bold and give their all. [...] Women are also hardworking—they braid and weave with great energy as if they were trying to conquer the world. As if they didn't already have it in their laps. But this is no longer sufficient. Today women compete with men in terms of skill and earning, they even overtake them and try to block their path."[22]

Today, Olga Wisinger-Florian would be called a "networker," cultivating contacts with artists like Marie von Ebner-Eschenbach, Rosa Mayreder, and Betty Paoli. She also had her own visitors' room with numerous pictures on easels.[23]

Descriptions of her person are generally positive, as, for example, in *Wiener Malerinnen*, a book written in 1895 by Karoline Murau, presumably for a female audience, because in the foreword she stresses the adversities that young female artists had to overcome. Some successful women have succeeded so that even "the most bitter enemies of women's emancipation can no longer deny [...] that there are women capable of significant achievements in all areas, of pursuing their career to the full."[24] Wisinger-Florian is described as "a frequently encountered and esteemed person whose multifaceted education, sparkling wit, and natural amiability ensure that she is always prominent wherever she is."[25] In an article in *Neue Freie Presse* on her eightieth birthday, Adalbert Franz Seligmann enthused about her intelligence, wit, and charm, although also not failing to mention her "almost fascinating ugliness".[26] Her inclination to seek out aristocratic circles was disapproved of by Marie Egner, "Incomprehensible that Wisinger chooses to frequent that band! Thank goodness (and I really mean it) I don't know any archdukes whom I have to kowtow to."[27]

In 1889, the artist met Bertha von Suttner at a reading of her book *Lay Down Your Arms* in the Verein für Schriftstellerinnen und Künstlerinnen. The two energetic women became friends, and Wisinger-Florian accompanied the peace activist to congresses in Rome, Bern, and Chicago.

Olga Wisinger-Florian was already having health problems in the 1890s—heart trouble and a stroke—and from 1910, weakened by breast cancer and a brain tumor that reduced her field of vision, began to withdraw from social life. After 1915 she lived permanently at her summer residence in Grafenegg, and she died practically blind on February 27, 1926.

The greater acceptance of female artists in Vienna toward the end of the nineteenth century is due to a large extent to her commit-

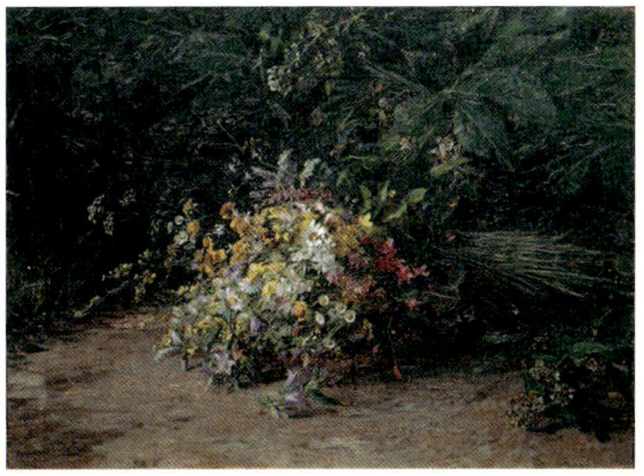

OLGA WISINGER-FLORIAN
Bunch of Wild Flowers, ca. 1906
Belvedere, Vienna

OLGA WISINGER-FLORIAN
Garden Path with Hortensias , 1902
Private collection

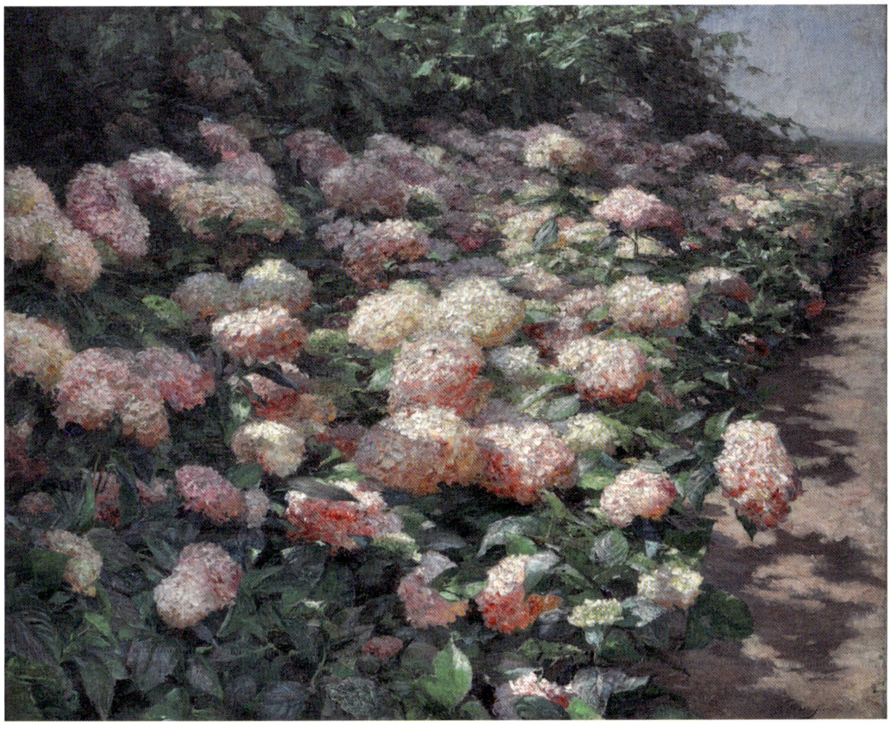

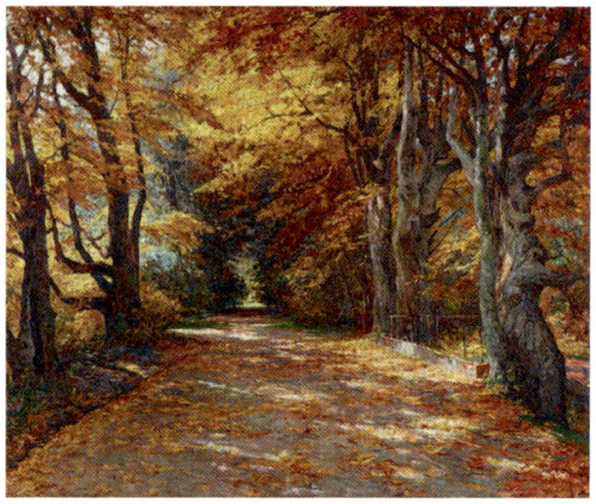

OLGA WISINGER-FLORIAN
Prater Alley in the Fall, ca. 1900
Belvedere, Vienna

ment and boldness, but also to her outstanding artistic talents.

1 Caroline Murau, *Wiener Malerinnen*, Dresden/Leipzig/Vienna 1895, p. 123.
2 Arthur Schnitzler, *Komtesse Mizzi oder Der Familientag. Komödie in einem Akt*, Berlin 1917, p. 33.
3 Ibid., p 25.
4 See Sabine Plakolm-Forsthuber, *Künstlerinnen in Österreich 1897–1938. Malerei, Plastik, Architektur*, Vienna 1994, pp. 25ff.
5 Cf. C. J. Hamilton, *Women Writers: Their Works and Ways*, London 1892, Foreword.
6 Cf. Renate Kassal-Mikula, "Wiener Malerinnen," in: *Die Frau im Korsett. Wiener Frauenalltag zwischen Klischee und Wirklichkeit 1848–1920* (exh. cat., Historisches Museum der Stadt Wien, Hermesvilla, Vienna, April 14, 1984–February 10, 1985), Vienna 1985, p. 78.
7 See Bärbel Holaus, "Olga Wisinger-Florian," in: Gerbert Frodl/Verena Traeger (ed.), *Stimmungsimpressionismus* (exh. cat. Österreichische Galerie Belvedere, March 3–July 4, 2004), Vienna 2004, p. 230.
8 Renate Berger, *Malerinnen auf dem Weg ins 20. Jahrhundert. Kunstgeschichte als Sozialgeschichte*, Cologne 1982, p. 78.
9 J. P. Hodin, *Oskar Kokoschka*, London 1968, p. 101, quoted from Kassal-Mikula 1985 (see note 6), p. 80.
10 Plakolm-Forsthuber 1994 (see note 4), pp. 23–25.
11 Andrea Winklbauer, "Als Frau und Künstlerin. Durchsetzungsstrategien weiblicher Kunstschaffender im 19. Jahrhundert," in: Ingried Brugger (ed.), *Jahrhundert der Frauen. Vom Impressionismus bis zur Gegenwart* (exh. cat.. Bank Austria Kunstforum, Vienna, October 7, 1999–January 2, 2000), Vienna 1999, p. 54.
12 Quoted from Bärbel Holaus, "Olga Wisinger-Florian (1844–1926). Arrangement mit dem 'Männlichen' in der Kunst," in: Brugger 1999 (see note 11), p. 88.
13 Ibid., p. 87.
14 See Edith Futscher, "Professioneller Dilettantismus? Zur Akzeptanz weiblichen Kunstschaffens im ausgehenden 19. Jahrhundert," in: Otmar Rychlik (ed.), *Natürlichere Natur. Österreichische Malerei des Stimmungsrealismus* (exh. cat., Kunsthaus Mürzzuschlag, Mürzzuschlag, summer exhibition 1994), Mürzzuschlag 1994, p. 215.
15 Ibid., p. 257.
16 "Die Internationale Jubiläumsausstellung in Wien," p. 257.
17 Quoted from Holaus 1999 (see note 12), p. 90.
18 *Erster Jahres-Bericht des Vereines der Schriftstellerinnen und Künstlerinnen in Wien*, Vienna 1886, p. 3.
19 Ibid.
20 Holaus 2004 (see note 7), p. 231.
21 Michaela Schwab, *Olga Wisinger-Florian (1844–1926)*, diss., Vienna 1991, pp. 114–115
22 Quoted from Futscher 1994 (see note 14), pp. 30–31.
23 Murau 1895 (see note 1), p. 122.
24 Ibid., p. IX.
25 Ibid., pp. 120–121.
26 Adalbert Franz Seligmann, "Olga Wisinger-Florian," in: *Neue Freie Presse*, November 2, 1924, p. 1.
27 Marie Egner, diary, January 1896, quoted from Winklbauer 1999 (see note 11).

ALFRED ZOFF
(1852 Graz – 1927 Graz)

A Painter of "Unsurpassed Truth to Nature"[1]

Peter Peer

To be honest, I never thought that much of myself as an artist, and only sometimes was I satisfied with this or that I had created and thought successful."[2] In fact, Alfred Zoff was one of the outstanding artist personalities in Austrian landscape painting in the transition period from the nineteenth to the twentieth century, combining traits from *Stimmungsrealismus* (Atmospheric Realism) and from Impressionism to produce an incomparable oeuvre of exceptional quality.

EARLY YEARS—DIFFICULT BEGINNINGS

Alfred Zoff's career path as an artist was certainly not mapped out. After working hard to pass his school-leaving exams, he studied law and later medicine, without graduating from either of these subjects. This was followed by years of searching—meaningless, wasted time, as he later commented. In 1869 he began studying at the Ständische Zeichnungsakademie (Styria's art academy) in Graz with Hermann von Königsbrunn. Although his own art tended to be conservative, Königsbrunn was an open-minded personality. He traveled widely, joining, for example, Franz Ritter von Friedau and zoologist Ludwig Karl von Schmarda as the artist on their expedition to Greece, Egypt, and Ceylon in 1853/54. As a topographer his draftsmanship was exceptional. In 1868 he was given the post of professor of landscape painting at Graz Academy, succeeding Ernst Christian Moser. It was in Königsbrunn's class that Zoff had the pivotal experience of his artistic career. On a study tour to Ičići[3] in the fall of 1878, he discovered his passion for the sea and the coast. These subjects were to become his specialism and laid the foundations for his artistic success. Yet this trip was important for Zoff in another respect, too. The following year, in an exhibition at Vienna's Künstlerhaus, he sold one of the paintings from the trip for a handsome sum.

In fall 1880, Zoff began studying at the Vienna Akademie der bildenden Künste (Academy of Fine Arts) with Eduard Peithner von Lichtenfels. The two artists did not see eye to eye. Zoff described his teacher as "really rigid and pedantic,"[4] and he rejected most of what Zoff had done before. Lichtenfels, successor of Albert August Zimmermann in the academy's landscape class but nowhere near as brilliant, subscribed to an outmoded view of painting. This placed an emphasis on drawing, while paint tended to be used only to color and fill in form, with an emphasis on pale and cool shades applied in thin glazes. "[…] Lichtenfels had a virtually monumental view of landscape; but he was a slave to paint, which he feared more than anything, not only on account of its color but also its thick and pasty consistency,"[5] Zoff observed. Under Lichtenfels's influence he toned down his brighter and fresher colors in favor of dark and pallid tones. During this time he studied works from the academy collection and visited other collections in Vienna wherever possible. He found the group study tours rewarding, one of which took him to Lundenburg an der Thaya[6] (also a source of subject matter for Emil Jakob Schindler, among others) and on another occasion to Pontafel.[7] In his own time, he also traveled time and again to the Adriatic coast.

Although this period studying with Lichtenfels was not very prolific and Zoff himself stated that his life was full of deprivations, he made many acquaintances in Vienna and was an admired painter who frequently sold his works. His contacts, especially with the Vienna Künstlerhaus, were very good, and the association finally accepted him as a member in 1883. That same year he received the academy prize that included a generous sum of money. A major success, which would turn out to be decisive for Zoff's future career, was Emperor Franz Joseph purchasing one of his paintings at the annual exhibition of the Vienna Küstlerhaus. Not only was this good for Zoff's reputation, but he also earned an impressive 800 Gulden. He seized his chance and abandoned the Vienna Academy and Lichtenfels's class.

ARTISTIC MATURITY AND SUCCESS

In 1884 Alfred Zoff attended the Großherzogliche Kunstschule (Grand Ducal School of Art) in Karlsruhe, where he continued his studies with Gustav Schönleber. The two artists had met in Munich back in 1878, when Zoff was living there for several months. "Yes, well, you first have to learn how to paint and handle color," was Schönleber's assessment, in a broad accent, on Zoff's arrival.[8] Schönleber's approach was similar to the artists of the Barbizon School, as reflected in his art's resemblance to the landscapes of Corot and Daubigny. (Zoff would remain friends with him for the rest of his life.) Zoff's years in Karlsruhe were important for him. He opened up to current trends in painting, his palette brightened, and he developed a loose, impasto painting style. All in all, it was during this time that he established his typical style, characterized by bold colors and broad brushwork.

Zoff stayed at Karlsruhe Kunstschule until 1890 when he and his wife moved to Munich. At the end of the nineteenth century, this city was the leading art metropolis in the German-speaking region. The Munich Academy enjoyed international acclaim and was most well-known as a center of history painting. Munich was also a melting pot of various modern art movements. It was here, for example, that Wilhelm Leibl and his circle were based, and a progressive movement in landscape painting had also been established that suited Zoff's style very well. The couple did not return to Austria until 1898, choosing to settle in the town of Krems on the Danube. (They probably also had considered Vienna, but the capital might have seemed too expensive.) By the 1890s at the latest, Zoff was a widely known and recognized artist. Emperor Franz Joseph was a great admirer of Zoff's marine paintings and acquired many examples. At the opening exhibition of the recently built Graz Landesmuseum, where several of

ALFRED ZOFF
Fishing boat on the Beach during Sunset, 1894
Private collection

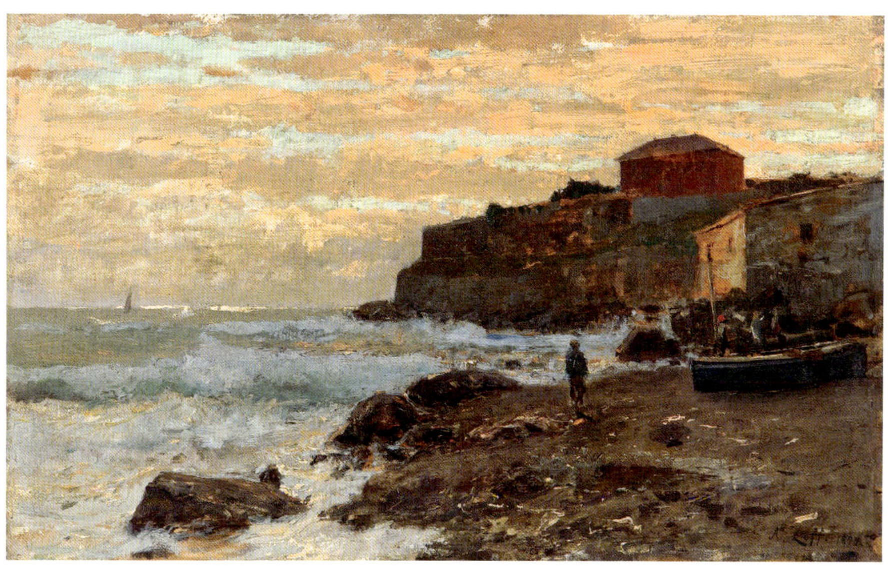

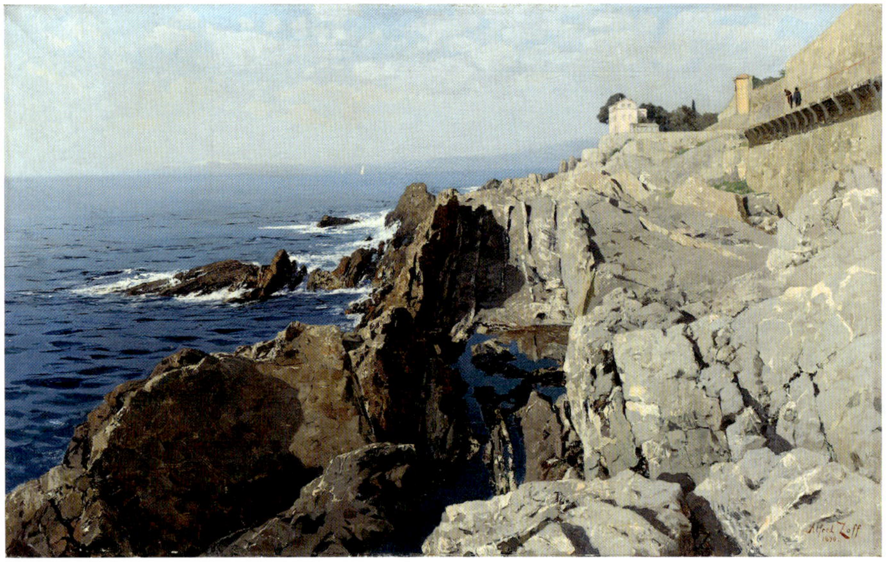

ALFRED ZOFF
Evening on the Coast near Nervi, 1890
Private collection

Zoff's pictures were on display, he was introduced to the Emperor, who happily came to the following conclusion, "Very nice, very nice, but your best pictures are owned by me."[9] Zoff sent work to many exhibitions in Germany, Austria, and countries in the Austro-Hungarian Empire; he received a number of awards and gave private tuition. In 1907 he moved to Graz, where he had been offered the post of professor of the master class for painting at the newly founded Steiermärkische Landeskunstschule (Styrian Art School), a post he would hold until his death in 1927. Yet this highly acclaimed artist still had scruples when correcting his students' drawings, "probably in the awareness of my own lack of drawing ability."[10] He held great importance for many Styrian painters, however, who assimilated and developed his style in one way or another. During these years he found his subjects in the surroundings of Graz and the region of Stainz in western Styria. Longer trips took him to Holland and Belgium in 1903 and 1910. But his preferred destinations were always to travel the coasts of Italy and Dalmatia, painting in Capri, Nervi, Camogli, Ragusa, and other Mediterranean coastal towns. These paintings met with great popular success as well as being highly acclaimed among art professionals.

THE MARINE PAINTER

Alfred Zoff's sea and coastal scenes are among the very best in Austrian painting). No other painter captured the different manifestations and movements of the sea so convincingly and with such mastery. Zoff often made it known that it was a rough sea that enthralled him most.[11] What is exceptional about his pictures is the perfect correlation between graphic and painterly passages, which, taken as a whole, convey the choppy surface of the sea with unique effect. The act of looking itself becomes a process of constant movement with the eye never coming to rest. He was brilliant at conveying the fleeting moment when the rolling breaker crashes and dispels, simultaneously heralding the next breaking wave. Commenting on the painting *Harbor on the Riviera (Hafen an der Riviera)*, one critic noted the "unsurpassed truth to nature" with which Zoff depicted the surf, "how beautifully the full light pours onto the frothing waters and the rocks on the shore, how lovely and clear is the aerial perspective, while the painter's technique stays well away from all the exaggerations of modern *plein air*."[12] One of Zoff's compositional traits was the closely cropped view,[13] often beginning in the immediate foreground. It is possible that this characteristic sometimes arose out of working from photographs.

ALFRED ZOFF
City on the Riviera, ca. 1897
Belvedere, Vienna

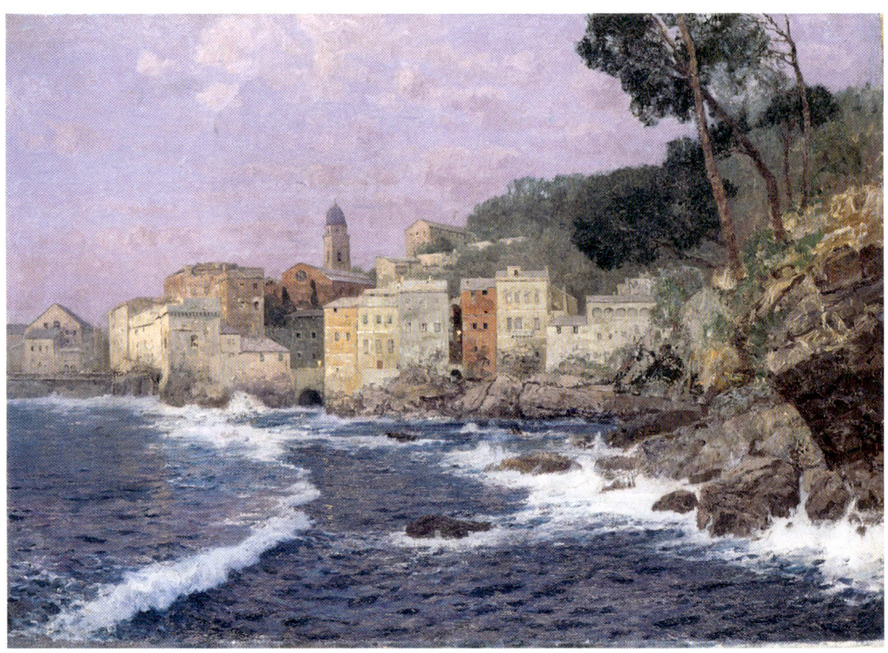

What is clearly apparent, however, is a lifelong exploration of Claude Monet's oeuvre, emerging especially in the compositional similarities to Monet's coastal scenes (see figs. pp. 56–60). Zoff's marine paintings always convey the impression of nature's tremendous power yet they never appear monumental, as is the case with the landscapes from previous generations.

ARTISTIC APPROACH

Although Alfred Zoff's work demonstrated an obvious resemblance to *Stimmungsrealismus* (Atmospheric Realism), from an aesthetic point of view, the painter developed this much further. The palette was now brighter and more luminous, the forms much freer, created with a feel for the spectacles of light. The bold coloring Zoff used to shape his objects using broad, impasto brushwork, always adhered to an overall color concept. But even though he ascribed maximum importance to the optical qualities in his representation of things, Zoff still remained close to the lyrical tone of Atmospheric Painting In his significance for Austrian landscape painting, he has also been compared to Emil Jakob Schindler, already regarded as the most important exponent of atmospheric realism in the 1890s.[14] His landscapes, somewhere between precise observation, felt reality, and an impression, were completely in tune with the tastes of his audience. He was thus appreciated as one of the few artists of his day, "who knew how to assimilate the good sides of modern naturalism in their technique without distancing themselves entirely from the ideal traits of the older school."[15]

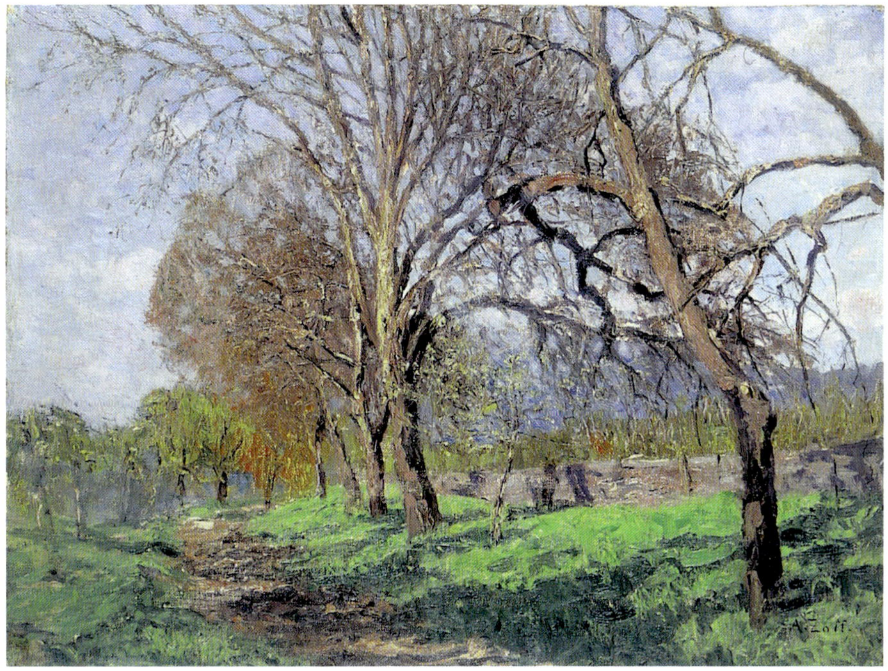

ALFRED ZOFF
Early Spring in Stainz, 1917
Neue Galerie am Universalmuseum Joanneum, Graz

1 Review of an exhibition at the Vienna Künstlerhaus in the *Wiener Sonn- und Feiertags-Courier* of May 12, 1890, quoted from Alfred Zoff, *Meine künstlerische Laufbahn*, 1922, unpublished manuscript by the artist, excerpts published in Martin Suppan, *Alfred Zoff. Ein österreichischer Stimmungsimpressionist. Landschaften, Marinen*, Vienna 1991, p. 45.
2 Zoff, quoted from Suppan 1991 (see note 1), p. 29.
3 On the Istrian coast between Opatija and Lovran.
4 Zoff, quoted from Suppan 1991 (see note 1), p. 32.
5 Zoff, quoted from Suppan 1991 (see note 1), p. 32.
6 Today Břeclav, Czech Republic.
7 Today Pontebba, Friuli, Italy.
8 Quoted from Suppan 1991 (see note 1), p. 37.
9 Quoted from Suppan 1991 (see note 1), p. 51.
10 Zoff, quoted from Suppan 1991 (see note 1), p. 72.
11 Zoff in Suppan 1991 (see note 1), p. 40.
12 Review of the exhibition at the Vienna Künstlerhaus in *Wiener Sonn- und Feiertags-Courier* of May 12, 1890, quoted in Suppan 1991 (see note 1), p. 45.
13 Wilfried Skreiner, "Alfred Zoff. Das unermüdliche Auge," in: Suppan 1991 (see note 1), p. 11.
14 *Hamburgischer Correspondent*, February 23, 1899, in Suppan 1991 (see note 1), p. 57.
15 N. N., "Wiener Skizzen. Die Jahresausstellung im Wiener Künstlerhause," in: *Hamburgischer Correspondent*, Feuilleton, April 25, 1889.

APPENDIX

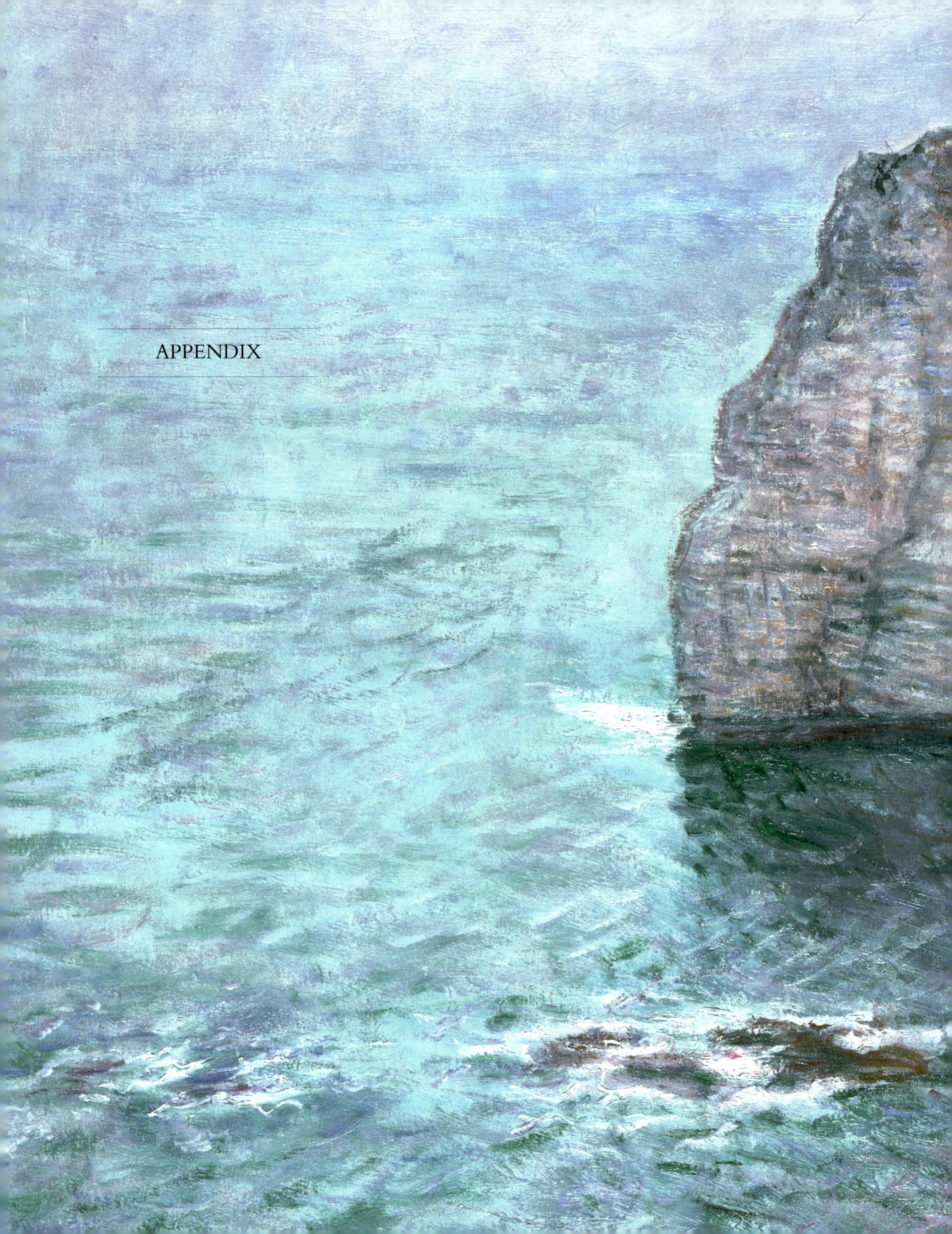

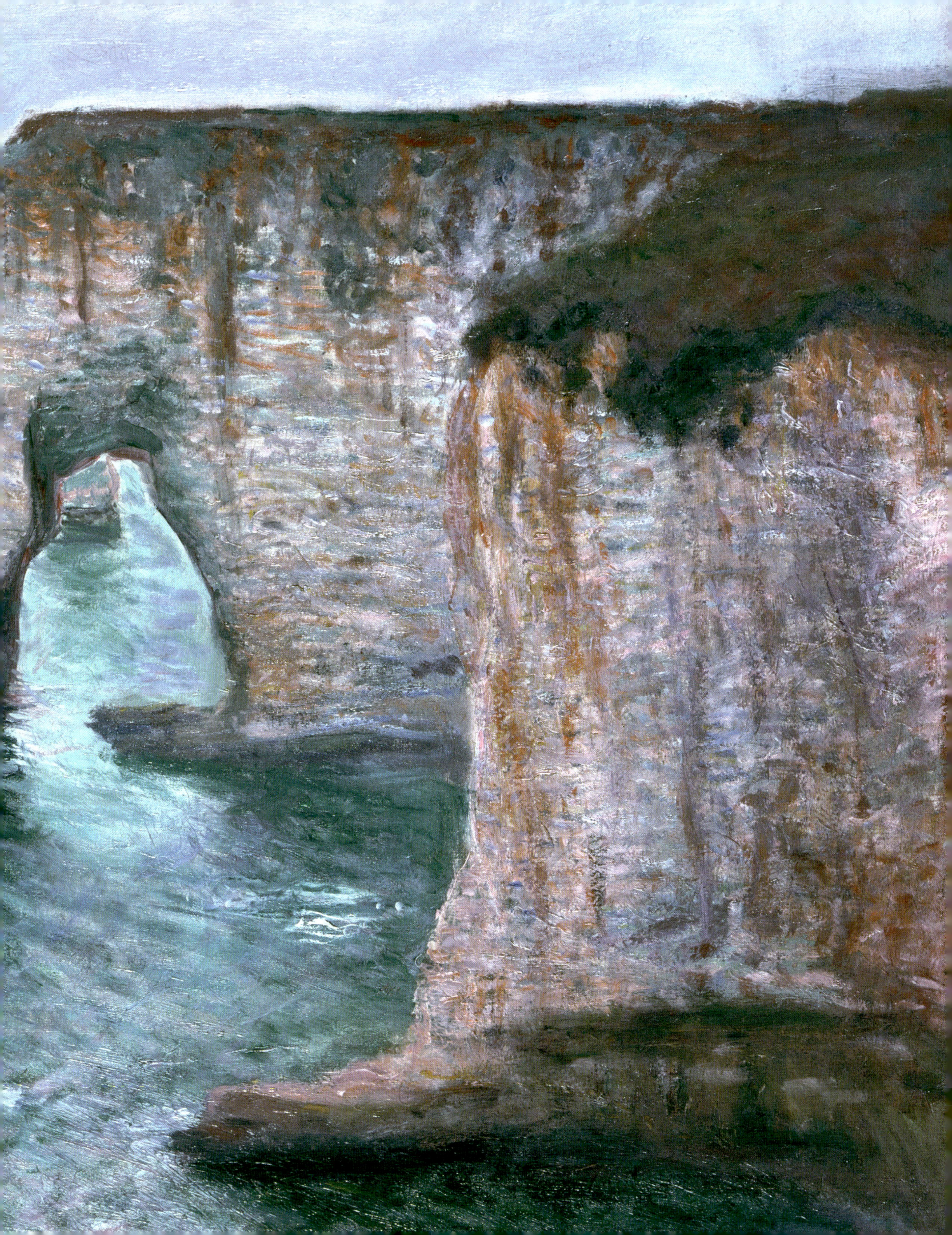

LIST OF WORKS AT THE EXHIBITION

The abbreviation W refers to:
Daniel Wildenstein, *Monet. Catalogue raisonné – Werkverzeichnis*, 4 vols., Cologne 1996

CLAUDE MONET
Houses at Argenteuil (Maisons d'Argenteuil), 1873
Oil on canvas, 54 x 73 cm
Staatliche Museen zu Berlin, Nationalgalerie
W 277

CLAUDE MONET
The Seine near Rouen (La Seine à Rouen), 1874
Oil on canvas, 50.5 x 65.5 cm
Staatliche Kunsthalle Karlsruhe
W 268

CLAUDE MONET
Sailing Boats, Regatta at Argenteuil (Les Barques, régates à Argentueil), ca. 1874
Oil on canvas, 60 x 100 cm
Musée d'Orsay, Paris
W 339

CLAUDE MONET
The Seine at Argenteuil (La Seine à Argenteuil), 1875
Oil on canvas, 60 x 80 cm
Private collection
W 373

CLAUDE MONET
*The Church at Vétheuil (L'*Église *de Vétheuil)*, 1878
Oil on canvas, 65 x 55 cm
Scottish National Gallery, Edinburgh
W 474

CLAUDE MONET
Courtyard of a Farmyard (Cour de ferme), 1878
Oil on canvas, 65 x 50 cm
Antoun Nabil Sehnaoui
W 494

CLAUDE MONET
The Seine at La Grande Jatte (La Seine à la Grande Jatte), 1878
Oil on canvas, 49.5 x 65 cm
Private collection, Vienna
W 454

CLAUDE MONET
View of Vétheuil (Sentier dans les coquelicots, île Saint-Martin), 1880
Oil on canvas, 80 x 60 cm
Lent by The Metropolitan Museum of Art, New York, bequest of Julia W. Emmons, 1956 (56.135.1)
W 592

CLAUDE MONET
Poppy Field (Champ de coquelicots), 1881
Oil on canvas, 58 x 79 cm
Museum Boijmans Van Beuningen, Rotterdam
W 677

CLAUDE MONET
Paul Antoine Graff *(Le Père Paul)*, 1882
Oil on canvas, 64.5 x 52.1 cm
Belvedere, Vienna
W 744

CLAUDE MONET
Anglers at the Seine at Poissy (Pêcheurs à la ligne sur la Seine à Poissy), 1882
Oil on canvas, 59.8 x 81.7 cm
Belvedere, Vienna
W 748

CLAUDE MONET
Cliffs at Dieppe (Sur la Falaise à Dieppe), 1882
Oil on canvas, 60 x 100 cm
National Gallery of Art, Washington, collection of Mr. and Mrs. Paul Mellon
W 754

CLAUDE MONET
Seascape at Pourville (Marine à Pourville), 1882
Oil on canvas, 60 x 100 cm
Columbus Museum of Art, Ohio, gift of Howard D. and Babette L. Sirak, the Donors to the Campaign for Enduring Excellence, and the Derby Fund
W 775

CLAUDE MONET
The Cliff at Dieppe (La Falaise à Dieppe), 1882
Oil on canvas, 66 x 82 cm
Kunsthaus Zürich, coalition Zürcher Kunstfreunde
W 759

CLAUDE MONET
Stormy Weather at Etretat (Gros temps à Étretat*)*, 1883
Oil on canvas, 65 x 81 cm
National Gallery of Victoria, Melbourne Felton Beqest, 1913
W 826

CLAUDE MONET
Poppy Field in a Hollow near Giverny (Champ de coquelicots, environs de Giverny), 1885
Oil on canvas, 65 x 81 cm
Museum of Fine Arts, Boston, Juliana Cheney Edwards Collection, 25.106
W 1000

CLAUDE MONET
Manne-Porte, Etretat (
La Manneporte, vue prise en aval), 1885
Oil on canvas, 65.4 x 81.3 cm
Philadelphia Museum of Art,
John G. Johnson Collection, 1917
W 1037

CLAUDE MONET
The Côte Sauvage (La Côte Sauvage), 1886
Oil on canvas, 65 x 81 cm
Musée d'Orsay, Paris
W 1100

CLAUDE MONET
Field of Tulips in Holland
(Champ de tulips, Hollande), 1886
Oil on canvas, 65.5 x 81.5 cm
Musée d'Orsay, Paris
W 1067

CLAUDE MONET
The Mediterranean (Cap d'Antibes)
(Rochers au bord de la Méditerranée), 1888
Oil on canvas, 65 x 81 cm
Columbus Museum of Art, Ohio,
bequest of Frederick W. Schumacher
W 1185

CLAUDE MONET
Valley of the Creuse (Sunlight Effect)
(Les Eaux semblantes, Creuse, effet de soleil)
1889
Oil on canvas, 65 x 92 cm
Museum of Fine Arts, Boston, Juliana
Cheney Edwards Collection, 25.107
W 1219

CLAUDE MONET
Rouen Cathedral, Façade
(Cathédrale de Rouen, effet de soleil), 1893
Oil on canvas, 100 x 65 cm
Museum of Fine Arts, Boston, Juliana
Cheney Edwards Collection, 39.671
W 1356

CLAUDE MONET
Path in Monet's Garden in Giverny
(Une Allée du jardin de Monet, Giverny), 1902
Oil on canvas, 89.5 x 92.3 cm
Belvedere, Vienna
W 1650

CLAUDE MONET
Waterloo Bridge, 1902
Oil on canvas, 65 x 100 cm
Kunsthaus Zürich, gift of Walter Haefner
W 1581

CLAUDE MONET
Waterloo Bridge, Sunlight Effect
(Waterloo Bridge, effet de soleil), 1903
Oil on canvas, 63.5 x 98.5 cm
Denver Art Museum Collection, funds from
Helen Dill bequest, 1935.15
W 1565

CLAUDE MONET
Waterloo Bridge, Sunlight
(Waterloo Bridge, effet de soleil), 1903
Oil on canvas, 65.1 x 100 cm
McMaster Museum of Art, McMaster
University, Hamilton, Ontario
W 1587

CLAUDE MONET
Waterloo Bridge, Sunlight Effect
(Waterloo Bridge, effet de soleil), 1903
Oil on canvas, 73 x 92 cm
Milwaukee Art Museum, bequest of
Mrs. Albert T. Friedmann, M1950.3
W 1567

CLAUDE MONET
Waterloo Bridge: the Sun in a Fog
(Waterloo Bridge, soleil dans la brouillard), 1903
Oil on canvas, 73.7 x 100.3 cm
National Gallery of Canada, Ottawa,
purchased 1914
W 1573

CLAUDE MONET
Houses of Parliament in London
(Le Parlement, couche de soleil), 1904
Oil on canvas, 80 x 91 cm
Kunstmuseen Krefeld
W 1602

CLAUDE MONET
Palazzo Contarini (Le Palais Contarini), 1908
Oil on canvas, 92 x 81 cm
Kunstmuseum St. Gallen, Ernst Schürpf-
Stiftung, erworben 1950
W 1767

CLAUDE MONET
Water Lilies (Nymphéas), 1914–1917
Oil on canvas, 150 x 200 cm
Fondation Beyeler, Riehen/Basel,
Sammlung Beyeler
W 1814

CLAUDE MONET
Water Lilies and Willow Branches
(Nymphéas avec rameaux de saule), 1916–1919
Oil on canvas, 160 x 180 cm
Lycée Claude Monet, Paris
W 1851

ANONYMOUS
Claude Monet in front of his House in Giverny
(Claude Monet devant sa maison à Giverny),
1921
Autochrome, 18 x 24 cm
Musée d'Orsay, Paris

ANONYMOUS
The Water Lily Pond in Giverny
(L' étange des nymphéas à Giverny), 1921
Autochrome, 18 x 24 cm
Musée d'Orsay, Paris

ANONYMOUS
The Rose Garden in Giverny
(La roseraie à Giverny), 1921
Autochrome, 18 x 24 cm
Musée d'Orsay, Paris

TINA BLAU
From the Tuileries – Sunny Day
(Aus den Tuilierien – Sonniger Tag), 1883
Oil on wood, 18 x 27 cm
Belvedere, Vienna

TINA BLAU
From the Tuileries – Gray Day
(Aus den Tuilierien – Grauer Tag), 1883
Oil on wood, 18 x 27 cm
Belvedere, Vienna

HERBERT BOECKL
Erzberg II, 1947
Oil on canvas, 103 x 121 cm
Artothek des Bundes – On permanent loan
to the Belvedere, Vienna

HERBERT BOECKL
Erzberg III, 1948
Oil on canvas, 92 x 112 cm
Lent by WIENER STÄDTISCHE
VERSICHERUNG AG Vienna Insurance
Group

HERBERT BOECKL
Erzberg IV, 1948
Oil on canvas, 82 x 99 cm
Private collection, Vienna

HERBERT BOECKL
Erzberg V, 1948
Oil on canvas, 81 x 97 cm
Private collection

MARIE EGNER
Stormy Sea in Dalmatia
(Meeresbrandung bei Dalmatien), 1884/90
Oil on canvas, 33.5 x 37.85 cm
Oberösterreichisches Landesmuseum, Linz

MARIE EGNER
Flowering Poppies (Blühender Mohn), um 1900
Oil on cardboard, 50 x 26.5 cm
Neue Galerie am Universalmuseum Joanneum, Graz

THEODOR VON HÖRMANN
In the Tuileries (In den Tuilerien), 1888
Oil on canvas, 38 x 55 cm
Belvedere, Vienna

THEODOR VON HÖRMANN
Houses on Jersey (Einzelstehende Häuser auf Jersey), 1888
Oil on wood, 13.5 x 29 cm
Belvedere, Wien

THEODOR VON HÖRMANN
Nighttime Paris with the Eiffel Tower (Paris bei Nacht mit Eiffelturm), 1889
Oil on canvas, 45.5 x 55 cm
Belvedere, Vienna

THEODOR VON HÖRMANN
View of Paris (Blick auf Paris), 1890
Oil on canvas, 46 x 81 cm
Belvedere, Vienna

THEODOR VON HÖRMANN
The Big Field of Sainfoins near Znojmo IV (Das große Esparsettenfeld in Znaim IV), 1893
Oil on canvas, 71 x 103.5 cm
Belvedere, Vienna

THEODOR VON HÖRMANN
Ice Skaters on the Thaya near Lundenburg (Eisläufer auf der Thaya bei Lundenburg), 1893
Oil on canvas, 70.5 x 103 cm
Belvedere, Vienna

FRANZ JASCHKE
At the Danube Canal (Am Donaukanal), 1903
Oil on canvas, 87.5 x 113 cm
Belvedere, Vienna

FRANZ JASCHKE
Danube Canal in Summer (Donaukanal im Sommer), 1903
Oil on canvas, 83.5 x 114 cm
Belvedere, Vienna

EUGEN JETTEL
Field Track in Winter (Hohlweg im Winter), 1895
Oil on canvas, 56 x 47 cm
Belvedere, Vienna

LUDWIG HEINRICH JUNGNICKEL
View of the Danube Valley from Aggstein (Blick von Aggstein auf das Donautal), ca. 1906
Tempera, spray technique on brown uncoated paper, 33.4 x 58.8 cm
Landesmuseum Niederösterreich, St. Pölten, Inv. 5856

MARIA KIRALY
Donaulandscape (Donaulandschaft), purchased 1957
Oil on hardboard, 45 x 57 cm
Artothek des Bundes im 21er Haus, Vienna

GUSTAV KLIMT
On Attersee (Am Attersee), 1900
Oil on canvas, 80.2 x 80.2 cm
Leopold Museum-Privatstiftung, Vienna

GUSTAV KLIMT
Park at Kammer Castle (Schlosspark in Kammer), 1909
Oil on canvas, 110 x 110 cm
Neue Galerie New York. This work is part of the collection of Estée Lauder and was made available through the generosity of Estée Lauder

GUSTAV KLIMT
Avenue to Schloss Kammer (Allee zum Schloss Kammer), 1912
Oil on canvas, 110 x 110 cm
Belvedere, Vienna

GUSTAV KLIMT
Schloss Kammer on Lake Attersee III (Schloss Kammer am Attersee III), 1909/10
Oil on canvas, 110 x 110 cm
Belvedere, Vienna

GUSTAV KLIMT
Flowering Poppies (Blühender Mohn), 1907
Oil on canvas, 110 x 110 cm
Belvedere, Vienna

JOHANN VICTOR KRÄMER
Taormina in the Sunshine (Taormina im Sonnenschein), 1897
Oil on canvas, 95 x 95 cm
Belvedere, Vienna

JOHANN VICTOR KRÄMER
Ascent to the Church at Senftenberg (Aufstieg zur Kirche von Senftenberg), ca. 1905/10
Oil on canvas, 90 x 90.2 cm
Landesmuseum Niederösterreich, St. Pölten, Inv.A 363/89

HEINRICH KÜHN
Southern Landscape (Südliche Landschaft), 1897
Gum print, 31.5 x 40.8 cm
ÖNB/Wien, Pk 3898, 1

HEINRICH KÜHN
Landscape in the South (Landschaft im Süden), 1897
Gum print, 46.9 x 73.9 cm
ÖNB/Wien, 3899, 1

HEINRICH KÜHN
Walther and Lotte Kühn in the meadow (Walther und Lotte Kühn in der Wiese) 1907-08
Autochrome, 18 x 24 cm
ÖNB/Vienna, Pk 3900, 94

HEINRICH KÜHN
Mary Warner in the landscape (Mary Warner in Landschaft), 1907-08
Autochrome, 24 x 18 cm
ÖNB/Vienna, Pk 3900, 12

HEINRICH KÜHN
Edeltrude and Miss Mary in a white and blue dress (Edeltrude und Miss Mary in weißem und blauen Kostüm), after 1907
Autochrome, 24 x 18 cm
ÖNB/Vienna, Pk 3900, 47

HEINRICH KÜHN
Still life with apples (Stillleben mit Äpfeln), ca. 1907
Autochrome, 18 x 24 cm
ÖNB/Vienna, Pk 3900, 91

HEINRICH KÜHN
Miss Mary and Lotte (Miss Mary und Lotte), after 1907
Autochrome, 18 x 24 cm
ÖNB/Vienna, Pk 3900, 51

HEINRICH KÜHN
Miss Mary in a blue dress (Miss Mary im blauen Kostüm), after 1907
Autochrome, 24 x 18 cm
ÖNB/Vienna, Pk 3900, 89

HEINRICH KÜHN
Imperial garden in Innsbruck (Hofgarten in Innsbruck), after 1907
Autochrome, 18 x 24 cm
ÖNB/Vienna, Pk 3900, 49

HEINRICH KÜHN
Miss Mary in the garden (Miss Mary im Garten), after 1907
Autochrome, 24 x 18 cm
ÖNB/Vienna, Pk 3900, 23

HEINRICH KÜHN
Still life with geraniums
(Stillleben mit Geranien), after 1907
Autochrome, 9 x 12 cm
ÖNB/Vienna, Pk 3900, 202

HEINRICH KÜHN
Hans and Edeltrude Kühn
(Hans und Edeltrude Kühn), 1908
Autochrome, 18 x 13 cm
ÖNB/Vienna, Pk 3900, 6

HEINRICH KÜHN
The painter's table
(Der Tisch des Malers), ca. 1910
Autochrome, 18 x 24 cm
ÖNB/Vienna, Pk 4893

HEINRICH KÜHN
Landscape with hikers
(Landschaft mit Wanderern), 1912
Autochrome, 9 x 12 cm
ÖNB/Vienna, Pk 3900, 218

HEINRICH KÜHN
Under the Trees at the River (In Summer)
(Unter den Bäumen am Fluss [Im Sommer])
ca. 1917
Bromoilprint, 43 x 31.6 cm
ÖNB/Wien, Pk 3898, 3

EMILIE MEDIZ-PELIKAN
Sea in the Midday Heat
(Meer in Mittagsglut), 1890
Oil on canvas, 24.5 x 32.5 cm
Private collection

EMILIE MEDIZ-PELIKAN
Fishing Boats on the Donaushore
(Fischerboote am Donauufer), 1890
Oil on canvas, 30 x 54 cm
Belvedere, Vienna

EMILIE MEDIZ-PELIKAN
The Blue Coast of Duino
(Die blaue Küste von Duino), 1898
Oil on canvas, 146 x 95 cm
Private collection

CARL MOLL
River Landscape (Flusslandschaft), ca. 1900
Oil on canvas, 60 x 60 cm
Austrian private collection

RUDOLF QUITTNER
Cargo railway (Frachtenbahnhof), ca. 1905
Oil on canvas, 150 x 168 cm
Belvedere, Vienna

RUDOLF RIBARZ
Ships in the Harbor (Schiffe im Hafen), 1882
Oil on wood, 13.5 x 23.5
Belvedere, Vienna

EMIL JAKOB SCHINDLER
Winter in the Park (Winter im Park), ca. 1880
Oil on canvas, 18 x 28 cm
Private collection, Vienna

EMIL JAKOB SCHINDLER
Coast at Sylt (Meeresküste von Sylt), 1892
Oil on canvas on wood, 16.5 x 30.5 cm
Belvedere, Vienna

MAX SUPPANTSCHITSCH
Stephanienbridge (Stephanienbrücke), 1901
Pastel on paper, 66 x 107 cm
Belvedere, Vienna

MAX WEILER
On the Far Right, Living Nature
(Ganz rechts lebendige Natur), 1973
Egg tempera on canvas, 256 x 608 cm
Bundesimmobiliengesellschaft m.b.H., Vienna

MAX WEILER
Nature with Caput Mortuum
(Natur mit Caput mortuum), 1974
Egg tempera on canvas, 256 x 608 cm
Bundesimmobiliengesellschaft m.b.H., Vienna

MAX WEILER
Above the Treeline (Über der Baumgrenze), 1976
Egg tempera on canvas, 256 x 580 cm
museum moderner kunst stiftung ludwig wien, purchased 1992

MAX WEILER
Skyscape (Himmelslandschaft), 1977
Egg tempera on canvas, 256 x 608 cm
museum moderner kunst stiftung ludwig wien, purchased 1992

OLGA WISINGER-FLORIAN
Railway in a Landscape (Landschaft mit Eisenbahn), ca. 1895
Oil on cardboard, 26.7 x 38.2 cm
Leopold Museum-Privatstiftung, Vienna

OLGA WISINGER-FLORIAN
Pergola near Mentone
(Pergola bei Mentone), ca. 1900
Oil on cardboard, 51.5 x 72.8 cm
Neue Galerie am Universalmuseum Joanneum, Graz

OLGA WISINGER-FLORIAN
Flowering Poppies
(Blühender Mohn), ca. 1895/1900
Oil on millboard, 70 x 98 cm
Belvedere, Vienna

OLGA WISINGER-FLORIAN
Garden Path with Hortensias
(Gartenweg mit Hortensien), 1902
Oil on canvas, 120 x 150 cm
Private collection

ALFRED ZOFF
Sea Coast (Meeresküste), 1893
Oil on paper board, 35 x 24.2 cm
Neue Galerie am Universalmuseum Joanneum, Graz

ALFRED ZOFF
Capri, 1905
Oil on canvas, 32 x 41 cm
Belvedere, Vienna

ALFRED ZOFF
The Harbor at Nieuwpoort
(Der Hafen von Nieuwpoort), 1910/12
Oil on canvas on artist's board, 42 x 54 cm
Private collection

ALFRED ZOFF
Coast near Pola (Küste bei Pola), undated
Oil on canvas on cardboard, 42.5 x 54 cm
Private collection

AUTHORS' BIOGRAPHIES

Agnes Husslein-Arco, Director of the Belvedere in Vienna since 2007, is an art historian, curator of numerous exhibitions dedicated to classical modernism and contemporary art, and author and editor of academic publications. In 1981, she opened the Viennese branch of Sotheby's, which she managed until 2000. From 1988 on, she was also the Managing Director of the Sotheby's branches in Budapest and Prague. In the 1990s, Agnes Husslein-Arco was Director of European Development at the Solomon R. Guggenheim Museum in New York, from 2001 to 2003 Director of the Rupertinum in Salzburg, and from 2003 to 2005 Founder-Director of the Museum der Moderne Salzburg. From 2002 to 2004, she organized the foundation of the MMKK–Museum Moderner Kunst Kärnten in Klagenfurt am Wörthersee.

Therese Backhausen spent several years in banking before beginning her studies of art history and archeology at the University of Salzburg from where she graduated with a thesis on the artist couple Emilie Mediz-Pelikan and Karl Mediz. During her period of study, she was active as an art communicator and collaborated on the *Origins and Modern* (*Ursprung und Moderne)* exhibition in the Neue Galerie in Linz, as well as *Masterworks from the Guggenheim Museum* (*Meisterwerke aus dem Guggenheim Museum*) shown at the Residenzgalerie in Salzburg. She subsequently worked for the Federal Monuments Office and St. Pölten Diocese in the area of monument inventory. Her activities as a freelance art historian included work for the im Kinsky auction house, collaboration on the production of numerous exhibitions for the Galerie Peithner-Lichtenfels in Vienna, and as a curator for exhibitions for *Vienna fabrics & design*. Therese Backhausen is the author of art-history publications (including *Der Traunsee. Der Mythos der Sommerfrische*, 2012). The main focus of her research is on villa architecture of the 19th century and female artists in the years around 1900.

Beatrice von Bormann studied art history, English language and literature and Romance philology in Freiburg, Paris, and Cologne. Since 1996, she has worked as a freelance curator and author and lectures regularly at the University of Amsterdam. *Max Beckmann in Amsterdam* (Van Gogh Museum, Amsterdam, 2007), *Oskar Kokoschka – Mensen en Beesten/ Rebell und Humanist)* (Museum Boijmans Van Beuningen, Rotterdam, Kunstmuseum Wolfsburg 2013/14) and *Mythos Welt: Otto Dix und Max Beckmann* (Kunsthalle Mannheim, Kunsthalle der Hypo-Kulturstiftung, Munich, 2013/14) are just three of the important exhibitions she has curated to date. Beatrice von Bormann is currently working as curator for modern art and head of collection at the Museum der Moderne Salzburg. The main areas of her research are the German and Austrian avant-garde before and after the First World War and the work of artists in exile between 1933 and 1945.

Regina Doppelbauer studied art history and German language and literature at the University of Salzburg before participating in the postgraduate course for museum and exhibition curators. She has been active in various fields in the Albertina, including research into the "Hortus Eystettensis" and the Albertina's holdings of prints, since 1990. Regina Doppelbauer was responsible for the research project "Max Weiler as a Draughtsman" (Jubilee Fund of the Austrian National Bank) from 2008 to 2011 and curated the exhibition *Max Weiler. The Draughtsman* in 2011. She is currently working on the catalog raisonné of Max Weiler's works on paper. Regina Doppelbauer has been in charge of the Albertina's online collection portal since 2012.

Dominique de Font-Réaulx is senior curator at the musée du Louvre and director of the musée Eugène Delacroix. She used to be in charge of the photographic collection of the musée d'Orsay. She curated many exhibitions, among them *Le Daguerréotype français : un objet photographique* (musée d'Orsay, The Metropolitan Museum of Art, 2003), *Gustave Courbet* (Grand Palais, The Metropolitan Museum of Art, musée Fabre, 2007–2008), *Jean-Léon Gérôme* (musée d'Orsay, The J.P. Getty Museum, 2010). In 2012, she published *Painting and Photography, 1839–1914*. She is professor at the École du Louvre and at the Institut de Sciences politiques in Paris.

Claus Jesina studied art history at the Universities of Graz and Vienna. After completing his studies, he participated in postgraduate training to become a museum and exhibition curator at the Institute for Cultural Sciences in Vienna. He has been active as an art dealer in Vienna since 1997 and founded the Edition Jesina publishing organization, which has Austrian art history as its main emphasis but also deals with other subjects, in the same year. In 1998, he conceived the postgraduate two-year course in art dealing with lectures by international experts from the exhibition and museum field, as well as the art business and the economy, which he has led since 1999. He has also been a registered mediator since 2004 and founded the Plattform für Mediation in Kunst und Kultur (MIKK) in the same year. Claus Jesina has been active as a researcher and curator for various museums and private projects on historical and art-historical themes. He is currently working together with Markus Fellinger, curator at the Belvedere in Vienna, on a catalog of paintings by Tina Blau.

Kerstin Jesse studied at the University of Vienna, the University of Applied Arts Vienna, and Freie Universität Berlin. She worked as an academic project assistant at the mumok–museum moderner kunst stiftung ludwig in Vienna during her university years. Since October 2008, she has been an assistant curator at the Belvedere's 20th-Century Collections Department, where she compiled the catalog raisonné on Herbert Boeckl and works on the catalog raisonné on objects by Curt Stenvert. She has been academically and curatorially involved in multiple exhibition projects.

Irina Katnik studied art history in Vienna. In 2014 she was curatorial assistant for the exhibition *Looking at Monet* in the Belvedere. Before she was working at the Conservation Department in the Belvedere for half a year.

Stephan Koja is curator of the 19th century and classical modern art collections at the Belvedere in Vienna. From 1995 to 2006 he was editor of *Belvedere–Zeitschrift für bildende Kunst*. He has curated numerous exhibitions, including *Georges Rouault* (1993), *Klimt – Kokoschka – Schiele. Un sueño vienés* (1995), *Claude Monet* (1996), *America – Die neue Welt in Bildern des 19. Jahrhunderts* (1999), *Gustav Klimt – Landschaften* (2002/03), *Nordlicht. Finnlands Aufbruch zur Moderne 1890–1920* (2005), *La destrucción creadora. Gustav Klimt, el Friso de Beethoven y la lucha por la libertad del arte* (2006), *Lovis Corinth. Ein Fest der Malerei* (2009), *Anton Romako. Tegetthoff in der Seeschlacht von Lissa* (2010), *Rodin und Wien* (2010/11) and *Carl Schuch. Ein europäischer Maler* (2012). Koja is the author of numerous books and two documentary films.

Peter Peer studied art history at the Karl-Franzens University in Graz and graduated with a dissertation on 19th-century Austrian Art. He then organized exhibitions and worked as a curatorial assistant in the Museum of the City of Graz and for the steirischer herbst festival. He began working as a research associate for the Neue Galerie Graz in the Universalmuseum Joanneum in 2000 and subsequently as curator for the graphic arts and photography collection from 2006 before being appointed Head of the Department for Modern and Contemporary Art at the Universalmuseum Joanneum (Neue Galerie Graz and Kunsthaus Graz) in 2011. His research and publications activities concentrate on Austrian painting and graphic arts from the 19th century to the period between the World Wars with particular emphasis on the art topography of Styria, as well as Austrian landscape painting in the 19th century. Since 2004, Peter Peer has held lectureships, especially on Austrian art in the 19th and first half of the 20th centuries at the Karl-Franzens University.

Bernadette Reinhold studied art history, history, and philosophy at the University of Vienna. Numerous publications, research and exhibition projects on art and architecture in the19th and 20th centuries, as well as on post-1918 Austrian art politics. Bernadette Reinhold was on the research staff of the Federal Monuments Office and collaborated on projects for the Austrian Academy of Sciences. She has been head of the Oskar Kokoschka Center of the University for Applied Arts inVienna; her most recent publication is a photo-biography on Kokoschka *Oskar Kokoschka–ein Künstlerleben in Lichtbildern. Aus dem Oskar Kokoschka-Zentrum der Universität für angewandte Kunst Wien* (edited together with Patrick Werner,Vienna, 2013).

Verena Perlhefter studied history and art history in Vienna and London. Her research focuses on the intellectual-historical problems of Humanism in the late Renaissance, on the one hand, and art history of the late 19th and early 20th centuries, on the other. In 2003, she collaborated on research for the exhibition *Gustav Klimt. Landscapes* in the Österreichische Galerie Belvedere. Verena Perlhefter has published on subjects as diversified as the phenomenon of the summer resort, Hans Tietze, Eugène Delacroix and George Sand, Tilla Durieux and Paul Cassirer.

Kathrin Wolf studied art history, Spanish, and French in Graz and Paris. Her master's thesis, for which she was awarded the Art History Prize of the Friends of the Art History Institute Graz, dealt with depictions of children in French art in the 19th century. This was followed by project-related activities as a research associate in the Belvedere in connection with the exhibition *Rodin and Vienna* (2010/11), for the Ponte Organisation for Cultural Management and the Albertina within the framework of the important digitalization project "Albertina online". Kathrin Wolf has worked as a curatorial assistant in the Belvedere's 19th and 20th Century Collection since April 2014. The main focus of her research is on French and Austrian painting in the late 19th century.

PICTURE CREDITS

© 2014 Kunsthaus Zürich, Schenkung Walter Haefner: p. 86 (a.); © 2014 Kunsthaus Zürich, Vereinigung Zürcher Kunstfreunde: p. 60 (54); © Archives Wildenstein Institute, Paris: pp. 160 (b.), 162 (m.), 164 (a.); © The Art Institute of Chicago, Mr. and Mrs. Lewis Larned Coburn Memorial Collection, 1933.443: p. 59 (53); © The Art Institute of Chicago, Mr. and Mrs. Martin A. Ryerson Collection, 1933.1158: p. 17; © Ashmolean Museum, University of Oxford, UK / Bridgeman Images: p. 41 (8); © Bel Etage, Wolfgang Bauer, Vienna: p. 225 (a.); © Belvedere, Vienna: pp. 6, 7, 39, 40 (b.), 43 (11, 12, 13, 14), 44 (18), 47 (26), 49, 50, 51 (a.), 52 (b.), 53 (a.), 54 (38), 56 (a.), 57, 59 (51), 62 (a.), 63 (b.), 64 (66), 67 (71, 72), 73 (83), 83 (110), 87, 91, 92, 93 (133), 111, 112 (a.), 118, 142, 144 (a.), 145, 146, 147, 149, 150, 152, 153, 158 (r. o.), 161 (b.), 179, 180 (b.), 182, 183 (l.), 184 (a.), 185, 187, 189 (b.), 192, 193, 195, 196 (a.), 197, 199, 202, 203, 204, 209, 210, 212, 220, 221, 222, 224 (a.), 228, 229, 231, 237, 239 (a.), 240, 242 (b.); © bpk / The Metropolitan Museum of Art / Heinrich Kühn: p. 81 (105); © bpk / Nationalgalerie, SMB: p. 207; © Christie's Images Limited [1996]: p. 46 (22); © Christie's Images Limited [1999]: p. 164 (b.); © Christie's Images Limited [2001]: pp. 66, 167 (b.); © Christie's Images Limited [2009]: pp. 41 (6, 7), 165 (m.); © Collection Société Générale de Banque au Liban c/o Sotheby's: p. 167 (a.); © Collection of the Speed Art Museum, Louisville, Kentucky: p. 156 (b.); © Columbus Museum of Art, Ohio: Bequest of Frederick W. Schumacher: p. 70 (79); © Columbus Museum of Art, Ohio: Gift of Howard D. and Babette L. Sirak, the Donors to the Campaign for Enduring Excellence, and the Derby Fund: p. 70 (80); © Conseil Général du Val d'Oise, Photo: J-Y Lacôte: p. 47 (25); © Courtesy Thomas Ammann Fine Art AG, Zurich: pp. 124, 164 (m.); © Courtesy Auktionshaus im Kinsky: pp. 44 (17), 226; © Courtesy Galerie bei der Oper: p. 241; © Courtesy Galerie Walfischgasse, Vienna: pp. 83 (109, 111, 112), 200 (a.); © Courtesy Kovacek Spiegelgasse: pp. 60 (57), 196 (b.); © Courtesy Kunsthandel Florian & Nikolaus Kolhammer, Plankengasse 7: p. 224 (b.); © Courtesy Kunsthandel Freller Antikhaus Ges.m.bh.: p. 242 (a.); © Dénes Józsa - Museum of Fine Arts, Budapest: p. 163 (b.); © Denver Art Museum Collection: Funds from Helen Dill bequest, 1935.15: p. 85 (a.); © digidall - Fotografie, Linz: p. 184 (m.); © Dorotheum Vienna: pp. 60 (55), 200 (b.), 227; © Dorotheum Vienna, Auktionskatalog 04.12.2001: p. 188; © Fondation Beyeler, Riehen/Basel, Beyeler Collection, Photo: Robert Bayer, Basel: p. 94; © Photo Incorporated, Toledo: p. 70 (78); © Photo: The Israel Museum, Jerusalem: p. 29; © Photo: Musée d'Orsay, Dist. RMN-Grand Palais/Patrice Schmidt: pp. 13, 19, 139, 172, 173; © Photo: RMN-Grand Palais/Daniel Arnaudet: p. 103; © Photo: RMN-Grand Palais (musée de l'Orangerie)/Michel Urtado: pp. 30, 31, 96, 97, 176, 177; © Photo: RMN-Grand Palais (musée d'Orsay) / Droits réservés: p. 169; © Photo: RMN-Grand Palais (musée d'Orsay)/Franck Raux: p. 53 (b.); © Photo: RMN-Grand Palais (musée d'Orsay) /Hervé Lewandowski: pp. 15, 21, 22 (a.), 27, 40 (a.), 58 (48), 64 (64), 69 (76, 77), 79 (b.), 95; © Fotostudio Otto, Vienna: p. 93 (131); © French Photographer, (20th century) / Musée Marmottan Monet, Paris, France / Bridgeman Images: p. 171; © Galerie 16 – Alexander Jesina, Vienna, Photo: Galerie 16, Vienna: p. 198; © Galerie Maier, Innsbruck: p. 184 (b.); © Gemäldegalerie der Akademie der bildenden Künste Wien: p. 223; © Henri Manuel / Collection Harlingue / Roger-Viollet: p. 174; © Harvard Art Museums/Fogg Museum, Friends of the Fogg Art Museum Fund, 1925.16, Photo: Imaging Department © President and Fellows of Harvard College: p. 166 (m.); © Harvard Art Museums/Fogg Museum, Gift of The Wertheim Fund, Inc., 1955.98, Photo: Imaging Department © President and Fellows of Harvard College: p. 158 (l. o.); © ISP Graz, C.Cichocki: pp. 76 (90, 91, 92), 78, 80, 81 (102, 103, 104), 82, 140 (10); © Johannesburg Art Gallery, Photo: John Hodgkiss: p. 157 (b.); © Kunstmuseum Bern, Legat Robert Vatter, Bern: p. 165 (b.); © Kunstmuseum St. Gallen, Ernst Schürpf-Stiftung, erworben 1950, Photo: Sebastian Stadler: p. 72 ; © Kunstmuseen Krefeld, Photo: Volker Döhne: p. 23; © Land Niederösterreich, Landessammlungen Niederösterreich, Photo: Peter Böttcher: p. 61 (b.); © Landesmuseum Niederösterreich, Photo: Peter Böttcher: p. 55 (b.); © Landesmuseum Hannover - ARTOTHEK: p. 47 (24); © Landessammlungen Niederösterreich, Photo: Christoph Fuchs: p. 232; © LENTOS Kunstmuseum Linz, Photo: Reinhard Haider: p. 208 (a.); © Leopold Museum, Vienna: pp. 37, 46 (21), 67 (70), 68 (a.); © Lycée Claude Monet, Paris: p. 102; © Matsukata Collection, The National Museum of Western Art, Tokyo: p. 167 (m.); © McMaster Museum of Art, McMaster University, Hamilton, Ontario, Gift of Herman Levy, Esq., O.B.E., 1984, Photo: John Tamblyn: p. 84 (b.); © Memorial Art Gallery of the University of Rochester, Gift of Marie C. and Joseph C. Wilson: p. 12; © The Metropolitan Museum of Art, New York, Bequest of Julia W. Emmons, 1956 (56.135.1), Photo: bpk / The Metropolitan Museum of Art: p. 74 (85); © The Metropolitan Museum of Art, New York, H.O. Havemeyer Collection. Bequest of Mrs. H.O. Havemeyer. 1929, Photo: bpk / The Metropolitan Museum of Art: p. 14; © Milwaukee Art Museum, Bequest of Mrs. Albert T. Friedmann M1950.3, Photo: John R. Glembin: p. 34, 35, 85 (b.); © Musée national des douanes, Bordeaux, Dépôt du Musée d'Orsay, Paris, Photo: Alban Gilbert, France: p. 161 (m.); © Musée Marmottan Monet, Paris, France / Giraudon / Bridgeman Images: pp. 11, 16, 18, 170; © Museum Boijmans Van Beuningen, Rotterdam, Photo: Studio Tromp, Rotterdam: p. 74 (86); © Museum of Fine Arts, Boston, Juliana Cheney Edwards Collection, 25.107: pp. 55 (a.), p. 63 (a.), 123; © National Gallery, London, UK/Bridgeman Images: p. 4, 158 (b.); © The National Gallery, London: p. 42 (b.); © National Gallery of Canada, Ottawa, purchased 1914: p. 86 (b.); © National Gallery of Victoria, Melbourne, Felton Bequest, 1913, Photo: NGV photo Services: pp. 104, 105, 158 (m.); © National Gallery of Victoria, Melbourne, Felton Bequest, 1937, Photo: NGV photo Services: p. 160 (m.); © National Gallery of Art, Washington, Chester Dale Collection, Photo: NGA images (open access): pp. 22 (b.), 24; © National Gallery of Art, Washington, Collection of Mr. and Mrs. Paul Mellon, Photo: NGA images (open access): pp. 79 (a.), 162 (a.); © National Gallery of Art, Washington, Gift of Janice H. Levin, in Honor of the 50th Anniversary of the National Gallery of Art, Photo: NGA images (open access): p. 159 (m.); © Neue Galerie Graz, Universalmuseum Joanneum, Photo: UMJ, N. Lackner: pp. 9, 43 (15), 62 (b.), 64 (65), 144 (b.), 151, 186, 190 (b.), 243; © Neue Galerie New York. This work is part of the collection of Estée Lauder and was made available through Estée Lauder : p. 73 (82); © The Norton Simon Foundation: p. 112 (b.); © Oberösterreichisches Landesmuseum, Photo: Alexandra Bruckböck: p. 180 (a.); © Oberösterreichisches Landesmuseum, Photo: Ernst Grilnberger: p. 58 (50); © Oblastní galerie Liberec, Photo: Jaroslav Trojan: p. 194; © ÖNB/Vienna, Pk 2539, 166: p. 119; © ÖNB/Vienna, Pk 2539, 167: p. 120; © ÖNB/Vienna, Pk 3898, 1: p. 75 (a.); © ÖNB/Vienna, Pk 3899, 1: p. 75 (b.); © ÖNB/Vienna, Pk 3898, 3: p. 76 (93) ; © ÖNB/Vienna, Pk 3900, 123: p. 133, 217; © Philadelphia Museum of Art: Gift of Mr. and Mrs. Hughs Norment in honor of William H. Donner, 1972: pp. 107, 166 (b.); © Philadelphia Museum of Art: John G. Johnson Collection, 1917: pp. 46 (23), 56 (b.), 244, 245; © Pola Museum of Art: p. 156 (a.); © Private collection c/o Sotheby's: pp. 44 (19), 159 (b.), 163 (m.); © Private collection, Vienna (Courtesy Kunsthandel Giese & Schweiger, Vienna): pp. 143, 225 (b.); © Pushkin Museum, Moscow, Russia / Bridgeman Images: p. 157 (a.); © Pushkin Museum, Moscow, Russia / Giraudon / Bridgeman Images: p. 110; © Sammlung Liaunig, Photo: Atelier Neumann / Stadler: p. 93 (132); © Sammlung Rudolf Staechelin, Deposit im Kunstmuseum Basel, Photo: Martin P. Bühler: pp. 154, 155, 161 (a.); © SCHÜTZ Kunst & Antiquitäten, Vienna: p. 238; © Scottish National Gallery: pp. 12, 61 (a.), 160 (a.); © Société française de photographie, Paris: p. 136; © Staatsgalerie Stuttgart: p. 77 (b.); © Staatliche Kunsthalle Karlsruhe: p. 60 (56); © Staatliche Museen zu Berlin, Nationalgalerie, Photo: Jörg P. Anders: pp. 77 (a.), 156 (m.); © Staatliche Museen zu Berlin, Preußischer Kulturbesitz, Nationalgalerie, Photo: Karin März: p. 51 (b.); © Sterling and Francine Clark Art Institute, Williamstown, Massachusetts, USA / Acquired in Memory of Anne Strang Baxter, 1967 / Bridgeman Images: p. 166 (a.); © Tiroler Landesmuseum: p. 191; © U. Edelmann- Städel Museum- ARTOTHEK: p. 157 (m.); © The Walters Art Museum, Acquired by Henry Walters, 1903, Photo: Susan Tobin: p. 140 (9); © Wien Museum: pp. 108, 109, 113, 211, 213, 230; © Verlag Galerie Welz: pp. 88, 89, 90, 208 (b.); © Worcester Art Museum (Mass.), Museum Purchase, 1910.37: p. 84 (a.); Herbert Boeckl: © Herbert-Boeckl-Nachlass, Vienna; Oskar Kokoschka: © Fondation Oskar Kokoschka/Bildrecht, Vienna 2014; Max Weiler: © Yvonne Weiler, 2014.

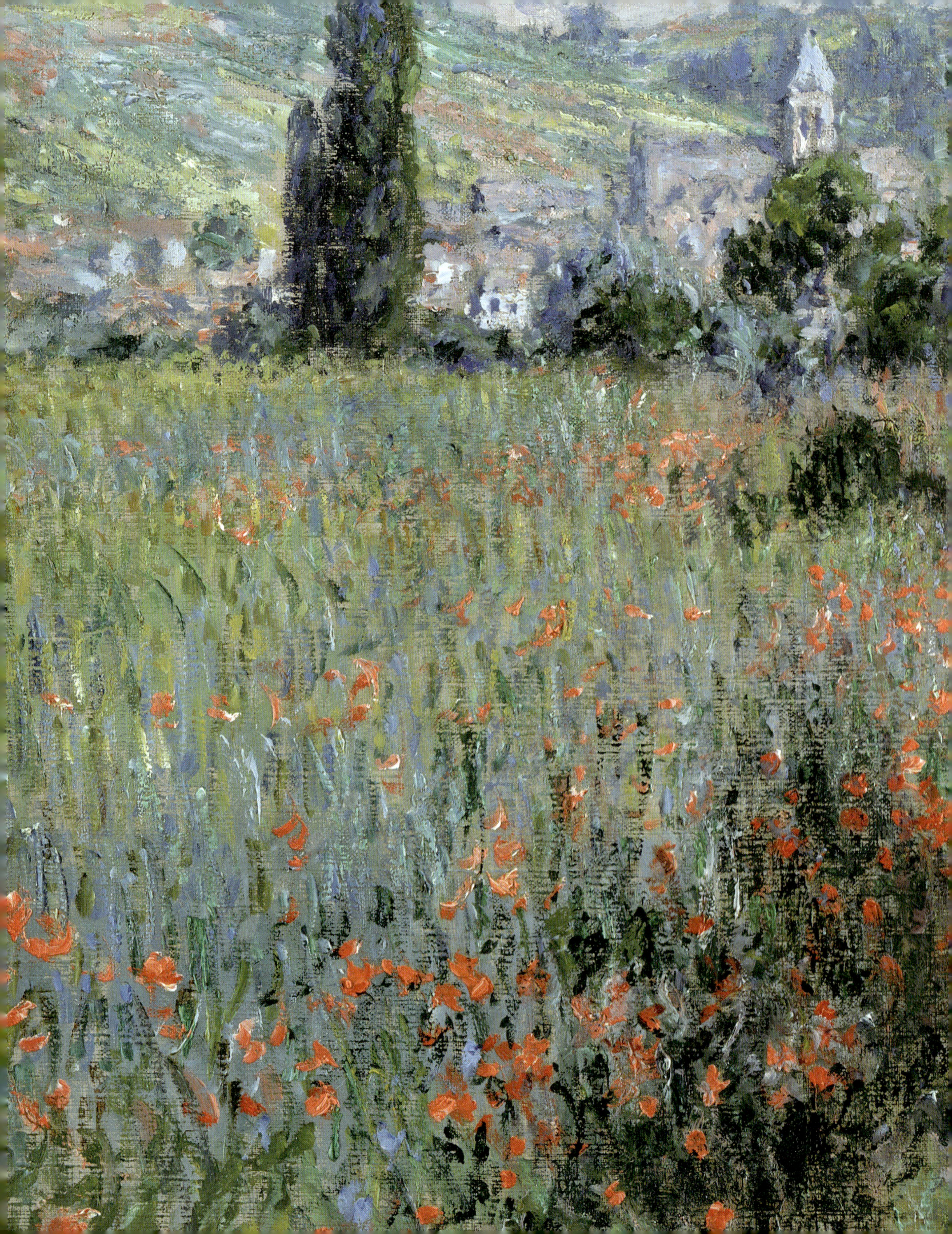

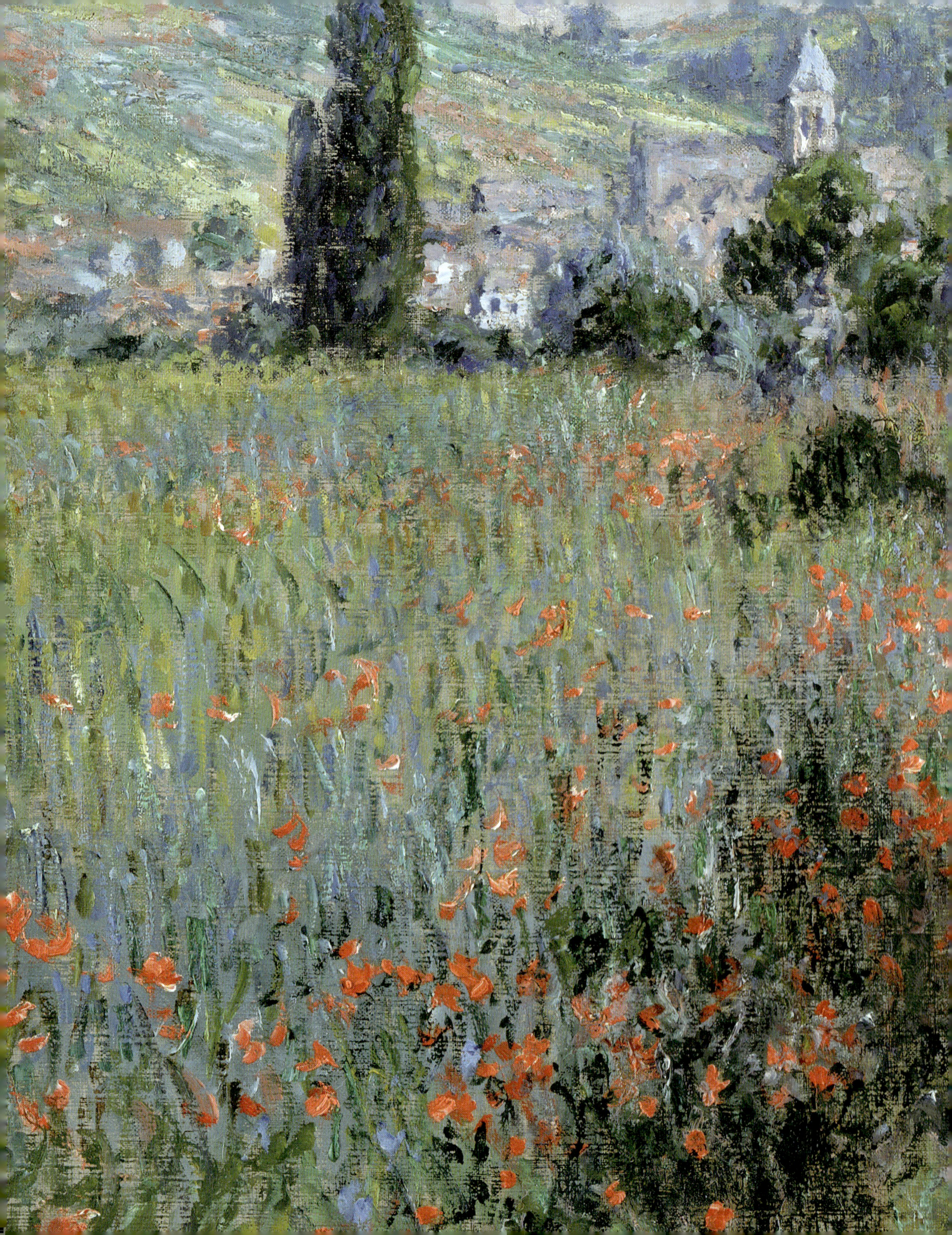

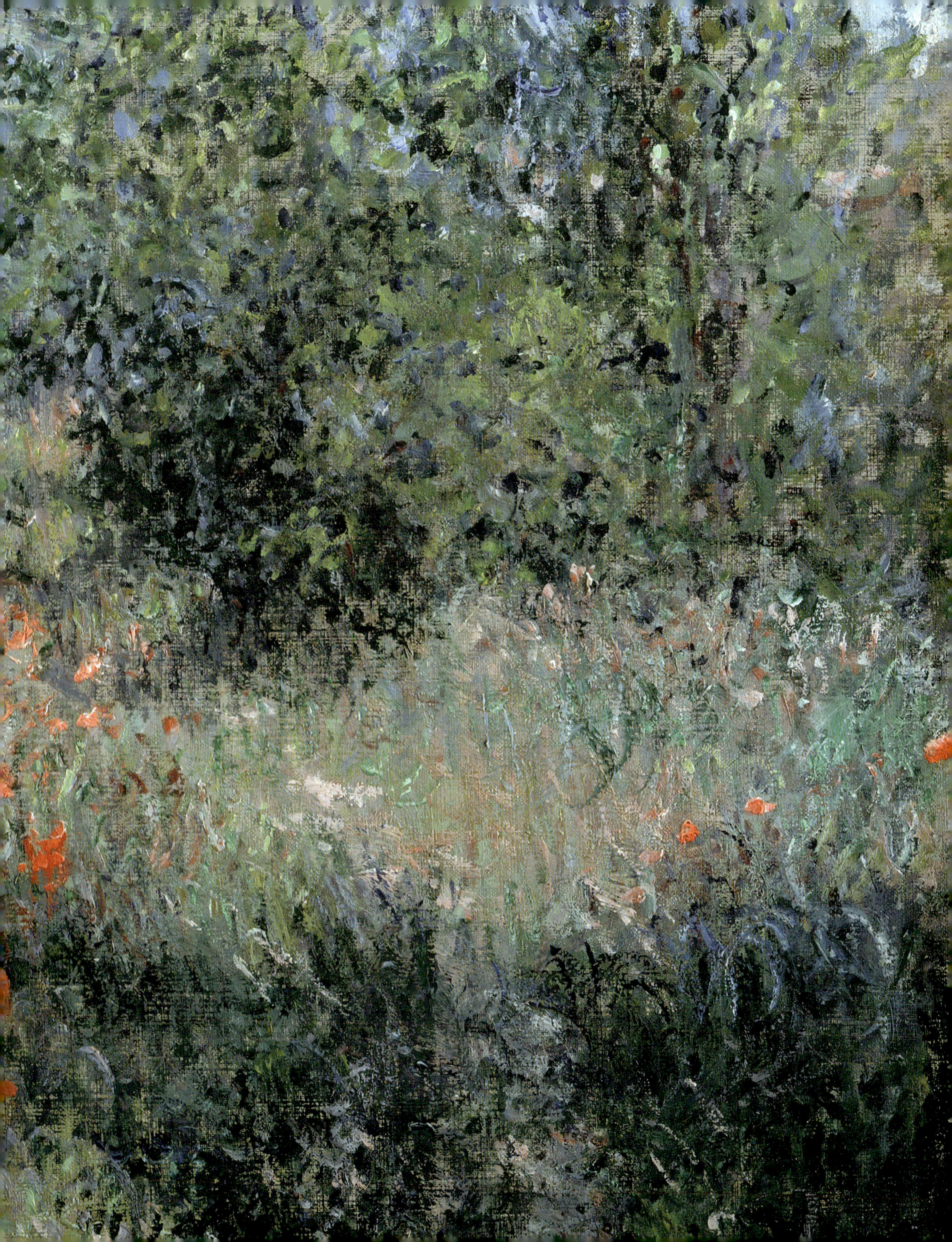

IMPRESSUM

This book is published on the occasion of the exhibition
Looking at Monet
The Great Impressionist and His Influence on Austrian Art
from October 24, 2014 to February 8, 2015 at the Lower Belvedere / Orangery, Vienna.

Director: Agnes Husslein-Arco
Curator: Stephan Koja
Curatorial Assistants: Kathrin Wolf, Irina Katnik

Belvedere
Prinz Eugen-Straße 27
1030 Vienna
www.belvedere.at

Publication
Editors: Agnes Husslein-Arco, Stephan Koja
Graphic Design: Peter Baldinger
Translation: Rebecca Law, Robert McInnes, Nick Somers
English-Proofreading: Louise Stein, Michaela Alex, Susanne Eder
Printed and bound by Grasl FairPrint, Bad Vöslau

www.hirmerpublishers.com

Printed in Austria

ISBN 978-3-7774-2364-7 (trade edition english)
ISBN 978-3-902805-56-0 (museum edition english)

Bibliographic information published by the Deutsche Nationalbibliothek
The Deutsche Nationalbibliothek lists this publication in the Deutsche Nationalbibliografie; detailed bibliographic data are available on the Internet at http://dnb.de

Cover illustrations:
Claude Monet, Waterloo Bridge, Sonne, 1903, Milwaukee Art Museum,
Bequest of Mrs. Albert T. Friedmann (museum edition english)
Claude Monet, Path in Monet's Garden in Giverny, 1902, Belvedere, Vienna (trade edition english)

If in spite of our thorough research any individual illustrations have not been correctly attributed or acknowledged, we offer our apologies and would appreciate any information that will allow us to rectify the matter in future editions.